THE NEW MEDIA
AND CYBERCULTURES
ANTHOLOGY

Edited by
Pramod K. Nayar

THE NEW MEDIA AND CYBERCULTURES ANTHOLOGY

WILEY-BLACKWELL

A John Wiley & Sons, Ltd., Publication

This edition first published 2010
© 2010 Blackwell Publishing Ltd except for editorial material and organization
© 2010 Pramod K. Nayar

Blackwell Publishing was acquired by John Wiley & Sons in February 2007. Blackwell's publishing program has been merged with Wiley's global Scientific, Technical, and Medical business to form Wiley-Blackwell.

Registered Office
John Wiley & Sons Ltd, The Atrium, Southern Gate, Chichester, West Sussex, PO19 8SQ, United Kingdom

Editorial Offices
350 Main Street, Malden, MA 02148-5020, USA
9600 Garsington Road, Oxford, OX4 2DQ, UK
The Atrium, Southern Gate, Chichester, West Sussex, PO19 8SQ, UK

For details of our global editorial offices, for customer services, and for information about how to apply for permission to reuse the copyright material in this book please see our website at www.wiley.com/wiley-blackwell.

The right of Pramod K. Nayar to be identified as the author of the editorial material in this work has been asserted in accordance with the UK Copyright, Designs and Patents Act 1988.

Library of Congress Cataloging-in-Publication Data is available for this title

9781405183086 (hbk) / 9781405183079 (pbk)

A catalogue record for this book is available from the British Library.

Set in Minion 10.5/13pt by SPi Publisher Services, Pondicherry, India
Printed and bound in Singapore by Fabulous Printers Pte Ltd

001   2010

CONTENTS

Preface   ix
Acknowledgments   x
Acknowledgments to Sources   xii

Introduction   1

PART ONE   THEORIES, POETICS, PRACTICES   7

1   Web Sphere Analysis and Cybercultural Studies   11
    Kirsten Foot

2   What Does it Mean to be Posthuman?   19
    N. Katherine Hayles

3   Digitextuality and Click Theory: Theses on Convergence
    Media in the Digital Age   29
    Anna Everett

4   The Double Logic of Remediation   46
    Jay David Bolter and Richard Grusin

5   The Database   50
    Lev Manovich

6   Making Meaning of Mobiles: A Theory of *Apparatgeist*   65
    James E. Katz and Mark A. Aakhus

PART TWO   SPACE, PLACE, COMMUNITY   77

7   Post-Sedentary Space   79
    William J. Mitchell

8   The End of Geography or the Explosion of Place?: Conceptualizing
    Space, Place and Information Technology   90
    Stephen Graham

9   Asphalt Games: Enacting Place Through Locative Media   109
    Michele Chang and Elizabeth Goodman

10 Thought on the Convergence of Digital Media, Memory, and
    Social and Urban Spaces   117
    Federico Casalegno

PART THREE   RACE IN/AND CYBERSPACE   129

11 Cybertyping and the Work of Race in the Age of
    Digital Reproduction   132
    Lisa Nakamura

12 Thinking Through the Diaspora: Call Centers, India, and a
    New Politics of Hybridity   151
    Raka Shome

13 Voices of the Marginalized on the Internet: Examples from a
    Website for Women of South Asia   166
    Ananda Mitra

PART FOUR   BODIES, EMBODIMENT, BIOPOLITICS   183

14 Hypes, Hopes and Actualities: New Digital Cartesianism
    and Bodies in Cyberspace
    Megan Boler   185

15 The Bioethics of Cybermedicalization   209
    Andy Miah and Emma Rich

16 Biocolonialism, Genomics, and the Databasing
    of the Population   221
    Eugene Thacker

PART FIVE   GENDER, SEX, AND SEXUALITIES   **251**

17   Assembling Bodies in Cyberspace: Technologies,
      Bodies, and Sexual Difference   254
      Dianne Currier

18   Lesbians in (Cyber)space: The Politics of the Internet in
      Latin American On- and Off-line Communities   268
      Elisabeth Jay Friedman

19   E-Rogenous Zones: Positioning Pornography in the Digital Economy   284
      Blaise Cronin and Elisabeth Davenport

20   Race, Gender and Sex on the Net: Semantic Networks of
      Selling and Storytelling Sex Tourism   307
      Peter A. Chow-White

PART SIX   POLITICS, POLITICAL ACTION, ACTIVISM   **325**

21   Internet Studies in Times of Terror   328
      David Silver and Alice Marwick

22   Free Labor: Producing Culture for the Digital Economy   335
      Tiziana Terranova

23   Ensuring Minority Rights in a Pluralistic and "Liquid"
      Information Society   357
      Birgitte Kofod Olsen

24   Hacktivism: All Together in the Virtual   369
      Tim Jordan

PART SEVEN   GAMES, GAMING, META-UNIVERSES   **379**

25   Games Telling Stories: A Brief Note on Games and Narratives   382
      Jesper Juul

26   WoW is the New MUD: Social Gaming from Text to Video   394
      Torill Elvira Mortensen

27   Women and Games: Technologies of the Gendered Self   408
      Pam Royse, Joon Lee, Baasanjav Undrahbuyan,
      Mark Hopson, and Mia Consalvo

28   To the White Extreme: Conquering Athletic Space, White
     Manhood, and Racing Virtual Reality   425
     David J. Leonard

29   Your Second Life?: Goodwill and the Performativity of
     Intellectual Property in Online Digital Gaming   441
     Andrew Herman, Rosemary J. Coombe, and Lewis Kaye

**PART EIGHT   THE DIGITAL, THE MOBILE,
               THE PERSONAL, AND THE EVERYDAY   465**

30   Taking Risky Opportunities in Youthful Content Creation:
     Teenagers' Use of Social Networking Sites for Intimacy,
     Privacy and Self-expression   468
     Sonia Livingstone

31   Dynamics of Internet Dating   483
     Helene M. Lawson and Kira Leck

32   Screening Moments, Scrolling Lives: Diary Writing on the Web   499
     Madeleine Sorapure

33   Your Life in Snapshots: Mobile Weblogs   515
     Nicola Döring and Axel Gundolf

34   Assembling Portable Talk and Mobile Worlds:
     Sound Technologies and Mobile Social Networks   526
     John Farnsworth and Terry Austrin

35   New Media, Networking and Phatic Culture   534
     Vincent Miller

Index   544

PREFACE

This eclectic collection of articles is intended as a point of entry into what has come to be called "digital cultures," "new media cultures," "Internet cultures, and, more often, "cybercultures."

Digital technology and new forms of media now inform all aspects of our life – from banking to online support groups, medical information to everyday communications, and recreation to research. The terrain is varied, complex, and shifting. Even as academic studies, reports, and critiques appear on digital cultures such as computer games and computer-mediated communication, the "object," process, or practice change. Thus cybercultures is a notoriously difficult and slippery "discipline" to theorize for the simple reason that it is arguably the fastest-growing set of practices in contemporary times.

The present volume draws together essays and studies that have appeared, in the main, since the 1990s. The topics covered include political economy and labor in the new media age, call-center work, medicalization, computer games, geographies, the body and identity, the gendered and racialized nature of cybercultures, sexualities, and mobile and personal communications. It has opted for diversity and range rather than intensive work. While there are a few empirical studies, these have by far been excluded. The contributions are also interdisciplinary, in keeping with the extremely amorphous and Protean nature of new media and cybercultural practices. The *Reader* does not propose any particular theoretical framework for "reading" cybercultures. As the articles in Part I demonstrate, there can be multiple approaches to and in this "discipline."

This anthology has chosen not to include the major, and now canonical, essays from the first wave of cyberculture theorists and commentators like Anne Balsamo, Donna Haraway, Howard Rheingold, and Sherry Turkle. Their work has been, quite rightly, anthologized enough and this particular anthology has chosen to present newer thinkers on cybercultures.

So now, click "Enter"!

PKN
Hyderabad, India

ACKNOWLEDGMENTS

When I offered *An Introduction to Cybercultures* to Jayne Fargnoli at Wiley-Blackwell, she came back with the idea for another book. This anthology began with a suggestion made to Jayne by her colleagues and who, with her capacious enthusiasm, decided it was a good thing to keep me busier. And I must admit, it has been fun. So thank you, Jayne.

Margot Morse at Wiley-Blackwell responded quickly to emails and offered suggestions at important moments. She got on the reviewer's case and ensured that there was no delay there. Her promptness is deeply appreciated. Also, I would like to thank Juanita Bullough for a careful editorial hand.

The *New Media and Cybercultures Reader* grew out of my work with the *Introduction* and has, since, acquired its own life, form, and voting rights in addition to, of course, its list of demands. It has also incurred its round of debts that I shall now proceed to list in great detail.

My parents deserve my interminable, unquantifiable gratitude for their support, love, and prayers. (They also deserve, as friends have pointed out, my sympathy for putting up with me.)

My parents-in-law, on their occasional visits, sneak in gentle reminders that I am mostly unavailable, but do so with great affection.

Nandini, who glances at the monitor to see what strange things I am working with *now*, puts on a brave, smiling face and reminds me that cyborgs *may* not eat, but those who write about them *must*.

Pranav (whose discovery of computer games and the Playmobil URL indicates that there will be keyboard battles in the future) has developed a rather unhealthy (if accurate) view that I am always working, and so proceeds, as remedy or restitution, to entertain me with endless and improbable battle sagas – or friendly encounters, depending upon his mood – staged between Transformers, dinosaurs, rescue helicopters, and Batman.

To friends who have stayed in touch – Panikkar, Ajeet, Ibrahim – I owe a good deal of healthy, non-profession-related emails and phone conversations.

Mysore Jagadish of American Information Resource Center, Chennai, supplied books and essays with what seems like ridiculous ease, and Thea Pitman at the University of Leeds generously sent me her work on Latin American cybercultures.

A special thanks to the School of Media, Critical and Creative Arts at Liverpool John Moores University, UK, for inviting me as Visiting Professor in February–March 2008, and to new friends there: Belle Adams, Timothy Ashplant, Elspeth Graham, and Joe Moran. But most of all, at Liverpool, thanks to Colin Harrison, who insisted that dinners included salads and who (rightly) believes I overwork.

I must also express my gratitude to the University of Dayton (UD), Ohio, USA, for inviting me as Visiting Professor in September–October 2008, a visit facilitated by the generosity of the Indian Council for Cultural Relations and the India Foundation (whose formidable Harish Trivedi ensured that everything went well). At UD, I must thank Sheila Hughes, Tina Manco, Tom Morgan, Sally Raymont, and Andy Slade, the staff of the Roesch Library and, for her enviable efficiency and generosity, Amy Anderson. Also at UD, my new friend, Akhila Ramnarayan, for her affection, the many lunches and coffees, and the unexpectedly long, if unplanned, drives (and, later, her supply of materials).

To Rita Kothari and Atul Tandan ("PAT") for inviting me to the Mudra Institute for Communications, Ahmedabad (MICA), where I spoke on cybercultures – a big thank you for your warm hospitality.

At the University of Hyderabad I am grateful for the presence of Narayana Chandran who, in sharp contrast/departure from established trends of thought and response there, is encouraging and affectionate, *and* interested in the things I do. Also at the University, Anindita Mukopadhyay, who surprises me with occasional phone calls, shares her most recent ideas and reading in philosophy, history, and literature and, when we do meet, is prone to infectious laughter that cheers the day.

Finally, I must embarrass my friend Anna Kurian by thanking her yet again, and declaring: "without your constant encouragement and limitless affection I would not do *this* kind (or quantum) of work."

ACKNOWLEDGMENTS TO SOURCES

Chapter 1: Kirsten Foot, "Web Sphere Analysis and Cybercultural Studies," pp. 88–96 from David Silver and Alexander Massanari (eds.), *Critical Cyberculture Studies* (New York: New York University Press). © 2006 by New York University Press. Reprinted with permission from NYU Press.

Chapter 2: N. Katherine Hayles, "What Does It Mean to be Posthuman?," pp. 283–91, 322–3 from N. Katherine Hayles, *How We Became Posthuman: Virtual Bodies in Cybernetics, Literature, and Informatics* (Chicago and London: University of Chicago Press, 1999). © 1999 by The University of Chicago. Reproduced by permission of the author and The University of Chicago Press.

Chapter 3: Anna Everett, "Digitextuality and Click Theory: Theses on Convergence Media in the Digital Age," pp. 3–28 from Anna Everett and John T. Caldwell (eds.), *New Media: Theories and Practices of Digitextuality* (London and New York: Routledge, 2003). © 2003 by Taylor & Francis Books, Inc. Reprinted by permission of the Copyright Clearance Center, www.copyright.com.

Chapter 4: Jay David Bolter and Richard Grusin, "The Double Logic of Remediation," pp. 3–15 from Jay David Bolter and Richard Grusin, *Remediation: Understanding New Media* (Cambridge, MA: MIT Press, 1999). © 1998, Massachusetts Institute of Technology. Reprinted with permission from The MIT Press.

Chapter 5: Lev Manovich, "The Database," pp. 218–36 from Lee Manovich, *The Language of New Media* (Cambridge, MA: MIT Press, 2001). © 2001, Massachusetts Institute of Technology. Reprinted with permission from The MIT Press.

Chapter 6: James E. Katz and Mark A. Aakhus, "Making Meaning of Mobiles – A Theory of *Apparatgeist*," pp. 301–18 from James E. Katz and Mark A. Aakhus (eds.), *Perpetual Contact: Mobile Communication, Private Talk, Public Performance*

(Cambridge: Cambridge University Press, 2003). © 2002 by Cambridge University Press. Reprinted with permission from the authors and CUP.

Chapter 7: William J. Mitchell, "Post–Sedentary Space," pp. 143–58, 240–1 from Mitchell, *Me⁺⁺: The Cyborg Self and the Networked City* (Cambridge, MA: MIT Press, 2003). © 2003, Massachusetts Institute of Technology. Reprinted with permission from The MIT Press.

Chapter 8: Stephen Graham, "The End of Geography or the Explosion of Place? Conceptualizing Space, Place and Information Technology," pp. 165–85 from *Progress in Human Geography* 22:2 (1998). © 1998 by SAGE Publications. Reprinted by permission of SAGE.

Chapter 9: Michele Chang and Elizabeth Goodman, "Asphalt Games: Enacting Place through Locative Media," from *Leonardo* 14:3 (July 2006) – *Leonardo Electronic Almanac*. © 2006 by Leonardo/ISAST. Reprinted with permission.

Chapter 10: Federico Casalegno, "Thought on the Convergence of Digital Media, Memory, and Social and Urban Spaces," pp. 313–26 from *Space and Culture* 7:3 (August 2004). © 2004 by SAGE Publications. Reprinted by permission of SAGE.

Chapter 11: Lisa Nakamura. "Cybertyping and the Work of Race in the Age of Digital Reproduction," pp. 1–30, 147–9, 159–61 from Lisa Nakamura, *Cybertypes: Race, Ethnicity, and Identity on the Internet* (London and New York: Routledge). © 2002 by Routledge. Reprinted by permission of the Copyright Clearance Center, www.copyright.com.

Chapter 12: Raka Shome, "Thinking Through the Diaspora: Call Centers, India, and a New Politics of Hybridity," pp. 105–23 from *International Journal of Cultural Studies* 9:1 (2006). © 2006 by SAGE Publications. Reprinted by permission of SAGE.

Chapter 13: Ananda Mitra. "Voices of the Marginalized on the Internet: Examples from a Website for Women of South Asia," pp. 492–510 from *Journal of Communication* 54:3 (2004). © 2004, International Communication Association. Reprinted with permission from Blackwell Publishing Ltd.

Chapter 14: Megan Boler, "'Hypes, Hopes and Actualities: New Digital Cartesianism and Bodies in Cyberspace," pp. 139–68 from *new media & society* 9:1 (2007). © 2007 by SAGE Publications. Reprinted by permission of SAGE.

Chapter 15: Andy Miah and Emma Rich, "The Bioethics of Cybermedicalization," pp. 107–16, 131–2 and references from Andy Miah and Emma Rich, *The Medicalization of Cyberspace* (London and New York: Routledge, 2008). © 2008 by Routledge. Reproduced by permission of Taylor & Francis Books UK.

Chapter 16: Eugene Thacker, "Biocolonialism, Genomics, and the Databasing of the Population," pp. 133–72 and notes from Eugene Thacker, *The Global*

Genome: Biotechnology, Politics, and Culture (Cambridge, MA: MIT Press, 2005). ©
2005, Massachusetts Institute of Technology. Reprinted with permission from The
MIT Press.

Chapter 17: Dianne Currier, "Assembling Bodies in Cyberspace: Technologies, Bodies,
and Sexual Difference," pp. 519–38 from. Mary Flanagan and Austin Booth (eds.), *Reload:
Rethinking Women+Cyberculture* (Cambridge, MA: MIT Press, 2002). © 2002,
Massachusetts Institute of Technology. Reprinted with permission from The MIT Press.

Chapter 18: Elisabeth Jay Friedman "Lesbians in (cyber)space: the politics of the
internet in Latin American on- and off-line communities," pp. 790–811 from *Media,
Culture & Society* 29:5 (2007). © 2007 by SAGE Publications. Reprinted by permission of SAGE.

Chapter 19: Blaise Cronin and Elisabeth Davenport, "E–Rogenous Zones: Positioning
Pornography in the Digital Economy," pp. 33–48 from *The Information Society* 17
(2001). © 2001 by Taylor & Francis. Reprinted with permission of the Taylor &
Francis Group, http://www.informaworld.com Table 19.2 reprinted by Permission
of Forbes Magazine © 2009 Forbes LLC.

Chapter 20: Peter A. Chow-White, "Race, Gender and Sex on the Net: Semantic
Networks of Selling and Storytelling Sex Tourism," pp. 883–905 from *Media,
Culture & Society* 28:6 (2006). © 2006 by SAGE Publications. Reprinted by permission of SAGE.

Chapter 21: David Silver and Alice Marwick. "Internet Studies in Times of Terror,"
pp. 47–54 from David Silver and A. Massanari (eds.), *Critical Cyberculture Studies*
(New York: New York University Press, 2006). © 2006 by New York University Press.
Reprinted with permission from NYU Press.

Chapter 22: Tiziana Terranova. "Free Labor: Producing Culture for the Digital
Economy," pp. 33–58 from *Social Text* 18.2 (Summer 2000). © 2000 by Duke
University Press. All rights reserved. Used by permission of the publisher.

Chapter 23: Birgitte Kofod Olsen, "Ensuring Minority Rights in a Pluralistic and 'Liquid'
Information Society," pp. 263–80 from Rikke Frank Jørgensen (ed.), *Human Rights in
the Global Information Society* (Cambridge, MA: MIT Press, 2006). © 2006, Massachusetts
Institute of Technology. Reprinted with permission from The MIT Press.

Chapter 24: Tim Jordan, "Hacktivism: All Together in the Virtual," pp. 119–35, 161
from Tim Jordan, *Activism! Direct Action, Hacktivism and the Future of Society*
(London: Reaktion Books, 2002). © 2006 by Joe Roman. Reprinted by permission of
Reaktion Books Ltd.

Chapter 25: Jesper Juul, "Games Telling stories? A brief note on games and Narratives,"
from *Game Studies: the international journal of computer game research* 1:1 (July
2001), http://www.gamestudies.org/0101/juul-gts/ © 2001 by Jesper Juul. Reprinted
by kind permission of the author.

Chapter 26: Torill Elvira Mortensen, "WoW is the New MUD: Social Gaming from Text to Video," pp. 397–413 from *Games and Culture* 1:4 (2006). © 2006 by SAGE Publications. Reprinted by permission of SAGE.

Chapter 27: Pam Royse, Joon Lee, Baasanjav Undrahbuyan, Mark Hopson, and Mia Consalvo, "Women and Games: Technologies of the Gendered Self," pp. 555–75 from *new media & society* 9:4 (2007). © 2007 by SAGE Publications. Reprinted by permission of SAGE.

Chapter 28: David J. Leonard, "To the White Extreme: Conquering Athletic Space, White Manhood, and Racing Virtual Reality," pp. 110–29 from Nate Garrelts (ed.), *Digital Gameplay: Essays on the Nexus of Game and* Gamer (Jefferson, NC: McFarland & Co., 2005). © 2005. Reprinted by permission of McFarland & Company, Inc., Box 611, Jefferson NC 28640. www.mcfarlandpub.com

Chapter 29: Andrew Herman, Rosemary J. Coombe, and Lewis Kaye, "'Your Second Life? Goodwill and the Performativity of Intellectual Property in Online Digital Gaming," pp, 184–210 from *Cultural Studies* 20:2–3 (March/May 2006). © 2006 by Taylor & Francis. Reproduced with permission from the authors and Taylor & Francis Group, http://www.informaworld.com.

Chapter 30: Sonia Livingstone, "Taking Risky Opportunities in Youthful Content Creation: Teenagers' Use of Social Networking Sites for Intimacy, Privacy and Self-expression," pp. 393–441 from *new media & society* 10:3 (2008). © 2008 by SAGE Publications. Reprinted by permission of SAGE.

Chapter 31: Helene M. Lawson and Kira Leck. "Dynamics of Internet Dating," pp. 189–208 from *Social Science Computer Review* 24:2 (summer 2006). © 2006 by SAGE Publications. Reprinted by permission of SAGE.

Chapter 32: Madeleine Sorapure, "Screening Moments, Scrolling Lives: Diary Writing on the Web," pp. 1–23 from *Biography* 26:1 (Winter 2003). © 2003, Biographical Research Center. Reprinted by permission of *Biography: An Interdisciplinary Quarterly*.

Chapter 33: Nicola Döring and Axel Gundolf, "Your Life in Snapshots: Mobile Weblogs," pp. 80–90 from *Knowledge, Technology, & Policy* 19:1 (Spring 2006). © 2006 by Springer. Reprinted with kind permission from Springer Science + Business Media.

Chapter 34: John Farnsworth and Terry Austrin, "Assembling Portable Talk and Mobile Worlds: Sound Technologies and Mobile Social Networks," pp. 14–22 from *Convergence: The International Journal of Research into New Media Technologies* 11:2 (2005). © 2005 by SAGE Publications. Reprinted by permission of SAGE and the authors.

Chapter 35: Vincent Miller, "New Media, Networking and Phatic Culture," pp. 387–400 from *Convergence: The International Journal of Research into New Media Technologies* 14:4 (2008). © 2008 by SAGE Publications. Reprinted by permission of SAGE.

INTRODUCTION

There is no one way of reading cyberculture or new media for the simple reason that cyberculture is not a unified, coherent phenomenon, space, or artifact. Cyberculture is a rapidly proliferating, multilayered, and complex space where different kinds of technology "work" and generate different kinds of interactions (with each other and with humans). Gaming, entertainment, blogging, hacking, news forums, radical subcultures, political mobilization, communication commerce, governance … the nature of "action" in cyberspace is diverse. Thus the number of terms used to describe academic studies of cyberculture are equally multiple: internet studies, new media studies, digital media studies, digital arts and culture studies, networked culture studies, information society studies, and contemporary media studies.

In this anthology, cyber*space* describes the worlds and domains generated by digital Information and Communications Technologies (ICTs). It is a set of relations and actions in electronic space. Cyberculture, as defined by the *Encyclopedia of New Media*, is "cultures formed in or associated with online social spaces" (Kendall 2007). To expand this definition, cyberculture is the electronic environment where various technologies and media forms converge and cross over: video games, the internet and email, personal homepages, online chats, personal communications technologies (PCTs, such as the cell phone), mobile entertainment and information technologies, bioinformatics, and biomedical technologies.

ICTs include the collection, processing, storage, retrieval, and transmission of information in the form of text, visuals (video), sound (audio), and graphics for economic, social cultural, scientific, and political applications among individuals, groups, institutions, and nations.

Cyberculture is, in Henry Jenkins's apposite term (2006), "convergence culture," where the PC, the telephone, the internet, and multimedia provide an integrated form of communication. Convergence is not just about platforms for the merger of these devices, but also the very functions where entertainment and information become "infotainment" or education and entertainment become "edutainment."

In what follows, I outline a series of propositions about new media or cybercultures. These are only signposts in our reading, for the essays in this volume suggest detailed steps in the cultural analysis of cybercultures.

1   The critique of technology is not to be left to technologists or software engineers alone because technology is co-constructed by users and within particular social, cultural, economic, and political contexts. Thus we need to see cell phones, software, search engines, broadband transmission, and Internet Protocols (IPs) as both emerging in (i.e., produced) and used within contexts.

2   The meaning of a technological device – its "semiotics" – is not inherent in the device: it is an attribute. The value of a device accrues to it from its acceptance, use, and circulation within a cultural context. Every society or culture bestows it with its own meanings, even as it modifies the device – or ensures that the producer modifies it – to suit its traditions, customs, and social values. That is, cybercultures and new media acquire values through a context-based "domestication."

3   Cybercultures emerge in the context of global flows – of people and finance. Cybercultures are both the driving force behind and the consequence of globalization where information technology enables the swift, constant, and unlimited movement of data.

4   Cybercultures and network cultures are situated within the context of globalization and technocapitalism where the distributed nature of production, finance, marketing, and consumption demands high-speed connectivity.

5   New media cultures extend and expand the possibilities of older forms of media (what Bolter and Grusin 2000 have termed "remediation"), but with increasing emphasis on both the hypervisibility of the medium (hypermediation) and the rendering invisible of the medium.

6   In cybercultures all media is *crossover media*, adapting, borrowing from, or echoing another format. Movies merge into computer games, and computer games generate fan sites, movie plots, and toys; advertisers use computer gameworlds.

7   As a result of this hybridization/convergence (or what I have called "crossover"), every medium is augmented. A cell phone serves as an email device, thus augmenting its "original" function. It also serves as a camera, a movie-making device, a conferencing facility, and a personal diary.

8   "Perpetual contact" and "augmentation" capture the spirit and logic of contemporary cyberculture.

9   The system (hardware–software–wetware) and the environment (cybernetic space) constitute each other, and it is becoming increasingly difficult to find the boundaries between the two. This is the dialectic of the virtual and the real. Cybercultures, approached via a Cultural Studies route, is an articulation between three crucial elements or actors: hardware (the machines, computers, cable networks), software (programs), and wetware (humans), all three of which are deeply embedded in the social and historical contexts of the technology.

10   Cybercultures – and the virtual worlds of cell phones, games, and cyberspace – are built through material labor. Real bodies working in different but real

material conditions of factories and the wage system provide the technologies that help others transcend bodies and real spaces.

11   Cyberspace must always return to the material because, thus far, citizenship, justice, emancipation, social welfare, and political responsibility rely on material bodies.

12   Cybercultures are at various points, and in different ways, attached to and connected with real-life material conditions, and they replicate, extend, and augment them.

13   Cybercultures, however, help generate a certain disembodiment and corporeal transcendence where bodies, geographies, and spaces become irrelevant when on a cell phone connecting different parts of the world, or in the game world of *Civilization* or *SIMCITY*.

14   Identity and subjectivity are no more restricted by skin or body – they are disseminated, dispersed, and augmented through connections facilitated by ICTs. The individual's identity is not restricted to her body or location, but can be simultaneously here and elsewhere, extending beyond immediate space and skin.

15   Cybercultures are not in and of themselves democratic, though they do facilitate greater connection between people and nations. A digital divide between "First" and "Third" Worlds, between classes and genders *within* the "First" World, and the quality of access within user communities does exist. Racial and class inequalities exist in terms of the access to and use of digital resources.

16   The consumption of cybercultures is increasingly a lifestyle choice too – especially in the case of personal communications technologies (PCTs).

17   Cybercultures empower communities to govern themselves or communicate with those who govern them. The increasing role of computers and ICTs in governance suggests that lines of communication with figures of authority or institutions are technologically mediated.

18   Civil society, too, is reconfigured. Rather than a "fragmentation of the social" (as Jenks 2005 characterized postmodern culture), we see a *reconfiguration* of the social where computer-mediated communication becomes the dominant form of social interaction. This might extend or substitute for face-to-face interaction.

19   Nongovernmental organizations and activists use ICTs for their radical, emancipatory, or subversive purposes. There is a marked escalation in the use of electronic spaces for political purposes (from election campaigns to counter-propaganda).

20   Activism via the Web, most commonly visible as "Hactivism" and electronic civil disobedience, has emerged as one of the most significant appropriations of the new media.

21   Subcultures that would otherwise find it difficult to communicate with their members find that ICTs and cyberspace provide an alternative forum. Queers, diasporic communities, and the differently-abled now find that distance, geography, and physical constraints do not pose the same degree of hindrance as before.

22   Identity – gender, racial, class, sexual orientation – is reconfigured in cybercultures. The disembodiment, corporeal transcendence, and augmentation result in a posthuman identity.

23   However, this transcendence of the body is a racialized, gendered, and class-inflected phenomenon because transcendence depends upon access, speed, the quality of technology, and the time available. In other words, the liberatory aspects of cyberculture are not always democratic.

24   Cybercultures are as prone to power struggles, inequalities, subversion, and appropriation, as any other cultures. Cybercultures are driven by material considerations of profit and power, and affect people in their day-to-day lives.

25   Cyberspace must be seen, therefore, as a *process* rather than an object, a series of actions, negotiations, and interactions in dynamic relations.

26   Cyberspace reflects and refracts real/material conditions where, for example, gameworlds reveal racial and gender stereotypes and search engines have their own politics that are, more and more, given to advertising and commercial space.

27   There is no *one* cyberspace or cyberculture because, like all social practices, it is a consequence of political economy, the human world, information, global finance, capitalism, the logic of the market, cables and wires, monitors, and SIM cards.

28   Several cybercultural developments have enormous economic potential – whether it is internet advertising or branding in games. The internet is big (for) business.

29   Contrary to commonly circulating myths, electronic spaces generated by ICTs are not "free." Controls exist over domain names, bandwidth, access, and speed even as surveillance technologies are put in place to monitor usage, and the internet is, in Alexander Galloway's terms (2004), a "protocological" space governed by protocols and systems of control.

30   Whereas moves to control the spaces of ICTs have accompanied the development of the technologies, Web 2.0 is marked by an increasing democratization, where users appropriate, alter, assimilate, and subvert these technologies.

31   Web 2.0 and the "next-gen" cybercultures are characterized by personalization, customization, and a sense of "play" with developments like wikis, blogging, social networking, customized games, and Personal Fabrication. To put it differently, ICTs are now technologies of creativity to be used and developed not by technoscience alone but by consumers, whom David Marshall (2004) correctly terms "prosumers."

32   Personalization in Web 2.0 will make ICTs more and more consumer-centered and individualist, or at least individualizable.

33   Cyberculture *studies* extends the work of cultural criticism and cultural studies by locating cybercultures as affected by and affecting these actual identities of individuals. Cyberculture studies explores the impact, consequence, context, and manifestations of computer technology and ICTs on the social, cultural, economic, and material (i.e., fleshly) conditions of real bodies. It explores the shifts in the nature of living for material bodies via ICTs and new media.

34   Cyberculture studies does (and should) constitute an important aspect of globalization studies, for the material structures and even the vocabulary of globalization show overlaps with that of cybercultures and ICTs. Cyberculture studies

calls attention to the raced, gendered, and classed nature of the "information revolution," the effects of this "revolution" on different sections of society, and the question of power that determines the course of the revolution.

35   Cyberculture studies foregrounds the ethical through questions of the racial, sexual, or gendered other in cybercultures.

36   Cyberculture studies explores the ways in which organizations, individuals, campaigns, and civil society in general have appropriated or resisted ICTs. The interest of cyberculture studies lies in the consequences and appropriation of new technologies – in this case, how they help formulate individual and collective identities.

OK, and that is just the beginning! Now read on …

REFERENCES

Bolter, J. D. and Grusin, R. (2000) *Remediation: Understanding New Media*. Cambridge, MA: MIT Press.

Galloway, A. (2004) *Protocol: How Control Exists after Decentralization*. Cambridge, MA: MIT Press.

Jenkins, H. (2006) *Convergence Culture: Where Old and New Media Collide*. New York: New York University Press.

Jenks, C. (2005) *Subculture: The Fragmentation of the Social*. London: Sage.

Kendall, L. (2007) http://sage-ereference.com/newmedia/Article_n55.html.

Marshall, P. D. (2004) *New Media Cultures*. London: Hodder Headline.

THEORIES, POETICS, PRACTICES

Introduction

The articles in this part of the book introduce various approaches to cybercultures.

Treating the Web as a collection of databases does not adequately capture the enormous, and changing, complexity of the "system." The Web – which continues to be the keystone of the cybercultural arch – must be seen as a dynamic but regulated, shifting but patterned set of processes. The Web can be studied as a collection of units that are interlinked, and may be generated by users as well. Databases are dynamic, complex entities that are constantly evolving and interminably (at least potentially) linked. The database becomes the defining form of the cybercultural age, and, as has been persuasively argued in Lev Manovich's article below, is opposed to the narrative form. Critics and theorists have sought to evolve modes of analyzing this complexity. New media *poetics* have involved studies of the integration of multiple media forms and platforms: the visual, audio, graphic, video, text. Theories of hypertexts, hyperlinkages, nodes, and "routes" explore the "terrain" of cyberspace in its various topoi (blogs, websites, social networking). Notions of "digitextuality," hypertextuality, hypermediacy, remediation, and convergence have informed and productively analyzed the poetics of digital cultures. The rise of new forms of art – commonly called "digital art" or even cyberart – has demanded new modes of analysis. The availability of new modes for writing has resulted in new textual practices. Electronic writing has great implications for the development and teaching of writing skills and seems to possess its own unique forms of rhetoric.

Yet cybercultural poetics also have other, more material consequences. Thus cyber- and networked cultures can also be examined for their effect on identity. Thus the networked, modified, and extended human would be the posthuman of cyberpunk fiction and the attenuated bodies of contemporary electronically linked lives. The rise of the posthuman who (seems to) transcend the limitations of the body is the congeries of software, hardware, and wetware where the borders of the human, the animal, and the machine merge.

Mobile and personalized communications redefine our relationship with space, geography, and our neighbors. Portable communication means, in simple terms, that one is always "connected." The "spirit" and logic of the new media age with email/surfing/communication/entertainment on the move seems to be that of "perpetual contact," as Katz and Aarhus's article (chapter 6) theorizes.

New forms of literacy have developed since the evolution of online games, and projects dealing with the potential of such cybercultural forms in education have been launched. The consequences of new media for the arrival of the stranger or the "Other" on our screens or in our ears via electronic media have resulted in, according to at least one prominent commentator, a "pop cosmopolitanism." Pedagogic practices and research methods will have (and already have) changed enormously since the arrival of such technology. ICTs disrupted traditional modes of knowledge acquisition, compilation, and dissemination when podcasts by students, indy-media, wikis, and other forms of knowledge work began to emerge in the late 1990s.

The articles collected here deal with particular aspects of cybercultures. None of them describe the new media in their entirety, nor is such a single theoretical text or approach desirable. What we have here is a series of suggestions and "tips" on how to navigate the amorphous, gargantuan, and still-evolving dynamic called digital culture.

Methods of studying the amorphous and diverse "discipline" of cyberculture studies have not been very easy to cobble together. Kirsten Foot proposes the *Web sphere* as a unit of analysis. The Web sphere is a collection of dynamically defined digital resources, including the websites related to a particular theme. The sphere changes with the addition of newer websites and resources. The concept enables the analysis of producer-generated as well as user-generated Web links, texts, and other materials. It involves preserving the Web links and sites (due to the ephemerality of websites) and the re-creation of the Web experiences for future analysis.

The cyborg – or the posthuman – invokes both pleasure and terror. Katherine Hayles begins by suggesting that the idea of transcendence causes terror, since embodiment is central to the human. The body is, she argues, "sedimented history," emerging from thousands of years of evolution. The articulation of the human with intelligent machines cannot be seamless because machines do not share the same history of embodiment. The pleasure of posthuman combinations with machines is driven by the sense of freedom it offers. Human awareness expands beyond consciousness. Consciousness itself is about random patterns evolving in specific contexts through permutations and combinations, trajectories, and play. Building on the idea of pattern and control, Hayles proposes that the older view of the auto-nomous, controlled self is an illusion because it ignores the processes through which consciousness emerges: with a distributed cognition and interaction with the environment and settings. The posthuman is a human with "extended embodied awareness." This means the self is now a networked one.

Anna Everett's article suggests a new conceptualization of new media. Building on Julia Kristeva's notion of "interextuality" and combining it with "digital," Everett's neologism is an attempt to address the interactive transmedia interfaces, the end-user role and the aesthetic features of new media. Thus where intertextuality refers to the multiple formats and registers crisscrossing every text, digitextuality captures the phenomenon where different signifying systems and materials are "translated and transformed into zeroes and ones for infinite recombinant signifiers." Thus television, film, computer games, and the internet all converge to create the digital text that generates a "hyperattentiveness." It is the interactive nature of this medium that makes it more attractive, argues Everett. Developing what she calls "click theory," she argues that services and pleasures are available at a click. This, she suggests, is a counter to the fantasy of disembodied subjectivity because click pleasure is inherent in the tactile nature of the click. It is her thesis that new media forms recycle and retool older forms and seek to heighten consumers' and users' affective responses.

Jay Bolter and Richard Grusin's influential thesis proposes that contemporary digital media has a double logic. On the one hand it seeks to erase all traces of mediation, making it immediate, "live," and "real." The re-creation of period costumes and the meticulousness of detail generate a reality effect that makes the medium itself invisible (what they term the "logic of immediacy"). On the other hand it seeks to multiply media itself. New forms of graphic designs, digitized photographs, animation, and video expand and recall the earlier media forms of television, cinema, print media, and the photograph. Multiple video streams, split-screen displays, the mix of text and graphics call attention to the excessive mediation and conflation of media forms that is digital culture. This constitutes a "logic of hypermediacy." "Remediation" is this dual logic where the desire to be as real as possible, to be "immediate," is what drives digital media to borrow from each other as well as from older forms. "New media," Bolter and Grusin conclude, are new because of the ways in which they refashion older media.

Lev Manovich proposes the database ("a structural collection of data," as he defines it) as the opposite of narrative. He proposes that the logic of the computer can be reduced to two software objects: data structures and algorithms. The database is a series of possibilities, any of which "work out" depending on the user's movement on the keyboard. Narrative is one of the many methods of accessing data. The narrative is the progression of movement through the database. Discussing computer games, Manovich notes that these are experienced as narratives by the players. He then proceeds to discuss how databases and narratives function in the cultural sphere. Manovich argues that any new media object is the creation of an interface to a database. The database is the paradigm of objects, data, and possibilities from which the user chooses. The narrative is the syntagm that emerges as the result, and the linear sequence of screens that the user follows is the syntagm.

Exploring the impact of cell-phone and communications technologies on users, James Katz and Mark Aakhus propose a theory of *Apparatgeist* – the *Geist* of an apparatus, its spirit, motive, and driving principle. In the case of the cell phone, they argue, the "spirit" is that of "perpetual contact." This principle or spirit is *social*, not merely individual. The spirit is made up of particular premises and presuppositions regarding preferences for social and communicative arrangements.

These premises generate a spirit which in turn informs research, design, and use of the technology. Technology in turn has a social impact, and the use of certain technologies – what they term "folk ways" – indicates social values. Katz and Aakhus develop a map of how *Apparatgeist* evolves through particular domains of individual decision-making based on an incentive–disincentive assessment of personal communication technologies. What is significant in *Apparatgeist* theory is that it sees *users* as contributing to developments in design and manufacture of personal communications devices.

1 WEB SPHERE ANALYSIS AND CYBERCULTURAL STUDIES

Kirsten Foot

One way of approaching cybercultural studies is to focus on the relations and patterns, means and artifacts of cultural production and exchange on-line. Viewed as an evolving set of structures that enable and manifest the production of cyberculture, the hyperlinked, coproduced, and ephemeral nature of the Web challenges traditional approaches to research of social, political, and cultural interchange. Cultural studies of the Web may benefit from new methods of analyzing Web form and content, along with processes and patterns of production, distribution, usage, and interpretation of Web-based phenomena. In this chapter, I propose the concept of a *Web sphere* as a unit of analysis for cybercultural studies, explain the value of Web archives, and discuss methods of Web sphere analysis that may be useful for understanding cybercultural phenomena. I illustrate these methodological reflections through two studies of personal expression on the Web in the wake of the attacks of September 11, 2001.

Borrowing a concept from the work of Taylor and van Every (2000) on the relationship between communication and organizing, we can view the Web as both a "site and surface" for communicative action. In order to conduct an analysis of both the "site" and "surface" of the Web, it is helpful to create and analyze an archive not just of Web sites but of a Web sphere. A Web sphere is a collection of dynamically defined digital resources spanning multiple Web sites deemed relevant or related to a central theme or object, in the sense of the *gegenstand* concept from classical German philosophy (Foot and Schneider 2002). The *gegenstand* notion of an object as a focal point embedded-in-activity (see Foot 2002; Leont'ev 1978) enables the identification of a Web sphere as a collaborative production. As a unit of analysis, a Web sphere is boundable by time and object-orientation, and it is sensitive to

Kirsten Foot, "Web Sphere Analysis and Cybercultural Studies," pp. 88–96 from David Silver and Alexander Massanari (eds.), *Critical Cyberculture Studies* (New York: New York University Press).

developmental changes. Within the sphere social, political, and cultural relations can be analyzed in a variety of ways.

The most crucial element in this definition of a Web sphere is the dynamic nature of the sites to be included. This dynamism comes from two sources. First, the researchers involved in identifying the boundaries of the sphere are likely to continuously find new sites to be included within it. Second, as will be discussed below, the notion of defining a Web sphere is recursive, in that pages that are referenced by other included sites, as well as pages that reference included sites, are considered part of the sphere under evaluation. Thus, as a Web sphere is archived and analyzed over time, its boundaries are dynamically reestablished by both the researchers and the sites themselves. The Web sphere can function as a macro unit of analysis, by which historical and/or intersphere comparisons can be made. For example, the Web sphere of the 2000 elections in the United States can be comparatively analyzed with the U.S. electoral Web sphere of 2002, as well as with electoral Web spheres in other countries. Alternatively and/or simultaneously, other, more micro units, such as features, links, or textual elements, can be employed in analyses of a Web sphere, as I explain below.

Web sphere analysis is an analytic strategy that, fully implemented, includes analysis of the relations between producers and users of Web materials, as potentiated and mediated by the structural and feature elements of Web sites, hypertexts, and the links between them (Schneider and Foot 2004, 2005). In a nutshell, the multi-method approach of Web sphere analysis consists of the following elements: Web sites related to the object or theme of the sphere are identified, captured in their hyperlinked context, and archived with some periodicity for contemporaneous and retrospective analyses. The archived sites are annotated with human and/or computer-generated "notes" of various kinds, which creates a set of metadata. These metadata correspond to the unit(s) and level(s) of analysis anticipated by the researcher(s). Sorting and retrieving the integrated metadata and URL files is accomplished through several computer-assisted techniques. Interviews of various kinds are conducted with producers and users of the Web sites in the identified sphere, to be triangulated with Web media data in the interpretation of the sphere.

From the perspective of Web sphere analysis, the essence of the Web is the link (Foot et al. 2003). Links provide the nutrients that give the Web the energy and nourishment necessary for growth and development. Links serve as the neural pathways through which the collective intelligences and performances of Web producers and users are created, displayed, and distributed. Several approaches have emerged that take hyperlink relationality into account in more nuanced ways. Lindlof and Shatzer (1998) point in this direction in their article calling for new strategies of media ethnography in "virtual space." Hine (2000) presents a good example of sociocultural analysis of cross-site action on the Web. Similarly, Howard's (2002) conceptualization of network ethnography reflects methodological sensitivity to processes of Web production. In these examples and in Web sphere analysis, attention is given to the hyperlinked context(s) and situatedness of Web sites, as well as to the aims, strategies, and identity-construction processes of Web site producers, as they are produced, maintained, and/or mediated through links.

In order to engage in any kind of developmental or retrospective study of cyberculture on the Web, it is helpful to capture Web materials in a time-sensitive way. The ongoing evolution of the Web poses challenges for scholars as they seek to develop methodological approaches permitting robust examination of Web phenomena. Some of these challenges stem from the nature of the Web, which is a unique mixture of the ephemeral and the permanent. There are two aspects to the ephemerality of Web content: First, Web content is ephemeral in its transience, as it can be expected to last for only a relatively brief time. From the perspective of the user or visitor (or researcher), specialized tools and techniques are required to ensure that content can be viewed again at a later time. Second, Web content is ephemeral in its construction – like television, radio, theater, and other "performance media" (Hecht, Corman, and Miller-Rassulo 1993; Stowkowski 2002). Web content, once presented, needs to be reconstructed or re-presented in order for others to experience it. Although Web pages are routinely reconstructed by computers without human intervention (when a request is forwarded to a Web server), it nevertheless requires some action by the producer (or the producer's server) in order for the content to be viewed again. In other words, the experience of the Web, as well as the bits used to produce the content, must be intentionally preserved in order for it to be reproduced (Arms et al. 2001). Older media – including printed materials, film, and sound recordings, for example – can be archived in the form in which they are presented; no additional steps are needed to re-create the experience of the original.

At the same time, the Web has a sense of permanence that clearly distinguishes it from performance media. Unlike theater or live television or radio, Web content must exist in a permanent form in order to be transmitted. The Web shares this characteristic with other forms of media such as film, print, and sound recordings. The permanence of the Web, however, is somewhat fleeting. Unlike any other permanent media, a Web site may regularly and procedurally destroy its predecessor each time it is updated by its producer. That is, absent specific arrangements to the contrary, each previous edition of a Web site may be erased as a new version is produced. By analogy, it would be as if each day's newspaper was printed on the same piece of paper, obliterating yesterday's news to produce today's.

The ephemerality of the Web requires that proactive steps be taken in order to allow a re-creation of Web experience for future analyses. The permanence of the Web makes this eminently possible. Although saving Web sites is not as easy as, say, saving editions of a magazine, archiving techniques are evolving in such a way to facilitate scholarly research of Web sites. In distinction to other ephemeral media, the Web can be preserved in nearly the same form as it was originally "performed" (Kahle 1997; Lyman 2002; Lyman and Kahle 1998) and analyzed at a later time. Web archiving enables more rigorous and verifiable research, as well as developmental analyses that are time sensitive (e.g., Foot et al. 2003).

Robust Web sphere analysis benefits from robust Web archives. Going further, I suggest that Web archives enable an expanded range of investigable questions and greater analytical rigor for social research on Web-based phenomena. In the remainder of this essay I illustrate the potential benefits of Web archiving and Web sphere analysis for cybercultural studies through a brief overview of the September 11

Web Archive project in general and two studies of personal expression in the post – September 11 Web sphere that exemplify some of quantitative and qualitative methods of analysis enabled by a Web sphere/Web archive approach.

The September 11 Web Archive consists of Web sites related to the airliner attacks in the United States on September 11, 2001, and archived between September 11, 2001, and December 1, 2001. During this period, Steve Schneider and I worked with the Pew Internet and American Life Project, the U.S. Library of Congress, the Internet Archive, and volunteers from around the world to identify and archive URLs that were likely to be relevant to the question of how Web site producers were reacting to the events of September 11. Twelve basic categories of site producers were identified that were expected to be responding to the attacks on the Web. The findings for the studies on personal expression summarized below were based on an examination of Web sites produced by nine of these: news organizations such as CNN, the *New York Times*, and Salon.com; federal, state, and local government entities; corporations and other commercial organizations; advocacy groups; religious groups, including denominations and congregations; individuals acting on their own behalf; educational institutions; portals; and charity and relief organizations.

To build the archive, systematic searches were conducted for URLs produced by these sets of actors, and links to other URLs were followed to find more sites with relevant content. In most cases, the salient feature of these sites was content referring to the attacks and/or their aftermath. In some cases, the absence or removal of such content was salient. These collection efforts identified nearly twenty-nine thousand different sites. Each site was archived on a daily basis from initial identification to the end of the collection period. The objective of the archiving activity was to preserve not only the bits and the content but also the experiential dimensions of this rapidly emerging Web sphere. By capturing pages and sites in their hyperlinked context, the archiving tools preserved not just the collection of Web pages but also an interlinked Web sphere, characterized and bounded by a shared object orientation or reference point, in this case, the September 11 attacks.

The first study on expression as one form of sociopolitical action (Foot and Schneider 2004) included analysis of the types of site producers that enabled Web users to contribute personal expression or access expression posted by others on their sites, as well as whether mechanisms of expression were produced autonomously on a site (onsite) or jointly across sites (coproduced). For this analysis, a sample of 247 sites was generated from the September 11 Web Archive. The sampling strategy, designed to include a broad representation of site producers and to focus on those sites that were captured closest to September 11, yielded a sample of three "impressions" or site captures of the different Web sites. A preliminary analysis of the site pages eliminated those without content relevant to the September 11 events, as well as those not captured in a readable format by the archiving tools. The refined sample of Web sites was then closely examined by trained observers for the range of social and political actions made possible by site producers, including personal expression.

TABLE 1.1   Percent of Sites, by Producer Type Enabling Expression

| | Type of Site Producer | | | | | | | | | |
Action Enabled	News	Government	Business	Charity	Advocacy	Religious	Personal	Educational	Portal	All Sites
Get Expression	54%	16%	47%	50%	55%	53%	86%	76%	37%	55%
Provide Expression	50%	42%	23%	44%	32%	26%	69%	47%	26%	44%
Number of Sites	24	38	30	18	22	19	59	17	19	247

TABLE 1.2   Mode of Production in Enabling Expression

| | Action Enabled | |
Mode of Production	Get Expression	Provide Expression
On-site	80%	75%
On-site and coproduced	13%	15%
Coproduced only	8%	11%

Based on analysis of 247 sites

Not surprisingly, we found that personal Web sites produced by individuals were most likely to both give Web users access to others' expression (typically the personal reactions of the site producers) and enable them to provide their own expression to the site (see table 1.1). More interesting was that at least a quarter of all sites and over 40 percent of sites in our sample produced by news organizations, government entities, charities, and educational institutions enabled the provision of personal expression by Web users. We interpreted these findings as suggesting an increased willingness in facilitating multivoiced discourse if not dialogue on the part of site producers who might normally have a vested interest in maintaining content control and a more singular voice on their sites.

In this study we also took note of the mode of production employed in enabling expression. We defined an autonomous or onsite mode of production as one in which the site producer provides the content directly. In contrast, a joint or coproduction mode is evidenced when a site producer links to another site to facilitate the user action, in this case accessing or providing personal expression. As table 1.2 illustrates, many site producers combined these modes of production, providing some of the content themselves and linking to another site for additional content or functionality.

Of those site producers whose sites enabled access to or provided personal expression by Web users, a strong majority did so autonomously. Most site producers who engaged in coproduction in enabling expression did so in addition to providing onsite access to expression and/or mechanisms for users to express themselves.

In the second study of online expression my coauthor and I employed textual analysis to explore the particular forms of expression manifested on the Web (Siegl and Foot 2004). This study shed light on the types of public expression evoked by personal or mediated exposure to a crisis and posted on the Internet, and it served as a case study in collective mourning on the Internet. The research questions guiding this analysis included: (1) What kinds of expression were posted on the Web after 9/11? and (2) How do these forms of online expression compare with public mourning and bereavement? Using the same sample of daily impressions of 247 sites from the September 11 Web Archive described above, we identified 84 sites that enabled site visitors to post their own textual expression and/or access the textual expression of others. As in the previous study, these Web sites represented a broad cross-section of Web site producers, including personal or individual sites, charity or civic organizations, businesses, and governments, as well as Web sites constructed for the sole purpose of memorializing the attacks. Due to the large variety of the Web sites, it was necessary to standardize the portion of expression observed on each site. This was accomplished by analyzing the first five discrete units of textual expression; a discrete unit was defined as a temporally bounded entry posted to the Web by an author.

Through close readings of the selected units of textual expression from archived impressions of each site, we identified nine forms of expression manifested on the Web in the three weeks following September 11 (September 11, 2001–October 2, 2001) and noted the changes in dominant forms of expression during that period that deserved further study. We then compared the post-9/11 Web expression with emotional phases identified in the literature on public mourning and bereavement, such as shock, anger, and grief. We demonstrated that post–September 11 Web expression included more than these emotions, suggesting that the functions of the Web-based post-9/11 expression went beyond public mourning and bereavement and included attempts at analysis, sense-making, and advocacy. We concluded by arguing that the broader range of expression on the Web after September 11 (in contrast with expression documented from offline/non-Web contexts in the public mourning and bereavement literature) is at least partially due to characteristics of the Web and processes/practices of Web production that distinguish it from traditional broadcast and print media.

The September 11 Web Archive and the two studies on post-9/11 online expression described here illustrate the usefulness of thematic Web archives and Web sphere analysis in facilitating investigations of some kinds of cybercultural phenomena. The demarcation of a Web sphere requires systematic identification of Web site producers as well as particular sites, which in turn creates a strong base for analyzing patterns and modes of Web (co)production, as demonstrated in the first study. An archive of the Web sphere, collected at regular intervals during a specific period, enables retrospective and developmental analyses of many aspects of online relations, as well as the means and artifacts of cybercultural production and exchange. Web sphere analysis can function as a framework for research on sociocultural phenomena manifested in Web texts, features, or links, at a micro or macro level, and employing a diverse range of methods. As scholars of cyberculture undertake broader and deeper studies of Web form and content, as well as processes and patterns of production, distribution, usage, and interpretation of Web-based phenomena, archive-based Web sphere analysis may provide a helpful foundation.

REFERENCES

Arms, W., Adkins, R., Ammen, C., and Hayes, A. (2001) Collecting and preserving the Web: The Minerva prototype. *RLG DigiNews*, 5 (2) (April 15). Available at http://www.rlg. org/preserv/diginews/diginews5-2.html.

Foot, K. A. (2002) Pursuing an evolving object: Object formation and identification in a conflict monitoring network. *Mind, Culture and Activity*, 9 (2): 132–149.

Foot, K. A., and Schneider, S. M. (2002) Online action in campaign 2000: An exploratory analysis of the U.S. political Web sphere. *Journal of Broadcasting & Electronic Media*, 46 (2): 222–244. Available at http://politicalweb.info/preElection.html.

Foot, K. A., and Schneider, S. M. (2004) Online structure for civic engagement in the post-9/11 Web sphere. *Electronic Journal of Communication*, 14 (3/4).

Foot, K. A., Schneider, S. M., Dougherty, M., Xenos, M., and Larsen, E. (2003) Analyzing linking practices: Candidate sites in the 2002 U.S. electoral Web sphere. *Journal of Computer-Mediated Communication*, 8 (4). Available at http://www.ascusc.org/jcmc/vol8/issue4/ foot.html.

Hecht, M. L., Corman, S. R., and Miller-Rassulo, M. (1993) An evaluation of the drug resistance project: A comparison of film versus live performance media. *Health Communication*, 5 (2): 75–88.

Hine, C. (2000) *Virtual ethnography*. Thousand Oaks, CA: Sage.

Howard, P. (2002) Network ethnography and hypermedia organization: New organizations, new media, new myths. *New Medio & Society*, 4 (4): 550–574.

Kahle, B. (1997) Preserving the Internet. *Scientific American*, 276 (3): 82–83.

Leont'ev, A. N. (1978) *Activity, consciousness, and personality*. Englewood Cliffs, NJ: Prentice-Hall.

Lindlof, T. R., and Shatzer, M. J. (1998) Media ethnography in virtual space: Strategies, limits, and possibilities. *Journal of Broadcasting and Electronic Media*, 42 (2): 170–189.

Lyman, P. (2002) Archiving the World Wide Web. *Building a National Strategy for Digital Preservation*, April. Available at http://www.clir.org/pubs/reports/pub106/web. html.

Lyman, P., and Kahle, B. (1998) Archiving digital cultural artifacts: Organizing an agenda for action. *D-Lib Magazine*, July. Available at http://www.dlib.org/dlib/july98/07lyman. html.

Schneider, S. M., and Foot, K. A. (2004) The Web as an object of study. *New Media & Society*, 6 (1): 114–122.

Schneider, S. M., and Foot, K. A. (2005) Web sphere analysis: An approach to studying online action. In *Virtual methods: Issues in social research on the Internet* (ed. C. Hine). Oxford, UK: Berg, 157–170.

Siegl, E., and Foot, K. A. (2004) Expression in the post–September 11th Web sphere. *Electronic Journal of Communication*, 14 (1/2).

Stowkowski, P. A. (2002) Languages of place and discourses of power: Constructing new senses of place. *Journal of Leisure Research*, 34 (4): 368–382.

Taylor, J. R., and van Every, E. J. (2000) *The emergent organization: Communication as its site and surface*. Mahwah, NJ: Lawrence Erlbaum.

2 WHAT DOES IT MEAN TO BE POSTHUMAN?

N. Katherine Hayles

What finally, are we to make of the posthuman?[1] At the beginning of this book [*How We Became Posthuman*] I suggested that the prospect of becoming posthuman both evokes terror and excites pleasure. At the end of the book, perhaps I can summarize the implications of the posthuman by interrogating the sources of this terror and pleasure. The terror is relatively easy to understand. "Post," with its dual connotation of superseding the human and coming after it, hints that the days of "the human" may be numbered. Some researchers (notably Hans Moravec but also my UCLA colleague Michael Dyer and many others) believe that this is true not only in a general intellectual sense that displaces one definition of "human" with another but also in a more disturbingly literal sense that envisions humans displaced as the dominant form of life on the planet by intelligent machines. Humans can either go gently into that good night, joining the dinosaurs as a species that once ruled the earth but is now obsolete, or hang on for a while longer by becoming machines themselves. In either case, Moravec and like-minded thinkers believe, the age of the human is drawing to a close. The view echoes the deeply pessimistic sentiments of Warren McCulloch in his old age. As noted earlier, he remarked: "Man to my mind is about the nastiest, most destructive of all the animals. I don't see any reason, if he can evolve machines that can have more fun than he himself can, why they shouldn't take over, enslave us, quite happily. They might have a lot more fun. Invent better games than we ever did."[2] Is it any wonder that faced with such dismal scenarios, most people have understandably negative reactions? If this is what the posthuman means, why shouldn't it be resisted?

Fortunately, these views do not exhaust the meanings of the posthuman. As I have repeatedly argued, human being is first of all embodied being, and the complexities

N. Katherine Hayles, "What Does It Mean to be Posthuman?," pp. 283–91, 322–3 from N. Katherine Hayles, *How We Became Posthuman: Virtual Bodies in Cybernetics, Literature, and Informatics* (Chicago and London: University of Chicago Press, 1999).

of this embodiment mean that human awareness unfolds in ways very different from those of intelligence embodied in cybernetic machines. Although Moravec's dream of downloading human consciousness into a computer would likely come in for some hard knocks in literature departments (which tend to be skeptical of any kind of transcendence but especially of transcendence through technology), literary studies share with Moravec a major blind spot when it comes to the significance of embodiment.[3] This blind spot is most evident, perhaps, when literary and cultural critics confront the fields of evolutionary biology. From an evolutionary biologist's point of view, modern humans, for all their technological prowess, represent an eye blink in the history of life, a species far too recent to have significant evolutionary impact on human biological behaviors and structures. In my view, arguments like those that Jared Diamond advances in *Guns, Germs, and Steel: The Fates of Human Societies* and *Why Sex Is Fun: The Evolution of Human Sexuality* should be taken seriously.[4] The body is the net result of thousands of years of sedimented evolutionary history, and it is naive to think that this history does not affect human behaviors at every level of thought and action.

Of course, the reflexivity that looms large in cybernetics also inhabits evolutionary biology. The models proposed by evolutionary biologists have encoded within them cultural attitudes and assumptions formed by the same history they propose to analyze; as with cybernetics, observer and system are reflexively bound up with one another. To take only one example, the computer module model advanced by Jerome H. Barkow, Leda Cosmides, and John Tooby in *The Adapted Mind: Evolutionary Psychology and the Generation of Culture* to explain human evolutionary psychology testifies at least as much to the importance of information technologies in shaping contemporary worldviews as it does to human brain function.[5] Nevertheless, these reflexive complexities do not negate the importance of the sedimented history incarnated within the body. Interpreted through metaphors resonant with cultural meanings, the body itself is a congealed metaphor, a physical structure whose constraints and possibilities have been formed by an evolutionary history that intelligent machines do not share. Humans may enter into symbiotic relationships with intelligent machines (already the case, for example, in computer-assisted surgery); they may be displaced by intelligent machines (already in effect, for example, at Japanese and American assembly plants that use robotic arms for labor); but there is a limit to how seamlessly humans can be articulated with intelligent machines, which remain distinctively different from humans in their embodiments. The terror, then, though it does not disappear in this view, tends away from the apocalyptic and toward a more moderate view of seriated social, technological, political, and cultural changes.

What about the pleasures? For some people, including me, the posthuman evokes the exhilarating prospect of getting out of some of the old boxes and opening up new ways of thinking about what being human means. In positing a shift from presence/absence to pattern/randomness, I have sought to show how these categories can be transformed *from the inside* to arrive at new kinds of cultural configurations, which may soon render such dualities obsolete if they have not already. This process of transformation is fueled by tensions between the assumptions encoded in pattern/randomness as opposed to presence/absence. In Jacques Derrida's performance of presence/absence, presence is allied with Logos, God, teleology – in general, with an originary plenitude that can act to ground signification and give order and meaning to the trajectory of history.[6] The work of Eric Havelock, among others, demonstrates how in Plato's *Republic* this view of originary presence authorized a stable, coherent self that could witness and testify to a stable, coherent reality.[7] Through these and other means, the metaphysics of presence front-loaded meaning into the system. Meaning was guaranteed because a stable origin existed. It is now a familiar story how deconstruction exposed the inability of systems to posit their own origins, thus ungrounding signification and rendering meaning indeterminate. As the presence/absence hierarchy was destabilized and as absence was privileged over presence, lack displaced plenitude, and desire usurped certitude. Important as these moves have been in late-twentieth-century thought, they still took place within the compass of the presence/absence dialectic. One feels lack only if presence is posited or assumed; one is driven by desire only if the object of desire is conceptualized as something to be possessed. Just as the metaphysics of presence required an originary plenitude to articulate a stable self, deconstruction required a metaphysics of presence to articulate the destabilization of that self.

By contrast, pattern/randomness is underlaid by a very different set of assumptions. In this dialectic, meaning is not front-loaded into the system, and the origin does not act to ground signification. As we have seen for multiagent simulations, complexity evolves from highly recursive processes being applied to simple rules. Rather than proceeding along a trajectory toward a known end, such systems evolve toward an open future marked by contingency and unpredictability. Meaning is not guaranteed by a coherent origin; rather, it is made possible (but not inevitable) by the blind force of evolution finding workable solutions within given parameters. Although pattern has traditionally been the privileged term (for example, among the electrical engineers developing information theory), randomness has increasingly been seen to play a fruitful role in the evolution of complex systems. For Chris Langton and Stuart Kauffman, chaos accelerates the evolution of biological and artificial life;[8] for Francisco Varela, randomness is the froth of noise from which coherent microstates evolve and to which living systems owe their capacity for fast, flexible response;[9] for Henri Atlan, noise is the body's murmuring from which emerges complex communication between different levels in a biological system.[10] Although these models differ in their specifics, they agree in seeing randomness not simply as the lack of pattern but as the creative ground from which pattern can emerge.

Indeed, it is not too much to say that in these and similar models, randomness rather than pattern is invested with plenitude. If pattern is the realization of a certain set of possibilities, randomness is the much, much larger set of everything else, from phenomena that cannot be rendered coherent by a given system's organization to those the system cannot perceive at all. In Gregory Bateson's cybernetic epistemology, randomness is what exists outside the confines of the box in which a system is located; it is the larger and unknowable complexity for which the perceptual processes of an organism are a metaphor.[11] Significance is achieved by evolutionary processes that ensure the surviving systems are the ones whose organizations instantiate metaphors for this complexity, unthinkable in itself. When Varela and his coauthors argue in *Embodied Mind* that there is no stable, coherent self but only autonomous agents running programs, they envision, pattern as a limitation that drops away as human awareness expands beyond consciousness and encounters the emptiness that, in another guise, could equally well be called the chaos from which all forms emerge.[12]

What do these developments mean for the posthuman? When the self is envisioned as grounded in presence, identified with originary guarantees and teleological trajectories, associated with solid foundations and logical coherence, the posthuman is likely to be seen as antihuman because it envisions the conscious mind as a small subsystem running its program of self-construction and self-assurance while remaining ignorant of the actual dynamics of complex systems. But the posthuman does not really mean the end of humanity. It signals instead the end of a certain conception of the human, a conception that may have applied, at best, to that fraction of humanity who had the wealth, power, and leisure to conceptualize themselves as autonomous beings exercising their will through individual agency and choice.[13] What is lethal is not the posthuman as such but the grafting of the posthuman onto a liberal humanist view of the self. When Moravec imagines "you" choosing to download yourself into a computer, thereby obtaining through technological mastery the ultimate privilege of immortality, he is not abandoning the autonomous liberal subject but is expanding its perogatives into the realm of the posthuman. Yet the posthuman need not be recuperated back into liberal humanism, nor need it be construed as anti-human. Located within the dialectic of pattern/randomness and grounded in embodied actuality rather than disembodied information, the posthuman offers resources for rethinking the articulation of humans with intelligent machines.

To explore these resources, let us return to Bateson's idea that those organisms that survive will tend to be the ones whose internal structures are good metaphors for the complexities without. What kind of environments will be created by the expanding power and sophistication of intelligent machines? As Richard Lanham has pointed out, in the information-rich environments created by ubiquitous computing, the limiting factor is not the speed of computers, or the rates of transmission through fiber-optic cables, or the amount of data that can be generated and stored. Rather, the scarce commodity is human attention.[14] It makes sense, then, that technological innovation will focus on compensating for this bottleneck. An obvious solution is to design intelligent machines to attend to the choices and tasks that do not have to be done by humans. For example, there are already intelligent-agent programs to sort email, discarding unwanted messages and prioritizing the rest. The programs work along lines similar to neural nets. They tabulate the choices the human operators make, and they feed back this information in recursive loops to readjust the weights given to various kinds of email addresses. After an initial learning period, the sorting programs take over more and more of the email management, freeing humans to give their attention to other matters.

If we extrapolate from these relatively simple programs to an environment that, as Charles Ostman likes to put it, supplies synthetic sentience on demand, human consciousness would ride on top of a highly articulated and complex computational ecology in which many decisions, invisible to human attention, would be made by intelligent machines.[15] Over two decades ago, Joseph Weizenbaum foresaw just such an ecology and passionately argued that judgment is a uniquely human function and must not be turned over to computers.[16] With the rapid development of neural nets and expert programs, it is no longer so clear that sophisticated judgments cannot be made by machines and, in some instances, made more accurately than by humans. But the issue, in Weizenbaum's view, involves more than whether or not the programs work. Rather, the issue is an ethical imperative that humans keep control; to do otherwise is to abdicate their responsibilities as autonomous independent beings. What Weizenbaum's argument makes clear is the connection between the assumptions undergirding the liberal humanist subject and the ethical position that humans, not machines, must be in control. Such an argument assumes a vision of the human in which conscious agency is the essence of human identity. Sacrifice this, and we humans are hopelessly compromised, contaminated with mechanic alienness in the very heart of our humanity.[17] Hence there is an urgency, even panic, in Weizenbaum's insistence that judgment is a uniquely human function. At stake for him is nothing less than what it means to be human.

In the posthuman view, by contrast, conscious agency has never been "in control." In fact, the very illusion of control bespeaks a fundamental ignorance about the nature of the emergent processes through which consciousness, the organism, and the environment are constituted. Mastery through the exercise of autonomous will is merely the story consciousness tells itself to explain results that actually come about through chaotic dynamics and emergent structures. If, as Donna Haraway, Sandra Harding, Evelyn Fox Keller, Carolyn Merchant, and other feminist critics of science have argued, there is a relation among the desire for mastery, an objectivist account of science, and the imperialist project of subduing nature, then the posthuman offers resources for the construction of another kind of account.[18] In this account, emergence replaces teleology; reflexive epistemology replaces objectivism; distributed cognition replaces autonomous will; embodiment replaces a body seen as a support system for the mind; and a dynamic partnership between humans and intelligent machines replaces the liberal humanist subject's manifest destiny to dominate and control nature. Of course, this is not necessarily what the posthuman *will* mean – only what it *can* mean if certain strands among its complex seriations are highlighted and combined to create a vision of the human that uses the posthuman as leverage to avoid reinscribing, and thus repeating, some of the mistakes of the past.

Just as the posthuman need not be antihuman, so it also need not be apocalyptic. Edwin Hutchins addresses the idea of distributed cognition through his nuanced study of the navigational systems of oceangoing ships.[19] His meticulous research shows that the cognitive system responsible for locating the ship in space and navigating it successfully resides not in humans alone but in the complex interactions within an environment that includes both human and nonhuman actors. His study allows him to give an excellent response to John Searle's famous "Chinese room." By imagining a situation in which communication in Chinese can take place without the actors knowing what their actions mean, Searle challenged the idea that machines can think.[20] Suppose, Searle said, that he is stuck inside a room, he who knows not a word of Chinese. Texts written in Chinese are slid through a slot in the door. He has in the room with him baskets of Chinese characters and a rulebook correlating the symbols written on the texts with other symbols in the basket. Using the rulebook, he assembles strings of characters and pushes them out the door. Although his Chinese interlocutors take these strings to be clever responses to their inquiries, Searle has not the least idea of the meaning of the texts he has produced. Therefore, it would be a mistake to say that machines can think, he argues, for like him, they produce comprehensible results without comprehending anything themselves. In Hutchins's neat interpretation, Searle's argument is valuable precisely because it makes clear that it is not Searle but the entire room that knows Chinese.[21] In this distributed cognitive system, the Chinese room knows more than do any of its components, including Searle. The situation of modern humans is akin to that of Searle in the Chinese room, for every day we participate in systems whose total cognitive capacity exceeds our individual knowledge, including such devices as cars with electronic ignition systems, microwaves with computer chips that precisely adjust power levels, fax machines that warble to other fax machines, and electronic watches that communicate with a timing radio wave to set themselves and correct their date. Modern humans are capable of more sophisticated cognition than cavemen not because moderns are smarter, Hutchins concludes, but because they have constructed smarter environments in which to work.

Hutchins would no doubt disagree with Weizenbaum's view that judgment should be reserved for humans alone. Like cognition, decision-making is distributed between human and nonhuman agents, from the steam-powered steering system that suddenly failed on a navy vessel Hutchins was studying to the charts and pocket calculators that the navigators were then forced to use to calculate their position. He convincingly shows that these adaptations to changed circumstances were evolutionary and embodied rather than abstract and consciously designed (pp. 347–51). The solution to the problem caused by this sudden failure of the steering mechanism was "clearly discovered by the organization [of the system as a whole] before it was discovered by any of the participants" (p. 361). Seen in this perspective, the prospect of humans working in partnership with intelligent machines is not so much a usurpation of human right and responsibility as it is a further development in the construction of distributed cognition environments, a construction that has been ongoing for thousands of years. Also changed in this perspective is the relation of human subjectivity to its environment. No longer is human will seen as the source from which emanates the mastery necessary to dominate and control the environment. Rather, the distributed cognition of the emergent human subject correlates with – in Bateson's phrase, becomes a metaphor for – the distributed cognitive system as a whole, in which "thinking" is done by both human and nonhuman actors. "Thinking consists of bringing these structures into coordination so they can shape and be shaped by one another," Hutchins wrote (p. 316). To conceptualize the human in these terms is not to imperil human survival but is precisely to enhance it, for the more we understand the flexible, adaptive structures that coordinate our environments and the metaphors that we ourselves are, the better we can fashion images of ourselves that accurately reflect the complex interplays that ultimately make the entire world one system.

This view of the posthuman also offers resources for thinking in more sophisticated ways about virtual technologies. As long as the human subject is envisioned as an autonomous self with unambiguous boundaries, the human-computer interface can only be parsed as a division between the solidity of real life on one side and the illusion of virtual reality on the other, thus obscuring the far-reaching changes initiated by the development of virtual technologies. Only if one thinks of the subject as an autonomous self independent of the environment is one likely to experience the panic performed by Norbert Wiener's *Cybernetics* and Bernard Wolfe's *Limbo*. This view of the self authorizes the fear that if the boundaries are breached at all, there will be nothing to stop the self's complete dissolution. By contrast, when the human is seen as part of a distributed system, the full expression of human capability can be seen precisely to *depend* on the splice rather than being imperiled by it. Writing in another context, Hutchins arrives at an insight profoundly applicable to virtual technologies: "What used to look like internalization [of thought and subjectivity] now appears as a gradual propagation of organized functional properties across a set of malleable media" (p. 312). This vision is a potent antidote to the view that parses virtuality as a division between an inert body that is left behind and a disembodied subjectivity that inhabits a virtual realm, the construction of virtuality performed by Case in William Gibson's *Neuromancer* when he delights in the "bodiless exultation of cyberspace" and fears, above all, dropping back into the "meat" of the body.[22] By contrast, in the model that Hutchins presents and that the posthuman helps to authorize, human functionality expands because the parameters of the cognitive system it inhabits expand. In this model, it is not a question of leaving the body behind but rather of extending embodied awareness in highly specific, local, and material ways that would be impossible without electronic prosthesis.

As we have seen, cybernetics was born in a froth of noise when Norbert Wiener first thought of it as a way to maximize human potential in a world that is in essence chaotic and unpredictable. Like many other pioneers, Wiener helped to initiate a journey that would prove to have consequences more far-reaching and subversive than even his formidable powers of imagination could conceive. As Bateson, Varela, and others would later argue, the noise crashes within as well as without. The chaotic, unpredictable nature of complex dynamics implies that subjectivity is emergent rather than given, distributed rather than located solely in consciousness, emerging from and integrated into a chaotic world rather than occupying a position of mastery and control removed from it. Bruno Latour has argued that we have never been modern; the seriated history of cybernetics – emerging from networks at once materially real, socially regulated, and discursively constructed – suggests, for similar reasons, that we have always been posthuman.[23] The purpose of this book has been to chronicle the journeys that have made this realization possible. If the three stories told here – how information lost its body, how the cyborg was constructed in the postwar years as technological artifact and cultural icon, and how the human became the posthuman – have at times seemed to present the posthuman as a transformation to be feared and abhorred rather than welcomed and embraced, that reaction has everything to do with how the posthuman is constructed and understood. The best possible time to contest for what the posthuman means is now, before the trains of thought it embodies have been laid down so firmly that it would take dynamite to change them.[24] Although some current versions of the posthuman point toward the anti-human and the apocalyptic, we can craft others that will be conducive to the long-range survival of humans and of the other life-forms, biological and artificial, with whom we share the planet and ourselves.

NOTES

1. I am grateful to Marjorie Luesebrink for conversations that stimulated me to think further about the ideas in this conclusion.
2. Warren McCulloch, quoted in Mary Catherine Bateson, *Our Own Metaphor: A Personal Account of a Conference on the Effects of Conscious Purpose on Human Adaptation* (1972; Washington, D.C.: Smithsonian Institution Press, 1991), p. 226.
3. Hans Moravec, *Mind Children: The Future of Robot and Human Intelligence* (Cambridge: Harvard University Press, 1988).
4. Jared Diamond, *Guns, Germs, and Steel: The Fates of Human Societies* (New York: Norton, 1997), and *Why Sex Is Fun: The Evolution of Human Sexuality* (New York: Basic Books, 1997).
5. Jerome H. Barkow, Leda Cosmides, and John Tooby, eds., *The Adapted Mind: Evolutionary Psychology and the Generation of Culture* (Oxford: Oxford University Press, 1992).
6. Jacques Derrida, *Of Grammatology*, translated by Gayatri C. Spivak (Baltimore: Johns Hopkins University Press, 1976).
7. Eric A. Havelock, *Preface to Plato* (Cambridge: Harvard University Press, 1963).
8. Chris G. Langton, "Computation at the Edge of Chaos: Phase Transition and Emergent Computation," *Physica D* 42 (1990): 12–37; Stuart A. Kauffman, *The Origins of Order: Self-Organization and Selection in Evolution* (New York: Oxford University Press, 1993).
9. Francisco J. Varela, "Making It Concrete: Before, During, and After Breakdowns," in *Revisioning Philosophy*, edited by James Ogilvy (Albany: State University of New York Press, 1992), pp. 97–109.
10. Henri Atlan, "On a Formal Definition of Organization," *Journal of Theoretical Biology* 45 (1974): 295–304. Michel Serres has a provocative interpretation of how this noise can give rise to human language, in "The Origin of Language: Biology, Information Theory and Thermodynamics," *Hermes: Literature, Science, Philosophy*, edited by Josué V. Harari and

David F. Bell (Baltimore: Johns Hopkins University Press, 1982), pp. 71–83. See N. Katherine Hayles, *Chaos Bound: Orderly Disorder in Contemporary Literature and Science* (Ithaca: Cornell University Press, 1990), pp. 56, 204–6, for a discussion of Atlan and Serres.

11. Gregory Bateson, quoted in Bateson, prologue to *Our Own Metaphor*, pp. 13–16.

12. Francisco J. Varela, Evan Thompson, and Eleanor Rosch, *The Embodied Mind: Cognitive Science and Human Experience* (Cambridge: MIT Press, 1991).

13. In Neal Stephenson's *Snow Crash* (New York: Bantam, 1992), his young white heroine, "Y.T.," is kidnapped, dumped aboard the Raft, and assigned to mess detail. She then has an insight into how small the fraction of the world's population is who ever believed they had a liberal humanist self. Once she gets over the shock and settles into a routine, she starts looking around her, watching the other fish-cutting dames, and realizes that this is just what life must be like for about 99 percent of the people in the world. "You're in this place. There's other people all around you, but they don't understand you and you don't understand them, but people do a lot of meaningless babble anyway. In order to stay alive, you have to spend all day every day doing stupid meaningless work. And the only way to get out of it is to quit, cut loose, take a flyer, and go off into the wicked world, where you will be swallowed up and never heard from again" (pp. 303–4).

14. Richard Lanham, *The Electronic Word: Democracy, Technology, and the Arts* (Chicago: University of Chicago Press, 1994).

15. Galen Brandt, "Synthetic Sentience: An Interview with Charles Ostman," *Mondo 2000*, no. 16 (winter 1996–97): 25–36. See also Charles Ostman, "Synthetic Sentience as Entertainment," *Midnight Engineering* 8, no. 2 (March/April 1997): 68–77.

16. Joseph Weizenbaum, *Computer Power and Human Reason: From Judgment to Calculation* (New York: W. H. Freeman, 1976).

17. Gilles Deleuze and Felix Guattari of course celebrate this very alienness in their vision of the phylum and "body without organs" in *Anti-Oedipus: Capitalism and Schizophrenia* (Minneapolis: University of Minnesota Press, 1983). For an ecstatic interpretation of the posthuman, see Judith Halberstam and Ira Livingston, eds., *Posthuman Bodies* (Bloomington: Indiana University Press, 1995).

18. Donna J. Haraway, "Situated Knowledges: The Science Question in Feminism and the Privilege of Partial Perspective," in *Simians, Cyborgs, and Women: The Reinvention of Nature* (New York: Routledge, 1990), pp. 183–202; Evelyn Fox Keller, "Baconian Science: The Arts of Mastery and Obedience," *Reflections on Gender and Science* (New Haven: Yale University Press, 1995), pp. 33–42; Sandra Harding, *The Science Question in Feminism* (Ithaca: Cornell University Press, 1986); and Carolyn Merchant, *The Death of Nature: Women, Ecology, and the Scientific Revolution* (San Francisco: Harper, 1982).

19. Edwin Hutchins, *Cognition in the Wild* (Cambridge: MIT Press, 1995).

20. John R. Searle, "Is the Brain's Mind a Computer Program?" *Scientific American* 262, no. 1 (1990): 26–31; see also John R. Searle, *Minds, Brains, and Science* (Cambridge: Harvard University Press, 1986), pp. 32–41, for the "Chinese room" thought experiment. Searle attempts to answer the analysis that it is the whole room that knows Chinese, saying there "is no way to get from syntax to semantics" (p. 34).

21. Hutchins, *Cognition*, pp. 361–62.

22. William Gibson, *Neuromancer* (New York: Ace Books, 1984). The narrator, after relating how Case has been exiled from cyberspace, comments: "For Case, who'd lived

in the bodiless exultation of cyberspace, it was the Fall. . . . The body was meat. Case fell into the prison of his own flesh" (p. 6).

23. Bruno Latour, *We Have Never Been Modern*, translated by Catherine Porter (Cambridge: Harvard University Press, 1993). Latour's important argument is that quasi-objects operate within networks that are at once in material real, socially regulated, and discursively constructed. Using different contexts, I have argued in this book for a very similar view regarding the history of cybernetics.

24. Dynamiting the system here alludes to Bill Nichols's seminal article on cybernetics, "The Work of Culture in the Age of Cybernetics," in *Electronic Culture: Technology and Visual Representation*, edited by Timothy Druckrey (New York: Aperture, 1996), pp. 121–44.

3

DIGITEXTUALITY AND CLICK THEORY
Theses on Convergence Media in the Digital Age

Anna Everett

The advent of the digital revolution in late-twentieth and early-twenty-first-century media culture apparently confirms both Jean-Luc Godard's belief in the "end of cinema" and other media critics' claims that we have even entered a posttelevision age.[1] Driving this ontological shift in the infrastructures of many Western media forms and practices is the near ubiquity of difficult-to-regulate satellites, cable TV, analog, and digital video recorders, computer camcorders, and other mass-market technologies outside the proprietary panopticon of big media corporations. Moreover, the rapid fin-de-siècle diffusion of such consumer-grade digital technologies as the CD-ROM, the DVD, the Internet, virtual reality, and wireless communications systems portends even more radical challenges to traditional media industries and their increasingly vulnerable representational hegemonies, as the symptomatic and infamous case of the Napster music-file-sharing system and other open-source code technologies have denoted. In response, big media corporations have begun a frenzied bout of high-profile megamergers, and concomitant new media colonization – or is it cannibalization? (We'll return to this later.)

Digital Matters: What Is Digitextuality?

Digitextuality. then, is a neologism that at its most basic combines two familiar word images: the overdetermined signifier *digital*. which denotes most of computer-driven media's technological processes and products, and Julia Kristeva's term *intertextuality*. (It also is indebted to John Caldwell's far-reaching work on televisuality.)

Anna Everett, "Digitextuality and Click Theory: Theses on Convergence Media in the Digital Age," pp. 3–28 from Anna Everett and John T. Caldwell (eds.), *New Media: Theories and Practices of Digitextuality* (London and New York: Routledge, 2003).

With the two terms conjoined in this way, digitextuality suggests a more precise or utilitarian trope capable at once of describing and constructing a sense-making function for digital technology's newer interactive protocols, aesthetic features, transmedia interfaces and end-user subject positions, in the context of traditional media antecedents. Moreover, digitextuality is intended to address, with some degree of specificity, those marked continuities and ruptures existing between traditional ("old") media and their digital ("new") media progeny and, especially, how new media use gets constructed. Given this explanatory agenda, it is useful at this point to invoke Kristeva's ideas about intertextuality to better clarify the term's influence on my thinking and theoretical formulation of digitextuality.

Where digitextuality departs from Kristeva's notion of intertextuality is that the former moves us beyond a "new signifying system" of quotations and transposition, to a metasignifying system of discursive absorption whereby different signifying systems and materials are translated and often transformed into zeroes and ones for infinite recombinant signifiers. In other words, new digital media technologies make meaning not only by building a new text though absorption and transformation of other texts, but also by embedding the entirety of other texts (analog and digital) seamlessly within the new. What this means is that earlier practices of bricolage, collage, and other modernist and postmodernist hybrid representational strategies and interary gestures of intertextual referentiality have been expanded for the new demands and technological wizardry of the digital age.[2] Nonetheless, our abilities to understand the new modes and codes of digital media texts today are still often predicated upon successfully decoding their semiotic densities and "semiotic polyvalence" in terms of earlier media structures, what Kristeva calls "an adherence to different sign-systems".[3]

Digitextuality, then, is not only concerned with digital media's *remediation* (to borrow Jay David Bolter and Richard Grusin's term) of our practices of intertextual reading and writing given our need to negotiate between radically different sign systems (historical and contemporary), but also explores digital media's own emerging aesthetics, ethics, and rhetorics in light of the media convergence phenomenon in this time of ascendant globalization and corporate media monopolization. An important part of digital media culture is bound up with the idea of interactivity and expectations for its functionality. As media convergence strategies evolve, a contest is now afoot to determine and delimit how this crucial feature will look and perform. The question is, Will interactivity achieve a political economy in terms of a proconsumerist idea of use value, or a procorporate, profit-motive imperative of exchange value? I return to this issue through a discussion of the significance of bits, sound bites, and digital media's computer determinism later on in the chapter.

Ontologies of Digitextuality

I suggest that digitextuality is a concept capable of bridging this epistemological chasm because it strives to understand digital media's technological proficiency at cannibalizing both media's modes of production and consumption techniques, particularly those of television. Whereas glance theory denigrates "television based on the viewer's 'fundamental inattentiveness'" (26), user practices of digitextuality, especially as practiced by that generation who have grown up with computer games, MTV-style television aesthetics,[4] and the Internet, suggest an alternative. Increasingly, today's sophisticated media consumers use television, the computer (the Internet, computer games), print material, and the telephone all at once. Such a radically transformed media environment suggests that perhaps we are witnessing media users' development of what might easily be described as a *fundamental hyperattentiveness*. Have apparatuses of convergence and new multimedia texts necessitated an activation of more than the proverbial 10 percent of new media consumers' brainpower when interacting with new technologies? It seems that consumer mastery of digital media's requisite multitasking behaviors and composite texts challenges accepted theories of cognition and spectatorship. Apparently we are becoming more adept at processing and appreciating the gestalt of digital technologies' multimedia barrage.

With this in mind, I propose we think about something approaching a *pixilated gaze* or *hyperattentive theory* of spectatorship, reception, and newmedia interaction more compatible with how people today actually engage with the emergent contours of digital encodings, semiotics, and aesthetics. Let us also consider, for example, the frequently changing and interchangeable semiotic systems and aesthetic codes that unquestionably redefine the look of television programs, commercial advertisements, Internet content, and special effects driven films that dominate our media topography these days. Talking about the reciprocal nature of film audiences' and especially reflexive films' "look back" at each other, Wheeler Winston Dixon offers an interesting perspective on reception and the apparatus. In *It Looks at You: The Returned Gaze of Cinema*, Dixon argues, "This is the gaze of the object returned – of the frame that possesses the object – of the projected image that possesses the viewer."[5] This certainly seems pertinent for the immersion thesis of new-media engagement.

Digitextual Semiotics and Aesthetics: Where Is Digitextuality?

Film

Since popular culture audiences today understand and expect that most contemporary media texts, including films, are produced with some degree of digital manipulation, processing, and computer generated images (CGI), expressions of cinematic realism, escapism, and formalism as representational incommensurabilities arguably become less significant, especially for digitextuality's *über*-real image constructs. For convergence media, fealty to "a unified set of related, interdependent elements," principles, and laws such as genres, narrative and nonnarrative categories matters less than a film's digitextual processing.[6] More important is its ability to technologize the sublime and convincingly render what was once considered unrepresentable.

Lev Manovich enables us to view such a situation as inhering in the fact that "[t]he iconic code of cinema is discarded in favor of the more efficient binary one. Cinema becomes a slave to the computer."[7] This remark may be hyperbolic, but the point remains. And from this perspective, the success of films like *Forrest Gump* (1994), *The Truman Show* (1998), *The Matrix* (1999), *Run Lola Run* (1999), *Crouching Tiger, Hidden Dragon* (2001), *Final Fantasy* (2000), and *Monsters, Inc.* (2001), among many others, does not hinge on the recognizable separations between representational strategies of realism or verisimilitude, artifice or animation, experimentation or virtuoso formalism to elicit spectators' willing suspension of disbelief. Rather, it is these films' ability to challenge the digital literacy and scopic competencies of contemporary media audiences more concerned with questions of technological magic ("How'd they do that?") than with believable representations of reality as markers of success.

Moreover, media-savvy audiences today apparently understand that the rhetoric of the real has, since modernity, been menaced and exterminated by new-media signifying systems.[8] Deftly simulating the real – an always already compromised state – therefore, is not the issue in digital media culture; overcoming reality's limitations and representing the sublime by any technique necessary apparently is. This is what I mean by *digitextuality's über-real* – an *overreal* or *grand real* construction with signifying powers beyond the simulacrum. Through digital-image manipulation we come to expect and enjoy talking pigs, as in *Babe* (1995), or cats and dogs, as in *The Truth about Cats and Dogs* (2001), in our popular family films. Digitextuality achieves its affective dimensions when it can seamlessly construct enthralling diegetic images of Tom Hanks as Forrest Gump greeting the late president John F. Kennedy in an unprecedented stroke of visual precision and acuity, or assist Natalie Cole in fabulations of "Unforgetable" music in a popular video with her deceased dad, Nat King Cole. Thus, digitextuality is the technological process whereby digital fabrications function as real-time experience of a sort to overcome not only time and space, but life and death.

Television

"I have seen the future of television, and it looks like Fred Astaire dancing with a vacuum cleaner – forever." When Zack Stentz made this memorable statement about digital technologies' obvious semiotic encroachments on analog television's representational regime, he was attending a conference of "movers and shakers in the computer, entertainment and legal industries" at Universal Studios.[9] The meeting concerned these industries' intentions to harness digital technologies' capacities to "'create' virtual humans'" as "a legion ot immortal pitchmen" and women. Consider this telling comment from Jeff Lotman, CEO of Global Icons: "'So, if you had the rights to a Michael Jordan ... you might not need him to appear personally at every promotional event or in each commercial. You can use his digital clone instead.'"[10] While there is neither need nor time to retread through scholarly and popular writing about virtual reality, or what Margaret Morse terms "virtualities as fictions of presence,"[11] it is interesting to get a glimpse of future plans for digital media's wide-ranging capacities from within the restricted spaces of the industry's managerial class.

Digitextuality's visual aesthetics and technological virtuosity are most recognizable on television in special-effects-driven texts such as: (1) commercials, many shot on film (e.g., the striking *Blade Runner*-inspired First Union Bank ad campaign or the Cingular Wireless' *2001: A Space Odyssey*-inspired depiction of unbound connectivity); (2) music videos (e.g., Jennifer Lopez's "Waiting for Tonight" and Korn's "Freak on a Leash"), and (3) science fiction shows like *The X-Files* and *Outer Limits*. What they all share is computerized textual production and image manipulation using high end digital editing, two- and three-dimensional painting and compositing software compatible with both film and video.[12]

Another important marker of digitextuality in the televisual flow of naturalistic, fantastic, and realistic images is the presence, especially, of commercial images that stand out due to their *sumptuous color saturation*, or that move from Technicolor to what I am calling "*techno*color." Where the exuberant coloring schemes in postwar 1940s Technicolor musicals countered the expressive but gloomly black-and-white chiaroscuro tones of mid- 1940s film noir, contenporary film and video production make use of digital paint tools to effectively and seamlessly merge these seemingly incommensurate modalities. For example, in commercials for luxury automobiles, makeup and hair products, and telecommunications and tourism businesses the color-saturation levels separating these income-generating texts from television's high-cost regular programming is stark. To capture the eyeballs of mass numbers of viewers, television ads use digital software tools like Amazon 2D and 3D (a digital paint system for film and high-definition TV) to intensify their products' look.[13] either as muted color intensities diffused with black or white tonalities, or fully enriched RGB (red, green, and blue) color filters that often seem to trump Technicolor's excesses in Hollywood musicals and melodramas from the 1940s to 1960s. Successful global soap operas like CBS's *The Bold and the Beautiful* and *The Young and the Restless* now simulcast in HDTV, and effects-driven prime-time shows such as CBS's hit drama *CSI* (*Crime Scene Investigation*) often hold their own against the digitally enhanced high production values of high-income-generating commercials. With the incredible allure of such lush, sumptuous, and compelling imagery, an assertion of one CBS promo for *CSI* makes us aware of the stakes involved here. Promoting the show's remarkable popularity and buzz, the promo states. "A lot's been said about *CSI*. One thing is certain: you can't look away."

To ensure that we don't avert our gaze, television producers are experimenting with several strategies to keep us looking, including the pervasive use of data-compression techniques, and program tie-ins with the Internet. Most characteristic in this regard is the obvious embrace of what I am calling the *congested* or *overwhelmed image* by cable networks such as CNN, MSNBC, Fox, and Court-TV. The fact that cable television's news and information programs increasingly construct new episte-mologies of the screen where images are frequently overrun by word texts indicates that some media critics' lamentations about "the rise of the image, the fall of the word" in modern culture apparently were premature.[14] Instead, the apparent parity between video image and text combinations on television is symptomatic of that industry's desperate mirnicry of the so-called information-rich look of commercial websites. Where CNN's *Headline News* was at the forefront, and continues to lead among all the others who followed in this practice, the events of September 11, 2001, upped the ante. Now virtually all networks and programs have transformed and redeployed the long-standing public service function of the emergency news crawl into a round-the-clock (24/7) attention-grabbing "ticker" device or contrivance. Shows like ABC's *The View* and others attempt to accommodate the industry's dis-comfiture with the early stages of television and Internet convergence, imploring audiences to "go to our website *after four o'clock*" for additional information covered on the program. To have it both ways, the shows promote their Internet content in the last minutes of the program to avoid competing with themselves and others for the dwindling television audience.[15]

A less successful approach to countering the Internet's poaching on its highly valued youth audience and its ideological "gatekeeping function" was the produc-tion of Generation X television shows like UPN's now defunct *Level 9* and *Freakylinks* – with messages implving that kids avoid the dangers of the Net by sim-ply watching it on TV-sutured to the programs' young, hip, and attractive hackers working as government agents. More explicit, however, were television's shrill demonizing and scapegoating of the Internet and video games in the 1999 Columbine High School shooting tragedy, which essentially indicted them "as virtual accom-plices to mass murder."[16] Traditional media messages of new media culpability con-tinue today with the profiting of of the Internet with child endangerment, pornography, and video games with excessive violence.

How We Experience Digitextuality

An important part ot our ability to experience digitextuality as a visual pleasure or as a potent force tor either good or ill seems intertwined with our expectations tor digital media's interactive capacities. No sooner had virtual communities' popu-larization of the Internet relay chat (IRC), bulletin boards, usencts, listservs, MUDs (multiuser domains), MOOs (multiuser object-oriented environments), and mul-tiplayer, text-based computer games oriented people toward a view ot interactivity that advances interpersonal communication and "rules of social interactions [that] are built, not received" than the corporate interests taking over the Web necessarily curtailed this vision.[17] In *Life on the Screen*, Sherry Turkle describes how these and other experiences of the web's interactivity continue to make it a formidable rival for traditional media concerns. Interactivity constructed by "old" media restricts its functioning through predetermined, binary logics (i.e. the ubiquitous "yes" or "no" survey/poll questions), or narrowly focused and limited e-mail commentary tied to TV and print texts. In contrast, Turkle observes, "it is on the Internet that our confrontations with technology as it collides with our sense of human identity are fresh, even raw" (10). A quote by an avid computer-games player articulates well the exchange-value problematic of tradiational media where digital media's version of interactivity is concerned: "This is more real than my real life" (10). Unfortunately, the current media-merger mania that holds the maturing information age in its grips signals nothing less than postmodern society's predictable return to the vertical integration schemes of the early film industry. This means that the corporation's vision of interactivity will eviscerate the more expansive vision of the Internet's early days. Convergence media determined by the economic realignment of big media conglomerates, the Federal Communications Commission's (FCC) 1996 Telecommunications Act, the 1998 Digital Millennium Copyright Act (DMCA), and deregulation policies are the true millennial (or Y2K-year 2000) threat that we should fear and fight.[18] In fact, as globalization gets further advanced by the tidal wave of actual and proposed corporate media mergers (creating such giants as AOL Time Warner and Disney ABC; the News Corporation and Twentieth Century Fox; Bertelsmann, Double-day Random House, and RCA Victor, Scagrams and Universal; General Electric and NBC, Viacom and CBS, and MCI and Spring), these mega-corporations threaten to usurp the societal reproduction function of the Althusserian ideological state apparatus (ISA) with an even more potent ideological corporate apparatus (ICA).

In support of my own transposition, I proffer Bill Gates's Microsoft empire as emblematic of the new media convergence industries' powerful role in ensuring the "ruling ideas" thesis through the political economy of the post-Marxist era ICA. When thinking about this idea of the ICA it is not difficult to view the congested and overwhelmed televisual images on CNN, MSNBC and Fox as visual renderings of Louis Althusser's elaboration on the Marxist base and superstructure metaphor lor capitalism. At the level of form and composition, for example, both the static and streaming text positioned at the bottom of the televisual frame that conveys stock market information and news headlines evokes the base. The top portion, containing live, in-studio images of reporters and videotaped images of current events, becomes an articulation of the superstructure. Such an image-text condensation of important news and information functions efficiently to reify or naturalize our economic mode of production and societal propagation. Finally, it is likely not an overstatement to say that the once attempted merger of MCI and Sprint (at $108 billion, the *New York Times* estimates it would have been "the largest acquisition in corporate history"[19]) heralds even more empire building, and power consolidation, by the ICA.

In shifting my discussion of digitextuality now to its most pervasive experiential phenomena in our contemporary society, I also argue for a reembodiment thesis in digital culture in terms of an intervention into the hype of new-media formalism. I would like to demonstrate how the hyperbolic discourse of the posthuman in the digital age might be rethought to recuperate a politics of the body in the wake of digital formalism's decade-long preoccupation with an art-for-art's-sake depoliticization imperative.

Click Theory and the Lure of Sensory Plenitude

An important part of understanding digitextuality centers on what I see as an emerging "click fetish" in the production and consumption of new-media discourses and practices. I propose that a fetishizing of the term *click*, and its attendant iconography (the ever-present computer mouse, its onscreen arrow or white finger icon), operate through new media's lure of a sensory plenitude presumably available simply, instantaneously, and pleasurably with any one of several clicking apparatuses. These newer apparatuses of click pleasure include video game joysticks, wireless cell phones with Internet connectivity, PDAs (personal digital assistants), and handheld computers, what David Pogue and others term "Internet appliances."[20] Also included here are the more familiar apparatuses of click, the TV remote control device and cable TV boxes, both newly adapted for MSN TV services, Replay, and the TiVo systems of convergence media applications, what "old" media executives call PVRs (personal video recorders.[21] As these new proliferating hardware devices saturate our physical spaces and consume our mental energies, they turn us, some argue, into either empowered posthuman cyborgs or disempowered lobotomized borgs in "the cult of information"[22] – that is, New Age couch potatoes. The question is, How can we better understand the emerging codes of digitextuality in our information society and our putative pleasurable situatedness therein? There must be some pleasure to be had – otherwise, why buy? Why buy the rhetoric of plenitude or the expensive machines and services of click culture?

Privileging the Body in the Nature-versus-Science Split in Click Culture

Relying on several observations found in Jean-François Lyotard's book *The Inhuman*, especially the chapters "Can Thought Go On without a Body?" and "Rewriting Modernity," I imagine click theory as a useful heuristic engagement with what Lyotard terms a "meta-function." For Lyotard, a meta-function is a "faculty of being able to change levels of referentiality" almost instantaneously.[23] Clearly, this idea of changing levels of referentiality corresponds to the operations of the Internet and web-based environments with their celebrated hypertext structures and linking functions, and even the channel surfing between television programs. However, its implications for our concerns will be manifest as we progress. As fruitful as the concept of bodily transcendence via the Gibsonian "consensual hallucination" of cyberspace has been for cyberculture and technoculture discourses – especially for imagining a breakout of postmodern society's prison house of socially constructed identities (race, gender, and class constraints) – not all new media theorists are satisfied with this utopian spin, this writer included. Following Lyotard, I too want to understand more precisely and problematize this seemingly reified sublation of body to mind, especially in digital culture and in practices of digitextuality.

The click fetish, then, signifies the persistence of the body despite the powerful rhetoric of the posthuman in new media figurations.[24] Click theory can be viewed as positing a counterpoint to a narratological privileging of disembodied subjectivity in cyberculture.[25] For click pleasure is predicated on an urge to retain the primacy of the body (or the meat), and to rescue it from the phenomenological scrap heap in much of the nature-versus-science debate of our technological era. The fetishizing of the click action, and click pleasure's lure of sensory plenitude, inhere in the bodily tactitity of the touch – touching the mouse, the keyboard, the touchpad and screens, and wireless keys. It is not so much that the desire to transcend the body is contested but that the sense of touch, on which this supposed transcendence is predicated, always returns the repressed body in a fort/da move of repression and recall. As voice, fingerprint, eyeball recognition and other biomechanical technologies develop, it seems to me that activating the click commands will only intensify a click pleasure – one rooted in the body, as the sensory aspect of speech and other kinesics call forth new modalities of corporeal interactive plenitude.[26] The bottom line for Lyotard, and I concur, is that "thought is inseparable from the phenomenological body" (23).

Double-click: on Hyperlinks and Rhizoplane Structures

Again, the new visual and aural representations that define digital texts, such as websites, CD-ROMs, DVDs, and computer games (arcade, console, handheld, and online varieties), construct new epistemologies of the screen that instantiate their own reading strategies, encodings, deciphering practices, and reception contexts. Click theory can allow us to think about the ontologies of new digital images and sound in terms of Immanuel Kant's exhortation to "let things come as they present themselves" (quoted in Lyotard, 32). And, in digital media, things present themselves most often as hypertexts, often designed according to a rhizoplane-like structure of links (the term *rhizoplane* means "the external surface of roots together with closely adhering soil particles and debris").[27] I find this particular terminology and definition metaphorically apt for characterizing the densely packed image, text, and soundscape combinations of websites, video-game menus and contemporary television programming content increasingly married to the Internet and other digital forms – in a word, *digitextuality*, as I have previously mentioned.

It is this promise of infinite narrative possibilies suggested by linkages in hypertexts and digitextuality that corresponds to my idea of sensory plenitude. Digital media texts are capable of simultaneously engaging our senses of sight, sound, touch, and now thought in a heightened manner that is different in degree, if not in kind, from more traditional media texts. Thus, not only do digital media hypertexts promise an immersive bodily experience, but they also present a point-and-click fetish object of unlimited choice and sensory experience. This raises the much debated issue of a presumed *new* media interactivity supposedly far superior to a putative *old* media passivity. But, if "Click Here" is the command gateway to the plenitude of the World Wide Web and global and local experiences, where do we position traditional and new televisual communication on this problematic active/passive media consumption continuum?

The Interactive/Passive Media Problematic and the Limits of Click

Because the rhetorics of *old* and *new* new media specifications have unsuitably constructed a binary system of media transmission and reception, I am compelled to question this situational logic by problematizing the construction of, say, TV viewership and traditional print readership as passive consumption in opposition to the view of computer usage as interactive. Again, it is Lyotard who offers me cover. I borrow from his concern about the "already thought" or the inscribed (20). Since the hypertexts' linking functions are delimited by an author's circumscriptions or choices, we can view computer *linking* as a form of interacting with the already thought – the author-programmers' preestablished inscriptions. (That said, it is the case that authors often abdicate their authorial function to those linked texts that escape their discursive control.) Be that as it may, the already thought is compelling. Lyotard argues, because "[t]the unthought hurts" and "we are comfortable with the already thought" (20).

I also find Lyotard's comments about our "faith in the inexhaustibility of the perceivable" (17) useful as I think through the sensory plenitude idea and the "mouse-over," or rollover applets of hypertexts and linking. As we become increasingly habituated to hypertexts' encodings of plenitude or "value added" content by "clicking here," for "more" data, I want to suggest that a Pavlovian effect charges the dynamics of mouse-overs and rollovers. Here, our gateway to unlimited sensory pleasures (or displeasures) seems assured as the ubiquitous arrow pointer icon gets immediately transformed into the white finger icon when rolled or "moused" over digital texts that activate supplements to the main texts that "radiate from it in the manner of branches from a tree."[28] In this way, I argue click theory's lure of sensory plenitude functions to affirm Lyotard's idea of our "faith in the inexhaustibility of the perceivable." In other words, by clicking on websites' embedded hotlinks we are instantly transported to other data fields within the site or to separate websites linked to the primary one.

Recently, one cable company advertisement promoted the telecommunications industry's new direct subscriber lines (DSL) service that sums up this idea perfectly.

A man is surfing the Internet when he gets a voiced computer message warning him that he has reached "the end of the Internet." He is told, "Please go back." We all recognize within this fictional scenario the essential utility of the "back" button when web surfing to reorient ourselves after going astray amid the inexhaustible information overload of the Internet's ever-increasing but always perceivable content. While we also recognize the fallacy of actually "reaching the end of the Internet," its symbolic or metaphoric relevance to our limited tolerance for experiencing the Web's "inexhaustibility of the perceivable" rings true. In fact, the success of Internet search engines like HotBot, Google, Yahoo, and others, despite the infamous dot-com bust, has been sustained precisely because of their reliable management of the web's daunting, inexhaustible data stream. Now they are what I term *information retailers*.

Unfortunately, today, with the corporate takeover of the web, the apparent unlimited choice of data distributed by these search engines is increasingly ordered and prioritized in ways analogous to the lucrative shelf ordering of retail commodities in supermarkets and superstores like WalMart and others. Google, at this writing, is in a legal dispute with Overture Services over a patent "that lets businesses, for a fee, have Web sites listed in the results of Internet queries."[29] While the outcome of this court-battle is uncertain, it is certain that businesses are not lined up to pay for a space on the *bottom* shelf of a search engine's popular "keyword" listings. The gravity of this situation becomes quite apparent when we consider the following context. The web's content may be inexhaustible, but our very human or bodily attention spans and leisure time are not. Thus it is here that the commercial discussed above captures and conveys the conflict between the Nietzscheian will to post-human power and the bodily limitations of physical possibility.

Another area of concern in my click theory argument focuses on some aesthetics of digital texts. When we stop to consider what makes websites alluring despite their semiotic densities and navigational mysteries, or "soil particles and debris," then Lyotard is again instructive, with his discussion of "the concept of the bit," the tyrannical unit of information restriction that characterizes the smallest, yet essential, component of computerized data and information systems. I want to contrast this computerized bit to the televisual "bite," and consider how these shorthand communicative cues engage with Lyotard's discussion of "pleasures in the beautiful" or "a promise of happiness" (33–34). I begin with Lyotard's statement that "Every discourse, including that of science or philosophy is only a perspective, a *Weltanschauuny*" (29). For Lyotard, this perspectivization is most acute and discernible through historical knowledge and writing that consists in a double-move of signification most familiar in the English form of "'putting down' – to write down and to repress," which also "suggests both inscription or recording and discredit" (29–30). For Lyotard, then this is a form of rewriting, "a double gesture, forwards and backwards" (30). What this means is that to construct a discourse, some information is foregrounded and some erased, some privileged and some discredited. But, most important for Lyotard, all this requires an anamnesis – a reminiscence and a working through, "a business of free imagination" and "the deployment of time between 'not yet,' 'no longer' and 'now'" (35). It is precisely these free-floating imaginative operations that the new technologies inhibit, in Lyotard's view. And that inhibition is most inherent in the basic unit of new technology information transfer, "the concept of the bit, the [basic] unit of information" (34); for as Lyotard puts it, "When we're dealing with bits, there's no longer any question of free forms given here and now to sensibility and the imagination. On the contrary, they are units of information conceived by computer engineering and definable at all linguistic levels – lexical, symbolic, syntactic, rhetorical and the rest. They are assembled into systems following a set of possibilities (a 'menu') under the control of the programmer" (34–35). Although Lyotard's deterministic logic miscalculates the breakout possibilities of hacking through the tyranny of the bit, his sober reflections on the limitations of new media's click culture and its attendant lure of sensory plenitude deserve contemplation. Beyond traditional media's ideologically inflected inscriptions, new-media encryptions get advanced along more restrictive lines of information codification, as anyone (other than hackers) attempting to manipulate or circumvent computerized information protocols quickly discovers via pop-up dialogue boxes alerting one to the errors of one's intent.

Remediating Classical Media Aesthetics through New-media Apparatuses of Click Culture

Finally, I would like to consider how the click fetish and sensory plenitude of new media production and consumption can be theorized as digitextual "remediations" of classical and traditional media aesthetics and forms.[30] The usefulness of articulating new-media practices' imbrication in old-media precedents is not to proffer a reduction of the former to mere rearticulations of the latter but rather to better outline new media's seductive allures. Moreover, this looking back enables us to grasp how contemporary media users and audiences decode and understand digital technologies' signifying practices and potent representational economies. In fact, Vivian Sobchack, following Martin Heidegger, makes the important observation that "technology is never merely 'used,' never merely instrumental. It is always also 'incorporated' and 'lived' by the human beings who engage it within a structure of meanings and metaphors in which subject-object relations are cooperative, co-constitutive, dynamic, and reversible."[31]

In constructing my click theory idea, I share Peter Lunenfeld's view that there are "new artistic communities, emergent technocultures, being built around computer-driven media," and "cybernetic tools" such as "word processors, nonlinear digital video editing systems, database managers, Web server softwares, interactive multimedia programs," and "virtual reality 'world-building' kits."[32] My concern, however, is with how these cybernetic tools recycle, recode, and redeploy classical-media modes and codes to heighten contemporary media users' and consumers' affective responses to new-media functions – especially the computer's immersive click functions. In his influential essay "The Myth of Total Cinema," André Bazin provides the most nuanced way of thinking about how old and new media practices intersect without simplistically conflating the two and thereby losing the specificities of either. He writes, "The cinema is an idealistic phenomenon. The concept men had of it existed so to speak fully armed in their minds, as if in some platonic heaven, and what strikes us most of all is the obstinate resistance of matter to ideas."[33] Here we easily recognize that the advent of what Lunenfeld calls digital media's "cybernetic tools" is the near fulfillment of the idealistic phenomenon that early cinema merely promised. Bazin writes that "it is clear that all the definitive stages of the invention of the cinema had been reached before the requisite conditions had been fulfilled"; what he is arguing here is that it had long been our desire to achieve "a total and complete representation of reality ... the reconstruction of a perfect illusion of the outside world in sound, color, and relief" (20). In mounting his refutation of the "absurd" belief that silent cinema somehow represented "a state of primal perfection" jeopardized or contaminated by the additions of sound, color, and three-dimensional technology, Bazin hyperbolically states, "In short, cinema has not yet been invented!" (21).

I propose that digital media's new technological advances bring us closer to a realization of Bazin's ideas in the myth of total cinema – in short, finally, cinema *has* been invented! Its invention is achieved through magical digital tools and our unending quest for "a recreation of the world in its own image, unburdened by the freedom of interpretation of the artist or the irreversibility of time" (21). Indeed, click culture now brings us the entire world through the Internet and the web, DVD and CD-ROM, Quick Time and RealPlayer technologies, and satellites where images do not suffer the ravages and degradations of time associated with analog image production. Additionally, MP3 and other digital sound technologies bring us pristine sounds, and cybernetic toolboxes give us sumptuous color, three dimensionaltiy, and virtual reality systems that Bazin could not fathom outside a mythological future vision.

In "What is Digital Cinema," Lev Manovich's observations that "digital filmmakers work with 'elastic reality'" due to digital technologies' "compositing, animating and morphing" features is nothing if not a confirmation of Rudolf Arnheim's 1933 prediction.[34] In "The Complete Film," Arnheim predicts that "The technical development of the motion picture will soon carry the mechanical imitation of nature to an extreme."[35] Although Arnheim is often judged as a silent cinema purist obsessed with denigrating the advances of sound and color (which is true to a certain extent), the reality is that he feared a one-dimensional cinematic hegemony. He writes, "In itself, the perfection of the 'complete' film need not be a catastrophe – if silent film, sound film, and colored sound film were allowed to exist along side it" (159). Despite his miscalculations, Arnheim was inadvertently prescient when he noted that with the arrival of the complete film, "Film will no longer be able in any sense to be considered as a separate art" (49). And with the digital technologies' engendering of convergence media, some of Arhneim's fears of the cinema's eclipse are being realized, if differently than he could have imagined in 1933.

For me, digital media technologies' abilities simultaneously to reproduce and manipulate reality with an unprecedented representational economy and efficacy turn traditional notions of mimesis and diegesis on their heads. And due to their abilities to construct new and synthetic representational strategies and possibilities seamlessly, they not only advance previously unimagined representations of ideas and desires, but are also able to portray the sublime, and that once believed-in idea of the unrepresentable. For click theory, this means that digital media's computerized hypertext structures and linking functions promise and convince us that clicking on hot links, RealPlayer and Quick Time movies embedded within digital texts virtually ensure that the complete film and total cinema have arrived, and that they are available on our desktops, our televisions, and in the numerous handheld computer devices that characterize our new cultural dominant – the age of ubiquitous computing via digitextuality.

As we all set out to articulate key aspects of digital technologies' medium specifities, the relevance of Jean Epstein and Germaine Dulac's elaborations on Jean Delluc's notion of *photogenie* – a conceptualization of the cinema's unique properties or "purest expression" – becomes increasingly apparent. In terms of click theory, I see its lure of sensory plenitude as a sort of recoding of the idea of the cinema of attractions. Again, the impulse here is not to posit an old-media restriction on new-media image processing, but rather to recognize the usefulness of previous critical and theoretical insights for thinking through what is truly new about new-media discourses and practices. At the same time, it is difficult not to see how the much hyped "bullet-time" and "hypertime" slow-motion, "Techno-slammin' visual" special effects of the films *The Matrix* (1999),[36] *Crouching Tiger, Hidden Dragon* (2001). and *Clock Stoppers* (2002) become new media iterations of Jean Epstein's photogenie ideal.

For her part, Germaine Dulac enables us to grasp the need to appreciate and approach a new medium on its own terms and in its own time. What Dulac advocates is the necessity of recognizing what she calls "the moral essence of the cinematic, an art born of our time, and for which we must make an effort, in order to avoid the misunderstanding which so often meets unexpected revelations."[37] (36) Like her contemporary Dziga Vertov, Dulac sees in cinema a second, more powerful eye available for mankind's benefit, "an eye more powerful than our own and which sees things we cannot see" (30).

In her desire to see the cinema "freed from its chains and be given its true personality" (37), Dulac points out a way for us to attend to what it is that digital media technologies bring to the changed moment and demands of our own twentieth- and twenty-first-century times. Unfortunately, the data merchants of digital cinema understand all too well the potentialities of a future cinema to tap human beings' thoughts and feelings, as Dulac desired. If you accept the premise that in many ways digital cinema's technological advancements fulfill Dulac's prediction of "pure cinema," Bazin's "total cinema," and Arnheim's "complete film" then you might more easily apprehend my click theory of new media's potent lure of sensory plenitude.

For now, not only are our thoughts, feelings and desires easily rendered and expressed through new media imaging, but our abilities to create and consume those once elusive imaginary ideals as Dulac sets forth are taken for granted and commodified through the various apparatuses of click technology. "Click Here" now means a new porousness of sorts, of such once rigidly constructed geopolitical, national, cultural, technological, economical, gendered, racial, class, and even temporal boundaries. Again, what motivates this brief detour through some key classical film theory ideas is the urge to temper the hype of the "new" in digital media aesthetics and formalist structures with a sober reflection on its similarities to discourses of the past. But the caveat, which Epstein, Dulac, Arnheim, and Bazin surely would have lamented, is that permeation of all these boundaries and the ability for media consumers to alter their spectatorial statuses (either as superconsumers or consumer-producers) is now available *only* if one possesses today's sophisticated (read: *expensive*) apparatuses of click.

I began this latter discussion by interrogating digital technologies' formidable impact on our increasingly mediated lives and technology-driven culture. I particularly wanted to point out some conceptual limitations within some of the much-touted posthuman logics and rhetorics, and I attempted to demonstrate how the very notion that the physical and material apparatuses that presumably make transcending the body possible ultimately fails. An important reality of digitextuality is that the apparatuses of click – the primal interfaces granting access to cyberspace, computer-enhanced television, pocket computers, wireless and handheld devices – *always return us to the body activating and making sense of the interface.*

NOTES

1. Wheeler Winston Dixon discusses Godard's views on the changing nature of the cinema in *The Films of Jean-Luc Godard* (Albany: State University of New York Press, 1997). Michael Nash elaborates on the notion of a posttelevision age in his article. "Vision after Television: Technocultural Convergence, Hypermedia, and the New Media Arts Field." in *Resolutions: Contemporary Video Practices*, ed. Michael Renov and Erika Suderburg (Minneapolis: University of Minnesota Press, 1996), 382–99.
2. In their books, both Lev Manovich and Peter Lunenfeld provide excellent and detailed treatises on some specifics of new media's debt to earlier visual media apparatuses, conventions, and philosophies. See Lev Manovich, *The Language of Digital Media* (Cambridge, Mass.: MIT Press, 2001) and Peter Lunenleld, *Snap to Grid: A User's Guide to Digital Arts, Media, and Cultures* (Cambridge, Mass.: MIT Press, 2000).
3. Julia Kristeva, "Revolution in Poetic Language," in *The Kristeva Reader*, ed. Toril Moi (New York: Columbia University Press, 1986), 111: hereafter, page numbers will be cited parenthetically in the text.
4. In *Growing Up Digital: The Rise of the Net Generation*. Don Tapscott provides an interesting look at how newer generations negotiate their changed status in the information age. As he puts it, "kids use computers for activities that seem to go hand-in-hand with our understanding of what constitutes traditional childhood. They use the technology to play, learn, communicate, and form relationships as children have always done. On the other hand, the digital media is creating an environment where such activities of

childhood are changing dramatically and may, for better or worse, accelerate child development"; Tapscott, *Growing Up Digital: The Rise of the Net Generation* (New York: McGraw-Hill, 1998).

5. Wheeler Winston Dixon. *It Looks at You: The Returned Gaze of Cinema* (Albany: State University of New York Press, 1995), 37.

6. David Bordwell and Kristin Thompson, *Film Art: An Introduction* (New York: Knopf, 1997), 78.

7. Lev Manovich. *The Language of New Media* (Cambridge, Mass.: MIT Press, 2001), 25.

8. Jean Baudrillard, *Simulations*, trans. Paul Foss. Paul Patton, and Philip Beitchman (New York: Semiotext(e), 1983), 142.

9. Stentz's full essay, "So Real They're Virtual," can be accessed online at the Metro paper's online archive <http://www.metroactive.com.../metro/09.03.98/virtual celeb-9835.htm>.

10. Jeffrey Lotman, quoted in Stentz, "So Real They're Virtual."

11. Margaret Morse, *Virtualities: Television, Media Art, and Cyberculture* (Bloomington: Indiana University Press, 1998), 1.

12. For specific technical information about the software systems used on these and many television and film texts, see the interactivefx company's website at <http://www.ifx.com>.

13. See interactivefx.at <http://www.ifx.com>.

14. Mitchell Stephens, *The Rise of the Image the Full of the Word* (New York: Oxford University Press, 1998).

15. Television has been competing with the Internet and other new media for nearly a decade, and the situation has destabilized the networks' traditional business model. In his article "Canceled, 'Adventures in Television': Was the Hook Too Quick?" (Los Angeles Times, June 22, 2002, F17) Allan Johnson reports that, "They're desperate at this point'. ... And desperation leads to shows being on for two weeks. ... With cable, the Internet, DVDs and more competing for viewers' attention, all networks usually can't wait for a show to find an audience, even if it might eventually be there."

16. Anna Everett, "P.C Youth Violence: What's the Internet or Video Gaming Got to Do with It?" *Denver Law Review* 77, no. 4 (2000): 690.

17. Sherry Turkle, *Life on the Screen: Identity in the Age of the Internet* (New York: Touchstone, 1995), 10; hereafter, page numbers will be cited parenthetically in the text.

18. Wayne Overbeck, a professor of communication, provides an important historical overview of the significance of the DMCA in his article "Let's Give a Toast to Prohibition, Circa 2000," *Los Angeles Times*, July 30, 2000, M5.

19. For details of this history-making deal and more, see Laura M. Holson and Seth Schiesel's article. "MCI to Buy Sprint in Swap of Stock for $108 Billion," *New York Times*. October 5, 1999, C13.

20. David Pogue, "Year of Living Geekely: Even the Dogs Evolved," *New York Time*, 27 December 2001, Dl.

21. For a complete discussion of the PVR revolution, see Staci D. Kramer's essay "Content's King" at *Cableworld* <www.inside.com/product/produn_p...0B8A11C30373&CONTENT=ARTK:LE&PRINT=triie>.

22. I am posing Donna Haraway's utopic cyborg vision against Theodore Roszak's more pessimistic view for argument's sake.

23. Jean-François Lyotard, "Can Thought Go On Without a Body?" in *The Inhuman*, trans. Geoffrey Bennington and Rachel Bowlby (Stanford, Calif.: Stanford University Press, 1991), 13; hereafter, page numbers will be cited parenthetically in the text.

24. See, for example, various positions espoused on the concept of the posthuman in Judith Halberstam and Ira Livingston's anthology *Posthuman Bodies* (Bloomington: Indiana University Press, 1995), especially the introductory essay "Posthuman Bodies."

25. *Wired* magazine's August 2001 edition has two articles promoting the posthuman ideal; see "The Next Brainiacs," by John Hockenberry (94–105), and "Let's Make Your Head Interactive." by Jennifer kahn (106–15).

26. *Kinesics* is defined as "the study of body movements, gestures, facial expressions, etc., as a means of communication"; "Kinesics," in *Random House Webster's College Dictionary* (New York; Random House, 2001), 731.

27. This term, *rhizoplane*, which is defined in the 1994 *Merriam-Webster's New Collegiate Dictionary*, does not appear in the later *Random House Webster's College Dictionary*, published in 2000. The 1994 *Merriam-Webster's New Collegiate Dictionary* – which is the later (and still most recent) edition of the 1977 dictionary – does indeed bear a definition (and still the **exact same** definition) for *rhizoplane* on p. 1005. The fact that the 2000 edition *Random House Webster's* does not include the term reflects only the fact that this book comes from a different publisher, and that this publisher chose not to include the term. Comparing dictionaries that bear the name *Webster* means little these days, as the name itself is no longer copyrighted and virtually **every** dictionary uses it to add an air of authority. What does this say about our ability to know word meanings and etymologies with any sense of certitude beyond a particular corporate reorganization of knowledge regimes? *Merriam-Webster's New Collegiate Dictionary*, 10th ed. (Spring-field, Mass.: Merriam-Webster, 1994), 1005.

28. George Landow, *Hyper/Text/Theory* (Baltimore: Johns Hopkins University Press, 1994), 23.

29. "Google Seeks to Void Overture's Patents," *Los Angeles Times*, June 20, 2002, C2.

30. I borrow this terminology from Jay David Bolter and Richard Grusin, *Remediation: Understanding New Media* (Cambridge, Mass.: MIT Press, 1999).

31. Vivian Sobchack, "The Scene of the Screen: Envisioning Cinematic and Electronic Presence," in *Electronic Media and Technoculture*, ed. John Thornton Caldwell (New Brunswick, N.J.: Rutgers University Press), 138.

32. Lunenfeld, *Snap to Grid*, 3, 5.

33. André Bazin, "The Myth of Total Cinema," (Berkeley and Los Angeles: University of California Press, 1967), 17: hereafter, page numbers will he cited parenthetically in the text.

34. Lev Manovich, "What Is Digital Cinema?" <http://www-apparitions.ucsd.edu/~manovich/text/digital-cinema.html>, 5.

35. Rudolph Arnheim, "The Complete Film," *Film As Art* (Berkeley and Los Angeles: University of California Press, 1957), 154: hereafter, page numbers will be cited parenthetically in the text.

36. These are some of the descriptive terms used on the packaging literature that comes with the DVD version of *The Matrix* now available at video retail stores.

37. Germaine Dulac, "The Essence, of the Cinema: The Visual Idea" (1925), reprinted in *The Avant-Garde Film: A Reader of Theory and Criticism*, ed. P. Adams Sitney (New York: New York University Press. 1978), 36; hereafter, page numbers will be cited parenthetically in the text.

4 THE DOUBLE LOGIC OF REMEDIATION

Jay David Bolter and Richard Grusin

"This is not like TV only better," says Lenny Nero in the futuristic film *Strange Days*. "This is life. It's a piece of somebody's life. Pure and uncut, straight from the cerebral cortex. You're there. You're doing it, seeing it, hearing it … feeling it." Lenny is touting to a potential customer a technological wonder called "the wire." When the user places the device over her head, its sensors make contact with the perceptual centers in her brain. In its recording mode, the wire captures the sense perceptions of the wearer; in its playback mode, it delivers these recorded perceptions to the wearer. If the ultimate purpose of media is indeed to transfer sense experiences from one person to another, the wire threatens to make all media obsolete. Lenny mentions television, but the same critique would seem to apply to books, paintings, photographs, film, and so on. The wire bypasses all forms of mediation and transmits directly from one consciousness to another.

The film *Strange Days* is less enthusiastic about the wire than Lenny and his customers. Although the wire embodies the desire to get beyond mediation, *Strange Days* offers us a world fascinared by the power and ubiquity of media technologies. Los Angeles in the last two days of 1999, on the eve of "2K," is saturated with cellular phones, voice- and text-based telephone answering systems, radios, and bill-board-sized television screens that constitute public media spaces. In this media-filled world, the wire itself is the ultimate mediating technology, despite – or indeed because of – the fact that the wire is designed to efface itself, to disappear from the user's consciousness. When Lenny coaches the "actors" who will appear in a pornographic recording, it becomes clear that the experience the wire offers can be as contrived as a traditional film. Although Lenny insists that the wire is "not TV only better," the film ends up representing the wire as "film only better."

Jay David Bolter and Richard Grusin, "The Double Logic of Remediation," pp. 3–15 from Jay David Bolter and Richard Grusin, *Remediation: Understanding New Media* (Cambridge, MA: MIT Press, 1999).

When Lenny himself puts on the wire and closes his eyes, he experiences the world in a continuous, first-person point-of-view shot, which in film criticism is called the "subjective camera."

Strange Days captures the ambivalent and contradictory ways in which new digital media function for our culture today. The film projects our own cultural moment a few years into the future in order to examine that moment with greater clarity. The wire is just a fanciful extrapolation of contemporary virtual reality, with its goal of unmediated visual experience. The contemporary head-mounted display of virtual reality is considerably less comfortable and fashionable and the visual world it generates is far less compelling. Still, contemporary virtual reality is, like the wire in *Strange Days*, an experiment in cinematic point of view. Meanwhile, the proliferation of media in 2K L.A. is only a slight exaggeration of our current media-rich environment, in which digital technologies are proliferating faster than our cultural, legal, or educational institutions can keep up with them. In addressing our culture's contradictory imperatives for immediacy and hypermediacy, this film demonstrates what we call a double logic of *remediation*. Our culture wants both to multiply its media and to erase all traces of mediation: ideally, it wants to erase its media in the very act of multiplying them.

In this last decade of the twentieth century, we are in an unusual position to appreciate remediation, because of the rapid development of new digital media and the nearly as rapid response by traditional media. Older electronic and print media are seeking to reaffirm their status within our culture as digital media challenge that status. Both new and old media are invoking the twin logics of immediacy and hypermediacy in their efforts to remake themselves and each other. To fulfill our apparently insatiable desire for immediacy, "live" point-of-view television programs show viewers what it is like to accompany a police officer on a dangerous raid or to be a skydiver or a race car driver hurtling through space. Filmmakers routinely spend tens of millions of dollars to film on location or to recreate period costumes and places in order to make their viewers feel as if they were "really" there. "Webcams" on the Internet pretend to locate us in various natural environments – from a backyard bird feeder in Indianapolis to a panorama in the Canadian Rockies. In all these cases, the logic of immediacy dictates that the medium itself should disappear and leave us in the presence of the thing represented: sitting in the race car or standing on a mountaincop.

Yet these same old and new media often refuse to leave us alone. Many web sites are riots of diverse media forms – graphics, digitized photographs, animation, and video – all set up in pages whose graphic design principles recall the psychedelic 1960s or dada in the 1910s and 1920s. Hollywood films, such as *Natural Born Killers* and *Strange Days*, mix media and styles unabashedly. Televised news programs featute multiple video streams, split-screen displays, composites of graphics and text – a welter of media that is somehow meant to make the news more perspicuous. Even webcams, which operate under the logic of immediacy, can be embedded in a hypermediated web site, where the user can select from a "jukebox" of webcam images to generate her own paneled display.

As the webcam jukebox shows, our two seemingly contradictory logics not only coexist in digital media today but are mutually dependent. Immediacy depends on hypermediacy. In the effort to create a seamless moving image, filmmakers combine live-action footage with computer compositing and two- and three-dimensional computer graphics. In the effort to be up to the minute and complete, television news producers assemble on the screen ribbons of text, photographs, graphics, and even audio without a video signal when necessary (as was the case during the Persian Gulf War). At the same time, even the most hypermediaced productions strive for their own brand of immediacy. Directors of music videos rely on multiple media and elaborate editing to create an immediate and apparently spontaneous style; they take great pains to achieve the sense of "liveness" that characterizes rock music. The desire for immediacy leads digital media to borrow avidly from each other as well as from their analog predecessors such as film, television, and photography. Whenever one medium seems to have convinced viewers of its immediacy, other media try to appropriate that conviction. The CNN site is hypermediated – arranging text, graphics, and video in multiple panes and windows and joining them with numerous hyperlinks; yet the web site borrows its sense of immediacy from the televised CNN newscasts. At the same time televised newcasts are coming to resemble web pages in their hypermediacy. The team of web editors and designers, working in the same building in Atlanta from which the television news networks are also administered, clearly want their technology to be "television only better." Similarly, one of the most popular genres of computer games is the flight simulator. The action unfolds in real time, as the player is required to monitor the instruments and fly the plane. The game promises to show the player "what it is like to be" a pilot, and yet in what does the immediacy of the experience consist? As in a real plane, the simulated cockpit is full of dials to read and switches to flip. As in a real plane, the experience of the game is that of working an interface, so that the immediacy of this experience is pure hypermediacy.

Remediation did not begin with the introduction of digital media. We can identify the same process throughout the last several hundred years of Western visual representation. A painting by the seventeenth-century artist Pieter Saenredam, a photograph by Edward Weston, and a computer system for virtual reality are different in many important ways, but they are all attempts to achieve immediacy by ignoring or denying the presence of the medium and the act of mediation. All of them seek to put the viewer in the same space as the objects viewed. The illusionistic painter employs linear perspective and "realistic" lighting, while the computer graphics specialist mathematizes linear perspective and creates "models" of shading and illumination. Furthermore, the goal of the computer graphics specialists is to do as well as, and eventually better than, the painter or even the photographer.

Like immediacy, hypermediacy also has its history. A medieval illuminated manuscript, a seventeenth-century painting by David Bailly, and a buttoned and windowed multimedia application are all expressions of a fascination with media. In medieval manuscripts, the large initial capital letters may be elaborately decorated, but they still constitute part of the text itself, and we are challenged to appreciate the integration of text and image. In many multimedia applications, icons and graphics perform the same dual role, in which the images peek out at us through the word ARKANSAS. This dual role has a history in popular graphic design, as a postcard of Coney Island from the early twentieth-century shows. Today as in the past, designers of hypermediated forms ask us to take pleasure in the act of mediation, and even our popular culture does take pleasure. Some hypermediated art has been and remains an elite taste, but the elaborate stage productions of many rock stars are among many examples of hypermediated events that appeal to millions.

[…]

Our primary concern will be with visual technologies, such as computer graphics and the World Wide Web. We will argue that these new media are doing exactly what their predecessors have done: presenting themselves as refashioned and improved versions of other media. Digital visual media can best be understood through the ways in which they honor, rival, and revise linear-perspective painting, photography, film, television, and print. No medium today, and certainly no single media event, seems to do its cultural work in isolation from other media, any more than it works in isolation from other social and economic forces. What is new about new media comes from the particular ways in which they refashion older media and the ways in which older media refashion themselves to answer the challenges of new media.

5 THE DATABASE

Lev Manovich

The Database Logic

After the novel, and subsequently cinema, privileged narrative as the key form of cultural expression of the modern age, the computer age introduces its correlate – the database. Many new media objects do not tell stories; they do not have a beginning or end; in fact, they do not have any development, thematically, formally, or otherwise that would organize their elements into a sequence. Instead, they are collections of individual items, with every item possessing the same significance as any other.

Why does new media favor the database form over others? Can we explain its popularity by analyzing the specificity of the digital medium and of computer programming? What is the relationship between the database and another form that has traditionally dominated human culture – narrative? These are the questions I will address in this section.

Before proceeding, I need to comment on my use of the word *database*. In computer science, *database* is defined as a structured collection of data. The data stored in a database is organized for fast search and retrieval by a computer and therefore, it is anything but a simple collection of items. Different types of databases – hierarchical, network, relational, and object-oriented – use different models to organize data. For instance, the records in hierarchical databases are organized in a treelike structure. Object-oriented databases store complex data structures, called "objects," which are organized into hierarchical classes that may inherit properties from classes higher in the chain.[1]

New media objects may or may not employ these highly structured database models; however, from the point of view of the user's experience, a large proportion of them are databases in a more basic sense. They appear as collections of items on

Lev Manovich, "The Database," pp. 218–36 from Lee Manovich, *The Language of New Media* (Cambridge, MA: MIT Press, 2001).

which the user can perform various operations – view, navigate, search. The user's experience of such computerized collections is, therefore, quite distinct from reading a narrative or watching a film or navigating an architectural site. Similarly, a literary or cinematic narrative, an architectural plan, and a database each present a different model of what a world is like. It is this sense of database as a cultural form of its own that I want to address here. Following art historian Ervin Panofsky's analysis of linear perspective as a "symbolic form" of the modern age, we may even call darabase a new symbolic form of the computer age (or, as philosopher Jean-François Lyotard called it in his famous 1979 book *The Postmodern Condition*, "computerized society"),[2] a new way to structure our experience of ourselves and of the world. Indeed, if after the death of God (Nietzche), rhe end of grand Narratives of Enlightenment (Lyotard), and the arrival of the Web (Tim Berners-Lee), the world appears to us as an endless and unstructured collection of images, texts, and other data records, it is only appropriate that we will be moved to model it as a database. But it is also appropriate that we would want to develop a poetics, aesthetics, and ethics of this database.

Let us begin by documenting the dominance of the database form in new media. The most obvious examples are popular multimedia encyclopedias, collections by definition, as well as other commercial CD-ROM (or DVD), that feature collections of recipes, quotations, photographs, and so on.[3] The identity of a CD-ROM as a storage media is projected onto another plane, thereby becoming a cultural form in its own right. Multimedia works that have "cultural" concent appear to particularly favor the database form. Consider, for instance, the "virtual museums" genre – CD-ROMs that take the user on a tour through a museum collection. A museum becomes a database of images representing its holdings, which can be accessed in different ways – chronologically, by country, or by artist. Although such CD-ROMs often simulate the traditional museum experience of moving from room to room in a continuous trajectory, this narrative method of access does not have any special status in comparison to other access methods offered by CD-ROMs. Thus narrative becomes just one method of accessing data among many. Another example of a database form is a multimedia genre that does not have an equivalent in traditional media – CD-ROMs devoted to a single cultural figure such as a famous architect, film director, or writer. Instead of a narrative biography, we are presented with a database of images, sound recordings, video clips, and/or texts that can be navigated in a variety of ways.

CD-ROMs and other digital storage media proved to be particularly receptive to traditional genres that already had a database-like structure, such as the photo album; they also inspired new database genres, like the database biography. Where the database form really flourished, however, is the Internet. As defined by original HTML, a Web page is a sequential list of separate elements – text blocks, images, digital video clips, and links to other pages. It is always possible to add a new element to the list – all you have to do is to open a file and add a new line. As a result, most Web pages are collections of separate elements – texts, images, links to other pages, or sites. A home page is a collection of personal photographs. A site of a major search engine is a collection of numerous links to other sites (along with a search function, of course). A site of a Web-based TV or radio station offers a collection of video or audio programs along with the option to listen to the current broadcast, but this current program is just one choice among many other programs stored on the site. Thus the traditional broadcasting experience, which consists solely of a real-time transmission, becomes just one element in a collection of options. Similar to the CD-ROM medium, the Web offered fertile ground to already existing database genres (for instance, bibliography) and also inspired the creation of new ones such as sites devoted to a person or a phenomenon (Madonna, the Civil War, new media theory, etc.) that, even if they contain original material, inevitably center around a list of links to other Web pages on the same person or phenomenon.

The open nature of the Web as a medium (Web pages are computer files that can always be edited) means that Web sites never have to be complete; and they rarely are. They always grow. New links are continually added to what is already there. It is as easy to add new elements to the end of a list as it is to insert them anywhere in it. All this further contributes to the antinarrative logic of the Web. If new elements are being added over time, the result is a collection, not a story. Indeed, how can one keep a coherent narrative or any other development trajectory through the material if it keeps changing?

Commercial producers have experimented with ways to explore the database form inherent to new media, with offerings ranging from multimedia encyclopedias to collections of software and collections of pornographic images. In contrast, many artists working with new media at first uncritically accepted the database form as a given. Thus they became blind victims of database logic. Numerous artists' Web sites are collections of multimedia elements documenting their works in other media. In the case of many early artists' CD-ROMs as well, the tendency was to fill all the available storage space with different material – the main work, documentation, related texts, previous works, and so on.

As the 1990s progressed, artists increasingly began to approach the database more critically.[4] A few examples of projects investigating database politics and possible aesthetics are Chris Marker's "IMMEMORY," Olga Lialina's "Anna Karenina Goes to Paradise,"[5] Stephen Mamber's "Digital Hitchcock," and Fabian Wagmister's "... two, three, many Guevaras." The artist who has explored the possibilities of a database most systematically is George Legrady. In a series of interactive multimedia works ("The Anecdoted Archive," 1994; "[the clearing]," 1994; "Slippery Traces," 1996; "Tracing," 1998) he used different types of databases to create "an information structure where stories/things are organized according to multiple thematic connections."[6]

Data and Algorithm

Of course, not all new media objects are explicitly databases. Computer games, for instance, are experienced by their players as narratives. In a game, the player is given a well-defined task – winning the match, being first in a race, reaching the last level, or attaining the highest score. It is this task that makes the player experience the game as a narrative. Everything that happens to her in a game, all the characters and objects she encounters, either take her closer to achieving the goal or further away from it. Thus, in contrast to a CD-ROM and Web database, which always appear arbitrary because the user knows additional material could have been added without modifying the logic, in a game, from the user's point of view, all the elements are motivated (i.e., their presence is justified).[7]

Often the narrative shell of a game ("You are the specially trained commando who has just landed on a lunar base; your task is to make your way to the headquarters occupied by the mutant base personnel ...") masks a simple algorithm well-familiar to the player – kill all the enemies on the current level, while collecting all the treasures it contains; go to the next level and so on until you reach the last level. Other games have different algorithms. Here is the algorithm of the legendary *Tetris:* When a new block appears, rotate it in such a way so char it will complete the top layer of blocks on the bottom of the screen, thus making this layer disappear. The similarity between the actions expected of the player and computer algorithms is too uncanny to be dismissed. While computer games do not follow a database logic, they appear to be ruled by another logic – that of the algorithm. They demand that a player execute an algorithm in order to win.

An algorithm is the key to the game experience in a different sense as well. As the player proceeds through the game, she gradually discovers the rules that operate in the universe constructed by this game. She learns its hidden logic – in short, its algorithm. Therefore, in games in which the game play departs from following an algorithm, the player is still engaged with an algorithm albeit in another way: She is discovering the algorithm of the game itself. I mean this both metaphorically and literally: For instance, in a first-person shooter such as *Quake* the player may eventually notice that, under such and such conditions, the enemies will appear from the left; that is, she will literally reconstruct a part of the algorithm responsible for the game play. Or, in a different formulation of the legendary author of Sim games, Will Wright, "playing the game is a continuous loop between the user (viewing the outcomes and inputting decisions) and the computer (calculating outcomes and displaying them back to the user). The user is trying to build a mental model of the computer model."[8]

... If in physics the world is made of atoms and in genetics it is made of genes, computer programming encapsulates the world according to its own logic. The world is reduced to two kinds of software objects that are complementary to each other – data structures and algorithms. Any process or task is reduced to an algorithm, a final sequence of simple operations that a computer can execute to accomplish a given task. And any object in the world – be it the population of a city, or the weather over the course of a century, or a chair, or a human brain – is modeled as a data structure, that is, data organized in a particular way for efficient search and retrieval.[9] Examples of data structures are arrays, linked lists, and graphs. Algorithms and data structures have a symbiotic relationship. The more complex the data structure of a computer program, the simpler the algorithm needs to be, and vice versa. Together, data structures and algorithms are two halves of the ontology of the world according to a computer.

The computerization of culture involves the projection of these two fundamental parts of computer software – and of the computer's unique ontology – onto the cultural sphere. If CD-ROMs and Web databases are cultural manifestations of one half of this ontology – data structures – then computer games are manifestations of the second half – algorithms. Games (sports, chess, cards, etc.) are one cultural form that require algorithm-like behavior from players; consequently, many traditional games were quickly simulated on computers. In parallel, new genres of computer games such as the first-person shooter came into existence. Thus, as was the case with database genres, computer games both mimic already existing games and create new game genres.

It may appear at first sight that data is passive and algorithms active – another example of the passive-active binary categories so loved by human cultures. A program reads in data, executes an algorithm, and writes out new data. We may recall that before "computer science" and "software engineering" became established names in the computer field, this was called "data processing" – a name which remained in use for the few decades during which computers were mainly associated with performing calculations over data. However, the passive/active distinction is not quite accurate because data does not just exist – it has to be generated. Data creators have to collect data and organize it, or create it from scratch. Texts need to written, photographs need to be taken, video and audio material need to be recorded. Or they need to be digitized from already existing media. In the 1990s, when the new role of the computer as a Universal Media Machine became apparent, already computerized societies went into a digitizing craze. All existing books and videotapes, photographs, and audio recordings started to be fed into computers at an ever-increasing rate. Steven Spielberg created the Shoah Foundation, which videotaped and then digitized numerous interviews with Holocaust survivors; it would take one person forty years to watch all the recorded material. The editors of the journal *Mediamatic*, who devoted a whole issue to the topic of "the storage mania" (Summer 1994) wrote: "A growing number of organizations are embarking on ambitious projects. Everything is being collected: culture, asteroids, DNA patterns, credit records, telephone conversations; it doesn't matter."[10] In 1996, the financial company T. Rowe Price stored eight hundred gigabytes of data; by the fall of 1999 this number rose to ten terabytes.[11]

Once digitized, the data has to be cleaned up, organized, and indexed. The computer age brought with it a new cultural algorithm: reality → media → data → database. The rise of the Web, this gigantic and always changing data corpus, gave millions of people a new hobby or profession – data indexing. There is hardly a Web site that does not feature at least a dozen links to other sites; therefore, every site is a type of database. And, with the rise of Internet commerce, most large-scale commercial sites have become real databases, or rather front-ends to company databases. For instance, in the fall of 1998, Amazon.com, an online bookstore, had three million books in its database; and the maker of the leading commercial database *Oracle* has offered *Oracle 8i*, fully integrated with the Internet and featuring unlimited database size, natural-language queries, and support for all multimedia data types.[12] Jorge Luis Borges's story about a map equal in size to the territory it represents is rewritten as a story about indexes and the data they index. But now the map has become larger than the territory. Sometimes, much larger. Porno Web sites exposed the logic of the Web at its extreme by constantly reusing the same photographs from other porno Web sites. Only rare sites featured the original content. On any given date, the same few dozen images would appear on thousands of sites. Thus, the same data would give rise to more indexes than the number of data elements themselves.

Database and Narrative

As a cultural form, the database represents the world as a list of items, and it refuses to order this list. In contrast, a narrative creates a cause-and-effect trajectory of seemingly unordered items (events). Therefore, database and narrative are natural enemies. Competing for the same territory of human culture, each claims an exclusive right to make meaning out of the world.

In contrast to most games, most narratives do not require algorithm-like behavior from their readers. However, narratives and games are similar in that the user must uncover their underlying logic while proceeding through them – their algorithm. Just like the game player, the reader of a novel gradually reconstructs the algorithm (here I use the term metaphorically) that the writer used to create the settings, the characters, and the events. From this perspective, I can rewrite my earlier equations between the two parts of the computer's ontology and its corresponding cultural forms. Data structures and algorithms drive different forms of computer culture. CD-ROMs, Web sites, and other new media objects organized as databases correspond to the data structure, whereas narratives, including computer games, correspond to algorithm.

In computer programming, data structures and algorithms need each other; they are equally important for a program to work. What happens in the cultural sphere? Do databases and narratives have the same status in computer culture?

Some media objects explicitly follow a database logic in their structure whereas others do not; but under the surface, practically all of them are databases. In general, creating a work in new media can be understood as the construction of an interface to a database. In the simplest case, the interface simply provides access to the underlying database. For instance, an image database can be represented as a page of miniature images; clicking on a miniature will retrieve the corresponding record. If a database is too large to display all of its records at once, a search engine can be provided to allow the user to search for particular records. But the interface can also translate the underlying database into a very different user experience. The user may be navigating a virtual three-dimensional city composed from letters, as in Jeffrey Shaw's interactive installation "Legible City."[13] Or she may be traversing a black-and-white image of a naked body, activating pieces of text, audio, and video embedded in its skin (Harwood's CD-ROM "Rehearsal of Memory.")[14] Or she may be playing with virtual animals that come closer or run away depending upon her movements (Scott Fisher et al., VR installation "Menagerie.")[15] Although each of these works engages the user in a set of behaviors and cognitive activities that are quite distinct from going through the records of a database, all of them are databases. "Legible City" is a database of three-dimensional letters that make up a city. "Rehearsal of Memory" is a database of texts and audio and video clips that are accessed through the interface of a body. And "Menagerie" is a database of virtual animals, including their shapes, movements, and behaviors.

The database becomes the center of the creative process in the computer age. Historically, the artist made a unique work within a particular medium. Therefore the interface and the work were the same; in other words, the level of an interface did not exist. With new media, the content of the work and the interface are separated. It is therefore possible to create different interfaces to the same material. These interfaces may present different versions of the same work, as in David Blair's *Wax Web*.[16] Or they may be radically different from each other, as in Olga Lialina's Last Real Net Art Museum.[17] This is one of the ways in which the principle of *variability* of new media manifests itself. But now we can give this principle a new formulation. *The new media object consists of one or more interfaces to a database of multimedia material.* If only one interface is constructed, the result will be similar to a traditional art object, but this is an exception rather than the norm.

This formulation places the opposition between database and narrative in a new light, thus redefining our concept of narrative. The "user" of a narrative is traversing a database, following links between its records as established by the database's creator. An interactive narrative (which can be also called a *hypernarrative* in an analogy with hypertext) can then be understood as the sum of multiple trajectories through a database. A traditional linear narrative is one among many other possible trajectories, that is, a particular choice made within a hypernarrative. Just as a traditional cultural object can now be seen as a particular case of a new media object (i.e., a new media object that has only one interface), traditional linear narrative can be seen as a particular case of hypernarrative.

This "technical," or "material," change in the definition of narrative does not mean that an arbitrary sequence of database records is a narrative. To qualify as a narrative, a cultural object has to satisfy a number of criteria, which literary theorist Mieke Bal defines as follows: It should contain both an actor and a narrator; it also should contain three distinct levels consisting of the text, the story, and the fabula; and its "contents" should be "a series of connected events caused or experienced by actors."[18] Obviously, not all cultural objects are narratives. However, in the world of new media, the word *narrative* is often used as an all-inclusive term, to cover up the fact that we have not yet developed a language to describe these new strange objects. It is usually paired with another overused word – *interactive*. Thus a number of database records linked together so that more than one trajectory is possible is assumed to constitute an "interactive narrative." But merely to create these trajectories is of course not sufficient; the author also has to control the semantics of the elements and the logic of their connection so that the resulting object will meet the criteria of narrative as outlined above. Another erroneous assumption frequently made is that, by creating her own path (i.e., choosing the records from a database in a particular order), the user constructs her own unique narrative. However, if the user simply accesses different elements, one after another, in a usually random order, there is no reason to assume that these elements will form a narrative at all. Indeed, why should an arbitrary sequence of database records, constructed by the user, result in "a series of connected events caused or experienced by actors"?

In summary, database and narrative do not have the same status in computer culture. In the database/narrative pair, database is the unmarked term.[19] Regardless of whether new media objects present themselves as linear narratives, interactive narratives, databases, or something else, underneath, on the level of material organization, they are all databases. In new media, the database supports a variety of cultural forms that range from direct translation (i.e., a database stays a database) to a form whose logic is the opposite of the logic of the material form itself – narrative. More precisely, a database can support narrative, but there is nothing in the logic of the medium itself that would foster its generation. It is not surprising, then, that databases occupy a significant, if not the largest, territory of the new media landscape. What is more surprising is why the other end of the spectrum – narratives – still exist in new media.

Paradigm and Syntagm

The dynamics that exist between database and narrative are not unique in new media. The relation between the structure of a digital image and the languages of contemporary visual culture is characterized by the same dynamics. As defined by all computer software, a digital image consists of a number of separate layers, each layer containing particular visual elements. Throughout the production process, artists and designers manipulate each layer separately; they also delete layers and add new ones. Keeping each element as a separate layer allows the content and the composition of an image to be changed at any point – deleting a background, substituting one person for another, moving two people closer together, blurring an object, and so on. What would a typical image look like if the layers were merged together? The elements contained on different layers would become juxtaposed, resulting in a montage look. Montage is the default visual language of composite organization of an image. However, just as database supports both the database form and its opposite – narrative – a composite organization of an image on the material level (and compositing software on the level of operations) supports two opposing visual languages. One is modernist-MTV montage – two-dimensional juxtaposition of visual elements designed to shock due to its impossibility in reality. The other is the representation of familiar reality as seen by a film camera (or its computer simulation, in the case of 3-D graphics). During the 1980s and 1990s, all image-making technologies became computer-based, thus turning all images into composites. In parallel, a renaissance of montage took place in visual culture, in print, broadcast design, and new media. This is not unexpected – after all, this is the visual language dictated by the composite organization. What needs to be explained is why photorealist images continue to occupy such a significant space in our computer-based visual culture.

It would be surprising, of course, if photorealist images suddenly disappeared completely. The history of culture does not contain such sudden breaks. Similarly, we should not expect that new media would completely replace narrative with database. New media does not radically break with the past; rather, it distributes weight differently between the categories that hold culture together, foregrounding what was in the background, and vice versa. As Frederick Jameson writes in his analysis of another shift, that from modernism to postmodernism: "Radical breaks between periods do not generally involve complete changes but rather the restructuration of a certain number of elements already given: features that in an earlier period of system were subordinate become dominant, and features that had been dominant again become secondary."[20]

The database/narrative opposition is a case in point. To further understand how computer culture redistributes weight between the two terms of opposition in computer culture, I will bring in the semiological theory of syntagm and paradigm. According to this model, originally formulated by Ferdinand de Saussure to describe natural languages such as English and later expanded by Roland Barthes and others to apply to other sign systems (narrative, fashion, food, etc.), the elements of a system can be related in two dimensions – the syntagmatic and paradigmatic. As defined by Barthes, "The syntagm is a combination of signs, which has space as a support."[21] To use the example of natural language, the speaker produces an utterance by stringing together elements, one after another, in a linear sequence. This is the syntagmatic dimension. Now let us look at the paradigmatic dimension. To continue with the example of the language user, each new element is chosen from a set of other related elements. For instance, all nouns form a set; all synonyms of a particular word form another set. In the original formulation of Saussure, "The units which have something in common are associated in theory and thus form groups within which various relationships can be found."[22] This is the paradigmatic dimension.

Elements in the syntagmatic dimension are related *in praesentia*, while elements in the paradigmatic dimension are related *in absentia*. For instance, in the case of a written sentence, the words that comprise it materially exist on a piece of paper, while the paradigmatic sets to which these words belong only exist in the writer's and reader's minds. Similarly, in the case of a fashion outfit, the elements that compose it, such as skirt, blouse, and jacket, are present in reality, while pieces of clothing that could have been present instead – different skirt, different blouse, different jacket – exist only in the viewer's imagination. Thus, syntagm is explicit and paradigm is implicit; one is real and the other is imagined.

Literary and cinematic narratives work in the same way. Particular words, sentences, shots, and scenes that make up a narrative have a material existence; other elements that form the imaginary world of an author or a particular literary or cinematic style, and that could have appeared instead, exist only virtually. Put differently, the database of choices from which narrative is constructed (the paradigm) is implicit; while the actual narrative (the syntagm) is explicit.

New media reverse this relationship. Database (the paradigm) is given material existence, while narrative (the syntagm) is dematerialised. Paradigm is privileged, syntagm is downplayed. Paradigm is real; syntagm, virtual. To see this, consider the new media design process. The design of any new media object begins with assembling a database of possible elements to be used. (Macromedia Director calls this database "cast," Adobe Premiere calls it "project," ProTools calls it a "session," but the principle is the same.) This database is the center of the design process. It typically consists of a combination of original and stock material such as buttons, images, video and audio sequences, 3-D objects, behaviors, and so on. Throughout the design process, new elements are added to the database; existing elements are modified. The narrative is constructed by linking elements of this database in a particular order, that is by designing a trajectory leading from one element to another. On the material level, a narrative is just a set of links; the elements themselves remain stored in the database. Thus the narrative is virtual while the database exists materially.

The paradigm is privileged over syntagm in yet another way in interactive objects presenting the user with a number of choices at the same time – which is what typical interactive interfaces do. For instance, a screen may contain a few icons; clicking on each icon leads the user to a different screen. On the level of an individual screen, these choices form a paradigm of their own that is explicitly presented to the user. On the level of the whole object, the user is made aware that she is following one possible trajectory among many others. In other words, she is selecting one trajectory from the paradigm of all trajectories that are defined.

Other types of interactive interfaces make the paradigm even more explicit by presenting the user with an explicit menu of all available choices. In such interfaces, all of the categories are always available, just a mouse click away. The complete paradigm is present before the user, its elements neatly arranged in a menu. This is another example of how new media make explicit the psychological processes involved in cultural communication. Other examples include the (already discussed) shift from creation to selection, which externalizes and codifies the database of cultural elements existing in the creator's mind, as well as the very phenomena of interactive links. As I noted in chapter one, new media takes "interaction" literally, equating it with a strictly physical interaction between a user and a computer, at the expense of psychological interaction. The cognitive processes involved in understanding any cultural text are erroneously equated with an objectively existing structure of interactive links.

Interactive interfaces foreground the paradigmatic dimension and often make explicit paradigmatic sets. Yet they are still organized along the syntagmatic dimension. Although the user is making choices at each new screen, the end result is a linear sequence of screens that she follows. This is the classical syntagmatic experience. In fact, it can be compared to constructing a sentence in a natural language. Just as a language user constructs a sentence by choosing each successive word from a paradigm of other possible words, a new media user creates a sequence of screens by clicking on this or that icon at each screen. Obviously, there are many important differences between these two situations. For instance, in the case of a typical interactive interface, there is no grammar, and paradigms are much smaller. Yet the similarity of basic experience in both cases is quite interesting; in both cases, it unfolds along a syntagmatic dimension.

Why does new media insist on this language-like sequencing? My hypothesis is that they follow the dominant semiological order of the twentieth century – that of cinema. As I will discuss in more detail in the next chapter, cinema replaced all other modes of narration with a sequential narrative, an assembly line of shots that appear on the screen one at a time. For centuries, a spatialized narrative in which all images appear simultaneously dominated European visual culture; in the twentieth century it was relegated to "minor" cultural forms such as comics or technical illustrations. "Real" culture of the twentieth century came to speak in linear chains, aligning itself with the assembly line of the industrial society and the Turing machine of the postindustrial era. New media continue this mode, giving the user information one screen at a time. At least, this is the case when it tries to become "real" culture (interactive narratives, games); when it simply functions as an interface to information, it is not ashamed to present much more information on the screen at once, whether in the form of tables, normal or pull-down menus, or lists. In particular, the experience of a user filling in an online form can be compared to precinematic spatialized narrative: in both cases, the user follows a sequence of elements that are presented simultaneously.

A Database Complex

To what extent is the database form intrinsic to modern storage media? For instance, a typical music CD is a collection of individual tracks grouped together. The database impulse also drives much of photography throughout its history, from William Henry Fox Talbot's *Pencil of Nature* to August Sander's monumental typology of modern German society *Face of Our Time*, to Bernd and Hilla Becher's equally obsessive cataloging of water towers. Yet the connection between storage media and database forms is not universal. The prime exception is cinema. Here the storage media support the narrative imagination.[23] Why then, in the case of photography storage media, does technology sustain database, whereas in the case of cinema it gives rise to a modern narrative form par excellence? Does this have to do with the method of media access? Shall we conclude that random-access media, such as computer storage formats (hard drives, removable disks, CD-ROMs, DVD), favor database, whereas sequential-access media, such as film, favor narrative? This does not hold either. For instance, a book, the perfect random-access medium, supports database forms such as photoalbums as well as narrative forms such as novels.

Rather than trying to correlate database and narrative forms with modern media and information technologies, or deduce them from these technologies, I prefer to think of them as two competing imaginations, two basic creative impulses, two essential responses to the world. Both have existed long before modern media. The ancient Greeks produced long narratives, such as Homer's epic poems *The Iliad* and *The Odyssey;* they also produced encyclopedias. The first fragments of a Greek encyclopedia to have survived were the work of Speusippus, a nephew of Plato. Diderot wrote novels – and also was in charge of the monumental *Encyclopédie*, the largest publishing project of the eighteenth century. Competing to make meaning out of the world, database and narrative produce endless hybrids. It is hard to find a pure encyclopedia without any traces of a narrative in it and vice versa. For instance, until alphabetical organization became popular a few centuries ago, most encyclopedias were organized thematically, with topics covered in a particular order (typically, corresponding to the seven liberal arts.) At the same time, many narratives, such as the novels by Cervantes and Swift, and even Homer's epic poems – the founding narratives of the Western tradition – traverse an imaginary encyclopedia.

Modern media is the new battlefield for the competition between database and narrative. It is tempting to read the history of this competition in dramatic terms. First, the medium of visual recording – photography – privileges catalogs, taxonomies, and lists. While the modern novel blossoms, and academicians continue to produce historical narrative paintings throughout the nineteenth century, in the realm of the new techno-image of photography, database rules. The next visual recording medium – film – privileges narrative. Almost all fictional films are narratives, with few exceptions. Magnetic tape used in video does not bring any substantial changes. Next, storage media – computer-controlled digital storage devices – privilege databases once again. Multimedia encyclopedias, virtual museums, pornography, artists' CD-ROMs, library databases, Web indexes, and, of course, the Web itself: The database is more popular than ever before.

The digital computer turns out to be the perfect medium for the database form. Like a virus, databases infect CD-ROMs and hard drives, servers and Web sites. Can we say that the database is the cultural form most characteristic of a computer? In her 1978 article "Video: The Aesthetics of Narcissism." probably the single most well-known article on video art, art historian Rosalind Krauss argued that video is not a physical medium but a psychological one. In her analysis, "Video's real medium is a psychological situation, the very terms of which are to withdraw attention from an external object – an Other – and invest it in the Self."[24] In short, video art is a support for the psychological condition of narcissism[25] Does new media similarly function to play out a particular psychological condition, something that might be called a "database complex"? In this respect, it is interesting that a database imagination has accompanied computer art from its very beginning. In the 1960s, artists working with computers wrote programs to systematically explore the combinations of different visual elements. In part, they were following art world trends such as minimalism. Minimalist artists executed works of art according to preexistent plans; they also created series of images or objects by systematically varying a single parameter. So when minimalist artist Sol LeWitt spoke of an artist's idea as "the machine which makes the work," it was only logical to substitute the human executing the idea with a computer.[26] At the same time, since the only way to make pictures with a computer was by writing a computer program, the logic of computer programming itself pushed computer artists in the same directions. Thus, for artist Frieder Nake, a computer was a "Universal Picture Generator," capable of producing every possible picture out of a combination of available picture elements and colors.[27] In 1967 he published a portfolio of twelve drawings that were obtained by successfully multiplying a square matrix by itself. Another early computer artist Manfred Mohr produced numerous images that recorded various transformations of a basic cube.

Even more remarkable were films by John Whitney, the pioneer of computer filmmaking. His films such as *Permutations* (1967), *Arabesque* (1975) and others systematically explored the transformations of geometric forms obtained by manipulating elementary mathematical functions. Thus they substituted successive accumulation of visual effects for narrative, figuration, or even formal development. Instead they presented the viewer with databases of effects. This principle reaches its extreme in Whitney's early film *Catalog*, which was made with an analog computer. In his important book on new forms of cinema of the 1960s entitled *Expanded Cinema* (1970), critic Gene Youngblood writes about this remarkable film: "The elder Whitney actually never produced a complete, coherent movie on the analog computer because he was continually developing and refining the machine while using it for commercial work. … However, Whitney did assemble a visual catalogue of the effects he had perfected over the years. This film, simply titled *Catalog*, was completed in 1961 and proved to be of such overwhelming beauty that many persons still prefer Whitney's analogue work over his digital computer films."[28] One is tempted to read *Catalog* as one of the founding moments of new media. As discussed in the "Selection" section, all software for media creation today arrives with endless "plug-ins" – the banks of effects that with a press of a button generate interesting images from any input whatsoever. In parallel, much of the aesthetics of computerized visual culture is effects-driven, especially when a new techno-genre (computer animation, multimedia, Web sites) is first becoming established. For instance, countless music videos are variations of Whitney's *Catalog* – the only difference is that the effects are applied to the images of human performers. This is yet another example of how the logic of a computer – in this case, the ability of a computer to produce endless variations of elements and to act as a filter, transforming its input to yield a new output – becomes the logic of culture at large.

NOTES

1. "Database," *Encyclopædia Britannica Online*. http://www.eb.com:180/cgi-bin/g?DocF=micro/160/23.html.
2. Jean-François Lyotard, *The Postmodern Condition: A Report on Knowledge*, trans. Geoff Bennington and Brian Massumi (Minneapolis: University of Minnesota Press, 1984), 3.
3. As early as 1985, Grolier, Inc. issued a text-only *Academic American Encyclopedia* on CD-ROM. The first multimedia encyclopedia was *Compton's MultiMedia Encyclopedia*, published in 1989.
4. See *AI and Society* 13.3, a special issue on database aesthetics, ed. Victoria Vesna (http://arts.ucsb.edu/~vesna/AI_Society/); *SWITCH* 5, no. 3, "The Database Issue" (http://switch.sjsu.edu/).

5. http://www.teleportacia.org/anna.

6. George Legrady, personal communication, 16 September 1998.

7. Bordwell and Thompson define motivation in cinema in the following way: "Because films are human constructs, we can expect that any one element in a film will have some justification for being there. This justification is the motivation for that element." Here are some examples of motivation: "When Tom jumps from the balloon to chase a cat, we motivate his action by appealing to notions of how dogs are likely to act when cats are around"; "The movement of a character across a room may motivate the moving of the camera to follow the action and keep the character within a frame." Bordwell and Thompson, *Film Art*. 5th ed., 80.

8. McGowan and McCullaugh, *Entertainment in the Cyber Zone*, 71.

9. This is true for a procedural programming paradigm. In an object-oriented programming paradigm, represented by such computer languages as Java and C++, algorithms and data structures are modeled together as objects.

10. *Mediamatic* 8, no. 1 (Summer 1994), 1860.

11. Bob Laird, "Information Age Losing Memory," *USA Today*, 25 October 1999.

12. http://www.amazon.com/exec/obidos/subst/misc/company-info.html/, http://www.oracle.com/database/oracle8i/.

13. http://artnetweb.com/guggenheim/mediascape/shaw.html.

14. Harwood, *Rehearsal of Memory*, CD-ROM (London: Artac and Bookworks, 1996.)

15. http://www.telepresence.com/MENAGERIE.

16. http://jefferson.village.virginia.edu/wax/.

17. http://myboyfriendcamebackfromth.ewar.ru.

18. Mieke Bal, *Narratology: Introduction to the Theory of Narrative* (Toronto: University of Toronto Press, 1985), 8.

19. The theory of markedness was first developed by linguists of the Prague School in relation to phonology, but subsequently applied to all levels of linguistic analysis. For example, "rooster" is a marked term and "chicken" an unmarked term. Whereas "rooster" is used only in relation to males, "chicken" is applicable to both males and females.

20. Fredric Jameson, "Postmodernism and Consumer Society," in *The Anti-Aesthetic: Essays on Postmodern Culture*, ed. Hal Foster (Seattle: Bay Press, 1983), 123.

21. Barthes, *Elements of Semiology*, 58.

22. Quoted in ibid., 58.

23. Christian Metz, "The Fiction Film and Its Spectator: A Metapsychological Study," in *Apparatus*, ed. Theresa Hak Kyung Cha (New York: Tanam Press, 1980), p. 402.

24. Rosalind Krauss, "Video: The Aesthetics of Narcissism," in John Hanhardt, ed. *Video Culture* (Rochester: Visual Studies Workshop, 1987), 184.

25. This analysis can also be applied to many interactive computer installations. The user of such an installation is presented with her own image; the user is given the possibility to play with this image and also to observe how her movements trigger various effects. In a different sense, most new media, regardless of whether it represents to the user her image or not, can be said to activate rhe narcissistic condition because they represent to the user her actions and their results. In other words, it functions as a new kind of mirror that reflects not only the human image but human activities. This is a different kind of narcissism – not passive contemplation but action. The user moves the cursor around the screen, clicks on icons, presses the keys on the keyboard, and so on. The computer screen acts as a mirror of these activities. Often this mirror does not simply reflect but

greatly amplifies the user's actions – a second difference from traditional narcissism. For instance, clicking on a folder icon activates an animation accompanied by sound; pressing a button on a game pad sends a character off to climb a mountain; and so on. But even without this amplification, the modern GUI functions as a mirror, always representing the image of the user in the form of a cursor moving around the screen.

26. Quoted in Sam Hunter and John Jacobus, *Modern Art: Painting, Sculpture, and Architecture*, 3d ed. (New York: Abrams, 1992), 326.

27. Frank Dietrich, "Visual Intelligence: The First Decade of Computer Art (1965–1975)," *IEEE Computer Graphics and Applications* (July 1985), 39.

28. Gene Youngblood, *Expanded Cinema* (New York: E. P. Dutton and Co., 1970), 210.

6 MAKING MEANING OF MOBILES
A Theory of Apparatgeist

James E. Katz and Mark A. Aakhus

[. . .]

Articulating the Neologism *Apparatgeist*

To convey the logic associated with our concept of communication technology more effectively, we coin the neologism *Apparatgeist* to suggest the spirit of the machine that influences both the designs of the technology as well as the initial and subsequent significance accorded them by users, non-users and anti-users. The neologism has its origins in Latin and is derived currently in the Germanic and Slavic word *apparat*, meaning machine, which includes both the technical and sociological aspects. English speakers are familiar with the term and concept, embodied in the word "apparatus." For instance, the American Heritage Dictionary (third edition) defines the primary meaning of the term as "the materials needed for a purpose such as a task." Another one of the meanings is "the totality of means by which a designated function is performed or a specific task is executed." "Equipment" is emphasized throughout the definitions of "apparatus."

Also, we often associate the term "apparatus" with gadgetry. In addition, it clearly means being able to accomplish a task, often an important or complicated one. The term also encompasses a social operation, an organized group that can achieve some end, often in an efficient way, and usually with a political objective.

We draw too upon the German word *Geist*, which denotes spirit or mind. We adopt Hegel's sense (Hegel, 1977) and use it to denote a directive principle within

James E. Katz and Mark A. Aakhus, "Making Meaning of Mobiles – A Theory of *Apparatgeist*," pp. 301–18 from James E. Katz and Mark A. Aakhus (eds.), *Perpetual Contact: Mobile Communication, Private Talk, Public Performance* (Cambridge: Cambridge University Press, 2003).

historical entities, and guiding their existence, that unfolds in historical time and expresses itself in the creations of the denizens of the society so animated (Rostenstreich, 1973, p. 491). Although the term has contested meanings, and is frequently misused, we find that Hegel's interpretation of terminology as stemming from the intellectual or rational, which defies empirical analysis, instead signifies a fundamental theme that animates the lives of human cultures. The term *Geist* is popularly associated with another Germanic philosophical thesis, namely the *Zeitgeist*. The *Zeitgeist* can be only indirectly observed. Although this spirit is actually directing human activities, in a broad sense, it can be only indirectly observed throughout the intellectual, moral and cultural climate of an era. Hence, folklore, poetry, popular myths and folk theories are all indicative of the more profound unified thesis of an era. The *Zeitgeist* transcends popular culture and other areas of a society, including religious beliefs, intellectual endeavors, social policy and political structures. Hegel himself asserted that the *Zeitgeist* was a spiritual and intellectual force that truly existed. With respect to our term *Apparatgeist*, we cannot embrace such an intangible concept.

The term *Geist* implies a sense of movement, a direction and a motive. This sense we encompass in our framework as well. The notion of goals connected to movement, though, is not included in our meaning. It does not have a sense of rational pursuit of ends, or *Zwecksrationalität*. Rather, it has only the rationality of means, the algorithms or rules that guide decisions on a moment-to-moment basis. It has then a sense of becoming rather than a sense of being, if we invoke the terms of the fascist philosopher Martin Heidegger (1996).

We also intend to link the word to the Hegelian notion of historical movement. Hegel (1977) argued that there were certain latent urges of each historical period that culminated in its idealized expression and manifestation; metaphorically speaking, much like a tree in autumn that sheds its leaves and revitalizes in the spring, the historical momentum decays, rebuilds and manifests itself in another time. He also argued that there was an underlying *Geist* to history, which he likened to the expansion of freedom. For our part, we use the term to imply spirit in the way of incremental change followed by occasional, unpredictable bursts of drastic change in history.

The term *Apparatgeist* ties together both the individual and the collective aspects of societal behavior. That is, the cultural situation and the limitations of extant technology determine individual behavior, which also takes place within a group or collective. Yet, it is not a term that requires technological determinism. In fact, we argue that technology does not determine what an individual can do; rather, it serves as a constraint upon possibilities. Much as a cafeteria menu will not offer infinite meal choices, but rather presents a finite selection of meal courses, so too historically bound technology offers us a flexible menu of extensive, but not infinite, choices. The *Apparatgeist* refers to the common set of strategies or principles of reasoning about technology evident in the identifiable, consistent and generalized patterns of technological advancement throughout history. It is through these common strategies and principles of reasoning that individual and collective behavior are drawn together.

The Logic of Perpetual Contact

We see that there is a logic, or nascent philosophy, about personal communication technology. It is both a logic that informs the judgments people make about the utility or value of the technologies in their environment, and a logic that informs the predictions scientists and technology producers might make about personal technologies. Our goal is to articulate this logic and to demonstrate the content of this spirit. The logic that informs the *Apparatgeist* is perpetual contact, at least in potential terms, or, as Emanuel Schegloff says, incipiency.

Perpetual contact is a socio-logic (Goodwin and Wenzel, 1979) of communication technology. A socio-logic is neither a formal logic nor the natural cognitive processes of an individual, but is located in the "socially developed sense of practical reasoning" that results from communities of people "thinking and acting together over time" (Goodwin and Wenzel, 1979, p. 289). The compelling image of perpetual contact is the image of pure communication, which, as Peters (1999) argues, is an idealization of communication committed to the prospect of sharing one's mind with another, like the talk of angels that occurs without the constraints of the body. Pure communication is the image deeply embedded in the logic of perpetual contact that underwrites how we judge, invent and use communication technology. Like the image of perpetual motion that has driven the technological development of machinery over the past two millennia (White, 1962), the development of personal communication technology presupposes perpetual contact. Whereas the idea of perpetual motion concerns the means of production, perpetual contact concerns the means to communicate and interact socially, which is fundamental to humans.

Although there is clearly a logic and pattern to people's reasoning, individually as well as collectively, about the adoption and use of PCTs, it is not always available for direct inspection. The chapters in this volume help solve this problem through empirical findings and illuminating analysis. Moreover, these contributions provide multiple convergent vantage points from which to understand perpetual contact as the logic of *Apparatgeist*. We see in the emergence of mobile communication, in a wide variety of nations, how the mobile phone initiates new questions about appropriate contact and renews contests over communication competence when new means for communicating require a new practical mastery of everyday activity. In the chapters on mobile communication in Finland, Israel, Italy, Korea, the United States, France, the Netherlands, and Bulgaria we see shifts in communicative habits to accommodate mobile communication that undermine long-standing routines and rituals in making contact with others. It is not that what went before stood in opposition to perpetual contact but that those rituals and routines were geared toward different capacities for achieving the ideal of perpetual contact. Indeed, the coming of the telephone to a Filipino village dramatizes the gap that can exist between extant communication rituals and routines and the needs and demands that stem from an ideal of perpetual contact.

The chapters on private talk and public performance go further in explicating the content of *Apparatgeist* as it is realized in the socio-logic of perpetual contact. Ling and Yttri (chapter 10) and Kasesniemi and Rautiainen (chapter 11) offer detailed analyses of how teens integrate the mobile phone into their lives. These reflect a common, though likely implicit, orientation among teenage user groups about communication competence now that mobile communication is a real part of their lives. This common orientation is given expression in the results of Skog's survey of Norwegian youth (chapter 16). The differences between gender in regard to mobile phones is built on an extraordinary similarity in orientation to both the technology design and the purpose of the technology as a means of communication and perpetual contact. Gergen's analysis (chapter 14) that the mobile phone presents a radically different solution to the phenomenon of absent presence than traditional mass media and the Internet (as an information retrieval tool) articulates aspects of the rationale implicit in the orientation identified in the empirical research on teens. The mobile telephone is a means to regulate one's social environment through integration of social contact rather than simply inviting socially dispersing media into one's life. The logic of perpetual contact makes it possible to take sensible action in the conditions of the contemporary societies.

Yet the logic of perpetual contact has other sides. As personal technology successively approximates the ideal of pure communication, it gives way to new behavior that is unanticipated, often objectionable, and open to redress. Rule, de Gournay, and Nafus and Tracey articulate the contests over the ideological and material conditions of communication precipitated by the media of perpetual contact, and highlighted by the national comparison chapters. In each case, extension of the logic of perpetual contact has an unanticipated consequence. Rule (chapter 15) outlines a paradoxical loss and gain for individual control over communicative environments afforded by the particularizing tendencies of the media of perpetual contact. The result is more personalized relations with entities such as firms and agencies. De Gournay (chapter 12) identifies how mobile telephones foster informal conversation at the expense of formal conversation and the etiquette necessary for generating a public sphere. Nafus and Tracey (chapter 13) show how perpetual contact helps people realize the traditional value of individuality while undermining social boundaries, such as the household, that in the past made individuality possible. These chapters put into perspective the frustration people experience with personal technologies. These authors may have also identified the by-products of a perspective that lead to its evolution. Thus, the cunning of the *Apparatgeist* may lie less in the current class of solutions it presents than in the class of frustrations it presents.

The contributions to this volume point in a direction that we choose to call *Apparatgeist*. However, we would like to go further in articulating and formalizing *Apparatgeist*. One reason this is important is that, although the family of structurational theories has brought people back into the picture of social and technological change, these theories emphasize the process of socio-technical environments and change at the expense of the content that animates socio-technical environments and change. We redress this balance here by focusing on the individual, with a full sensitivity that individuals and their relationship to their media are embedded in a social context and history.

The investigations of perpetual contact bolster our position that there is a socio-logic of perpetual contact. Katz (1999), for instance, has shown that people regard telecom technologies in a coherent conceptual way. Moreover, in our own unpublished research with student focus groups, we find that, in describing their decision-making processes, subjects oscillate between explicit reasons (form, function, price) and implicit ones (how others perceive them, beliefs about the usefulness, appropriateness to one's concept of "self"). Both these levels, which Merton tagged as manifest and latent functions, are required for a full understanding of PCT's role in people's lives, or what we call *Apparatgeist*.

In table 19.1, we present both the manifest and latent salient points in people's reasoning, further breaking them down into technological and social aspects of PCTs. These reasonings or functions move along an upward vector of, say, 45 degrees, representing the increased capabilities of PCTs. Imagine, if you will, the vector encased in a spiral spring, representing the movement of people's thinking and needs listed in each cell in table 19.1.

The premises in each cell in table 6.1 (identified in italics) have a dual quality. On the one hand, these premises can be used to generate empirical predictions about communication technology. They enable the individual, and, in turn, collective entities, to make predictions about the performance of and uses for a technology. On the other hand, these premises are used to formulate normative judgments about communication technology, its uses and its users. The premises refer to presuppositions about preferences for the social and communicative arrangements technology makes possible. The fact that these premises are both empirical and normative justifies the creation and utilization of the perhaps inherently paradoxical term *Apparatgeist*.

The direction of the *Apparatgeist* is evident in the premises of perpetual contact. *Apparatgeist* can be broadly vocalized because universal features exist among all cultures regarding PCT; technology itself tends to assume certain standard features independent of place or time. Regardless of culture, when people interact with their PCTs they tend to standardize infrastructure and gravitate towards consistent tastes and universal features. Throughout the history of technological advancement, the tendency is for people to operate by identifiable, consistent and generalized patterns, and to rely on a common set of strategies or principles of reasoning despite individual creativity and worldwide cultural diversity. For instance, people and corporations worldwide create and gravitate toward common designs for airports, cars, bicycles and computers, regardless of cultural diversity. Another vital point is that users operate within a networked environment. That is, behavior relative to the system is affected by who else is available, currently and potentially. Though this can be seen most clearly with the telephone, it is useless when there is only one person with a telephone. Its value increases as does the number of potential users. Decisions about adoption and use are carried out with at least latent recognition of this quality.

TABLE 6.1 Premises supporting the drive toward perpetual contact

	Technology	*Social relationships*
MANIFEST REASONING	**Qualities of attractive technology (design)**	**Qualities of technology's potential social role (social context)**
	These are specific and manifest attributes that are sought after in the design process, and what potential users might want	*These are the manifest qualities and processes of the local social context of the potential user, hence, to the extent the technologies can "fit," they will be of interest*
	Smaller	
	Faster	
	More places	
	More functions if cheap and easy to operate	Efficient information seeking
	Lower cost	Social roles
	Higher status or luxury marker	Personal needs
		Local interests
	Easier to use	Norms (patterns of behavior)
	Better control of information	Values (principles of what is desirable and worth pursuit)
	Better filtering of outsiders	
	Control over others	Social system's action – reward/punishment matrix
	Escape control of others	
	Efficiency in personal life	Network externalities (changing character as more users and activities added to system)
	Automate routine and repetitive tasks	
LATENT REASONING	**Qualities of attractive uses of technology (performance and personal applications)**	**Social setting in which technology will be used (social applications)**
	These are the latent issues concerning the technology that potential users weigh in their adoption and use of technology	*These are latent social dimensions that factor into decisions about adoption and usage*
	Symbolic affirmation of values	Reference group (attraction/avoidance)
	Socially appropriate behavior of relevant technology	Perspectives (*Weltanschauung*)
		Network of social ties based on:
	Exploit to loosen monitoring over self	Sentiment
		Interest
		Obligation
	Exploit to increase monitoring over others	Predicates of action folk theories
		Advancement of self within group, but retention of affiliation and integration
	Reproduction of moral regime	
	Selective access	Advancement of group within society, but avoidance of conflict
	Media exposure	
	Social learning	Advancement of values within culture, diminution of values of others
		Synergies of additional participants in network

Having addressed *Apparatgeist* content from the perspective of the individual, we look now at how *Apparatgeist* moves forward through history. Systematic reinforcements (and dissuasions) affect the directions of technological development as well as the filters through which people see these technologies. Table 6.2 illustrates how *Apparatgeist* evolves through several domains of incentives and disincentives by an individual's assessment of PCT. Some of the reinforcements that give life to *Apparatgeist* include folkways and folk theories, social learning and the mass media's tendencies to advertise technology in terms of the new, the dramatically changing, the threatening and, most of all, the entertaining. It is important to note that the individual in this model is firmly rooted in a social context.

The Pertinence of the *Apparatgeist* Theory

Through our theory of *Apparatgeist* we intend to advance the state of communication theory concerning personal technologies. Understandably, much of communication theory draws from face-to-face interpersonal communication and mass media modes. Beginning in the 1970s, a third and increasingly visible branch of theory was evolving, centered on understanding human–computer interaction. Although these lines of inquiry have been fruitful, we see that it is now appropriate to speak of a fourth form of communication mediated through personal technologies. Although it is an intangible concept in terms of the horizon of the communication discipline, we anticipate it represents the shape of things to come.

[...]

For our part, we seek to introduce the rudiments to establish a formal theory. However, these are only modest first steps in a long and complex journey. The task we set for ourselves is to create statements that enable us to investigate the nature of social reality and change as adequately as possible. We see that mobile phones are used in many facets of life. Yet despite the great variation in cultures – from teen dating to family arrangements and from economic bases to social hierarchies – the use and folk understanding of the mobile phone seem to be pressing toward conformity and uniformity. Because PCT affects so many facets of life, we cannot avoid calling it something, and we find *Apparatgeist* a viable term.

People seldom pursue one prevailing interest; instead, they seek to work several avenues of interest at one time. They apply a variety of perspectives to any given issue. In our research on folk theories and attitudes toward the mobile phone, we note that people's multiple perspectives are often simultaneously logically incompatible. There is no reason to think that the mobile phone is unique in this regard. These perspectives constrain and guide people's behavior; however, we also realize that many of these perspectives are constructed retrospectively to justify behavior in which the actor was engaged.

Social actors must constantly perform a series of ever-changing and highly complex social roles. They must also deal with other actors who themselves are performing

TABLE 6.2 Evolution of *Apparatgeist* through domains of individual decision-making

		Individual's assessment of personal communication technology		
	Disincentives	Incentives		
Level of analysis	Avoidance motives	Individual psychological domain	Material contingencies	Social symbolic/affiliative aspects
Symbolic	Anti-symbolic	Cultural/social location of individual	Technology possibilities	Pro-symbolic
Usability	Perceived difficulty using	Self-image/ competence	Ease of use	Mastery in social settings
Affirms group affiliation	Anti-reference groups	Relational	Family and friends ties/ co-workers	Reference groups and social class
Economics	Cost	Reallocation of disposable income	Promotions and ads, social learning, media exposure	Relationship to body and self
Operational environment	Desire not to complicate environment	Immediate control of environment	Demands on individual; network size and externalities	Perceived social role
Folklore	Negative folk theories	Personal values	Positive folk theories	Cultural ideals
Body orientation	Physical discomfort	Physical needs	Personal and economic resources	Physical pleasure

a series of ever-changing and highly complex social roles. This in itself represents an uncertain and complex scenario in which communication takes place. Indeed, PCT is powerful enough to affect national leadership. Take for instance, the drama that occurred during the US election of 2000 when heavily utilized mobile phones and pager devices delivered timely information and strongly affected serious decisions. Vice President Albert Gore had been en route in a motorcade with the intention of delivering a concession speech, when an aide in another vehicle in the motorcade received the breaking news via a pager system. The aide used his mobile phone to contact the staffer, who in turn revealed that the margin between the presidential candidates was becoming slimmer. Based on a rash of mobile phone calls, the Vice President decided not to deliver his concession speech on November 8, 2000. Thus, the sequence of communication via PCT served as a critical intervention tool in light of the fact that massive public confusion would have prevailed if Gore had given his concession speech. According to an Associate Press wire story, Gore policy adviser Greg Simon said, "We had no TVs. Everyone was on their cell phones. People were calling us from everywhere, telling us, "Don't concede" " (Sobieraj, 2000). Because of PCT, intervention was possible and helped to avoid embarrassment and confusion. The anecdote illustrates how these technologies can alter the course of American and, indeed, world history.

Conclusion

The chapters in this book seek to make sense of the phenomenon of mobile communication by analyzing its many manifestations and meanings. By assembling these insights, we wish to lay a foundation that could serve many different theoretical perspectives. Yet we also see them in service of a specific perspective, which we call *Apparatgeist*. We see emerging from it the rudiments of a theory that explains, and that makes testable predictions about, the phenomenon of personal communication technology. Thus, in Popper's (1963) sense, we seek to migrate the insights captured in this book from a context of discovery to one of justification where ideas must stand the test of theoretical and empirical refutation.

To summarize, we have suggested how the functionalist and structuration theories, though they deal with important issues and provide valuable insight, fail to deal with or account for what we see as some core aspects of the way people use mobile and other personal communication technologies and the way they make meaning from them and their use. Functionalist theories emphasize instrumental, goal-oriented rationality at the expense of the symbolic. Structuration theories emphasize process at the expense of the values that animate processes. With our approach, *Apparatgeist*, we wish to draw attention to several issues that we feel are insufficiently dealt with by these approaches. These issues include the way that people use mobile technologies as tools in their daily life in terms of tools-using behavior and the relationship among technology, body and social role. They also include the rhetoric and meaning-making that occur via social interaction among users (and non-users). That is, unlike the functionalist approach, we do not just see mobile phones as a narrow way to achieve a specific purpose. Rather, they are both utilitarian and symbolic. Indeed, the symbolic importance is often paramount. And, unlike the structuration approach, we do not see that, as technologies become institutionalized, they are rendered invisible. Instead, a technology's being taken for granted is the result of a large amount of prior evaluation and resolved choices of people concerning technology. Their evaluations and choices are based not only on the function of the technology but on their own social roles, status and values. An important aspect of this process is the competition for status and prestige as well as public perceptions of competence and the management of social roles and commitments. Moreover, we do not take for granted the axiom that the habituation and institutionalization of personal technologies flow from exploitation or conspiracy. Rather we regard these as matters for investigation and demonstration, which indeed may very well show that the exploitation can flow in the opposite direction than would have been predicted by these models, and that conspiracies can take place on many levels, for many ends. In this regard, *Apparatgeist* also spotlights how personal technology can be used creatively to empower some individuals, often at the expense of others.

We see a consistent interaction between the functional and social needs of potential users, their perceived values and status concerns, and their choice of which technologies to use and where to use them. This interaction has directionality in the sense that there is a consistent strain to manage competing needs for connection and autonomy and the various boundaries people construct to manage the social world. These competing demands and the struggle to define appropriate boundaries between public and private are evident in the design and use of personal technology and the folk discourse praising and blaming personal technology. As a result, we see that a certain degree of predictability can be attained in terms of who uses which types of new technologies. Because these tools have a life of their own, people must deal with the tools in their social environments even if they do not adopt the tools themselves. This extends not only to new users, but to those who will be "drop-outs" or active rejecters, or who will simply ignore technology. These stances toward technology are grounded in deeper communicative principles outlined in *Apparatgeist* theory and should be reflected in the personal theories of technology that people develop and their routine and ritual behaviors relevant to the technology.

Given the extraordinary impact of communications technology on virtually all cultures, there is a need to understand still better how people fit these new devices into their lives and to what effect. Certainly these issues have been explored with insightful results using perspectives drawn from, among others, world systems, postmodern, developmental, feminist and ethnomethodological perspectives. However, although these perspectives can be used to create post hoc explanations of how people's technology use changes over time, they have had only limited success in predicting future states (Cummings and Kraut, forthcoming). For instance, the above theories, to the extent they offer predictions at all, suggested that work uses would expand at the cost of social uses. After their initial inception, this certainly does not appear to have been the case with mobile phones. Hence it seems we could benefit from a theory that would predict uses and meanings within a social setting and in light of potential connectivity.

We believe our proposed perspective, *Apparatgeist*, is helpful in this regard. Our theory sets parameters that may aid in explaining and understanding the role of the machines we choose as "intimate partners" in our daily lives. The perspective should facilitate understanding the role of communication devices such as the mobile within the complex realm of social interaction as well as from the multifaceted perspectives of users. This is especially true as new forms and uses of PCTs inevitably arise.

In conclusion, it seems that certain conceptual perspectives arise in people's minds as a result of their interaction with technologies, and these are remarkably consistent across cultures. If this is indeed the case, future research should continue to detect this phenomenon. It then becomes the job of theorists to provide a conceptual justification. We have offered our own theory that might account for this process and result. Further investigation may be merited on the heuristic value of this theoretical perspective in terms of understanding the social dimensions and reciprocal path dependencies of these new personal communications technologies. The empirical findings of this volume doubtless are valuable since they add to the extraordinarily slender literature on the human uses and meanings of mobile communication technology.

REFERENCES

Cummings, Jonathon N., and Kraut, Robert E. (forthcoming). "Domesticating Computers and the Internet." *The Information Society.*

Goodwin, M., and Wenzel, J. (1979). "Proverbs and Practical Reasoning: A Study in Sociologic." *Quarterly Journal of Speech* 65: 289–302.

Hegel, G.W.F. (1977). *Hegel's Phenomenology of Spirit.* Trans. A.V. Miller. New York and London: Oxford University Press.

Heidegger, Martin (1996). *Being and Time: A Translation of Sein und Zeit.* Trans. Joan Stambaugh. New York: State University of New York Press.

Katz, James (1999). *Connections: Social and Cultural Studies of the Telephone in American Life.* New Brunswick, NJ: Transaction.

Peters, J. (1999). *Speaking into the Air: A History of the Idea of Communication.* Chicago: University of Chicago Press.

Popper, K. (1963). *Conjectures and Refutations: The Growth of Scientific Knowledge.* London: Routledge.

Rostenstreich, Nathan (1973). "Volksgeist." *Dictionary of the History of Ideas*, vol. 4. New York: Scribner's, 490–496.

Sobieraj, Sandra (2000). "The Story behind the Near-Concession." Associated Press Wire story, November 8, 16:33 EDT.

White, Lynn, Jr. (1962). *Medieval Technology and Social Change.* Oxford: Clarendon Press.

APPENDIXES

Whereas the exploration of perpetual contact and mobile communication in the previous chapters has been contingent primarily on comparison across cultures and nations, across the micro–macro divide, and across time, these appendixes provide a different vantage point from which to understand mobile communication. In a rigorous, searching examination, *Emanuel Schegloff* discusses the interplay between technology and social science with particular reference to the way the telephone set in motion a substantial interest in what today has become known as conversation analysis. The field arose out of a need to analyze the fossil residues of human communication – namely, naturally occurring telephone conversations – and this has led to insight into both human behavior and the way people use technology in their everyday life. As part of his analysis, a heretofore unpublished essay written more than a quarter-century ago is presented, along with an intertextual interpretation. This analysis illumines what is a constant in human intention despite the proliferation of electronic forms of those contacts through cellular phone and other mobile and increasingly semi-automatic communication technologies.

SPACE, PLACE, COMMUNITY

Introduction

Cyberspace has been seen and touted as an entirely new ageographic, unrestricted space. The articles in this part of the book deal with cyberspace as spatial, but also as a mode of negotiating everyday, material spaces.

Digital technology transforms our interaction with the environment, buildings, streets, and space through GPS, mapping, and other technologies. Electronic networks and material infrastructures mediate the human body's orientations and work in space in a recursive linkage. "Locative media" and "emotion mapping" that map real spaces onto digital ones and record emotional responses to spaces in digital cartographic systems provide an entirely different "view" of physical space through the use of computer technologies. Mapping cyberspace includes all of these: mapping user spread and demographics, community systems of linkages, transnational bonds, wired spaces of home, and emotional mapping. Communities mapping memory into digital formats extend their community into cyberspace even as subsequent experiences of the real are mediated through the digitized memories. As a result of the recursive linkage between real and cyber- spaces, the latter are as open to control and regulation as any space. Different cultures perceive cyberspace differently and, as a consequence, produce different forms of access, use, and regulation.

Space is cultural, and cyberspace represents a new form of cultural space where subcultures, resistant cultures, and mainstream cultures exist. Home spaces are transformed with the external world and social relations – both being spatial – altered through online work and socializing. Wired homes and wired communities represent another space where a lot of time is spent online rather than in face-to-face interactions. Cell phones enable people to occupy different spaces simultaneously – both here and elsewhere – even as unfamiliar places are experienced differently because one is elsewhere. Remote-control mothering and family time, the intrusion of office into the home via electronic networks, and cell phones mean that the distinction between private and public are altered significantly. Personal music and communications systems "enclose" the user in a moving envelope of privacy, even in public space. Computer games present gameworlds that offer a different order of space in the experience of play, the player's perception of the fictional world of the game narrative, and the interaction between players in massive networked games.

William Mitchell's article proposes that networks and portable devices create continuous "fields" of presence that extend throughout buildings and locations. There is greater spatial indeterminacy nowadays because we can be connected to our homes, banks, and offices via electronic networks. This means we use space differently and access resources differently. Regimes of separation and control are also significantly altered through such networks. Public space itself becomes "blanketed" by fields of such networked presences. As for users, the way we use public and private places has changed radically owing to the extended fields of presence.

Stephen Graham's article looks at two major spaces: that of the material world and that of information. Analyzing the various approaches to cyberspace and its connections with/embeddedness in real spaces, Graham identifies three main approaches: that of technological utopianists who see cyberspace as transcending material spaces, that of cultural studies that sees cyberspace and material spaces as co-evolving, and finally, the view from actor-network theory which sees the two spaces as "recombinant," resulting from the social construction of technology. Graham proposes that space, place, and technologies must be seen as relational assemblies. Global financial markets, channels of flows, and technological structures are parts of networks that bring some distant places into proximity and physically push away adjacent spaces.

With digital technology, our experience of place has been significantly altered. In their article Michael Chang and Elizabeth Goodman explore the role of locative media – digital technologies that mediate and represent our experience of place. The online map becomes a digital equivalent of New York city in this game. When players "conquer" or explore the real streets, a corresponding conquest of the online space on the map also occurs. The players seek objects, explore streets, make social causes and comments, and make simultaneous "moves" digitally. They argue that such a representational and experiential mode marks an interplay of the social and the spatial plays.

Federico Casalegno's article explores the merging of the virtual and the real. Studying the Living Memory project, he demonstrates how a community's collective memory is acquired, digitized, and stored. Their interfaces occur in public spaces such as bus shelters and parks. This kind of linkage develops social and civic networks between people and administrative units, and people within a community. He sees the emergence of a new "social aesthetic" through such a project where everybody contributes to and shares the collective – and what he terms "connective" – memory.

7 POST-SEDENTARY SPACE

William J. Mitchell

Antonello da Messina's famous picture of Saint Jerome in his study shows how the attachment of atoms, in the most literal way, adds inertia to information.[1] It depicts the scholar surrounded and encumbered by his heavyweight personal information environment; he pores over a manuscript on the inclined desk before him, and his precious accumulation of books, papers, and writing instruments is gathered around, within the enclosure of his room. It is a tightly bounded assemblage of physical materials at a particular location. If he wants to keep it at hand, rather than rely upon fallible memory, its bulk and mass tightly tether him to that particular place.

Dilbert wasn't so different. Like most office workers of the 1980s and 1990s, he occupied a cube containing a PC.[2] His information environment was more digital than paper – some of it residing on his local disk, and some of it on distant servers. Although he did not need physical proximity to the servers, he still had to be near the delivery point. He was as tied to his computer as Saint Jerome had been to his book-shelves. Furthermore, his telephone was physically attached to the cubicle; you could only call him when he was in. In other words, desktop computers, telephones, and wired networks provided fixed *points* of presence. These favored points were like oases in a digital information desert; they were powerful attractors of human presence and activity.

The cubicle farms of the era were grids of such points. As networks became faster and more sophisticated, and as more and more information moved from local storage to servers, it ceased to matter which cubicle Dilbert occupied. He could log in from wherever he happened to be in the building, and he could have his calls electronically redirected. This was good for the boss, who could make more efficient use of his stock of cubicle space by shuffling cubicle-dwellers around at will, but it did not help Dilbert's quality of life. He still had to be at *some* point of presence, and the new cube-to-cube mobility gave him even less opportunity to personalize his surroundings.

William J. Mitchell, "Post-Sedentary Space," pp. 143–58, 240–1 from Mitchell, *Me++: The Cyborg Self and the Networked City* (Cambridge, MA: MIT Press, 2003).

But wireless connections and portable access devices create continuous *fields* of presence that may extend throughout buildings, outdoors, and into public space as well as private. This has profound implications for the locations and spatial distributions of all human activities that depend, in some way, upon access to information.

Fields of Presence

By selectively loosening place-to-place contiguity requirements, wired networks produced fragmentation and recombination of familiar building types and urban patterns.[3] For example, the local bank or branch bank largely disappeared in the early digital era; it was replaced by more decentralized access points distributed throughout the city – that is, ATM machines and electronic home banking on desktop computers, combined with centralized back office facilities and call centers that provided economics of scale. Similarly, by selectively loosening *person*-to-place contiguity requirements, wireless networks and portable devices have created an additional degree of spatial indeterminacy; you can now electronically "home" bank from a wireless laptop, and if you can rely upon credit cards, debit cards, or some form of electronic cash, you never need to go looking for an ATM location. From the customer's perspective, banking no longer has any particular place in the city.

In the short-lived dot-com era, Amazon and other online retailers fragmented and recombined retail functions and provided an alternative to stores and malls; you would order goods online, and they would be delivered from a warehouse to your home or office. Thus the retail store functions of advertising and enticement, browsing, and completing the sale transaction were fragmented and dispersed, while the functions of storage and dispatch of stock were highly centralized at monster-box (often national) distribution centers that offered economies of scale, and back-office functions – supported by ecommerce technology – could be located just about anywhere. This turned out to work well for compact, high-value items like books and electronics, but for dog food, delivery costs were a killer. Now, wireless fields of presence are beginning co provide yet another alternative – one that returns advantage to highly differentiated, place-based retailers. Location-based advertising, maybe combined with electronic urban navigation, can tell you the nearest point of availability of some specialized thing that you want – such as a funghi porcini risotto at a good Italian restaurant – and guide you to it. ...

Location-based advertising can also guide you to scarce commodities available at dynamically varying locations, such as urban parking spaces and unoccupied machines in laundry rooms. ...

Some activities, such as stock trading and gambling on horse races, depend upon highly time-sensitive information. Before highspeed telecommunication, this meant that you had to be right at the site of production of that information – the stock exchange floor or the racetrack, for example. With telecommunication, and electronic information and transaction services, the action began to shift to distributed points of presence; we saw the decline (and sometimes disappearance) of centralized exchanges and clusters of bookies on the rails, accompanied by the rise of electronic trading floors, day-trading at PCs, and off-track betting shops. Today, even those distributed sites are no longer technically necessary – though they may sometimes be preserved by regulators who want to confine activities to particular locations; trading and gambling can readily shift to wireless, portable devices.

Yet other activities have begun to depend upon clandestine, wirelessly distributed information and indeterminate locations. Where prostitution is legal (or at least tolerated), for example, brothels and red-light districts can be at fixed, well-known, maybe even advertised locations; where it is frowned upon, and telecommunication is not readily available, you get mobile streetwalkers; and where a wired telephone network is available, you get call girl operations – effectively mobilizing and distributing the actual sites of service but leaving the headquarters vulnerable to raids. But where clients, pimps, and sex workers have access to pagers, cellphones, and instant messaging, locations are temporary, mobile, and indeterminate. It becomes much harder to regulate the sex industry – and to protect workers.

[...]

Pornographers, as they always managed with new technology, have been particularly fast on their feet. Photography and print facilitated the production of pornography but generated a distribution problem; the obvious, site-specific option of a porn store was vulnerable to busts and shakedowns, might embarrass the customers, and might be resisted by neighbors. Pornographers quickly turned to the smut magazine format, the mail, and plain brown wrappers, but they still had to contend with mail regulators and customs officials. (Even today, don't try smuggling skin pix into Saudi.) They swiftly took advantage of the Internet, offshore servers, encryption, and anonymous remailers, but the authorities immediately countered by raiding server locations and looking for downloaded nasties on PC hard drives. Now it is possible to create highly redundant, decentralized, peer-to-peer porn networks (that is, to Napsterize smut), and to distribute to wireless devices at mobile locations. As broadband wireless develops, delivery of high-resolution pornographic images and videos (may be captured live by wireless camera/transmitters) will undoubtedly be a killer app.

[...]

Remobilizing Services

The simplest of transportation networks allowed itinerant poets and scholars to visit communities and doctors to make house calls. However, as educational and medical services increasingly depended upon accumulations of specialized equipment, supplies, and expertise, they were centralized at large-scale, purpose-built facilities – particularly modern schools, university campuses, and hospitals. Sometimes students and patients became long-term inmates of these facilities, sometimes they visited them on regular schedules (school days and school hours), sometimes they went by appointment, and sometimes they made emergency visits – but always they had to remove themselves from the contexts of their communities and enter particularized environments to access the services they needed. The ivory tower and the magic mountain came to symbolize this system's reliance upon separation, the invigilated exam room and the Nurse Ratchet its engagement with structures of control.

Throughout the twentieth century, educational and medical complexes (sometimes combined) grew and coevolved with urban networks. Sometimes they were simply concentrations of specialized facilities within the urban fabric, as at University College London or New York University, and sometimes they were discrete, clearly bounded, even walled and gated campuses. Increasingly extensive transportation networks enabled them to serve larger populations, provided their personnel with access to housing, and encouraged them to take advantage of scale to develop specializations. They evolved into major urban elements and important nodes in transportation networks. The UCLA campus, at the edge of the Los Angeles basin, may be the mature masterpiece of the genre; there is a pretty piazza at the center, the pavilions of the arts and humanities occupy the green and hilly northern end, big-footprint medical and engineering buildings cluster at the more urban southern end, and the perimeter is defined by a ring road studded with huge parking structures and card-key access points. Daily commuters converge on campus from throughout the basin, the San Fernando Valley to the north, and Orange County to the south.

[...]

At the macro scale, during the 1980s and 1990s, wired interconnections encouraged division of labor among campuses, increasingly ambitious and long-distance campus-to-campus collaborations, and formation of geographically distributed professional communities. Much as designers of the Arpanet had focused on long-distance sharing of computational resources, college, university, and medical center administrators became increasingly interested in the possibility of sharing specialized human resources through classrooms and lecture halls equipped for videoconferencing, telemedicine suites, and Web sites. At the micro scale, though, wired networks tied teachers and students to fixed points of presence – often to the detriment of face-to-face community; they tended to keep faculty members (like Dilbert) in their offices and students in wired dormitory rooms. As local and distributed communities competed for mindshare, local began to lose ground; professors and medical specialists often discovered that they had more valuable and satisfying exchanges with colleagues on the far side of the world than with those just down the hall.

Meanwhile, the Internet had expanded far beyond its ancestral heartland in academia – making not only on-campus sites, but also homes and offices generally, potential delivery points for remote education and telemedicine services. In their most elementary form, remote service sites simply pumped out information that might otherwise have been delivered through print, lectures, or face-to-face consultations – maybe personalized according to the stored needs profiles of clients. With higher bandwidth and more sophisticated software, these sites could efficiently provide interactions that approximated face-to-face; you might take a test online from the comfort of your home, or if you lived in a remote community, you might get a reasonably good medical examination through videoconferencing.

Finally, wireless networks superimposed continuous fields of service presence onto this pattern of major and minor points of presence. In particular, the introduction of campus wireless networks in the early 2000s, combined with portable wireless devices and the growth in electronic distribution of educational material, quickly began to break down the rigid person-to-place connections that had hitherto characterized campus life; students did not need to be at fixed network drops or computer clusters to download or electronically interact, they did not have to go to the library to pick up texts, they no longer required desks or carrels to write, and they did not need to show up in person for videocast lectures.[4] They could form ad hoc discussion and collaboration clusters, wherever and whenever they wanted, without losing access to online resources or contact with their geographically extended communities. The classically minded recalled that the Greek philosophers did not have offices and classrooms elaborately organized into departments and schools; they strolled freely through the groves and stoas of academe – but, as Plato vividly emphasized, they had to rely upon their memories. Now, while a scholar stands in line for a sandwich, she can wirelessly search the *TLG* for a passage from Plato to clinch an argument with her lunch companion.

As wireless education serves the mind, wireless medical care attends to the body – and the effects of the resulting service continuity are, potentially, even more dramatic. When monitoring and emergency summoning devices began to migrate from the hospital to the networked home, continuity of service could be increased, and separation of patients from their families and communities could be decreased. Now further migration, to wearable and implanted, wirelessly connected devices, is taking that process a step further. And more active care, through wirelessly operated implants and medication delivery devices, is an obvious possibility.[5] All this is not so different from continuously monitoring the conditions and dynamically responding to the biological needs of deep-sea divers or astronauts but without the cumbersome suits and the tethers back to the ships.

Marketers of goods and services can potentially make use of wireless, context-aware devices to monitor customer needs continuously and respond to them appropriately, thus gaining a competitive advantage.[6] If you are in a theater, for example, your cellphone might discreetly vibrate in your pocket instead of ringing loudly and disturbing your neighbors. …

The advantages of wireless fields of presence are accompanied by subtle and not-so-subtle challenges to the regime of separation and control that has long been built into schools, campuses, and medical facilities. Schoolteachers were among the first to notice this, as kids equipped with wireless devices began to order pizzas in class, pass SMS notes, and clandestinely circulate answers to test questions. Retailers began to worry that customers in their stores might scan the barcodes on products and wirelessly search for competitors with better prices. Professors delivering lectures began to wonder if they had the undivided attention of students crouched over their wireless laptops and were surprised in seminars as their interlocutors silently downloaded salient information to interject into the discussion. The immediate authoritarian response, of course, was to try to banish personal wireless devices – but this was doomed to failure. When the dust settled, few would willingly give up the benefits of continuous connection.

Restructuring Live/Work

Before the emergence of large-scale networks, dwellings and workplaces were often intermingled in fine-grained spatial patterns. Shepherds slept with their flocks, peasants lived among their fields, craft specialists both lived and worked in urban professional quarters, and merchants resided above their shops. But as Engels so vividly observed in Manchester, industrial cities changed that. Factory owners provided work space, the urban proleteriat provided labor, and the workers lived outside the factory gates. The separation of noisy, polluted industrial zones from leafy garden suburbs, and their linkage by commuter transportation networks, became one of the great triumphs of enlightened urban planning.

In a parallel development, telegraph and telephone networks enabled the spatial separation of management from industrial production and allowed managers and clerical workers to cluster with others of their kind in downtown central business districts. The focusing of transportation networks on these centers, and the concentration of network infrastructure there, drove up land values and encouraged high-density development. Steel, concrete, glass, and electrically powered systems provided the means, and the high rise office tower emerged in response to these conditions; it became the characteristic business workplace of the twentieth century.

There were numerous variations on the theme of the coarsegrained industrial city, with its separated industrial, commercial, and residential zones linked by commuter transportation networks. You might get suburban office parks with parking lots instead of high-density, transit-serviced cores, secondary and tertiary centers, clusters of towers at edge-city locations, and vast, multicentered urban regions such as that of Los Angeles. But in major cities the principle of spatial separation into discrete zones, combined with that of commuter linkage among zones, obtained with remarkable consistency throughout the twentieth century.

As the capabilities of wired telecommunication networks developed and their service areas expanded, though, there was increasing speculation that telecommunication might substitute for travel within this sort of urban structure.[7] ... One version of this idea was the concept of home telecommuting; the cubicle might become a study in a suburban house.[8] Another was that of the electronic cottage ... if you no longer had to commute to work, you might move your residence out beyond suburbia to a distant recreational or scenic area. ... And another, again, was motivated by urban workspace costs; employers realized that they could save on rent by relocating employees to less expensive, suburban satellite locations instead of keeping them all at expensive downtown sites, with the added advantage that employees could save on commute time and costs.

But these strategies merely substituted one fixed workplace for another, and forced a tradeoff between them. As a result, they met with mixed success. There have been some interesting examples of live/work televillages in attractive locations, such as Richard Rogers's design for ParcBIT in the Balearic Islands,[9] and Giancarlo De Carlo's rehabilitation of the Ligurian mountain village of Colletta di Castelbianco,[10] and electronically serviced live/work has certainly played a role in the revitalization of urban areas such as Manhattan's SoHo, San Francisco's SoMa, and Singapore's China Square. Telecommuting has also proved to be crucial to rapid disaster recovery in the wake of events such as the 1994 Northridge earthquake in Southern California, and the September 11 attack on New York, which destroyed workplaces and disrupted commuter travel.

[...]

By contrast, wireless networks, portable electronic devices, and online work environments now allow information workers to move freely from location to location as needs, desires, and circumstances demand. By the early 2000s, many workers (and their employers) had discovered that they just needed a cellphone and a laptop to operate effectively at their nominal workplaces, on commuter trains, in airplane seats and airport lounges, in hotel rooms, at the sites of clients and collaborators, at home, and on vacation. Anyplace was now a potential workplace. And this condition would only intensify as the technology of nomadics developed and proliferated.

So the emerging, characteristic pattern of twenty-first-century work is not that of telecommuting, as many futurists had once confidently predicted; it is that of the mobile worker who appropriates multiple, diverse sites as workplaces.[11] As architects are rapidly discovering, this breaks down rigid functional distinctions among specialized spaces, and makes provision for varied and sometimes unpredictable functions increasingly critical; a home must serve as an occasional workplace, a hotel room must also be an office, a café table must accommodate laptops, and a workplace must adapt to more complex and dynamic patterns of use. Special places, with particularly desirable qualities, become powerful attractors when traditional person-to-workplace linkages are loosened; if you have your wireless connections, a seat under a tree in spring beats an interior office cubicle. And electronically arranged, ad hoc meeting places – where you can most conveniently form the human clusters you need at a particular moment, while remaining in wireless contact – dominate the fixed locations and inflexible schedules that had once been necessary to enable interaction and coordination.

Hertzian Public Space

Public spaces have traditionally worked best at nodes in transportation networks. The central crossroad is typically the focus of rural village life, and in larger settlements this crossroad often grows into a village green, a piazza, or a town square. Still more extensive cities – among them Rome, Georgian London, Haussmann's Paris, and Cerdá's Barcelona – have frequently been organized around multiple public spaces embedded in networks of streets and avenues.

These spaces become even more effective when they superimpose nodes of different networks. The village crossroad, for example, may not only play a role in local pedestrian circulation, it may also serve as a stop in a regional bus transportation network and the site of a public telephone box. A piazza may be activated by a well of fountain – that is, a public node in a water supply network. And multiple transportation networks may converge, as at Sydney's Circular Quay, where ferries, trains, buses, taxis, and urban pedestrians come together at a bustling, café lined interchange and meeting point.

In many contexts, wired telecommunication nerworks have both taken advantage of the activity genetated by this superimposicion and added an important component to it. Central intersections and squares were natural sites for post and telegraph offices, and before private telephones were common and toll calls were inexpensive, these often expanded to provide banks of booths for long-distance phone service. Similarly, in the early Internet era, before network connections had become commonplace and computers had dropped to insignificant cost relative to income levels (a shift still under way in developing countries and areas), networked computer clusters emerged as new foci of public spaces – much like the traditional village well, but supplying a different type of scarce resource. At MIT, for example, Athena clusters unexpectedly developed into important meeting and socializing points. Public libraries also got connected and introduced computer clusters. Then, as the necessary infrastructure spread throughout urban areas, Internet cafés began to take root. It was not surprising that, when telecommunications infrastructure began to return to war-torn Afghanistan in 2002, one of the first points of Internet availability was an Internet café in the basement of Kabul's Intercontinental Hotel.

Just as the social role of the village well began to fade with the introduction of domestic piped water supply, though, so did that of the public point of network presence as domestic space got wired and computers got cheaper. If you had a networked computer at home, you didn't need an Internet café, and the point of presence that really mattered to you was the switching node that connected your domestic line (the "last mile" of the network) to your service provider.[12] Public access points hung on longer in specialized contexts – where they provided significant technological advantage (in particular, faster and more reliable connection), as in India, where infrastructure is sparse and often unreliable and private connection remained beyond the reach of many, in China, where Internet cafés also served as connections to a wider world and rallying points for the intelligentsia, and in Korea,[13] where PC *baangs* allowed kids to escape from crowded domestic space and strict parental supervision and had a particular cultural resonance in the land of consumer electronic gadgets – but by the early 2000s it was clear that they would eventually shrink to niche roles at best. They would go the way of other hopeful space mutations, such as the telegraph station and the drive-in movie theater, which had emerged in response to particular technological conditions and were left behind by further technological change.

Meanwhile, continuous fields of network presence had begun to blanket public spaces. This began with cellular technology, which brought phones out of seclusion like bees from a hive and rapidly transformed public behavior and space use – most obviously by inserting the essentially private activity of phone conversation into space governed by the conventions of public conduct. This created frictions, which had to be resolved by the development of new rules of etiquette. Miss Manners had her work cut out for her: continuous phone accessibility was part of the point, but this produced rings at inappropriate times and places. You might call from a public place to avoid being overheard at home or in the office, but you might end up annoying strangers with your chatter; you might be so engrossed in your private conversation that you lost track of your immediate surroundings and walked into someone; your phone might inconveniently ring while you were in company, forcing you to find a quick and graceful way to excuse yourself; and, if you couldn't help overhearing an embarrassing private conversation, you had to avert your eyes and compose your face.

A more profound outcome was the new capacicy of mobile urbanites, at unknown locations, to arrange ad hoc meeting places.[14] In the past, meetings had depended upon explicit prearrangement (leaving you at a loss if, for some reason, your party didn't show up as expected), upon random encounter, and upon standard meeting places and regular schedules that increased the probability of random encounter. Italian piazzas, for example, had traditionally depended for their social efficacy upon their central locations and ingrained conventions of showing up there at established times; now, Italians simply call one another and arrange meetings on the fly. Piazzas still look the same and still work superbly as public space, but their patterns of use have become far more flexible.

With the emergence of 802.11 wireless networks in the early 2000s, a new field of functional possibility superimposed itself on public space. This hub-and-card technology provided convenient connectivity for wireless laptops, and enthusiasts set about creating public wireless hotspots. These first emerged in semipublic spaces – such as cafés, bars, lobbies, waiting rooms, and airport lounges – which suddenly became much more useful as ad hoc workplaces and online interaction points; instead of reading a newspaper, you could download your email or surf the Web. (If you wanted privacy, you learned to take the seat against the wall, and keep the back of your screen to the public). Then hotspots migrated outdoors. Midtown Manhattan's Bryant Park was one of the first outdoor public places to provide for 802.11 surfing under the trees and email from a park bench. A latterday Manet might paint laptop users on the grass.

In general, as these transformations of public space illustrate, there is a strong relationship between prevailing network structure and the distribution of activities over public and private places. Where essential urban networks have relatively few access points, as with public transportation and water supply networks, the access points are often in public places, attract activity to those places, and thus strengthen their roles as meeting and interaction points. When networks become more ramified – as with domestic water supply and sewer, automobile transportation, electrical, and communication networks – they tend to decentralize functions and move them into private spaces – the public bathhouse gives way to the private bathroom, the public theater to the private home entertainment center. And where networks go wireless, they mobilize activities that had been tied to fixed locations and open up ways of reactivating urban public space; the home entertainment center reemerges as the Walkman, the home telephone as the cellphone, and the home computer as the laptop.

Virtual Campfires

In traditional nomadic societies, regularly rekindled eampfires provided mobile focal points for social life. With urbanization, social life became more commonly focused by fixed attractions – village wells, domestic hearths, and computer network drops. In the mobile wireless era, a third alternative has emerged; we can use our portable communication devices to construct meeting points and gathering places on the fly – places that may only be known within particular, electronically linked groups, and which may only play such roles for fleeting moments.

NOTES

1. The image is, of course, anachronistic. It shows a fifteenth-century scholar rather than a fourth-century one. But this does not affect my point.
2. Jerome's cube was illustrated by many medieval and Renaissance artists, including Antonello and Dürer. Dilbert's was chronicled by Scot Adams in a popular syndicated strip.
3. Early descriptions of the process of digital fragmentation and recombination, as it had begun to unfold, were provided in William J. Mitchell, *City of Bits: Space, Place, and the Infobahn* (Cambridge: MIT Press, 1994), and William J. Mitchell, *E-topia: Urban Life, Jim – But Not As We Know It* (Cambridge: MIT Press, 1999).
4. For an early snapshot of this transformation in progress, see Josh McHugh, "Unplugged U," *Wired*, October 2002, <www.wired.com/wired/archive/10.10/dartmouth.html> (accessed December 2002).
5. See, for example, Dadong Wan, "Magic Medicine Cabinet: A Situated Portal for Healthcare," *Proceedings of International Symposium on Handheld and Ubiquitous Computing* (Karlsruhe, September 1999).
6. Andrew Fano and Anatole Gershman, "The Future of Business Services in the Age of Ubiquitous Computing," *Communications of the ACM* 45, no. 12 (December 2002): 83–87.
7. For an introduction to telecommuting, live/work, and the associated literature, see William J. Mitchell, "Homes and Neighborhoods," chapter 5 in *Etopia*. A more recent

and detailed overview is provided by Penny Gurstein, *Wired to the World, Chained to the Home: Telework in Daily Life* (Vancouver: University of British Columbia Press, 2001).

8. For a useful typology of live/work space configurations, see Gurstein, *Wired to the World*, pp. 138–45.

9. <www.parcbit.es> (accessed December 2002).

10. Ian Wylie, "La Dolce Vita, Internet Style," *Fast Company*, 20 August 2002, p. 76. See also <www.colletta.it> (accessed December 2002).

11. For an analysis of the potential advantages and disadvantages of mobilizing information work, see Gordon B. Davis, "Anytime/Anyplace Computing and the Future of Knowledge Work," *Communications of the ACM* 45, no. 12 (December 2002): 67–73.

12. On the complex set of issues related to domestic connection, see National Research Council, *Broadband: Bringing Home the Bits* (Washington, D.C.: National Academy Press, 2002).

13. For a lively discussion of Seoul's PC *baang* culture, in the early 2000s, see J. C. Hertz, "The Bandwidth Capital of the World," *Wired* 10, no. 8 (August 2002), <www.wired.com/wired/archive/10.08/korea.html> (accessed December 2002). See also Howard W. French, "Korea's Real Rage for Virtual Games," *New York Times*, 9 October 2002, p. A8.

14. This creates a demand for software to help arrange ad hoc meetings among mobile participants and to perform meeting follow-up functions. See, for example, Mikael Wiberg, "Roam Ware: An Integrated Architecture for Seamless Interaction in between Mobile Meetings," *ACM Group '01* (Boulder, September 2001).

THE END OF GEOGRAPHY OR THE EXPLOSION OF PLACE?

Conceptualizing Space, Place and Information Technology

8

Stephen Graham

I   Introduction: Cyberspace, Spatial Metaphors, Space and Place

It is now widely argued that the 'convergence' of computers with digital tele-communications and media technologies is creating 'cyberspace' – a multi-media skein of digital networks which is infusing rapidly into social, cultural and economic life. Cyberspace is variously defined as a 'consensual hallucination, a graphic representation of data abstracted from the banks of every computer in the human system' (Gibson, 1984: 51); a 'parallel universe' (Benedikt, 1991: 15); or a 'new kind of space, invisible to our direct senses, a space which might become more important than physical space itself [and which is] layered on top of, within and between the fabric of traditional geographical space' (Batty, 1993: 615–16).

Interestingly from the view point of geographers, the recent growth of discourses on 'cyberspace' and new communications technologies, even the very word 'cyber-space' itself, have been dominated by spatial and territorial metaphors (Stefik, 1996). 'Cyberspace', suggests Steve Pile (1994: 1817), 'is a plurality of clashing, resonating and shocking metaphors'. The expanding lexicon of the Internet – the most well-known vehicle of cyberspace – is not only replete with, but actually *constituted* by,

Stephen Graham, "The End of Geography or the Explosion of Place? Conceptualizing Space, Place and Information Technology," pp. 165–85 from *Progress in Human Geography* 22:2 (1998).

the use of geographical metaphors. Debates about the Internet use spatial metaphors to help visualize what are, effectively, no more than abstract flows of electronic signals, coded as information, representation and exchange. Thus, an Internet point-of-presence becomes a web *site*. The ultimate convergent, broadband descendant of the Internet is labelled the information super*highway*. A satellite node becomes a tele*port*. A bulletin board system becomes a virtual *community* or an electronic *neighbourhood*. Web sites run by municipalities become virtual *cities* (see Graham and Aurigi, 1997). The whole society-wide process of technological innovation becomes a wild-west-like electronic *frontier* awaiting colonization. Those 'exploring' this frontier become Web *surfers*, virtual *travellers*, or, to Bill Mitchell (1995: 7), electronic *flâneurs* who 'hang out on the network'. The Internet as a whole is variously considered to be an electronic *library*, a medium for electronic *mail* or a digital market*place* (Stefik, 1996). And Microsoft seductively ask '*Where* do you want to go today?' And so the list goes on and on.

Such spatial metaphors help make tangible the enormously complex and arcane technological systems which underpin the Internet, and other networks, and the growing range of transactions, social and cultural interactions, and exchanges of labour power, data, services, money and finance that flow over them. While many allege that networks like the Internet tend to 'negate geometry', to be 'anti-spatial' or to be 'incorporeal' (Mitchell, 1995: 8–10), the cumulative effect of spatial metaphors means that they become visualizable and imageably reconstructed as giant, apparently territorial systems. These can, by implication, somehow be imagined similarly to the material and social spaces and places of daily life. In fact, such spatial metaphors are commonly related, usually through simple binary oppositions, to the 'real', material spaces and places within which daily life is confined, lived and constructed.

Some argue that the strategy of developing spatial metaphors is 'perhaps the only conceptual tool we have for understanding the development of a new technology' (Sawhney, 1996: 293). Metaphor-making 'points to the process of learning and discovery – to those analogical leaps from the familiar to the unfamiliar which rally the imagination and emotion as well as the intellect' (Buttimer, 1982: 90, quoted in Kirsch, 1995: 543). ...

But the metaphors that become associated with information technologies are, like those representations surrounding the material production of space and territory (Lefebvre, 1984), active, ideological constructs. Concepts like the 'information society' and the 'information superhighway' have important roles in shaping the ways in which technologies are socially constructed, the uses to which they are put, and the effects and power relations surrounding their development. ... As Nigel Thrift (1996a: 1471) contends, 'in this form of [technological] determinism, the new technological order provides the narrative mill. The new machines become both the model for society and its most conspicuous sign'.

[...]

In this article I aim to explore some of the emerging conceptual treatments of the relationships between information technology systems and space and place.

Building on my recent work with Simon Marvin on the relationships between telecommunications and contemporary cities (Graham and Marvin, 1996), and on conceptualizing telecommunications-based urban change (Graham, 1996; 1997a), I identify three broad, dominating perspectives and explore them in turn. First, there is the perspective of *substitution* and *transcendence* – the idea that human territoriality, and the space and place-based dynamics of human life, can somehow be replaced using new technologies. Secondly, there is the *co-evolution* perspective which argues that both the electronic 'spaces' and territorial spaces are necessarily produced *together*, as part of the ongoing restructuring of the capitalist political-economic system. Finally, there is the *recombination* perspective, which draws on recent work in actor-network theory. Here the argument is that a fully *relational* view of the links between technology, time, space and social life is necessary. ...

II Substitution and Transcendence: Technological Determinism, Generalized Interactivity and the End of Geography

Both the dominant popular and academic debates about space, place and information technologies adopt the central metaphor of 'impact'. In this 'mainstream' of social research on technology (Mansell, 1994), and in the bulk of popular and media debates about the Internet and 'information superhighway', new telecommunications technologies are assumed directly to cause social and spatial change, in some simple, linear and deterministic way. Such technological determinism accords with the dominant cultural assumptions of the West, where the pervasive experience of 'technology is one of apparent inevitability' (Hill, 1988: 23). Here technology is cast as an essential and independent agent of change that is separated from the social world and 'impacts' it, through some predictable, universal, revolutionary wave of change. Thus, that central purveyor of cyberspace rhetoric, *Wired* magazine, proclaimed in their 1996 (pp. 43–44) 'Manifesto for the digital society' that:

> the Digital Revolution that is sweeping across society is actually a communications revolution which is transforming society. When used by people who understand it, digital technology allows information to be transmitted and transmuted in fundamentally limitless ways. This ability is the basis of economic success around the world. But it offers more than that. It offers the priceless intangibles of friendship, community and understanding. It offers a new democracy dominated neither by vested interests of political parties nor the mob's baying howl. It can narrow the gap that separates capital from labour; it can deepen the bonds between people and planet.

In terms of the 'spatial impacts' of current advances in communications technologies, two broad and related discourses have emerged from the loosely linked group of technological forecasters, cyberspace commentators and critics who found their commentaries on simple technological determinism (that is, extrapolating the 'logic' of the spatial impacts of telecommunications from the intrinsic qualities of the technologies themselves). First, there are widespread predictions that concentrated urban areas will loose their spatial 'glue' in some wholesale shift towards reliance on broadband, multimedia communications grids. Advanced capitalist societies are thus liberated from spatial and temporal constraints and are seen to decentralize towards spatial and areal uniformity. Secondly, there are debates about the development of essentially immersive virtual environments, which, effectively, allow the immersive qualities of geographical place to be transmitted remotely.

1   Areal Uniformity, Urban Dissolution and Generalized Interactivity

... As technologies of media, computing and telecommunications converge and integrate; as equipment and transmission costs plummet to become virtually distance independent; and as broadband integrated networks start to mediate all forms of entertainment, social interaction, cultural experience, economic transaction and the labour process, distance effectively *dies* as a constraint on social, economic and cultural life (*The Economist*, 1995). Human life becomes 'liberated' from the constraints of space and frictional effects of distance. Anything becomes possible anywhere and at any time (see Graham and Marvin, 1996). All information becomes accessible everywhere and anywhere. The 'logic' of telecommunications and electronic mediation is therefore interpreted as inevitably supporting geographical dispersal from large metropolitan regions, or even the effective dissolution of the city itself (Gillespie, 1992; Graham, 1997a).

Most common here is the assumption that networks of large metropolitan cities will gradually emerge to be some technological anachronism, as propinquity, concentration, place-based relations and transportation flows are gradually substituted by some universalized, interactive, broadband communications medium (the ultimate 'Information Superhighway'). To Baldwin and colleagues (1996), for example, this all-mediating network, this technological Holy Grail of fully converged telephony, TV, media and data flow, embellished with virtual shopping and interactive video communications, is already in sight, with the trials of so-called full-service networks (FSNs) in cities like Orlando, Florida. 'We now have', they write (1996: 1),

a vision of an ideal broadband communication system that would integrate voice, video and data with storage of huge libraries of material available on demand, with the option of interaction as appropriate. The telephone, cable, broadcast, and computer industries, relatively independent in the past, are converging to create these integrated broadband systems.

... 'In urban terms', writes Pawley (1995), 'once time has become instantaneous, space becomes unnecessary. In a "spaceless city", the whole population might require no more than the 30 atom diameter light beam of an optical computer system.'

Such substitutionist arguments, in fact, have a long lineage. ...

... Marshall McLuhan argued that the emergence of his 'global village' meant that the city 'as a form of major dimensions must inevitably dissolve like a fading shot in a movie' (McLuhan, 1964: p. 366, quoted in Gold, 1990: p. 23). ...

Such technologically determinist predictions also resonate surprisingly strongly with some of the more critical recent perspectives of the relationships between space, place and technological change. For example, Paul Virilio (1993), a French urban theorist and philosopher, recently suggested that a culture of 'generalized interactivity' is emerging, based on pervasive, ubiquitous and multipurpose telematics grids, through which 'everything arrives so quickly that departure becomes unnecessary' (Virilio, 1993: 8). Such a transition, suggests Virilio, will amount to nothing less that a 'crisis in the notion of physical dimension' (1993: 9) of space, place, the region and the city. ...

2 'Mirror Worlds', the Transmission of Place and World Transcendence

Virilio's predictions of the evaporation of the material, physical dynamics of space and place find support in the more optimistic perspectives of 'cyber-gurus' like Nicholas Negroponte (1995) and Bill Gates (1995). Again, the substitution ethos dominates here, with the assumption that sophisticated VR technologies, switched over broadband global grids, will allow immersive, 3D environments to become so life-like that 'real' places will easily become substitutable. David Gelerntner (1991) imagined that such technological trends will lead to the construction of 'mirror worlds', immersive electronic simulations tied into real-time monitoring apparatus which would allow us to 'look into a computer screen and see reality. Some part of your world – the town you live in, the company you work for, your school system, the city hospital – will hang there in a sharp colour image' (Gelerntner, 1991: 1; see also Graham, 1998). ...

Such technologically evangelistic debates about 'digital living' therefore suggest that we are on the verge of accessing a technological infrastructure which will do little less than provide some single, immersive system to mediate all aspects of human life. ... Human societies, cultures and economies are seen simply to *migrate* into the electronic ether, where identities will be flexibly constructed, any services might be accessed, endless fantasy worlds experienced and any task performed, from any location and at any time, by human agents acting *inside* the limitless domains of constructed electronic environments.

Presumably, as human life becomes more and more dominated by what Thu Nguyen and Alexander (1996: 117) call 'participation in the illusion of an eternal and immaterial electronic world', the material world of space and place would become gradually eviscerated. Pascal's shift towards 'complete areal uniformity', of homes and buildings providing equally-spaced entry points into the pure and liberating cyberspace realm, would be underway. Many cyberspace enthusiasts do, indeed, proclaim the need for what Schroeder (1994) has termed 'world rejection'. Here cyberspace is seen to offer an *alternative* territoriality, an infinitely replenishable and extendible realm of spatial opportunity that counters the finitudes and problems of the increasingly crowded and problematic material spaces on earth. Don Mapes, for example, urges us 'to do away with our territoriality'. ... (Mapes, 1994, in Channel 4, 1994).

[...]

III   Co-evolution: the Parallel Social Production of Geographical Space and Electronic Space

... In proffering new technologies as some complete and simple *substitutes* for the material body, the social world, and for space and place, its proponents do little to advance understanding of the complex *co-evolutionary* processes linking new information technologies and space, place and human territoriality. In allocating technologies almost magical transformative powers, in implying the easy emergence of universal social and spatial access to computer networks, and in radically overestimating the degree to which such networks can simply substitute for, and transcend, place-based, face-to-face interaction, Kevin Robins (1995: 139) has argued that they say more about their own (usually masculine) 'omnipotence fantasies' than about how complex combinations of place-based and telemediated interactions co-evolve. ...

Fortunately, however, a much more sophisticated understanding has been developed recently through our second broad perspective which explores how the social production of electronic networks and 'spaces' *co-evolves* with the production of material spaces and places, within the same broad societal trends and social processes (see Mosco, 1996: 173–211). Three strands of work have emerged here: analysing the articulation between place-based and telemediated relationships; addressing the linkages between telecommunications and the city; and theoretically analysing the broader roles that new telecommunications and information technologies play in supporting the production of new types of spatial arrangements.

1   Articulations between Place-Based and Telemediated Relationships

Rather than assuming some simple substitutional relationship, our second perspective suggests that complex *articulations* are emerging between interactions in geographical space and place, and the electronic realms accessible through new technologies. The argument here is that, because cyber-evangelists are naively obsessed with the abstract *transmissional* capabilities of information technologies, technologically determinist debates usually neglect the richness and embeddedness of human life within space and place. Sawhney (1996: 309) criticizes the 'very transmission-oriented view of human communication [in cyberspace debates]. The purpose of human communication is reduced to transfer of information and the coordination of human activity. The ritual or the communal aspect of human communication is almost totally neglected'.

Technologically determinist commentators are accused of failing to appreciate the social, cultural and economic dynamics of place and space that cannot be simply telemediated no matter how broadband, 3D or immersive the substitutes. Quite the reverse, in fact, because the human construction of space and place is seen actually to ground and contextualize applications and uses of new technologies. 'The urban world networked by [Bill] Gates' technologies "strung out on the wire"', argues Denis Cosgrove (1996: 1495), 'is not disconnected, abstract, inhuman; it is bound in the places and times of actual lives, into human existences that are as connected, sensuous and personal as they ever have been'. ...

2   Telecommunications and the City

This 'state of suspension' or articulation between place-based and electronically mediated realms is especially evident in the contemporary metropolis, which, despite some trends towards the decentralization of routine service functions (OTA, 1995), shows no sign of simple, wholesale evisceration. ... New communications technologies are not simply substituting for the experience of, or reliance on, metropolitan places. Rather, a complex co-evolution, articulation and synergy between place-based and telemediated exchange seem to be emerging. ...

Drawing on McLuhan, Castells (1996: 373) similarly posits that the new, integrated media systems will bring with it what he calls a 'culture of real virtuality' drawing diverse participants and fragmented communities into new symbolic environments in which 'reality itself (that is, people's material/symbolic existence) is entirely captured, fully immersed in a virtual image setting, in the world of make believe, in which appearances are not just seen on the screen through which experience is communicated, but they become the experience'. While increasingly encompassing, however, such exchanges do not simply substitute for place-based material social worlds. Rather, they embody complex global–local articulations between the 'space of places' and the 'space of flows' (Castells, 1996: 423–28).

After all, as with television, radio and printing technologies, any cursory examination of the Internet and World Wide Web shows that much of the traffic actually *represents and articulates* real places and spaces, supporting and generating physical mobility, tourism, transport and trips for the highly mobile, élite groups that currently use it in the process. ...

As I show with Simon Marvin in a recent book (Graham and Marvin, 1996), cyberspace is, in fact, a predominantly metropolitan phenomenon which is developing *out of* the old cities. ...

The work of Jean Gottmann (1982) has clearly demonstrated that the incorporation of computer networks into the economic, administrative and sociocultural dynamics of the city merely intensifies and adds further capability to the older functions of the post, the telegraph and the telephone. ...

New information technologies, in short, actually resonate with, and are bound up in, the active construction of space and place, rather than making it somehow redundant. William Mitchell's notion of 'recombinant architecture' is especially relevant here, because it demonstrates how constructed and produced material spaces are now being infused with cyberspace 'entry points' of all kinds (Mitchell, 1995). Material space and electronic space are increasingly being produced together. The power to function economically and link socially increasingly relies on constructed, place-based, material spaces intimately woven into complex telematics infrastructures linking them to other places and spaces. 'Today's institutions', argues Mitchell (1995: 126), 'are supported not only by buildings but by telecommunications and computer software.' Thus the articulation between widely stretched telematics systems, and produced material spaces and places, becomes the norm and is a defining feature of contemporary urbanism. 'Constructed spaces', he suggests,

> will increasingly be seen as electronically-serviced sites where bits meet the body – where digital information is translated into visual, auditory, tactile or otherwise sensorily perceptible form, and vice versa. Displays and sensors for presenting and capturing information will be as essential as doors (Mitchell, 1994).

Bookstores, libraries, universities, schools, banks, theatres, museums and galleries, hospitals, manufacturing firms, trading floors and service providers increasingly become embodied through their presence in both material spaces and electronic spaces. While some substitution is evident – for example, with the closure of banking branches paralleling the growth of telebanking – much of the traditional, nonroutine face-to-face activity within constructed spaces, and the transportation that supports it, seems extremely resilient to simple substitution. In other words, the contemporary city, while housing vast arrays of telematic 'entry points' into the burgeoning worlds of electronic spaces, is a cauldron of emotional and personal worlds and attachments, an engine of reflexivity, trust and reciprocity (Amin and Graham, 1998).

The usefulness of the co-evolution perspective is that it underlines the fact that materially constructed urban places and telecommunications networks stand in a state of *recursive interaction*, shaping *each other* in complex ways that have a history running back to the days of me origin of the telegraph and telephone. ...

The complex articulations between the local and global dynamics of both material places and electronic spaces have recently been explored by Staple (1993). He believes that the Internet and other communications technologies, far from simply collapsing spatial barriers, actually have a dialectic effect, helping to compress time and space barriers while, concurrently, supporting a localizing, fragmenting logic of 'tribalization'. Far from unifying all within a single cyberspace, the Internet, he argues, may actually enhance the commitment of different social and cultural interest groups to particular material places and electronic spaces, thus constituting a 'geographical explosion of place' (Staple, 1993: 52). This 'new tribalism', exemplified by the use of the Internet to support complex diasporas across the globe, and to draw together multiple, fragmentary special interest groups on a planetary basis, 'folds' localities, cities and regions into 'the new electronic terrain' (Staple, 1993: 52).

But it is important to stress that the ways in which places become enmeshed into globally stretched networks like the Internet will be a diverse, contingent process. A wide diversity of relations seems likely to exist between the urban structures and systems, and indeed the particularities of culture, of different spaces and the growth of telemediated interaction. ...

3   Telecommunications, 'Spatial Fixes' and the Production of Space

Theoretical perspectives drawing on critical political economy serve to exemplify further the ways in which new telecommunications systems are materially bound up with the production of complex new social and economic geographies. Reacting against the all-encompassing and overgeneralized concepts of the 'global village' and 'time-space compression', Scott Kirsch (1995: 544, emphasis in original) argues that 'by resorting to the rather cartoonish shrinking world metaphor, we lose sight of the complex relations ... between capital, *technology*, and space, through which space is not "shrinking" but rather must be perpetually recast'.

While new information and telecommunications technologies support more flex-ibility in the way production interests, services and media firms, tourists and investors treat space, they do not herald some simple shift to a world of pure, absolute mobility. Rather, time and space barriers become reconstituted and reformed within global geometries of flow, incorporation and exclusion. ...

Perhaps the clearest exploration of how telecommunications become woven in to the production of new geographical landscapes of production, consumption and distribution at all spatial scales comes from Eric Swyngedouw (1993: 305). Building on the work of Harvey (1985), he argues that every social and economic activity is necessarily geographical. It is '*inscribed in space and takes place*' (emphasis in origi-nal). Human societies 'cannot escape place in the structuring of the practices of everyday life' (p. 305). Within an internationalizing economy, capitalist firms and governments must continually struggle to develop new solutions to the tensions and crisis tendencies inherent within capitalism, between what David Harvey calls 'fixity' and the need for 'motion', mobility and the global circulation of information, money, capital, services, labour and commodities (Harvey, 1985). Currently, such tensions and crises arise because increasingly widely dispersed areas of production, con-sumption and exchange, befitting of the internationalizing economy, need to be integrated and co-ordinated into coherent economic systems. Space thus needs to be 'commanded' and controlled, on an increasingly international scale.

To do this, relatively immobile and embedded fixed transport and telecommuni-cations infrastructures must be produced, linking production sites, distribution facilities and consumption spaces that are tied together across space with the transport and communications infrastructure necessary to ensure that a spatial 'fix' exists that will maintain and support profitability. Without the elaboration of ever more sophisticated and globally stretched transport and communications infrastructures, Harvey (1993: 7) argues that 'the tension between fixity and mobility erupts into generalized crises, when the landscape shaped in relation to a certain phase of development ... becomes a barrier to further [capital] accumulation'. Thus, new telecommunications networks 'have to be immobilised in space, in order to facilitate greater movement for the remainder' (Harvey, 1985: 149). ...

Crucially, then, the political economic perspective underlines that the development of new telecommunications infrastructures is not some value-neutral, technologically pure process, but an asymmetric social struggle to gain and maintain social power, the power to control space and social processes over distance. ...

By demystifying, and unpacking, the social and power relations surrounding telecommunications and the production of space, the political economic perspective does much to debunk the substitutionist myths of technological determinism discussed above. It allows us to reveal the socially contingent effects of new technologies, the way they are enrolled into complex social and spatial power relations and struggles, and the ways in which some groups, areas and interests may benefit from the effects of new technologies, while others actually lose out. Thus, 'the increased liberation and freedom from place as a result of new mobility modes for some may lead to the disempowerment and relative exclusion for others' (Swyngedouw, 1993: 322).

An excellent example of this is the current transformation of utility markets, under pressures of competition and liberalization, and the experiences of consumers at different ends of the market (Graham, 1997b). On the one hand, affluent consumers will have 'smart meters' which use telematics to allow them to access supplies for many, distant, competitors in a 'virtual market' for energy, from the comfort of their own homes. On the other, over 4 million poorer UK electricity consumers have already had their electromechanical utility meters turned into electronic 'prepayment' meters. These lock consumers into one supplier and need to be 'topped up' electronically before use, necessitating a physical journey to the post office – a major problem for many with already poor mobility, health problems, and poor physical services.

Building on Giddens' (1990) work on time-space distanciation, Paul Adams (1995) uses the concept of 'personal extensability' to capture how a subject's (telemediated and physical) access to distant spaces, services and places may allow him or her to extend his or her domination over excluded groups and so support the production of divided spaces and cities. 'One person's (or group's) time-space compression', he writes, 'may depend on another person's (or group's) persistent inability to access distant places.' As Adams states, 'the variation of extensability according to race, class, age, gender, and other socially-significant categories binds microscale biographies to certain macro-level societal processes' (Adams, 1995: 268; see Massey, 1993: 66).

Thus, within cities, forms of 'telematics super-inclusion' (Thrift, 1996b) emerge for élite groups, who may help shape cocooned, fortified, urban (often now walled) enclosures, from which their intense access to personal and corporate transport and telematics networks allows them global extensability. Meanwhile, however, a short distance away, in the interstitial urban zones, there are 'off-line' spaces (Graham and Aurigi, 1997), or 'lag-time places' (Boyer, 1996: 20). In these, often-forgotten places, time and space remain profoundly real, perhaps *increasing*, constraints on social life, because of welfare and labour market restructuring and the withdrawal of banking and public transport services. It is easy, in short, to overemphasize the mobility of people and things in simple, all-encompassing assumptions about place-transcendence (Thrift, 1996c: 304), which conveniently ignore the splintering and fragmenting reality of urban space.

To Christine Boyer (1996: 20), the highly uneven geography of contemporary cities, and the growing severing of the 'well designed nodes' of the city from the 'blank, in-between places of nobody's concern', allows fortunate groups to 'deny their complicity' in the production of these new, highly uneven, material urban landscapes. But perhaps the most extreme example of the complex interweaving of new technologies, power relations, and the production of space and place comes with the small, élite group who run the global financial exchanges in world cities. Here, we find that 'the extensible relations of a tiny minority in New York, London, and Tokyo, serve to control vast domains of the world through international networks of information retrieval and command' (Adams, 1995: 277).

IV Recombination: Actor-Network Theory and Relational Time-Spaces

Our third and final perspective takes such *relational* views of the social construction of technology further. Anchored around the actor-network theories of Michel Callon (1986; 1991) and Bruno Latour (1993), and drawing on recent theorizations of Donna Haraway on the emergence of blended human-technological 'cyborgs' (or 'cybernetic organisms' – see Haraway, 1991), a range of researchers from the sociology of science, science, technology and society, cultural anthropology and, increasingly, geography have recently been arguing for a highly contingent, relational perspective of the linkage between technology and social worlds. Actor-network theory emphasizes how particular social situations and human actors 'enrol' pieces of technology, machines, as well as documents, texts and money, into 'actor-networks'.

The perspective is fully relational in that it is 'concerned with how all sorts of bits and pieces; bodies, machines, and buildings, as well as texts, are associated together in attempts to build order' (Bingham, 1996: 32). Absolute spaces and times are meaningless here. Agency is a purely relational process. Technologies only have contingent, and diverse, effects through the ways they become linked into specific social contexts by linked human and technological agency. What Pile and Thrift (1996: 37) call a 'vivid, moving, contingent and open-ended cosmology' emerges. The boundaries between humans and machines become ever more blurred, permeable and cyborgian. … Nigel Thrift (1996a: 1468) summarizes the approach:

> no technology is ever found working in splendid isolation as though it is the central node in the social universe. It is linked – by the social purposes to which it is put – to humans and other technologies of different kinds. It is linked to a chain of different activities involving other technologies. And it is heavily contextualised. Thus the telephone, say, at someone's place of work had (and has) different meanings from the telephone in, say, their bedroom, and is often used in quite different ways.

… The growing *capabilities* of telecommunications, for supporting action at a distance and remote control, do not therefore negate the need for the human actors which use them to struggle to enrol passive technological agents into their efforts to attain real, meaningful remote control. … Such 'heterogeneous work involving programmers, silicon chips, international transmission protocols, users, telephones, institutions, computer languages, modems, lawyers, fibre-optic cables, and governments to name but a few, has had to be done to create envelopes stable enough to carry [electronic information]' (Bingham, 1996: 31).

Thus there is not one single, unified cyberspace; rather, there are multiple, heterogeneous networks, within which telecommunications and information technologies become closely enrolled with human actors, and with other technologies, into systems of sociotechnical relations across space. …

'Cyberspace' therefore needs to be considered as a fragmented, divided and contested multiplicity of heterogeneous infrastructures and actor-networks. For example, there are tens of thousands of specialized corporate networks and intranets. The Internet provides the basis for countless Usenet groups, Listservers, corporate advertising sites, specialized Web sites, multi-user dungeons (MUDs), corporate intranets, virtual communities and increasingly sophisticated flows of media and video. Public switched telephone networks (PSTNs) and the many competing telecoms infrastructures support global systems of private automatic teller machine (ATM) networks, credit card and electronic clearing systems, as well as blossoming applications for CCTV, tele-health, teleshopping and tele-banking, global logistics, remote monitoring, back office and telesales flows, electronic data interchange (EDI), electronic financial transactions and stock market flows, as well as data and telephony flows. And specialized systems of satellite, broadband, cable and broadcasting networks support burgeoning arrays of television flow. Each application has associated with it whole multiplicities of human actors and institutions, who must continually struggle to enrol and maintain the communications technologies, along with other technologies, money and texts, into producing some form of functioning social order. These, and the hundreds of other actor-networks, are always contingent, always constructed, never spatially universal, and always embedded in the microsocial worlds of individuals, groups and institutions. Such sociotechnical networks 'always represent geographies of enablement and constraint' (Law and Bijker, 1992: 301); they always link the local and nonlocal in intimate relational, and reciprocal, connections.

Such a fully relational perspective has important implications for the ways in which we conceptualize place, space and time. For actor-network theory suggests that, rather than simply being space and time *transcending* technologies, telecommunications systems actually act as technological networks within which new spaces and times, and new forms of human interaction, control and organization are continually constructed (Latour, 1987).

Similarly relational rather than absolute theories of time-space are rapidly gaining influence in geography and urban studies (Harvey, 1996: Thrift, 1996a). The unthinking acceptance within urban studies that time and space act simply as objective, unvariant, external containers for the urban scene is now collapsing (Harvey, 1996: 256). Harvey draws on Whitehead's relational theories to suggest that the heterogeneous experience and construction of time within cities is a very real phenomenon. 'Multiple processes', he writes, 'generate multiple *real* as opposed to Leibniz's ideal differentiation in spatio-temporalities' (Harvey, 1996: 259, emphasis in original). Crucially for the conceptualization of place is his notion of 'cogredience' or 'the way in which multiple processes flow together to construct a single consistent, coherent, though multi-faceted time-space system' (Harvey, 1996: 260–61). Thus 'place' becomes an embedded and heterogeneous range of time-space processes; neighbourhoods, cities and regions, by implication, 'cannot be examined independently of the diverse spatio-temporalities such processes contain' (Harvey, 1996: 263–64). As Nigel Thrift (1996a: 2) puts it, drawing on his long-standing work on time geography (Thrift *et al.*, 1978), 'time is a multiple phenomenon; many times are working themselves out simultaneously in resonant interaction with each other.'

The continual recombination of the world, within actor-networks and their specific 'different spaces and different times', is possible because the Internet and other information and communications systems are based on 'technological networks'; these, despite the rhetoric of universality, are always specific and contingent in linking one place to another.

[...]

Work by Thrift (1996a; 1996b; 1996c) has used actor-network theory to show how highly concentrated urban spaces like the City of London, far from suffering some simple dissolution, have, over the past century, actually been continually recombined with new technological networks: the telegraph, telephone and, most recently, the telematics trading system. Such new technologies, he writes, do not produce some 'abstract and inhuman world, strung out on the wire' (Thrift, 1996a: 1480); they are subtly recombined with the spatial and social practices of workers and managers, operating within the complex, material and social spaces of the City.

Often, the use of faster and faster telematics systems actually *increases* the demands for face-to-face contact so that the interpretive loads surrounding information glut can be dealt with rapidly and competitively. 'The major task in the information spaces of telematic cities like the City of London', writes Thrift (1996a; 1481), 'become interpretation and, moreover, interpretation *in action* under the pressure of real-time events'. Thus the production of new material spaces, and the social practices that occur in them, is neither some technological cause-and-effect, nor some simple political-economic machination. Rather, it is

> the hybrid outcome of multiple processes of social configuration processes which are specific to particular differentially-extensive actor-networks (made up of people and things holding each other together) and generate their own space and own times, which will sometimes, and sometimes not, be coincident. There is, in other words, no big picture of the modern City to be had but only a set of constantly evolving sketches (Thrift, 1996a: 1485).

V   Conclusions: Space, Place and Technologies as Relational Assemblies

Two clear conclusions for how we might address the linkages between space, place and information technology emerge from our discussion of the three broad substitution, co-evolution and recombination perspectives.

First, we need to be extremely wary of the dangers of adopting, even implicitly, deterministic technological models and metaphors of technological change. The choice of words here is important. For example, the very notion of a technological 'impact', so long a central feature of mainstream technological debates in urban and regional studies (e.g., Brotchie *et al.*, 1987), is problematic, because of its attendant implications of simple, linear, technological cause and societal effect. In their extreme form, deterministic approaches deliver little but the 'logic' of apparent technological inevitability, naive assumptions about simple, cause-and-effect, social and spatial 'impacts', and even messianic and evangelistic predictions of pure, technological salvation.

The co-evolution perspective teaches us that such perspectives fail to capture the ways in which new technologies are inevitably enrolled into complex social power struggles, within which *both* new technological systems and new material geographical landscapes are produced. The recombination perspective, on the other hand, teaches us that such broad-brush transition and 'impact' models ignore the full, contingent and relational complexity surrounding the social construction of new technologies, within and between specific places. It argues powerfully that, outside such contingencies, the meaning and effects of new information technologies can never be fully understood or simply generalized. To draw again on Thrift's (1996a: 1474) recent work:

> seen in this light, electronic communications technologies are no longer an economic, social or cultural earthquake, but rather a part of a continuing performative history of 'technological' practices, a complex archive of stances, emotions, tacit and cognitive knowledges, and presentations and re-presentations, which seek out and construct these technologies in certain ways rather than others.

Secondly, however, we need to be equally wary of the dangers of adopting simplistic concepts of *space* and *place*. Following the arguments of such authors as Giddens (1979), Massey (1993) and Harvey (1993; 1996) we need to reject the extremely resilient 'Euclidean' notions, still implicitly underlying many treatments of the geographies of information technology, that treat spaces and places simply as bounded areas, as definable, Cartesian spatial objects, embedded within some wider, objective framework of time-space. As Doreen Massey (1993: 66) suggests, places need to be defined *in relational terms, too*, as 'articulated moments in networks of social relations and understandings' rather than as 'areas with boundaries around'.

The message, then, is clear. Only by maintaining linked, relational conceptions of *both* new information and communications technologies *and* space and place will we ever approach a full understanding of the inter-relationships between them. For Latour's 'skein of networks' (1993: 120) involves *relational assemblies* linking technological networks, space and place, and the space and place-based users (and non-users) of such networks. Such linkages are so intimate and recombinatory that defining space and place separately from technological networks soon becomes as impossible as defining technological networks separately from space and place.

The example of the contemporary city helps illustrate the point. Here, propinquity in material space has no *necessary* correlation with relational meaning, as was always assumed with the social physics concept of 'distance decay', with positivist urban simulations like the gravity model, and with many traditional planning treatments of the unitary, integrated city (Webber, 1964). Complex place and transport-based relational meanings – such as access to physical infrastructure, property, labour markets, an 'innovative milieu', social interaction and the use of cultural facilities – are constantly being recombined with local and nonlocal relational connections, accessed via technological networks (telecommunications, long-distance transport networks and, increasingly, long-distance energy supplies too).

The 'urban' thus can now be seen as a locus for many sociocultural, economic, and institutional networks and practices, spread out over diffuse and extended regions, and mediated by complex combinations of physical 'copresence' and technological mediation (see Healey *et al.*, 1995). In some, the interlinkage and superimposition within physical urban space form meaningful nodes and connections – economic, social, cultural, physical. In others, the place-based relations are outweighed by the technologically mediated links to far-off places. Thus, neighbours may or may not know each other's names and have meaningful social relations. Adjacent firms may or may not create meaningful linkages (adjacent back offices are likely to be tied intimately into their own distant corporate telematics networks but poorly linked to each other). Urban public spaces may or may not emerge as common cultural arenas in their articulations with global media flows and exchanges. Complex, subtle and contingent, combinations of electronic propinquity in the 'nonplace urban realm' (Webber, 1964) and place-based relational meanings based on physical propinquity and transport therefore need to be considered in parallel.

Such recombinations of 'technology' and 'place' represent merely the latest processes of urbanism and not some simple post-urban shift (Graham and Marvin,

1996). 'Cities cannot be seen as places which are leaking away into space of flows', writes Thrift (1996b: 6).

> This is to fundamentally misunderstand the ways in which new information technologies have normally acted as a supplement to human communication rather than as a replacement. Innovations like the telephone, the fax, and the computer are used to extend the range of human communication, rather than act as a substitute. It is not either/or but both/and.

Complex relational webs emerge here. As the global financial networks linking London, Paris or New York, or the TGV train networks linking Paris and the French provincial capitals demonstrate, the technological networks that support these distant linkages, while always local and always embedded in space and place, may actually provide 'tunnel effects' which bring certain spaces and places closer together, while pushing physically adjacent areas further away (Graham and Marvin, 1996). The global divisions of labour and telecommunications networks of transnational corporations (TNCs) provide another perfect example. For, as Paul Adams (1995: 277) suggests, 'in this milieu of globalization, the buildings housing the various functions of a transnational corporation [headquarters, control, research and development, manufacture, etc.], although dispersed around the globe, are intimately connected, yet they may have little or no connection with offices or housing that are directly adjacent'.

The relationships between the USA, UK and Japanese urban systems to the global financial capital that is sited within their nation are characterized by similar network – territory tensions. Some of the world's most sophisticated telematics networks now underpin such cities, linking them, 24 hours a day, through trillions of dollars of submillisecohd global financial transactions, into a global financial marketplace (and, not uncoincidentally, the hubs of the global airline systems). One *individual office building* in Wall Street, New York, houses a computer system which supports global electronic financial trading of $1 trillion per day (UNRISD, 1995). Meanwhile, however, the immediate, provincial 'hinterlands' and domestic urban systems surrounding global financial capitals often fail to integrate closely into such global technological networks, despite the fact that they actually pass materially through or by them. Such relational actor-networks strewn across the planet mean, effectively, that 'the centres of two cities are often for practical purposes closer to each other than to their own peripheries' (Mulgan, 1991: 3).

But while cities are often spreading out to be vast, multicentred urban regions linked into global networks, place-based relational webs that rely on adjacency, propinquity and physical flows remain central to the experience of human social, economic and cultural life. The two rely on each other; they recursively interact. For, as Storper (1996) suggests, shifts towards growing reliance on telemediated information, image, electronic transactions and financial flow, as well as the continuing importance of fashion, art, the media, dance, consumption, leisure, research, play, collective consumption, travel, tourism, education and governance (Thrift, 1996b), place a premium on reflexivity, interpretation and innovation – the key assets of urban areas. As he argues, 'the worlds of action which make up the [reflexive] city economy and society are hybrids, constrained by the machine-like forces of late modern capitalism, but themselves enabled by the ways that system not only permits, but in certain ways, thrives on social reflexivity' (Storper, 1996: 32).

REFERENCES

Adams, P. 1995: A reconsideration of personal boundaries in space-time. *Annals of the Association of American Geographers* 85, 267–85.

Amin, A. and Graham, S. 1998: The ordinary city. *Transactions, Institute of British Geographers,* Forthcoming.

Baldwin, T., McVoy, D. and Steinfield, C. 1996: *Convergence: integrating media, information and communication.* London: Sage.

Batty, M. 1993: The geography of cyberspace. *Environment and Planning B: Planning and Design* 20, 615–61.

Benedikt, M. 1991: Introduction. In Benedikt, M., editor, *Cyberspace: first steps,* Cambridge, MA: MIT Press, 1–18.

Bingham, N. 1996: Object-ions: from technological determinism towards geographies of relations. *Environment and Planning D: Society and Space* 14, 635–57.

Boden, D. and Molotch, H. 1994: The compulsion of proximity. In Friedland, R. and Boden, D., editors, *Now/here: space, time and modernity,* Berkeley, CA: University of California Press, 257–86.

Boyer, C. 1996: *Cybercities: visual perception in an age of electronic communication.* Princeton, NJ: Princeton University Press.

Brotchie, J., Hall, P. and Newton, P., editors, 1987: *The spatial impact of technological change.* London: Croom Helm.

Buttimer A. 1982: Musing on helicon: root metaphors and geography. *Geografiska Annaler* 64B, 89–96.

Callon, M. 1986: Some elements of a sociology of translation: domestication of the scallops and the fisherman of St Brieuc bay. In Law, J., editor, *Power, action and belief: a new sociology of knowledge,* London: Routledge, 196–232.

Callon, M. 1991: Techno-economic networks and irreversibility. In Law, J., editor, *A sociology of monsters: essays on power, technology and domination,* London: Routledge, 196–233.

Castells, M. 1996: The rise of the network society. Oxford: Blackwell.

Channel 4 1994: *Once upon a time in cyberville.* London: Channel 4 (programme transcript).

Cosgrove, D. 1996: Windows on the city. *Urban Studies* 33, 1495–98.

The Economist 1995: Telecommunications survey, 30 September–6 October.

Gates, W. 1995: *The road ahead.* London: Viking.

Gelerntner, D. 1991: *Mirror worlds: the day software puts the universe in a shoebox … How it will happen and what it will mean.* New York: Oxford University Press.

Gibson, W. 1984: *Neuromancer.* London: Harper and Collins.

Giddens, A. 1979: *Central problems in social theory.* London, Macmillan.

Giddens, A. 1990: *The consequences of modernity.* Oxford: Polity Press.

Gillespie, A. 1992: Communications technologies and the future of the city. In Breheny, M. editor, *Sustainable development and urban form*, London: Pion, 67–77.

Gold, J. 1990: A wired society? Utopian literature, electronic communication, and the geography of the future city. *National Geographic Journal of India* 36, 20–29.

Gottmann, J. 1982: Urban settlements and telecommunications. *Ekistics* 302, 411–16.

Graham, S. 1996: Imagining the real-time city: telecommunications, urban paradigms, and the future of cities. In Westwood, S. and Williams, J., editors, *Imagining cities: scripts, signs and memories*, London: Routledge, 31–49.

Graham, S. 1997a: Cities in the real-time age: telecommunications as a paradigm challenge to the conception and planning of urban space. *Environment and Planning A* 29, 105–27.

Graham, S. 1997b: Liberalized utilities, new technologies, and urban social polarization: the UK case. *European Urban and Regional Studies* 492, 135–50.

Graham, S. 1998: Spaces of surveillant-simulation: new technologies, digital representations, and material geographies. *Environment and Planning D: Society and Space*, forthcoming.

Graham, S. and Aurigi, A. 1997: Virtual cities, social polarisation and the crisis in urban public space. Journal of Urban Technology 4, 19–52.

Graham, S. and Marvin, S. 1996: *Telecommunications and the city: electronic spaces, urban places*. London: Routledge.

Haraway, D. 1991: A manifesto for cyborgs: science, technology, and socialist-feminism in the late twentieth century. In Haraway, D., editor, *Simians, cyborgs and women: the reinvention of nature*. New York: Routledge, 149–81.

Harrison, M. 1995: *Visions of heaven and hell*. London: Channel 4 Television.

Harvey, D. 1985: *The urbanization of capital*, Oxford: Blackwell.

Harvey, D. 1993: From space to place and back again: reflections on the condition of postmodernity. In Bird, J., Curtis, B., Putnam, T., Robertson, G. and Tickner, L., editors, *Mapping the futures: local cultures, global change*, London: Routledge, 3–29.

Harvey, D. 1996: *Justice, nature and the geography of difference*. Oxford: Blackwell.

Healey, P., Cameron, S., Davoudi, S., Graham, S. and Madani Pour, A., editors, 1995: *Managing cities: the new urban context*. London: Wiley.

Hill, S. 1988: *The tragedy of technology*. London: Pluto.

Kirsch, S. 1995: The incredible shrinking world? Technology and the production of space. *Environment and Planning D: Society and Space* 13, 529–55.

Latour, B. 1987: *Science in action: how to follow scientists and engineers through society*. Oxford: Oxford University Press.

Latour, B. 1993: *We have never been modern*. London: Harvester Wheatsheaf.

Law, J. and Bijker, W. 1992: Postscript: technology, stability and social theory. In Bijker, W. and Law, J., editors, *Shaping technology, building society: studies in sociotechnical change*, London: MIT Press, 290–308.

Lefebvre, H. 1984: *The production of space*. Oxford: Blackwell.

Mansell, R. 1994: Introductory overview. In Mansell, R., editor, *Management of information and communication technologies*, London: ASLIB, 1–7.

Massey, D. 1993: Power-geometry and a progressive sense of place. In Bird, J., Curtis, B., Putnam, T., Robertson, G. and Tickner, L., editors, *Mapping the futures: local cultures, global change*, London: Routledge, 59–69.

McLuhan, H. 1964: *Understanding media – the extension of man*, London: Sphere.

Mitchell, W. 1994: Building the bitsphere, or the kneebone's connected to the I-Bahn. *ID Magazine* November.

Mitchell, W.1995: *City of bits: space, place and the infobahn*. Cambridge, MA: MIT Press.

Mosco, V. 1996: *The political economy of communication*. London: Sage.

Mulgan, G. 1991: *Communication and control: networks and the new economies of communication*. Oxford: Polity Press.

Negroponte, N. 1995: *Being digital*. London: Hodder & Stoughton.

Office of Technological Assessment 1995: *The technological reshaping of metropolitan America*. Washington DC: Congress of the United States.

Pawley, M. 1995: Architecture, urbanism and the new media. Mimeo.

Pile, S. 1994: Cybergeography: 50 years of *Environment and Planning A. Environment and Planning A* 26, 1815–23.

Pile, S. and Thrift, N. 1996: Mapping the subject. In Pile, S. and Thrift, N., editors, *Mapping the subject: geographies of cultural transformation*, London: Routledge, 13–51.

Robins, K. 1995: Cyberspace and the world we live in. In Featherstone, M. and Burrows, R., editors, *Cyberpunk/cyberspace/cyberbodies*, London: Sage, 135–56.

Sawhney, H. 1996: Information superhighway: metaphors as midwives. *Media, Culture and Society* 18, 291–314.

Schroeder, R. 1994: Cyberculture, cyborg postmodernism and the sociology of virtual reality technologies. *Futures* 26, 519–28.

Staple, G. 1993: Telegeography and the explosion of place. *TeleGeography, Global Traffic Statistics and Commentary*, 49–56.

Stefik, M. 1996: *Internet dreams: archetypes, myths and metaphors*. Cambridge, MA: MIT Press.

Storper, M. 1996: The world of the city: local relations in a global economy. Mimeo, School of Public Policy and Social Research, University of California, Los Angeles.

Swyngedouw, E. 1993: Communication, mobility and the struggle for power over space. In Giannopoulos, G. and Gillespie, A., editors, *Transport and communications in the new Europe*, London: Belhaven, 305–25.

Thrift, N. 1996a: New urban eras and old technological fears: reconfiguring the goodwill of electronic things. *Urban Studies*, 33, 1463–93.

Thrift, N. 1996b: 'Not a straight line but a curve': or, cities are not mirrors of modernity. Mimeo.

Thrift, N. 1996c: Inhuman geographies: landscapes of speed, light and power. In Thrift, N., editor, *Spatial formations*, London: Sage, 256–310.

Thrift, N., Carlstein, T. and Parkes, D. 1978: *Timing space and spacing time*. London: Edward Arnold.

Thu Nguyen, D. and Alexander J. 1996: The coming of cyber space-time and the end of polity. In Shields, R., editor, *Cultures of Internet: virtual spaces, real histories, living bodies*, London: Sage, 125–32.

UNRISD 1995: *States of disarray: the social effects of globalization*. London: United Nations Research Institute for Social Development.

Virilio, P. 1993: The third interval: a critical transition. In Andermatt-Conley, V., editor, *Rethinking technologies*, London: University Of Minnesota Press, 3–10.

Webber, M. 1964: The urban place and the nonplace urban realm. In Webber, M., Dyckman, J., Foley, D., Guttenberg, A., Wheaton, W. and Whurster, C, editors, *Explorations into urban structure*, Philadelphia, PA: University of Pennsylvania Press, 79–153.

Wired Magazine 1996: The *Wired* manifesto, October, 42–6.

9 ASPHALT GAMES
Enacting Place Through Locative Media

*Michele Chang and
Elizabeth Goodman*

Beyond the Grid

In maps or satellite photographs, the New York City street grid appears as crisp as when first built nearly two centuries ago. Yet then as now, the order seen from above collapses into the noise and tumult of street level life. Until the 1980s, New York streets, though sometimes dangerous and derelict, were often playgrounds[1]. Now, street games such as stickball, marbles, and hopscotch are no longer as prevalent. New York's children still play in the streets, but the recreational activity of choice is now likely to be shopping.

Attempts to "reclaim the streets" as a site for non-commercial play have flourished recently, as evidenced by the international Reclaim the Streets movement's slogan of "celebration as direct action; dance as resistance"[2]. The Cacophony Society, self-proclaimed "dada clowns rewiring the neural circuits of the community" have branches in several American cities[3]. Following McKenzie's theory of performance as at once artistic practice and technological imperative[4], public play makes alternatives to the norm of efficiency visible.

Beginning in the 1950s, a group of artists and intellectuals in France decided that utopian ideologies of urban planning concealed a metropolis of regimentation. They called themselves the Situationists. As one slogan put it in 1967, "The guarantee that we will not die of starvation has been purchased with the guarantee that we will die of boredom"[5]. In wandering the streets according to game-like rules or momentary whims, they sought to revitalize urban experience by constructing new "situations". Situationist interventions employed randomness and satire. The most prominent of these experiments was the dérive, or "drift", in which individuals

Michele Chang and Elizabeth Goodman, "Asphalt Games: Enacting Place through Locative Media," from *Leonardo* 14:3 (July 2006) – *Leonardo Electronic Almanac*.

abandon normal everyday practices in favor of alternate acts dictated by the urban terrain and encounters found therein[6].

Inspired by the Situationist techniques of dérive[6] and détournement[7] as well as contemporary psychogeographic experiments in algorithmic walks[8], we designed and built *Asphalt Games*, first as students at New York University's Interactive Telecommunications Program in 2003 and then with the sponsorship of Intel Research in 2004. *Asphalt Games* is a location-based game in which players vie for territory on an online map of New York City by playing their own, modern day "street games" on real-world street corners. Gameplay started with "friends-only" trials at New York University and continued through open invitations on weblogs and New York events mailing lists such as the nonsensenyc list[9]. By the end of active play in October 2004, the game had over 80 registered players.

The game was intended to encourage "ordinary" New Yorkers to imagine, perform, document and share physical responses to an increasingly regulated and surveilled public sphere. As designers, we hoped to change the way both active players and the physical and online onlookers understood public spaces in New York. By linking game success to exploration of territory, we also hoped players would explore new neighborhoods.

We define locative media as the representation and experience of place through digital interfaces. The ever-advancing geographic positioning capabilities of mobile devices and the embedding of geographic location into online experience are both changing the way we experience the world around us. Embedded in mobile devices, technological capabilities are especially changing the way we experience public spaces. As the physical and digital become ever more entwined, we cannot evade the responsibility to describe location beyond physical coordinates. Grounded in the human experience of play, hybrid games such as ours acknowledge that spatial knowledge becomes social, and the social can become spatial.

How to Play

Based on techniques for improvisational theater games, game moves ("stunts") have three components: an object, an action, and a theme.[10] The stunt generation engine randomly selects these components from a database, and the player may "roll again" as often as she chooses until an exciting combination presents itself. An object can be any item often found in a city, such as coffee cups, newspapers, and fire hydrants. An action can be any traditional American outdoor game such as hopscotch, hide-and-go-seek, and tag. A theme is an event or situation prevalent in metropolitan life, such as "happy hour", "vice", or "hailing a cab." It is a wild card altering the interpretation of the other components.

As in charades, players must imaginatively communicate all three components through props, setting and a sequence of actions. We generated the original set of components from research into the history of street games as well as our own experience (as long-time New Yorkers) of the city. However, after the first iteration of the game interface, we added a suggestion feature so that players could enrich our list and take more ownership of the game.

Each stunt is associated with a node, which is the street corner in New York where the stunt took place. Nodes are marked on the virtual map with their owners' tags. Stunts are always situated within a specific neighborhood or even street corner, so they must be judged in context. The same behavior that is amusing in a children's park might be less so on a deserted residential street. Imaginative performances – and thus game standing – are improved by clever use of the surrounding landscape.

Players document their stunts through digital photographs uploaded to the website. The photographs and accompanying description inspire community ratings. Players may only rate a stunt once, but they can comment as much as they like. The comments become a more nuanced counterpoint to the flat ratings, and often record debates over the meaning and value of a player's actions.

If a player wishes to take over a corner already owned by another player, s/he must create and document another stunt using the same elements as the first. The whole game community must then decide which stunt wins the "rumble". There is no final disposition of the city, so one street corner may change hands as many times as there are players who want it.

Hybrid Games

The ability to link location to digital devices, coupled with an increasing interest of urbanites in mass public events (such as Flash Mobs[11] and, in the U.S., the bicycle crowds of Critical Mass [12]) have sparked the development of games that bridge the online and "real" worlds. Hybrid games - sometimes called "mixed-reality games" [cite Benford] – that combine physical and digital play arise from this recent cultural and technological watershed.

Asphalt Games exists within a growing movement of New York-based hybrid games addressing Manhattan's characteristic grid. The first, 2002's *Noderunner*[13], uses the invisible wireless spectrum as its field. As played in Manhattan, it sent players racing from north to south on a treasure hunt for access points. In comparison, *Asphalt Games*, designed in 2003, uses street corners as territory markers for players to capture and control. And in the case of 2004's *PacManhattan*[14], Manhattan's gridded streets stand in for PacMan's maze.

Like many other physical-digital games, *Asphalt Games* is based on a familiar mode of play. For example, Blast Theory's *Can You See Me Now?*[15] is an updated chasing game (like Tag) in which offline players attempt to catch their online counterparts. *Asphalt Games* is a mix of traditional turf games (like Capture the Flag) and performance games (like charades).

Compared to day-length games such as *Noderunner*, *Asphalt Games*' social component moved in slow motion. Without a set beginning or end, there was no incentive for intense, frequent participation. Stunts were initiated and conducted within a week, but a month could go by between stunts for some players. In such a long-running game, momentum is created through a scarcity of space, not time. If games are inherently driven by competition, then *Asphalt Games'* competitive spirit suffered from too much time and too large a gameboard.

As game designers, we took a risk in not verifying the spatial location of play. Unlike most other location-based games, *Asphalt Games* is based on self-reported positioning. Players' decisions to 'cheat' prompted online dialogue about the nature of play. Have you really played the game if you weren't in New York City? Have you really played the game if you used Photoshop? The self-policing nature of the player community determined the answers. Through individual votes and comments, the community of players controlled the course of the game.

Risk and Public Play

As adults, powerful sets of social norms regulate our behavior at nearly all times. Games, however, can excuse adults (and certainly children) from adhering to ordinary customs. Games create their own worlds that temporarily overwrite everyday rules. For that reason, most public games for adults advertise themselves *as games* to excuse potential transgressions. Often, games require distinctive clothing or equipment and are played in a special zone (a park or court). These safeguards legitimize otherwise abnormal behavior.

But playing invented games on street corners – and then uploading documentation to the Internet – can be socially uncomfortable or even dangerous, especially for people who may not identify themselves as risk-takers. Players are required to act unusually in places often unsanctioned for anything but transportation, commerce or (in the case of a fire station) public safety. In Lower Manhattan, succeeding generations of youthful rebellion have permanently altered neighborhood norms. We hoped that introducing *Asphalt Games* in there would minimize any fears. However, interviews with selected players revealed that social anxiety about self-exposure significantly deterred play. One player would only participate on her rooftop (a dubiously "public" place). She feared a loss of professional credibility if acquaintances witnessed odd behavior.

The rumble between Parade and Monkey exemplifies this tug-of-war between verve and social convention[16]. Monkey staged a stunt on his rooftop, which happened to be on a street corner. He wore a tank top made from an "I heart NY" plastic bag (used to "take out" food from restaurants) and played a game of "kick the can" to satisfy the elements: "I heart NY", "Kick the Can", and "Take Out." A few weeks later, challenger Parade staged a more elaborate performance[17] and defeated him. Wearing restaurant workers' uniforms and carrying restaurant take-out bags, she and a partner played "Kick the Can" on bicycles, watched by neighborhood children. The last image of her stunt depicts a chalk drawn mural on the street depicting an "I heart New York" drawn along with a monkey figure with X'd out eyes. In an interview, Parade told us that Monkey's retreat to the roof, which she saw as cheating, inspired her challenge.

When locative media leaves the gallery, it leaves behind the social safeguards surrounding designated art spaces. Because we cannot control the crowds around us in public places, we must consider the role of bystanders, police officers, and other people outside the game. Given the time, effort, and potential risk involved, *Asphalt Games'* active players (as opposed to those who only visited the site) tended to be socially confident, with little fear of police attention and spare time to coordinate elaborate stunts. We suspect that the game's demands excluded those feeling less secure, whether about police attention or from loss of social status online and off.

Asphalt Games exposes participants on the street *and* on the website. Photographs from the website could be easily copied and repurposed, continuing the visibility of transgressive actions. One player even reused a stunt photo for an emailed party invitation, thus extending the reach of his stunt into the rest of his social life. *Asphalt Games* took place within a wider context of players' social life; the photographs and stories that were its products served multiple purposes for groups of friends. For some players, the photograph was the end of the game. Carefully composed and shot, it promoted their cleverness and creativity. For others, the photograph was secondary. Blurry and often confusing, the photographs taken by these players reveal not showmanship but the opposite: an experience deliberately left inaccessible for those who were not physically there.

Player interviews suggested two divergent models of public behavior, technology, and spectatorship. One group saw the dual public spaces of street and website as sites of performance/applause: stunt as opportunity to win social status. For another group, the street/website represented surveillance/punishment: every stunt as dangerous loss of control over self-representation. The game design does not favor either model, giving players power over planning stunts, reporting location, and documenting actions. Though players in Asphalt Games cannot control who witnesses their behavior, they are ultimately the instigators and actors in their own plays[18].

What We Learned

Like other hybrid games, such as *Can You See Me Now?*, *PacManhattan*, and *Noderunner*, *Asphalt Games* takes place both online and on the physical streets of a city. Yet *Asphalt Games* moves beyond location as constant – a stable set of coordinates that unambiguously 'locates' us on a gameboard – to consider how player activity constructs 'place' out of data.

Ironically, we had spent considerable time designing the map as both a spatial overview of game activity, and as a visual introduction to the game for newcomers. We imagined that our coordinate-based map would serve as a kind of canvas or wall for players to tag, much as graffiti writers leave their names on city walls to prove their presence. And some of that behavior happened. One group of players systematically took over a string of subway stops on the L line – a joke visible only on a map.

However, visitors to the site did not often use the map. Instead, they navigated through lists of most recent or most highly ranked stunts. Due to technological limitations in the pre-Google Maps days, players had to manually enter cross streets into web form – not click on the map – to initiate stunts. Text entry moved the focus of interaction off the map. However, one unexpected result of the freeform text entry was that players began to play "off the map." They ignored the implicit boundaries of the map viewing area and instead created private stunts that never reached the gameboard.

The tension between a general diagram and the specificity of human experience is a common theme in hybrid media. Maps can rework the complexity and occasional ugliness of the territory they represent into abstracted beauty. Through them, we run the risk of masking the complexity of embodied experience with well-intentioned simplification. Maps are clear, which is why they are so useful in navigation. Maps are clear, which is why they often lead us astray. Focusing on building and maintaining a spatially organized gameboard distracted us from supporting the social games motivating the activity.

Through the comments and ratings, the stunt pages play out negotiations around the meaning of neighborhoods and spaces. They also play out deeper conversations about fairness, friendship, and artistic merit. Though we as creators are responsible for the website, this partial loss of control proved unexpectedly fruitful. Instead of communicating our own vision for New York neighborhoods we loved, the game revealed aspects of the city that we could never have imagined.

Enacting Place

Many genres of locative media structure interaction with places through information delivery. Consider "place-based storytelling" or "tour guide" applications[19] in which participants uncover a pre-existing set of stories as they move through space. In tour guide projects, the creator(s) link pre-determined content to specific locations, which their audience access through geographic movement. Tour guide projects rely upon an ownership model for location-based experience, in which the creator becomes the sole storyteller or "owner" of a place, and the audience passive spectators. In contrast, *Asphalt Games* and other collaboratively generated locative media projects function as a medium through which people tell their own stories.

When we start to tell stories is not merely a series of coordinates, but rather a medium for expression. One player's (Dface) use of the Roosevelt Island Tram in a stunt requiring 'Manpurse', 'Jumprope', and 'Hangover' reflects an understanding of a particular place and an interest in performing this knowledge within the space of the game[20]. In the player's stunt, we see him board the tram (which links Midtown Manhattan to Roosevelt Island). He rides across with his manpurse (a Samsonite overnight traveler) strapped over his shoulder. Advancing through the images, we then see that he has reached the other side and begins to jumprope through the strap of the man-purse. In the background, we see the air tram hovering above the ground as it makes its return journey, standing in for 'Hangover.' This stunt rated high in the eyes of the community, receiving a 4.7 out of a possible 5 (at time of writing; stunt ratings continually change) when it was first judged. We believe that its popularity is based on its linguistic and locative play.

The distinction between embedded versus emergent experiences of place calls into question the very nature of designing locative media for public spaces. If digital interventions are to have an affect on the physical world, it is crucial to address the ways humans understand and enact the limitations and constraints of public places. Indeed, as we came to understand, the medium's power ultimately resides in changing everyday movement through space.

Combining ordinary street corners and random stunt elements into a funny or exciting stunt can be difficult. When we work hard at locative play, we reflect on the historical, social, and spatial dimensions of well-known neighborhoods and practices. When we are acting out these reflections, we reveal something about ourselves through the places in which we act them. Location becomes a communicative medium in its own right.

Many locative applications treat location as a canvas – a place to tell; a place to mark; a place to store. The dynamism of *Asphalt Games* as a locative experiment comes from the active interpretation of familiar places, or better still, manipulation of their attributes. Embodied play, like the 'cheating' of the system itself, is perhaps best seen as a metaphor for the way in which locative media can be enacted, as something to be gamed, misused, or perhaps overthrown. Location no longer as notebook, frame, text, or coordinate, but a medium reshaping itself and the people who invoke it.

NOTES

1. K. Malone, "Street life: youth, culture and competing uses of public space", in *Environment & Urbanization*, Vol. 14, No. 2 (October 2002).
2. J. Jordan, "The Art of Necessity: The Subversive Imagination of Anti-Road Protest and Reclaim the Streets", G. McKay (ed.), *DiY Culture: Party and Protest in Nineties Britain* (London: Verso, 1998) pp. 129–151.
3. http://www.cacophony.org.
4. Jon McKenzie, *Perform or Else: Discipline to Performance* (New York: Routledge, 2001).
5. Greil Marcus, *Lipstick Traces: A Secret History of the Twentieth Century* (Cambridge: Harvard University Press, 1990).
6. Guy Debord, "Theory of The Dérive, Internationale Situationniste #2", Trans. Ken Knabb. *Situationist International Anthology* (1958).
7. Guy Debord and Gil J. Wolman, "A User's Guide to Detournement", in 'Les Lèvres Nues', No. 8 (May 1956). Trans. Ken Knabb. *Situationist International Anthology* (1958).
8. Joseph Hart, "A new way of walking", *Utne Reader*, (July/August 2004).
9. http://www.nonsensenyc.com/

10. Violet Spolin, *Improvisation for the Theater: A Handbook of Teaching and Directing Techniques* (Northwestern University Press; 3rd edition, 1999).

11. Paul McFedries, "Mobs R Us", in *IEEE Spectrum*, Vol. 40, No. 10, pp. 56–56 (October 2003).

12. Susan Blickstein and Susan Hanson, "Critical mass: forging a politics of sustainable mobility in the information age", in *Transportation*, Volume 28, pp. 347–362 (November 2001).

13. Yuri Gitman and Carlos Gomez de Llarena, *Noderunner*, (http://noderunner.omnistep. com/play.php, accessed March 2005).

14. http://www.pacmanhattan.com/

15. Steve Benford and others, "Coping with uncertainty in a location-based game", in *IEEE Pervasive Computing Journal*, July–September (2003).

16. Monkey, *I heart NY, kick the can, take out* (http://www.asphalt-games.net/play/ ViewStunt.aspx?StuntId=274, accessed March 2005).

17. Parade, *I heart NY, kick the can, take out* (http://www.asphalt-games.net/play/ ViewStunt.aspx?StuntId=383, accessed March 2005).

18. M. Chang and E. Goodman, "Digital Street Game: Location-Based Game as Research Probe", in *Poster Proceedings of the 2004 conference on Ubiquitous Computing*, (Nottingham, UK, 2004).

19. Reinhold Grether, *Dr. Reinhold Grether's directory to mobile art and locative media* (http://www.netzwissenschaft.de/mob.htm, accessed March 2005).

20. Dface, *man-purse, jumprope, hangover*, (http://www.asphalt-games.net/play/ViewStunt.aspx?StuntId=271, accessed March 2005).

THOUGHT ON THE CONVERGENCE OF DIGITAL MEDIA, MEMORY, AND SOCIAL AND URBAN SPACES

10

Federico Casalegno

In the following pages, the phenomenon of the evolution of memory, communication, and community is discussed; these are the key elements for a complete understanding of the societies in which we live. These concepts also lie at the basis of an important evolution: As we are going through a moment of great changes, their boundaries have never been so permeable and vague. Telecommunications and information technology have modified the process of accessing and storing data, and consequently, they have also modified our relationship toward knowledge and memory. Our communities are expanding on a planetary scale, and in the meantime, they are getting local. And then there is communication, defined by Albert Einstein as the third bomb of the 20th century (after the atomic and the demographic ones), and its unpredictable evolution. In a reciprocal relationship, these concepts lie at the core of our complex social forms: Nowadays, with the development of telecommunication systems, we are facing a new definition of these concepts and of their mutual combinations.

In the following pages, the different perspectives connected with this phenomenon will be analyzed while focusing on a theoretic sensitivity toward the complex synergy between memory, community, and communication. Such perspectives are based on the research carried out within the Living Memory[1] project.

Federico Casalegno, "Thought on the Convergence of Digital Media, Memory, and Social and Urban Spaces," pp. 313–26 from *Space and Culture* 7:3 (August 2004).

It should be noted that since the beginning, the intention was not that of empha-sizing the existence of a structural approach, and according to this approach, it is enough to insert a communication system within a social group to cause the effects we desire. In a sense, we move away from a cybernetic perspective, according to which communication is just a leading and commanding means (from the Greek *kybernìtiké* (*téchnì*), "art of leading," art of control). Within this cybernetic perspec-tive, the spreading of a simple software would be sufficient to create virtual com-munities and lead to the birth of new electronic agoras; in the same way, it would be enough to wire cities to give birth to smart communities.[2] Taking these perspectives into account, it is essential to underline the importance of experience and human passions, thanks to which a communication system exists only when it is inhabited and adopted by users; in this sense, we have a cybersociality perspective rather then a cybernetic approach.

Social liveliness and human passions cannot be confined within linear and causal perspectives. That is the reason I propose an ecological approach that draws inspi-ration from the classical definition of the term *ecology*: the study of the relation-ships between living beings and the environment in which they live in (*oikos*, from the Greek "home," in the holistic sense as geophysical and social environment, and *logos*, "speech, reasoning"). From this starting point, the definition of memory must be intended as a living system (Living Memory) within its mutual interactions with a social, technological, and territorial environment. In the following pages, I will discuss the points of views and the utopias that, according to my opinion, have gone through the Living Memory project and that lie at the basis of this communi-cation system, which is still at a prototype stage. I will therefore propose an eco-logical approach to memory that considers the close relationship between communication technologies and memory, knowledge and information, and net-works and societies.

The Origins of the Ecological Approach to Memory

Toward the end of the 1960s, Ulric Neisser proposed an ecological approach to memory within the psychological field (Neisser, 1982; Neisser & Winograd, 1988; Winograd, Fivush, & Hirst, 1999; for this analysis, see also Maldonado, 2000). In the debate concerning the study of memory, he maintained that memory cannot be studied in a laboratory starting from ad hoc built-up cases. He therefore suggested the existence of two different approaches to the study of the psychology of memory: The former concerns those approaches that aim at understanding the mental mech-anisms that can be controlled and demonstrated (high road); the latter concerns those that aim at understanding memory through human experience (low road). Neisser thought that it was important to know how people use their experiences when they have to face the present and when they are under natural conditions. It is interesting to emphasize the desire to let memory out from laboratories and observe it in the light of everyday interactions. The Living Memory system embodies this perspective in the sense that it tried to design a communication environment that favored everyday life (concerning the analysis on everyday life, see Maffesoli, 1996) and, at the same time, could be used by everyone within the community and not only by a computer-literate cyber elite.

The system must be viewed under this perspective, and it aims at promoting the sharing of usual and informal memory and at providing access not only to historical, formal memory (of absolute importance undoubtedly) but also to the memory lived and experienced by human beings. In this sense, we are dealing with an open communication system that exists thanks to the support of the individuals. Within this perspective, we can presume that communal memory is nourished by social communities and individuals rather than by official institutions.

Furthermore, we can speak of a communal memory when the community as a whole can access it and nourish it in a constant process: As Maurice Halbwachs (1950) stated,

> It is not enough to rebuild piece after piece the image of a fact in order to obtain a memory. It is necessary that this reconstruction is based upon data or common notions that are to be found both in our spirit and in that of the others, as these memories are continuously passed on from one to the other and vice-versa; and therefore this can only happen if they are or were part of the same society. (p. 12)

Halbwachs emphasized some of the general concepts concerning communal memory: The aim of Living Memory was that of designing a communication system that allowed this constant flow of information.

[…]

… nowadays, after a period of a slight disinterest at the beginning of the 1990s, the issues concerning the local and territorial dimension of the technological development are regaining favor. …

[…]

[O]ne of the assumptions of the Living Memory system is that of accompanying informal and near communication, trying to make communities' lives easier. In the end, the system – even though it concerns urban spaces (public squares and buildings' facades with a screen), social places (cafes, schools, or public libraries with interactive tables), and people (with a coin or through other systems that are still being studied) – does not intend to upset the existing social dynamics regulating social relationships. But it tries to accompany them. At least in its premises, the system aims at promoting a kind of relational memory between man and environment. Its diffusion in cities, with its urban and relational tissue, does not take place in a frontal way, yet it defines itself as an ecological, homeopathic integration.

Superimposition between Physical Places and Digital Information in Cyberspace

The environment is both co-present and co-organizer. ... Therefore the basic idea: the environment constantly makes up all the beings that get nourishment in it; it constantly cooperates with their organization. These beings and this organization are thus constantly eco-dependant. (Morin, 1997)

If on one hand the ecological vision of memory brings our attention to the universal access, then on the other hand, it shifts our attention to the superimposition of the real territory with the digital information of cyberspace. We are dealing with a superimposition and not with a mutual exclusion between real spaces and cyberspace. We are aware that the techno-pessimists (Sale, 1994), rebels against the future, think of a dark universe where "internauts," prisoners of the electric virtual sphere, tend to confine themselves in the golden cages of the electronic bits – net slaves (Lessard & Baldwin, 1999) – and to be disconnected from the world. ... the posthumanistic raves of the "Extropians" leave us skeptical when they wish that the (con)fusion between technological and human could be the excuse for freeing us from our ability of processing information, leaving the task of generating and managing our memory to computers.[3]

Being that my point of view is distant from these extremes, I think that the real dimension of the city and information cybernetics are superimposing and supporting each other. The growing number of available digital information that is scattered throughout the territory emphasizes the element of physical places; the environment becomes a real interface of memory, a connective tissue. As Irene McWilliam (2002) and Marco Susani (2000) underlined, our objective in the Living Memory project is not that of substituting the real with the virtual but rather to integrate the real with digital information. This is not what the French artist Chris Marker (2002; see also Roth & Bellour, 1999) defined the optional world link, that is, a world in which the virtualization of life reaches a paroxysm and real life, in the real world, becomes an option. Instead, we think that cyberspace superimposes with the space, and real and virtual do not reject each other but make up a bigger topography of places and coexist, creating a new form of city topology, as W. J. Mitchell (1999) explained in *E-Topia*. ... E-Topia is therefore a kind of new configuration that considers the superimposing of physical space and interconnected electronic environments.

Discussing this issue with Edgar Morin and speaking about how the human brain works, he made me realize that according to K. H. Pribram,[4] our memory works in the same way as the waves provoked by a stone thrown into a small lake: They create a series of concentric circles. During our recollection process, the motion of the waves is upset: The memory goes out of the brain just like the stone would go out of the water; as if we were watching a film in the reverse order, we would first see the waves converging and then the stone coming out of the water.

In the same way, metaphorically, the remembrance that our memory induces in our spirit is, first of all, these trembling waves that are generated in the distance and then converge into a memory. This is an interesting idea that shows us how the human brain works as an ecosystem of scattered memories and that memories exist only within this ecosystem. This scenario suggests to us what the eventual dynamics on the social level within a communication system like Living Memory could be. Social information and memory exist thanks to the synergy between physical places and people who make them come alive. …

Memory as an Appropriating Event

In Living Memory, we have several nodes of memory that create a unique system; within this complex, cosystemic, and coevolutionary environment, the members of a local community send out information, make communal memory pulse by nourishing it with contents they think relevant for themselves and for their social and cultural environment. In this way, we are introduced into a new virtual-real scenario, which allows social actors to enrich social memories, to express and interiorize individual, communal, living, and past memories. The postmodern city is covered with a new connective tissue; just like we all decorate our houses with objects and memories, members of the community can decorate their social interaction spaces, thus taking part in the construction of their collective memory.[5] Memories of an individual join another individual's memories, and they link together in constant dynamics.

[…]

Sharing a memory means sharing a common experience. However, the lack of sharing of a "co-presence in real time" can be compensated by narration (telling): In fact, it is narration (as a form of a gift from the one to the other) that allows us to get the experience back and that allows us to overcome space and time barriers. Narration is fundamental as it replaces the shared experience of taking part in the creation of communal memory. Therefore, thanks to narration, we can elaborate common sense – sharing past experiences that have not been experienced together in the same moment. The Living Memory environment aims at favoring this kind of communication. Within this context, the concept of memory as a system of interrelations of individual memories, a synergy of personal memories that join the others' memories in a flow of everlasting motion, is very important. Man continuously appropriates memory, starting a cyclical and noncumulative process of social knowledge, because by appropriating memory, it is forged within man's comprehension schemes and stock of knowledge. … We therefore find … the idea that memory is "responding" rather than "recording." … Memory exists only through this constant and permanent alteration. Living memory does not have a precise, fixed, and static boundary.

> because its form and its structure depend on an outside circumstance, even if its content (the missing detail) is its. Its mobilization cannot be separated from an alteration. But there is more here than meets the eye. Memory draws its power of intervention from its capability of being altered – shifted, mobile, without a fixed point. Permanent

trait: it creates itself (and its capital) being born from the other (a circumstance) and then losing it (now it is only a memory). (de Certeau, 1990, p. 131)

With Living Memory, we therefore focused our attention onto forms of interactions between people that use the system everyday and on the study of the dynamics of sedimentation of memory. Memory does not have a fixed and static point; in a sense, it is a "memory without record," as von Foester (1981) put it when he questioned the learning of computers and inductive inferences: a living, mobile memory made up of precise events and floating roots in the social corpus that are generated by a trivial and founding experience.

A New Social Aesthetics

The definition of the term *community* is always changing shape and meaning. Nowadays, the term *community* is probably used in a far too imprecise and disenchanted way; in the Living Memory project, it is always used in connection with a specific space and place. The starting point was that a community needs to share a memory to exist and that the social tie needs communication and sharing information to exist.
[...]
On the social impact of new communication technologies, there are several perspectives. Our attention is focused on the critics on the progressive creation of a society of the individual (Scheer, 1998) or on any community that does not communicate but rather commutes (Agamben, 1990). In this prospect, far from a communal dynamics and from a communal memory supported by online computers, we would face an "autistic form of shared memory." A paradox indeed, but it forces us to consider what these critics emphasize: Man paradoxically uses communication technologies to build societies that do not communicate in the distance but that build a distance in communication. Actually, it is clear that having a Web site or sending messages to a forum does not automatically make us members of a community. ...
Once we accept this condition, and are aware of the fact that new technologies can participate in both the creation and the destruction of the social tie, to understand how technologies can determine communal aggregation, I will make reference to the *Society of Mind* by Minsky (1987, chap. 8). The father of artificial intelligence showed us in his theory about memory that we have lines of knowledge, the so-called knowledge-lines (K-lines): We can memorize what we do by making a list of all the agents involved in the activity in question. For example, we can consider the action of fixing a bicycle, and we can mark with a red pen all the tools we need to fix the bicycle. When we have finished mending the bicycle, all the tools we have used will have a red mark, and this will remind us that "red" is the color of "fixing the bicycle." Next time, it will be enough to take those tools marked in "red." In a word, we have to activate this *K-line*. Anyway, it could also happen that

certain tools, being used for other works, have marks of more colors. In any case, when we have a new work to do, all we need to do is to activate the appropriate K-line, and we will automatically find all the tools we have used in the past for similar works. Thus, the K-lines we build go through a continuous evolution: A K-line can connect with other K-lines and create "societies."

This reasoning seems pertinent to me, and without entering the debate on neurosciences but using the theory of memory by Minsky as a source of inspiration, we can notice the remarkable contribution of the Internet and other networks to the realization of these social knowledge lines. Exchanges happening in cyberspace allow the creation of virtual communities and provide K-lines on all kinds of issues. Several Internet sites and forums are typical of this process and explain their dynamics. Furthermore, we can make reference to civic nets whose aim is that of providing these K-lines to a community so that people can have means to act in the society in a form of civic intelligence.[6]

As a consequence, we have civic nets favoring the contact with administrations or other institutions, with commerce and work, with different neighborhood associations, and with the others. … The social capital is made up of particular resources provided to a social actor that is defined by the actor's role in the society (Coleman, 1988, p. 98). Like other capital forms, it is a productive resource. Furthermore, reading the work of Putnam (1995), we realize that the social capital is a network of ability and relationships based on mutual trust between individuals. … In a sense, solidarity comes from a technical structure that acts as a guarantee of the positive functioning of communal life of the community, even though this functioning seems to be determined from the above rather than by the feeling of community. In *La Condition Postmoderne*, Lyotard (1979) explained the nature of the social tie according to a conception of modernity and emphasized how this is based on a technocratic vision in which

> the harmony of needs and hopes of individuals or groups with the functions that the system provides is now a part of the functioning of the system itself; the real target of the system that is self-programmed as an intelligent machine, is the optimization of the global relationship between its input, that is its efficiency. (p. 25)[7]

[…]

Anyway, I would suggest we associate the K-lines that build up structured communities to the metaphor of sociality lines (S-lines). So, telematic networks allow us to find forms of "organic solidarity,"[8] to share memories and affinities without following forms of rational aggregation. … In cyberspace webs, we face forms of societies that are mainly empathic that consequently would oppose contractual societies, even if their copresence were impossible. We are far from of a mechanicalistic and calculated logic. Emotion and spontaneity become essential parameters of "being together." The Web and its intrinsic dynamics give us many examples of this phenomenon of community as an aesthetic accident. Therefore, we observe the creation of a community whose strongest tie is based on the empathy between its own members, passion, and emotion. Michel Maffesoli clearly explained this communal aesthetics that differentiate modernity and postmodernity:

> The proletarian, the bourgeois could be "historical subjects" with a duty to carry out. Any theoretic genius, artist and politician could send out a message whose content showed the direction to be followed. Both existed as abstract and inaccessible entities, that proposed an objective. ... This is the difference between abstract and rational periods, and emphatic periods. The former are based upon the principle of individuating, separating, the latter are based upon melting within a communal theme, that I would define neo-tribalism. (Maffesoli, 1988, p. 22)

Maffesoli's thought allows us to theorize new forms of aggregation: The phenomenon of new tribalism does not have a mechanic and targeted structure in which individuals play social roles and congregate according to the logic of contract. Instead, we have more complex, organic, and open societies in which people play parts and come together in affective tribes. Rather than merely considering our communal participation in connection to social capital, we can also think of it in terms of *dépense* (G. Bataille); we let ourselves go and live in a sort of osmosis with the tribes we belong to.

This belonging is not stable, but it is at the same time glittering; the tribe is an event, a temporary materialization born to the sharing of passions. And if in the case of a community we have a strictly structured society, when we speak of tribalism, we speak of a floating society, imbued with a vitality that defines human unions. Maffesoli defined this process by using the expression *ethics of aesthetics*: You observe sociality forms based on an ethos, that is, a relative behavior that is grounded on the sharing of an aesthesis, of emotions and passions.

Through the interactions taking place in cyberspace, we face the creation of several communities: The Internet, a matrix for new human relationships, allows the encounter – virtual and/or real – between people who share some affinities. Yet these forms of social aggregation do not necessarily turn into tribes that are an expression of a fusion, a "warm sociality." Therefore, new communication technologies allow, at the same time and in a synergic and contemporary movement, the creation of "communities" – that is, structured aggregations between individuals, which are targeted, hierarchical, and instrumental – and the materialization of "tribes" – that is, more ephemeral forms of association transversal and emphatic among people who play in the theatre of everyday life. Communities are made up of K-lines; tribes are made up of S-lines. They are different forms that can live together but that do not coincide. That is why it is necessary to distinguish them.[9]

Sharing Communal Memory for a Poetical Existence

Cyberspace is an underlining foundation to social alchemies. The opportunity of establishing K-lines and S-lines with the people you share interests and passions with leads to the creation of this tribe and to the simultaneous union with our physical and social environment. Lévy (1995, 2000) spoke about a "collective intelligence" and De Kerckhove (1997) of a "connective intelligence," paving the way for a social structure with a more complex functioning that becomes a communal substrate and that allows people to communicate and cooperate; this is exactly what is already happening within scientific communities that have actually created this communication network that is the Internet.

The World Wide Web, we have to bear in mind, developed as a consequence of scientists at the CERN (http://www.cern.ch) in Geneva who felt the need to share a communal memory and to share individual memories. This basic structure becomes the foundation for a substrate of how social aggregations work and allows technology to favor connections and ties.

Moscovici (2002) reminded us that it is man's nature to be a "myth maker": We all take part in the creation of small daily myths and gossips, and we have to be able both to act and to rationalize our actions through speech. …

In this sense, new interactive communication technologies distance us from the society of the spectacle that is typical of media. Or, rather, online technologies allow us to add the spectacular and participating dimension to this society. The society of the spectacle is not just a simple group of confused images but a system of complex social relationships conveyed by media through images.

[…]

This relationship between what has been experienced and representation is evolving with online communication. The ecological approach to memory leads us to take into consideration a postmodern logic of the entertainment society in which the hypothesis we mentioned before can be true as well as its contrary: With interactive media, the representation is lived by every single internaut, by every individual. They create a memory by sending out information, accessing knowledge, and creating real tribe belongings. We therefore face the realization of a "responding" rather than "recording" memory. In this sense, not only is experience confined in representations, but representations are experienced in "the first person."

The research carried out by Sherry Turkle (1995, 2002) shows how internauts in virtual environments, in the MUD or in other virtual communities, are the main characters; they experience and live different aspects of their personalities.

This form of online expressing and sharing of sensations and information shapes the communal and living memory of the community we belong to, and it allows in the last place to give a meaning to our existence: to create associations, form communities, and share common and shared emotions. If sharing a memory is one of the sine qua non conditions for the creation of a community, the ways in which this process takes place evolve together with the transformation of those means in which memory settles in. The ecological vision of memory allows every single member of a community to send information, thus nourishing communal memory.

[…]

This allows us, or at least this is what we hope for, to create what Edgar Morin (2002) called a poetical vision of existence. He reminded us that we have the necessity of keeping a cultural heritage so that we can conquer the present, that is, to live not only in a useful and functional way but also in a poetical way. The several forms of empathy, from love to celebrations, from parties to communions, are paths that lead man to this state of poetical existence.

Therefore, among the birth of human relationships and cyber networks, we have a varied example of expressions coming from current cyber socialities, like pictures of a new social paradigm of the synergy between community, memory, and communication. Thus, "new technologies" are old man-made creations. Use and experience give them a value and a sense; it is the task of mankind to use them to make this poetical vision come true.

NOTES

1. For more information about the research, see http://www.memoire-vivante.org (all Web sites mentioned in this article were verified as of May 19, 2004).
2. Smart communities according to the Canadian government (see http://smart-communities. ic.gc.ca/).
3. On the Internet, see http://www.extropy.org/ as well as http://www.trashuman.org/. "Extropy Institute acts as a networking and information center for those seeking to foster our continuing evolutionary advance by using technology to extend healthy life, augment intelligence, optimize psychology, and improve social systems" (http://www.extropy.org/). See also Moravec (1994, 2000). For an analysis on this issue, see Dery (1997).
4. Edgar Morin (1996) dealt with the issue of knowledge in the third book of the *Méthode, la connaissance de la connaissance*. See also Pribram (1977, 1981).
5. It is interesting to note that for Heidegger, inhabiting meant building, farming the land (*bauen*).
6. This is civic intelligence according to Douglas Schuler (see http://www.scn.org/ip/commnet/ Presentations/capetown-2000.html).
7. A very interesting book concerning this issue is Neil Postman's (1992) *Technopoly*. The author explained the dynamics characterizing the shift from a society that uses technology toward a society shaped by technology itself, the Technopoly. It is about the submission of any form of cultural life in front of the supremacy of technique and technology. It is a self-justifying and self-producing system, in which technology reigns over institutions and social life.
8. I quote Maffesoli's (1979/1999) analysis that upset the Durkheimian vision on organic and mechanic society.
9. Human and social sciences, from the end of the past century, are questioning the issue of community, and Tönnies's (1988) work, *Community and Society*, is indeed a point of reference. In 1887, the German author differentiated the Gemeinschaft (community) from the Gesellschaft (society). When speaking about the Gemeinschaft, he made reference to the farmers' community in which interpersonal relationships are based on simple and straightforward relations. The members of the community have affective and sentimental relationships. In the Gesellschaft, on the contrary, we face impersonal interactions within the modern city, in which relationships are cold and mechanic. Therefore, the differentiation described here between community and tribe aims at underlining some patterns that are useful for our explanation.

REFERENCES

Agamben, G. (1990). *La comunità che viene* [The community that comes]. Turin, Italy: Einaudi.

Coleman, J. S. (1988). Social capital in the creation of human capital. *American Journal of Sociology, 94*, 95–120.

De Certeau, M. (1990). *L'invention du quotidien: Arts de faire* [The invention of daily newspaper: Arts to make]. Paris: Edizioni Gallimard.

De Kerckhove, D. (1997). *Connected intelligence: The arrival of the Web society.* Toronto, Canada: Somerville House Books.

Dery, M. (1997). *Velocità di fuga: Cyberculture a fine millennio* [Escape velocity: Cyberculture at the end of the century]. Milan: Feltrinelli.

Halbwachs, M. (Ed.). (1950). *La mémoire collective* [The collective memory]. Paris: Presse Universitaire de France.

Lessard, B., & Baldwin, S. (1999). *NetSlaves.* New York: McGraw-Hill. Retrieved from http://www.disobey.com/netslaves/

Lévy, P. (1995). *L'intelligence collective: Pour une anthropologie du cyberspace* [Collective intelligence: For an anthropology of cyberspace]. Paris: La découverte.

Lévy, P. (2000). *World Philosophie: La planète, le marché, le cyberespace, la conscience* [World philosophy: The planet, the market, cyberspace, conscience]. Paris: Odile Jacob.

Lyotard, J. F. (1979). *La Condition Postmoderne* [The postmodern condition]. Paris: Les éditions de minuit.

Maffesoli, M. (1988). *Le temps des tribus: Le déclin del'individualisme dans les sociétés de masse* [The time of the tribes: The decline of individualism in mass society]. Paris: Meridiens Klincksieck Editor.

Maffesoli, M. (1996). *The ordinary knowledge.* Cambridge, UK: Polity.

Maffesoli, M. (1999). *La violence totalitaire* [Totalitarian violence]. Paris: Desclée de Bouwer. (Original work published 1979).

Maldonado, T. (2000). Il futuro della memoria in rete [The future of memory in the Net]. In G. Boccia Artieri & G. Mazzoli, *Tracce nella rete.* Milan: Franco Angeli Editore.

Marker, C. (2002). *Immemory* [CD-ROM]. Cambridge, MA: Exact Change.

McWilliam, I. (2002). La storia del gatto perso [The story of the lost cat]. In F. Casalegno, *Memorie quotidiane.* Milan: Le Vespe.

Minsky, M. (1987). *Society of mind.* New York: Touchstone.

Mitchell, W. J. (1999). *E-topia.* Cambridge, MA: MIT Press.

Moravec, H. (1994). Il robot universale [The universal robot]. In H. Moravec, *Il corpo tecnologico.* Bologna, Italy: Ed. Baskerville.

Moravec, H. (2000). *Robot: Mere machine to transcendent mind.* Oxford, UK: Oxford University Press.

Morin, E. (1996). *La méthode: Tome 3. La connaissance de la connaissance* [The method: Volume 3]. The knowledge of knowledge. Paris: Seuil.

Morin, E. (1997). *La nature de la nature* [The nature of nature] (I. Tome, Ed.). Paris: Seuil.

Morin, E. (2002). Memorie vissute per un'esistenza poetica [Lived memory for a poetic life]. In F. Casalegno, *Memorie quotidiane.* Milan: Le Vespe.

Moscovici, S. (2002). Memorie, rituali e cyber-rappresentazioni [Memory, rituals and cyber-representation]. In F. Casalegno, *Memorie quotidiane.* Milan: Le Vespe.

Neisser, U. (1982). *Memory observed.* San Francisco: Freeman.

Neisser, U., & Winograd, E. (Eds.). (1988). *Remembering reconsidered: Ecological and traditional approaches to the study of memory*. Cambridge, UK: Cambridge University Press.

Postman, N. (1992). *Technopoly: The surrender of culture to technology*. New York: Knopf.

Pribram, K. H. (1977). *Languages of the brain: Experimental paradoxes and principles in neuropsychology*. Englewood Cliffs, NJ: Prentice Hall.

Pribram, K. H. (1981, November). *Non-locality and localisation: A review of the place and memory of the holographic hypothesis of brain function in perception and memory*. Paper presented at the 10th International Conference on the Unity of the Sciences, Seoul, Korea.

Putnam, R. (1995). Bowling alone: America's declining social capital. *Journal of Democracy*, 6(1), 65–78.

Roth, L., & Bellour, R. (1999). *Qu'est-ce qu'une Madeleine? À Propos du CD-Rom Immemory de Chris Marker* [What's a Madeleine? About the CD-ROM *Immemory* by Chris Marker]. Paris: Centre George Pompidou.

Sale, K. (1994). *Rebels against the future: The Luddites and their war on the industrial revolution*. Reading, MA: Addison-Wesley.

Scheer, L. (1998). *Hypothèse sur la singularité* [Hypothesis on singularity]. Paris: Sens & Tonga.

Susani, M. (2000). Citizen media: lieux sociaux et transmission de la connaissance [Citizen media: Social places and transmission of knowledge]. *Sociétés, 2*.

Tönnies, F. (1988). *Community and society*. New Brunswick, NJ: Transaction Publishing.

Turkle, S. (1995). *Life on the screen: Identity in the age of the Internet*. New York: Simon & Schuster.

Turkle, S. (2002). Memorie sullo schermo [Memories on the screen]. In F. Casalegno, *Memorie quotidiane*. Milan: Le Vespe.

von Foester, H. (1981). *Observing systems*. Seaside, CA: Intersystems Publications.

Winograd, E., Fivush, R., & Hirst, W. (1999). *Ecological approach to cognition*. London: Lawrence Erlbaum.

III RACE IN/AND CYBERSPACE

Introduction

Cyberspace is as raced as the "real." The cultures of informational capitalism are racialized in the sense of labor, markets, and capital.

Reading the nature of cyborg bodies, the distribution of internet use, and the politics of representation in cyberspace – from games to internet porn – thinkers have argued for the racialized nature of cyberspace. Race theorists "reading" cyber-cultures also argue that the hype around the transcendence possible through the new technologies is also racialized. For the marginal – people of color, women, minorities – when identity, welfare, affirmative action, and political rights are embodied (and are therefore about skin color and ethnic identity), transcendence is really not desirable or possible. Disembodiment would thus be a white fantasy.

Further, questions of access to the new technologies are racialized – even if things are changing in terms of internet use among minorities and nonwhite races. Finally, ICT-linked technologies such as pharmacogenomics and projects such as the Human Genome Project and the "genetic turn" have racial dimensions. Questions about whether medicines in the future would be linked to ethnic gene pools – and thereby exclude some populations – and the commercial use of data from such projects must be addressed. The "digital divide" remains a keystone in the racialized areas of cyberspace.

Race and internet studies also address issues of racialized labor. With Business Process Outsourcing (BPO), labor from South-East Asian nations, and Silicon Valley's high Asian immigrant software professional population, critical cyberculture studies must explore the racialized political economy of ICTs. This means paying attention to the regional, geopolitical variations in and concentrations of ICTs and, in some cases, seeing cyberculture as yet another racialized technology that reinforces the divide between races and ethnic groups.

In some cases the new technologies have enabled those traditionally denied the space to speak to find a means of articulation. However, questions of authenticity and trust remain at the forefront of debates, even in cybercultures.

The articles in this part of the book look at cyberspace as a racialized space. They range from studies of political economy to issues of stereotyping (i.e., representations) in cyberspace.

Proceeding from the assumption that cyberculture does not erase issues of race in a transcendence of the body or subjectivity, Lisa Nakamura argues that the human/computer interface, the dynamics of access, and the means by which users express themselves online interact with ideologies of race – a process she terms cybertyping. Nakamura draws attention to the very material conditions of cyberculture – bodies with or without access to the internet, telecommunications, and computers, and bodies without basic health care. Cyberspace, she argues, seeks to stabilize a sense of the white self and identity. Cybertypes are therefore images of race scripted into the digital domain. People of color, women, and minorities are seen as potential markets rather than coalitions. Nakamura is emphatic that "fluid identities aren't much use to those whose problems exist strictly … in the real world if they lose all their currency in the realm of the real." We should be aware of the westernization of global media and of the fact that a "cosmetic multiculturalism" – the technological Diaspora of black, brown, and yellow foreign high-tech workers absorbed into America's high-tech industry – results in distant global identities while masking the racialized nature of local ones.

Diaspora studies has come to occupy both postcolonial studies and globalization studies in a big way. Raka Shome's article explores the newest hybrid spaces in a globalized world: the offshore call center. Shome suggests that traditional notions of hybridity as espoused and developed by Homi Bhabha, James Clifford, and others have to be recast. The Asian call center produces racial hybridity, transnational crossings, and dislocations. But because these occur without geographical and physical displacements – and occur only in virtual environments while being physically located in India – the cultural politics of hybridity and Diaspora play out in different ways. "New regimes of hybridity" emerge in the accent and cultural training of call-center recruits, and produce a "de-Indianization," argues Shome. Further, the hybrid identity will never reach the level of a "public" and will forever remain privatized, as call-center employees play American roles, speak in American accents, and have American names. This is a "privatized dis-appearance" in this "virtual migration" through which their hybrid identity speaks, because they cannot ever reveal their Indian identity in the global public sphere. They are also unable to return the many "gazes" they are subject to as call-center workers. Shome concludes that a transnational "refraction" is at work here, and the violence of the call centers that creates such subjects is an imperial/national violence that is more insidious than the earlier colonial one. Shome's article foregrounds the politics of race and the material contexts of virtual communications and global electronic business and financial flows.

Cyberspace and internet technologies are used by the marginalized and the dispossessed. Denied other forums for voicing their grievances and claims, they take to the internet as a space for this articulation. Ananda Mitra's article suggests that "voice" is the crucial component of this use of the internet. Voice, for Mitra, is what enables a speaking individual to acquire agency. However, the wide-open spaces of the internet mean that multiple voices clash for what Mitra identifies as the two key components of internet cultures: trust and authenticity. "Netizens" have to decide on which voice to trust in this cacophony of competing voices. These voices try to generate trust through a representation of experiences that convey authenticity. Mitra studies SAWNET (the South Asian Women's Network) in order to see how women seek to assert voice and agency in their self-representations and how even conditions of anonymity – the names of the speakers are not always given on the discussion forum – contribute to a collective "hypervoice."

11 CYBERTYPING AND THE WORK OF RACE IN THE AGE OF DIGITAL REPRODUCTION

Lisa Nakamura

[...]

In an attempt to transcode the language of race and racialism that I observed online. I coined the term *cybertype* to describe the distinctive ways that the Internet propagates, disseminates, and commodifies images of race and racism. The study of racial cybertypes brings together the cultural layer and the computer layer: that is to say, cybertyping is the process by which computer/human interfaces, the dynamics and economics of access, and the means by which users are able to express themselves online interacts with the "cultural layer" or ideologies regarding race that they bring with them into cyberspace.

[...]

Cybertypes are more than just racial stereotypes "ported" to a new medium. Because the Internet is interactive and collectively authored, cybertypes are created in a peculiarly collaborative way: they reflect the ways that machine enabled interactivity gives rise to images of race that both stem from a common cultural logic and seek to redress anxieties about the ways that computer enabled communication can challenge these old logies. They perform a crucial role in the signifying practice of cyberspace; they stabilize a sense of a white self and identity that is threatened by the radical fluidity and disconnect between mind and body that is celebrated in so much cyberpunk fiction. Bodies get tricky in cyberspace; that sense of disembodiment that

Lisa Nakamura, "Cybertyping and the Work of Race in the Age of Digital Reproduction," pp. 1–30, 147–9, 159–61 from Lisa Nakamura, *Cybertypes: Race, Ethnicity, and Identity on the Internet* (London and New York: Routledge).

is both freeing and disorienting creates a profound malaise in the user that stable images of race work to fix in place.

Cybertypes are the images of race that arise when the fears, anxieties, and desires of privileged Western users (the majority of Internet users and content producers are still from the Western nations) are scripted into a textual/graphical environment that is in constant flux and revision. As Rey Chow writes in "Where Have All the Natives Gone?" images of raced others become necessary symptoms of the postcolonial condition. She writes that "the production of the native is in part the production of our postcolonial modernity" (30), and that "we see that in our fascination with the 'authentic native' we are actually engaged in a search for the aura even while our search processes themselves take us farther and farther from that 'original' point of identification" (46). The Internet is certainly a postcolonial discursive practice, originating as it does from both scientific discourses of progress and the Western global capitalistic project. When Chow attributes our need for stabilizing images of the "authentic native" to the "search for the aura," or original and authentic object, she is transcoding Walter Benjamin's formulation from "The Work of Art in the Age of Mechanical Reproduction" into a new paradigm. In a subsection to her essay entitled "The Native in the Age of Discursive Reproduction," Chow clarifies her use of Benjamin to talk about postcolonialism and the function of the "native." While Benjamin maintained that technology had radically changed the nature of art by making it possible to reproduce infinite copies of it – thus devaluing the "aura" of the original – Chow envisions the "native" himself as the original, with his own aura. When natives stop acting like natives – that is to say, when they deviate from the stereotypes that have been set up to signify their identities – their "aura" is lost: they are no longer "authentic." Thus, a rationale for the existence of racial cybertypes becomes clear: in a virtual environment like the Internet where *everything* is a copy, so to speak, and nothing has an aura since all cyberimages exist as pure pixellated information, the desire to search for an original is thwarted from the very beginning. Hence the need for images of cybertyped "real natives" to assuage that desire. Chow poses a series of questions in this section:

> Why are we so fascinated with "history" and with the "native" in "modern" times? What do we gain from our labor on these "endangered authenticities" which are presumed to be from a different time and a different place? What can be said about the juxtaposition of "us" (our discourse) and "them"? What kind of *surplus value* is created by this juxtaposition? (42)

The surplus value created by this juxtaposition (between the Western user and the discourses of race and racism in cyberspace) lies precisely within the need for the native in modern times. As machine-induced speed enters our lives – the speed of transmission of images and texts, of proliferating information, of dizzying arrays of decision trees and menus – all of these symptoms of modernity create a sense of unease that is remedied by comforting and familiar images of a "history" and a "native" that seems frozen in "a different time and a different place."

This is the paradox: In order to think rigorously, humanely, and imaginatively about virtuality and the "posthuman," it is absolutely necessary to ground critique in the lived realities of the human, in all their particularity and specificity. The nuanced realities of virtuality – racial gendered, othered – live in the body, and though science is producing and encouraging different readings and revisions of the body, it is premature to throw it away just yet, particularly since so much postcolonial, political, and feminist critique stems from it.

The vexed position of women's bodies and raced bodies in feminist and postcolonial theory has been a subject of intense debate for at least the past twenty years. While feminism and postcolonial studies must, to some extent, buy into the notion of there being such a thing as a "woman" or a "person of color" in order to be coherent, there are also ways in which "essentialism is a trap," (89) to quote Gayatri Spivak. Since definitions of what counts as a woman or a person of color can be shifting and contingent upon hegemonic forces, essentialism can prove to be untenable. Indeed, modern body technologies are partly responsible for this: gender reassignment surgery and cosmetic surgery can make these definitions all the blurrier. In addition, attributing essential qualities to women and people of color can reproduce a kind of totalizing of identity that reproduces the old sexist and racist ideologies. However, Donna Haraway, who radically questions the critical gains to be gotten from conceptualizing *woman* as anchored to the body, takes great pains to emphasize that she does not "know of any time in history when there was greater need for political unity to confront effectively the dominations of 'race,' 'gender,' 'sexuality,' and 'class'" (157). Though she replaces the formerly essential concept of "woman" with that of the "cyborg," a hybrid of machine and human, she also acknowledges that feminist polities must continue "through coalition – affinity, not identity" (155). Both she and Spivak write extensively about the kinds of strategic affinities that can and must be built between and among "women" (albeit in quotation marks), racial and other minorities, and other marginalized and oppressed groups.

Is it a coincidence that just as feminist and subaltern politics – built around affinities as well as identities – are acquiring some legitimacy and power in the academy (note the increasing numbers of courses labeled "multicultural," "ethnic," "feminist," "postcolonial" in university course schedules) MCI Worldcom, and other teletechnology corporations are staking out their positions as forces that will free us from race and gender?

[…]

Increasing numbers of racial minorities and women are acquiring access to the Internet – a hopeful sign indeed. Ideally, this equalizing of access to the dominant form of information technology in our time might result in a more diverse cyberspace, one that doesn't seek to elide or ignore difference as an outmoded souvenir of the body. Indeed, sites such as ivillage.com, Oxygen.com, Salon.com's Hip Mama webpages, and NetNoir, which contain content specifically geared to women and to African Americans, indicate a shift in the Internet's content that reflects a partial bridging of the digital divide. As women of color acquire an increasing presence online, their particular interests, which spring directly from gender and racial identifications (that is to say, those identities associated with a physical body offline), are being addressed.

Unfortunately, as can be seen from the high, and ultimately dashed, feminist hopes that new media such as the Oxygen Network would express women's concerns in a politically progressive and meaningful way, gender and race can just as easily be co-opted by the e-marketplace. Commercial sites such as these tend to view women and minorities primarily as potential markets for advertisers and merchants rather than as "coalitions." Opportunities for political coalition building between women and people of color are often subverted in favor of e-marketing and commerce. (NetNoir is a notable exception to this trend. It is also the oldest of these identitarian websites, and thus was able to form its mission, content, and "look and feel" prior to the gold rush of dot-com commerce that brought an influx of investment capital, and consequent pressure to conform to corporate interests, to the web).[1] Nonetheless, this shift in content which specifically addresses women and minorities, either as markets or as political entities[2] does acknowledge that body-related identities such as race and gender are not yet as fluid and thus disposable as much cybertheory and commercial discourse would like to see them.

However, such is the stubborn power of cybertyping that even when substantial numbers of racial minorities do have the necessary computer hardware and Internet access to deploy themselves "fluidly" online they are often rudely yanked back to the realities of racial discrimination and prejudice. For example, on March 13, 2000, in what was called "the first civil rights class action litigation against an Internet company," the Washington-based Equal Rights Center and two African-American plaintiffs sued Kozmo.com for racial "redlining" because of what was perceived as geographic discrimination (Katz n.p.). Kozmo.com, an online service that delivers convenience foods and products, claims to deliver only to "zip codes that have the highest rates of Internet penetration and usage" (Hamilton n.p.); however, the company's judgment of what constitutes an Internet-penetrated zip code follows racial lines as well. African-American Washingtonians James Warren and Winona Lake used their Internet access to order goods from Kozmo, only to be told that their zip codes weren't served by the company. Kozmo.com also refused to deliver to a neighborhood of Washington, D.C., occupied primarily by upper-class African Americans with equal "Internet penetration" as white neighborhoods (Prakash n.p.).[3] It seems that these African-American Internet users possessed identities online that were too firmly moored to their raced bodies to participate in the utopian ideal of the Internet as a democratizing disembodied space. Unfortunately, it would appear that online identities can never be truly fluid if one lives in the "wrong" zip code.

As the Kozmo.com example shows, actual hardware access is a necessary but not sufficient component of online citizenship. All of the things that citizenship implies – freedom to participate in community on an equal basis, access to national and local infrastructures, the ability to engage in discourse and commerce (cyber- and otherwise) with other citizens – are abrogated by racist politics disguised as corporate market research. This example of online redlining, or "refusing to sell something to someone due to age, race or location" puts a new spin on cybertyping. Rather than being left behind, bracketed, or "radically questioned" the body – the raced, gendered, classed body – gets "outed" in cyberspace just as soon as commerce and discourse come into play. Fluid identities aren't much use to those whose problems exist strictly (or even mostly) in the real world if they lose all their currency in the realm of the real.

[...]

The Internet generates both images of identity and afterimages. The word *after-image* implies two things to me in the context of contemporary technoscience and cyberculture.

The first is its a rhetorical position as a "Y2Kism," part of the millennial drive to categorize social and cultural phenomena as *post-*, as *after*. It puts pressure on the formerly solid and anchoring notion of identity as something we in the digital age are fast on our way to becoming "after." This notion of the posthuman has evolved in other critical discourses of technology and the body, and is often presented in a celebratory way.[4]

The second is this: the image that you see when you close your eyes after gazing at a bright light: the phantasmatic spectacle or private image gallery that bears but a tenuous relationship to "reality." Cyberspace and the images of identity that it produces can be seen as an interior, mind's-eye projection of the "real." I'm thinking especially of screen fatigue – the crawling characters or flickering squiggles you see inside your eyelids after a lot of screen-time in front of a television, cathode ray tube (CRT) terminal, movie screen, or any of the sources of virtual light to which we are exposed every day. How have the blinding changes and dazzlingly rapid developments of technology in recent years served to project an altered image or projection of identity upon our collective consciousness? This visual metaphor of the afterimage describes a particular kind of historically and culturally grounded seeing or misseeing, and this is important. Ideally, it has a critical valence and can represent a way of seeing differently, of claiming the right to possess agency in our ways of seeing – of being a subject rather than an object of technology. In the bright light of contemporary technology, identity is revealed to be phantasmatic, a projection of culture and ideology. It is the product of a reflection or a deflection of prior images, as opposed to afterimages, of identity. When we look at these rhetorics and images of cyberspace we are seeing an afterimage – both posthuman and projectionary – that is the product of a vision rearranged and deranged by the virtual light of virtual things and people.

Similarly, the sign-systems associated with advertisements for reproductive and "gendered" technologies reveal, in Valerie Hartouni's words, "the fierce and frantic iteration of conventional meanings and identities in the context of technologies and techniques that render them virtually unintelligible" (51). According to this logic, stable images of identity have been replaced by afterimages. When we look at cyberspace, we see a phantasm that says more about our fantasies and structures of desire than it does about the "reality" to which it is compared by the term *virtual reality*: Many of cyberspace's commerical discourses, such as the television and print advertisements I examine in closer detail in chapter 4, work on a semiotic level that establishes a sense of a national self. However, in a radically disruptive move they simultaneously deconstruct the notion of a corporeal self anchored in familiar categories of identity. Indeed, this example of "screen fatigue" (commercials are great examples of screen fatigue because they're so fatiguing) projects a very particular kind of afterimage of identity.

The discourse of many commericals for the Internet includes gender as only one of a series of outmoded "body categories" like race and age. The ungendered, deracinated self promised to us by these commercials is freed of these troublesome categories, which have been done away with in the name of a "progressive" politics. The goal of "honoring diversity" seen on so many bumper stickers will be accomplished by eliminating diversity.

It's not just commercials that are making these postidentitarian claims. Indeed, one could say that they're following the lead or at least running in tandem with some of the growing numbers of academics who devote themselves to the cultural study of technology. For example, in *Life on the Screen* Sherry Turkle writes,

> When identity was defined as unitary and solid it was relatively easy to recognize and censure deviation from a norm. A more fluid sense of self allows for a greater capacity for acknowledging diversity. It makes it easier to accept the array of our (and others') inconsistent personae – perhaps with humor, perhaps with irony. We do not feel compelled to rank or judge the elements of our multiplicity. We do not feel compelled to exclude what does not fit. (261)

According to this way of thinking, regulatory and oppressive social norms such as racism and sexism are linked to users' "unitary and solid" identities offscreen. Supposedly, leaving the body behind in the service of gaining more "fluid identities" means acquiring the ability to carve out new, less oppressive norms, and gaining the capacity to "acknowledge diversity" in ever more effective ways. However, is this really happening in cyberspace?

I answer this question with an emphatic no in chapter 2. I have coined the term *identity tourism* to describe a disturbing thing that I was noticing in an Internet chat community. During my fieldwork I discovered that the afterimages of identity that users were creating by adopting personae other than their own online as often as not participated in stereotyped notions of gender and race. Rather than "honoring diversity," their performances online used race and gender as amusing prostheses to be donned and shed without "real life" consequences. Like tourists who become convinced that their travels have shown them real "native" life, these identity tourists often took their virtual experiences as other-gendered and other-raced avatars as a kind of lived truth. Not only does this practice provide titillation and a bit of spice: as bell hooks writes, "one desires a 'bit of the Other' to enhance the blank landscape of whiteness" (29), it also provides a new theater in cyberspace for "eating the Other." For hooks, "the overriding fear is that cultural, ethnic, and racial differences will be commodified and offered up as new dishes to enhance the white palate – that the Other will be eaten, consumed, and forgotten" (39). Certainly, the performances of identity tourists exemplify the consumption and commodification of racial difference; the fact that so many users are willing to pay monthly service fees to put their racially stereotyped avatars in chat rooms attests to this.

Remastering the Internet

The racial stereotype, a distinctive and ongoing feature of media generally, can be envisioned in archaeological terms. If we conceive of multimedia, in particular what's been termed the "new media" engendered by the Internet, as possessing strata – layers of accretions and amplifications of imageries and taxonomies of identity – then it is possible (and indeed, for reasons I will show shortly, *strategic*) to examine the structure of these layerings. Old media provide the foundation for the new, and their means of putting race to work in the service of particular ideologies is reinvoked, with a twist, in the new landscape of race in the digital age. Visions of a "postracial democracy" evident in much discourse surrounding the Internet (particularly in print and television advertisements), are symptomatic of the desire for a cosmetic cosmopolitanism that works to conceal the problem of racism in the American context.

I could put this another way: Where's the multi(culturalism) in multimedia? or Where is race in new media? What is the "work" that race does in cyberspace, our most currently privileged example of the technology of digital reproduction? What boundaries does it police? What "modes of digital identification" or disidentification are enabled, permitted, foreclosed vis-à-vis race? Has the notion of the "authentic" been destroyed permanently, a process that Benjamin predicted had begun at the turn of the century with the advent of new means of mechanical reproduction of images? How do we begin to understand the place of authenticity, in particular racial and cultural authenticity, in the landscape of new media? Digital reproduction produces new iterations of race and racialism, iterations with roots in those produced by mechanical reproduction. Images of race from older media are the analog signal that the Internet optimizes for digital reproduction and transmission.

On the one hand, Internet use can be seen as part of the complex of multimedia globalization, a foisting of a Western (as yet) cultural practice upon "third world," minority, and marginalized populations. Recent protests in the Western world against the International Monetary Fund critique global capitalism and globalization as not only economically exploitative of the "third world," but also culturally exploitative as well, essentially creating a "monoculture of the mind."

[…]

Ziauddin Sardar characterizes cyberspace itself as a monoculture, the West's "dark side" and thus a powerful continuation of the imperialist project. The discourse of agribusiness and the bioengineering of crops is central here: monocultures are economies of scale, an erasure of diversity under current attack by the fashionable as offering little resistance to disease. But where does the hybrid, specifically the "hyphenated" American of color, stand in relation to this?

[…]

Does the Internet indeed create a monoculture? Is there space within it for the subaltern to speak? How do representations of the subaltern in reference to the Internet preserve or deny diversity? How is the paradigm of tourism invoked to stabilize threatened ideas of the authentic native Post-Internet?

The Internet has a global sweep, a hype (hysteria?) attached to it; it makes distinctive claims to a radical postracial democracy that other media have failed to employ effectively. Racial cybertyping is at work on the Internet today, and its implications both *for* its "objects" and for the cultural matrix it is embedded in generally are far reaching. Groups such as racial and ethnic minorities, who are prone to being stereotyped in older media, are now being "remastered" to use more digital terminology, ported to cybertyping. Remastering, the practice of converting an analog signal – for instance, from a vinyl record, to a digital one like a digital video disc (DVD), or compact disk (CD), or to hypertext markup language (HTML) – preserves the "content" of the original piece while optimizing it for a new format. Remastering fiddles with sound levels and timbre, erases scratchy silences, smoothes roughnesses, and alters signal-to-noise ratios in such a way that the same song is made infinitely available for reproduction, replay, and retransmission. But with a difference: variations in tone, timbre, and nuance are detectable; while the song remains the same, some of its qualities are altered, as are the possibilities for different audiences, different occasions for capture, replay, and transmission. The weblike media complex of images of the racialized other as primitive, exotic, irremediably different, and fixed in time is an old song, one that the Internet has remastered or retrofit in digitally reproducible ways. I wish to get back in the studio, so to speak, and to see how this remastering happens and what its effects are upon social formations and readings of race in the age of digital reproduction. When you feed racism into this machine, what you get are images of "exotic" non-American racial minorities (but not American minorities) using technology.

The Internet is the fastest, most effective image-reproduction machine this world has yet seen. Just as the stereotype machine, that clumsy mechanical device that produced multiple but imperfect copies of an original image, has been replaced by more efficient and clearer, cleaner modes of image reproduction, so too are racial stereotypes being replaced by cybertypes. While racial stereotypes can now be perceived by our ever more discerning eyes as crude and obvious, and have thus have been appropriated as camp (as in Bill Cosby's collection of racist black memorabilia), or parody (black humor, like Chris Rock's, turns upon this) or incorporated into a history of oppression, cybertypes have as yet managed to sneak under the radar of critical and popular scrutiny.[5] The digital images of natives, others, and the "raced" that proliferate on and around the Internet are clean, nonmechanical, and carried upon a beam of fiber-optic light. Cybertyping's phantom track can be traced in a Cisco television advertisement, produced as part of a series entitled "The Internet Generation" that participates in a subtle blend of racism and racialism. Rather than stereotyping different races, it cybertypes them. The children in the first ad, "Out of the Mouths of Babes," repeat statistics about the Internet's improvements about older media (i.e., "The Web has [*sic*] more users in the first five years than television did in the first thirty") in distinctively accented voices while they are depicted in "native" dress in "native" settings, such as a temple pool, a mosque, and a rural schoolyard. In addition, their dialogue is fractured, as each sentence is continued or repeated by a different child in a different locale. Thus, the ad tries to literalize the smaller world that Benjamin predicted audiences accustomed to proliferating mechanical images, and, by extension, digital images, would come to desire and expect. One child tells us that "a population the size of the United Kingdom joins the Internet every six months. Internet traffic doubles every one hundred days." This depiction of the Internet as a population one joins, rather than a service one purchases and consumes or a practice one engages in, significantly uses the ur-imperial nation, the United Kingdom, as the yardstick of measurement here. This language of a "united kingdom" of multiracial "generations" seems utopian, yet polices the racial and ethnic boundaries of this world very clearly. Global capitalism is envisioned as a United Nations of users from different countries united in their praise of the Internet, yet still preserved in their different ethnic dress, languages, and "look and feel."[6] Despite the fact that international Internet users are likely to be city dwellers, these ads depict them in picturesque and idealized "native" practices uncommon even in rural areas.

Cybertyping's purpose is to representatively bracket off racial difference, to assuage fears that the Internet is indeed producing a monoculture. The greater fear, however, which cybertyping actively works to conceal, is the West's reluctance to acknowledge its colonization of global media, and ongoing racist practices within its own borders. The ad's claims that "soon, all of our ideas will be free of borders" tries to stake out the notion that America's responsibility for its own problems with race, the greatest problem of our age in W. E. B. Du Bois's terms, will be erased when "borders" (between nations, between the mind and the raced body) are figuratively erased. The subtlety of this argument is necessary in our postcolonial, postmodern age: scenarios that invoke the scramble for Africa, an emblematic episode of the West's division and exploitation of the non-Western world, just will not "play" any- more. However, porting the imperialist impulse to a commercial like Cisco's "Generations" series, which cybertypes race as useful rather than divisive sneaks it under the surveillance cameras.

This commercial remasters race. Remastering implies subjugation, the recolo- nization of otherness in a "postcolonial" world, and its method rests upon the ideological rock of cultural "authenticity." On the contrary, rather than destroying authenticity, cybertyping wants to preserve it. Just as intellectuals in ethnic studies and women's studies are starting to radically question the efficacy of "authenticity" as a flag to rally around, a way to gain solidarity, the commercial discourse of the Internet (that is, the way it figures itself *to* itself) scrambles to pick up that dropped flag.

The Internet must contain images of authentic natives in the service of militating against particular images of cultural hybridity. The Internet functions as a tourism machine; it reproduces digital images of race as other. Missing from this picture is any depiction of race in the American context. The vexed question of racism here and now is elided. Racism is recuperated in this ad as cosmetic multiculturalism, or cos- metic cosmoplitanism. In this ad and others like it, American minorities are discur- sively fixed, or cybertyped, in particular ways to stabilize a sense of a cosmopolitan, digeratiprivileged self, which is white and Western.

Postracial Cosmopolitanism

In "The Unbearable Whiteness of Being: African American Critical Theory and Cyberculture," Kalí Tal writes that "in cyberspace, it is possible to completely and utterly disappear people of color," and that the elision of questions of race in cyberspace has led to its "whitinizing" (n.p.). On the contrary, race is far from elided in these narratives; instead it is repurposed and remastered, made to do new work.

This article [James Fallows] refers to the technological (and in this case Internet-driven) diaspora of brown, black, and yellow foreign high-tech workers into America's technology industry. This contributes to a cosmetic multiculturalism, a false sense of racial equality – or postracial cybermeritocracy – that I would term *cosmetic multiculturalism*. As Fallows notes, this cosmetic multiculturalism actively works to conceal "the entrenched racial problems of black and white America." The presence of black and brown faces from other countries, notably Asian ones, encourages white workers to inhabit a *virtually* diverse world, one where local racial problems are shuffled aside by a *global* and disaporic diversity created by talented immigrants as opposed to "hyphenated Americans." This is a form of tourism, benefiting from difference in order to make the American/Western self feel well-rounded, cosmopolitan, *postracial*. This is not digital identification, but digital *dis*identification – disavowal of the recognition of race in local contexts in favor of comfortably distant global ones. In the new landscape of cyberspace, other countries (i.e., markets, and sources of cheap expert immigrant labor in information fields) exist, but not American minorities. It only seems commonsensical, as Reed Koch, a manager at Microsoft, puts it, that "if you go ten years [in the high-tech corporate world] and extremely rarely in your daily life ever encounter an American black person, I think they disappear from your awareness" (Fallows 95). One of the symptoms of cybertyping is this convenient "disappearance from awareness" of American racial minorities, a symptom that "multiculturalist" Internet advertising and the discourse of technology work hard to produce.

Cybertyping and the American Scene

In Vijay Prashad's important work *The Karma of Brown Folk*, he poses a question to Asian readers: "How does it feel to be the solution?" In this volume, Prashad invokes Du Bois's rhetorical question to African Americans – "How does it feel to be a problem?" – and repurposes it in order to trace the construction of the Asian, in particular the South Asian, as a model minority. The figure of the Asian as model worker is inextricably tied to this stereotype, which has been reiterated as a particular cybertype of the Asian as an exemplary information worker. If one sees race as a major "problem" of American digital culture, an examination of these cybertypes reveals the ways in which Asians prove to be the "solution." Different minorities have different functions in the cultural landscape of digital technologies. They are good for different kinds of ideological work. And, in fact, this taxonomy of work and identity has been remastered: seeing Asians as the solution and blacks as the problem is and has always been a drastic and damaging formulation which pits minorities against each other and is evident in the culture at large.

On the contrary, in a fascinating twist, cybertyping figures both Asians and blacks as the solution, but for different problems. While Asians are constructed as anonymous workers, an undifferentiated pool of skilled (and grateful) labor, African Americans serve as a semiotic marker for the "real," the vanishing point of cyberspace in particular and technology in general.[7]

The New New Thing: Head-Hunting the South Asian Cyborg

The issue of the *New York Times Magazine* that contains Michael Lewis's article "The Search Engine" features a cover graphic that repeats the words "The New New Thing" hundreds of times. The subtitle is "How Jim Clark taught America what the technoeconomy was all about." Clark, the founder of Netscape, Silicon Graphics, and Healtheon is described as "not so much an Internet entrepreneur as the embodiment of a new kind of economic man." This article reveals that the "new kind of economic man," specifically an American man, attains preeminence partly by his ability to repurpose the discourse of racism, to create new cybertypes of Asian technology workers, in ways which at first seem unobjectionable because they have become so common.

Clark spent a great deal of energy recruiting Indian engineers from Silicon Graphics (like engineer Pavan Nigam) to work for his new start-up Healtheon. As Lewis writes, "Jim Clark [of Netscape] had a thing for Indians. 'The Indian outcasts of Silicon Valley,' he usually called them, 'my Indian hordes' in less sober moments. 'As a concentrated group,' he said, 'they were the most talented engineers in the valley ... *And they work their butts off*'" (Lewis 82).

These "less sober moments" reveal cybertyping in action. This idea of Indians as constituting a horde devoid of individuality, a faceless mob, reveals both a fear of their numbers and a desire to become the head of the horde, their leader.[8] These "Indian outcasts" are seen as a natural resource to be exploited – valuable workers, like Chinese railroad laborers. What's more, they're a racial group characterized "naturally" as always-already digital, like Asians as a whole. In 1997, Bill Gates indulged in a moment of foot-in-mouth cybertyping when he declared during a visit to India that "South Indians are the second-smartest people on the planet (for those who are guessing, he rated the Chinese as the smartest; those who continue to guess should note that white people, like Gates, do not get classified, since it is the white gaze, in this incarnation, that is transcendental and able to do the classifying!)" (Prashad 70). Asian technology workers are thought not to need a "personal life," just like Chinese railroad workers were thought to have nerves farther away from the skin. This characterization of Asians as being superior workers because of inherent, near-physiological differences, seeing them as impervious to pain, in their butts or elsewhere, places them squarely in a new, digital "different caste": the outcasts of Silicon Valley. This term repurposes the old language of caste, an ancient system that preserves hierarchical distributions of privilege and oppression, for use in the digital age. Keeping to this logic, no amount of work can make them a part of the digital economy as "entrepreneurs" or "new economic men"; they are figured as permanent outcasts and outsiders.[9] Yet, such is the power of cybertyping that Clark's and Gates's comments are not viewed as racist but as strategic, a canny recognition of the rightful work of race in the digital age: this is what makes Clark the "new economic man."

As Lisa Lowe writes, "stereotypes that construct Asians as the threatening 'yellow peril,' or alternatively, that pose Asians as the domesticated 'model minority,' are each equally indicative of these national anxieties" (18). Clark's figuration of South Indian engineers, his "thing," cybertypes them as simultaneously, rather than alternatively, the threatening horde *and* the model minority: both threatening as a quasi-conspiratorial "concentrated group" and enticing because of their engineering talents. This cybertype of the South Asian seeks to fix the "unfixed liminality of the Asian immigrant – geographically, linguistically, and racially at odds with the context of the 'national' – that has given rise to the necessity of endlessly fixing and repeating such stereotypes." (Lowe 19).

Indeed, the discourse of Internet technology has a "thing" for Asians. In the article noted above, Jim Clark describes himself as a *headhunter*, and the term is appropriate in at least two senses of the word. A headhunter, in the language of the cultural digerati, is an entrepreneur who locates professional "talent" and lures it away from one job to another. Much of the tension in this story has to do with Clark's quest to acquire Asian engineers he'd previously worked with for his new venture. A high-tech headhunter facilitates the flow of human capital and labor, often across national borders.[10] The term has roots in colonial discourse: a headhunter is a mythologized figure, like the cannibal, constructed by colonists to embody their notions of the native as savage, a creature so uncivilized and unredeemable that he cannot be broken of his habit of collecting humans as if they were trophies; thus he must be exterminated or civilized. The figure of the headhunter was a justification for colonization. Envisioning South Asians as if they were trophies, outcasts, or hordes, having a "thing for Indians," is a form of cybertyping; it homogenizes South Asians as a group in such a way that they constitute both the familiar model-minority paradigm as well as a resource for global capital. And what's more, cybertyping permits this kind of speech, even allows it to signify as "cool," or "new" in a way that Jimmy "the Greek" Synodinos's better-intentioned comments about the superiority of black athletes could not be.

As Lewis writes, "By 1996 nearly half of the 55,000 temporary visas issued by the United States government to high-tech workers went to Indians. The definitive smell inside a Silicon Valley start-up was of curry" (82). This insistence upon the smell of curry in the context of global commerce and capitalism works to discursively fix Asians as irredeemably foreign in order to stabilize a sense of a national self. This smell, here invoked as a stereotyped sign of South Asian identity, is figured as a benefit of sorts to white workers, a kind of virtual tourism: they need never leave their start-up offices (a frowned-upon practice in any event) yet can conveniently enjoy the exotic cuisine and odors of "another" world and culture.

At the dawn of the twenty-first century, cultural digerati live lives composed of these "less sober moments"; culturally and economically, Americans are living in intoxicating times, a gold rush of sorts. The fever of acquisition, creation, and entrepreneurship engendered by dot-com culture licenses specific forms of racialism, if not overt racism, that are no more descriptive of the lived realities of Asian immigrants or Asian Americans than earlier colonialist or racist ways of speaking were. Just as the gold rush depended upon the exploited labor of Chinese immigrants, black slaves, and Mexican workers and consequently created racial stereotypes to justify and explain their exploitation as "Western expansion," so too does our current digital gold rush create mythologies of race that are nostalgic. That is, they hark back to earlier narratives of race and racialism which were always-already "virtual" in the sense that they too were constructed narratives, the product of representational labor and work. As Susan Stewart defines nostalgia, it is a "sadness without an object." Nostalgia is "always ideological: the past it seeks has never existed except as narrative, and hence, always absent, that past continually threatens to reproduce itself as a felt lack" (23). The construction of postracial utopias enabled by the Internet, and so prominently troped in television advertising for the Internet, seeks to fill that "lack" by supplying us with new narratives of race that affirm its solidity in the face of global culture, multiracialism, and new patterns of migration. Cybertyping keeps race "real" using the discourse of the virtual. The object of digital nostalgia is precisely the idea of race itself. As Renato Rosaldo defines it, nostalgia is "often found under imperialism, where people mourn the passing of what they themselves have transformed," and is "a process of yearning for what one has destroyed that is a form of mystification" (quoted in hooks 25). Cybertyping works to rescue the vision of the authentic raced "native" that, first, never existed except as part of an imperialist set of narratives, and second, is already gone, or "destroyed" by technologies such as the Internet.

African-American Digital Divides: Bamboozled by the Myth of Access

The year 2000 was a banner year, for "Web use became balanced between sexes for the first time year with 31.1 million men and 30.2 million women online in April, according to Media Metrix. In some months this year [...] female users have significantly outnumbered their male counterparts" (Austen D7). The digital divide between the genders is shrinking, which is not to say that there isn't gender cybertyping occurring online. (This contradicts prior predictions from the early and mid-1990s that a mas-culinist web would repel women from logging on: on the contrary, as in television, sexism didn't repel women from the medium). The hegemony of the web is still emphatically male. However, the article from which these statistics come, entitled "Studies Reveal a Rush of Older Women to the Web," also notes that "lost in the rush to use the Web, however, are the nation's poor."

While the article provides graphs and statistics to track web use by gender, nationality, income, and whether users log on from home or work, it neglects to mention race as a factor at any point. This elision of race in favor of gender and class is symptomatic of what Radhika Gajjala sees as the tendency of "this upwardly mobile digiterati class to celebrate a romanticized 'multiculturalism' and diversity in cyberspace" (6).

It is widely assumed that the digital divide is created by inequities in access; indeed, institutional efforts to address this divide seem solely focused on getting everyone online as quickly as possible. African Americans are cybertyped as infor-mation "have-nots," occupying the "wrong" side of the digital divide; it tropes them as the "problem." This fallacy – that access equals fair representation in terms of race and gender – can be traced by examining the ways that race has worked in other media.

No sane person would contend that once everyone has cable, television will become a truly democratic and racially diverse medium, for we can see that this has not come to pass. Mainstream film and television depicts African Americans in con-sistently negative ways despite extremely high usage rates of television by African Americans.[11] Hence, the dubious goal of 100 percent "penetration" of African-American communities by Internet technologies cannot, by and of itself, result in more parity or even accuracy in representations of African Americans. How does the Internet perpetuate this myth of access-as-ultimate-equalizer? Cyberspace's rhetor-ics make claims that are distinctively different from those of other media: its claims to "erase borders" and magically produce equality simply via access can be seen nowhere else. However, Internet usage by racial minorities is a necessary, but not sufficient, condition of a meaningfully democratic Internet. As Spike Lee's brilliant film parody *Bamboozled* (2000) makes all too clear, even the presence of black writ-ers or content producers in a popular medium such as television fails to guarantee programming that depicts "dignified black people" if audiences are unwilling to support the show in large numbers. In *Bamboozled*, the Harvard-educated black television writer Pierre Delacroix produces the most offensive, racist, "ignorant" variety show he can come up with as a form of revenge against his white boss. He fully intends that the show, which depicts blacks as Topsys, Aunt Jemimas, Sambos, and Little Nigger Jims, will be a resounding flop. He entitles it the *Man Tan New Millennium Minstrel Show* and requires the African American performers to appear in authentic blackface made of burnt cork. Of course, it is a major hit with the net-works and the audience. This can be seen as an object lesson to people interested in the Internet's potential as a space for activism and antiracist education: what needs to happen on the Internet to ensure that it doesn't become the newest of the new millennium minstrel shows? The film contains a clip from Lee's earlier film.

Malcolm X, in which the protagonist addresses a crowd of African Americans, crying out, "You been hoodwinked, bamboozled." Until we acquire some insight into racial cybertypes on the Internet, we are quite likely to be hookwinked and bamboozled by the images of race we see on the Net, images that bear no more relation to real people of color than minstrel shows do to dignified black people.

Due to the efforts of black activists and scholars working in older media studies, we can better see what's at stake in this limited range of representations of racial minorities. Studies of race and the Internet are just now beginning to catch up (which is not surprising, considering the familiar lag time in media criticism when it comes to critical readings of race).

We should wish Internet access for the betterment of material and educational conditions of African Americans, but ought not expect that the medium itself is going to represent them fairly without any strategies or plans put into place to encourage this direction.

Postracial Digerati? Cybertyping the Other

Some studies claim that the Internet causes depression. A 1998 Carnegie Mellon University study posits that this is so because the Internet reduces the number of "strong social ties" that users maintain in "real life" and replaces them with "weak" or virtual ties, which don't have the same beneficial psychological effects as face-to-face social interactions (Kraut and Lundmark 1029). The Internet's ability to produce depression in its users (at least in me) can be traced at least in part to cybertyping, a kind of virtual social interaction that constructs people of color as "good" workers or "bad," on the "right" or "wrong" side of the digital divide. The Internet's claims to erase borders, such as gender, class, and racial divisions, and the ways in which public policy makers' attentions to bridging the "digital divide" that is erroneously attributed as being the source of these problems in representation, overshadow these more subtle varieties of cybertyping. This dynamic is indeed depressing, all the more so because largely silent and undiscussed.

Radhika Gajjala writes,

> Race, gender, age, sexuality, geographical location and other signifiers of "Otherness" interact with this class-based construction of "whiteness" to produce complex hierarchies and contradictions within the Digital Economy. While we can continue to call this[4] "whiteness" because the status quo is still based upon a cultural hegemony that privileges a "white" race, it might be more appropriate to refer to this up wardly mobile subject as a "privileged hybrid transnational subject" who is a member of the "digiterati" class. (6)

Here, Gajjala(6) posits that "privileged hybrid transnational subjects" such as Clark's coveted South Asian programmers can be read, for all intents and purposes, as "white" since they participate in the "cultural hegemony that privileges a white race." While they are no doubt part of that hegemony, as is every person of color who consumes, produces, and becomes the object of representation of information technologies, I contend that they are put to work in that hegemony in distinctively raced ways. The "work" that they do in this hegemony, their value-added labor in the system of information practices dubbed "global capitalism," is this: their cybertypes work to preserve taxonomies of racial difference. The nostalgia for race, or visions of racial "authenticity" invoked by the Cisco advertisements, assuages a longing. The espoused public desire for technological uplift, in the discourse of science-fiction narratives, the desire to create a new class of "digiterati" that is in some sense postracial, is matched by a corresponding longing for "race" as a spectacle of difference, a marker to function as the horizon to the vanishing point of postmodern identities.

Contemporary debates about the digital divide tend to be divided roughly into two camps. The first of these maintains that the master's tools can never dismantle the master's house, to paraphrase Audre Lorde's formulation. In other words, if people of color rush to assimilate themselves into computer culture, to bridge the digital divide, they are simply adopting the role of the docile consumer of Microsoft, Intel, and other products, and are not likely to transform the cyberspace they encounter. Like feminists who adopt the values of the patriarchy, they may succeed as isolated individuals in what has thus far been a privileged white male's domain – technology and the Internet – but cannot bring about the kind of change that would bring about true equality. As Lorde writes, taking up the master's tools "may allow us to temporarily beat him at his own game, but they will never allow us to bring about genuine change. And this fact is only threatening to those women who still define the master's house as their only source of support" (99).

The second camp maintains that people of color can only bring about "genuine change" in the often imperialistic images of race that exist online by getting online. Envisioning cybertechnologies as less the master's tools than tools for discourse that can take any shape is an optimistic ways of seeing things.

While it is impossible to say, definitively, which path is correct, there is no question that the digital divide is both a result of and a contributor to the practice of racial cybertyping. It is crucial that we continue to scrutinize the deployment of race online as well as the ways that Internet use can figure as a racialized practice if we are to realize the medium's potential as a vector for social change. There is no ignoring that the Internet can and does enable new and insidious forms of racism. Whether the master's tools present the best way to address this state of affairs has yet to be seen.

NOTES

1. In an article entitled "Survivor: As Internet Industry Plays Survival of the Fittest, Netnoir.com celebrates 5th Anniversary," which appeared in Netnoir.com's online newsletter in 2000, the company announced that San Francisco mayor Willie Brown had proclaimed June 22 "Netnoir.com day in the city and county of San Francisco." In 1994,

Netnoir.com's E. David Ellington received an award from the AOL Greenhouse Project to fund information technology entrepreneurs, and "soon after, AOL backed NetNoir with a 19.9 percent equity stake." Currently, NetNoir has partnered with AOL, Syncom Ventures, and Radio One. NetNoir's slogan – "Taking you there. Wherever there is" – stands as an interesting contrast to Microsoft's "Where do you want to go today?" in the sense that it is far more openended about the web's topography and structure.

2. Since the incredible dominance of the Internet by the World Wide Web in the 1990s, it has consistently supported this construction of women *as* bodies. The notion that the Internet is 90 percent pornography and advertising, while it may be a slight exaggeration, gestures toward the Internet's role as an extremely efficient purveyor of exploitative images of women. Similarly, the Internet's current bent toward merchandising and selling online constructs women as either "markets" or more commonly as scantily clad figures in commercials for products.

3. Kozmo.com has since gone out of business, for reasons unrelated to this lawsuit.

4. See *Posthuman Bodies*, edited by Judith Halberstam and Ira Livingston, as well as Scott Bukatman's *Terminal Identity: The Virtual Subject in Postmodern Fiction*.

5. Guillermo Gomez-Peña's work is a notable exception. In *Dangerous Border Crossers*, he describes how responses from live audiences and Internet users became the inspiration for a "series of performance personae or 'ethno-cyborgs' co-created (or rather 'coimagined') in dialogue with gallery visitors and anonymous net users" (49). These ethno-cyborgs are collaboratively constructed by canvassing and melding together Internet users' "projections and preconceptions about Latinos and indigenous people." (46). This performance project, *Mexterminator*, was constructed from the "majority of responses we received [that] portrayed Mexicans and Chicanos as threatening Others, indestructible invaders, and public enemies of America's fragile sense of coherent national identity" (49). Thus, these ethno-cyborgs are synthesized cybertypes of Mexican American identity.

6. Just as computer users become accustomed to the "look and feel" of particular interfaces (the loyalty of Macintosh users to the desktop metaphor is legendary), so too do consumers of popular discourse become strongly attached to particular images of race. As software designers and webmasters have learned, users are quick to protest when familiar websites, such as Amazon.com's, are redesigned, and these designers have often responded to consumer protests by changing them back to their original appearance. This is also the case for the ways that the "native" is portrayed in popular culture.

7. See Alondra Nelson and colleagues' essay collection *Technicolor: Race, Technology and Everyday Life* for a critique of this formulation; their work posits a reframing and redefinition of the "technical" to include sampling, sound technologies, and communications technologies such as the beeper, cellphone, and pager in ways that would "count" African Americans as innovators and users of note.

8. This is akin to Neal Stephenson's cyberpunk novel *The Diamond Age*, which represents Chinese girls as members of a faceless "horde" of model minorities.

9. Growing attention has been paid to the existence of a "glass ceiling" for Asian engineers in the high-technology industry, particularly in Asian-American publications and newspapers. However, despite this glass ceiling, R. Mutthuswami asserts that "highly educated Indians [...] serve as CEOs of 25 percent of the companies in Silicon Valley" (quoted in Kumar 81).

10. One can see the headhunter's analogue in the more down-market image of the "coyote." Coyotes are "smugglers of workers and goods ... for the farms of South Texas, the hotels

of Las Vegas and the sweatshops of Los Angeles" (Davis 27). They guide people across the U.S. Mexican border, and there are often casualties along the way.

11. Despite the existence of black-oriented programming on smaller cable networks such as the WB and UPN, the majority of African Americans, as well as Asians and Latinos (groups even less depicted on television as primary characters), understandably feel that their lived realities are entirely unrepresented on television. Of course the same is true for whites: few possess the limitless leisure and privilege enjoyed by the characters on the show *Friends*, for example; but they might at least aspire to these roles. What African-American woman truly would want to be the "hoochie mama" depicted on Rikki Lake's "reality" programming or the noble black mammy Oracle in the film *The Matrix*?

REFERENCES

Bukatman, Scott. *Terminal Identity: The Virtual Subject in Postmodern Fiction*. Durham, NC: Duke University Press, 1998.

Davis, Mike. *Magical Urbanism: Latinos Reinvent the U.S. Big City*. London: Verso, 2000.

Fallows, James. "The Invisible Poor." *New York Times Magazine*, March 19, 2000, 8–78, 95, 111–12.

Gajjala, Radhika. "Transnational Digital Subjects: Constructs of Identity and Ignorance in a Digital Economy." Paper presented at the Conference on Cultural Diversity in Cyberspace, College Park, MD, May 2000.

Gomez-Peña, Guillermo. *Dangerous Border Crossers*. London and New York: Routledge, 2000.

Halberstam, Judith, and Ira Livingston, eds. *Posthuman Bodies*. Bloomington: Indiana University Press, 1995.

Hamilton, Martha. "Web Retailer Kozmo Accused of Redlining: Exclusion of D.C. Minority Areas Cited." *Washington Post*, April 14, 2000. Online at http://www.washingtonpost.com/wp-dyn/articles/A9719-2000Apr13.html.

Haraway, Donna. *Simians, Cyborgs, and Women: The Reinvention of Nature*. New York: Routledge, 1991.

Hartouni, Valerie. "Containing Women: Reproductive Discourse in the 1980s." *Technoculture*. Ed. Constance Penley and Andrew Ross. Minneapolis: University of Minnesota Press, 1991.

Katz, Frances. "Racial-Bias Suit Filed Against Online Delivery Service Kozmo.com." *KRTBN Knight-Ridder Tribune Business News: The Atlanta Journal and Constitution*, April 14, 2000.

Kraut, Robert, and Vicki Lundmark. "Internet Paradox: A Social Technology That Reduces Social Involvement and Psychological Well-Being?" *American Psychologist*, 53.9 (1998):1017–31.

Kumar, Amitava. "Temporary Access: the Indian H1-B Visa Worker in the United States." *Technicolor: Race, Technology, and Everyday Life*. Ed. Alondra Nelson and Thuy Linh N. Tu with Alicia Headlam Hines. New York: New York University Press, 2001.

Lewis, Michael. "The Search Engine." *New York Times Magazine*, October 10, 1999, 77–83+.

Lorde, Audre. "The Master's Tools Will Never Dismantle the Master's House." *This Bridge Called My Back: Writing by Radical Women of Color*. Eds. Cherríe Moraga and Gloria Anzaldúa. New York: Kitchen Table Press, 1981.

Nelson, Alondra, Thuy Linh N. Tu, and Alicia Hines, eds. *TechniColor: Race, Technology, and Everyday Life*. New York: New York University Press, 2001.

Netnoir.com Newsletter. Online mailing list.

Prakash, Snigdha. *All Things Considered*. National Public Radio. May 2, 2000. http://search. npr.org/cf/cmn/cmpd01fm.cfm?PrgDate=05%2F02%2F2000&PrgID=2.

Prashad, Vijay. *The Karma of Brown Folk*. Minneapolis: University of Minnesota Press, 2000.

Sardar, Ziauddin. "Alt.Civilizations.FAQ: Cyberspace as the Darker Side of the West." *The Cybercultures Reader*. Ed. David Bell and Barbara Kennedy. New York: Routledge, 2000.

Spivak, Gayatri Chakravorty. *In Other Worlds: Essays in Cultural Politics*. New York: Routledge, 1988.

Stephenson, Neal. *The Diamond Age*. New York: Bantam, 1995.

Tal, Kalí. "The Unbearable Whiteness of Being: African American Critical Theory and Cyberculture." Online at http://www.kalital.com/Text/Writing/Whitenes.html.

12 THINKING THROUGH THE DIASPORA

Call Centers, India, and a New Politics of Hybridity

Raka Shome

This article is an attempt to think through and against some dominant assumptions and trends that have informed theories of hybridity and diaspora in postcolonial cultural studies in the western academy. ...

In recent times, however, there has been a growing discussion of the scope and possibilities of what may count as diasporic in our transnational moment and what new transnational conditions are emerging which can also be captured by the concept diaspora, and which may throw into crisis many of the North Atlantic-centered frameworks and logics through which hybridity has typically been conceptualized. (See for example, the special issue of *Interventions* [2003], the introductory essay on diaspora in Abbas and Erni, [2005]; Axel, 2004; Ong, 1998). Some of these frameworks have typically included the following: a privileging of movement or territorial migration of formerly colonized people towards western geographies and their metropolitan centers (Ong, 1998; Walsh, 2003); a dialectic of 'home' and 'away' (Axel, 2004), that is, for something to be recognized as diaspora, it usually has to be a condition of transnational movement of people to disparate geographies in other nations; a stabilization of a particular modality of temporality in which hybridity is often conceptualized through a linear framework of time as in concepts such as the 'third space' which assumes a linear chronology of a first and second instead of also recognizing the possibility of diasporic exist-

Raka Shome, "Thinking Through the Diaspora: Call Centers, India, and a New Politics of Hybridity," pp. 105–23 from *International Journal of Cultural Studies* 9:1 (2006).

ence in a simultaneity of times; the framing of the diaspora in a relation of 'other-ness' to the nation (Tololyan, 1996) in which the diaspora is seen as a post-national interruption to nationalist discourses of any kind of 'ethnic absolutism' (as in Appadurai, 1996 or Gilroy, 1991);[1] an attachment to regimes of visuality through which to theorize race and hybridity; and a privileging of North Atlantic geographies through which to theorize hybrid identity politics and related issues of multiculturalism, difference, and race.

However, as scholars (Abbas, 1997; Axel, 2004; Brah, 2003; Erni, 2001; Ong, 1998; Walsh, 2003) now begin to question and unsettle many of these North Atlantic-centered logics, the recognition being invited is that 'the old meaning of diaspora – of being scattered or in dispersion … is too limiting an analytical concept to capture the multiplicity of vectors and agendas associated with the majority of contemporary border crossings' (Ong, 2004: 87). There is thus a turn towards acknowledging that the analyses of a 'more nuanced critical genealogy of terms equivalent to diaspora in *different cultures and communities* is a path yet hardly taken' (Liao, 2005: 508, emphasis added). …

This article turns to an analysis of the cultural politics of call centers in India to provide an example of an emerging diasporic formation in an 'other' modernity that may move our understanding of hybridity and diaspora in new directions. Indian call centers are part of the recent phenomenon of Business Processing Outsourcing (called BPO in economic parlance), primarily from the US and the UK. Major US corporations such as Dell, Citibank, AOL, Delta, General Electrics, AT&T, Goldman Sachs, among numerous others, routinely remote source telematics work to India. Hundreds of thousands of Indians are employed in call centers and a typical entry-level worker in India earns around US$250 month, which by the standards of the Indian economy would be a significant entry-level salary for a fresh college graduate. Consequently, as the premier magazine *India Today* (2002) notes it is now 'the electronic housekeeper to the world, taking care of a host of routine activities for multinational giants' such as credit card inquiries, invoices and payrolls, medical transcriptions, applications, billings and collections.[2]

Indian call centers provide a rich case study that demonstrates that when the critical gaze is turned away from North Atlantic geographies (which has usually characterized studies of diaspora and hybridity) to Asian geographies and their emerging modernities under neoliberal globalization, the prevailing theoretical maps of hybridity and diaspora demonstrate ruptures and tensions that manifest new logics and formations of race that require new theoretical lenses and frameworks. Specifically, the cultural politics of Indian call centers point to the need for recognizing the importance of information and technology flows as constituting important sites upon which new and alternate relations of hybridity are being reworked in neoliberal globalization.

In recent times we have witnessed a growing attention to global flows of information and telematics, and their postcolonial implications (Castells, 1996; Freeman, 2000; Sassen, 1998; Sundaram, 2005). Scholars are grappling with the question: what are the new politics of modernity and colonialism being produced by the global flows of 'techno-space (Sundaram, 2005) or 'informatics' (Freeman, 2000)? In an attempt to contribute to this discussion, this article focuses on forms of high-tech and virtualized disciplining of the 'worker' in Indian call centers from far away geographies in the West that produce unpredictable and emerging logics of transnational encounters in the current global moment. To a certain extent, this line of inquiry has been pioneered by the groundbreaking study by Carla Freeman (2000) of the informatics industry in Barbados where she examined how outsourcing of informatics represents new gendered complexities of surveillance of the 'third world' worker by global information regimes. While Freeman's study focuses on gender as a primary category of analysis, my interest is in the new politics of race, hybridity, and diaspora which are being produced by global regimes of telematic virtuality that characterize our moment of digitalized capitalism.

In particular, this article argues that the culture of the call centers manifests a rich and complex situation that reflect many of the logics of diaspora – such as the production of racial hybridity, transnational crossings, being inside and outside (the nation), displacements and dislocations, and more. But these logics do not play out in expected ways; rather, we find these tropes and trends being rearticulated in new ways. We find the occurrence of complex productions of racial formations, of living in the inbetween, of replacements and displacements, of being both outside and inside multiple nations and geographies that intersect at the collision of multiple times. Taken together, such rearticulations unsettle many of the dominant frameworks of diaspora that have characterized postcolonial studies in the western academy. In particular, this article is interested in the question: when transnational physical migration of people and territorial departures are not the centerpiece of our theoretical frames, what new insights about diasporic belonging and hybrid border crossings are produced? The article is divided into two related sections. The first section addresses the new politics of race and hybridity that the culture of call centers manifest. The second section focuses on the rearticulation of time, space, and belonging that point to new logics of diasporic productions. My discussion will also largely focus on the American clientele whom call center agents have to serve (although the global clientele comprises British, Australians, and Europeans as well).

Race and the Disappearance of the Visual: Accent Training, Role Playing, and New Regimes of Hybridity

Race has always been central in studies of diaspora and hybridity. However, in studies of Anglo colonial modernities, race has been typically tied to visuality. As the works of Frantz Fanon, Richard Dyer, Koebena Mercer, Stuart Hall, among others have shown, racism tends to be predicated on the hatred of the *visible* and *interruptive* presence of the racial body that produces tensions of hybridity. In the culture of call centers and outsourcing of telematics, we see a crisis of this logic of race.

We see a shift from a regime of visuality to aurality where the racism occurs through a control of language, voice, and accent all carried out under the label of 'cultural neutralization'. Sneja Gunew (2000) has noted that while the 'register of the visible permeates much current theory [of race] … the aural dimension, including the category of voice and, for example, accent has remained somewhat undertheorized' (2000: 146). The cultural politics of call centers provides a rich case study through which to rethink the politics of race from the perspective of aurality and disembodiment instead of visuality and embodiment. And this is centrally seen in the regimes of 'accent training' through which call agents are required to take on an American linguistic identity. Such requirement manifests how in globalization, as Walter Mignolo (2000) has noted, language becomes a site upon which we see the collisions of multiple modernities – and language is intricately tied to the politics of modernity – albeit never in equal ways.

Call center agents have to undergo rigorous training in American culture, which is usually anywhere between six to eight weeks. Accent training is central to this; one must sound like an American when one is handling American customers, be able to chit chat about everyday American issues, and be knowledgeable in American etiquette so as to conduct casual conversation with the American customer on the other end while a request is being processed. Accent trainers, sometimes comprising Indians who may have lived in the US, are often used for this purpose. Vikam Paul, an accent trainer in a small classroom in Hero Mind Mine, a cultural training center for aspiring call center agents, makes this introductory comment to his students: 'We are here to teach you to speak global English. We are here to teach you how to speak English correctly so that they can understand you.' Inside the training school students learn how to roll their R's, emphasize their Ps, and perform facial exercises to help them feel the difference between Indian English and the 'global English' required by the call centers.

[…]

Terms such as accent neutralization, de-Indianization, voice neutralization, global English, safe international accents, are regularly used by trainers to describe the desired goal of this training where 'accent interference has to be regulated', so that the customer calling from the West has no way of recognizing that the voice on the other end is not American (or British, as the case may be). For example, a report in the *Financial Times* of London (2003) stated: 'a neutral accent enhanced with idiomatic phrases and local colloquialisms of the particular country allows the agent to focus solely on the problem' that the agent is handling. The implication is that the 'accent' could take away from a focus on the client's problem, leading to reduced efficiency. But at another level, the struggle in the regime of 'accent training' is not only over language per se – since English is an official language in India. That is, the training is not just about teaching English. It is about the control and regulation of 'voice', tone, phonology, (American) 'speech codes' (word choices, inflections, emotions, affects, stresses, etc.), and thus behavior itself that provides an example of what Ferguson and Gupta (2002: 989), following Foucault, have termed 'transnational governmentality'.

Transnational governmentality constitutes transnational mechanisms and organizations through which the conduct (of the third world subject) is regulated and disciplined from macro levels (for example, regime changes, environmental planning) to micro levels of personal behavior and social identity (for example, cultivating a taste for Coke or McDonald's) in order to maximize profit and efficiency in the global economy. Here language functions as an apparatus of transnational governmentality through which the voice of the third world subject is literally erased and reconstructed in the servicing of the global economy. In this regime of 'accent training' the presence of the 'modern' technologized Indian subject, servicing the global economy, is produced through the 'death of the subject'. The linguistic identity of the Indian subject has to be first erased before s/he can enter the virtual, modern, high-tech space of call centers and data entry. This is indeed a new politics of race where the racist erasure occurs not *after* the racial subject's *physical presence* has *visually* interrupted the dominant culture and geopolitical spaces. Rather, the racist erasure is geared towards not allowing any visual marking, recognition, and interruption of the racial subject. The visual non-existence of the racial subject and her/his transformation as a virtual, unseen figure is the logic informing this racial formation of hybridity.

In much of the current literature on the global IT culture, the metaphor of body shopping is often used (see van der Veer 2005) to discuss the recruitment of cheap 'technocoolies' from third world countries into tech cities such as Silicon Valley. With the culture of call centers, however, the issue is not simply body shopping but one of voice shopping. At the time of recruitment, agents consider questions such as: How does a recruit speak English (read: global English)? How thick is her/his regional accent and can it be modified and trained into 'American-ness'? What is her/his familiarity with American spoken styles and exposure to American media? Voice and accent become the prime commodities in this global body politics.

This manifests a new logic of race that is predicated upon what Sneja Gunew (2000: 151) calls the 'splitting of the visible and audible' – that what you see or think you see is not what you really get that poses complex questions about racial identification in flows of global technology (see also Nakamura, 2002). In this scenario, while the visible is erased and the aural is foregrounded, the visible is also imaginatively reconstructed in that the aural is now attached to a different but imagined (American) body, especially by the customer on the other side. It is this splitting and re-attachment of the voice to a different imagined body that produces the racism but at the same time hides it in that the customer hears the voice, imagines a different body, and goes along with it, until this splitting erupts into recognition – as when the accent 'slips' and the customer furiously recognizes that the agent is some third world tele-worker.

In fact, this is the point on which major controversies have arisen in the US regarding outsourcing of work to India. For example, US customers of Dell (and Dell employs close to 3000 call center workers in India) have been aggrieved about 'accent interference' and the agents' inability to engage in efficient American-style conversational English, which interferes with their requests and communication. The escalation of hostility finally caused Dell to move much of its customer inquiry services back to Texas from Bangalore, India.

Such new racial formations thus significantly intersect with and are regulated by transnational flows of (American-centric) legal regimes. This is especially seen in the case of unwritten legal (American) prescriptions that inform the communication and voice performance of Indian call center agents. For example, American legal maps informing 'proper' speech implicitly extends to the call center agent who – however much the training – may not fully be aware of what is and is not appropriate speech in America, given that speech codes are so heavily and legally regulated in the US. Trainers note for instance that 'thank you' is frequently said at the wrong moment, or 'tonight' may be rendered 'today', or the faster speed of spoken Indian English (which can surface from time to time despite rigorous training) can sound rude or unsophisticated compared to the slower American speech patterns (Merchant, 2003). At issue here is the (racist) recognition by companies (such as Dell) of the potential legal troubles (as well as economic fall out) that may surface when customers are offended by a different use and accent of English (which can quite literally change the meaning of a communication) or feel that their requests are not understood adequately.

The issue of global outsourcing, then, raises fascinating questions about the (unequal) global flows of particular legal values and frameworks driving the global corporate sphere and its 'electronic spaces' (Sassen, 2000). The Indian agent becomes virtually reconstructed as a 'modern subject' (i.e. able to 'speak' to a 'modern' clientele) by the presence of an impending legal apparatus of a far away country that monitors her/his speech and language use that the American customer can always resort to in terms of complaints of misconduct by the agent. Voice, speech, language, technology, race, space, and legality all intersect to produce and articulate the hybrid racial subject through a logic of disembodiment in which the hybrid subject virtually 'crosses over' through the performance of language and voice while physically 'hiding' her/his body.

Beyond language control and 'accent training', a significant part of the training is geared towards learning how to role play an American, including different regional American behaviors and mannerisms. For instance, Ms. Prabhu, a trainer, role plays a person from Brooklyn. In her demonstration, she speaks in Brooklyn English – 'you can walk the walk and you talk the talk'. Such role playing often occurs by watching hours of sitcom and Hollywood movies in order to learn how to 'sound like the girl or boy next door' (CBS, 2004). Agents discuss how they are made to watch hours of shows such as *Friends* and *Ally McBeal* (*New York Times*, 2001). Further, some reports note that in some training centers, teetotalers learn how to sip wine 'properly' by sipping Coke out of their wine glasses. It should be noted that in some Indian communities, individuals may not be regular consumers of alcohol for religious or other faith based reasons (*International Herald Tribune*, 2003).

[…]

An especially remarkable aspect of such role playing is the taking on of Western aliases in the servicing of customers on the other side of the globe. Traditional Indian names become replaced by anglicized names: Suman may become Susan, Nishara may become Naomi, or Amit may become Alex or Alan. Agents not only talk like an

American but even perform the identity of one through chit chatting with clients about American culture. The pressure to come across as an 'authentic' American is tremendous, since call centers may run the risk of losing the franchise with the parent company if the agent does not convincingly come across as an American.

In the current literature on electronic space and cyberspace, the issue of racial passing has received much attention. Lisa Nakamura (2002) has discussed the notion of 'identity tourism' whereby individuals of different ethnicities often take on the persona of another (often non-whites taking on a white persona or sometimes a white person playing a non-white role). Similarly, in much of postcolonial literature on race and hybridity, passing has been a central area of investigation (e.g. Ahmed, 1999; Bhabha, 1994; Young, 1996) and has often been associated with resistance and transgression (as in Bhabha's discussion of colonial mimicry). And yet, as Sara Ahmed (1999: 96) has rightly suggested, it is important to be careful about this association for 'passing is not becoming ... it is not a painless merger'; rather it has to be seen 'in relationships of social conflict and antagonisms'.

With call centers (especially in the taking on of personas), the otherwise useful notion of identity tourism does not work as well, for tourism at some level implies a voluntarism (that is, someone chooses to take on the role of another ethnicity in cyberspace and chatrooms) that call center agents do not have. Their very employment – and the larger unequal global economic structures that it supports – are based upon being 'required' to play another role – a role playing that is filled with stresses, tensions, mental health problems and anxieties which I discuss later. Nor is their role playing – and the mimicry informing it – productive of resistance or transgression. If anything, this 'mimicry' feeds into the further colonization and disciplining of the 'third world' worker by global flows of capital and information.

This speaks to a new politics of hybrid racial 'passing' in which the passing is predicated not only upon the split of the visual and the aural, sight and sound, voice and body, but 'passing' itself functions as a disembodied phenomenon. ... this is a disembodied passing in which the disembodiment is located at and produced through complex connections and dis/connections of space, geographies, and time.

Aihwa Ong and others have focused on diasporic formations that occur through internet and information technology. Ong (2004) has brilliantly discussed the concept of diasporic 'cyber publics' that are formed through online connections and affiliations. Indeed, there is now enough of a recognition in cultural studies that global flows of technology are enabling new forms of diasporic *publics*. With the case of call centers, however, while some of this is certainly relevant, the hybrid subject produced does not rise to the level of a 'public'. Public-ness assumes some level of visiblity in the public sphere and a public presence. But the very peculiarity of this hybridity is that it *is privatized*. The call center agents playing American roles and simultaneously traversing multiple times and spaces are private underground subjects in the global economy as they cannot disclose their true identities to the global public sphere that they serve through hundreds of calls a day. It is a privatized dis-appearance (sustained by tropes such neutralization, de-Indianization) through which their hybridity comes into being.

Rethinking Time and Diasporic Belonging: Between Virtuality, Personas, Erasures, and the Transnational

In dominant trends of diaspora studies, time has always been a central component of interrogation – the time of the nation left behind (the past) and the time of the new present (the host nation) to which the hybrid subject has dislocated. And while to be sure, the diasporic subject in the immigrant land may and does continue to invoke and mythically recreate the nation left behind (the past) through cultural rituals and practices (as in the South Asian diaspora), the time of the nation (left behind) is still an imagined time that is rearticulated in the present (host nation). But with the situation of call centers, the hybrid subject is recreated at the intersection, collision, and simultaneity of multiple times that defy the temporal dialectic or framework of an imagined 'past' (left behind) and a real 'present' (signifying a new national world). The present itself is multiply extended across geographies, nations, and spaces through telematic communication and it is this collision of times stretched over multiple geographies and spatial relations in one moment that creates the diasporic tension and articulates the subject as hybrid. Consider the following examples.

A report in *India Today* describes the life of Meghna, a 23-year-old arts graduate. As a worker for the midnight shift, also called the 'graveyard shift', she enters the glass and concrete building in Gurgaon late in the night. Walking into the bright hall crowded with rows of computer consoles and telephones, she slips on her designer headset and settles into her cubicle. As the telephone rings, her persona within minutes undergoes a transformation. She becomes Michelle, with an American accent, talking to her caller who is a JC Penney customer in Philadelphia. Although she has never been inside a large department store the size of Penney, she handles the caller with confidence that she has acquired by watching hours of Hollywood blockbusters and reading American fictions. Her computer screen flashes the weather conditions in Philadelphia and she is able to chat with the caller about the perfect day in Philly. She then hangs up saying 'have a good day'. As she looks outside the glass building in the Gurgaon (Delhi) office, it is pitch dark and she is reminded of where she is. The spatiality and temporality of Gurgaon/Philadelphia blur and collide in her virtual world, as she finds herself at the messy intersection of multiple times and multiple spaces articulating each other in the transnational regime of telematics and global economy.

Employees describe their lives as living India by day and America by night; thinking like an Indian by day and an American by night, given that they work through the night when business hours are active in the day time in the US. The stress of living dual lives stretched across multiple times and geographies often takes the form of emotional toll and a transnational identity crisis of an unique nature. *Business World*, a weekly Indian magazine, wrote about an young Indian man, who after pretending at work that he was Arnold sitting in a New York office for 10 hours in the night into the early morning, had problems adjusting to his Indian family and lifestyle when he reached his home in Bombay where he switched back to being Indian and his Indian name – Anand (in Dhillon, 2003: 2). 'He kept finding fault with everything we did and then fumed, "that's so typical of you Indians"', stated his family members. Arnold/Anand defended himself in the interview stating:

> How can I switch identities? I am Arnold for eight hours and then Anand for the rest. I've learned to speak like a foreigner now and I'm beginning to feel like one too. What's wrong with that?

A senior medical consultant in Delhi notes that 'this is altogether a new culture affecting the lives of the young people who take up these jobs for the initial attraction of the money without being aware of the precautions they should take' (quoted in Roy, 2004) Reports of constant pattern of ailments, fatigue-related diseases and psychological conditions amongst call center employees are also noted by many doctors. By working at night the body clock is upset. When family members prepare to go to work in the morning, agents return home to get sleep for the rest of the day. And when the family returns home in the early evening, employees get ready to go to work. Ali, a female employee, talks of high stress levels. She states that 'I can't help but sleep all day till an hour before I have to leave for work … In fact, I oversleep most days' (*India Today*, 2002). Reports describe how those who have problems adjusting to sleep manifest numerous illnesses such as body aches, nausea, insomnia, depression, and anxiety. Several Indian psychiatrists state that over time call center agents often begin to treat their transnational job identity as an extension of their own identity, resulting in all kinds of personality problems caused by the con/fusion of temporal belonging.

This is a fascinating case of a postcolonial switch of flows. In studies of South Asian diaspora the focus for the most part has been on the tension that arises when the 'immigrant' situated in the metropolitan West is unable to let go of her/his 'long distance nationalism' (Anderson, 1998) or nationalist affiliations with the 'home' left behind. There is the nostalgia, the desire, the myth of return through which many diasporic experiences have been discussed. And this nostalgia has been usually framed through a West–East logic – that is, it is a nostalgia for a time and homeland left behind by immigrants in the wake of de-colonization. But, as in the case of Arnold/Anand, 'home' and 'away', 'return' and 'nostalgia', and 'past' and 'present' are turned on their heads. Arnold, having never been physically 'away', nonetheless identifies more with the 'virtual away' of America that he lives in, in the technology parks, for several hours a day. When he says 'that's typical of you Indians' he implicitly manifests a desire for 'return' to (a virtual life of) a nation that he is geographically disconnected from. While surrounded by the physical topography of Mumbai, his identity has been re-projected onto an America, through virtual technology, that he will probably never visit. The nostalgia (if one can even use this trope) manifest in his anger, is a nostalgia *not* for a past and homeland left behind, but a never-to-be homeland to which he is only imaginatively, telematically, and virtually connected.

Further, while there is no physical/transnational territorial migration at work in these hybrid formations, there is a *virtual migration* in which the body both departs into another national world and time in the performances of American-ness through virtual technology but also simultaneously remains geographically and temporally situated in India. Additionally, the diasporic logic of 'home' and 'away' exists here but the 'away' into which the subjects move becomes the technology parks, the glassy futuristic buildings, open work stations, and cafeterias with television sets showing American programs – reflecting what one report called 'Manhattan mores' – that virtually transport the agents into the space of American-ness (while their bodies are still fixed within the territory of India). The spatial landscapes of these technology parks – where call centers are often housed – are deliberately designed to assert the physicality of a new modernity and cosmopolitanism (read: Americanization) brought about by global technology, and to distinguish that modernity from the rest of the city (and the nation). For example, on the one hand, Bangalore, India's Silicon Valley, has posh technology parks that could be in Palo Alto or Austin (*New York Times*, 2001). On the other hand, the city outside continues to exhibit terrible traffic conditions, potholes, and an overburdened airport with few international flights. Narayan Murthy, the head of Infosys, a premier Indian software and IT company, states that 'we live in a make believe world. ... Right now, when you come to our campus, *you are leaving India behind*' (*New York Times*, 2001, emphasis added). The campus of Infosys has a putting green, aerobics studio, and basketball court, reflecting an American ambience. Similarly Gurgaon, which is a major technology hub outside Delhi, constitutes not only technology parks but a maze of glossy and glassy malls, plush offices, multiplexes, pubs, and eating places, all of which together create the 'international' atmosphere that these technology parks signify.

The complex articulations and collisions of temporalities is also manifest in the way in which the third world worker's body is colonized through the colonization of the body's clock and its biological functioning. Hardt and Negri (2000) have theorized the current regime of 'empire' as being constituted through biopolitical power and control. Whatever the limitations of their theorization of the empire might be, the landscape of call centers can be seen as manifesting an example of biopolitical invasion of the body's natural time by global communication networks and the colliding temporalities and spatialities through which they operate.

This is an egregious instance of a new postcolonial re-colonization of the body where the body's biological functioning is invaded and its innermost recesses intruded upon. Fatigue, exhaust, stress, sleep deprivation, constipation, heart diseases, acidity, indigestion, and mental health problems plague some workers and constitute the potential and, in some cases, the real price paid by call center agents (Roy, 2004). In earlier dispensations of colonialism, at least the body's time was not invaded. The colonizer and the colonized inhabited the same physical time. In this case, however, the reversal of day and night brought about by the collision of time results in a biopolitical violence towards the health of the third world body that parallels, with differences to be sure, other ways in which the global economy today invades the third world body through toxic dumping, pharmaceutical distribution, reduced funding for AIDS, forced contraception, and more.

[...]

The issue of memory is also central in this postcolonial reconfiguration. This memory is not of the 'past' – the remembrance of a time no more – but the necessary and even anxious remembrance (through details about a non-existent family) of a fiction whose plot is geographically situated in an 'other world', but whose narration and authorship occurs in a world both disconnected from yet telematically connected to that geography. In fact, a situation such as Bala's raises complicated issues about the politics of memory in the culture of call centers and global flow of telematics. What does the agent have to remember about lives in America in terms of spinning an 'authentic' fiction of American-ness for over 10 hours a day and, in that process, what other memories (of her Indian-ness) have to be suppressed or put on hold? Memory, space, time, technology, globalization, and identity intersect to recreate the 'modern' worker of the global service economy and its cross-border flows.

Gender is also central to this transnational politics. Much of the call center work force comprises women who face special challenges. Sometimes, women employees, who are often in a young age group, find themselves subject to sexual harassment from the customer at the other end. There is additionally the challenge of dealing with the social stigma for women who are out of the house in the night. An agent named Ali stated in an interview that 'my mother worries a lot about my future, my marriage prospects in particular' (*India Today*, 2002). She discussed how frustrated her parents become when they have to explain their daughter's late night absences and absences from family functions, which are often sites for potential match-making. Here we have an example of gender operating at the nexus of multiple times stretched over colliding spaces. Ali's gendered and sexual identity is transnationally articulated at the intersection of colliding national patriarchies that demonstrate once again, as works of scholars (Bhattacharjee, 1997; Freeman, 2000; Grewal, 2005; Mohanty, 1997) have asserted in different contexts, how the female body and sexuality function as a central terrain upon which the collisions and alliances of national modernities are occurring in globalization. Such transnational collisions and alliances throw into crisis the very public/private dichotomy that has characterized much of gender studies in the West.

A complex politics of race (and its intersection with gender) also plays out in other ways – especially in the culture of surveillance and performativity of American-ness. Carla Freeman (2000)'s work has discussed the surveillance of informatics workers in Barbados through the Foucauldian trope of the 'panopticon'. The 'gaze', Freeman notes, is central in the informatics industry in the Caribbean. Freeman discusses the panoptic mechanisms at work: 'the gaze of computer, the gaze of supervisor, the manager, the fellow production worker, and finally the internal gaze of self' (2000: 258).

In the Indian call centers, the 'gaze' is similarly located at complex intersections of the local, national, and global, and at the nexus of technology, virtual time, real time, gender, sexuality, family, and spaces that are both colliding as well as seamless. We have the gaze of the accent and cultural trainers, the gaze of the computer screen that flashes weather descriptions and cultural conditions of a particular city in which the customer whom the agent is talking to may be located and in the process virtually interpellating the agent into the community of the local city. Then there is the gaze of the customer who may not 'see' the worker, but certainly imagines her/him through an 'imagined community' (Anderson, 1983) of American-ness that the call center worker has to live up to. There is also the gaze of the worker upon her/himself and the pressure to perform American-ness in the 'correct' way, otherwise her/his job may be at stake. Added to all this is the gaze of the futuristic building and their landscapes that house these call centers and that transform the agents into a different world as they enter its 'modern' technologized ambience. There is also the gaze of the family – one's own family and social networks – as in the examples of the young women who experience scrutiny from their families for working late in the night. And finally, there is the unseen sexual gaze of the male customer on the other end who may try to engage in sexual flirtation with, and sometimes even harassment towards, female employees.

The gaze has always implicitly informed discussions of the diasporic subject. Traversing the world of the 'host' nation as well as the 'nation' left behind, the ethnic hybrid subject (as demonstrated in works of Anzaldua, Gilroy, among others) is a split (*mestiza*) subject because s/he traverses dual worlds and the colliding gaze of those worlds. In the case of the call centers, however, the gaze takes on a greater complexity as it is globally refracted and collides across multiple times and spaces, multiple screens and languages, multiple modernities and their desires, multiple social networks and familial (fictional and real) be/longing, and multiple body politics, all of which are geographically and temporally connected and disconnected in the same 'moment'.

It is this complex transnational refraction, collision, and splintering of the 'gaze' that makes the imperial/national violence of the call centers and the neoliberal engines that drive it much more insidious than earlier colonial operations, and yet that much harder to resist or negotiate. There is no clear identifiable gaze located in one site at which the third world subject in the call centers can look back in anger. There is no way to return the gaze for the gaze is multiply situated at numerous trans/national nodes. The resistive element that has typically been associated with the diaspora is thus subsumed and consumed through, and across, globally dis/connected spaces and times. This calls attention to the fact that assumptions of diaspora and hybridity need to be delinked from their taken for granted association with disruption and resistance (as has been the trend in postcolonial cultural studies). The politics of hybridity is finally and always a 'politics without guarantees' (to use Stuart Hall's famous phrase). In the emerging neo-liberal modernities in Asia, what shape, form, and logics such politics acquires is an open issue whose contours are just only beginning to emerge – as in the case of IT and call center cultures.

There are some other reversals of the diasporic logic that are also worth mentioning. In usual theorizations of the diaspora, as noted earlier, the diasporic subject is an 'other' of the nation. But here, the 'away' into which the agents travel into the night is not an 'other' of the nation. While the performances and nocturnal existence of call center workers lodged in high-tech buildings for hours are instrumental in producing the hybrid tensions and complexities that mark their lives, the 'away' that these call centers and IT parks signify – that the head of Infosys had described as sites for 'leaving India' – (*New York Times*, 2001) is not really about leaving India. These places and the hybrid subjects populating them are not India's far away 'others' who have abandoned the nation. Rather, they function as highly efficient sites through which the nation – that is, the Indian nation – asserts its presence in the global market, harnesses global capital into the country, and reconstitutes itself as a 'modern' country with emerging global recognition. Rama Bijapurkar, a Bombay-based consultant who sits on the board of Infosys Technologies, describes the young IT and call center kids as 'liberalization children … [who have] a hunger in the belly for achievement and all the good things that money can buy' (Ottawa Citizen, 2004). This demonstrates an example of how the frequently oppositional binary of diaspora/nation is unsettled here as the hybrid space is put into the service of the nation and functions as a site through which global capital flows into India. As a headline in a report in *India Today* put it, the IT and call center culture in Gurgaon represent the 'globally mobile citizens of Gurgaon, the newest subspecies of the yuppies, who are creating a city within a city in a maze of malls, multinationals, and Manhattan mores' (*India Today*, 2003).

We also see how the binaristic logic of West/Rest that has informed some trends in diaspora studies is reconfigured here. The Indian nation is an active participant in the production of this racial formation of hybrid subjects, who are forced into a virtual invisibility in the global economic sphere as their voices are outsourced and their bodies erased. As the globally situated IT and informatics workers constitute a prime group through which the nation barters its population to global finance, the nation encourages the logic of cultural neutralization and de-Indianization – given that many of these call centers are run by Indian owners who recognize the importance of neutralizing an Indian subjectivity if their call center businesses are to survive. This exemplifies a powerful case of how in neoliberal globalization, multiple modernities often working together in 'the financialization of the globe' – to use Spivak's (1999) phrase – may produce and articulate new global racial formations in the process. The 'enemy' (the colonizer) thus becomes a little confusing to identify.

Finally, the diasporic and hybrid landscape of call centers also calls attention to the fact that today many new relations of diaspora are emerging that cannot just be mapped through an East–West flow (or displacement of peoples) or be centered in North Atlantic geographies. Today the flows are being reconfigured. As financial and technological centers proliferate in Asia, producing new dynamics of mobile Asian cosmopolitanisms, new frameworks of hybridity are being produced where the linear logic of East–West, or for that matter even West–East, simply does not hold. West–East, East–West, flows all come together in unpredictable ways in recreating new hybrid spaces of modernity in Asia such that the very issue of 'movement' and the temporal linearity that that has characterized it needs to be rethought.

We live in a time when global technology and information systems are producing such complex cultural dynamics that the politics of colonialism, race, nation, and belonging are undergoing massive shifts. New insights and lenses are continually needed to rethink the diaspora and hybridity. Such work has already begun as documented at the beginning of this paper. Minimally, we need to continue to turn our critical attention seriously towards Asian modernities in order to map the emerging connections and disconnections, reversals and reconfigurations, of contemporary postcolonial politics in relation to earlier times. The postcolonial landscape in many

Asian contexts for the last ten years is being recreated and rearticulated in new ways and information technology functions as a central vehicle for such rearticulation. This article constitutes a small attempt to provide one glimpse of such rearticulation and the new relations of diaspora and hybridity that are unfolding in the process.

NOTES

1. For a powerful discussion of how this logic is reversed in particular diasporic politics, see Drezewiecka and Halualani (2002).
2. 'Housekeepers to the World', *India Today*. November 18, 2002.

REFERENCES

Abbas, A. (1997) *Hong Kong: The Cultural Politics of Disappearance*. Minneapolis, MN: University of Minnesota Press.

Abbas, A. and J. Erni, eds (2005) *Internationalizing Cultural Studies*. Malden, MA: Blackwell.

Ahmed, S. (1999) 'She'll Wake Up One of These Days and Find She's Turned into a Nigger: Passing through Hybridity', *Theory, Culture, & Society* 16(2): 87–106.

Anderson, B. (1983) *Imagined Communities: Reflections on the Origin and Spread of Nationalism*. London: Verso.

Anderson, B. (1998) *The Spectre of Comparisons*. London: Verso.

Appadurai, A. (1996) *Modernity at Large*. Mineappolis, MN: University of Minnesota Press.

Axel, B. (2004) 'The Context of Diaspora,' *Cultural Anthropology* 19(2): 26–60.

Bhabha, H. (1994) *The Location of Culture*. New York: Routledge.

Bhattacharjee, A. (1997) The Public/Private Mirage: Mapping Homes and Undomesticating Violence Work in the South Asian Immigrant Community', in J. Alexander and C. Mohanty (eds) *Feminist Genealogies, Colonial Legacies, and Democratic Futures*, pp. 308–29. New York: Routledge.

Brah, A. (2003) 'Diaspora, Border, and Transnational Identities', in R. Lewis and S. Mills (eds) *Feminist Postcolonial Theory: A Reader*, pp. 613–34. New York: Routledge.

Castells, M. (1996) *The Rise of Network Society*. Malden, MA: Blackwell.

CBS News Transcripts (2004) 'Out of India', *60 Minutes*, 11 January.

Dhillon, A. (2003) 'Indian Shift Is Leading to Culture Shock in the Call Centre', *South China Morning Post*, 20 January.

Drzewiecka, J. and R.T. Halualani (2002) 'The Structural–Cultural Dialectic of Diasporic Politics,' *Communication Theory* 12(3): 340–66.

Erni, J. (2001) 'Like Postcolonial Culture: Hong Kong Reimagined', *Cultural Studies* 15(3–4): 389–418.

Ferguson, J. and A. Gupta (2002) 'Spatializing States: Towards an Ethnography of Neoliberal Governmentality', *American Ethnologist* 29(4): 981–1002.

Freeman, C. (2000) *High Tech and High Heels in the Global Economy*. Durham, NC: Duke University Press.

Gilroy, P. (1991) 'It Ain't Where You're From, It's Where You're At … The Dialectics of Diasporic Identification' *Third Text* 13(Winter): 3–16.

Grewal, I. (2005) *Transnational Americas*. Durham, NC: Duke University Press.

Gunew, S. (2000) 'Operatic Karaoke and the Pitfalls of Identity Politics: A Translated Performance', in S. Ahmed et al. (eds) *Transformations: Thinking through Feminism*, pp. 145–58. New York: Routledge.

Hardt, M. and A. Negri (2000) *Empire*. Cambridge, MA: Harvard University Press.

India Today (2002) 'Untitled Article', 18 November: 36.

India Today (2003) 'Untitled Article', 3 November: 70.

International Herald Tribune (2003) 'Indian Companies Are Adding a Western Flabor', 20 August: 14.

Liao, P. (2005) 'Introduction: Global Diasporas', in A. Abbas and J. Erni (eds) *Internationalizing Cultural Studies*, 501–10. Malden, MA: Blackwell Publishing.

Merchant, Khozem (2003) 'India's Call Centres Drop the Face Accents', *The Financial Times*, 8 December: 13.

Mignolo, W. (2000) *Local Histories/Global Designs*. Princeton, NJ: Princeton University Press.

Mohanty, C. (1997) 'Women Workers and Capitalist Scripts: Ideologies of Domination, Common Interests, and the Politics of Solidarity', in J. Alexander and C. Mohanty (eds) *Feminist Genealogies, Colonial Legacies, and Democratic Futures*, pp. 3–29. New York: Routledge.

Nakamura, L. (2002) *Cybertypes: Race, Ethnicity and Identity on the Internet*. New York: Routledge.

New York Times (2001) 'Hi, I'm in Bangalore (But I Can't Say So)', 21 March.

Ong, A. (1998) *Flexible Citizenship*. Berkeley, CA: University of California Press.

Ong, A. (2004) 'Cyberpublics and Diaspora Politics among Transnational Chinese', *Interventions* 5(1): 82–100.

Roy, B. (2004) 'Woes at Call Centres', *Times of India*, 22 February.

Sassen, S. (1998) *Globalization and its Discontents*. New York: The New Press.

Sassen, S. (2000) 'Whose City Is It? Globalization and the Formation of New Claims', in F. Lechner and J. Boli (eds) *The Globalization Reader*, 70–7. Malden, MA: Blackwell.

Spivak, S. (1999) *A Critique of Postcolonial Reason*. Cambridge, MA: Harvard University Press.

Sunandaram, R. (2005) 'Recycling Modernity: Pirate Electronic Cultures in India', in A. Abbas and J. Erni (eds) *Internationalizing Cultural Studies*. Malden, MA: Blackwell.

Tololyan, K. (1996) 'Rethinking Diaspora(s): Stateless Power in the Transnational Moment', *Diaspora* 5(1): 3–36.

Van der Veer, P. (2005) 'Virtual India: Indian IT Labor and the Nation-State', in T.B. Hansen and F. Stepputat (eds) *Sovereign Bodies*, pp. 276–90. Princeton, NJ: Princeton University Press.

Walsh, R. (2003) 'Global Diasporas: Introduction', *Interventions: International Journal of Postcolonial Studies* 5(1): 1–3.

Young, L. (1996) *Fear of the Dark: 'Race', Gender and Sexuality in the Cinema*. New York: Routledge.

VOICES OF THE MARGINALIZED ON THE INTERNET

Examples from a Website for Women of South Asia

Ananda Mitra

The Internet has transformed popular culture by providing a virtual forum in which different communities and groups can produce a "presence" that might have been denied to them in the "real world." This presence can be obtained in cyberspace by appropriate use of one's voice to articulate the specific narratives and discourses about one's group or subculture. In this article, I demonstrate the importance of having a voice on the Internet by using illustrations from the subculture of women of South Asia,[1] who have had various discriminatory vectors constantly working to marginalize them in real life. ...

Silencing of voices is one of the primary consequences of forced and oppressive invisibility in the real-life public sphere. However, new digital technologies are transforming the sense of "silence" by offering opportunities for traditionally invisible groups, such as the women of South Asia, to find a new discursive space where they can voice themselves and thus become visible and make their presence felt. ...

Voice and the Internet

Although the focus here is not necessarily on the development of the idea of voice, it remains the case that voice has been a well-explored construct, and there are several approaches that can be utilized to expand on the theories of voice. Within

Ananda Mitra. "Voices of the Marginalized on the Internet: Examples from a Website for Women of South Asia," pp. 492–510 from *Journal of Communication* 54:3 (2004).

the tradition of communication scholarship, the notion of voice was opened up for careful investigation when Black (1978) raised questions about the significance of voice within a larger context of the social world. Subsequently, several different approaches have emerged within different contexts of communication. When considered by rhetoricians, the idea of voice has been considered on one hand from a primarily performative perspective, as explained by Appelbaum (1990), in which the focus has been on the coded relationships between signifying systems and the autonomous sound of the speaking subject. Others have considered voice as it relates to the larger realm of social discourse in which one's voice allows one to connect with a larger social body, as suggested by Smith and Hyde (1991) and Scruton (1983), who all contended that how one feels about the other is often actualized in one's voice, making voice a central phenomenon within establishing the self with the other. The way in which voice brings forth the connection between the self and society is also considered within the context of organizations in which a metaphor of voice (Putnam, Phillips, & Chapman, 1996) can be mobilized to demonstrate how the access to voice or lack thereof can produce specific relations of power within an organization. Specifically, the relationship between empowerment and voice was considered by Mumby (1988) and Haslett (1990), who argued that different subgroups speak in different voices, thus ensuring the structurations within an organization. ...

In this particular case, voice has been conceptualized as acquiring agency by which the speaker can take on the position of the speaking agent to produce a specific voice for him- or herself. Watts (2001) has made the argument that to have a voice an agent must find a space where the voice can be concretized. The connection between voice and space becomes particularly critical when such a space is denied in the real life through marginalizing forces and a new space needs to be carved out. It is precisely the notion of discovering the new spaces that allows for the connection between the idea of the voice and the Internet as a space (Mitra, 2001; Mitra & Watts, 2003). Being a "discursive space," the effectivity of a voice on the Internet is implicated by the way in which the discourse has been constructed and presented as a voice in cyberspace. Here the term "discourse" refers to a system of representations that has developed socially to produce a specific set of meanings around which structures of popular culture are constructed (Fiske, 1987). ... Two of the key issues that voice, as a theoretical construct, opens up are trustworthiness and authenticity of discourses and texts on the Internet.

Trust and Authenticity

The issue of trust becomes critical because anyone with access to the Internet, and with a little technological savvy, is able to create a presence on the Internet. Therefore, within such a "free for all" discursive space, it is important to be able to constantly judge which voice is trustworthy and which must be treated with a degree of caution. In the case of the Internet, the question of whose voice is trustworthy is further complicated by the fact that there can be many voices speaking together through portals of information, such as the home pages of thousands of people belonging to a particular group.

In many ways this is similar to the phenomenon Bakhtin (1981, 1986) suggested in the notion of *heteroglossia*, in which many voices come together to create a discourse that encompasses the variation in the voices. There are many ways in which such heteroglossic systems can appear on the Internet. For instance, the work of Gurak (1997) demonstrated the way in which the employees of a major corporation were able to produce a unified voice to bring forth significant changes. Such situations have been true of many different groups, ranging from immigrants to obscure fan clubs (see, e.g., Mitra, 1997; Shaw, 1997).

Indeed, it is the presence of many voices that makes the question of trust particularly complex. ...

The issue of trust thus remains a slippery yet important aspect of the presence of voices on the Internet. The tension between what is trustworthy and what appears to be trustworthy needs to be resolved by the audience. In the end, the way in which this tension is resolved could have a significant impact on the consequences of the presence of marginalized groups in cyberspace. ...

Although the question of trust remains critical when considering the voices on the Internet, it is also important to consider the tension between voices that can be trusted and voices that are authentic. It can be argued that a voice would be considered authentic when the speaker(s) can claim to have an experience that offers them the background to speak about an issue. An analogous condition can be identified in the way in which voices manifest themselves within the organizational context in which people who are traditionally lower in a hierarchy are empowered by being given their own voice so they can speak of their own conditions without editorialization (Bormann, 1988; Pacanowsky, 1988). This is not necessarily a matter of credibility but is related to the fact that the speaker is producing socially located discourse that is always already influenced by the baggage the speaker carries. Authenticity is thus related to the specific social, political, and cultural history that a speaker may have that offers the speaker a claim to being "authentic," not necessarily credible, about what the speaker has to say. In other words, it can be argued that an Afghan woman speaking of her experiences under the Taliban rule could be more authentic than a Western female reporter writing about Afghan women. In cyberspace, where many voices contend to be heard, some can claim to have a greater legitimacy to speak about something because of their unique history and background.

In considering the question of authenticity, it is also important to consider the role played by the Netizen reader. I argue that the reader of the Internet text needs to be considered as an active reader whose decoding practices could be understood from the perspective offered by Hall's (1980) argument that readers actively decode messages in dominant, negotiated, and oppositional ways. ... In looking at Usenet groups in cyberspace, I have argued for the empowerment of the reader in suggesting that Netizens are always already active individuals who can be conceptualized as the "reader-author" and not just a passive reader, as is often the case for traditional media scholarship (Mitra, 1999). Within such a discursive arena, the interaction between the reader and the author opens up questions about the way in which the perceived trust and authenticity of the speaker implicates the power attributed to the speaker by the reader.

Power and Voice in Cyberspace

In the real world, those who had the financial and cultural capital to have the power to speak through their media wielded the power to shape global opinion. ... Foucault (1972) made this point in arguing that discourse and power are intimately related because those who have access to voice can wield power within a system, as demonstrated in some systems such as organizations where access to voice itself remains contested (Cheney, 1995). In the discursive space of the Internet, the power of a voice is not necessarily dependent on the traditional determinants of power, such as economic wealth, military prowess, or industrial development, although having all those powers is certainly not a disadvantage. At the same time, anyone with moderate technological savvy and minimal financial capital now can have a voice and speak for him- or herself in cyberspace. It is no longer the case that any particular subculture needs to remain silenced, or merely spoken for; now they can speak for themselves. ...

The issue here is not unlike the argument made by Poster (1990), who suggested that electronic communications offers a new "mode of information" exchange in which the medium allows one to simultaneously speak within or outside of the structures of power. Indeed, the power of a voice is often implicated by the ability to mobilize the various representational strategies – the "bells and whistles" of technology – available to the speaker. Thus websites of traditionally powerful institutions, such as Cable News Network (http://www.cnn.com) or the British Broadcasting Corporation (http://www. bbc.co.uk), spare little expense to voice themselves in a technologically attractive way. The existing financial and consequent technological power of the CNNs and BBCs makes it easier for them to put up appealing websites that make them stand out in cyberspace. Yet, it is also only in cyberspace where the traditionally less powerful, such as regional non-English language newspapers like *Ananda Bazaar Patrika* from Kolkata, India (http://www.anandabazar.com/index.htm), can appear to be equally powerful and appealing. What emerges is a veritable paradox of power because the traditionally powerful, based on their conventional sources of power (financial, political, etc.), are competing against those who have been conventionally powerless but have begun to gain a sense of discursive power because they can now find a speaking space on the Internet.

In this analysis the notions of voice-trust-authenticity-power-agency are explored through the specific example of a website that relates to issues important to women of South Asia. It is important to note that the focus here is not necessarily on the particular website, or the subculture it wants to represent, but how that website helps to illustrate and support the claims about trust, authenticity, power, and discursive strategies being made here. However, having selected to work with this particular group, it is important to ponder the traditional means used by this group to voice themselves and then examine the discursive and textual strategies used by the digital voices to become powerful by gaining trust as authentic voices of the group.

Voices of Women of South Asia

Traditionally, women of South Asia have voiced themselves through protests. Indian women, for instance, participated in rallies, strikes, and demonstrations prior to independence (Gandhi & Shah, 1992). After independence, Indian women let their voices be heard in protests over issues such as land reform regulations, antidowry movements, rights of Muslim women, and deforestation practices. Such attempts at making a presence felt and having a voice were, however, geographically restricted and did not have far-reaching implications given the fact that the powerful – primarily the mainstream media – often chose not to cover these events in great detail for a national or international audience.

A second way of voicing their concerns can be traced in the way that women of South Asia have pursued a form of guerilla warfare to get their resistance message across to those who previously perceived them as passive and submissive. In areas like Telgangana, India, women fought against their landlords for the right to own property (Kumar, 1993). Women also used guerrilla warfare tactics to voice their resistance to wife beating. Domestic assault movements were directly linked with the liquor protests in India. ...

The third method of voicing resistance, unions, began as women started to gain employment. Women were no longer forced to live in the private background, and for the first time, issues of equal pay and employment rights became a cause worth fighting for. One of the first recorded attempts of women of South Asia participating in trade unions was in 1972 in Ahmedabad, India. ...

However, although trade unions offered women a voice in the workplace, they did little to challenge the role of women in society (Forbes, 1996). Shortly after the creation of women's unions, a fourth mechanism of voicing resistance was created: women's organizations (Vecchio & Ray, 1998). Many historians argue that the first Indian women's organization was founded in Hydrabad, India, and called the Progressive Organization of Women (POW). POW served as a model, and soon women's organizations were surfacing all over India. Although the earlier forms of resistance revolved around a single issue, women's organizations focused on women's role as a whole. These groups helped focus on the conditions that created women's oppression primarily by a mode of cooperative action through empowering communication as illustrated by Papa, Singhal, Ghanekar, and Papa (2000).

Over time, women of South Asia also have begun to get their voice heard through the mass media. For instance, in India between 1982 and 1987, Doordarshan, the official state-run television system in India, began to commission programs aimed at creating a social conscience in the way Indian viewers saw women. These programs had a large viewing audience and became a modern voice for Indian women. These programs led to the production of popular films that changed the image of a woman from house-wife to an independent individual. However, what is important to note here is the transformation of the voices from the realm of the "real" to the "mediated," where the speaking power is now negotiated through a state-controlled organization such as the Indian television system. It is no longer the case that the women's organizations are out in the "trenches" working with the marginalized but are now in the process of creating a mediated text that would represent the material existence of the marginalized.

This is a significant change and brings with it the baggage of shifting relations of power. As suggested by Fiske and Hartley (1978), the very process of migrating to the media can result in a co-opting of voices within the mainstream and dominant and can begin to "claw back" the voices within the folds of the hegemonic system. Specifically, the process of claw back refers to the way in which the dominant forces disempowered the marginal and oppositional voice by claiming it within the main-stream. … the process by which the media system has developed in India has caused sufficient concerns with respect to the hegemonic system that has been supported by the state-controlled system. Mitra (1993) and Singhal and Rogers (1989) have pointed out the unevenness of the effects of television on Indian society and the ways in which certain patriarchal messages have prevailed within the content of tel-evision in India. Thus, the migration to television might not necessarily have been the solution that the women's movements were seeking.

However, now it is possible to argue that the Internet can begin to modify the direction and modality of the struggles precisely because the voice on the Internet can take on characteristics that neither the real nor the mediated voices could. The crux of this claim lies in the fact that the Internet provides a "low cost/high reward" environment for voicing oneself. For marginalized groups, gaining access to a space that exists in the virtual with implications in the real could have far-reaching social and political consequences (see, e.g., Mitra, 2001; Mitra & Watts, 2003). … I demon-strate and elaborate this argument by drawing upon a set of webpages that relate to the issues of women of South Asia. It is important that throughout the analysis pre-sented here it is implicitly acknowledged that not all women from South Asia have easy access to the Internet. Indeed, most do not. However, in this analysis the focus is on the numerous texts that are produced by those women of South Asia who have direct or indirect access to the Internet and have thus been able to voice themselves.

The Defining Parameters of the Voice of South Asian Women on the Internet

Methodology

Doing research with websites poses several significant methodological challenges. Two of the most important challenges relate to the starting point of the analysis and the number of websites that could be included within the scope of the analysis. It has been pointed out that the Web is increasingly shaping up as a scale-free network system that is unlike a random network in which any starting point can be considered to be a reasonable point to begin an analysis. The notion of scale-free suggests that there are specific hubs that can be quantitatively or qualitatively identified as the "busy" nodes in a specific network. In this case, a specific decision has been made to begin with such a node, which qualitatively offers a starting point for the analysis. As suggested in the work of Mitra and Cohen (1999), there are many possible criteria that can be used as the point of entry into the Internet discourse. Several different criteria have been suggested, and one of them is to look for a webpage that appears to have a sufficient number of links; this ultimately allows for analysis at up to three degrees of separation.[2]

Using the criteria described above, it is better to start with a page with an adequate number of links so that it is possible to use the links to move to other pages that also deal with the issues regarding the women of South Asia. One such page is called "SAWNET," an acronym for South Asian Women's Network (http://www.umiacs. umd.edu/users/sawweb/SAWNET/).[3] SAWNET is made up of different components such as the moderated mailing list that is primarily a place where the members of the SAWNET can post messages that only members can access. Membership is restricted and moderated. The mailing list is not the focus of the analysis here, but SAWNET also maintains a website that provides a variety of links. This website represents a pioneering action because the creators of the site were some of the first to bring issues relating to women of South Asia to cyberspace. Indeed, this particular page has attracted scholarly attention because of its potential to transform the identity of women of South Asia (see, e.g., Gajjala, in press). There surely are other websites about women of South Asia but most often they address specific groups or specific issues related to these women of South Asia. SAWNET considers a comprehensive and broad set of issues. The initial webpage, begun in 1996, has grown over the years to become an important Web portal for the discussion of issues surrounding South Asian women. The growth and relevance are evident in the fact that a mailing list with 40 subscribers in 1991 now reaches about 700 subscribers.

[...]

The second methodological challenge is the decision regarding the depth to which to conduct the discourse analysis. Again using the idea of the scale-free network and Mitra and Cohen's (1999) approach of selecting specific degrees of separation from the starting point, it is possible to claim that typically three degrees of separation provide the textual material necessary for making an argument. In this case, most of the analysis has been conducted within three degrees of separation from the starting point.

[...]

Whose Voice Is It?

On opening the page, the reader is greeted with a list of possible links from the starting point of SAWNET. There is no particular reference to authorship of the webpage except for the disclaimer that the page is devoted to issues about South Asian women; South Asia is defined as the collection of several countries in the subcontinent.[4] The opening page offers a computer-drawn picture of faces representing women from different parts of South Asia. The page then offers a list of links to various other pages that deal with specific themes relevant to women of South Asia, such as domestic violence, marriage, and organizations of South Asian women. The page also offers a search capability and a way to contact the Web master of SAWNET. Finally, there are links to other pages that cite SAWNET, such as the reference by British Broadcasting Corporation (BBC) to SAWNET in stories that deal with South Asian women on the BBC website (Lak, 1998).

The first key point about the opening page is that there is no clear indicator of whose voice is being heard in this discourse. There is no specific mention of the name of a person or organization responsible for SAWNET, its authoring, or its maintenance. In most cases, websites attempt to showcase the author or "webmaster" in its opening page, offering the visitor a sense of whose voice is being heard. This is absent on the opening page, although the names of the "founders" of SAWNET as an Internet discussion forum can be found one degree of separation from the opening page. It is important to note that even though these same people are responsible for maintaining the website, they do not display that information in the opening page, but that information is embedded nearly four degrees of separation away from the home page. This is significant because it has to do with the way in which authorship is problematized by the technology of the Internet. Usually the speaking capital needed to have a voice on the Internet is less than the capital needed when speaking in the more traditional public sphere created by mass media. This is because of the ease with which one can produce and maintain a website. Other forms of media, such as television or radio, make a deliberate attempt to highlight authorship because the speaker's identity as the author becomes particularly, carrying with it the traces of the speaking capital that focuses on who has the capability of speaking for whom, as demonstrated in the case of diasporic voices on the Internet (Mitra & Watts, 2003). However, the SAWNET authors recognize that speaking capital can be thought of differently on the Web. It can be argued that, to the people responsible for creating and circulating SAWNET, the very fact that the website exists is authority and legitimacy enough, and question of agency is provisionally deferred. In most other speaking situations, authorship is coveted and sometimes required. However, this absence of author information has many consequences.

The author(s) of the page are not compelled to say who they are, but find it sufficient to claim that it is a forum for those interested in issues important to women of South Asia. This could suggest that the ability to have a voice is considered more important than who is speaking. It is indeed a forum where agency is supplanted, as evidenced by the fact that there is a forum available where several speakers can voice their opinions and experiences. In thinking of the importance of considering the idea of voice on the Internet, Mitra (2001) claimed that having the ability to speak is often more important than considering whether the voice is heard. The open-ended potential of technology offers the opportunity to many who simply could not speak before to now have a voice. Bakhtin (1981) made the distinction between the authoritative discourse that belongs to the dominant and the internally persuasive discourse that allows the powerless to challenge the authoritative discourse. In the case of the Internet, it is this discourse of the powerless that now gains the ability to speak, making that moment of speaking a determinate moment in the discursive process. To a large degree, this claim can be substantiated in the strategy adopted by members of SAWNET who are mostly interested in being able to speak. Miller (1995) made a similar argument using the work of Goffman (1981), suggesting that having a Web presence can itself be a liberating experience. This is partly attributed to the fact that there is little fear of rebuff in some regimes of cyberspace such as websites.[5] Indeed, this argument underscores the importance of presenting a voice without necessarily looking for a response or focusing on whether the voice is eventually heard. In traditional forms of communication, the need for response has always been critical, but on the Internet, where personal voices operate within the public sphere, it is possible to get beyond the desire of being "heard" and focus on being "able to speak."

Although such an argument appears contrary to the traditional way of thinking of communication, the argument is more plausible for the Internet because it presents a unique and different media environment. Consider, for instance, the claim that "SAWNET also has no philosophy or goals, except as a medium of communication by and for South Asian women" (Chacko, Narayanan, & Rao, 2002). This amorphous structure and the emphasis on being a medium of communication are announced publicly on the Internet, and the statement makes no claim about who the specific audience is. All that is highlighted, in what appears to be a mission statement, is the emphasis on being able to communicate, have a voice, independent of who might be hearing the voice.

The lack of concern with the audience is also demonstrated by the fact that there is not even the customary "hit counter" to keep track of how many times the page has been visited. Although it is possible that some form of invisible tracking is in place, at least on the surface, this website does not appear to be interested in who is hearing what is being said. The voices on the website are more interested in the determinate moment of speaking. Indeed, by going against the grain of the emerging insistence on keeping track of visitors and number of visits, this page plays up the importance of gaining the ability to speak.[6] To be sure, what is important is whether a safe space exists for the many voices to be uttered.[7] ...

Within the safe space of the SAWNET website, the numerous voices all connected together eventually produce a "hypervoice" of the women of South Asia on SAWNET. The notion of the hypervoice extrapolates the idea of voice on the Internet by focusing on the fact that the inherent hypertextuality of the Internet, when mobilized properly, offers the opportunity of connecting the voices of many speakers independent of who the reader is. The proper mobilization of the Internet stems primarily from the fact that hypertext has the potential of connecting disparate voices, thus creating a hypervoice that could in unison call for recognition within the public sphere of cyberspace. The seminal work of Landow (1992) and others (see, e.g., Mitra, 1999) constantly have pointed out that the fundamental characteristic of hypertext is its ability to create seamless and nonlinear connections that offer Netizens a variety of texts to explore. When considered from the perspective of voice, each of these texts also can be considered to carry traces of an author's work. Yet, no single author might emerge. Several authors produce an amorphous whole in which each author is empowered by the fact that he or she has been able to find a place on the table, along with similar others, and thus has been able to utter a point of view and become a part of the hypervoice. The idea of the hypervoice can also be compared to the notion of heteroglossia as suggested by Bakhtin (1986), with a significant point of difference. It is possible that the heteroglossic process could create a disjointed Babel of voices unable to accomplish much. The hypervoice of many, however, is expected to bring forth changes that can have an impact on those who produce the hypervoice. The work of Gurak (1997) demonstrated the possibilities that can be achieved by hypervoices.

In the case of SAWNET, the empowering characteristic of hypervoice is apparent in the list of options offered by the opening page of the SAWNET website with links that cover issues ranging from domestic violence to children's books. Included within that range are issues about weddings, news about South Asian women, news about charities, and several other links that become elements of the hypervoice. The links offer the visitor a series of opportunities and textual potentials so that the hypervoice is not co-opted by a single author, but rather the openended potential of the Internet is used to bring together the voices of many, who all belong to a single marginal group – women of South Asia. It is no longer the case that the speech of the women of South Asia is co-opted by trade unions, POWs, and other "speakers" who have earlier claimed legitimacy to speak for the marginalized. In the traditional modes of speaking, each speaker could make a contribution in moving forward the cause of the women of South Asia, but they ultimately remained disjointed voices that never were effectively connected together in the public sphere. However, in the discursive space of the Internet, any speaker, whether a traditional group such as POW or a woman experiencing the trauma of a failed marriage, all reside next to each other, empowering each other and utilizing the opportunity offered by the Internet to create a singular hypervoice whose authorship eventually becomes impossible (and hopefully unimportant) to pinpoint. To be sure, this tendency can be thought of in terms of Nakamura's (2002) arguments about the absence of the problematic of race on the Internet. Here some similar "invisible" problematics are indeed addressed.

The significant outcome of the emergence of the hypervoice as a product of many individual voices is a recasting of the way in which a marginalized group can obtain discursive power. ...

There are thus two key interrelated characteristics of the cyber discourse produced by the hypervoice of women of South Asia on SAWNET. First, the voices do not represent authoritative and institutional authorship, and second, these individual speakers obtain a discursive purchase by being able to create a hypervoice that is all connected together. Eventually it is the ambiguous authorship of the hypervoice that opens up the questions of trust, authenticity, and power.

Which "Authentic" Voice to "Trust"?

First, the strategy of creating a collection of links that collate the voices of many different speakers is perhaps the most significant way in which SAWNET fosters trust. The fact that the webpage does not have its singular monolithic voice, but instead attempts to empower the voices of many speakers, is a strategy to deflect any questions about the trustworthiness of a single institutional speaker who would want to speak authoritatively on issues related to women of South Asia. The stress on individuals as opposed to institutions remains a significant strategy for generating trust by giving the individual voices a chance to "stand on their own," as well as in the company of many other individual voices. This individuality of the "unknown," we argue, is an element of the SAWNET page that can generate a sense of trustworthiness for the page.

Trust is generated by the process by which the voices of the atomized individuals are not refracted through the dominant ideological lenses of the institutions. For example, the individuality of the voices, and their freedom from control by the hegemonic voices that have spoken for South Asian women, are particularly evident in the links offered one degree of separation from the portal page. Consider the page where several stories about South Asian weddings are collected. Here, using all the tools of hypertext, various speakers describe their authentic experiences of weddings in South Asia. These stories appear trustworthy because they are not edited and constructed by systematic processes of textual construction, but in their somewhat random arrangement take on an "amateurish" look that eventually suggests an honesty that has not been abandoned for the bells and whistles of the institutional page. Witness, for instance, the series of pictures and the brief commentary about the pictures on the page titled, "A Wedding in India" (http://www.umiacs.umd.edu/users/sawweb/SAWNET/wedding.html). This link offers a collection of pictures of a wedding in Kolkata, India, of an Indian woman to an American man. The pictures, photographed by the author of the page, are accompanied by brief commentaries that do not attempt to "dress up" the text. Indeed, one of the commentaries says, "I can't remember what we were laughing about." In that confession, we would argue, lies the seeds of building a cyberspace that has not been colonized by dominant institutions, but where individuals can still continue to be able to speak for themselves. The confession of "not remembering," although antithetical to professional journalistic writing, offers a breath of fresh air to what is an authentic personal experience that has not gone through the ever-increasing "spinning" that has become the mainstay of contemporary popular mass media (see, e.g., Shields & Goidel, 1998).

The relatively invisible creators of the page do not underscore the selection process either. The absence of a systematic selection process is evident in the minimal attempts to seek thematic unity. Indeed, this is a departure not only from tendencies seen in traditional mass media (e.g., radio and television), but also from the textual strategies adopted in institutional webpages, which often attempt to collate together various hyperlinks on similar topics. The collation process constructs the page in a way that carries traces of the ideological stance of those who created the page. Consider, for instance, the authoritative voice of an institution such as CNN, which would typically categorize and collate information in "logical" groups that indicate what the institutional authors would consider to be logical. In the case of SAWNET, however, the collation does not carry any visible traces of the individuality of the people who began the Web portal, but it is indeed the hypervoices of many people who have been brought together in the discursive space created by the various hypertextual links. In a discursive cyberspace where the "construction" of webpages is a booming industry by itself, the way in which the members of SAWNET have chosen to leave the portal somewhat "unconstructed" could itself become a means for generating trustworthiness.

The textual strategy of leaving out any editorialization also can generate trust by bringing together marginalized individuals who can speak in the company of similar others, without having their voices co-opted and transformed by institutions. Consider, for instance, the story of Ameena Meer, who says in her own voice, "I think the hardest part of getting divorced is the social thing – explaining to everyone why you're not together" (Meer, n.d.). Although the statement could have been editorialized out by the process of construction on a different webpage because of the inherent obviousness of the statement, on SAWNET it is allowed a space along with many other such individual voices that coexist with the voice of Meer. It is now possible to consider how the issue of authenticity is addressed by SAWNET, and how specific textual strategies connect trust with authenticity.

The textual strategies that generate trust also are the ones employed to encode authenticity in the SAWNET discourse. Following the conventions of hypertextual discourse, this page invites the visitor to examine the various hypertextual options provided by the portal page. Links from this page are labeled, "Articles," "News About South Asian Women," the "Khush Page" dedicated to lesbian issues, "Domestic Violence," "South Asian Women's Organizations," and "Divorce," among others. SAWNET thus utilizes the open-ended potential of hypertextuality and allows the visitor to experience a multitude of voices that SAWNET does not claim as its own. Witness the link that takes the visitor to the "Articles" page. There are articles here that all congeal around the central theme of "articles by and about South Asian women." In a textual sleight, the page claims authenticity simply by using the terms "by and about" and not on the basis of SAWNET's own authority. This textual strategy legitimizes the presence of such diverse voices as the Guardian newspaper's Internet edition and an article written by an author called Arundhathi Subramaniam (n.d.), who is described as "poet, dance critic, a regular freelance journalist on the arts." The latter article, whose location is recognizable only as a link from SAWNET, occupies a discursive space along with the more traditionally authentic sources, such as the Internet edition of a major newspaper or a reprinted story from *Newsweek* magazine (Narayan, 2000).

Similar to the way in which trust is generated, authenticity is also built around hypertextuality rather than on the basis of SAWNET's authorship. Indeed, in stories of specific experiences of specific women, it is their own individual voices that are reproduced and recirculated without leading the visitor off to the original source. This process is important because it attempts to reclaim the authenticity of the voice on its own merit rather than by its association with any traditionally authoritative voice. …

As indicated in these examples from the voices of South Asian women on SAWNET there are specific textual strategies that create a sense of authenticity and trust. The lack of obsession with authorship and the creation of hypervoice are specific representational strategies that have been employed by the SAWNET facilitators. It can be argued that these strategies help to provide a sense of trust and authenticity to these hypervoices that in turn can gain discursive power in the global public sphere created by the Internet. Indeed, this power could transcend the power of unions, protests, and the surrogate voice on institutional media. The path of the transition from gaining speaking capital and discursive power to obtaining political, social, cultural, and economic power could be an uneven and rocky one. However, there is some precedence to suggest that when specific new powers are provided, the ripple effect can be remarkably positive. The women-operated bank system in Bangladesh is a significant example of the way in which providing minimal financial freedom to marginalized women can result in far-reaching changes in the social and cultural system.[8] Similar transitions, which could be witnessed as discursive power and freedom, are achieved by marginalized groups. It is thus important to recognize that the questions that arise about the voices of women from South Asia also can be raised about other marginalized groups who are gaining purchase in cyberspace. To be sure, the questions of trust and authenticity when related to the idea of voice on the Internet can be applied to a large set of issues that are debated on and about the Internet.

Conclusion

It takes just a brief perusal of cyberspace to see the presence of the multitude of voices that espouse their particular points of views to the increasing number of Netizens. Very often the voices are articulated in a textually attractive and persuasive fashion, making them appear to be trustworthy and authentic. However, there are no clear directions for the reader to negotiate this space and develop a "cyberspace literacy" to be able to make sense of the plethora of voices. Furthermore, there is also a lack of discussion about theoretical means of understanding what to make of the numerous hypervoices that are on the Internet and the consequences of the existence of these voices in the public sphere.

The examples from SAWNET used here begin to demonstrate that there are some critical issues to consider when looking at the voices on the Internet. It is clear that marginalized groups such as women of South Asia have embraced the virtual and developed strategies of voicing that include the ones identified here, such as distancing of authorship and inclusion of personal voices. Such illustrations help to develop some arguments about the ways in which trust, authenticity, and power could be negotiated discursively in cyberspace. Surely some of the negotiations are reminiscent of past discussions on power and discourse, as suggested, for instance, by Foucault (1972). Ultimately, it might be possible to develop a lexicon of strategies of voicing that would show how discursive empowerment could occur on the Internet. To some degree, there needs to be an urgency to this project because the Internet can be shaped to become what the various Netizens want it to become, but by not voicing, it is likely that the Internet will become what many other media of mass communication have become: bastions of the powerful where the relatively powerless have remained silent and silenced. Perhaps the Internet could take a different trajectory. There does remain one limitation to this process that merits attention. The analysis represented here demonstrates how the notion of voice, as a rhetorical and textual construct, allows for an interpretation of a website. The analysis eventually attempts to show how a hypervoice can be created by the website. However, the analysis does not attempt to consider the conditions of production of the website. The focus here is on the text and how the text could become a voice of a group of people.

It also needs to be noted that there are specific ways of going about analyzing the discursive presence of the marginalized. As demonstrated here, it is important to be able to locate a relevant starting point for the analysis and then follow a specific protocol to decide how much will be analyzed using which specific analytic strategies. Keeping in mind that the analysis is of discourse, it is critical to be able to apply specific methods of discourse analysis while keeping in sight the fact that such analysis has to be rethought in view of the hypertextuality of the material being examined. A systematic process such as that can begin to yield useful and interesting information about the way in which the cybernetic space could be used by those who have been powerless in the real world.

NOTES

1. South Asia is loosely defined to include the entire Indian subcontinent as well as Afghanistan.
2. The idea of degrees of separation, as suggested by Mitra and Cohen (1999), measures the "the number of 'clicks' necessary to go from one WWW page to another" (p. 195). Here the term is used in a similar manner by considering how far a Netizen has to travel to stay within the boundaries of the discursive domain opened up by a portal page.
3. SAWNET includes a moderated mailing list where members can post their comments. This is a "closed" domain and is not the focus of the current analysis. Additionally, SAWNET also includes a website that links together many different webpages that deal with issues related to women in general and women of South Asia in particular. The current effort is to analyze the public domain texts available at the website. The website space is donated by one of the members of SAWNET, and there is no funding for SAWNET. According to the webpage, all the people involved with SAWNET squeeze in volunteering time to maintain the page. The SAWNET webpage provides no specific guidelines about how links are selected for inclusion.
4. The page claims, "South Asia is taken to include Bangladesh, Bhutan, India, Maldives, Nepal, Pakistan, Sri Lanka."

5. It is important to note that within some regimes of the Internet, as in the case of the SAWNET discussion group, there is a significant amount of inclusiveness and attempts to exclude those who do not appear to "belong." This is particularly true for Usenet discussion groups, as noted in Fredrick's (1999) work with women and by Mitra (1997) for ethnic groups.

6. I would argue that the popularity of hit counters on pages represents a tendency to align the Internet discourse with traditional mass media. In the case of television and radio, it is extremely important to know who consumes what. The hit counters and tracking software attempt to do the same for the Internet. However, when that is absent, as in the case of SAWNET, it can be argued that the "hearing" part of the communicative process becomes less important to these speakers.

7. The idea of the Internet as a safe place to have a voice has been demonstrated in the case of other marginal groups such as gays and lesbians as well (Hyde & Mitra, 2000).

8. Details of the way in which the women-operated bank system in Bangladesh works and how it has benefited many can be seen at their website, http://www.grameen-info.org/.

REFERENCES

Appelbaum, D. (1990). *Voice*. Albany: State University of New York Press.

Bakhtin, M.M. (1981). *The dialogic imagination*. Austin: University of Texas Press.

Bakhtin, M.M. (1986). *Speech genres and other late essays*. Austin: University of Texas Press.

Black, E. (1978). *Rhetorical criticism: A study in method*. Madison: University of Wisconsin Press.

Bormann, E.G. (1988). "Empowering" as a heuristic concept in organizational communication. In J.A. Anderson (Ed.), *Communication Yearbook, 11*, 391–404. Newbury Park, CA: Sage.

Chacko, S., Narayanan, L., & Rao, K. (2002). *About SAWNET*. Retrieved June 6, 2003, from http://www.umiacs.umd.edu/users/sawweb/SAWNET/about.html

Cheney, G. (1995). Democracy in the workplace: Theory and practice from the communication perspective. *Journal of Applied Communication Research, 23*, 167–200.

Fiske, J. (1987). *Television culture*. London: Methuen.

Fiske, J., & Hartley, J. (1978). *Reading television*. London: Methuen.

Forbes, G. (1996). *The new Cambridge history of India IV.2: Women in modern India*. Cambridge, UK: Cambridge University Press.

Foucault, M. (1972). *The archaeology of knowledge and discourse on language*. New York: Harper & Row.

Fredrick, C.A.N. (1999). Feminist rhetoric in cyberspace: The ethos of feminist Usenet newsgroups. *Information Society, 15*(3), 187–197.

Gandhi, N., & Shah, N. (1992). *The issues at stake: Theory and practice in the contemporary women's movement in India*. New Delhi, India: Kali for Women.

Goffman, E. (1981). *Forms of talk*. Oxford, UK: Basil Blackwell.

Gurak, L. (1997). *Persuasion and privacy in cyberspace*. New Haven, CT: Yale University Press.

Hall, S. (1980). Encoding/decoding. In S. Hall, D. Hobson, A. Lowe, & P. Willis (Eds.), *Culture, media, language* (pp. 128–139). London: Hutchinson.

Haslett, B. (1990). Discourse, ideology and organizational control. In J. A. Anderson (Ed.), *Communication Yearbook, 13*, 48–58. Newbury Park, CA: Sage.

Hyde, M., & Mitra, A. (2000). On the ethics of constructing a face in cyberspace: Images of a university. In V. Berdayes & J.W. Murphy (Eds.), *Computers, human interaction, and organizations* (pp. 197–206). Westport, CT: Praeger.

Kumar, R. (1993). *The history of doing: An illustrated account of movements for women's rights and feminism in India 1800–1990.* New Delhi, India: Kali for Women and Verso.

Lak, D. (1998). *Child brides marry in Rajasthan.* Retrieved June 6, 2003, from http://news.bbc. co.uk/1/low/despatches/85708.stm

Landow, G.P. (1992). *Hypertext: The convergence of contemporary critical theory and technology.* Baltimore: Johns Hopkins Press.

Meer, A. (n.d.). *My first divorce was a lot harder than my second.* Retrieved June 6, 2003, from http://www.umiacs.umd.edu/users/sawweb/SAWNET/divorce/p3.html.

Miller, H. (1995). *The presentation of self in electronic life: Goffman on the internet.* Paper presented at the Embodied Knowledge and Virtual Space Conference, June 1995, London, UK.

Mitra, A. (1993). *Television and popular culture in India.* New Delhi, India: Sage.

Mitra, A. (1997). Virtual commonality: Looking for India on the internet. In S. Jones (Ed.), *Virtual culture: Identity and communication in cybersociety* (pp. 55–79). Thousand Oaks, CA: Sage.

Mitra, A. (1999). Characteristics of the WWW text: Tracing discursive strategies. *Journal of Computer-Mediated Communication, 5*(1).

Mitra, A. (2001). Marginal voices in cyberspace. *New media and society, 3*(1), 29–48.

Mitra, A., & Cohen, E. (1999). Analyzing the web: Directions and challenges. In S. Jones (Ed.), *Doing internet research* (pp. 179–202). Thousand Oaks: Sage.

Mitra, A., & Watts, E. (2003). Theorizing cyberspace: The idea of voice applied to the internet discourse. *New Media and Society, 4,* 479–298.

Mumby, D.K. (1988). *Communication and power in organizations: Discourse, ideology and domination.* Norwood, NJ: Ablex.

Nakamura, L. (2002). *Cybertypes: Race, ethnicity, and identity on the internet.* Bristol, PA: Taylor & Francis.

Narayan, S. (2000). *Was it me or was it my sari?* Retrieved June 6, 2003, from http://www. umiacs.umd.edu/users/sawweb/SAWNET/misc/sari.html.

Pacanowsky, M. E. (1988). Communication in the empowering organization. In J. A. Anderson (Ed.), *Communication Yearbook, 11,* 356–379. Newbury Park, CA: Sage.

Papa, M.J., Singhal, A., Ghanekar, D.V., & Papa, W.H. (2000). Organizing for social change through cooperative action: The [dis]empowering dimensions of women's communication. *Communication Theory, 10,* 90–123.

Poster, M. (1990). *The mode of information: Poststructuralism and social context.* Chicago: University of Chicago Press.

Putnam, L.L., Phillips, N., & Chapman, P. (1996). Metaphors of communication and organization. In S. R. Clegg, C. Hardy, & W. Nord (Eds.), *Handbook of organization studies* (pp. 375–408). London, UK: Sage.

Scruton, R. (1983). *The aesthetic understanding: Essays in philosophy of art and culture.* Manchester, UK: Carcanet.

Shaw, D.F. (1997). Gay men and computer communication. In S. Jones (Ed.), *Virtual culture: Identity and communication in cybersociety* (pp. 133–145). Thousand Oaks, CA: Sage.

Shields, T.G., & Goidel, R.K. (1998). Taking credit and avoiding blame: Good news, spin control, and democratic accountability. *Political Communication, 15,* 99–115.

Singhal, A., & Rogers, E.M. (1989). *India's information revolution.* New Delhi, India: Sage.

Smith, C.R., & Hyde, M.J. (1991). Rethinking the "public": The role of emotion in being with others. *Quarterly Journal of Speech, 77,* 446–466.

Subramaniam, A. (n.d.). *Why on earth would an Indian choose to write English poetry?* Retrieved June 6, 2003, from http://www.umiacs.umd.edu/users/sawweb/SAWNET/books/arundhathi_semicerchio.html

Vecchio, N., & Ray, K.C. (1998). *Poverty, female-headed households, and sustainable economic development.* Westport, CT: Greenwood Press.

Watts, E. K. (2001). Voice and voicelessness in rhetorical studies. *Quarterly Journal of Speech, 87,* 179–196.

IV BODIES, EMBODIMENT, BIOPOLITICS

Introduction

The body has been at the center of debates in cyberculture studies. From individuals who experience a sentimental, affective relation with the computer to the larger projects of databasing entire populations based on their genetic makeup, ICTs have transformed the way we see the body.

Hagiographers of cyberspace and cybertechnology have praised them as a "technology" of corporeal transcendence and identity-switching. Critics have seen new forms of embodiment emerging in this "medium." Subjectivity, ontology, and identity are all altered in the age of networked human beings and computer technology. Cognitive abilities of the body have also been altered significantly by technologies that now mediate our relationship with the world and our environment. Bodies are networked, wired, and modified with implants, circuitry, and biomedical interventions that enhance, alter, or restore the bodies' functions and abilities. Experiments in cryogenics seek to change the parameters of aging, disability, and death. Aestheticization now also involves computerized beauty treatments, and new art forms that work at the interface of body–beauty–art–technology are now commonplace. Cyborg bodies have been the subject of fantasy and film, and are increasingly visible in real, material lives.

Certain kinds of bodies find the anonymity and identity-switching "facility" of cyberspace attractive. "Disembodiment" is a viable option for those who believe their bodies are socially marginalized. Otherwise unacceptable bodies – fat, disabled, gay, anorexic – find cyberspace a site where they can meet other such bodies, develop communities, exchange information, and engage in meaningful relationships. This mediation marks a radical redefinition of both the individual subjectivity and her/his social experience, where the face-to-face is replaced by the face-to-screen body-image.

The articles in Part IV deal with various body-phenomena in the age of cybertechnology. They explore subjectivity, identity, aesthetics, medicalization, and the biopolitics of populations.

Megan Boler explores the hype around corporeal transcendence – what she terms "new digital Cartesianism" – that informs much of digital cultures. She argues that much of the talk about the purity of consciousness, the fluidity of identity, and the absence of geographical–spatial restrictions in cyberspace is misplaced. Using pedagogy as a point of departure, Boler suggests that embodied pedagogy remains central, even in the age of computer-mediated communications. She notes how, in the age of hypes about disembodied communication, there remains a strong emphasis in CMCs on gender and age. In fact, users often make connections between the stereotype of race or gender and the views that other user is expected to hold.

Medical discourses and practices have taken to cyberspace in a big way – for disseminating information, databasing, helplines, and scholarly work. In their book, *The Medicalization of Cyberspace*, Andy Miah and Emma Rich study this new phenomenon. In this particular chapter from the book they focus on bioethics and its new configurations in medicalized cyberspace. Looking at pro-anorexia groups (called "Pro-Ana"), Miah and Rich suggest that cyberspatial narratives may not be only discursive but can have very real material and bodily consequences for users. This brings the issue of ethics to the fore. Miah and Rich note that Pro-Ana cyberspaces challenge the medicalized notions of anorexia when they draw upon gendered and embodied experiences. They read Pro-Ana as a type of cyberfeminist theory, but which provokes debates about ethics. Miah and Rich see online blogs about bodies as transformative, where gender categories are reworked.

Eugene Thacker notes the increasing "databasing" of the human body via projects such as the Human Genome Diversity Project (HGDP). Treating this informatization of the body as a new form of biocolonialism, Thacker argues that biopolitics now moves from territory to population. Noting the involvement of biotech companies in this databasing project, he suggests that the governmental and medical concerns over the health of the population will shift from sex and sexuality to a notion of population defined in terms of genetics and informatics. Population genomics shifts the focus from a more traditional anatomo-politics of the human body to a biopolitics of the human race. And this commodification of the human population, argues Thacker, has consequences for the pharmaceutical industry.

14 HYPES, HOPES AND ACTUALITIES

New Digital Cartesianism and Bodies in Cyberspace

Megan Boler

'New Digital Cartesianism' investigates the virtual vapor trails of existing socio-material power inequities in text-based computer-mediated communication (CMC). While marketing hypes and cyber-enthusiast hopes actively mythologize the potentials of disembodied CMC with promises of anonymity and fluid identities, the actualities of the way in which users interpret and derive meaning from text-based communication often involve reductive bodily markers that re-invoke stereotypical notions of racialized, sexualized and gendered bodies. Ironically, this new digital Cartesianism, initiated by a rhetorical cheerleading of the mind/body split as a desirable aim of CMC, ultimately results in the invocation of stereotyped bodies in order to confer authenticity and signification to textual utterances.

At stake is not just whether we can achieve a new adaptation of Descartes' disembodied dream or not, but how the imagined construction of online spaces functions as a material productive force that reinscribes existing social relations.[1] Evoking Henri Lefebvre, David Harvey writes, 'spaces of representation ... have the potential not only to affect representation of space but also to act as a material productive force with respect to spatial practices' (1990: 196; see also Lefebvre, 1981). This article makes the case that in digital Cartesianism, although the body is allegedly 'transcended' in virtual environments according to the hypes and hopes, it actually functions as a necessary arbiter of meaning and final signifier of what is accepted as 'real' and 'true'. To illustrate this paradox, it summarizes the 'hypes' of the technology advertisers and the 'hopes' of cyber-enthusiasts, then outlines the 'actualities' of CMC which contradict these very hypes and hopes.

Megan Boler, "'Hypes, Hopes and Actualities: New Digital Cartesianism and Bodies in Cyberspace," pp. 139–68 from *New Media & Society* 9:1 (2007).

... the aim is to substantiate that, despite the hypes and hopes of the freedom offered by transcending usual images of the other, there comes a point at which users crave information about traditional markers of the body – to know the 'meat' that accompanies the textual bones (see Gibson, 1984).

... this inquiry is situated at the intersection of several nascent disciplines. First, feminist poststructuralist and postcolonial analyses of the importance of material and embodied experience (Fanon, 1967[1952]; Grosz, 1993; Probyn, 1993) and how this has been prematurely dismissed (Adam, 1998; Balsamo, 2000; Boler, 2002).[2] Second, cultural geographies that analyse the 'time–space compression' and 'death of distance' arguments within the context of globalization, which also signal the necessary intersections of theorizations of 'space and place' alongside analyses of discourses and experiences of cyberculture (Harvey, 2000; McDowell, 1999; Massey, 1994; Robins and Webster, 1999). Third, the implications of these socio-theoretical shifts in relation to educational theory and practice (Boler, 2002; De Castell and Jenson, 2004; Zembylas and Vrasidas, 2005). The central question underpinning this critique of digital Cartesianism is: whose goal is it to transcend the body and what may be lost in this migration to new spatial imaginaries? ...

This analysis focuses on text-based CMC. ...

Important distinctions need to be made between social MUDs and MOOs and other environments such as web-enhanced educational environments, for example where threaded discussions or instant messaging (IM) is used to complement F2F education. Some may challenge that critiques of social CMC are not applicable to educational uses of CMC (or to newsgroups, listservs or other chat environments) because adopting a 'fictional' identity in these latter spaces is unlikely. However, in web-enhanced education (i.e. where part of the course is experienced in F2F and the rest is conducted online through threaded discussions), there is a greater likelihood, especially in large class sizes, that users will 'fill in' an image of the other. Further, in educational environments that are entirely online, users do 'fill in' identity markers, often with stereotyped conceptions of others' age, sex and location, just as in other environments (Boler and Vellenga, 2000).[3]

This article is organized in five sections. First, the relation of the body to CMC and education will be discussed, followed by the discourse of hypes. The discourse of hopes is then addressed, followed by the actualities. Finally, the implications of new digital Cartesianism for progressive pedagogies are considered.

What's the Problem? CMC, Bodies and Social Change

Some educators place a premium on the pedagogical significance of the body. Text-based, computer-mediated digital culture repackages the Cartesian desire to transcend the 'truth-polluting' body. As such, this apparent disembodiment created in cyberculture poses a genuine dilemma for critical, feminist and progressive educators who have invested decades in ensuring that 'the body' be recognized as essential to knowledge production (Grosz, 1993; Probyn, 1993; Senft, 1996).

In an article published in the *Chronicle of Higher Education*, Ingrid Banks argues that her body is a central aspect of the curriculum and pedagogy:

> As a black female teaching African-American Studies, I am troubled by the prospect of being asked to teach Online or televised courses. I fear that they would obscure or even erase my presence in the classroom. When I walk into class on the first day of the term, I know that my presence there sends a political message. By standing in front of my students, I challenge not only their conception of the typical – that is, white and male – professor, but also their images of black people. (1998: B6)

Yet other educators, equally committed to progressive pedagogies, argue that the relative anonymity of online interaction encourages students to participate more freely in dialogue and conversation.[4] Some studies suggest that students who are typically silent in the F2F classroom participate more frequently in online environments. The relative anonymity of disembodiment may encourage freedom of expression, emboldening students to express politically incorrect views that warrant discussion. As Banks further expresses,

> some colleagues have told me that certain students are willing to say things online that they would not mention in the classroom. Given that I teach sensitive material that challenges students to think critically, the Internet could be a great way of pushing students to discuss why they think the way they do. (1998: B6)

There are also strong counter-arguments in favour of having these difficult conversations in person. Banks states clearly:

> I don't like the idea of students hiding behind a computer monitor. I want to engage them and I want them to engage each other, face to face. Over the course of the semester, I want to see their uncomfortable facial expressions and body language change. Of course, some expressions and gestures won't change, which is also information that I want to have. (1998: B6)

This value of an embodied pedagogy has been developed by a range of progressive, radical and feminist theorists, points which are taken up in the concluding section of this article (Boler, 1997, 1999; Ellsworth, 1989). Does disembodiment allow for growth and transformation? No doubt, to express difference in the absence of F2F may be more comfortable. But is comfort a goal of education? Given the aims of pedagogies of discomfort (see Boler, 1999), of learning to *witness* rather than *spectate* in order to understand the social responsibilities inherent to seeing differently, what is the cost of replacing discomfort with the convenience of anonymity? At present, there exists a significant gulf between the research undertaken about instructional technologies and how CMC can be used towards liberatory pedagogical goals.[5] A scrutiny of digital Cartesianism has implications for how we develop a critical digital pedagogy.

The Hypes

'Hypes' refers to the marketing discourses employed to promote and sell software, hardware and other CMC technologies. Surveying the images and texts of advertisements used to target consumers from around 2000 reveals several, frequently recurring themes: transcending bodies, transcending differences and transcending space and place. To discern the rationale and narrative thrust behind these hypes, let us begin by illustrating how the socio-historical frame of neo-liberalism functions as a cornerstone for advertising hypes.[6]

Neo-liberal Cartesianism

A neo-liberal version of the Cartesian binary of mind and body sells differences by simultaneously highlighting difference of race and nation while erasing them; differences or bodies are recognized, situated within the discourse as an obstacle of some sort and 'displaced' through a re-emphasis of mind or transcendence of difference or body.[7]

The neo-liberal discourse of simultaneously marking difference in order to erase it is well exemplified in a series of World.com television advertisements for Generation Digital.[8] This series depicts a series of seemingly multicultural, ambiguously categorized bodies against high-speed backdrops of urban landscapes. In rapid succession seven diverse persons repeat, in different accents, the phrase 'I was born into a new generation', or in the case of the one older white man, 'I was *reborn* into a new generation'. Then one person states, 'It isn't about country', another, 'It isn't about culture', and then a white (Australian) girl states emphatically, 'It's about attitude'. Finally, a distinctly 'other' voice or body speaking in a heavy accent utters, 'But we speak the same language'. We're told, 'You've come to the right generation. Generation Digital'. World.com depicts a utopian, globalized world where 'you can be whomever you want to be'. Country and culture do not matter.

What defines Generation Digital is a 'shared language'. In 'Gen D', whatever our color or nationality, we all speak 'digital'. The implication is that digital is cleansed of any cultural determinants. In reality, digital is English, thus revealing an imperialism which governs much of the internet and software (Adam, 1998). In addition, Gen D bodies do not merely transcend; they transcend through a mediated language. Language as a technology and technologies themselves are not neutral (Castells, 2000; King, 2003), and in this instance we are able to see the dialectic of difference concurrently, produced and erased.

The World.com commercial reveals the hypocrisy in the claim that on the internet there is neither 'race', nor class, nor gender. Rather, these racialized and gendered identities are necessary placeholders of difference which enable the vision of the idealized community of neo-liberal sameness. Difference is actually required for a world to exist in which differences do not matter. In short, these selves are variations of a sovereign liberal individual.⁹ Jodi O'Brian words this succinctly: '[On the internet,] can I really expect to be treated just like everyone else? Does "just like everyone else" mean "just like one of the [white] guys?"' (1996: 56). A 'white global consumer' who transcends the body, local space and time in their fundamentally interchangeable nature has replaced Descartes' 'man of reason'.

Hype 1: Transcending Bodies

This advertisement for 'ThinkAd' explicitly represents one form of digital Cartesian hype. 'Free the body', states the text of the original advertisement, 'and the mind will happily follow'. Shown in the foreground is a white male professional. A white woman is in the background, seated on a desk, next to a computer, her bare legs seductively crossed, and her gaze turning 'demurely' downward (at what? her ankle?), and away from us. Both represent workers as consumers/producers, in an ambiguous space–part office, part yuppie loft–where technology allows people to be 'free to roam' from their desks. (ThinkAd) gives people (read 'bodies') and ideas (read 'minds') extra space to roam (read 'transcend') … beyond the realm of their desk (read 'space and place').

Here again, stereotyped bodies are crucial for meaning-making (see Hall, 1997, ch. 4). The woman's body is classically eroticized, even in her 'free' relation to the machine and her implied ability to 'roam' from the desk. However, her position is all-too familiar in its fixed and static position as appendage, subservient and subordinate, while the 'older, wiser, white man' roams in the foreground. Arguably, she is a bonus prize; a fringe benefit of the freedom afforded to him through technology.

Hype 2: Transcending Differences

Closely related the hype of transcending the *body* is the hype of transcending *difference*. Each requires the other. However, within advertising discourses, often the two hypes are represented as distinct from one another. The classic MCI commercial proclaims: 'There is no race. There is no gender. There are no infirmities. There are only minds'.¹⁰ Pure and unsullied communication can take place regardless of embodied differences – in this case, an African-American man in formal attire and a bright-faced, corn-fed, freckled, ambiguously gendered youth can communicate across differences, thanks to new technologies. Picture Tel asks, 'Who will your students meet today?' and shows a colorful line up of what appears to be a Thai princess, an astronaut, a ballerina and a Japanese geisha. These advertising hypes express a world in which difference is transcended by technology; difference, first seen and experienced, is then bridged or erased. The neo-liberal, concurrent erasure or dependence on difference is foundational for each of these hypes. The differently marked bodies are indispensable as a backdrop against which to sell technologies that bridge or transcend.

... A voyeuristic 'experience' of otherness is replicated, working against the explicit aims of radical pedagogies, postcolonial critiques and feminist post-structuralism that have worked for decades to establish the importance of embodied difference encountered not through reductive notions of otherness, but through careful recognition of precisely how difference is constructed and perceived (Boler, 1999; Lugones, 1989; Mohanty, 1989–90). In educational practice, drive-by difference may result in superficial CMC about difference that fails to challenge deeply the kinds of prejudice and stereotypes that people hold about others (Riel, 1996). For example, in one account, two groups of young children had been interacting online between Louisiana and New York for some months. When the Louisiana group received a photograph of their penpals, they expressed shock and asked 'Where are the brothers?' (Riel, 1996) They had assumed their penpals to be 'black like them'. In this case, the gaze brought to bear appears not necessarily to be the dominant cultural gaze but the gaze of the self-seeking itself. In short, while there is a promise of freedom in the anonymity of text-based virtual communities and a promise that we transcend assumed differences in our online interactions, in fact, users may tend to reproduce themselves in imagined others.

There is no guarantee that F2F classrooms will ensure that beliefs and assumptions about others are profoundly challenged, but certainly one must question whether packaging multicultural encounters through technology achieves the kinds of interactions, communities and education envisioned as progressive, feminist or liberatory. The 'actualities' of these educational uses of technology will be discussed further in the final section of the article.

Hype 3: Transcending Space and Place

A persistent illustration of the new digital Cartesianism involves hype about transcending space and place.[11] [In a parodic advertisement for iSell,] we are told that, 'Redesigning a campus is easy. You just knock down a few walls'. Brick and mortar universities and traditional walls are replaceable with the connectivity of computer wireless systems. The original image depicts a male and female couple happily seated outdoors on a campus looking at a laptop screen together. The text of the original ad describes creating a classroom from the entire world, following the instructed wishes of a particular university, with the promise that staff as well as students will be connected via the internet at all places and times.

In another ad from this series (not depicted visually here due to interesting copyright issues faced by this author as might now be clear), the same software company depicts parents and teachers seated in children's school chairs in a classroom, apparently at a meeting with one frustrated parent raising their hand.

This advertisement builds on the discourse of 'time–space compression'[12] – that technology closes the gap of both space and time through its capacity to transcend the limitations of material communication and bodies. It also exemplifies the hype about the efficiency of CMC in relation to education. Not only do we find the discourse that F2F communication in traditional space and place is failing us in matters of education, but that schools need to model themselves after business management to achieve success. ... the assumption is that educational software promises efficiency and frees up the 'economy of attention' (De Castell and Jenson, 2004). Teachers can be 'more accessible' to their students. ... Moreover, this implication begs the question of access to technology, whether on the part of teachers or the parents.

The hypes represented in educational technology advertisements reflect the new digital Cartesianism. Promises are made that by transcending the body and difference, the mind will be accentuated, freed and enhanced. We can escape the trappings and limitations of bodies and place through the promises of technology. Efficiency and time are rewarded in exchange for bodies and space.

The Hopes

Social theorists of cyberculture recognize the potential for challenging notions of fixed and static identities, for fluidity of identity though gender play and an escape from binaries. Such analyses have tended to focus on the social interactions that take place in MOOs and MUDs.[13]

Whereas the primary impetus here is to show the overlap of the new digital Cartesianism common to both the advertising hypes and these sociotheoretical hopes, there is a key difference between the hypes and the hopes: for the most part, cybertheorists do not want to ignore differences of ethnicity, class, gender and sexual orientation. In fact, many are painfully aware of these realities. Rather, their expressed desire to transcend the body appears to reflect a yearning to change how we think about, experience and envision social identities. The hopes reflect a desire to challenge static notions of identity, engage fluidity and break down traditional binaries.

Although cyber-enthusiast motives are quite different from the neo-liberal hype discussed in the previous section, the outcome remains the same. In advocating transcendence of the limiting aspects of embodiment, we nonetheless carry the 'virtual vapor trails' of stereotyped notions of difference embedded in our language, social imaginaries and practices. We reinscribe the stereotypes that we sought to undo and lose the embodied differences that feminists and poststructuralists see as precious aspects of subjectivity and epistemology.

Hope 1: Transcending Bodies and Difference

Can we challenge stereotypic experiences or perceptions of identity in CMC environments? In 1993, Amy Bruckman wrote:

> MUDs are an identity workshop ... Gender swapping is an extreme example of a fundamental fact: the network is in the process of changing not just how we work, but how we think of ourselves–and ultimately, who we are. (1996: 5)

Over a decade later, we find similar hopes echoed: 'On the Net, race and gender distinctions dissolve' (Gray, 2001: 188) The hopes invested in cyborgs that transcend traditional binaries suggest, somewhat optimistically, that 'bodies and persons are things that can be made' (Gray, 2001: 191). These hopes are reiterated sometimes within cyberwritings in language not very different from the MCI commercial hype. To seek spaces in which we can engage dialogue without having our utterances dismissed and foreclosed by presuppositions is an admirable and worthy hope.

Progressive thinkers hold out the utopian hopes of transcendence, a hope that in digital environments identities may be fluid and 'queer', neither fixed nor in static form and may avoid the traps of binary and oppressive assumptions about identities. The transcendence of bodies and difference is achieved through two primary avenues: fluidity of online identities and transcending binaries (e.g. of human/machine).

Fluidity of Online Identities

According to the hopes, one promise of online spaces is that users have freedom to construct virtual, 'fictional' identities that allow them to move beyond the constraints of the usual social markers of ethnicity, class, gender, age and ability. The 'queer' hope, as it might be called, beholds cyberspace as potential for emergent identities. In this idealized view, cyberspace promises fluid subjectivities; uninhibited gender play where 'real life' men, for example, can 'try on' the experience of being a woman and vice versa, or where anyone can experiment with homosexual experiences without fear of ostracization.

As one cybertheorist describes the hope for moving beyond static identities:

> The greatest freedom cyberspace promises is that of recasting the self: from static beings, bound by the body and betrayed by appearances, Net surfers may reconstruct themselves in a multiplicity of dazzling roles, changing from moment to moment according to whim. (Stallabrass, quoted in Wakeford, 1999: 179)

Sherry Turkle's work was one of the early studies to demonstrate users' desire to experience a fluidity of social class identity. The hopes for fluidity often specifically address gender, particularly within social use of MUDs and MOOs, advocating the possibilities of gender fluidity usually in terms of users adopting gender-neutral avatars or a name or persona of the opposite sex. (Bruckman, 1996; Stone, 1995; Turkle, 1995)

[…]

The hope of such 'queered' spaces is not merely that such play occurs online, but that somehow this online gender-play may affect offline social relations.

[…]

Transcending Binaries

Closely related to the desires for fluid identities are the hopes of transcending binaries. To make sense of our conceptual and linguistic world, we rely on the differences created through these binaries – i.e. we understand male in relation to female, etc. However, binaries are not only a problem in terms of their apparent intractability in our conceptual grasp of the world, but they have very real material effects on how people experience themselves in the world. The trouble with binaries is that the two named terms of binary pairs – e.g. male/female, good/bad, black/white – are not equal; one becomes privileged over the other. The privileged term of the binary pair translates into social values, norms and power that marginalize those marked by the 'lesser' of the binary term. Binaries not only torment feminist and poststructural theorists but also represent a seemingly intractable foundation of traditional western thinking.

Cyber-hopefuls extol the possibility of transcending binaries and dualisms through cyber-morphing. Poster, in even stronger terms, suggests that the ability of MUDders to adopt a 'fictional role that may be different from their actual gender … drastically calls into question the gender system of the dominant culture as a fixed binary' (quoted in Kendall, 2002: 11). For example, a cyborg is itself both human and machine, thus defying that binary opposite. In Stone's vision, virtual interactions allow us to enact our cyborg identities. Cyberspace represents the potential for 'emergent behavior, for new social forms that arise in a circumstance in which body, meet, place and even space mean something quite different from our accustomed understanding' (1995: 37).

[…]

Hope 2: Transcending Space and Place

Echoing the advertising hype of transcending the limitations of material space and F2F communication, cyber-discourse invokes notions of a 'postgeographical world'. Such utopian hopes envision digital worlds where we connect across differences of national and geographic boundaries: 'the new technologically-mediated world will be a post-geographical world, "profoundly anti-spatial" in its nature' (Mitchell, quoted in Robins and Webster, 1999: 240–1).

The hope discourse offers a transspatial, transcendental vision; a world less defined by violent boundaries of nations or segregated communities. But it also may harken a 'postmodern' version of the classical wish to go beyond this world and arrive into God's:

> The postmodern will to virtuality parallels the medieval religious will to transcendence … Cyberspace is socially constructed as the postmodern paradise and all our hopes for virtuality express our desire to escape the limitations of our bodies and the ills of our society. (Fisher, 1997: 122).

'Virtual paradise' discourses bear more similarity to Cartesian desires to transcend 'polluting' bodies and the impermanence of space and time.[14] This discourse is illustrated in popularized form in *Wired* magazine, in which a cover story in 2002 advertised computers as theology: 'computation seems almost a theological process. It takes as its fodder the primeval choice between yes and no, the fundamental state of 1 or 0' (Kelly, 2002: 180).

[…]

The Actualities

Cartesianism with a Twist

While the hypes and hopes suggest that we can inhabit a communicative world where anonymity reigns and freedom of expression rules regardless of one's bodily identity, the actualities evidence that in fact, users rely on markers such as age, sex and location to make sense of online communication. The mythologies of anonymity and fluidity appear to have their limits: users require that the other offers 'essential' data about their 'real life' identity so that sense can be made of textual utterances. In short, we seem to be able to go only so long without asking or imagining these familiar social markers and cues.

Hence 'digital Cartesianism with a twist': the online context promising pure, disembodied communication and the 'twist' of the body required to make sense of textual communications. This 'twist' is well illustrated by the frequency with which users inquire about others' 'age/sex/location' ('asl') in order to interpret communication and/or to confirm one's projection of the other's identity.[15] In many environments users are obsessively concerned with 'asl'. As O'Brian in her study 'Writing in the Body: Gender (Re)production in Online Interaction' succinctly puts it,

> even when the body is anchored elsewhere and unavailable as the source of symbolic cueing, central distinctions that reference the body as connected to self will still be evoked as the basis of meaningful communication. (O'Brian, 1999: 85)

[…]

Curiously, the users themselves interrogate the significance of the 'asl' practice, revealing their own perception of the tension between the promise of disembodied exchange and this reinvocation of stereotyped bodies. These debates about the practice of requiring that users declare their age, sex and location illustrate the concerns of critics:

> [T]here remains persistent and apparent cultural resistance to gender model change ... Whatever social construction is, it is not something that appears to be easily made malleable or ambiguous even in the rapidly changing world of technological civilization. (Ihde, 2002: 31)

This *reinscription* of stereotypes of the body occurs not only in purely social online environments but also in other discussion groups such as Usenet. In an article titled 'Reading Race Online: Discovering Racial Identity in Usenet Discussions', Burkhalter demonstrates that in his studies of newsgroup users:

> Discussion between groups, which progressive people might hope would alleviate racial stereotypes, instead is a site where previously held stereotypes are made into self-fulfilling prophecies ... In online discussions, readers treat racial identities as entailing particular perspectives ... A discrepancy arises when a person identified as a member of a particular racial group by his or her physical characteristics offers a perspective that is inconsistent with the stereotype of that group. (1999: 72–3)

Readers make an essentialized link between a user's racial identity and the views that this person is expected to hold. For example, the following post responds to an author who was troubled by blacks she had seen on a talk show and finds a discrepancy between the author's identity as black and the perspective that she offers:

> It is a shame that you even have to ask these questions because I would hope that you see more blacks on Ricki Lake, whether you are black or white. But being black, I am truly amazed at what you have asked. I will just guess that you are still a teen (as opposed to a hick that has never seen a black person) and haven't been out in the world and exposed to much. (1999: 72–3)

The Usenet member is confused by how a 'black' person could express a particular view that does not conform to a stereotyped notion of 'the perspective that 'should be' held by a black person. The user reconciles the dissonance by 'filling in' and attributing the discrepancy to the other's age and ignorance:

> [R]esolving these puzzles by modifying the author's identity allows readers to maintain the connection between racial identities and perspectives ... perspective and race are made to conform online. Far from being a site where race, racism, ethnocentrism or stereotyping are banished, these phenomena flourish in newsgroups. (Burkhalter, 1999: 73)

Despite the hypes and hopes that online interaction might open up new spaces of communication, there is ample evidence that users invoke habitual assumptions and stereotypes about bodies in order to make sense of the other.[16] As Stone ascribes,

> for symbolic exchange originating at and relating to the surface of the body, narrowing the bandwidth has startling effects. A deep need is revealed to create extremely detailed images of the absent and invisible body … Frequently in narrow-bandwidth communication the interpretative faculties of one participant or another are powerfully, even obsessively, engaged. (1995: 93)

Following Lacan, Stone argues that desire

> theorized as a response to perceived lack, arises as a product of the tension between embodied reality and the emptiness of the token, in the forces that maintain the preexisting codes … for body … that are absent from the token. (1995: 95)

And Baym reiterates:

> Because computer-mediated interactants are unable to see, hear and feel one another they cannot use the usual contextualization cues conveyed by appearance, nonverbal signals and features of the physical context. With these cues to social context removed, the discourse is left in a social vacuum quite different from face to face interaction. (1995: 139–40)

The body's role as final arbiter of authentic identity is evident across studies of online interaction. One of the most revealing crises of interaction in which the body plays a most decisive role is one user's experiences of 'deception' at the hands of another user.[17]

The anger expressed towards the deception turns on the body as being the final arbiter of authenticity. As O'Brian argues:

> Ultimately, one has either a vagina or a penis and the presence of one or the other of these physical attributes marks an 'authentic' immutable presence in time and space. Or so we will continue to believe. (1999: 95–6)

In the case of 'deception', the physical attribute of one's 'real', biological identity functions to determine the 'real' person. Stone notes that

> the societal imperative with which we have been raised is that there is one primary persona or 'true identity' and that in the off-line world – the 'real' world – this persona is firmly attached to a single physical body. (1995: 73)[18]

Even so, computer-mediated relationships still may have the potential to transcend these limited and stereotyped conceptions of the self and its relationship to an essentialized body. But as O'Brian (1996, 1999) emphasizes, for online relationships to represent and inhabit truly 'queer' or 'transgendered space', the social meanings shared by those inhabitants both on and offline must be social meanings unconstrained by omnipresent and dominant assumptions about such categories as gender and ethnicity. Unfortunately, there is not yet evidence that the majority of users inhabiting online spaces represent a demographics of democracy, much less a population who share 'queered' understandings of the relationship of sex to gender. And the question remains: 'How might these narrow bandwidth educational interactions disrupt fixed assumptions?' One must examine the complexity of people's social networks and cannot examine solely 'whether and how an individual transforms her ideas in an online educational environment'. Any person's experience is occurring in myriad spaces, places and interactions. It is not at all clear that the disembodied, anonymous space of online communication can ensure that users will challenge fixed notions of gender and racial identities in any way:

> [T]he metaphor of the internet as space masks the disassociation of Netters from their bodies, masks the fact that bodies are elsewhere, real, material – invested with a responsible subjectivity. Here it is clearest that gender is information, discourse rather than nature – and sexuality, offline or on it, functions linguistically. But the deployment of this potentially dematerialized information has material effects and historically, they have been to the detriment of women. We appropriate technology to our own physiques and resolutely refuse to change our perceptions to fit the parameters of our inventions. We may indeed be becoming cyborgs, as Haraway suggests, but if so, we are cyborgs who perform traditional biography, *Blade Runner* androids passing as standard human bodies and the standard body, the subject's body, is male. (Gilbert, 1996: 137)

Instances in which users 'deceive' others through misleading online self-representations illustrate precisely how the body functions as the final arbiter of truth, authenticity and meaning. You can be whomever you want to be online, but quite often you will be asked to reveal your 'true' identity – i.e. a shorthand reference to your gender or ethnicity. And once you have uttered 'male' or 'female', 'black' or 'white', there is little fluidity or ambiguity about what this nomenclature means.

Implications for Digital Pedagogy

Whose desire is it to transcend the body? What sense do we make of the coincidence that, just as feminist poststructuralists, postcolonial theorists and neo-Marxist accounts had begun to establish the significance of the body to epistemology and signification, we encounter a new version of Descartes' disembodied fantasy? In this concluding section, new digital Cartesianism is read against some of the educational aims outlined by radical, progressive and feminist educators. There persists a gulf within educational theory between the discourses of cognitive psychology and social constructionism that frame the development of instructional technologies and the critical theorists who are beginning to articulate what would count as 'creative' and 'critical' digital pedagogies. While there is no space to outline this vast discrepancy here, the discourses of digital Cartesianism align with the learning models of the emphasis of instructional technology on 'scaffolded learning' and 'banking education' long eschewed within progressive and radical educational practices.

The feminist philosopher Susan Bordo's critique of Descartes and her suggested goal of 'dynamic objectivity' offers an initial answer to the question: 'Whose desire is it to transcend?' She elaborates:

> If the key terms in the Cartesian hierarchy of epistemological values are clarity and distinctness – qualities which marked each object off from the other and from the nowhere – the key term in this alternative scheme of values might be designated as sympathy … [Sympathetic understanding] means granting personal or intuitive response a positive epistemological value, even (perhaps especially) when such response is contradictory or fragmented. 'Sympathetic' thinking, Marcuse suggests, is the only mode which truly respects the object, that is, which allows the variety of its meanings to unfold without coercion were too focused interrogation. (1987: 102–3)

Bordo outlines Evelyn Fox Keller's notion of 'dynamic objectivity' and argues that:

> [I]n contrast to the conception of dynamic objectivity, Descartes' program for the purification of the understanding … has as its ideal the rendering impossible of any such continuity between subject and object. The scientific mind must be cleansed of all its 'sympathies' toward the objects it tries to understand. It must cultivate absolute detachment. (1987: 103–4)

Sandra Harding calls this a supreme characterization of modern science and a 'super masculinization of rational thought' (quoted in Bordo, 1987: 104). Worthy of note is that, in striving to transcend binaries, some of the discourses of hope outlined earlier actually reinscribe potential binary divisions between subject and object.

Feminists and others have extended these worries about the dismissal of embodied subjectivity directly to their analyses of digital identities. As Anne Balsamo reflects:

> Upon analyzing the 'lived' experience of virtual reality, I discovered that this conceptual denial of the body is accomplished through the material repression of the physical body. The phenomenological experience of cyberspace depends upon and in fact requires the willful repression of the material body … From a feminist perspective is clear that the repression of the material body belies a gender bias in the supposedly disembodied (gender free) world of virtual reality. (2000: 493)

Balsamo's argument confirms the longstanding feminist critique of Cartesian rationality. Namely, that the ideal of a reality 'free from bodies' reflects the masculinist ideal which entails a repression of materiality and the body. In a moving story ('Come in CQ') that echoes this concern, Ullman writes:

> Ironically those of us who most believe in physical, operational eloquence are the very ones most cut off from the body. To build the working thing that is a program, we perform 'labor' that is sedentary to the point of near immobility and we must give ourselves up almost entirely to language … Software engineering is an oxymoron: we are engineers, but we don't build anything in the physical sense of the word. We think. We type. It's all grammar.
>
> And, cut off from the real body, we construct a substitute body: ourselves online. We treat it as if it were our actual self, our real life. Over time, it does indeed become our life. (Ullman, 1996: 12)

These notions of dynamic objectivity and insistence on the importance of embodiment as part of epistemology and education are in strong tension with the constrained imaginations of bodies and differences outlined in new digital Cartesianism.

What educational experiences lead to growth and transformation? How do we comprehend self and other as situated in a lived, embodied and material environment? In *Experience and Education*, Dewey cautions:

> A primary responsibility of educators is that they not only be aware of the general principle of the shaping of actual experience by environing conditions, but that they also recognize in the concrete what surroundings are conducive to having experiences that lead to growth. Above all, they should know how to utilize the surroundings, physical and social, that exist so as to extract from them all that they have to contribute to building up experiences that are worthwhile. (1997[1938]: 40)

Dewey emphasizes the educator's responsibility to consider the concrete surroundings that shape educational experience. Educational growth and transformation cannot be divorced from the material environment:

> [W]e live from birth to death in a world of persons and things which in large measure is what it is because of what has been done and transmitted from previous human activities. When this fact is ignored, experience is treated as if it were something which goes on exclusively inside an individual's body and mind. It ought not to be necessary to say that experience does not occur in a vacuum. (1997[1938]: 39–40)

Dewey's urging to consider the distributed experience of the self suggests a fundamental epistemological and ontological problem for online education. Why discourage users from engaging difference through computer-mediated forms? As the problem of 'drive-by difference' was described earlier, the concern is that in CMC we encounter the other only through voyeuristic perception as opposed to a radical encounter with embodied difference that leads to self-reflexive change.

Foreshadowing the work of thinkers such as Foucault as well as contemporary analyses of how space is defined not merely in terms of its absolute, physical stasis, but more importantly, how spaces dynamically construct social experience and vice versa, Dewey's critique of traditional education parallels contemporary concerns about online education:

> Traditional education ... could systematically dodge this responsibility. The school environment of desks, blackboards, a small school yard, was supposed to suffice. There was no demand that the teacher should become intimately acquainted with the conditions of the local community, physical, historical, economic, occupational, etc., in order to utilize them as educational resources. (1997[1938]: 40)

Dewey's insistence on the local, physical, historical conditions as fundamental to a progressive pedagogy suggests that, at minimum, education that is conducted entirely online needs to revisit what it might look like to invoke this material historicity as part of the educational exchange.[19] In contemporary terms, Alison Adam asks in *Artificial Knowing: Gender and the Thinking Machine*:

> [H]ow far is the body or embodiment necessary for having knowledge[?] ... [A]t least two aspects of situatedness are of interest – being physically situated in an environment (which relates to the embodiment problem) and being socially situated in a culture. (1998: 129)

For many educators – as illustrated by Ingrid Banks' comments earlier – the body represents a kind of shared 'text' within a physically proximate environment and is recognized as part of the subject who experiences growth or transformation. The risk of losing the body as part of transformative pedagogy in web-enhanced education is a real one.

More systematic studies are needed to investigate precisely what is gained when users feel more 'freedom' to speak in online discussions and what this means about our ability to engage in productive F2F dialogue (Boler, 2004). We need to know how and when students feel recognized or heard during online discussions about volatile questions regarding gender, ethnicity, sexual orientation and disabilities. For example, in an article titled 'Type Normal Like the Rest of Us', Alison Regan analyzes the pedagogical and ethical dilemmas that she faces when, in an online chat in her composition course, a student expresses death threats towards homosexuals and in the ensuing discussion the students use the pronoun 'we', revealing the assumption that all the participants were heterosexual. Regan analyzes how such homophobic expressions easily result in the silencing and 'exclusion of lesbian and gay participants from networked conversation' (1994: 118). As Gilbert puts it:

The Net is not 'just words' ... but a space of social action, in which subjects are responsible for their utterances and performances and in which discursive actions can mobilize material effects. Like other social spaces, it is not safe ... That these spaces are discursive rather than material does not lessen their phenomenological reality. (1996: 137)

Finally, given that one of the primary arguments about digital participation is that users feel freer to participate because of the safety offered by relative anonymity, how can we measure dialogue in its transformative sense as engaged in CMC? Paulo Freire contends that dialogue

cannot exist unless the dialoguers engage in critical thinking – thinking which discerns an indivisible solidarity between the world and the people and admits of no dichotomy between them – thinking which perceives reality as process, as transformation, rather than as a static entity-thinking which does not separate itself from action, but constantly immerses itself in temporality without fear of the risks involved. (1970: 92)

Freire's vision seems in part antithetical to the distanced anonymity of interaction in digital environments. This sense of safety is not the kind of risk-taking Freire calls for: rather, he envisions a risk-taking based in action, self-reflexive praxis and dialogue that recognizes the body, the word and world as material constituents of identity and change.

Conclusion

In conclusion, it is possible to imagine engaging CMC in ways that do not promote new digital Cartesianism. It is possible to imagine web-enhanced education that engages bodies in F2F environments in ways that can be taken up with complexity in CMC environments. Nevertheless, the risks are great. We live in an era of time–space compression where attention is at a premium and the economy is fueled by oversaturated attention. We have invested decades of theory, practice and politics to create physical and theoretical spaces in which bodies and differences are recognized – in all of their complexities – as fundamental to the production of meaning. Bodies are messy and differences fraught. What would it take to preserve messiness and conflict as foundational values, rather than being tempted by neat and tidy drive-by difference, as we shape the digital future in all its material significance?

NOTES

1. This notion of materiality is referenced in Sofoulis, in which she writes that the 'objects and bodies studied/produced by technoscience ... are ... "material/semiotic actors",

whose boundaries are not predefined but 'materialize in social interaction' (2003: 6). To some extent this portrait drawn from Latour and Haraway characterizes the needed understanding of communication (even in so-called 'disembodied' spaces) as materially productive. Similarly, in *Technologies of Gender* (1987), De Lauretis addresses how technology shapes and mediates our relationships in the physical and material world.

2. Here I signal two distinct fields: feminist poststructuralism and postcolonialism that consider the centrality of the body to epistemology and perception, and more recent critiques of cyberculture that raise worries about the 'disembodiment' discourses that threaten the inroads made by earlier decades of feminist and postcolonial work. For example, Fanon's considerations of how the body is perceived through the gaze of the other and how that look is then internalized into the self, is not a theoretical issue widely considered by cyber-enthusiasts that I discuss in the 'hopes' section. There are a handful of feminist analyses of the representation of bodies in cyberculture that have begun to develop the urgently needed 'materialist' analyses of the body in relation to technology – a concern certainly initiated in Haraway's (1991[1985]) 'A Cyborg Manifesto'. King (2003) references Haraway's notion of technology as 'frozen social relations', which may be another way of talking about the intractability of stereotyped notions of bodies in relation to lived practices. The representation of the body has been taken up by some cultural and certainly literary studies (Foster, 1999; Joyce, 1999; Nakamura, 2000; O'Brian, 1999); but there is far less to be found in the way of a neo-Marxist or feminist analysis of the relationship of the body to technology in everyday practices.

3. For example, I co-directed a documentary about a women's studies class that had been conducted entirely online during a summer session (Boler and Vellenga, 2000). This project developed when one of the students came to me at the end of the class and described the 'wow' experience that she and other students had during the entirely online course. Many of the students had experienced some measure of transformative growth. As we interviewed students on camera, it was revealed that it was the frequency and 'intimacy' of IM exchange with the professor, who was conducting the course from hundreds of miles away, that established the basis for this sense of transformative 'wow'. The student who originally approached me told me that students were prepared to rent a car and take a road trip to meet the professor who was in Kansas: in fact, they were obsessed with meeting this fabulous professor 'face to face'.

4. Yet others argue, to the contrary, that degrading and harmful norms and stereotypes are reinscribed within the social spaces of digital relations (Burkhalter, 1999; O'Brian, 1996; Regan, 1994).

5. In, 2002, I conducted a study with James Dwight of 10 top tier journals in education and educational technology (see also Dwight et al., 2006). Striking in these findings of journals between 1997–2002 was that in journals devoted to educational theory, only about 5 percent of the articles addressed critical theories of technology or new media in relation to education. A corresponding absence was found in top information technology journals: only a very small percentage addressed questions of social context, ethnicity, class, gender or critical perspectives on technology. This signals a serious gap in the way that the field of education is conversing about the progressive uses of new media.

6. For discussions of globalization and neo-liberalism as relevant to an analysis of information technology, see for example, Castells (2000), Harvey (2000) and Sassen (1998).

7. Particularly fascinating within cyberculture hypes as well as hopes, is the association of body–space–femininity. The philosophical roots of the masculinist repudiations of the

body as polluting knowledge and truth are discussed extensively in numerous feminist critiques (Benjamin, 1988; Bordo, 1987; Kaufman-Osborn, 1997, to signal a few). In a forthcoming work I draw on feminist cultural geography to analyze how space is represented and recreated in 'nostalgic' forms within online discourses.

8. This advertisement can be seen as Quick time online at http://it.stlawu.edu/uglobal/pagessemiotics/montagewcom.html

9. Discussing avatars, Nicola Green states that the 'digitized bodies' represent the historically constructed western individualist subject whom Grosz suggests is a historical abstraction because it evokes sameness, similarity and continuity. As Robins notes in the case of virtual systems … all identities can be rendered as one of these 'universal' (masculine) digital identities, thus suppressing the material effects of difference in digital interaction. (2001: 154)

10. The MCI ad can also be seen at http://www.brillomag.net/NO3/erasism.htm

11. Frequently, in traditional philosophy 'space' is considered something to be transcended and has been associated with femininity (McDowell, 1999). Correlated with 'being', space is understood traditionally as a fixed and static materiality. Thus space is often opposed to time or the masculine progress associated with 'becoming'. Feminist geographer Doreen Massey (1994) makes a powerful case that we need to understand space not as fixed and static, but as dynamic and changing. She defines 'place' in part as 'localities' which are shared social spaces. Places are defined as a locality of shared space, dynamic and changing because they are defined not by 'boundaries and containment' but by social interactions.

12. This refers in part to the effect of information technologies and the creation of the so-called 'global village'. Massey (1994) points out that the recent emphasis and anxiety expressed by theorists regarding time–space compression reflects two aspects of patriarchal ethnocentrism. First, the ethnocentric or colonizer's view that this compression of time–space is 'new'. In fact, many ethnic groups and communities have been exiled, forced to move or colonized for centuries and so have experienced time–space compression for generations. The anxieties associated with time-space compression are new only for the colonizer. Second, the depiction of time–space compression as creating much greater 'global movement' ignores the fact that mobility – say, for women and many poor persons – is still greatly constricted and highly dependent on 'power geometry' or access to social and economic class and power. In short, while time–space compression affects many persons across socioeconomic classes, it creates 'increased mobility' only for the few 'jetsetters' who fly business class from one country to another calmed by the presence of Starbucks in every international airport and city.

13. There is, by 2005, a well-established trajectory of sociological and ethnographic literature studying the experience of identities online. I conceptualize the early work in this field as having established its own unique perimeters (Rheingold, 1994; Stone, 1995; Turkle, 1995). There was then an influx of feminist analyses that both embraced the potential for gender-shifting as well as critiquing the 'hopes' for reasons similar to those I pose in this article (Baym, 1995; Bruckman, 1996; Herring, 1994; Kendall, 2002).

14. The theme of transcendence as connected to religious discourses occurs frequently both in reflective and unreflective forms in cyberculture literature. The range of writings that discuss explicitly the religious elements of the discourses include Heim (1993) and Wertheim (1999). In another forthcoming article I analyze the significance of the

invocation of transcendence from space and place, reading cultural geography against these 'religious' cyberculture discourses to examine the gendered nature of the repudiation of space and place.

15. In another example, the purpose of the online chat is advertised precisely to search for people on the basis of their 'asl':

> Communities.com is an international online community where people from all over the world (184 countries) meet, chat, flirt and interact every day. There are loads of things to do and it's FREE to join!
>
> *Make new friends*
>
> Whether you're looking for new friends in a different part of the world or in your local area you should be able to find them here. If you're looking for someone in particular you can search for members by age, sex, location, etc. When you find someone that seems interesting you simply send them a message and start chatting. And who knows, maybe you'll even find the love of your life inside!

16. To the extent that this is accurate, psychoanalytic analyses of self–other relations constructed in online communities is promising (Benjamin, 1988). Unfortunately, there is no evidence yet that the majority of users inhabiting online spaces represent a demographics of democracy, much less a population who share 'queered' understandings of the relationship of sex to gender. How are educators, in particular, to challenge cultural habits, values and norms within the narrowed bandwidth on text-based interactions?

17. One of the more famous is the incident of Joan, the 'wheelchair therapist'. Despite that he was 'in fact' a man, the user Alex presented himself online (or was misperceived once and then came to assume this continuing identity) as a disabled, wheelchair-bound female therapist. As an online persona, over the course of several months 'Joan' developed numerous highly intimate relations with other women. When eventually 'some of the online friends wanted to meet her in person', real-life Alex freaked out and decided that online Joan needed to die. Joan's fictitious husband then gets online and tells the friends that Joan is deathly ill in a hospital. When the online friends offer an outpouring of financial and emotional assistance, real-life Alex finally decides Joan needs to recover. However, when 'real' cards and flowers are sent to the supposed Manhattan 'hospital', the fiction unraveled and Joan is revealed to be Alex.

    There are numerous accounts of this particular event. Joan's friends were furious with the deception. As Sherry Turkle summarizes, some of the anger is simply anger at being lured into intimacy by a man who posed as a woman to win their secret confidence. Some of the anger

    > centers on the fact that Joan had introduced some of her online women friends to lesbian netsex and the women involved felt violated by Joan's virtual actions [when in fact he was a man] ... In other accounts, Joan introduced online friends to Alex, a Manhattan psychiatrist, who had real-life affairs with several of them. (1995: 229)

18. In social theories of online identities and communities, there is debate about what constitutes the 'real' persona and disagreement about what such ethics must be based upon; for example, when this crisis occurred in the CompuServe community,

    > the hackers ... just smiled tiredly ... All of them had understood from the beginning that the net presaged radical changes in social conventions, some of which would go unnoticed. That is, until

an event like the disabled woman who is revealed to be 'only' a persona – not a true name at all – along with the violated confidences that resulted from the different sense in which various actors understood the term person, all acted together to push these changes to the foreground. (Stone, 1995: 80–1)

At what point did the transgression of acceptable ethical norms occur? Where does one draw the line regarding which self counts as real in online interactions? However, these questions are beyond the scope of this article. My focus is simply to recount how the body functions as an emergent 'metaphysics of presence'.

19. The materiality of the body is ignored also in the hype of the 'accessibility' of online education for certain populations: for example, offering homebound women with children access to online education reinscribes women's isolation from the public sphere. Alternatives include providing women with the option of adequate childcare so they can engage in face-to-face education. To isolate certain bodies geographically may deliver less on the promise of 'connection' across borders and instead reinscribe women's exclusion from the public sphere. Further, a concern expressed by many is that engaging with others via digital representations of language and images atomizes and isolates social experience. Whether or not one sees time spent online as socially isolating or not, relatively few studies exist that take as a central question the body's material relationship to computing practices through a materialist or phenomenological frame.

REFERENCES

Adam, Alison (1998) *Artificial Knowing. Gender and the Thinking Machine*. London and New York: Routledge.

Balsamo, Anne (2000) 'The Virtual Body in Cyberspace', in David Bell and Barbara Kennedy (eds) *The Cybercultures Reader*. London: Routledge.

Banks, Ingrid (1998) 'Reliance on Technology Threatens the Essence of Teaching', *Chronicle of Higher Education*, 16 October, p. A24.

Baym, Nancy (1995) 'The Emergence of Community in Computer-Mediated Communication', in Steven G. Jones (ed.) *Cybersociety*. Thousand Oaks, CA: Sage.

Benjamin, Jessica (1988) *The Bonds of Love*. NY: Pantheon.

Boler, Megan (1997) 'Disciplined Emotions: Philosophies of Educated Feelings', *Educational Theory* 47(3): 203–27.

Boler, Megan (1999) *Feeling Power: Emotions and Education*. NY: Routledge.

Boler, Megan (2002) 'The New Digital Cartesianism: Bodies and Spaces in Online Education', *Philosophy of Education Society 2002* (ed. Scott Fletcher). Champaign, IL: Philosophy of Education Society).

Boler, Megan (2004) (ed.) *Democratic Dialogue in Education: Troubling Speech, Disturbing Silence*. New York: Peter Lang.

Boler, Megan and Vellenga, Amber (2000) womensstudies@vt.edu (video).

Bordo, Susan (1987) *The Flight to Objectivity*. New York: SUNY Press.

Bruckman, Amy S. (1996) 'Gender Swapping on the Internet', in Peter Ludlow (ed.) *High Noon on the Electronic Frontier. Conceptual Issues in Cyberspace*, pp. 317–26. Cambridge, MA: MIT Press.

Burkhalter, Byron (1999) 'Reading Race Online: Discovering Racial Identity in Usenet Discussions', in Mark A. Smith and Peter Kollock (eds) *Communities in Cyberspace*, pp. 60–75. London: Routledge.

Castells, Manuel (2000) *The Rise of the Network Society*. London: Blackwell Science.

De Castell, S. and J. Jenson (2004) 'Paying Attention to Attention: New Economies for Learning', *Educational Theory* 54(4): 381–98.

De Lauretis, Teresa (1987) *Technologies of Gender*. Bloomington, IN: Indiana University Press.

Dewey, John (1997[1938]) *Experience and Education*. New York: Macmillan.

Dwight, James, Megan Boler and Pris Sears (2006) 'Reconstructing the Fables: Women on the Educational Cyberfrontier', in Joel Weiss, Jason Nolan, Jeremy Hunsinger and Peter Trifonas (eds) *International Handbook of Virtual Learning Environments*, pp. 1107–29. New York: Springer.

Ellsworth, Elizabeth (1989) 'Why Doesn't This Fell Empowering? Working Through the Repressive Myths of Critical Pedagogy', *Harvard Educational Review* 59(3): 297–324.

Fanon, Frantz (1967[1952]) *Black Skin, White Masks*. New York: Grove Press.

Fisher, Jeffrey (1997) 'The Postmodern Paradiso: Dante, Cyberpunk and the Technosophy of Cyberspace', in David Porter (ed.) *Internet Culture*, pp. 111–32. London: Routledge.

Foster, Thomas (1999) '"The Souls of Cyber Folk": Perfomativity, Virtual Embodiment and Racial Histories', in Marie-Laure Ryan (ed.) *Cyberspace Textuality, Computer Technology and Literary Theory*, pp. 137–63. Bloomington, IN: Indiana University Press.

Freire, Paulo (1970) *Pedagogy of the Oppressed*. New York: Continuum.

Gibson, William (1984) *Neuromancer*. New York: Ace Books.

Gilbert, Pamela (1996) 'On Space, Sex and being Stalked', in Theresa M. Senft and Stacy Horn (eds) *Women & Performance: A Journal of Feminist Theory*, pp. 125–50. New York: Women and Performance Project Inc.

Gray, Chris Hables (2001) *Cyborg Citizen*. New York: Routledge.

Green, Nicola (2001) Strange yet Stylish Headgear: Virtual Reality Consumption and the Structure of Gender', in Eiteen Green and Alison Adam (eds) *Virtual Gender: Technology, Consumption and Identity*, pp. 151–7. New York: Routledge.

Grosz, Elizabeth (1993) 'Bodies and Knowledges; Feminism and the Crisis of Reason', in Linda Alcoff and Elizabeth Potter (eds) *Feminist Epistemologies*, pp. 187–216. London: Routledge.

Hall, Stuart (1997) *Representation: Cultural Representations and Signifying Practices*. London: Sage.

Haraway, Donna (1991[1985]) 'A Cyborg Manifesto', in *Simians, Cyborgs and Women: the Reinvention of Nature*. New York: Routledge.

Harvey, David (1990) *The Condition of Postmodernity*. London: Blackwell.

Harvey, David (2000) *Spaces of Hope*. Berkeley and Los Angeles, CA: University of California Press.

Heim, Michael (1993) *The Metaphysics of Virtual Reality*. Oxford: Oxford University Press.

Herring, Susan (1994) 'Gender Differences in Computer-Mediated Communication: Bringing 'Familiar Baggage to the New Frontier', paper presented at 'Making the Net *Work*: Is There a Z39.50 in Gender Communication?', American Library Association Annual Convention, Miami, 27 June (available at: http://cpsr.org/cpsr/gender/herring.txt).

Ihde, Don (2002). *Bodies in Technology*. Minneapolis, MN: University of Minnesota Press.

Joyce, Michael (1999) 'On Boundfulness: the Space of Hypertext Bodies', in Mike Crang, Phil Crang and Jon May (eds) *Virtual Geographies*, pp. 222–43. London and New York: Routledge.

Kaufman-Osborn, Timothy V. (1997) *Creatures of Prometheus*. Lanham, MD: Rowman & Littlefield.

Kelly, Kevin (2002) 'God Is the Machine', *Wired Magazine* 10(12), available at: http://www. wired.com/wired/archive/10.12/holytech.html

Kendall, Lori (2002) *Hanging Out in the Virtual Pub*. Berkeley, CA: University of California Press.

King, Katie (2003) 'Women in the Web', in Marc Bousquet and Katherine Wills (eds) *The Politics of Information*, pp. 303–14, URL (consulted 23 May 2006): http://www.altx.com/ebooks/infopol.html

Lefebvre, Henri (1981) *The Production of Space*. Paris: Anthropos.

Lugones, Maria (1989) 'Playfulness', "World" Traveling and Loving Perception', in Ann Garry and Marilyn Pearsall (eds) *Women, Knowledge and Reality*, pp. 275–90. Boston, MA: Unwin Hyman.

Massey, Doreen (1994) *Space, Place and Gender*. Minneapolis, MN: University of Minnesota Press.

McDowell, Linda (1999) *Gender, Identity, and Place: Understanding Feminist Geographies*. Minneapolis, MN: University of Minnesota Press.

Mohanty, Chandra Talpade (1989–90) 'On Race and Voice: Challenges for Liberal Education in the 1990s', *Cultural Critique* 14(winter): 179–208.

Nakamura, Lisa (2000) *Race in Cyberspace*. New York: Routledge.

O'Brian, Jodi (1996) 'Changing the Subject', in Theresa M. Senft and Stacy Horn (eds) *Women & Performance: A Journal of Feminist Theory*, pp. 55–68. New York: Women and Performance Project Inc.

O'Brian, Jodi (1999) 'Writing in the Body: Gender (Re)production in Online Interaction', in Mark A. Smith and Peter Kollock (eds) *Communities in Cyberspace*, pp. 76–106. London: Routledge.

Probyn, Elspeth (1993) *Sexing the Self: Gendered Positions in Cultural Studies*. London: Routledge.

Regan, Alison (1994) 'Type Normal Like the Rest of Us: Writing, Power and Homophobia in the Networked Composition Classroom', in Linda Garber (ed.) *Tilting the Tower*, pp. 154–67. New York: Routledge.

Rheingold, Howard (1994) *The Virtual Community*. Amherst, MA: MIT Press.

Riel, Margaret (1996) 'Cross-Classroom Collaboration: Communication and Education', in Timothy Koschmann (ed.) *CSCL: Theory and Practice of an Emerging Paradigm*. Mahwah, NJ: Lawrence Erlbaum Associates.

Robins, Kevin and Frank Webster (1999) *Times of the Technoculture*. London: Routledge.

Sassen, Saskia (1998) *Globalization and its Discontents*. New York: New Press.

Senft, Theresa M. (1996) 'Introduction: Performing the Digital Body – A Ghost Story', in Theresa M. Senft and Stacy Horn (eds) *Women & Performance: A Journal of Feminist Theory*, pp. 9–34. New York: Women and Performance Project Inc.

Sofoulis, Zoé (2003) 'Cyberquake: Haraway's Manifesto', in Darren Tofts, Annemarie Jonson and Alessio Cavallaro (eds) *Prefiguring Cyberculture: an Intellectual History*, pp. 9–34. Cambridge, MA: MIT Press.

Stone, Allucqu`ere Rosanne (1995) *The War of Desire and Technology at the Close of the Mechanical Age*. Cambridge, MA: MIT Press.

Turkle, Sherry (1995) *Life on the Screen: Identity on the Age of the Internet*. New York: Simon and Schuster.

Ullman, Ellen (1996) 'Come In, CQ: the Body on the Wire', in Lynn Cherny and Elisabeth Weise (eds) *Wired_Women*, pp. 3–23. Seattle, WA: Seal Press.

Wakeford, Nina (1999) 'Gender and the Landscapes of Computing in an Internet Café', in Mike Crang, Phil Crang and Jon May (eds) *Virtual Geographies*, pp. 178–202. London: Routledge.

Wertheim, Margaret (1999) *The Pearly Gates of Cyberspace: a History of Space from Dante to the Internet*. New York: W.W. Norton.

Zembylas, M. and C. Vrasidas (2005) 'Levinas and the "Inter-face": the Ethical Challenge of Online Education', *Educational Theory* 55(1): 61–78.

15 THE BIOETHICS OF CYBER-MEDICALIZATION

Andy Miah and Emma Rich

Our posthumanist reading of Pro-Ana communities is a confrontation with biomedical models of health, though it is necessary to elaborate on this reading more fully to explain our intentions in offering posthumanism as an analytical device. One of the central themes of our discussion on the medicalization of cyberspace has been an exploration of the relationship between ethical and social scientific analyses of medical or pseudo-medical practices that stretch the limits of medicine's traditional goals. While medicalization generally has been inscribed with sociological assumptions and developed in the context of cultural and social studies, it has clearly implied a concern that can be described as moral and ethical. Morally, the concern over medicalization involves the degree to which it limits the enjoyment of a fulfilling and enriched life, through its relegation of social problems to the surveillance of medical expertise. Ethically, there are concerns that the practice of medicine is stretching beyond its prescribed role and that this can diminish both the integrity of medicine and, ultimately, patient care.

In this chapter, we make this ethical context more explicit and offer explanations and responses to the positioning of ethics within medicalization work. To reiterate one of our earliest statements, we do not presume that medicalization is inherently negative or undermining of autonomy. We agree with Rose (2007: 700), who observes that 'since at least the 18th century in developed countries, medicine played a constitutive part in making up people'. Consequently, our ethical objection to it would be to object to the very conditions of existence that allowed the derivation of a medicalization discourse. Thus, Rose states that 'medicine has been fully engaged in making us the kinds of people we have become' and that 'this is not in itself grounds for critique'. We refer back to our earlier note on the comment of bioethicist Eric Juengst, who defines medicalization as *inherently* negative, since it is 'the mistake of applying the medical

Andy Miah and Emma Rich, "The Bioethics of Cybermedicalization," pp. 107–16, 131–2 and references from Andy Miah and Emma Rich, *The Medicalization of Cyberspace* (London and New York: Routledge, 2008).

model to the wrong problem' (1998: 43). Our difficulty with this view is that there is considerable disagreement about whether a particular set of circumstances is, indeed, the wrong problem. So, if one were to talk about sexual dysfunction as a medicalized condition, the point of contention is often over whether a given set of circumstances is the effect of a treatable biological dysfunction rather than a social or psychological condition, for which the legitimacy of medical intervention is more dubious.

Anorexia and eating disorders more generally are often met with mixed responses to this matter. A range of conflicts of interest that are latent within the allied medical sciences and professions accompany these concerns. Thus, it is naïve to ignore the interest of pharmaceutical companies to support medicalization in so far as it leads to the utilization of their products. Also, one must take into account the interests of health care services to seek the most economical adequate solution to a given problem, given the limitation of resources. Finally, it is necessary to recognize that it is in the interest of patients to seek the least burdensome treatments. These factors strengthen the position of those who are concerned about medicalization, though the challenge seems to be more about how one discusses medicalization in the context of practices that might be described as lifestyle choices. To elaborate on this, it will be helpful to pursue more fully how one situates ethical concern in the context of Pro-Ana websites.

The Ethics within Pro-Ana

Pollack's (2003: 249) recent work on what a feminist response to Pro-Ana might involve alludes to the dangers that 'postmodern feminists may romanticize these spaces as political statements and thus, in essence, condone the inherent self-destructiveness that such a protest entails'. She warns against 'the possibilities for the pro-anorexic subject becoming a symbolic martyr'. These concerns arise partly because the anorexic body enacts *the cyborg ritual* discussed earlier: 'a paradoxical situation in which the development of increasingly "natural" and embodied interfaces leads to "unnatural" adaptations or changes in the user' (Biocca 1997). Indeed, claims continue to be made that some Pro-Ana support groups have been found to foster rather negative competitions for weight loss (Chesley *et al.* 2003):

> [H]ow many of you thin hotties want to prove yourself ang gain personal satisfaction (not weight) by showing you are the best at getting rid of that shit that pull your self-steem even more down? well guess what? the best way of doing that is to compete!!! so lets do this, starting AUGUST 21 i am competing against anyone who will challenge me (friendly competition of course), for a chance to prova myself ... if you think you can keep up, reply before the 21 and let me know ... this will help as motivation for you to lose more weight and reach your beloved numbers (lowest weight) so we will have fun!) we will be eating 500 or less calories ONLY IN FOOD THAT IS FRUIT OR VEGETABLE FOR THREE WEEKS STRAIGHT. the person who wins picks another competition. so if you are in, reply. ... YOU HAVE NOTHING TO LOSE IF YOU TRY TO COMPETE, ONLY POUNDS!!!! (Anonymous user, Pro-Ana blog)

Thus, the sort of ethical concerns about the Pro-Ana movement reflect a position that construes cyberspatial narratives not merely as discursive transformations, but as sites that may prompt material and bodily change. Part of the critique levelled at these communities is driven by concerns that they may foster competition and secrecy among users. We would be cautious of drawing parallels between virtual communities and the observations that within real-time support groups, members may negatively evaluate each other (see Walstrom 2000). Instead, we emphasize the need for further online ethnographies of Pro-Ana and other health-related communities.

Work on cybercommunities has already informed some of these discussions. Numerous papers in this area discuss how social hierarchies of the body are established in computer mediated communication contexts, even without the presence of actual visual body cues (see Wakeford 1999). Hierarchies connect with what is valued and, in this sense, certain sets of meanings are created and sustained as having value *across* the narratives of these young women, affording them not only alternative subjectivities but relations of power and knowledge. As Mitra (1997: 59) suggests, 'Since the Internet user is empowered to play an active role in the production of the discursive community, identity and community are formed around the discourses that are shared by members.'

The juxtaposition of this potentially liberalizing movement with potentially harmful implications is central to discussions concerning the gendered ethics of medicalized cyberspace. These Pro-Ana cyberspaces challenge the medicalized notions of anorexia, drawing upon embodied, gendered experiences. In particular, they refute the traditional 'sick role whereby there is an obligation to seek and comply with medical treatment, reducing the ill person to patient' (Frank 1997: 31).

In this sense, Pro-Ana may be a significant case for the development of cyberfeminist theory, since it occupies such a transgressive space (Dias 2003: Ferreday 2003). In part, this is also why we adopt a posthumanist reading of medicalized cyberspace. The cases we outline provoke questions about how discursive practices and power over women's bodies and ill health are theorized. They draw attention to the rewritings of, and on, the body, associated with particular subjectivities. However, the problem of the anorexic body, the Pro-Ana body, is that it mediates liberal and radical feminisms in a way that might be negatively plural. The idea of reconstituting one's subjectivity, of reconstituting the anorexic body outside of psychiatric and biomedical discourse, is marred by the manner in which such control is conducted and accepted. It is marred by the dangerous and perhaps, even life-threatening possibilities around body modification via self-starvation. This is the basis on which these alternative narratives become rejected as a legitimate discourse.

Fox *et al.* (2005: 947) make a critical point in this discussion when noting that Pro-Ana differs from other explanatory frameworks in rejecting the position that anorexia is a wholly negative condition that must always be 'remedied through medical treatments or psychosocial intervention'. Pro-Ana explicitly challenges this and raises a critical question for the ethics of health care: should the recourse to recovery be considered an absolute criterion by which we assess the expectations of these cyberspaces? Relativism may allow us to consider the biological property rights of minority or subjugated groups, including the often silenced voices of these young anorectics. These cyberspatial voices draw attention to the need for young women to have safe environments within which they can construct the often chaotic, embodied, and painful stories of anorexia. However, this should not imply a retreat to an epistemology of solipsism or absolute relativity on the ethics of anorexia. Drawing upon Braidotti (2002: 228), we do not wish to fall into either 'moral relativism [n]or the suspension of ethical judgement'.

To endorse the Pro-Ana position of supporting the rights of an individual to sustain anorexia at any stage of an eating disorder would be to support a position of extreme relativism characterized by a lack of shared understanding of treatment or prognosis and, perhaps, poststructural nihilism (Squires 1993). A position of absolute relativity, while supporting the Pro-Ana position, would preclude any shared understanding of how one should treat anorexia, if at all. Much like the Pro-Ana notion of *lifestyle choice*, rationality in this sense is determined by an individual's own experiences of the world. Conversely, as Pollack (2003: 249) suggests,

> a pedagogical solution of 'enlightening' these women about the oppressive nature of their embodied protest implicitly undermines their agency and thus perpetuates the current interplay of dominant cultural discourses that enticed the anorexic to take a pro-eating disorder stance in the first place.

Yet the contested terrain of this subject is about 'whether someone in the grip of an eating disorder can actually make competent decisions about their quality of life' (Draper 2000: 120). After all, Pro-Ana is a movement that embraces the idea that one can make competent decisions to live with anorexia and refuse treatment. However, as Draper (ibid.: 126) cautions, 'we should be wary of confusing irrational reasons with reasons with which we simply do not agree. Furthermore, we should be wary of confusing either irrationality or strong disagreement with incompetence'. Draper goes on to suggest that a biomedical model of health asserts that those with anorexia 'are not competent to make decisions that relate in any way to food and withdrawing therapy or treating palliatively effectively entails withdrawing feedings' (ibid.: 122). Certainly, there are legitimate moral and ethical reasons why medical intervention in the decisions that a young woman makes about her health is appropriate. But what of those individuals, like many of the cases outlined above, who are not 'broadly incompetent', who 'are studying for school leaving exams or degrees' (Draper 2000: 122) but choose to live their life in a state of starvation? Cyberspatial narratives highlight many of the complexities that mediate these discussions around ethics and the choice to engage in what are seen as problematic practices (such as self-starving). In large part, our medicalization of cyberspace is characterized by this phenomenon. By reading these narratives *along-side* wider cultural scripts about health and illness, they provide new cultural significations about the body and facilitate a dialectical relationship between the social and ethical. Exploring these narratives as alternative features of recovery is particularly important when we consider that despite massive study of and resources available for treating these potentially fatal conditions [eating disorders], they remain pervasive. ... The slow progress made in alleviating eating disorders becomes even more frightening, considering that these conditions are grossly underreported – both their occurrences and fatalities. (Walstrom 2000: 762)

However, as Dias (2003) notes, most studies on recovery from eating disorders have been conducted within a biomedical model, exploring causes and treatments, focusing on the negative factors that might prevent recovery. She argues that what seems absent from the literature is a focus on positive outcome indicators, which are most likely to come in narrative form, rather than measurable indicators. Some authors are beginning to speculate on whether voicing one's desire to retain and embrace anorexia may be a productive aspect of the recovery process:

[A] statement that he [*sic:* the therapist] agrees that the patient is probably better off, all things considered, remaining anorexic, can be the most helpful and often totally new experience for the anorexic. She [*sic*] can approach the task of limited weight gain with much more confidence under such circumstances. (Crisp, *anorexia nervosa, let me be,* cited in Draper 2000: 129)

These are uncomfortable and ethically complex circumstances to accept, requiring an unusual form of empathy with the experience of the sufferer.

Posthumanism: The Absent Present

These interpretations of the online Pro-Ana movement must be seen in the context of broader cybermedicalization issues. It is one example of how the virtualization of identity has led to a prostheticization of the body, which is revealed as a removal process towards an artificial prosthetic – a prosthetic that is designed to *not* fit, to be burdensome. This notion of a prosthetic burden returns us to the main theoretical premises of the book, where the medicalization of cyberspace encompasses the consideration of health outside of the traditional medical environment and within the multi-faceted, non-regulated (rather than unregulated) space of the Internet.

The medicalization of cyberspace embodies the way that medical practice is developing in the contested conditions of postmodernity, where ethical discourse takes place within a space of ambiguous realness. As Braidotti (2002: 2) observes, 'we live in permanent processes of transition, hybridization and nomadization, and these in-between states and stages defy the established modes of theoretical representation'. In keeping with these observations, we have not attempted to assert a single, comprehensive view of the body in cyberspace. Instead, we have explored how questions of materiality and humanness emerge via the context of medicalized cyberspaces. Through our examples, various modes of enacting what Sandberg (2001) describes as 'morphological freedom' have been articulated. The auctioning of a human kidney on eBay, the proanorexia movement and the rhetoric of the first human clone each clarify the broadening base of ethical concern and its challenge to social science.[1] This confrontation takes two forms, the first of which is most clearly espoused by Fuller's (2006) critique of 'bioliberalism,' as fundamentally antithetical to sociology's socialism. Fuller's concern is that the legitimization of such practices leads to a diminishing respect for human subjectivity, and his views are not unlike Fukuyama's (2002) attack on technoprogressive or transhumanist claims. Fuller's encounters with bioethics are part of a series of inquiries by social scientists who have become critical of the politics of bioethics. Over the past few years, a number of other sociologists have offered similar critiques of how bioethics should engage more fully with sociological issues (Haimes 2002; Hedgecoe 2004; de Vries *et al.* 2006; López 2004).[2]

The second confrontation involves the operable mode of sociology, as the study of societies. This is explained usefully through another example. In 2002, designers from the Royal College of Art in London developed a prototype of a telephone tooth implant that would sit permanently lodged in the tooth, rather like a cavity filling.[3] These designers had no intention of developing the product, and so in one sense the episode was a hoax (Metz 2006). Yet the media treated the concept as a genuine product that might arrive soon on the market. The imaginary artefact took on a life of its own and came to constitute the conditions within which such prospects came to matter to previously unengaged communities.[4] Indeed, with the increasing miniaturization of technology to the nano scale, the concept is difficult to dismiss outright, although such applications are nowhere near realization. Again, this reminds us of the examples discussed earlier in the context of David Cronenberg's film *The Fly* (1986). This provocation appeals to the kinds of blurred space that are now characteristic of discussions about the future, where technological possibility is treated as technological probability or inevitability.[5] Perhaps the height of the success for these designers was making the front cover of *Time* magazine, which confirmed the extent of their provocation.

Such future-casting advances the sociological criticisms of futurology in quite interesting ways, and these provocations are inextricable from an analysis of medicalized cyberspace.[6] Indeed, imagining the (ethical) future has become a more legitimate practice for sociologists via the recent trend towards upstream public engagement on science and technology issues, which has, in turn, provoked discussions about the value of *empirical ethics*.[7] While one might discuss the politics and sociology of these possible futures – bioliberalism versus bioconservativism – what seems uncontested is the rebiologization of sociology that the debate presumes. Indeed, Delanty (2002) takes stock of the challenge this provokes by considering how the science of genetics is inevitably socially constructed by individual agency, and so we must look to the social sciences to make sense of this. He goes on to locate these discussions in the context of a public discourse that resembles the upstream engagement debates about science.

Accompanying these conversations is the emerging conceptual lens of *mobility*, which Urry (2000) offers to explain how sociologists must work in a period that is characterized by the absence of societies. We will return to this concept in the conclusion, though it is useful to mention that an integral aspect of this work attends to the digital dimensions of mobile cultures. It offers further support for considering online health discourses as mechanisms through which to make sense of technological identity and its relationship to the officialdom of medicine. However, it is also important to link these ideas with other contemporary health care debates, such as the notion of *medical tourism,* where clients travel the world in search of medical laws that accommodate their particular need or desire. One can include our earlier discussions about body and organ trafficking within such debates.

Like Zylinska (2005), we also revert from the cyborg paradigm in order to apply a more precise, theoretical claim about the medicalization of cyberspace. This is because our claim is only partially connected to the cyborg metaphor (as *cyborg ritual*), which has become only one form of various ways of conceptualizing the implications of machinic interfaces with biology.[8] We also consider that Haraway's cyborg has often entered contemporary academic parlance without taking into account how non-central were her aspirations to talk about the imminence of the cyborg as a posthuman entity.[9] Rather, Haraway's ideal sits comfortably with the idea that there are fewer and fewer reasons to accept clarity over ontological distinctions.[10] Indeed, Haraway suggests as much when proclaiming that 'the cyborg is our ontology; it gives us our politics' (1991: 150), thus invoking our earlier claim about the presence of the anorexic body in Pro-Ana movements. In each of the cases we discuss, the cybernetic organism cannot be reduced to mere information: yet the body is both absent and present in cyberspace.

The concept of presence is a crucial, though contested, notion in studies of digital cultures. Stories of suicide chat rooms (Rajagopal 2004) suggest that communication about sensitive or private issues online can often be accompanied by a weak sense of responsibility in participants that works to counter the quality of the experience. This has implications for what we call the *bioethics of cybermedicine.* Discussions about physical presence are accompanied by criticisms of bioethics as an industry of sorts, which lacks a demonstrated ability to prioritize social needs – such as welfarist conceptions of health care (Purdy 2001; Turner 2003; Zylinska 2005).[11] To this, we also add the commercialization of ethical culture – shopping, eating, energy, tourism, etc. – as further evidence of how the ethical has become *hyphenated* in the sense offered by Žižek (2004), as a surrogate for *genuine* ethical concern. In this manner, the absent presence within bioethics is characterized by its overwhelming presence within the public sphere, and lacking any ability to argue on behalf of basic health care needs. We are both overwhelmed and unassisted by bioethics, to the point where key scholars in the midst of discussions about medicine's future are beginning to think 'beyond bioethics' (Fukuyama and Furger 2007). This situation also explains why our construction of the absent present is ethical: it is the presence of an ethical commitment within cultural studies, which is constituted by an absence of the capability to scrutinize judgements. This is not a criticism of pluralism as such, nor wholly a criticism of those who have pioneered bioethics. Indeed, it is more carefully an appeal to consider what literature should inform bioethical deliberations and to support Callahan (1993: S9) in his counsel that bioethics must continue to 'expand its own horizons'.[12]

Textual Bodies

We have explored the complex interplay that occurs between embodied forms of subjectivity in cyberspace and have endeavoured to show how identities are medicalized through the Internet. We have offered various types of examples that achieve this. Some of our examples reveal how identities are medicalized through their reconfiguration of the relationship between old and new media and the expectations of each as truth makers and truth fakers. Other examples reveal a similar occurrence through their constituting counteractions to legitimate medicalizing phenomenon, as is suggested by the Pro-Ana communities, where self-help and community support are ambiguously read by expert discourses.

Theoretical notions of the textual human, which have been discussed in cyberspatial literature, are intimated by Hayles' (1999) suggestive notion of the posthuman, which privileges informational pattern over material instantiation. However, Hayles' notion may appear to misrepresent how medicalized identities are formed in cyberspace, particularly in relation to the cases of medicalization presented above. Cyberspace is an environment impoverished of flesh and yet, it is a space within which there is a continual engagement with body matters, including health, reproduction, body disorder, and so on. In this sense, cyberspace is the body reincarnate, with essential missing or transformative ingredients. As processes of medicalization operate in cyberspace, one is drawn into a perpetual engagement with body matters, though in an environment where the body is sometimes considered to be missing. As such, these processes invoke and embody an ongoing sentimental search for bodily attributes. As Kroker and Weinstein (1994) deseribe,

> Why be nostalgic? The old body type was always OK, but the wired body with its micro-flesh, multi-media channeled ports, cybernetic fingers, and bubbling neuro-brain finely interfaced to the 'standard operating system' of the Internet is infinitely better. Not really the wired body of sci-fi with its mutant designer look, or body flesh with its ghostly reminders of nineteenth-century philosophy, but the hyper-texted body as both: a wired nervous system embedded in living (dedicated) flesh.

Prosthetic Burdens

Our analysis claims that the body is neither obsolete, as Stelarc (1997) proclaims, nor does it 'no longer exist' (Kroker and Kroker 1987); the digital form does not obscure the body. Instead, it enables the development of an alternativee, *prosthetic* body to emerge, which brings with it both new and old burdens. As Braidotti (2002: 227) notes, 'today's body is immersed in a set of technologically mediated practices of prosthetic extension'. However, before we explain this further, it is necessary to clarify the meaning of prosthesis and why we claim that a new form of prosthetic – to replace the last prosthesis, Viagra – is a useful articulation of cyberspace's medicalization, compared with cyborg manifestos.

Prostheses are artificial devices that replace absent (body) parts, though virtual bodies lack no visual parts. The 'missing part' is imag(in)ary, again, and the (ab) users pursue some truth of being that is entirely fabricated. The sites of these medicalized, prosthetic identities are hypothetical cyberspace communities. Notably, however, the Web does *not* play a constructive role here. Rather, the underlying ideologies embodied by cyberspaces reflect the mediatory nature of cyberspace. The images are indicative of a broader synthetic that is valued because it defies its designation as *virtual,* as non-reality. This is the discourse that drives Hayles' (1999) informational human. The cyberspatial prosthetic is an informational prosthetic, necessarily a mask for some*one* rather than some*thing.*

In this sense, the body-self narratives of young anorectics operate within a 'mediated co-presence, where the real and the virtual enmesh and interact' (Mules 2000). Thus, our language for engaging the cybermedical problematic resists the complete overcoming of cyborgisms in favour of an emerging prosthetic, outlined in various recent texts (see Smith and Morra 2006). We do not advance the idea that online discussion boards or blogs are indicative of bodies becoming less *fleshy,* or neutralized into mere information. Rather, we articulate them as ambiguously transformative, absent but present. As Wright (1999: 24) indicates, '"I" may become text, seemingly free of gender or racial identity, but both text and fluid identity remain prosthetic'. Extending Wright (1999: 23), we have argued that the cybermedicalization of the body is a further 'step towards the depoliticisation of gender'. In this sense, it can be characterized as *post*-gender, but not *past*-gender. It is a critical reworking of gender boundaries, rather than the complete effacing of them. It also provides a reason for scepticism over the distinctiveness of cyberfeminism as a discrete discourse. To reiterate our earlier point, prostheticization does not lead to the effacing of gendered discourses, but is the means through which to rework some of the boundaries.

NOTES

1. Indeed, the convergence of these areas is made evident by the existence of both scholarly studies of and political will to support work on the 'public engagement with ethics' (see Miah 2005). Ashcroft (2003) describes this as the 'empirical turn' within bioethics.
2. For more general ethics and social science papers see the September 2006 issue of *Sociology of Health and Illness.*
3. Thanks to James Auger for sharing this story at one of the Royal College of Art's Design Interactions sessions in October 2006.

4. This is reminiscent of Žižek's story about the filming of 'David Lean's *Doctor Zhivago* in a Madrid suburb in 1964'. As part of the performance, local inhabitants were gathered to 'sing the "Internationale" in a scene of mass demonstration' (Žižek 2004: xii). The happening developed to a point where other residents thought it genuine and believed that it signalled the fall of Franco. As Žižek writes, 'these magic moments of illusory freedom' constitute what we articulate here as the 'reality of the virtual' (ibid.: 3).

5. Indeed, the bioethics community can be quite neatly divided into those who accept this premise and try to rewrite ethics on this basis, and those who contest it.

6. For examples of this broader digital paradigm through which to understand emerging technology, see Nayar (2004).

7. One might also invoke the concept of 'public sociology' (Burawoy, cited in Brewer 2007: 176) as indicative of this trend within the social sciences to address future issues. Delanty (2002) also makes explicit this problematic by noting that, in the context of genetics, 'scientific knowledge must be mediated by civic cultures of knowledge' (p. 288).

8. An alternative 'mundane cyborg' is articulated by Peterson (2007). This emphasizes the everyday function of the Internet in a way that is analogous to other household machines, such as refrigerators and coffee makers.

9. Indeed, at NYU in 2006, Haraway made explicit her rejection of this kind of posthumanism, which she more precisely wants to replace with 'ahumanism' a la Bruno Latour (personal communication, 2007, see also Haraway 2006b).

10. As Sobchack (2006) notes when discussing the prosthetic of below-the-knee amputee athlete/actress/model Aimee Mullins: the legs 'confuse such categories as human and animal and animate and inanimate in precisely the ironic way that Donna Haraway's cyborg was originally meant to do' (p. 35).

11. It is interesting to note that Zylinska's chapter on bioethics is titled '*Bio-ethics and cyberfeminism*', thus unavoidably being drawn into questions raised by Žižek in his 'Against hyper-ethics' (2004: 123). Zylinska's use of italics within her title suggests a similar concern about making ethics provisional in an era where new technology appears to raise new ethical questions, if not new ethical theories.

12. In more detail, Callahan notes the rise of bioethics in the United States as connected to liberal ideology. Perhaps the increasing need for new horizons reveals something about politics within the United States, though this has no necessary bearing on other political contexts. However, it is relevant to consider how the US approach to bioethics and medical ethics has informed other geographical regions.

REFERENCES

Biocca, F. 1997. The Cyborg's Dilemma: Progressive Embodiment in Virtual Environments. *Journal of Computer-Mediated Communications* 3(2). Available at http://www.ascusc.org/jcmc/Vol3/Issue2/Biocca2.html.

Braidotti, R. 2002. *Metamorphoses: Towards a Materialist Theory of Becoming*. Cambridge: Polity Press.

Brewer, J.D. 2007. Review: *The New Sociological Imagination* by Steve Fuller. *European Journal of Social Theory* 10: 173–6.

Butler, J. 1993. *Bodies that Matter: On the Discursive Limits of "Sex"*. London: Routledge.

Callahan, D. 1993. Why America Accepted Bioethics. *Hastings Center Report* 23: S8–S9.

Chesley, E.B., J.D. Alberts, J.D. Klein, and R.E. Kreipe. 2003. Pro or Con? Anorexia Nervosa and the Internet. *Journal of Adolescent Health* 32: 1123–4.

Coyle, F. 2006. Posthuman Geographies? Biotechnology, Nature and the Demise of the Autonomous Human Subject. *Social and Cultural Geography* 7: 505–23.

Delanty, G. 2002. Constructivism, Sociology and the New Genetics. *New Genetics and Society* 21(3): 279–89.

de Vries, R., L. Turner, K. Orfali, and C. Bosk. 2006. Social Science and Bioethics: The Way Forward. *Sociology of Health and Illness* 28: 665–77.

Dias, K. 2003. The Ana Sanctuary: Women's Pro-Anorexia Narratives in Cyberspace. *Journal of International Women's Studies* 4(2): 31–45.

Douglas, M. 1965. *Purity and Danger*. London: Routledge.

Draper, H. 2000. Anorexia Nervosa and Respecting a Refusal of Life-Prolonging Therapy: A Limited Justification. *Bioethics* 14(2): 120–33.

Ferreday, D. J. 2003. Unspeakable Bodies: Erasure and Embodiment in Pro-Ana Communities. *International Journal of Cultural Studies* 6(3): 277–95.

Fox, N.J., K.J. Ward, and A.J. O'Rourke. 2005. Pro-Anorexia, Weight-Loss Drugs and the Internet: An 'Anti-recovery' Explanatory model of Anorexia. *Sociology of Health and Illness* 27(2: 944–71.

Frank, A. 1997. Illness as a Moral Occasion: Restoring Agency to Ill People. *Health: An Interdisciplinary Journal for the Social Study of Health, Illness and Medicine* 1: 131–48.

Fukuyama, F. 2002. *Our Posthuman Future: Consequences of the Biotechnology Revolution*. London: Profile.

Fukuyama, F., and F. Furger. 2007. *Beyond Bioethics: A Proposal for Modernizing the Regulation of Human Biotechnologies*. Washington, DC: Paul H. Nitze School of Advanced International Studies.

Fuller, S. 2006. *The New Sociological Imagination*. London: Sage.

Gray, C.H. 2002. *Cyborg Citizen: Politics in the Posthuman Age*. London: Routledge.

Haimes, E. 2002. What can the Social Sciences Contribute to the Study of Ethics? Theoretical, Empirical and Substantive Considerations. *Bioethics* 16: 89–113.

Haraway, D. 1991. A Cyborg Manifesto: Science, Technology, and Socialist-Feminism in the Late Twentieth Century. In *Simians, Cyborgs and Women: The Reinvention of Nature*. New York: Routledge.

Haraway, D. 2006. 'When We Have Never Been Human, What Is to be Done?' Interview with Donna Haraway. *Theory, Culture and Society* 23(7–8): 135–58.

Hayles, N.K. 1999. *How We Became Posthuman: Virtual Bodies in Cybernetics, Literature, and Informatics*. London: University of Chicago Press.

Hedgecoe, A.M. (2004). Critical Bioethics: Beyond the Social Science Critique of Applied Ethics. *Bioethics* 18: 120–43.

Juengst, E.T. 1998. What Does *Enhancement* Mean? In E. Parens (ed.), *Enhancing Human Traits: Ethical and Social Implications*. Washington, DC: Georgetown University Press, pp. 29–47.

Kroker, A., and M. Kroker. 1987. Body Digest: Theses on the Disappearing Body in the Hyper-Modern Condition. *Canadian Journal of Political and Social Theory* 11: i–xvi.

Kroker, A. and M. Weinstein. 1996. The Hyper-Texted Body, or Nietzsche Gets a Modem. *CTHEORY*. Available at http://www.ctheory.net/articles.aspc?id=144.

López, J. 2004. How Sociology Can Save Bioethics. Maybe. *Sociology of Health and Illness* 26: 875–96.

Metz, R. Lying through their Teeth. 2006. *Wired*. Available at http://www.wired.com/culture/lifestyle/news/2006/04/70601?currentpage=all.

Mitra, A. 1997. Virtual Commonality: Looking for India on the Internet. In S. G. Jones (ed.), *Virtual Culture: Identity and Communication in CyberSociety*. London: Sage, pp. 55–79.

Mules, W. 2000. Virtual Culture, Time and Images: Beyond Representation. *M/C: A Journal of Media and Culture* 3(2). Available at http://journal.media-culture.org.au/0005/images.php (accessed July 2003).

Nayar, P.K. 2004. *Virtual Worlds: Culture and Politics in the Age of Cybertechnology*. New Delhi: Sage.

Peterson, S.M. 2007. Mundane Cyborg Practice: Material Aspects of Broadband Internet Use. *Convergence* 13: 79–91.

Pollack, D. 2003. Pro-Eating Disorder Websites: What Should Be the Feminist Response? *Feminism and Psychology* 13(2): 246–51.

Purdy, L.M. 2001. Medicalization, Medical Necessity, and Feminist Medicine. *Bioethics* 15: 248–61.

Rajagopal, S. 2004. Editorial: Suicide Pacts and the Internet. *British Medical Journal* 329: 1298–9.

Rose, N. 2007. Beyond Medicalization. *The Lancet* 369: 700–1.

Sandberg, A. 2001. Morphological Freedom: Why We Not Just Want It, but Need It. Paper given at the TransVision Conference, Berlin, June 22–24.

Smith, A.D., and D. R. Manna. 2004. Exploring the Trust factor in e-Medicine. *Online Information Review* 28: 346–55.

Sobchack, V. 2006. A Leg to Stand On: Prosthetics, Metaphor, and Materiality. In M. Smith and J. Morra (eds.), *The Prosthetic Impulse: From a Posthuman Present to a Biocultural Future*. Cambridge, MA: MIT Press, pp. 7–41.

Squires, J. 1993. Introduction. In J. Squires (ed.) *Principled Positions: Postmodernism and the Rediscovery of Value*. London: Lawrence & Wishart, pp. 1–16.

Stelarc. 1997. From Psycho to Cyber Strategies: Prosthetics, Robotics and Remote Existence. *Cultural Values* 1: 214–49.

Turner, L. 2003. Has the President's Council on Bioethics Missed the Boat? *British Medical Journal* 327: 629.

Urry, J. 2000. *Sociology beyond Societies: Mobilities for the Twenty-First Century*. London: Routledge.

Wakeford, N. 1999. Gender and the Landscapes of Computing in an Internet Café. In M. Crang, P. Crang, and J. May (eds.), *Virtual Geographies: Bodies, Space and Relations*. London and New York: Routledge, pp. 178–201.

Walstrom, M.K. 2000. "You Know, Who's the Thinnest?": Combating Surveillance and Creating Safety in Coping with Eating Disorders Online. *CyberPsychology and Behavior* 3(5).

Wright, A. 1999. Partial Bodies: Re-establishing Boundaries, Medical and Virtual. In Cutting Edge: The Women's Research Group (ed.), *Desire by Design: Body, Territories and New Technologies*. London: I. B. Tauris.

Žižek, S. 2004. *Organs without Bodies: On Deleuze and Consequences*. London: Routledge.

Zylinska, J. 2005. *The Ethics of Cultural Studies*. London: Continuum.

16

BIOCOLONIALISM, GENOMICS, AND THE DATABASING OF THE POPULATION

Eugene Thacker

The Map, the Territory, and the Population

When in the early 1990s the U.S. government – funded Human Genome Diversity Project (HGDP) drafted plans for a large genetic database of distinct ethnic populations, it was met with a great deal of controversy and criticism.[1] Led by scientists such as Luca Cavalli-Sforza and Allan Wilson – both pioneers in the field of population genetics – the HGDP's original aim was to collect DNA from individuals of genetically isolated populations around the world in order to reconstruct the evolutionary path of humankind.[2] But the initial planning sessions, which were funded by the U.S. National Science Foundation, the National Human Genome Research Center, the National Institute for General Medical Sciences, and the DoE, quickly became mired in disagreements over which populations to choose for sampling and the best way to define what *population* means in this context, a context that is as much cultural and anthropological as it is scientific. In addition, groups such as the Rural Advancement Foundation International (RAFI) and Third World Network voiced their concern over the possible implications of such research for those largely indigenous communities who would have their genetic material housed in cell lines in U.S. institutes. Although HGDP committee members denied that there is any economic motive behind their proposal, critics expressed concern over the way in which indigenous communities were effectively cut out of the planning process.

... Native American groups in the United States accused the HGDP of practicing *biocolonialism*, a term that has been used frequently in describing the practice

Eugene Thacker, "Biocolonialism, Genomics, and the Databasing of the Population," pp. 133–72 and notes from Eugene Thacker, *The Global Genome: Biotechnology, Politics, and Culture* (Cambridge, MA: MIT Press, 2005).

of sampling genetic material for potential genes of value (be it medical or economic value).[3] The governments of Panama and the Solomon Islands separately protested to the international community over the patents (one of which was subsequently dropped), and indigenous communities, nongovernmental organizations, and South Pacific governments lobbied for a "lifeforms patent protection treaty."[4]

... Such concern and dissent forced the HGDP committee to draft up a set of "model ethical protocols" (MEPs), and in 1993 the HGDP formed the North American Regional Committee, whose aim was to come up with acceptable criteria for the collection of genetic material from human populations.[5] ... Since that time, however, the HGDP has been conspicuously silent, and there has been relatively no news or updates on the HGDP's progress.[6]

Much of the HGDP's curious disappearing act has to do, certainly, with the bioethical ties in which the HGDP has been involved and with the combination of criticism being voiced by groups such as RAFI and the HGDP's having been "marked" by the media.[7] ... Problem parallel developments within biotech and genetics have emerged, more or less taking up the "diversity problem" that the HGDP dealt with in the 1990s: bioinformatics and genomics. As we have seen, bioinformatics involves the use of computer and networking technologies in the organization of updated, networked, and interactive genomic databases being used by research institutions, the biotech industry, medical genetics, and the pharmaceutical industry.[8] ...

One of this chapter's arguments is that these two trends – the decrease in the HGDP's visibility, and the rise of bioinformatics – are inextricably connected. ... Genomics – the technologically assisted study of the total DNA, or genome, of organisms – currently commands a significant part of the biotech industry's attention. In economic as well as scientific terms, genomics has for some years promised to become the foundation on which a future medical genetics and pharmacogenomics will be based.[9] This chapter attempts to draw out some of the linkages between the biotech industry and the emphasis within genomics programs on diversification and the collection of particular populations' genomes into computer databases. ...

Blood, Sex, Data

With the sheer quantity of material being generated by such globalized science endeavors as the human genome projects, the need for a biotech-infotech science has become the more prominent, if only for organizational and managerial reasons. Biotech corporations such as Affymetrix, Incyte, and Perkin-Elmer not only specialize in research and development, but also emphasize product development.[10] Bioinformatics promises to deliver the tools that will make genomic science an information science and propel the human genome projects into the next phase of "post-genomic science."[11] With the aid of bioinformatics technologies, the "public" genome project, originally cast by the NIH as a 15-year endeavor, was shortened to a 3-year effort, with a "working draft" presented – not without a great deal of fanfare – during the summer of 2000.[12] Biotech corporations such as Celera and Incyte have initiated their own corporate-framed and privately run human genome mapping projects. …

The recent rise in genomics projects, especially those geared toward unique gene pools and genetic difference, has implied the hybridization of a new practice of statistics and medicine, combining studies in population genetics and new techniques in genomic mapping. This application of the genetic study of the genomes of specific populations – what has been called *population genomics* – brings together a lengthy tradition in the study of populations, hereditary patterns, and inherited characteristics with the contemporary development of large-scale genomic sequencing and analysis for clinical medicine.[13] … The field of population genomics thus contrasts itself to the universal human genome projects. Its focus is an entity whose definition is still in some dispute – the "population." Its emphasis is on those genetic elements that make a human population distinct from "the human" itself: genetic markers, STSs, haplotypes (HAPs), and SNPs.[14]

Biotech companies such as deCODE, Myriad Genetics, and Gemini Genomics are focusing on the genomes of populations with histories of a low degree of migration and a low frequency of hybridity (Icelandic, Mormon, and Newfoundland communities, respectively).[15] Other companies, such as DNA Sciences Inc., are focusing on building a volunteer-based genetic health database to aid in the fight against disease. DNA Science's Gene Trust databank uses the GenBank model to archive medical, genetic, and health-related data (GenBank holds the IHGSC's human genome data).[16] … Still other companies and research labs are focusing on the minute genetic sequence differences between individuals – polymorphisms, SNPs, and HAPs – which may be the keys to individual genetic susceptibility to disease and, by extension, to pharmacogenomic approaches to drug development.[17] …

These and other population genomics projects (see table 16.1) have met with a great deal of controversy, most notably from the populations that are the object of study and data agglomeration. For instance, in Iceland a group of scientists, physicians, and citizens called Mannvernd continues to contest the ethical implications behind the IHSD.[18] Contentious ethical issues have also arisen in relation to the Tonganese genome (where Autogen had aimed to begin a genomics project), the government-sponsored Estonian genome, and efforts to establish a Korean genome (headed by Macrogen).[19] … Such concerns have prompted many population genomics projects to take on responsibility for ethical issues. For instance, the U.K. BioBank has established an independent ethics and governance council to, oversee ethical, policy, and legal issues that will inevitably arise with such broad genetic sampling endeavors.[20] … In 2002, the World Medical Association (WMA), along with the WHO, announced the "Declaration on Ethical Considerations Regarding Health Databases," which would, among other things, give priority to the individual patient's right in such databasing ventures.[21]

TABLE 16.1 Population Genome Projects

Institute	Subjects
Estonian National Gene Bank Project (Estonian Genome Foundation, Estonian government)	Estonian volunteers
The Gene Trust (DNA Sciences, Inc.)	More than 100,000 U.S. volunteers via the Internet
Genomic Research in African-American Pedigrees (G-RAP; Howard University)	African American volunteers
Icelandic Health Sector Database (IHSD, deCODE Genomics)	More than 280,000 Icelanders
Korean Gene Bank (Macrogen)	Korean volunteers
Mormon Gene Bank (Myriad Genetics)	Mormon communities (United States)
Newfoundland Gene Bank (New-found Genomics, a spin-off of Gemini Genomics)	Half a million Newfoundlander volunteers
P3G (Public Population Program in Genomics)	Includes U.K. BioBank, CARTaGENE (Quebec), Estonian National GeneBank Project, and GenomEUtwin Project (Finland)
Swedish Gene Bank (UmanGenomics)	More than 250,000 Swedes from Väterbotten
Tonga Gene Bank (Autogen)	More than 180,000 Tonganese in Australia
U.K. BioBank (Wellcome Trust, Medical Research Council, and the U.K. Department of Health)	Half a million U.K. volunteers

... But perhaps the most noteworthy distinction is not between population genomics projects, but between recent projects that emphasize finding specific-population genomes and the earlier "biocolonialist" projects such as the HGDP. Whereas the HGDP proposal was an example of Western scientists gathering or appropriating genetic material from mostly indigenous populations around the world, the newer population genomics projects are by and large in-house operations. Population genomics projects such as the IHSD or the U.K. BioBank are examples of "national" genomics programs exercised reflexively: Icelandic scientists sampling Icelandic citizens to gain knowledge about the Icelandic genome and, perhaps, to aid in the health of common diseases affecting the Icelandic body politic (or so the story goes). If this is biocolonialism, it is arguably a very different sort of exploitation: government sanctioned, driven by national industry, and completely voluntary. As Michael Fortun notes, the study of such projects must therefore "trace how these rhetorics of exoticism and national difference are deployed not only by 'foreign' commentators and media outlets, but also have more 'domestic' origins."[22] What is produced in such projects is not only a database, but, in a sense, a new concept of what *population* may come to mean in the context of a genetics-based medicine and health-care paradigm. Fortun adds that such population databases "are like value-added export products designed to circulate in a global rhetorical economy."[23]

... In this sense, population genomics is part of a much broader process constituting what Michel Foucault calls "bio-history," or "the entry of life into history." For Foucault, new scientific techniques, along with specific governmental modes of intervention and regulation, culminate in the inclusion of "phenomena peculiar to the life of the human species into the order of knowledge and power, into the sphere of political techniques."[24]

How is the bio-history of population genomics constituted? Foucault, as is well known, argues that the nineteenth century saw a passage from a bio-history centered around blood (kinship) to one centrally concerned with sex and sexuality. As Foucault notes, the blood relation was closely tied to "a society in which the systems of alliance, the political form of the sovereign, the differentiation into orders and castes, and the value of descent lines were predominant." Although many of these elements did not disappear completely, the nineteenth century marks, for Foucault, a shift in emphasis: "Through the themes of health, progeny, race, the future of the species, the vitality of the social body, power spoke of sexuality and to sexuality." The emergence of new scientific disciplines (psychopathology, germ theory, evolutionary biology) as well as a set of new social concerns (deviancy, hygiene, poverty, homosexuality) culminated in this shift "from a symbolics of blood to an analytics of sexuality."[25]

In the case of population genomics, it is clear that the concerns of "health, progeny, race" within a national context are still relevant. The particular challenge to population genomics endeavors – a challenge that marks them out as being unique – is that they must redefine the genomic "population" in ways that are congruent with the technical paradigm of the computer database. ... If this is the case, then the governmental and medical concern over the health of the population will shift emphasis from sex and sexuality to a notion of population defined in genetic and informatic terms: *blood, sex, data.*

In order to investigate these claims, it will be helpful to consider how *population* is defined within population genetics, paying particular attention to the biohistorical and biopolitical aspects of which Foucault speaks.

The Genome Race

Many of the discomforts with population genomics and DNA sampling become clearer when we look at how *race* and *population* are articulated according to modern population genetics.[26]

[...]

Luca Cavalli-Sforza, who originally headed the HGDP and is a leading researcher in population genetics, provides us with the following statement concerning race: "A race is a group of individuals that we can recognize as biologically different from others. To be scientifically 'recognized,' the differences between a population that we would like to call a race and neighboring populations must be statistically significant according to some defined criteria."[27]

Consider this definition in light of a similar one given by early population geneticists such as Theodosius Dobzhansky: "Races may be defined as Mendelian populations of a species which differ in the frequencies of one or more genetic variants, gene alleles, or chromosomal structures."[28] As historians of biology note, part of the debate in the early twentieth century between American Mendelians and British population geneticists lay in the disagreement over how to define a population.[29] ...

The first thing to note is that in this formulation race is, implicitly, biologically determined: as Cavalli-Sforza indicates, a race is a human collectivity defined by biological properties (be those phenotypic or genotypic). Race, for population geneticists, is biological. ...

On the phenotypic, or visible, level, the concept of race has long been tied to a biological determinism that initially grew out of early colonial travel narratives to Africa and the Americas. ...

In many ways, it is difficult to discuss the concept of race without some reference to the role that modern science has played in the legitimizing articulation of racial and ethnic difference. Many early modern travel narratives depicted bizarre natives and races from Africa or the Americas and often relied on the discourse of the fantastic or the monstrous, describing others who were both debased and repulsive.[30] Darwinism and natural history during the nineteenth century helped to give such fantastic accounts a certain basis in scientific fact.[31] They also helped to explain, through evolutionism and classificatory biology, the basis and reasons for such differences. This basis in visible characteristics is such a core element of our everyday notions of race that it is difficult to think otherwise. Through the sciences, elements such as skin color became the set of characterizing morphologies that defined a given race and that explained that race's evolutionary development according to such factors as natural habitat and climate.[32]

[...] A biological definition of race makes use of an abstracting biological science to explain away the social and cultural dimensions of race.

This also means that race must be scientifically defined, which is my second point. That race is something recognized is in itself significant; that race is scientifically defined, or recognized through science, means that the possibilities of other forms of communal recognition are excluded. ...

On the genotypic level, or the contemporary level of genetic codes and sequences, race has been further articulated along its biological determinist lines. This articulation has not only added further scientific "truth" to the difference of races, but also brought to light differences that are exclusively genetic (that is, which are not seen but exist only as differences in genetic code). ...

In one sense, the genetic basis for racial identification further extends the explanatory power of Darwinism and modern biology, but it also initiates a new type of biological determinism with regard to race. If, in projects such as population genome databases, race can be identified genetically – that is, according to sequences of genetic code – then the urgency of clear phenotypic markers between races is simply displaced by an emphasis on genetic markers. These genetic markers of difference can be visible and nonvisible (expressed and unexpressed), but with this unique mode of racial identification race becomes not only biologically determined but informatically determined.

Without a doubt, this approach is still biological determinism; the emphasis on abstract genetic code in no way liquidates the role that race and racism play in modern science's study and classification of populations. If anything, a genetic-based approach to race provides a mathematical proof (an informatic proof, as in DNA fingerprinting) of racial identification. It also provides a new means of quantifying racial hybridity, according to varying gene frequencies (a method used in population genetics but also applicable to individuals). ...

This scientific approach implies a methodological approach, which is that race is articulated through numbers. That scientific recognition is a bioscience of mathematics. More traditional population genetics approaches focus on frequencies of traits, demographic distribution of traits, and probability of gene migrations or inheritance of traits. But, as Cavalli-Sforza shows, the rise of genomics, new mathematical methods, and computer technology means that populations and races become informatic objects of analysis: "Within genetics itself, we want to collect as much information about as many genes as possible, which would allow us to use the 'law of large numbers' in the calculation of probabilities."[33] ...

From the population genetics perspective, particular populations – be they objects of archaeological study or of the study of Third World collectivities – are tied to nationality not only through social and political linkages, but also through biological ones. According to the biological determinism of early race theories and the discourses of monstrosity, if one was born into a certain nation, one was also born into a certain race and even into a certain culture extending from that race.[34] This connection between biological race and the geopolitics of nationality can become the opportunity for a range of situations, from colonial expansion to First World aid to economic globalization.

From Population Genetics to Population Genomics

Population geneticists traditionally look to a theory called the Hardy-Weinberg equilibrium to assess the degree to which a population can be defined as such, and the degree to which knowledge about that population will be minimally affected by the noise of other influences The Hardy-Weinberg theory, first developed in 1908, makes the broad claim that although genes may shuffle and recombine within a population, the total genetic makeup of the population remains the same.[35]

[...]

[T]he Hardy-Weinberg theory isolates all those elements that deter a population from maintaining a homeostasis with its overall gene pool or genetic frequency. A population thus defined is not only entirely removed from environment, external influence, or context, but such a definition also recuperates biological dynamics within an overarching static framework. This emphasis on information sciences such as statistics gives rise to specific techniques, a few of which can be mentioned here.

Population geneticists use the concept of "genetic distance" to study human collectivities and their evolutionary histories.[36] For modern evolutionary biology, genetic alterations happen for one of four reasons: mutation, or a random alteration in the genetic sequence, which is passed on to subsequent generations (and which may or may not affect the organism); natural selection, or changes in the organism (genetic and otherwise), usually in response to environmental conditions; genetic drift, or the complex fluctuations of particular genetic traits or genes within a stable population; and genetic migration, or the geographical movement of peoples out of one collectivity and into another.

[...]

Within the concept of genetic distance is a strong linkage between territory, population, and biology. Scientists such as Cavalli-Sforza explain race in terms of biological determinism and biological necessity. The reasons Cavalli-Sforza gives for migration – overpopulation, food shortages, low reproductive rates – are based on a biological pragmatism. But can this teleological, determinist framework adequately explain genetic variation, especially when at the genetic level many variations appear to have no connection to biological survival?

With this in mind, we can see that the field of population genetics has left several areas unconsidered, areas that at first glance are nonbiological, but that on closer inspection are intimately related to the concerns of population genetics. For instance, if a great deal of genetic change occurs via unexplained or random processes, do not these warrant some radically new approaches to the study of population, instead of accounting for random variation simply by mathematical analysis? If a great deal of our polymorphisms in SNPs reside in "junk DNA," does this not this suggest a more complex network of genetic differences, working to produce a wide range of qualitatively different polymorphisms?

Furthermore, if for a moment we accept Cavalli-Sforza's biological determinism, changes within populations would be the result of a response to environmental changes (climate changes for instance). This conclusion suggests that the human organism has a great deal of adaptability at the genetic level, and, indeed, much of evolutionary biology supports the idea (though through a long-term, gradualist approach). But what about horizontal biological adaptability, not through generations, but between individuals and collectivities? To some extent, we adapt all the time in new contexts, new environments. Are these adaptations simply elements of synchronic genetic adaptability?

In this perspective, genetic variation, biodiversity, and gene recombinations may occur; indeed, they even define the internal character of a population. But they are constrained by the fact that they should maintain the population's overall genomic makeup. From a biosocial perspective, a pure population, or a healthy population, is one that maintains a regularity in its genetic makeup (and assumedly in its phenotypic makeup), allows for conservative internal recombination, and can be studied using statistical and probabilistic means – isolated, static, and ahistorical.

Each and Every

Thus far, we have seen how the controversies surrounding biocolonialism stem in part from the way in which genetic science inscribes *race* biologically and from the way in which population genetics and genomics reinscribes *population* mathematically. If these fields view their object of study – the "population" – through genetic and informatic lenses, then what social and political effects might such approaches have?

One result is that population genomics, in the way it stitches together genomes, governments, and corporations, forms a novel type of biopolitical power, one in which the biological – and social – population is reconstituted through the high technologies of genomics and bioinformatics. This biopolitical dimension to population genomics is not simply the exercise of sovereign power, as if genome projects are an attempt to instill top-down apparatuses of power. Rather, what is at stake is "the biological existence of a population," the point at which the health of a population becomes isomorphic with the health of a nation and the wealth of the nation.[37]

For Foucault, *biopolitics* was this technoscientific incorporation of the "life" of a population into a set of political and economic concerns. In its most assertive forms, biopolitics was not a negative, repressive power, but a power that "exerts a positive influence on life, that endeavors to administer, optimize, and multiply it, subjecting it to precise controls and comprehensive regulations." At the very least, biopolitics was a political relation in which state and economic forces took up the "task of administeting life."[38] ...

Biopolitics, then, implies some political and economic incorporation of scientific and technological notions of the "life of the population." Foucault distinguishes biopolitics from "anatomo-politics," the latter that type of power relation that dealt primarily with individuated bodies of subjects, which were rendered docile within a range of social institutions. Whereas anatomo-politics worked through institutional disciplinarization (in the prison, the military barracks, the school, the hospital), biopolitics "focused on the species body, the body imbued with the mechanics of life and serving as the basis of the biological processes: propagation, births and mortality, the level of health, life expectancy and longevity, with all the conditions that can cause these to vary."[39] Whereas the disciplinary mechanisms of anatomo-politics were addressed to the individual, anatomical body, the regulatory mechanisms of biopolitics were addressed to the species body, or to the population. "Their supervision was effected through an entire series of interventions and regulatory controls: *a biopolitics of the population.*"[40] The difference between these two types of power relations – anatomo-politics and biopolitics – is thus also a difference in two approaches to the "power over life." For Foucault, they are historically overlapping, rather than opposed to each other: "After the anatomo-politics of the human body established in the course of the eighteenth century, we have, at the end of that century, the emergence of something that is no longer an anatomo-politics of the human body, but what I would call a 'biopolitics' of the human race."[41]

This shift in power relations had a number of consequences. One is that a biological and medical notion of "population" became the primary concern for state and economic interests.[42] Though the "life" of a body politic is an implicit concern in all political thinking, the emergence of biopolitics, for Foucault, is a specific concern with the population as a biological entity, such that "biological existence was reflected in political existence."[43] The notion of a biologically defined population gained much currency in the eighteenth century from political economists such as Thomas Malthus and, later, Adam Smith, David Ricardo, and John Stuart Mill. Malthus's *Essay on the Principle of Population* (first published in 1798, then modified in 1803) put forth the famous and largely discounted argument that a population grows at a geometrical rate (1, 2, 4, 8), but the resources to sustain that population grow only at an arithmetical rate (1, 2, 3, 4). If this argument is accepted, then the population, if unchecked, will outgrow the resources that can sustain it. For Malthus, the concern was that this discrepancy would lead not only to overpopulation, but potentially to an increase in poverty and subsequently moral degradation.[44] For this reason, Malthus acknowledged the negative controls of nature (e.g., famine), while also promoting the positive controls of "moral restraint" (e.g., birth control). In combining mathematical analyses of population growth with a social and moral concern for the health of a population, he formulated a biopolitical concern of political economy. The population is not only biological at its basis, but, as a social entity, it is constantly threatened by "misery and vice," or by overpopulation, unchecked reproduction, and promiscuity.[45] Furthermore, the population is not just a biological or social entity, but, more important, a political and economic one. In his *Principles of Political Economy*, Malthus acknowledged a relation between population and wealth, but that "population alone cannot create an effective demand for wealth."[46] For Malthus, production is not always the same as reproduction; the practical application of political economy in this period was thus to regulate, modulate, and control the population, rather than simply to promote its growth as a source of production itself. "The question really is, whether encouragements to population, or even the natural tendency of population to increase beyond the funds destined for its maintenance, will, or will not, alone furnish an adequate stimulus to the increase of wealth."[47]

In addition to this biological – but also political – definition of *population*, a second consequence follows from biopolitics: the emphasis on mathematical and informatic-based approaches to studying the population. In his discussion of biopolitics, Foucault makes frequent reference to the fields of statistics, demographics, and other mathematical methods used in political economy to account for birth and death rates, the spread of epidemics, and the monitoring of citizens' well-being by health officers. Ian Hacking, in his history of statistics during the nineteenth century, suggests that the rise of such mathematical fields occurred in conjunction with a medical view of human norms as regulated by "laws of dispersion" rather than with a deterministic view of "human nature." The development of statistics and probabilistic methods to measure risks, dangers, and tendencies was part of the long process whereby "society became statistical."[48] The statistical assessment of the health of a population was among the first areas to be affected by these methods. Hacking argues that statistical and probabilistic methods played a central role in the expansion of information regarding populations. Whereas such information for much of Great Britain prior to 1815 had been limited largely to births, deaths, and marriages, by the mid-nineteenth century a number of professional committees and societies dedicated themselves to articulating the "statistics of sickness": that biological processes such as health or illness could be accounted for through mathematical techniques. "Statistical law was on the march, conquering new territory," such as the role of occupation, poverty, age, and frequency of illness.[49] As Hacking notes, "a new type of law came into being, analogous to the laws of nature, but pertaining to people."[50] In this process, the indeterminacy of natural selection, combined with strict laws of biological selection, would produce a tension-filled zone in which statistical and informatics-based methods reconfigured the population as a nondeterministic yet regulatory entity. Hacking's historical context is nineteenth-century industrialism, but his comments resonate with contemporary population genomics: "The avalanche of numbers, the erosion of determinism, and the invention of normalcy are embedded in the grander topics of the Industrial Revolution. The acquisition of numbers by the populace, and the professional lust for precision in measurement, were driven by familiar themes of manufacture, mining, trade, health, railways, war, empire."[51]

Finally, a third consequence of biopolitics is that this combination of a biological definition of a "population" and a set of statistical and informatic approaches for studying (indeed, producing) the "population" culminates in a flexible, variable, differentiated body politic. On the one hand, Foucault's description of biopolitics places emphasis on the mass quality of population, the result of "collective phenomena which have their economic and political effects, and that they become pertinent only at the mass level."[52] Yet – and this is equally important for Foucault – this massification of the population also implies a set of techniques for differentiating within the population. This "biologization of the state" involves approaching the population on the biological level as a particular kind of species with defined characteristics, for Foucault a significant move away from earlier notions of the state grounded in territory.[53] As a defined unit, the population-species can not only be studied and analyzed (for health/medical reasons), but also be extrapolated, its characteristic behaviors projected into plausible futures (birth/death rates, etc.). The proto-information sciences of demographics and statistics provided a technical ground for a more refined, mathematically based regulation and monitoring of the population (and thus of the state's prime resources). The sciences of statistics and demographics are tools "to intervene at the level at which these general phenomena are determined," to inscribe a specificity within a generality.[54] More important, this internal differentiation is the point at which biological notions of race become relevant: by folding biological notions of race (difference) onto biological notions of population (sameness), biopolitics treats "the population as a mixture of races, or to be more accurate, to treat the species, to subdivide the species it controls, into the subspecies known, precisely, as races." In its most extreme cases, this biopolitics of race results in forms of "race war." Thus, "racism makes it possible to establish a relationship between my life and the death of the other that is not a military or warlike relationship of confrontation, but a biological relationship."[55]

Foucault is clearly thinking of the use of medicine in the service of racial purity and of ethnic-cleansing programs, and, as such, his statements may seem extreme in the case of population genomics projects. But there is also a more "liberal" (or, perhaps, neoliberal) side to biopolitics in this regard: by creating internal differentiations within the population, biopolitics opens up new ways of monitoring and regulating the political and economic health of the population. David Arnold notes this tendency in the nexus between colonialism and biomedicine when he states that "colonial rule built up an enormous battery of texts and discursive practices that concerned themselves with the physical being of the colonized," attempting to use this medicalized body "as a site for the construction of its own authority, legitimacy, and control."[56] … groupings do not make sense, however, without a means of defining the unit of grouping – not just the individual subject (and in Foucault's terminologies *subject* is also a verb), but a subject that can be defined in a variety of ways, marking out the definitional boundaries of each grouping.

This dual character of governmentality directly applies to current approaches to genetic difference in the biotech industry, especially in fields such as genomics, bioinformatics, and population genomics. Although the various efforts to map the human genome have been concerned with constructing a universal, representative genome (in which specifics as to race are left out of its description), genomics has also become a thriving business in terms of genetic differences, population genomes, or polymorphisms. According to some reports, pharmaceutical companies are realizing that the real money to be made and the most powerful discoveries to be made are not within the universal, single human genome, but in the minute markers that distinguish different human genomes from each other. This pharmacogenomics, or "personalized medicine," promises a tailor-fit drug program in place of the "one size fits all" methods traditionally used.

[…]

Decoding the Population

If population genetics is an extension of the informatic and biological aspects of Foucauldian biopolitics, then how might this connection change the definition of *population* in genomics projects such as those in the United Kingdom or Iceland? In most cases, what population genome databases promise to provide is an extensive, computer-driven, data-mining analysis of the genetic basis of disease as well as the development of treatments, cures, and preventive practices. A database such as deCODE's IHSD has become a paradigmatic example from a scientific point of view in that it brings together three types of data: phenotypic data and health-care information, genotypic data (genomic sequence information), and genealogical and hereditary data (gene pool and statistical information).[57] In 1998, the Icelandic parliament approved deCODE Genomics's proposal for the development of the IHSD, an agreement that would give deCODE exclusive rights to control the access privileges to the IHSD for up to twelve years. Under this agreement, even Icelandic physicians would be forced to pay a fee to access health data that was previously freely available. At the same time, deCODE also established a multimillion-dollar alliance with pharmaceutical giant Hoffman-LaRoche for carrying out basic drug R&D on the IHSD.

[...]

At the same time that deCODE's proposal was approved, a collection of concerned scientists, activists, and citizens gathered together to voice dissent over many of the ethical questions raised by the IHSD. This group, known as Mannvernd, and the Icelandic Medical Association continue to emphasize the importance of ongoing, truly democratic debate, not just on the IHSD, but on the trend of genomics databases generally.[58]

The main criticisms of the IHSD are fourfold. First, there is the issue of the commodification of health-care data. ... rights to Second, there are also concerns over information privacy and the confidentiality of medical data; although deCODE controls database access, it does not claim any responsibility for how patient information would be used by third parties. ... Third, there is the more scientific controversy over the efficacy of such population genome projects: many scientists claim that they are of benefit only regarding direct disease-causing genes (e.g., in cystic fibrosis or Huntington's disease), where single-point mutations or variations in a population can be targeted for the development of drugs. ... Fourth, a central area of dispute is deCODE's notion of "presumed consent": that, by default, Icelanders will be included in the database unless they voluntarily opted out. The assumption is that a visit to the doctor is as good as signing a consent form, an assumption that groups such as Mannvernd strongly contravene. ...

In any science-based project where human biological materials are being taken by a corporation, the issue of commodification is foremost in the social debate and ethical considerations. Although it is true that projects such as the IHSD are ostensibly aimed at providing positive models for the future of health care, the organizations that run them, such as deCODE, are also, when it comes down to it, businesses. This connection thus involves a consideration of what a particular biotech company's product is. In genomics, the product is most often, not surprisingly, information. But in genomics and in biotech generally, the rise of informatics has shown that many types of valuable information are available on the biotech market – universal genome data, gene pool data, disease profiling, SNP databases, and so on. A company's success depends on "having" not only the most valuable data, but also the most accurate (this is Celera's claim over the public consortium), the most technically sophisticated (thus the importance of tech companies), and the most articulate, or data that are shown to have a direct, immediate impact on health care and the fight against disease (the search for pragmatic genetic data). The challenge put forth by those critical of corporations and businesses handling health-related issues is that the research conducted and the projects undertaken be in the best interests of public health and not be determined by commercial concerns.

However, even when public projects attempt to assemble biological databases, there is still discomfort over the very process of sampling, extraction, and utilization of one's own body for medical research. In the case of genomics, this is a very abstract process, but also a very simple one, moving from a blood sample to a DNA archive in a computer. Contemporary issues of privacy have such a resonance in biotech, however, because of the central importance of new computing technologies in the biotech and biomedical lab. There have been disputes concerning the ownership of one's own DNA, in which, for instance, a company such as deCODE develops novel patents based on research done on individual human DNA samples. For this reason, many companies require complex disclaimers, and they also make an important further distinction between a person's own lived body and health-related data generated from a person's body. This reduction of the debate to a distinction between blood and data may solve the patenting and ownership issue, but it still does not address that fundamental gap: the ontological difference between one's own, proper body and the genetic data extracted from one's body. Many of the debates concern the handling of genetic data (for some projects, such as Celera's, individual donors are anonymous, and for others, such as deCODE's, individual identification is required to correlate genealogical with medical data).

Because these two issues of privacy and commodification are present in virtually every endeavor to create a genetic database, it is common for differing levels of informed consent to be an imperative for the research carried out. Informed consent mandates became especially important in so-called biopiracy cases, either involving the appropriation of Third World natural resources or the sampling of genetic material from indigenous populations around the world by First World science organizations. Similar issues apply to genetic sampling within a nation or community. Although there are different levels of consent, ranging from individual informed consent to the broadly applicable "presumed consent," they all contain clauses that permit certain types of activities and enable others. The IHSD, for instance, requires three levels of consent because there are three basic levels of appropriation of genetic material: consent for the blood/DNA sample extraction, consent for the genotyping, and consent for the analysis and diagnosis of the sequence and of its potential range of uses in research and clinical practice. As may be guessed, the ambiguities in different consent clauses have led to disputes over issues such as patentability, the buying and selling of genetic data, and so on.

As a unique technoscientific approach to race and ethnicity, population genomics also undertakes a unique type of biological or genetic surveillance. First World big science projects (such as the HGP) that harvest biological materials from Third World communities are an explicit form of *biocolonialism* in the more common usage of the term. The HGDP's controversy surrounding the extraction of cell lines from a New Guinea community is an example. Even with the now-mandatory clause of informed consent (again, there are many, often ambiguous levels of informed consent, including "presumed consent"), the appropriation of biological materials by First World science more often than not feeds into First World health-care economies (principally drugs). This situation, it should be said, becomes more complex when we consider the level of involvement or compromise of those who are the object of biocolonialism. Whereas some instances do involve the veritable plunder of biological materials, with little or highly falsified information given, other instances, in which the colonized community demands some economic reimbursement, are more complicated because such negotiations play into the commodification of the body.

But biocolonialism is also a phenomenon within First World countries, where the pharmaceutical industry stands to gain the most returns. This "endocolonization" – not only of the body but of medical practice itself – focuses on the ways in which the biological body can be turned into a value generator, either in drug development or through novel medical techniques such as gene therapy.[59] With a very straightforward pipeline of capital investment, R&D, products and services, and finally medical application, the biotech industry has transformed the First World into a giant molecular laboratory. The human genome database is only the most explicit manifestation of this literal data mining of precious, valuable genes. The patenting of biological materials and new technologies feeds back into an economy that operates largely at the level of finance capital.

What these four issues illustrate is that the question of genomics has much to do with institutional control and the level of biopolitical practices within societies, be those practices handled by governments or corporations. [...]

For instance, in articles written by Kari Stefansson, CEO of deCODE, the potentials of informatics technologies transform science research from a linear, hypothesis-driven approach to a semiautomated data mining agent that completes computations far beyond what was possible prior to the use of parallel processing computers and data mining algorithms.[60] ...

In considering this complex of life science business models, new computer tools, and a genomics-based approach to populations and disease, we can actually differentiate several strategies within contemporary genomics. One strategy has to do with the utilization of a universal reference in genomics. Generalized human genome projects, such as that undertaken and first completed by Celera, emphasize their universality as models for the study of disease, for treatment, and for a greater understanding of life at the molecular level. They also highlight the backdrop against which all genetic difference and deviations from a norm will be assessed. Indeed, part of the reason why genomic projects by Celera, Incyte, and the public consortium have received so much attention is that they are in the process of establishing the very norms of genetic medicine. Their practices and techniques themselves are the processes of establishing a genomic norm, what will or will not exist within the domain of consideration for genetic medicine, and what will or will not be identified as anomalous, excessive, or central to genetic knowledge and pharmacogenomic drug design. A company such as Celera, though it assembles its sequences from a number of anonymous individuals, constructs one single, universal human genome database. That database becomes the model for all sorts of research emerging from genomics – proteomics, genetic drug design, functional genomics, population genetics, gene therapy, and genetic profiling.

The utilization of a universal reference also implies a high degree of individualization within targeted population groups. At the opposite pole of Celera's universal model of the human genome is a field of research that deals with the minute, highly specific base-pair changes that differ from one individual to another.[61] However, many SNPs are phenotypically nonexpressive; that is, they are base-pair changes that do not effect the organism in any way – they are simply differences in code sequence. Many large-scale genome projects, such as Celera's, also contain information on polymorphisms, and many bioinformatics applications are designed to provide analysis of polymorphisms. But specific projects, such as Genaissance Pharmaceutical's HAP series of database tools and the Whitehead Institute's SNP database, focus exclusively on these minute base-pair changes.[62] For Genaissance in particular, the study of single-case base-pair changes in themselves are less productive than a total chromosomal perspective of SNP positioning. Genaissance uses its proprietary bioinformatics tools to assemble the given SNPs within a given chromosome or gene, thus offering a more distributed map sample of the interrelationships of SNPs. These databases of individual point changes form linkages between variations within a gene pool and a flexible drug-development industry that operates at the genetic, molecular level.

From the combination of a universal reference and minute differences within the universal, population genomics, specific modes of integrating biology and race are woven. Whereas Celera's human genome database attempts to establish itself as a general, universal model for genetic research, other genomics projects are focusing on collectivities within a universal gene pool. The projects from deCODE, Genaissance, Myriad, and others focusing on genetically isolated populations move somewhere between the *universality* of Celera and the *individuality* of the SNP databases. Often combining the usual genotypic data with data from demographics, statistics, genealogy, and health care, these projects are both new forms of health-care management and paths toward understanding the effects of disease within genetically homogenous groupings. This is perhaps the main discomfort with projects such as deCODE's IHSD; they promise the ability to perform large-scale computational analysis on entire genomes, but in this they also threaten to abstract genetic data from real, physical communities. They take a genetics-based, or genotypic, view of race and make connections to the functioning of norms within medicine and health care. In doing this, they establish an intermediary space of negotiation between the universality of a human genome project (which claims a uniformity under the umbrella of a distinct species) and the high-specificity of SNP or HAP databases (which claim difference within a general category). This intermediary space is precisely the space of racial (mis)identification and ethnic boundary marking; it is the space where collectivities form, composed of individuals united under a common species categorization. These population genomics projects, with their primary aim as medical (specifically in drug development and genetic diagnosis), are involved in the rearticulation of race and ethnicity through the lens of bioscience research and corporate biotechnology.

[…]

"On the Surface of Life, to Be All Open Wounds"

In the specific context of molecular biotechnology and biomedicine,[63] biocolonialism brings together the discourses and practices of contemporary bioscience with a colonialist approach to specific bodies and populations.[64] This approach involves the application of the ideologies of expansion, technological development, and appropriation of natural resources to modern medicine. It also brings in the critical perspectives of postcolonial theory, especially as it pertains to the complexities of the relationships between colonizer and colonized, of hybridity, and of the relationship between conceptions of race and the body.[65]

… We should recognize several things about biotech in relation to biocolonialism. To begin with, biotech is founded on Western bioscience research and Western medical practice. As a technical practice, it emerges from a discontinuous tradition of Western science. This also means that it has a more or less defined position on what counts as legitimate scientific research (that is, which kinds of research will form linkages to medical practice).

But as is well known, biotech is as much a business as it is science research. Along with its growth in the finance capital sector and its use of government funding, biotech is partaking in the broad processes of economic and technological globalism. The result is that the gap between the knowledge of the patient and the black-boxing of biomedicine becomes greater and greater. This global perspective has meant a series of problematic scientific and political relationships between First World and Third World countries. The expansion of "Big Pharma" to other countries, the sampling and patenting of biological materials from Third World populations, and the influence of Western medical practices are all instances of an asymmetrical conflict of interests.

This appropriationist approach to Western medicine is applied equally within technologically advanced sectors of the First World, especially in the United States. The globalization process of biotech means, first and foremost, an expansion and reconfiguration of the (mainly U.S. and British) medical and health-care landscape. The agglomeration of genetic databases, high-tech drug development, and high-pressure clinical trials combine to transform the United States into a biotech-infotech laboratory.

If, generally speaking, *colonialism* refers to the process whereby one collectivity (usually geographically and nationally defined) forcibly or coercively appropriates the land and resources of another collectivity, then some important issues can be brought up concerning the current influence of global biotechnology. However it is not exactly accurate to speak of biotech as a colonial instance, despite explicit examples of biological sampling and patenting. Rather, we should ask how biotech, as a technology-driven practice networked into a globalizing economy, approaches, transforms, and encodes different kinds of culturally specific bodies. In particular, we need to consider the relationships between the science of biotechnology and the concept of race as manifested within the biosciences.

Bearing in mind Foucault's emphasis on the population as a biologically defined entity and on the proto-informatic forms of regulation of the population, we can discern three primary issues with respect to biocolonialism and population genomics: informatics, biodiversification, and the notion of "genethnicities."

First, informatics is a key factor in considering contemporary power relationships in biotech because it works as a medium for transforming bodies and biologies into data. But those data are understood in many different ways, not simply as the liquidation or the dematerialization of the body. The case of population genomics suggests that databases are anything but "just data." Networked into drug development, medical records, and health-care services (including health insurance), genome databases are literally information that "matters." ...

Second, and in a similar vein, *biodiversity* is a term most often reserved for debates concerning the preservation, conservation, or sustainability of natural resources, which depends a great deal of natural diversity, as opposed to the advantage of natural diversity that transnational corporations take to produce monocultures as product.[66] In the context of genomics, biodiversity becomes a signifier for genetic difference and for the ways in which genetic difference gets translated into cultural difference. Biopiracy (the attack on biodiversity) is not simply about the destruction of natural resources; it is about a complex reframing of "nature" and the use of diversity toward commercial ends. As Vandana Shiva argues, the discourse of biodiversity is actually less about sustainability than it is about the conservation of biodiversity as a "raw material" for the production of monocultures.[67] The same can be said of biotechnology, especially in the case of genome projects, genome databases, cell and tissue banks, DNA sample collections, and other instances of accumulating biological information.

A third point of controversy regarding many such projects is the issue of genetic discrimination, which is, in the case of bioinformatics and genomics, a kind of data-based discrimination. With molecular genetics, a unique type of identification and differentiation has come about in which individuals and populations can be uniquely analyzed and regulated. Discussing recent genetic screening of African Americans in the United States for sickle-cell anemia, Troy Duster observes how the argument for genetic screening changes when dealing with specific racial or ethnic groups. Whereas general medical tests can be proposed as being "transparently in the general public interest," this "ceases to be the case when screening is aimed at a specific population with its 'own' health problem, and when the cost effectiveness of such screening is assessed by those not in the screened population."[68] This twofold process of molecular genetics (genetic essentialism) and informatics (population databases) paves the way for a new type of data filtering, or, in some cases, discrimination. Such discrimination is based not on race, gender, or sexuality, but rather on information (genetic information). Bioinformatics – an apparently neutral technical tool – thus becomes manifestly political, negotiating how race and ethnicity will be configured through the filter of biotech, constituting a unique type of *genethnicity*.

These biopolitical features of population genomics – informatics, diversification, genethnicities – point to the ways in which the object of such practices is the molecular body itself. If colonialism historically involved the forced or coerced appropriation of people, land, and economy, *bio*colonialism presents us with a situation in which the bodies of the colonized *are* the land and economy. ...

Biocolonialism takes the molecular body and biological processes as the territory or the property to be acquired, *but insofar as this body can be modulated at the level of informatics.* ...

Postgenomic Collectivities

[...]

The most important issue brought up by population genetics and related fields is the future of genetic difference. Is this a new form of racism for the "biotech century"? With the widespread use in science of informatics and computers, will biotechnical forms of racism also become informatic forms of discrimination?

As a way of addressing this question, we can point to three possible directions that a biocolonial critique might initiate. A starting point would be a consideration of the population within a temporal – and not just spatial or statistical – framework. A population should be taken as *dynamic*. Although traditional population genetics aims to study an "ideal" population – static, closed, predictable – human collectivities of all sorts are embedded in heterogeneous, fluctuating, and dynamic environments. As such, they cannot help but also be dynamic and, above all, adaptive. Bioscience has yet to consider seriously this notion of an adaptive, flexible population. Doing so would mean integrating, in a transdisciplinary manner, other perspectives – distributed pattern-recognition systems, autopoietic theories, systems biology, non-linear dynamics, and molecular epidemiology.

A second guideline would take into account the way in which populations are dynamic; that is, a population should be taken as a *hybrid*. Again, the ideal population for study is coherent; it forms a closed system in a vacuum, with no new genetic material coming in and the overall gene frequency remaining stable, though internal fluctuations may occur. But – as this guideline points more directly to the notion of race – populations not only are dynamic, but can be incredibly diverse, even to the point of internal fragmentation. This hybridity is not a deviation from a biologically pure ideal; it is the very substance that composes the population. A mode of articulating and understanding difference at the biological and genetic level is needed, one that does not define difference as deviation, but, in a more constitutive manner, as something without which a population cannot form.

Finally, although there are a number of problematic points concerning the conception of race and ethnicity in population genomics, a critique of such points should not be taken as antiscience. The biological should be integrated into the cultural, the social, and the political. Population genetics – and biotech generally – cordons off the biological determinism of bioscience from cultural processes, but we might question, from the point of view of the biosciences, whether the biological is all that containable. Our definitions of the biological domain also need to be more flexible and more articulate. The biological should not simply determine or explain race; it should be a core part of the cultural experience of race. This quasi-dialectical move would also require that cultural issues be a central part of science projects such as the HGDP. It is through this perspective that non-Western viewpoints on race and population can be seriously considered.

Given these starting points, we can reconsider now the apparent contradiction with which we began. Recall that I noted the simultaneous disappearance of the issues associated with the HGDP and the rapid rise of bioinformatics and the use of computer technologies in genomics generally. So, then, what has become of the original issue put forth by the critics of the HGDP? Part of the problem is that the issues dealt with in this criticism have been handled in the same way that criticism of genomic mapping and human embryonic cloning have been handled: they have been filed under the worrisome category of "bioethics" (which commands a mere 3 percent of the HGP's budget). As postcolonial critiques have pointed out, the HGDP came to a relative standstill because it could not reconcile Western scientific assumptions and intentions with non-Western perspectives toward agriculture, population, medicine, culture, and so forth. The sheer gap between the HGDP's bioinformatic colonialism and those predominantly non-Western cultures who were to be the source of biomaterial for the HGDP database illustrates the degree to which *global* once again means "Western" (and, increasingly, "economic"). *One of the meanings of the decrease in the presence of the HGDP and the rise in bioinformatics developments and applications is that the issues of ethnicity and cultural heterogeneity have been sublimated into a paradigm in which they simply do not appear as issues.* That paradigm is, of course, one based on the predominance of information in understanding the genetic makeup of an individual, population, or disease. When, as geneticists repeatedly state, genetic information is taken as one of the keys to a greater understanding of the individual and the species (along with protein structure and biochemical pathways), the issue is not ethnicity but rather how to translate ethnicity into information. In such propositions, ethnicity becomes split between its direct translation into genetic information (a specific gene linked to a specific disease) and its marginalization into the category of "environmental influence" (updated modifications of the sociobiological imperative).

The biopolitics of genomics is that of an informatics of the population in which cultural issues (ethnicity, cultural diversity) are translated into informational issues (via either a universal, generalized map of the human genome or individualized maps of genetic diversity). As with numerous other sciencetechnology disciplines, the apparent neutrality of abstract systems and purified information needs to be questioned. As Evelyn Fox Keller, Donna Haraway, and others have pointed out, information is not an innocent concept with regards to issues of gender and race.[69] The question that needs to be asked of bioinformatics, online genomic databases, and genome mapping projects, is not just "Where is culture?" but rather "How, by what tactics, and by what techniques is bioinformatics reinterpreting and incorporating cultural difference?"

Coda: Fanon's Database

As a closing note, I should point out that despite the increasing visibility of the more "neutral" technical fields of genomics, bioinformatics, and population genomics, the HGDP's broad initiative has not disappeared. In fact, it can be observed alongside the high-tech fields of genomics in contemporary media culture. For instance, consider the 2003 *Nova* documentary *The Journey of Man*. Narrated by population geneticist Spencer Wells, *The Journey of Man* attempts to show how all races – no matter how different culturally, economically, or politically – are united by a common genetic heritage. This heritage is, of course, "the" human genome, which genetic archaeologists claim can be traced back to the earliest human beings on the African continent. Using both high-tech genomics and "old-fashioned" ethnography, *The Journey of Man* shows us cultural difference at the same time that it posits genomic unification. *The Journey of Man*, in its ethnographic representation of Wells visiting a range of cultures, even purports that this common genetic heritage can be the basis for a greater cultural understanding. The question is, of course, Understanding for whom and dictated by what criteria? *The Journey of Man* makes a number of alarming claims, such as Wells's closing comments that "we are all literally 'African' under the skin." And the documentary is made more volatile by the fact that Wells is a former student of Cavalli-Sforza.

Frantz Fanon's essay "Medicine and Colonialism" offers a counterpoint to what may be the new face of population genomics. Fanon's text situates the tensions between colonizer and colonized within the framework of medicine. Although more recent developments in postcolonial studies have complicated and tempered Fanon's position – one thinks of Homi Bhabha's work on the colonial encounter, or Gayatri Spivak's work on the subaltern – Fanon's essay still has great import in thinking about the problem of biocolonialism. Writing in the midst of the Algerian revolution, Fanon's essay is instructive for colonialisms of all kinds, for it attempts to do two things: remain decisive in a critique of colonialism and, at the same time, remain open to the transformative and empowering aspects of a science and technology that serve the people or "the population." Fanon is adamant about the impermeable barrier between a colonized society and the colonizing one, "the impossibility of finding a meeting ground in any colonial situation." In addition, the biopolitical concerns of a population's health make the colonial imperative immune to critique: "When the discipline considered concerns man's health, when its very principle is to ease pain, it is clear that no negative reaction can be justified."[70] For Fanon, the introduction of European medicine into the colonies is part and parcel of the colonial program. Not only are local knowledges and practices delegitimized, but, in the case of colonial medicine, the gift of health care always leads to an indebtedness.[71] The figure of the colonial doctor is, for Fanon, a figure that represents the most insidious form of colonialism because it is precisely "life itself" and bodily health that cannot be questioned. At the end of the day, Fanon sees political and economic interests behind this imperative of health. As he notes, "in the colonies, the doctor is an integral part of colonization, of domination, of exploitation." Furthermore, "in the colonial situation, going to see the doctor, the administrator, the constable or the mayor are identical moves."[72] Thus, "this good faith is immediately taken advantage of by the occupier and transformed into a justification of the occupation."[73]

[...]

If in colonial medicine the native doctor is effectively alienated, this situation is reversed by the condition of revolutionary conflict. Fanon notes how in the context of Algeria's war of liberation the native doctor, nurse, and technician went from being an ostracized third party to becoming a constitutive part of the anticolonization movement. Certain key events served as the impetus for this transition, such as the French government's decision, throughout 1954–55, to place an embargo on all medicines entering Algeria for the Algerian people. Although the people were barred not only from seeing the European doctors, but also from receiving vaccines and medicines, the native medical professionals, occupying an intermediary position, were able to create an infrastructure for the flow of medicines and medical knowledge into Algeria. Fanon describes the Algerian National Liberation Front's controversial medical program:

> These medications which were taken for granted before the struggle for liberation, were transformed into weapons. And the urban revolutionary cells having the responsibility for supplying medications were as important as those assigned to obtain information as to the plans and movements of the adversary. ... It [the National Liberation Front] found itself faced with the necessity of setting up a system of public health capable of replacing the periodic visit of the colonial doctor. This is how the local cell member responsible for health became an important member of the revolutionary apparatus.[74]

The preventive practices, hygiene plans, and routine examinations that were shunned by the Algerian people were suddenly now put into place with great fluency. Native medical professionals; previously alienated as constituting part of the problem rather than a solution, were now brought into the fray of colonial struggle. "The war of liberation introduced medical technique and the native technician into the life of the innumerable regions of Africa."[75] There are many examples like these, but what Fanon shows us in the case of Algeria is the degree to which politics is biopolitics and how colonialism is never far from biocolonialism.

[...]

Thus, although Fanon's generalizations may be questioned on particular historical grounds, the general lesson he points to is worth thinking about in the context of biopiracy and biocolonialism. Fanon is militant about the irresolvable conflict between colonizer and colonized, but he adopts a more complex approach on the issue of bio-politics – the "health of the population," of the body politic. The example of the native Algerian doctor, nurse, and medical technician is an example of reappropriating the benefits of medical practice and knowledge, but without the political and economic imperatives set on them by colonial interests. Political, economic, and cultural issues will certainly come up in such situations, and, indeed, we are seeing such issues play themselves out in the ongoing efforts to offer American governmental and corporate financial aid to combating AIDS and tuberculosis in Africa (most notably, from the Gates Foundation). Writing in the midst of Algeria's colonial struggle, Fanon offers the possibility of a deeply committed critique of colonialisms of all kinds, along with an equal commitment to the social and political empowerment of medical knowledge and practice. However, Fanon's overall point still retains a degree of ambiguity, despite his vehement voice against colonialism. As he notes, "science depoliticized, science in the service of man, is often non-existent in the colonies."[76] ...

In the case of contempotary biocolonialism and biopiracy, we see a situation sig-nificantly different from the examples of Algeria, India, and other sites of colonial struggle. As I have noted, it is not the territory that is at stake, but rather the biological population – the population is the territory in biocolonialism. Moreover, this popula-tion is configured as a biological and a genetic entity, and in this sense the body of the population is separated from the body of a culture. Blood, protein, and DNA samples do not contest their status as items of property, especially when they are extracted and abstracted from the particular bodies of individuals. This biological-genetic defini-tion of the population is coupled with an informatic approach to the population, as we see in the discipline of population genetics and in the techniques of population genomics. Both approaches – the genetic and the informatic – are approaches that Foucault implicitly points to in his discussions on biopolitics.[77] Finally, biocolonial-ism is also unique in that, by shifting the emphasis from territory to population, it makes possible layered forms of "endocolonization": population genomics and pros-pecting within a given population or nation (for example the U.K. BioBank, or the Gene Trust in the United States). Thus, biocolonialism raises not only cultural issues (as in the case of the HGDP), but also, in its endocolonial form, issues pertaining to medical surveillance, the privacy of health-related information, and economically driven health-care practices in technologically advanced countries.

Although the potential medical benefits from fields such as population genomics are still being debated, the economic and civil liberties issues have prompted many individuals and groups (such as RAFI) to speak out against biocolonial practices. Is there a space, within the *biocolonial* encounter, for negotiation? As Fanon notes,

> Specialists in basic health education should give careful thought to the new situations that develop in the course of a struggle for national liberation on the part of an underdeveloped people. Once the body of the nation begins to live again in a coherent and dynamic way, everything becomes possible. The notions about "native psychology" or of the "basic personality" are shown to be in vain. The people who take their destiny into their own hands assimilate the most modern forms of technology at an extraordinary rate.[78]

For Fanon, the political and military program of occupation is also a medical program of occupation. But his twofold position – a critique of colonial imperatives and an openness to tactical innovation – can be seen as one example of how to avoid simply demonizing science and medicine en masse. This model – difficult as it may be to carry out – can be of great benefit for confronting the issues raised by, for example, population genomics. In fact, such biobanking efforts demand at the minimum a sort of "critical genomic consciousness," or, as Fortun notes, a "genomic solidarity": "experimenting with the idea of genomic solidarity and working to imagine and invent its social practice seems increasingly necessary to me. One way or another, we are going to find ourselves grouped into some kind of population that has some kind of value, commercial or otherwise. … So why should any of us become scientifically and commercially consolidated, but remain socially and politically isolated?"[79] In the colonial context of Algeria, Fanon notes that "the Revolution and medicine manifested their presence simultaneously."[80] Perhaps, in the genome era, we can complicate Fanon's terms without losing his critical acuity: revolution and biotechnology manifest their presence simultaneously, as that which is always about to arrive.

NOTES

1. Many press releases and news items can be found at the Rural Advancement Foundation International (RAFI) archives Web site at http://www.rafi.org. Also see Patricia Kahn, "Genetic Diversity Project Tries Again," *Science* 266 (November 4, 1994): 720–722.

2. The idea for the HGDP came to Cavalli-Sforza as a postdoc at Cambridge University under the eugenicist Ronald Fisher, who was then applying mathematical techniques to studying Mendelian laws in human characteristics such as height, weight, and intelligence (e.g., IQ scores). Fisher's book *The Genetical Theory of Natural Selection*, published in 1930, reiterated late-nineteenth-century fears about the degeneration and deterioration of the population from the overbreeding of the lower classes. Cavalli-Sforza soon became a leading figure in population genetics. In the 1980s, he and his colleagues collected DNA samples in Africa to use statistics to study human genetic differences in select populations. For an excellent analysis of the HGDP, see Jennifer Reardon, "The Human Genome Diversity Project: A Case Study in Coproduction," *Social Studies of Science* 31.3 (2001): 357–388.

3. See Debra Harry, *Biocolonialism: A New Threat to Indigenous Peoples*, a report from the Indigenous Peoples Council on Biocolonialism (1998), available at http://www.foel.org/LINK/LINK93/biocolonialism.html.

4. See Vandana Shiva, *Biopiracy: The Plunder of Nature and Knowledge* (Toronto: Between the Lines, 1997), pp. 65–85. Also see the GeneWatch report *Privatising Knowledge, Patenting Genes: The Race to Control Genetic Information*, GeneWatch Briefing no. 11 (June 2000), available at http://www.genewatch.org.

5. See Reardon, "The Human Genome Diversity Project."

6. The former HGDP is now based at Stanford University's Morris Institute for Population Studies.

7. Other organizations instrumental in lobbying against biopiracy include the Foundation for Economic Trends (FET) and the Institute for Science in Society (I-SIS).

8. On bioinformatics, see Ken Howard, "The Bioinformatics Gold Rush," *Scientific American* (July 2000): 58–63.

9. On pharmacogenomics, see Julio Licino and Ma-Li Wong, eds., *Pharmacogenomics: The Search for Individualized Therapies* (Weinheim, Germany: Wiley-VCH, 2002). Also see chapter 1 in this book.

10. For instance, Affymetrix's "GeneChip" technology, Incyte's "LifeSeq" databases, Perkin-Elmer's automated genetic sequencing computers.

11. On bioinformatics and post-genomics, see Diane Gershon, "Bioinformatics in a Post-Genomics Age," *Nature* 389 (September 27, 1997): 417–418.

12. For reportage on the human genome projects, see the news articles "Genetic Code of Human Life Is Cracked by Scientists," *New York Times*, June 26, 2000; "Special Issue: Genome – The Race to Decode the Human Body," *Newsweek* (April 10, 2000); and "Special Issue: Cracking the Code," *Time* (July 3, 2000).

13. On developments in population genetics, see Aravinda Chakravarti, "Population Genetics – Making Sense out of Sequence," *Nature Genetics* 21 (January 1999): 56–60. Also see Steve Olson, "The Genetic Archaeology of Race," *The Atlantic Online* (April 2001), http://www.theatlantic.com.

14. For example, the two most common genetically based components of difference include SNPs, or the minute sequence differences from one individual to another, and HAPs, or the physical arrangement of SNPs on a chromosome. See Nicholas Wade, "In the Hunt for Useful Genes, a Lot Depends on Snips," *New York Times*, August 11, 1998, available at http://www.nytimes.com.

15. See Vicki Brower, "Mining the Genetic Riches of Human Populations," *Nature Biotechnology* 16 (April 1998): 337–340; and Gary Taubes, "Your Genetic Destiny for Sale," *MIT Technology Review* (April 2001): 41–46.

16. Both the Gene Trust and the First Genetic Fund borrow the rhetoric of investment banking to contextualize genetic research as long-term investments, benefitting not just the individual, but the species as a whole. GenBank is one of the first online databases to be established by the U.S. government – funded HGP. The Gene Trust Web site makes this explicit in its Web-based advertising (e.g., the DNA you donate now could save lives in the future).

17. A Web site dedicated to HAP research is Hapcentral, http://www.hapcentral.com. Along with the myriad of genomics databases now online, a centralized, U.S. government – funded SNP database exists at the Whitehead Institute, http://www.genome.wi.mit.edu/SNP/human/index.html.

18. See Michael Fortun, "Towards Genomic Solidarity: Lessons from Iceland and Estonia," *Open Democracy* (October 7, 2003), available at http://www.open democracy.net.

19. See Taubes, "Your Genetic Destiny for Sale."

20. See the UK BioBank Web site at http://www.ukbiobank.ac.uk.

21. WMA, "Declaration on Ethical Considerations Regarding Health Databases," adopted by the WMA General Assembly (2002), available at http://www.wma.net/e/policy/d1.htm.

22. Michael Fortun, "Experiments in Ethnography and Its Performance," on the Mannvernd Web site at http://www.mannvernd.is.

23. Ibid.

24. Michel Foucault, *The History of Sexuality*, vol. 1, *An Introduction*, trans. Robert Hurley (New York: Vintage, 1978), pp. 141–142.

25. Ibid., 1: 147, 148 (italics removed).

26. Much of this analysis is predicated on textbooks in population genetics, including A. J. Ammerman and Luigi Luca Cavalli-Sforza, *The Neolithic Transition and the Genetics of Populations in Europe* (Princeton, N.J.: Princeton University Press, 1984); Luigi Luca Cavalli-Sforza, *The History and Geography of Human Genes* (Princeton, N.J.: Princeton University Press, 1994); and Luigi Luca Cavalli-Sforza and F. Cavalli-Sforza, *The Great Human Diasporas* (Menlo Park, Calif.: Addison-Wesley, 1995).

27. Luigi Luca Cavalli-Sforza, *Genes, Peoples, and Languages* (New York: North Point, 2000), p. 25.

28. Quoted in Reardon, "The Human Genome Diversity Project," p. 362. The full reference is Theodosius Dobzhansky, *Genetics and the Origin of Species* (New York: Columbia University Press, 1951 [orig. 1937]), p. 138.

29. See Reardon, "The Human Genome Diversity Project," pp. 361–362. Also see Daniel Kevles, *In the Name of Eugenics: Genetics and the Uses of Human Heredity* (Cambridge, Mass.: Harvard University Press, 1995), pp. 164–175.

30. See Elaine Daston and Katherine Park, *Wonders and the Order of Nature, 1150–1750* (New York: Zone, 1998), pp. 25–39.

31. See Zakiya Hanafi, *The Monster in the Machine: Magic, Medicine, and the Marvelous in the Time of the Scientific Revolution* (Durham, N.C.: Duke University Press, 2000). See also Daston and Park, *Wonders and the Order of Nature*, pp. 201–215.

32. See Cavalli-Sforza, *The History and Geography of Human Genes*.

33. Cavalli-Sforza, *Genes, Peoples, and Languages*, p. 20.

34. See Dudley Wilson, *Signs and Portents: Monstrous Births from the Middle Ages to the Enlightenment* (New York: Routledge, 1993). See Daston and Park, *Wonders and the Order of Nature*, pp. 177–190.

35. See G. H. Hardy, "Mendelian Proportions in a Mixed Population," *Science* 28 (1908): 49–50. Also see the sections in Daniel Hartl and Andrew Clark, *Principles of Population Genetics* (Sunderland, Mass.: Sinauer Associates, 1997). The Hardy-Weinberg principle is by no means universal to all population genetics approaches, but it is being taken here as emblematic of the kind of complicated interweaving of statistics and culture that constitutes the field.

36. See Cavalli-Sforza, *Genes, Peoples, and Languages*, pp. 66–73.

37. Foucault, *History of Sexuality*, 1: 137.

38. Ibid., 1: 137, 139.

39. Ibid., 1: 139.

40. Ibid., 1: 139, emphasis in original.

41. Michel Foucault, *"Society Must Be Defended": Lectures at the Collège de France, 1975–76*, trans. David Macey, ed. Mauro Bertani and Alessandro Fontana (New York: Picador, 2003), p. 243.

42. "The great eighteenth-century demographic upswing in Western Europe, the necessity for coordinating and integrating it into the apparatus of production, and the urgency of controlling it with finer and more adequate power mechanisms cause 'population,' with its numerical variables of space and chronology, longevity and health, to emerge not only as a problem but as an object of surveillance, analysis, intervention, modifications, and so on." Michel Foucault, "The Politics of Health in the Eighteenth Century," in *Power: The Essential Works of Michel Foucault 1954–1984*, vol. 3, trans. Robert Hurley et al., ed. James Faubion (New York: New Press, 2000), p. 95.

43. Foucault, *History of Sexuality*, 1: 142.

44. Malthus notes that "it follows necessarily that the average rate of the actual increase of population over the greatest part of the globe, obeying the same laws as the increase of food, must be totally of a different character from the rate at which it would increase *if unchecked*. The great question, then, which remains to be considered, is the manner in which this constant and necessary check upon population practically operates." Thomas Malthus, "A Summary View of the Principle of Population," in *An Essay on the Principle of Population* (New York: Penguin, 1985 [orig. 1798]), p. 242.

45. Regarding threats to the population, Malthus observes that "a foresight of the difficulties attending the rearing of a family acts as a preventive check; and the actual distresses of some of the lower classes, by which they are disabled from giving the proper food and attention to their children, act as a positive check." *An Essay on the Principle of Population*, p. 89.

46. Thomas Malthus, *Principles of Political Economy* (New York: Augustus M. Kelly, 1964 [2d ed. 1836]), p. 313.

47. Malthus, *An Essay on the Principle of Population*, pp. 313–314.

48. Ian Hacking, *The Taming of Chance* (Cambridge: Cambridge University Press, 1990), p. 1.

49. Ibid., p. 52.

50. Ibid., p. 1.

51. Ibid., p. 5.

52. Foucault, *"Society Must be Defended,"* p. 246.

53. See Michel Foucault, "Security, Territory, and Population," in *Ethics: Subjectivity and Truth: The Essential Works of Michel Foucault 1954–1984*, vol. 1, trans. Robert Hurley et al., ed. Paul Rabinow (New York: New Press, 1997), pp. 67–72.

54. Foucault, *"Society Must be Defended,"* p. 246.

55. Ibid., p. 255.

56. David Arnold, *Colonizing the Body: State Medicine and Epidemic Disease in 19th Century India* (Berkeley: University of California Press, 1993), p. 8.

57. More information on the IHSD can be found at the deCODE Web site at http://www.decode.com.

58. See the Mannvernd Web site at http://www.mannvernd.is.

59. On the concept of "endocolonialism," see Paul Virilio, *The Art of the Motor* (Minneapolis: University of Minnesota Press, 1995), pp. 99–133.

60. See Kari Steffanson and Jeffrey Gulcher, "The Icelandic Healthcare Database and Informed Consent," *New England Journal of Medicine* 342.24 (June 15, 2000). Other articles are available through the deCODE Web site (see note 57).

61. Accounting for approximately 0.1 percent of the total genome (or roughly one million base-pair variations per individual), these SNPs are thought to contribute to a range of phenotypic characteristics, from the physical markers that make one person different from another to the susceptibility to single base pair mutation conditions (such as sickle-cell anaemia or diabetes).

62. For an example of a HAP database, see Genaissance's Web site at http://www.genaissance.com. For the SNP database, see http://www.genome.wi.mit.edu/SNP/human.

63. The quotation given in the section heading is from "Madrigal IV" by Ulver, ©1997 Magic Arts Publishing. Quoted in G. B. Della Potta, "Vitalism and the Role of Physicians in Early Modern Expansionism," *Renaissance Studies* 4 (2002), p. 19.

64. See Harry, "Biocolonialism." Also see Jeremy Rifkin, *The Biotech Century: Harnessing the Gene and Remaking the World* (New York: Tarcher/Putnam, 1998).

65. On postcolonialism and technoscience, see Donna Haraway, *Modest_Witness@Second_Millennium.FemaleMan©_Meets_OncoMouse™: Feminism and Technoscience* (New York: Routledge, 1997); and Sandra Harding, *Is Science Multicultural? Postcolonialisms, Feminisms, and Epistemologies* (Bloomington: Indiana University Press, 1998).

66. See Vandana Shiva, "Biodiversity, Biotechnology, and Profits," in *Biodiversity: Social and Ecological Perspectives*, ed. Vandana Shiva (New Jersey: Zed Books, 1991), pp. 43–58.

67. Ibid., 44–45.

68. Troy Duster, *Backdoor to Eugenics* (New York: Routledge, 2003), p. 40. Duster notes two significant trends in modern genetic screening practices: first, the fact that "genetic screening programs, already in place throughout most of the United States, can be distinguished from all previous health screening in the degree to which 'risk-populations' to be identified have frequently been linked to ethnicity and race" (p. 5), and, second, "state and national registries for information received from newborn genetic screening programs are already in place, collecting data on the chromosome and genetic trait status of millions of infants" (p. 5).

69. See Evelyn Fox Keller, *Reflections on Gender and Science* (New Haven, Conn.: Yale University Press, 1995). Also see Haraway, *Modest_Witness*.

70. Frantz Fanon, "Medicine and Colonialism," in *A Dying Colonialism*, trans. Haakon Chevalier (New York: Grove, 1965), pp. 121, 125.

71. Fanon paraphrases this more familiar view of colonial intervention: "Colonialism obviously throws all the elements of native society into confusion. The dominant group arrives with its values and imposes them with such violence that the very life of the colonized can manifest itself only defensively, in a more or less clandestine way" (ibid., p. 130). This view has, of course, been complicated more recently by Homi Bhabba's psychoanalytic reading of the colonial encounter.

72. Ibid., pp. 134, 139. Fanon also notes that "in centers of colonization the doctor is nearly always a landowner as well" (p. 133).

73. Ibid., p. 122. In his psychological analysis, Fanon notes the attitude of the colonial doctor that produces this debt: "This is what we have done for the people of this country; this country owes us everything; were it not for us, there would be no country" (p. 122).

74. Ibid., pp. 140–141.

75. Ibid., p. 142.

76. Ibid., p. 140.

77. In light of recent trends to emphasize the role of information technology and computers in biotech, Fanon's comments are especially prescient: "All the efforts exerted by the doctor, by his team of nurses, to modify this state of thing encounter, not a systematic opposition, but a 'vanishing' on the part of the patient." Ibid., p. 129.

78. Ibid., pp. 144–145.

79. Fortun, "Towards Genomic Solidarity."

80. Fanon, "Medicine and Colonialism," p. 142.

V GENDER, SEX, AND SEXUALITIES

Introduction

Is the use of cyberspace or cybertechnology gendered? How are women represented in cyberspace? Does cyberspace become another realm where the stereotyping of women, gays, and alternative sexualities continues from the real, material world? Sexuality studies in cyberculture addresses these several related themes.

Enthusiasts, especially those with a feminist view, see cyberspace and the cyborg as an emancipatory and liberating figure. Embodiment, disembodiment, and re-embodiment in cyberspace mean different things for men and women. Those who wish to be free of their bodies find cyberspace useful for inventing new gender identities, even though this does not alter their material lives.

For people with different and socially "aberrant" sexualities, the realm of cyberspace is a safer forum in which to meet other people with similar interests, and studies have shown how gays have found relationships and support online, with no reference to their geographical location. For others, it is an anonymous space where sexual experimentation, flirtation, transgression, and relatively safe adventures can be experienced. Online diaries, chatrooms, and blogs have emerged as spaces of freedom for women.

Studies of internet sexuality reveal that stalking, sexual stereotyping, and the objectification of women continue in cyberspace. Games, science fiction dealing with digital technology, websites, and pornography continue to treat women as sexual objects and, in many cases, raced sexual objects.

Sex is, as studies in the politics and economy of cybercultures show, a major commercial dimension of ICTs. Sex tourism and pornography constitute a major source of revenue.

The articles in Part V explore the many dimensions of cybersexuality, from embodiment to stereotyping to political economy. They deal with different cybergenres: online romances, pornography, computer games, and community networking.

Cyberspace and cybercultural technologies are as much about power relations as the "real world" they inhabit. Dianne Currier's article begins with this assumption in order to explore the gendered nature of cyberbodies. Noting that bodies are sites of difference and subjectivity and also the points of contact with technology, Currier argues that the emphasis on disembodiment (in cybercultures) actually operates on the logic of identity. The older binary of mind/body and immaterial/material frames such discourses about cyberspace identity. Currier argues that insofar as gender can "float free of bodies, it possesses an informational status in opposition to the matter of the bodies onto which it is inscribed." For Currier this is severely problematic, for it assumes gender is "detachable information" where we assume there is primarily a body, and then there is the technological prosthesis. Turning to Deleuze and Guattari's formulation of "assemblages," Currier reframes the logic of identity. Body and technology is not a 1+1 binary identity. Instead, we need to see bodies as "articulated or actualized, within complex assemblages of other bodies, objects, institutions, technologies, regimes of signs, and relations of power." She suggests that we need to track the configurations of bodies that emerge in such assemblages. Once we see these configurations embedded in social-technological formations, feminists can be alerted to the power relations at work, and thereby hope to reverse the assemblages or make new configurations within it. Currier's is a call to a feminist appropriation of the cultural and technological as well as social structures of cyberculture.

The internet has provided a space for thus-far marginalized peoples. Elizabeth Friedman maps the ways in which lesbians have appropriated the internet and used it to form communities that have also significantly affected their offline lives. In her study of Latin American lesbian communities in cyberspace Friedman notes that a more enduring presence in the public sphere is made possible with websites. However, she does not focus entirely on cyberspace lesbian movements and communities. Rather, she locates lesbian cyberspace within a larger material and social context of lesbian communities. Moving from a history of the regional lesbian movement in Latin America to cyberspace, Friedman is able to ground virtual subcultures within a material context. She sees the presence of lesbians in cyberspace as providing a supplementary space for social action. Community building in cyberspace, she discovers, brings solutions as well as problems to real-life organizing. Far from an international and global solidarity enabled by the internet, Friedman notes, what we see is a regional community-making even in cyberspace. This article is a useful corrective to the now-fashionable notions of cyberspace as a space of freedom, which too often treat cyberspace as disjunctive from material structures of social lives.

Blaise Cronin and Elisabeth Davenport shift the focus of internet sexuality from the realm of psychology and bodies to commerce. They propose that the social shaping of technology approach could provide a theoretical framework for studying the economic and commercial profits gained from online sexualities and behavior. They see a link between the online sex industry and the entertainment sectors. They also propose that new forms of linkage are emerging between consumer culture and online sex services. Consumers, therefore, have a significant role to play in the development of online sex products and services. Cronin and Davenport see a greater internationalization of the online sex industry, as well as a more professional and strategic focusing.

Peter Chow-White's article studies the massive industry of internet sex tourism, which he sees an extension of global mass-tourism flows. Using computer-aided content analysis of discussion boards and homepages, he examines the reproduction of the myths and stereotypes of sex workers and of race and masculinities in sex tourism websites. He discovers that information exchange involves discussion of health and safety matters and pricing. In the discourse of these websites Chow-White unpacks a dual process of "remasculinization" – where buying cheap sex for money is seen as possessing power – and racialization, but also the facilitation of transgressive sexualities.

17 ASSEMBLING BODIES IN CYBERSPACE
Technologies, Bodies, and Sexual Difference

Dianne Currier

As women engage the emergent technological matrix of cyberspace, a new sphere of social practice, communication activities, alignments, and theories is taking shape. New alliances between women are being forged across traditional barriers of time and geography, and new modes of political organizing, campaigning, and information dissemination are being developed. In addition women in the new social communicative spaces generated by these technologies are exploring the crucial questions of feminism, identity, sexual difference, communication, social and cultural institutions, community, power, and knowledge. Emerging from these explorations and activities have been equal measures of suspicion and expectation. Exploring the possibilities that the technologies and social spaces commonly known as cyberspace might signal for women is a vast and complex project that has generated responses across a variety of registers. For feminist respondents it means posing the same general questions that underpin all feminist investigations of technologies. That is, how are relations of power distributed across and actualized through human-technology interactions, and how do women fare in this distribution? Further how can such relations, where they prove to be detrimental to women, be challenged and transformed? Clearly these are complex questions that demand investigation on multiple levels from the everyday encounters of women with technological objects and practices in the workplace, and in domestic and social arenas to the broader theoretical frameworks and modes of knowledge through which understandings of technology, woman, and man are articulated and function. These are not two distinct fields of study; rather I would argue that every investigation of the everyday is framed, if not explicitly, by broader theoretical questions. Thus to inquire as to

Dianne Currier, "Assembling Bodies in Cyberspace: Technologies, Bodies, and Sexual Difference," pp. 519–38 from. Mary Flanagan and Austin Booth (eds.), *Reload: Rethinking Women+Cyberculture* (Cambridge, MA: MIT Press, 2002).

what avenues of transformation the technologies and social spaces of cyberspace offer women is also to inquire as to the nature of those technologies, technology in general, women and man – to ask how they are configured and how this has an impact on the understanding of the relations between them.

In this essay I track the formulations of technology and woman as they are articulated through the operations of a particular epistemological structure – the logic of identity and the associated structure of binary opposition – across the field of transformational discourses of cyberspace. Using bodies as a conduit, explore how this logic gives rise to particular understandings of technologies and the modes of engagement with them that are often ultimately counterproductive to the transformational claims for cyberspace being made by a range of feminists. Finally, I indicate an alternative mode of thinking technologies drawn from Deleuze and Guattari which, I would claim, effects a conceptual shift that counters this problematic logic of identity.

[…]

Identity in Cyberspace: Information Minds and Bodies

From the proliferation of accounts of cyberspace emerging from the academy, the arts, and online communities have emerged a number of core tropes that are so pervasive that they have achieved commonsense status. Two such tropes that dominate discussions of bodies and cyberspaces are the disembodied mind and the virtual body. Both propose that the information-based nature of cyberspace renders it inaccessible to physical bodies and find in this exclusion the means for achieving transformation.[1] I want to trace the articulation of bodies through these two configurations in order to demonstrate how, in both, bodies become confined and defined exclusively within the logic of identity through the operations of various binary oppositions. An examination of the founding assumptions underpinning these two tropes, regarding the nature of bodies and their encounters with the technologies that support cyberspace, demonstrates clearly the pervasive operations of the binary structure.

Informed by a dual lineage drawn from cybernetics and science fiction, the notion of free-floating consciousness released from a redundant physical body is one of the earliest and most pervasive tropes in the discourses of cyberspace. The possibility of such a radical separation depends largely on the foregrounding of information as the engine of cyberspace. The consequences of the intersection of information with bodies is vividly elaborated by cybernetic researcher Hans Moravec. The most exemplary advocate of radical disembodiment, Moravec envisioned a postbiological age where the increasing power and sophistication of computer technologies eventually facilitate the downloading of consciousness into computer memory that would survive the mortal physical body. For Moravec, the subject is located and constituted within the pattern of information in the brain, and as such the body is only ever a mechanical conveyance and often an inconvenience. Consciousness, as brain pattern, is understood to be of the order of cybernetic feedback loops and information-processing systems and, on this basis, is completely compatible with other information patterns and processing devices such as computers. According to Moravec's "transmigration" scenario, a downloaded data-based consciousness could be temporarily relocated or downloaded into a variety of robotic vehicles pragmatically selected to accomplish any number of tasks.

Moravec's thought experiment may propose a fanciful imagined future; nevertheless, in his insistence on the precedence of information as the decisive factor governing the relations between embodied individuals and technologies, he gestures toward an epistemological shift whereby information processing becomes the principal function and defining mode of existence for a subject to the detriment of embodied existence: "Body-identity assumes that a person is defined by the stuff of which a human body is made. … Pattern-identity, conversely, defines the essence of a person, say myself, as the pattern and the process going on in my head and body, not the machinery supporting that process. If the process is preserved, I am preserved. The rest is mere jelly" (Moravec 1988, 116).

The human organism becomes a particular distribution of information that can be exchanged, intermeshed, and mingled with other information-processing systems. As N. Katherine Hayles (1994) explains, this seamless interface between information systems is predicated on the disassociation of information from the physical markers that embody it.

This fundamental duality can be seen in operation in the two moments of disconnection from material bodies that occur with the foregrounding information patterns in the cybernetic paradigm. In the first moment, minds are disconnected from bodies. Consciousness is downloaded and bodies are redundant. In this case, bodies are considered entirely distinct from mind, as information, in a straightforward reiteration of the mind/body split. In the second instance, information processes belonging to bodies, such as DNA sequences and the feedback loops of the central nervous system, are disconnected from a residual bodily materiality. While seemingly more inclusive of bodies, this second moment does not however escape the binary structure. To the degree that bodies are permeated by information, a material/immaterial dichotomy established between the informational systems of the bodies that can enter the cybernetic loop and a physical substrate that cannot. Insofar as a residual material body remains excluded from the circuits of information, the elaboration of an information body simply offers another route to disembodiment.

[…]

The point is not only that abstracting information from a material base is an imaginary act but also, and more fundamental, that conceiving of information as a thing separate from the medium instantiating it is a prior imaginary act that constructs a holistic phenomenon as an information/matter duality.

Thus what appears as a straightforward mind/body dichotomy in Moravec's transmigration scenario actually turns on this more central opposition between information and physical matter – a material/immaterial binary. This distinction pervades everyday conceptions of cyberspace in which information is clearly the privileged term of the pair and matter is subordinated to it. It is within this horizon that information functions as the determining principle in theorizing the encounters between organic embodied subjects and the technological devices and social spheres of cyberspace. As such, it delimits the horizon within which the range and modalities of relations are articulated and underpins any subsequent propositions of transformation. We can see this in operation by tracing how the two moments of disconnection of information from the material, indicated by Moravec, function as the basis for the tropes of disembodiment and the virtual body and also predicate any associated transformative claims.

Disembodiment

From its first appearance in the science-fiction novels of Gibson, Sterling, and Stephenson, and across the proliferating field of critical and popular commentary, cyberspace has been figured consistently as a purely informational zone generated within global communication networks. On these grounds, it seems a perfectly reasonable assumption that cyberspace is the exclusive province of disembodied information-based consciousness – the materiality of bodies being simply unable to access it. Rather than this exclusion being regarded as a technical, or theoretical, limitation, the banishment of the material body becomes the privileged means of subjective transformation. The shared immaterial social spaces of the Internet are hailed as a realm where physical attributes such as sex, race, infirmity, and age are displaced and rendered irrelevant, thereby allowing more egalitarian virtual communities to emerge. According to Howard Rheingold: "Race, gender, age, national origin, and physical appearance are not apparent unless a person wants to make such characteristics public. … People whose physical handicaps make it difficult to form new friendships find that virtual communities treat them as they always wanted to be treated – as thinkers and transmitters of ideas and feeling beings, not carnal vessels with a certain appearance and way of walking and talking (or not walking and not talking)" (1993, 26).

While clearly based on the disconnection and dislocation of material bodies wrought by information technologies, this model of transformation turns on a more sophisticated notion of the body than that of Moravec. Bodies here are not simply an amalgam of information systems and material structures but surfaces of inscription. While race, age, and infirmity may be cast as physical realities – in line with a broadly constructivist framework – it is more commonly understood that such characteristics are not simply and solely biological givens. Rather they are constituted as viable and active categories and attributed meaning through the inscription of social and cultural values and expectations onto bodies. Thus bodies are not simply mute physical objects merely incapable of entering the informational realm, but are irretrievably inscribed and shaped by social categories and values that constrain and oppress the embodied subject. The movement of transformation offered by disembodiment is in transcending these marked and compromised bodies.

For feminists, this scenario of disembodied social interaction offers an avenue for exploring the possibilities of identity not constrained by conventional representations of sexual difference, gendered identity being understood as the socially constructed identity that inscribes a subordinate position onto sexed bodies. The movement of disembodiment relegates gendered identity to the material realm, ostracized from cyberspace with the physical sexed body, and thus frees individual women to construct their own sexual identity.

By providing women with an opportunity to express their ideas in a way that transcends the biological body, this technology gives them the power to redefine themselves outside the historical categories of "women," "other," or "object" (Shade 1996).

Such a complete disconnection of consciousness and material body is of course the limit case; many shades and degrees of disembodiment are explored in feminist analyses of cyberspace. Feminists, such as Stone and Turkle, while they consider transgressive possibilities to exist in adopting a self-created gender-free identity within cyberspace, also contend that there remains an inescapable bond to a physical "real" life body. Feminists of this school of thought demand a more sophisticated understanding of the relationship between bodies and identity. For example, Allucquère Rosanne Stone insists that "no matter how virtual the subject may become, there is always a body attached. It may be off somewhere else … but consciousness remains firmly rooted in the physical. Historically, body, technology and community constitute each other" (1991, 111).

She considers the relationship between a disembodied entity in cyberspace and an embodied computer user as one continually mediated by social formations and hierarchies that envelop technology and subjectivity and articulate each in relation to the other. However complex Stone's understanding of the constitution of embodied subjectivity, it nevertheless remains one articulated within a binary framework – that of mind/body. Within such a formulation a clear demarcation remains between the immaterial realm of cyberspace and the materiality of bodies. Consciousness might inhabit both realms; however, to the extent that the materiality of bodies cannot participate in the immaterial realm of cyberspace where consciousness can, a clear-cut opposition between body and mind persists. Thus we can see any scenario where the possibility of subjective transformation via a disembodied postgender identity activated in cyberspace is proposed affirms, either implicitly or explicitly, a mind/body binary in alignment with an immaterial/material opposition.

Virtual Bodies

If disembodied consciousness reflects the first moment of dislocation suggested by the cybernetic account of bodies, then the trope of the virtual bodies takes up the second, that of the demarcation of an informational body. It draws on this notion of the informational aspect of bodies, as well as constructivist understandings of embodiment, in order to speculate on possible modes of embodiment in cyberspace.

The notion of virtual embodiment suggests that instead of debarring the body entirely from information space, the body can be translated or (re)constructed via technology into an entity capable of inhabiting these spaces. During the process of radical modification in the passage into cyberspace, the potential for transformation exists. This model is taken up across a range of virtual embodiment scenarios, the two most prominent being within the electronic social spaces of the Internet and through virtual reality technology.

In the case of the Internet, it is within the context of primarily text-based (though sometimes graphic) social environments that one notion of the virtual body is deployed. In the multiuser real-time interactive spaces of the Internet, individuals engage in a variety of activities, some of which (particularly erotic encounters) draw heavily on a textual articulation and representation of a body. These virtual bodies are constructed as an informational representation of locale, physical characteristics, adornment, comportment, expression, and function as the site for interaction with other such virtual bodies. The construction of these bodies is entirely along the lines of individual desires. Likewise, the visual avatars adopted by participants in more sophisticated graphical social environments present not simply a graphic icon manipulated by the individual user but a figure that is self-imagined and created. In terms of transformation, these virtual bodies operate along the same lines as disembodiment. As the product of the individuals' independent choice and self-directed representation, a virtual body promises to deliver the participant from the bondage of social cultural constraints that inhere in the "real-life" body. As Lyn Cherney explains, "Bodies in virtual space can be created with a bit of programming. "Real life" gender can be switched, skin colour can be forgotten temporarily, age or infirmity can be escaped" (1996).

This "reprogramming" of bodies is also the premise of the other schema of the virtual body as generated by virtual-reality technology. Such technology locates subjects within a real-time visual representation of spatial surrounds in which they occupy a graphically represented "virtual" body able to move and interact with other informational objects in the simulated environment. Virtual bodies in this instance have a direct relation to "actual" bodies insofar as movement and perspective are generated by the actual body and then experienced via visual immersion, and to a limited degree tactile sensation, in the virtual environment. However, this virtual body is no ethereal doppelgänger or electronic shadow that transports a mirror image of the body into an information environment. In passing through the process of electronic reconstruction into a virtual body, bodies are able to take any form within information space. Once again we see the possibility of reshaping bodily attributes, abilities and functions by manipulating their information patterns. ...

Running through both these conceptions of virtual bodies is the desire to maintain, albeit in modified ways, a relationship between the virtual and the real-life body. The real-life body is that which must be translated and refigured along the lines of individual desires to provide a more accurate representation of identity as conceived by themselves. As such, the virtual body does not require discarding the body entirely; rather, it is an attempt to rearticulate certain attributes of bodies into another context and in the process reshape its representations, meanings, and functions. While bodies may be transported into cyberspace, it is only on the basis of the extraction of an information body from a material body that remains excluded. As in the more complex accounts of disembodied identity, irrespective of the complexity or degree of relations between virtual and real bodies, the underlying assumption remains that the material is excluded from a purely informational realm. Again this barrier answers the desire to transcend the limitations of the material body by filtering out unwanted cultural and social inscription in the transition from real to virtual. Insofar as this formulation presumes that consciousness, once free from the restrictions of the marked materiality of the body, can autonomously articulate its own identity, the construction of virtual bodies enacts the same movement of dispensation and distancing of the physical body as disembodiment scenarios.

As we have seen, the tropes of disembodied consciousness and virtual bodies both turn on the premise of the privilege of information in an information/matter binary. Within this theoretical horizon an immaterial/material binary operates as the governing distinction of cyberspace in the light of which all attempts to explain embodiment and bodies are inevitably drawn. This results in either the clear-cut separation of immaterial mind/material body, or a preliminary division of information-body/material-body that likewise supports a mind/body distinction in which mind remains distinct from both bodies but able to manipulate the information body. In this manner, the logic of identity through the binary structures of mind/body, immaterial/material frames a particular understanding of bodies that pervades these transformational accounts of cyberspace. Bodies are denied difference insofar as they are constrained within the binary structure within which they are figured only in terms of their opposition, lack, negation, or diminution of the privileged term – immaterial mind. Their particular specificities and differences, including sexual difference, are obliterated as is any consideration of their excessive and transgressive potential. Thus we can see that any account of embodiment that invariably results in the reinstallation of a mind/body dichotomy is clearly counterproductive for feminists. Further, this saturation of cyberspace with binary oppositions works to limit opportunities for transformation rather than effect them.

Gendered Bodies and Prosthetic Technologies

If bodies are articulated across discourses of information space entirely through a immaterial/material binary structure, consistent with a generalized logic of identity, I want to briefly trace how this logic is activated in the sites where transformation is pursued. Many such sites exist; however, two key sites or avenues of transformation are particularly prevalent to discourses of cyberspace. The first is gender, which figures as the moment of reconfiguring prevailing social constructions of sexual identity. And second is prosthesis as a mode of interaction with technology, which marks it as an agent for effecting change.

The persistence of mind/body dualism and the associated immaterial/material binary is, I would suggest, due to its compatibility with a certain configuration of gender as an information pattern distinct from the materiality of the sexed body. In the transformative scenarios of cyberspace, gender becomes a key site of transformation insofar as it is understood to be information inscribed onto a material body that can be transcended through disembodiment or virtual rearticulation. In such a formulation, gender as information operates in two modes. First, it is distinct from yet affixed to materially sexed bodies, such that the two cannot be readily detached in the real world; however, through disembodiment or virtuality gender patterns may be eluded. Second, within pure information cyberspace, it is a free-floating pattern that as, Sherry Turkle describes, individuals can take up and rescind at will: "As MUD players talked to me about their experiences with gender swapping, they certainly gave me reason to believe that through this practice they were working through personal issues that had to do with accepting the feminine and/or masculine in their own personalities" (1994).

Gender has become a fraught concept in feminist theory in recent years, and as deployed in discourses of cyberspace it is problematic on a range of levels. Although such a configuration of gender suggests powerful bonds between bodies and gender – bonds that only drastic technological intervention can dislocate – this model of gender is clearly embedded in the information/matter binary. Insofar as gender can, in less socially saturated environments such as cyberspace, float free of bodies, it possesses an informational status in opposition to the matter of the bodies onto which it is inscribed. Framing gender as a socially generated information pattern that does not impinge on consciousness once that consciousness has disassociated itself from the body likewise turns on a binary opposition, in this case between mind information/body matter. This formation also underpins any scenario whereby consciousness can interact with various gender patterns at will within information space.

For some years feminists have been complicating this model of detachable gender precisely on the basis of its recourse to mind/body and other dichotomies. Gatens (1983) has convincingly shown that sexed bodies and socially inscribed masculinity and femininity are by no means neatly detachable or interchangeable. She insists that such inscriptions are deeply involved in the way bodies are lived, and that sexed bodies are inextricable from the way femininity or masculinity is experienced. However, in the desire for cybertransformation, these complexities invariably become simplified to a degendered consciousness that negotiates new (or not) relations with gender other than those of the physically sexed embodied subject. Even those such as Stone, who disdain any neat bisection of materially sexed body and socially gendered mind in favor of more complex interrelations between subjectivity and embodiment, entertain the possibility of virtual gender swapping and thus reiterate this gender-mind/sex-body binary. Thus any account that takes an unproblematic formulation of gender as detachable information pattern as the locus of transformation, such as those expressed by Turkle, Cherney Shade, or Rheingold, remains bound by binary logic, unable to think bodies in cyberspace, confined to an economy of identity and ultimately unable to pursue the transformational possibilities of articulating difference.

The second conceptual model that I have suggested is key to the installation of the logic of identity at the heart of many cybertransformation scenarios is that of prosthesis. By prosthesis, I mean a particular conceptualization of the field and mode of encounter between subjects and technologies. In the simplest terms, a prosthetic understanding of technologies holds that a technological object, or practice, meets a subject's body and affects it in some way – enhancing it, reshaping it. Eyeglasses meet the eyes and extend the range of vision, pacemakers regulate the heart, telephones extend the range of the voice. A more sophisticated version of prosthesis is of course Donna Haraway's famous cyborg that celebrates the mutations wrought upon bodies through their intermeshing with technologies. In the case of the cyborg, the human is transformed as this intermeshing works to dislodge the socially constructed human subject. I claim that whatever permutations arise from a prosthetic encounter between bodies and technologies, they remain bound within the logic of identity or sameness that structures all binary oppositions.

The logic of identity pervades the prosthetic model of interaction and, in doing so, negates any possibility of autonomy and difference of bodies or technologies. The prosthetic equation is 1 + 1. It begins with an original self-identical entity being added to by some exterior element that has some effect upon it. The element that is added to the original is understood only in terms of its difference from the original as not-original. In the instance of embodied subjects and technologies, it is a self-identical and unified self upon which technology as not-self (or object) impacts and instigates some alteration. Regardless of the novelty of the resultant entity, this original binary demarcation of self/not-self grounds the entire process within the logic of sameness. Sameness is insinuated in the proposition of a singular, stable, identifiable 1 as the basis for all such encounters. We have seen this logic of sameness running through the accounts of bodies and cyberspace offered above. The technologies of cyberspace – the computer screens and keyboards, chips and cables, which generate a field of information on the other side of the screen – on encountering the body either relegate it entirely to one side of the screen or bisect it into an informational virtual body and a material body, one of which functions on the other side of the screen. Irrespective of the outcome, the fundamental encounter between bodies and technologies is elaborated in terms of a unified body acted upon by some "not-body" force or entity in a straightforward reiteration of binary logic. Thus any account of cyberspace that begins with a prosthetic understanding of the interaction of technologies and subjects is already situated within the binary structure, and thus the possibilities of thinking transformation are already circumscribed.

Transformation based on both or either of these frameworks is impossible to the extent that they are embedded within the epistemological structures of identity that preclude any articulation of autonomous difference, including sexual difference. For those feminisms concerned with thinking sexual difference in its specificity, any investigation of the transformative possibilities of cyberspace requires, in the first instance, reconceptualizing bodies, technologies, and their modes of interaction such that the question never begins with the unified self-identical body of prosthesis, or an understanding of gender as detachable from bodies. It is at this point that I turn to Deleuze and Guattari for a fundamentally different account of the meetings between technologies and individuals, one that develops an alternative understanding of bodies and technologies that affirms difference instead of insinuating identity and sameness.

… In thinking of the interactions between bodies and technologies in terms of assemblages, I would claim that we are able to frame an account that is not contained within the logic of identity. Rather it opens a field of inquiry that has as its basis "difference." Clearly such an endeavor is of great benefit for feminists concerned with articulating autonomous sexual difference and tracing how it might be elaborated across various technological formations of cyberspace. The process of establishing difference as the basis of the operations of assemblages is elaborated in great detail and complexity across the corpus of Deleuze and Guattari's work.

[…]

Assemblages are functional conglomerations of elements, but most important, the component elements are not understood as unified, stable, or self-identical entities or objects. In each assemblage the forces and flows of components meet with and link to the forces and flows of other elements; the resultant distribution of these meetings constitutes the assemblage. While concerned with the meetings of various objects and entities, this is not simply a prosthetic model of connection by addition. For Deleuze and Guattari, a self-identical body or object does not exist as origin, prior to or outside the field of encounters that articulate it within any specific assemblage. There is no original whole body that divides into organs, movements, pieces, forces, or information flows, which are then complied into assemblages. Rather bodies and other components are fields of multiplicities that make transitory connections and alignments within each assemblage.

[…]

If the elements of the assemblage are multiplicities that intersect with other multiplicities, clearly each intersection will produce other multiplicities that differ in nature from any of those preceding. As such each element becomes something other with each new connection and within each assemblage. Thus when referring to the elements or components of an assemblage, we must remember that these contents of assemblages are never enduring, stable, individuated, and self-identical. Rather, multiplicities of flows and partial fragments of information, matter, ideas, particles, movements, and intensities coalesce into particular recognizable forms and functions within the context of particular assemblages. As such, the meetings between elements of assemblages do not proceed on the basis of a prosthetic encounter. Rather the flows, forces, and intensities of multiplicities link and connect with other flows and forces, and different multiplicities are elaborated. These are not hybrids, or variations; they differ in kind and cannot be traced back to a single original entity.

If the movement of differing constitutes an assemblage, and its components are not organized along the lines of identity, binary oppositions are no longer adequate as a means of establishing the status of any one element. For example, minds and bodies can no longer be explained in a binary relation where one is understood in terms of the other – bodies being characterized as the absence or lack of consciousness. Rather each is considered different in and of itself, and thus relation between the two no longer turns on any founding hierarchy. Both elements are equally operational in a productive mode. The forces of each meet and mix such that it is impossible to figure one as the diminution of the other as the privileged term. Clearly a new conception of bodies emerges within this field of differing. Instead of an organized, unified object subordinated to consciousness, bodies are collections of disparate flows, materials, impulses, intensities, and practices. They take shape within a complex field of relations with the flows and intensities of surrounding objects, knowledges, geographies, and institutional practices in transitory, functional assemblages. Grosz describes such bodies as "discontinuous, nontotalizable series of processes, organs, flows, energies, corporeal substances and incorporeal events, speeds and duration" (1994, 164).

The concept of assemblage, then, suggests a two-pronged approach to understanding bodies. First, that while they are undeniable concoctions of material, chemical, and electrical impulses, these are not fixed into any immutable pattern; they are continually in flux, open to the circumstances and fields of objects and discourses through which they circulate. Second, particular bodies are articulated or actualized, within complex assemblages of other bodies, objects, institutions, technologies, regimes of signs, and relations of power that may move to unify and stabilize them but can never entirely succeed in doing so.

Insofar as my discussion of assemblage draws on the terminology of construction and constitution, caution must be exercised so as not to conflate assemblages with a generalized constructivism. Assemblages propose an entirely different mode of understanding the constitution and functions of bodies (and other objects) than constructivist models. A brief examination of how each model responds to the question of the relation of the whole to the parts illustrates another of the theoretical shifts flagged earlier that Deleuze and Guattari make. Constructivist accounts propose an overarching system or structure that orders component parts. This whole not only transcends the parts but also determines them insofar as they are interpolated into it. For example, in the case of bodies the "biologically" female body is interpolated into the social institutions, discourses, and practices of an overarching systemic whole – such as patriarchy – to become a body constructed and experienced as feminine. Assemblages, in contrast, turn on a different understanding of the relation of the whole to the component elements, whereby the parts constitute the whole. Because it is composed of the links and connections between multiplicities, an assemblage is only ever the sum of its component elements and is not governed or ordered by any transcendent organizing structure. Given this composition, within an assemblage any change or shift in a constituent element brings about a new assemblage, whereas changes within the component parts in a constructivist model are permissible only within a limited sphere of variation, beyond which they become excluded, unintelligible, or rehabilitated while the whole remains intact.

[…]

Feminism and Assemblages

For feminists investigating cyberspace, these theoretical shifts that Deleuze and Guattari make suggest the possibility of engagements with the technologies and practices of cyberspace that are not always already contained within the logic of identity that, as I have shown, forecloses transformation. Exploring and analyzing such engagements is a vast and complex task that is clearly beyond the bounds of this essay. At most what I hope to accomplish here is to indicate the directions and theoretical tools that feminists taking up such projects might draw from Deleuze and Guattari. I would claim that the redrawn theoretical horizon that Deleuze and Guattari elaborate is useful to feminists on a number of levels. First, in theorizing assemblages as temporary aggregations of multiplicities, in which component elements find their local and specific articulation through their linkages with other elements, it offers an alternative to prosthesis as the mode of encounter between bodies and technologies: in the first instance because there is no assumption of a stable identified body prior to the encounter, and in the second because the encounters between bodies and technologies take place within a field of other intersections. The mode of meeting is never one of simple addition, of 1 + 1; rather, each instance gives rise to a new configuration of bodies and technologies and all the other elements of an assemblage. The task then becomes not to measure what effects technologies have on unified stable bodies, but to track what configurations of bodies, technologies, practices, objects, and discourses emerge within particular assemblages.

Thus instead of concluding that beyond the contact of fingers with keyboards and eyes with screen the body is effectively excluded from cyberspace, it would be a matter of tracing what kinds of bodies are elaborated in the activities, exchanges, and circuits of the particular practices. For example in the instance of the cyberspace of a MOO, a body is not simply split into a materiality that is excluded and an electronic / informational body that is activated in the social environs of the MOO. Rather the energy and impulses of bodies and electronic circuitry combine and find new forms, and they are traversed by flows of light, information, signs, sociality, sexuality, conversation, and contact that give rise to differing meanings, experiences, and configurations of bodies and technologies. It becomes a question of tracing out these differing configurations not by beginning with an already established model of the body but by mapping the assembled field in order to track very specifically what bodies come into being and how.

This points immediately to the second useful aspect of Deleuze and Guattari's model of assemblage and multiplicity for feminists. It offers a diagnostic tool with which to begin mapping how assembled bodies and technologies and social spaces and practices intersect with systems of knowledge and power. Why and how do certain bodies and models of interaction with technology such as prosthesis emerge and predominate? It becomes possible to map how certain understandings of woman are formulated in conjunction with certain understandings of the technological and the social. Further, it is possible to trace this process in a tangible way across particular practices discourses, such as those of cyberspace, in order to map the complex ways in which power and knowledge intersect with these formulations. For example, feminist concerns, such as those voiced by Renate Klein (1999), as to the risks posed to women in their engagements with "techno-patriarchy" (210) of cyberspace can be assessed such that they are not premised on an essential alienation of women from technologies. While not denying the very real inequities operational in many practices associated with cyberspace, Deleuze and Guattari offer a more sophisticated and less teleological approach to analyzing the operations of power within such practices. If, following Deleuze, we approach technology, masculinity, femininity, technoscientific discourses, and military-industrial complexes as a series of interconnected assemblages, we can begin to delineate more clearly how such associations of masculinity with technologies of computing function and on what basis women are articulated as incompatible with those technologies. Through such a process, the very tangible operations of power should become apparent. Further, within such an analysis no individual technological formation is automatically foreclosed to women on the basis of an essential masculinity, but the relations and operations of power that render it oppressive to women can be more acutely discerned and its responses then formulated.

The third aspect of Deleuze and Guattari's model of assemblage that is of importance to feminists is the shift whereby structures of knowledge and power such as the economics of identity are repositioned as functional elements of an assemblage rather than as overarching and transcendent structures. It is on this basis that the above diagnostic exercise can proceed. Deleuze and Guattari begin with a different question – asking what an object, assemblage, practice, institution, discourse *does* rather than what it *is*. In making such an initial reorientation, our inquiries are no longer directed toward uncovering or defining an essential identity of these elements, which as we saw earlier most often leads to an installation of the epistemological structures of identity. Rather, it is to begin to (1) trace the processes through which identity is installed, and (2) consider what configurations of forces and objects are relegated to outside the limits of this identity that might suggest other formulations of bodies, subjects and technologies.

Thus in taking up a Deleuzian approach to cyberspace, two immediate tasks present themselves to feminists. First, we must understand cyberspace itself as not simply a technologically generated information space or place, but as a series of assemblages comprised of elements of the technical, social, discursive, material, and immaterial. It then becomes necessary to map such assemblages in order to discern how relations of power traverse them, how discourses and practices of femininity and masculinity intersect with those of technology and technological artifacts, what hierarchies are functional, and through what particular and local linkages are bodies and technologies articulated. Though this mapping process, a more nuanced and complex understanding of the operations of prevailing power relations and modes of knowledge will emerge. Such a mapping process will alert feminists to any exclusionary and oppressive practices, arrangements, and structures of knowledge that, while frequently circumscribing women's encounters with the technological, never completely foreclose transformative possibilities. Second, having traced out these fields of intersection among bodies, technologies, information flows, power relations, social institutions, and practices, we can begin to investigate the lines of flight and movements of differing that also always traverse an assemblage. It is these movements that are creative in their own right and that raise the possibility that new connections and configurations of technologies and bodies might generate a field within which new autonomous unrestricted articulations of woman might emerge.

NOTE

1. Landmark examples of this position can be found in Stone 1991 and Rheingold 1991.

REFERENCES

Cherney, Lyn. "Objectifying the Body in the Discourse of an Object-Oriented MUD." 1996. Available online at <http://bhasha.stanford.edu/~cherny/charley.tx>. 1 March 2000.

Deleuze, Gilles, and Felix Guattari, *A Thousand Plateaus: Capitalism and Schizophrenia*. Trans. Brian Massumi. Minneapolis: University of Minnesota Press, 1987.

Gatens, Moira. "A Critique of the Sex/Gender Distinction." In *Interventions after Marx*, ed. J. Allen and P. Patton, 18–33. Sydney: Intervention, 1983.

Grosz, Elizabeth. *Volatile Bodies. Toward a Corporeal Feminism*. St. Leonards: Allen & Unwin, 1994.

Hayles, N. Katherine. "Boundary Disputes: Homeostasis, Reflexivity and the Foundation of Cybernetics." *Configurations: A Journal of Literature, Science & Technology* 2, no. 3 (1994): 441–467.

Klein, Renate. "If I'm a Cyborg Rather Than a Goddess Will Patriarchy Go Away?" In *Cyberfeminism: Connectivity, Critique and Creativity*, ed. S. Hawthorne and R. Klein. Melbourne, Australia: Spinifex Press, 1999.

Moravec, Hans. *Mind Children: The Future of Robot and Human Intelligence*. Cambridge: Harvard University Press, 1988.

Rheingold, Howard. *Virtual Communities: Homesteading on the Electronic Frontier*. New York: Addison–Wesley Publishing Company, 1993.

Shade, Leslie Regan. "Gender Issues in Computer Networks." 1996. Available online at <http://www.vcn.bc.ca/sig/comm-nets/shade.html>. 1 March 2000.

Stone, Allucquère Rosanne. "Will the Real Body Please Stand Up? Boundary Stories about Virtual Cultures." In *Cyberspace: The First Steps*, ed. M. Benedikt. Cambridge, MA: MIT Press, 1991.

Turkle, Sherry. "Constructions and Reconstructions of Self in Virtual Reality: Playing in the MUDs." 1994. Available online at <http://www.mit.edu/people/sturkle/constructions.html>. 1 March 2000.

18 LESBIANS IN (CYBER)SPACE

The Politics of the Internet in Latin American On- and Off-line Communities

Elisabeth Jay Friedman

Two women, heads close together, beam at the camera, with a caption in Portuguese that reads 'Stable Union: Luciana and Kátia made their declaration with us! You do it too!'[1] A magenta book cover, illustrated with one Renaissance woman gazing at another, proclaims in Spanish 'Compilation of the 3rd Competition of Lesbian Erotic Poetry'. Two rainbow-striped, rotating women's symbols draw attention to announcements about lesbian publications and organizations, separated by rainbow ribbons. In Spanish, the name 'GALF: Group of Feminist Lesbian Activists' headlines a page swirling with pastel colors, evocative paintings of women, and twinned women's symbols.

These images represent lesbian political and social action in Latin America: out, proud and visible, in cities from São Paulo, Brazil, to Lima, Peru. ...

Since the mid-1990s, although lesbians have achieved greater visibility and, in some countries, increased equality, they are routinely discriminated against in the Latin American region – as are gay men, bisexuals and transsexuals, transvestites and transgendered people. This discrimination all too often takes the form of social denigration and physical violence. Recent reports reveal the vicious murders of lovers who dared to hold hands in public; legislators considering public funding for 'conversion therapy' for homosexuals; the arrest of lesbian activists for producing television programs on sexual rights; 'pro-masculinity' and right-wing counter-demonstrations at lesbian marches; heavy-handed

Elisabeth Jay Friedman "Lesbians in (cyber)space: the politics of the internet in Latin American on- and off-line communities," pp. 790–811 from *Media, Culture & Society* 29:5 (2007).

Catholic Church opposition to LGBT (lesbian, gay, bisexual, and transgender)[2] organizations in schools; and law after law restricting a panoply of social benefits to heterosexuals.

[…]

This article argues that cyberspace – the dense web of information and communication created by email, chat, distribution lists and websites – is a virtual public sphere especially useful for Latin American lesbian communities. The internet addresses the central problems impeding the effectiveness of lesbian organizing: isolation, repression, resource restriction and lack of community cohesion. Lesbians can find each other via the internet even if they are isolated in their daily lives; and if they can find a reasonably private place to go online, they can be out without fear of stigma or violence. Compared to the often-transient spaces of 'women's nights' at bars or cafés, or the expense of keeping up an office, websites offer a more stable and inexpensive platform for socializing and activism. Email, distribution lists and websites are relatively accessible sources of alternative information, crucial for communities ignored or criticized in the mass media. Finally, the internet cannot end contentious regional debates over political practice, but it provides new possibilities for communication within and across national boundaries.

[…]

This study brings together insight gathered from three sources: secondary material on the history of Latin American lesbian organizing and the impact of the internet on LGBT communities; original interviews with members of six lesbian feminist organizations in Argentina and Mexico; and analysis of a representative sample of lesbian feminist websites from Mexico, Chile, Argentina, Peru, and Brazil.[3] The sites are:[4]

LeS VOZ (LeS[bian] VOICE; www.lesvoz.org.mx/): This website, started in 2000, is the online counterpart of *LeS VOZ* magazine, a Mexico City-based publication dedicated to 'lesbian feminist culture' from arts to politics. . . .

Rompiendo el Silencio (Breaking the Silence; www.rompiendoelsilencio.cl/): Begun in 2002 in Santiago de Chile, this website is an internet-only lesbian magazine that supports 'whatever group, creation or idea that wants to develop through the internet and has as its goal the respect and dignity of lesbian women'. …

Safo Piensa (Sappho Thinks; http://www.rimaweb.com.ar/safopiensa/): This 'Lesbian Feminist Network' is a page of the website for RIMA: Information Network of Argentine Women. …

Grupo de Activistas Lesbianas Feministas (Activist Lesbian Feminist Group or GALF; www.galf.org/): This Peruvian organization's goal is 'to struggle for the construction of inclusive societies with social justice and gender equality, based in a culture of peace and exercise of human rights for everyone and, in particular, for lesbians'. …

Um *Outro* Olhar (An *Other* Look; http://www.umoutroolhar.com.br/): This website, started in 2004, forms part of the off-line lesbian feminist documentation center of this Brazilian organization, which also publishes a print magazine. […]

Come Out, Come Out? The Delights and Dangers of Real-time Community-building

... Regional activist Alejandra Sardá (2002) has written, before lesbians began to mobilize on their own behalf, in the Latin American 'social imaginary the homosexual was male and the lesbian was practically inconceivable'. Nevertheless, over the last three decades lesbian movements have expanded across the region.

The emergence of independent lesbian activism can be traced to four influences: political dynamics at the macro-level, the left, and the mixed gay/lesbian and women's liberation movements. Given the tumultuous political history of the region, including long periods of authoritarian repression as well as drawn-out democratization processes, LGBT organizing has been marked by the political context of different countries (Mongrovejo, 2000: 63). Region-wide political liberalization in the 1980s allowed more room for LGBT social movement activity (Green and Babb, 2002), but democratic politics have been no guarantee of LGBT rights.

Many early lesbian activists came out of communist, socialist or anarchist parties, through which they struggled for national (socialist) and sexual liberation. Nevertheless, left parties and movements often rejected homosexuality as contrary to revolutionary morality. Revolutionary regimes in Cuba and Nicaragua were actively hostile to homosexuals. Castro promoted re-education until the 1990s, and the revolutionary Nicaraguan Sandinistas forbade even stalwart cadres from forming an LGBT organization (Babb, 2003; Mongrovejo, 2000).

[...]

It is hard for women to procure information about lesbianism, let alone attend meetings, given the lack of resources groups have to communicate about their existence and efforts. Most rely on word of mouth to publicize issues and events. Some groups have published a newsletter or journal in order to share information and political, literary, and artistic work, but the publications have had limited circulation. In the 1980s, for example, the handmade Peruvian bulletin, *Al Margen* (On the Margin) was passed out in discotheques and in a few women's centers (Jitsuya and Sevilla, 2004; Mongrovejo, 2000: 309).

Lesbian groups, whether social or political, have found it almost impossible to maintain physical spaces. ...

The repression of lesbians and their organizing efforts, sometimes sanctioned by the state, has not been limited to authoritarian governments. ... As Alejandra Sardá argues, even in democracies lesbians' degree of citizenship is 'tenuous, limited and fragile', considering their non-existent protection from discrimination; their overall lack of legal recognition as parents or partners; and their risk of physical attack if they come out, particularly outside the major cities (Sardá, 1998, 2002).

Some challenges are internal. Lesbians disagree, sometimes bitterly, over the meaning of political autonomy and what it implies for political practice ... The growth of international lesbian networking and (limited) external funding from international foundations, and even some governments, has further complicated internal politics. Are leaders and groups responsive to the government or international foundations and networks' agendas, or to local demands?[5] International intervention, while a key source of resources and ideas, intensifies the already complex politics of autonomous lesbian organizing.

Clearly, Latin American lesbian organizations face a host of challenges. They struggle to reach out to (isolated) others in a situation of resource restriction. They endeavor to organize while facing social denigration, governmental repression and internal divisions. And they seek to balance the benefits of international networking with the complications external influences bring to local groups. Can the internet help activists face these challenges? A brief survey of the literature reveals a very positive answer.

Cyberspace: a 'Virtual Lifeline' for the GLBT Community

The relatively inexpensive medium of the internet offers a unique virtual public sphere open to a wide range of actors and expressions (Dilevko, 2002; Leon et al., 2001; Warkentin, 2001). This range is clearly restricted by traditional sources of exclusion, such as race/ethnicity, gender, class and geographical location (Ebo, 1998; Hafkin and Taggart, 2001). But the increasing accessibility of travel within cyberspace, whether from public locales such as community telecenters or private means such as wired (or WiFi) cafes, helps to mediate restrictions. As a result, the internet 'may be of particular importance to small or marginal groups with limited finances or expectation of mainstream support for their views' (Friedman, 2005: 5).

Studies from various countries demonstrate that the internet is being used to end the 'social isolation of homosexuals', since online they can 'try out behavior that is socially labeled as deviant and ... fulfill personal and political needs' (Burke, 2000: 593; see also Haag and Chang, 1997; Koch and Schockman, 1998; Weinrich, 1997). One comparison of LGBT websites in the US, Germany, China and Japan claimed that 'there is no other forum in which so many people of so many different backgrounds have safely disclosed, and felt comfortable disclosing, their sexual identities' (Heinz et al., 2002: 109). Cyberspace is crucial for 'sexual minorities', according to legal scholar Edward Stein (2003), because of social and legal discrimination that either compels them to be closeted or punishes them should they emerge. In sharp contrast to mainstream society, cyberspace is 'an ideal environment and a "virtual lifeline"' (2003: 183).

According to some, the benefits of cyberspace include the expansion of queer communities within and across national boundaries (Alexander, 2002b). Whereas homophobia and political subjugation have isolated LGBT individuals from others in their own societies, and geography and politics have kept them separated from others elsewhere, 'cyberspace promises, at least in theory, an emancipatory and community-building realm that transcends intranational boundaries and international borders' (Heinz et al., 2002: 108). This potential 'globalization' of communication and connection may allow a virtual escape from the repression and rejection of real-time interactions into a place of acceptance and solidarity.

[...]

The fact of the internet's (potential) existence in all space, and thus, in some way, no place, may also exacerbate issues of accountability and representation in LGBT communities. ...

Finally, the very globality offered by internet-mediated communication carries with it the risks inherent in boundary crossing. Transnational organizing efforts have made excellent use of the internet, but the speed and range made possible by virtual communication can also jeopardize or compromise carefully negotiated local or national strategies and discourses (Friedman, 2005). Reaching across geographical expanses does not guarantee cross-cultural understanding, and the ever-larger audiences available for 'transmission' do not promise appreciation for the reality of grounded experiences. As Nina Wakeford reminds us, 'There is a risk that ... geographically located experiences and the local politics of boundary markers become lost in the rush to claim the Internet as a vehicle of a global (lesbian) community' (cited in Alexander, 2002a: 103). Internet-based community building may well trample over local problems and politics.

The literature on internet use by LGBT individuals and communities offers potential answers to the dilemmas of Latin American lesbian organizing – answers that are mostly upheld by the evidence below. Online interaction mitigates social isolation for Latin American lesbians and a web presence eases resource restrictions for organizations. The internet does act as a 'virtual lifeline' in the face of widespread oppression, allowing lesbians to connect, express their ideas, broadcast news and mobilize. Although inherently transnational virtual reality complicates the politics of local lesbian communities, it also permits more voices to participate in regional discussions. Establishing regional connections through the internet is more vital to these communities than achieving international ones. Rather than creating virtual ghettos, lesbian feminist websites and individuals are busy strengthening their identities and traversing (some) borders.

Safe (Cyber)space: out Online

Why have a website? To show that a group of lesbian mothers exists here in Argentina. In the interior [of the country] there are women who are mothers who have feelings for other women ... how are they going to know who they are? (A founder of Argentine Autonomous Feminist Lesbian Mothers)

The role of the internet in ending – or at least alleviating – the isolation of lesbians is undeniable. The non-territorial nature of the community, and the threat of violence that isolated members face, make the refuge provided by online exchange critical. Because lesbian organizations concentrate in the major cities and rural areas tend to be much more traditional, women living in the 'interior' of countries such as Argentina and Mexico depend on the internet to make contact. . . .

Interviews and messages to websites confirm the significance of putting lesbians in touch with each other, or providing them with hard-to-come-by information. Martha Patricia Cuevas Armas, the co-coordinator of the Mexico City-based New Generation of Young Lesbians, received regular email messages from lesbians from different states seeking information about local groups (interview, 2002). According to Mariana Pérez Ocaña, editor of the *LeS VOZ* lesbian magazine and website, also based in the capital, there may not have been much to tell them: 'we get a lot of email from women from the provinces because in the provinces there is nothing! No magazines, nowhere to go ... but if there are groups, we publish what they are doing' (interview, 2002). The founders of the Argentine Autonomous Feminist Lesbian Mothers group, located in Buenos Aires, have been active distributing information via the internet to reach isolated women 'not only in our country, but also to countries such as Paraguay, Mexico – to women who don't belong to a group, but are lesbian mothers' (interview, 2001). Email allows those who are wary of revealing their identities to remain anonymous when making contact, and facilitates the sharing of crucial information such as the location of local lesbian organizations.

Gabriela de Cicco and Irene Ocampo, co-founders of Safo Piensa, note that in Argentina, the internet is 'quite a resource for women who have trouble finding each other' (interview, 2002) – wherever they live. The safe space provided by websites is at once local, national, and regional, as revealed by recent posts to Safo Piensa's 'guest book.' A Buenos Aires woman reflected on the importance of the website for community creation and political change:

> [i]t seems really important to have a place to go when we are eager for information. Society is quite hard and makes an effort to make difficult a life that, particularly, I think is beautiful. In this way I can learn, socialize, try to change situations and share moments and ideas. Simply for that, THANK YOU.

... While this area of the webpage may not be a place to find support, the fact that a Dominican woman posted her distress on an Argentine site reveals how the internet can create at least tangential connections across vast distances.

Although the provision of internet personal ads may seem to be peripheral to creating social change, this web-based service is an integral part of creating community (Burke, 2000). Placing or answering a personal ad is a direct affirmation of lesbian identity; simply reading them can also foster a sense of belonging. The realization that others are 'out' there is particularly significant for women who are struggling to accept their own identity in a hostile environment. Personal contacts are fostered by four of the websites, and are in high demand. Safo Piensa runs a discussion list in which around 70 lesbian, lesbian feminist and bisexual women participate. LeS VOZ accepts personal ads via email (which are then printed in their print magazine). Um *Outro* Olhar has about 500 personals listed. Rompiendo el Silencio hosts 13 different discussion forums, the largest of which (with nearly 3500 messages) is for 'contacts', and provides a chat service for instant interaction. It also offers psychological counseling, a boon for women unable to discuss issues related to their sexuality elsewhere.

The lines between personal contact, community development and political mobilization can easily blur. Rompiendo el Silencio provides a page for the public denunciation of acts of discrimination 'so that others might know about the injustices that continue to be committed in our country and in the world because of our sexual orientation'. One entry on the 'Denouncing Silences' page presents a pointed and poignant example of the importance of online contact in the face of off-line abuse:

> I'm a faithful visitor of this page, and I wanted to tell you my story: last year through chat I met the person that I love the most in my life (along with my son), and I started on an adventure, I never thought that I would meet the most beautiful person in the world. … I had her live with me without thinking that I would make her suffer so much, thanks to the people that are around me, my family, my work and friends, in general, they have humiliated us, they have singled us out, it is an immense sorrow what is happening to us, they are threatening to take my son away, we've been beaten, we've been threatened with death in general it is a forbidden love. MY CITY IS A HELL. I ask myself what is wrong with our loving each other. I love you, *negra*, my greatest joy was meeting you, you were the most important person, I will fight for you even if they've mistreated us, if they've told us that we are the most horrible and sinful people, if loving you is a sin I want to die sinning, I will endure the beatings for you only for you …

As this message reveals, this woman not only met her partner in cyberspace, but the internet offers a way for her to denounce their mistreatment – and to proclaim her love. This personal testimony serves as a potential spur for others to get involved in social action, or at the very least reassures readers that they are part of a larger community that continues to love despite societal sanction. This level of visibility for lesbian reality would be impossible in Latin America without virtual reality.

Building Community Online

> *Lesbian kiss becomes police case in USP East:* Two girls, 22 and 18 years old, who kissed, on October 7, in the cafeteria of the University of São Paulo in the East Zone, had their kiss registered, as an obscene act, in the [local police station], where they were detained for three hours to give 'explanations.' The complaint was filed by a military policeman who argued that the University is a place for mothers and serious people who do not condone that kind of activity. (report posted on website Um *Outro* Olhar)

As inexpensive platforms for expression and exchange comparatively free from censorship, Latin American lesbian websites and distribution lists address ongoing problems with resources and repression. They distribute distinct kinds of information – political, social, even artistic – that promote community and frame individual actions as part of the fight for lesbian human rights. News about LGBT politics reminds lesbians that they face common problems along with other GBT people and offers ways to get involved; scholarly articles and personal testimonies enable deeper reflection on what it means to be a lesbian; interviews, reviews and artistic presentations reflect other facets of lesbian life; and erotic images and lesbian symbols stand as visual rebukes to the repression of lesbian desire and existence.

Although the internet cannot erase – and may even exacerbate – ongoing tensions around accountability and representation within lesbian communities, it also serves to expand participation in region-wide debates. But this global tool does not eliminate every boundary. While it does seem to be creating Heinz et al.'s 'emancipatory and community-building realm that transcends intranational boundaries', it does not fully traverse 'international borders' (2002: 108). Judging by the intended audience of the websites, as well as information available about website usage, the communities woven together by this virtual web are national and regional. Latin American lesbians are largely reaching out to each other.

Of course, 'digital divides' exist along the region's deep divisions of class, race, and geographical position (Hilbert, 2001). Internet cafes provide commercial access for those who cannot go online at home, school or work. Nevertheless, the majority of the population has neither regular entry into cyberspace nor the 'digital literacy' to facilitate navigation. This means that lesbians from lower-middle-class, working-class and poor backgrounds, whose class position may already limit their exposure to lesbian feminist organizations, also have difficulty entering virtual community spaces. Some may be helped by community organizations that run telecenters and offer basic internet skills training for lower-income people. But outing oneself in the real world while seeking information in the virtual one, given the public nature of many access points, remains a problem. Even these seemingly enormous barriers may be breached, as 'chains of access' connect those who can travel into cyberspace to those cannot, facilitating information transmission in real time in real communities (Friedman, 2005). While the most isolated women cannot take advantage of others' access, those who have trusted contacts who can go online may not need direct access to take advantage of digital resources.

Getting the Word/s out

Supplying readers with current information about LGBT politics is a key feature of all the websites. Rompiendo el Silencio republishes articles from other news sources about international LGBT news and offers original articles and editorials. Um *Outro* Olhar posts Brazilian lesbian groups' events and gives readers information on their rights and how to protect them. Safo Piensa publishes reports on the lesbian and feminist movements in Argentina and pertinent legislative initiatives. LeS VOZ also advertises political and cultural events on their website. GALF goes farthest in providing in-depth, often scholarly, articles in a convenient format: its website hosts a virtual documentation center with pdf versions of a wide range of analytical and provocative articles. The website is also the home of GALF's online lesbian feminist magazine, *Labia*. While the offerings of GALF's 'virtual library' are quite impressive, the diverse array of information available from different websites informs and enriches lesbian community.

Each website finds other ways to present material that increases lesbian visibility and solidarity. ...

Several of these websites, as well as many other lesbian organizations, also use electronic distribution lists as a potent tool for political work. While websites reach a greater audience than the hand-distributed bulletins of earlier organizing periods, a largely anonymous audience makes information hard to target. Distribution lists – a regular transmission of news and events of interest sent directly to subscribers – enable organizations to reach out directly to many people in a timely fashion. LeS VOZ sends its bimonthly electronic bulletin to 900 subscribers; Rompiendo el Silencio's list has nearly 700 subscribers. Other lesbian organizations, faced with severe political and/or resource restrictions, rely on distribution lists to reach supporters. The Mexico City-based, all-volunteer Lesbians in Collective group believed agents of the federal government were spying on their email account because of the group's involvement with radical political movements. Despite this disturbing setback, which forced them to close one account and open another, anonymous account on a free server, in 2002 the collective distributed information to 150 contacts, half in Mexico and half international (Corona Tinoco interview, 2002). Gloria Carreaga Pérez, a founding member of Mexico City-based The Closet of Sor Juana – which has served as the Women's Secretariat of the International Lesbian and Gay Association – explained that the group's lack of resources led to the use of the internet, since it is inexpensive, and 'allows us to be in contact with people at all levels, in practically the whole world' (interview, 2002). Carreaga Pérez herself distributes several lists on lesbian and gay issues at the national, regional and international levels, which reach up to 100 people. These groups do not only send out information; distribution lists also incorporate them into larger networks of progressive action. Safo Piensa's coordinators easily named nearly 40 lists to which they subscribed.

[...]

The importance of the internet in getting broad content into circulation is clear to Pérez Ocaña. She explained that the website and distribution list reached far more people than the relatively small run of the magazine. While it was hard to get magazine stands to carry the *LeS VOZ* magazine and many lesbians could not afford a subscription, the website had a very different life:

It's very good, because we've really developed, lots of people know us, the magnificent thing of having a permanent page there, it's a communications media that everyone can access, that is very economical, whereas other media are very expensive, or even blocked. [And] it's always there! So for us it's magnificent, and we can put whatever we want. Nobody's going to censor us, to tell us what we can and can't put on it. There it is, because we want it. (Interview, 2002)

Escaping censorship to present a rich array of resources to a wide audience – in Latin America, only the internet can make this possible. Cyberspace presents lesbians with opportunities to break free from social, economic and political constraints on their freedom of expression and action to foster community-building and political change.

Tensions between the Virtual and the Real

Community-building online does not solve the long-term conflicts over accountability and representation, and the distributional power and anonymity of the internet add new levels of complexity to these issues. However, the openness of cyberspace means that different points of view – not just those of established groups or well-connected leaders – can find wide audiences. In addition, some organizations are implementing mechanisms of 'virtual' accountability so that the internet can be a more transparent and responsible tool for activism.

Wakeford's concern about losing 'the local politics of boundary markers' in using the internet to build (supranational) community is evident in some instances – although this loss may also be a gain. In a 2001 interview, members of the Argentine Autonomous Feminist Lesbian Mothers claimed that a virtual presence sometimes represented no one on the national level. They referenced groups that were known to Dutch funders:

> ... that aren't known here. They exist online but don't know people in the next block. [It's] a fantasy image. They can use the web, they can use English, write projects, but they doesn't exist as groups. Except they exist on the web so they exist for the rest of the world. (Interview, 2001)

In a community that fiercely values accountability, the web can exacerbate the already loaded politics of international funding when newcomers change the boundary markers of the community itself. What one organization sees as a 'fantasy image' with no local interlocutors could well be a web-based group that is building community among its internet-based interlocutors. Given the difficulty of face-to-face meetings, virtual interaction is a crucial resource for lesbians located down the block – or elsewhere in the region.

In some cases, the web has exposed difficult internal debates to a much wider audience, exacerbating local tensions. Several lesbian groups in Mexico described how a national debate over the representational legitimacy of a lesbian who won a seat in Congress became known throughout Latin American lesbian feminist networks. When some organizations felt shut out of the representative's nomination process, they circulated an email message around the region declaring that they did not consider this woman their representative. Another group responded via an email message, also aired regionally, denouncing what they saw as a personal attack against the woman, who had a long history of activism. A second acute disagreement between Mexican activists over the ownership of a set of archives achieved regional notoriety after one side posted its claims on a webpage. Although the other side saw this action as defamation, they were unable to persuade the server to take down the page.

Fierce national debates reached regional audiences prior to the use of email and websites, but the transmission was slower and more limited. Rapid regional spread can have serious national fall-out; for example, the exchange over the Mexican representative had such negative repercussions within the Mexican lesbian feminist community that at least one organization swore off using the web politically. Still, there is no denying the communicative power that websites give to voices that might otherwise lack a platform, as they can now offer whole websites detailing their particular positions.

Attempts to restore or create mechanisms of accountability have begun to surface in cyberspace. Rompiendo el Silencio posts 'Principles' that clarify it 'is not an organization and only acts as a medium of truthful communication within the internet'. It maintains its independence from any political, religious or occupational organization (and refuses to publish political candidates' platforms, no matter how lesbian-friendly). While its collaborators may use the space to share information about their organizations, the website offers only the director's editorials. The moderators of Safo Piensa's distribution list responded to some subscribers' anger at being 'observed' by other subscribers who 'wouldn't show their "faces"' (i.e. never wrote in, only read) by instituting a more inquisitive registration process. They ask potential subscribers to provide their names; how they heard about the list; why they want to subscribe to a list of lesbian feminists; how they self-identify; what they think the list will offer them – or what they can offer the list; and whether they are interested in face-to-face meetings. Through this process the coordinators of Safo Piensa attempt to infuse their online community with some of the personal relations and responsibility off-line communities can more easily demand.

The Regionality of Virtual Reality

Much has been made of the potential for global community-building in cyberspace, and certainly Latin American lesbians use the internet to establish and nourish connections outside their home countries and region. The International Gay and Lesbian Human Rights Commission's website, for example, regularly posts information and action alerts about LGBT status in the region. International solidarity via email has also been credited with positive intervention during incidents of flagrant discrimination. But analysis of the websites' intended audiences and actual usage reveals a national and regional perspective rather than a focus on international concerns. This perspective could be seen as somehow limiting the 'inherent' globality of cyberspace. But this 'globality' has been premised, if implicitly, on the use of English – still the leading language of the internet – and the primacy of US-based websites and organizations. Thus, defiance of the US and English-language domination of the internet shows the potential of this 'global' tool to foster Latin American and Spanish-speaking solidarity.

Hyperlinks are a central mechanism through which websites foster solidarity. Hyperlinks out of each website indicate where it locates itself with respect to others within cyberspace – a type of travel recommendation – making them a telling element for analysis. Hyperlinks into each website indicate which other guidebooks include that destination. The hyperlink maps created by the websites under study illuminate the largely national and regional communities – lesbian, LGBT, feminist, progressive – within which the organizations situate themselves and are located by others. Hyperlinks are virtual pathways for readers, helping them find organizations they may not have been aware of.

Extra-regional hyperlinks account for only a small percentage of all the hyperlinks from the websites, with most to and from Spain and Puerto Rico. When these websites link to international human rights, gay rights and women's rights websites, they usually select sites that have Spanish translations available. US representation is confined to funders, magazines, one portal and two universities, with the Mexican website responsible for a majority of these links. These websites collect and then publish information that their regional readers can use, rather than working to speak to a global audience. A combination of language and politics trumps a complete internationalization of lesbian community.

An examination of the individual websites attests to a national, and to some extent regional, use of online connections. Written in Portuguese, Um *Outro* Olhar is definitively directed at Brazilian lesbians. The website designers are so sure that users will be Brazilians that the site registration offers a pulldown menu of Brazilian states rather than other countries. Nearly all of its links are to Brazilian LGBT organizations. Not surprisingly, the links into the site are Brazilian or Portuguese-language LGBT sites. Um *Outro* Olhar's privileging of national community no doubt reflects its decades of publication and activism in Brazil, but it also indicates the sheer size of the country and, of course, its use of Portuguese rather than Spanish.

Like Um *Outro* Olhar, LeS VOZ assumes a national audience, though not for language reasons. …

The information on the Safo Piensa page focuses mainly on Argentina, though it includes coverage of regional issues and general lesbian themes. Its hyperlinks are to Argentine and Latin American lesbian organizations, as well as a gay Argentine news source. It also links to international foundations that give grants to lesbian organizations. …

Rompiendo el Silencio takes a different approach. While designed for Chilean lesbians, its news and resources encompass all of Latin America and beyond. It has international collaborators, from Argentina, Canada, Mexico, Spain and the US, and covers events of regional interest, such as the third annual lesbian march in Mexico, as well as offering international LGBT news. Its neatly organized list of links includes many Chilean lesbian organizations and blogs, and other Latin American, Spanish, and international lesbian and progressive organizations. …

More than the other websites, GALF has a regional, if not an international, audience in mind. While the events page focuses on Peru, the article database offers work from Latin America and elsewhere (in Spanish translation), and the electronic journal *Labia* (published in Spanish and, recently, Portuguese) is intended for the entire region and possibly elsewhere. According to its first edition, it seeks 'to reach large numbers of lesbians, already organized or not, from the region of the Americas, and if possible, lesbians from around the world; to communicate, debate and develop regional/global strategies [for the recognition of lesbian rights as human rights]'. GALF links include Peruvian groups but also many from Latin America, Spain and Puerto Rico. Although the majority of the links are to lesbian organizations, there are plenty that focus more generally on the LGBT community, as well as some progressive and human rights organizations. Although the website builds on GALF's more than 20 years of political and social activism in Peru, its online presence seems largely intended as a regional resource for reflection on the lesbian condition.

Though created as national resources, each website also serves to link lesbians across the region – with some notable exceptions. Most markedly, the language division between Brazil and the rest of Latin America is a near-complete barrier. Given Brazil's considerable size, Um *Outro* Olhar's national focus is understandable, but the barrier does show a limitation of regional networks. Indeed, Um *Outro* Olhar neither links to, nor is linked by, any of the other websites under study here. Given the language division, GALF's effort to translate *Labia* into Portuguese is a worthy bridging attempt.

The regional connections created by the sites are largely South American and Mexican, with Central American countries completely absent, and Andean countries, with the exception of Peru, scarcely represented. Of course these 'omissions' may reflect the absence of online lesbian organizing in those areas. But absences are worth considering. For example, the four non-Brazilian websites under study here do not all link to each other: Rompiendo el Silencio, GALF, and Safo Piensa link to each other, and Safo Piensa additionally links to LeS VOZ, but LeS VOZ only connects to (a previous version of) Safo Piensa. Although there is a risk of over-interpreting the meaning of links, this pattern may well reflect off-line political divisions, as well as LeS VOZ's choice to focus on national issues. When these sites decide which websites to list as additional resources, they are creating – and circumscribing – paths for their readers to follow.

Although divisions and omissions exist, the potential for the internet to create 'ghettos' does not seem to be realized in this case. In societies where it is often dangerous to assert lesbian identity, the internet can hardly be the primary reason for lesbian isolation. Moreover, given the difficulty of lesbian organizing in the region, having online spaces dedicated to the community is vital. All the websites do provide links to non-lesbian sites within Latin America, a sign that they see their demands for lesbian rights and their efforts at community-building as a part of a larger progressive effort. If any ghettoization is in process, it seems more from the outside world. Given the extensive resources provided on these sites, the fact that there are few hyperlinks into them attests to the continuing marginalization that lesbians experience.

The geography of Latin American lesbian community in cyberspace is one that reflects regional realities. Largely circumscribed by the shared language of Spanish, with Portuguese marking a distinct border, the territory also reflects uneven distribution of resources and organizational capacity. ...

Latin American Lesbians: Weaving a Homespun Web

Like other LGBT communities, lesbians in the Latin American region have found the internet to be a kind of (cyber)shelter, distant enough from the difficulties of their off-line existence to enable their own and their communities' development and visibility. The relatively safe arena of cyberspace counters a sense of social isolation, including from family, and the sometimes dangerous consequences of coming out. Lesbians who are not able, for social or geographic reasons, to make connections with others in real time can make those connections online. Through submitting personal ads or posting to discussion lists, or simply reading about lesbian identity and looking at images celebrating lesbian life, women can explore their sexuality and its social context.

Cyberspace also provides a vital place for lesbians to build their community and carry out political action. Websites transmit news, events, ideas and whole publications of general interest to lesbians, making them less dependent on an oblivious or biased mass media, or the more narrowly circulated alternative print media, for information. Distribution lists allow political organizers to target audiences for pertinent and timely updates on issues of concern. The rapid and extensive distribution of information and opinion by more and less established activists complicates the question of who represents lesbian communities to themselves and outsiders, but this complication is the result of a democratization of communication – increased visibility of divergent and minority views – enabled by the internet.

Latin American lesbians have used this global tool to assert the centrality of the region to their identity and political practice. Although hyperlinks, users and information flow over regional boundaries, the websites and lists target national and regional audiences, often filtering international information on their behalf. The text basis of the internet is doubtless partially responsible for this finding, as well as for the intraregional division along language lines. But, overall, Latin American lesbians are weaving a homespun web.

NOTES

1. All translations by author.
2. In Latin American organizing, LGBT or GLBT is used widely; however some movements and organizations opt for variations, including 'Transsexual', 'Transvestite', 'Intersex' and/ or 'Queer' and their respective initials.
3. The field research for this article was made possible by a Fulbright-Hays Faculty Research Abroad Fellowship. I want to thank the interviewees and websites for their contributions and inspirational work, Kathryn Hochstetler for her astute commentary and Kathryn

Jay for her tireless editorial efforts. This article was enriched by participants at the 2005 Western Political Science Association Annual Meeting and the DeWitt Wallace Center for Media and Democracy at Duke University.

4. The information from these websites was collected in January 2006, and may have changed since.

5. Babb (2003) explains that in Nicaragua, lesbian organizing was stimulated by international influences: those with experience abroad, or international solidarity workers themselves, founded local nonprofits. But competition over international funding may be contributing to the current decline in LGBT visibility.

REFERENCES

Alexander, J. (2002a) 'Homo-pages and Queer Sites: Studying the Construction and Representation of Queer Identities on the World Wide Web', *International Journal of Sexuality and Gender Studies* 7(2/3): 85–106.

Alexander, J. (2002b) 'Queer Webs: Representation of LGBT People and Communities on the World Wide Web', *International Journal of Sexuality and Gender Studies* 7(2/3): 77–84.

Babb, F.E. (2003) 'Out in Nicaragua: Local and Transnational Desires after the Revolution', *Cultural Anthropology* 18(3): 304–28.

Burke, S.K. (2000) 'In Search of Lesbian Community in an Electronic World', *CyberPsychology & Behavior* 3(4): 591–604.

Dilevko, J. (2002), 'The Working Life of Southern NGOs: Juggling the Promise of Information and Communications Technologies and the Perils of Relationships with International NGOs', pp. 67–94 in P.I. Hajnal (ed.) *Civil Society in the Information Age*. Burlington, VT: Ashgate.

Ebo, B. (ed.) (1998) *Cyberghetto or Cybertopia? Race, Class, and Gender on the Internet*. Westport, CT: Praeger.

Friedman, E.J. (2005) 'The Reality of Virtual Reality: The Internet and Gender Equality Advocacy in Latin America', *Latin American Politics and Society* 47(3): 1–34.

Green, J.N. and F.E. Babb (2002) 'Introduction', *Latin American Perspectives* 29(123): 3–23.

Haag, A.M. and F.K. Chang (1997) 'The Impact of Electronic Networking on the Lesbian and Gay Community', *Journal of Gay & Lesbian Social Services* 7(3): 83–94.

Hafkin, N. and N. Taggart. (2001) *Gender, Information Technology, and Developing Countries: An Analytic Study*. Global Bureau: United States Agency for International Development.

Heinz, B., L. Gu, A. Inuzuka and R. Zender (2002) 'Under the Rainbow Flag: Webbing Global Gay Identities', *International Journal of Sexuality and Gender Studies* 7(2/3): 107–24.

Hilbert, M.R. (2001) *Latin America on its Path into the Digital Age: Where Are We?* Santiago, Chile: CEPAL/ECLAC.

Jitsuya, N. and R. Sevilla (2004) 'All the Bridges that We Build: Lesbophobia and Sexism Within the Women's and Gay Movements in Peru', *Journal of Gay and Lesbian Social Services* 16(1): 1–28.

Koch, N.S. and H.E. Schockman (1998) 'Democratizing Internet Access in the Lesbian, Gay, and Bisexual Communities', in B. Ebo (ed.) *Cyberghetto or Cybertopia? Race, Class, and Gender on the Internet*. Westport, CT: Praeger.

Leon, O., S. Burch and E. Tamayo (2001) *Social Movements on the Net*. Quito: Agencia Latinoamericana de Información. URL (consulted May 2004): http://alainet.org/publica/msred/en/index.html

Mongrovejo, N. (2000) *Un amor que se atrevió a decir su nombre: la lucha de las lesbianas y su relación con los movimientos homosexual y feminista en América Latina*. Mexico, DF: Plaza y Valdes Editores/CDHAL.

Sardá, A. (1998) 'Lesbians and the Gay Movement in Argentina', *NACLA* 31(4): 40–2.

Sardá, A. (2002) 'Avances y retrocesos en el reconocimiento de los derechos de lesbianas y mujeres bisexuales', *Cuadernos Mujer Salud* 5:107–12. URL (consulted January 2006): http://www.reddesalud.org/espanol/datos/ftp/sarda.pdf

Stein, E. (2003) 'Queers Anonymous: Lesbians, Gay Men, Free Speech, and Cyberspace', *Harvard Civil Rights-Civil Liberties Law Review* 38(1): 159–213.

Warkentin, C. (2001) *Reshaping World Politics: NGOs, the Internet, and Global Civil Society*. Lanham, MD: Rowman and Littlefield.

Weinrich, J.D. (1997) 'Strange Bedfellows: Homosexuality, Gay Liberation and the Internet', *Journal of Sex Education & Therapy* 22(1): 58–66.

INTERVIEWS

Argentine Autonomous Feminist Lesbian Mothers – Founders, Buenos Aires, 25 October 2001.

Carreaga Pérez, Gloria, founder of El Closet de Sor Juana, Mexico City, 5 June 2002.

Corona Tinoco, Maria de Jesus, general coordinator of Lesbians in Collective, Mexico City, 24 May 2002.

Cuevas Armas, Martha Patricia, coordinator, New Generation of Young Lesbians, Mexico City, 28 May 2002.

De Cicco, Gabriela and Irene Ocampo, co-founders of RIMA and Safo Piensa, Rosario, Argentina, 26 September 2002.

Pérez Ocaña, Mariana, editorial and design director of LeS VOZ, Mexico City, 31 May 2002.

19 E-ROGENOUS ZONES

Positioning Pornography in the Digital Economy

Blaise Cronin and Elisabeth Davenport

A Brief History of Eros, Representation, and Technology

Eros and technology have combined historically to produce publicly available erotic representations. ... Pornography thus offers one of the most enduring corroborations of the observation that technology and the uses to which it is put are shaped by prevailing social values and consumers' life-style choices, as much as by the original intentions of the artifact's designer (Kling, 1996). With the advent of the Internet and the proliferation of Usenet usegroups, the popularity of sex as a discussion topic, and the suitability of the medium as a marketplace for sexual partners and pornographic goods and services of every conceivable kind, became quickly apparent. ...

With almost 50 subgroups, ranging from bondage to swingers, alt.sex, now saturated with personal and commercial advertisements, has long been the most trafficked and discussed newsgroup of all. ... In the United States (the main focus of this article), the battle lines between the various stakeholders (e.g., religious organizations, conservatives, libertarians, vendors) and their myriad representatives are firmly drawn, as the contesting of the ill-fated Communications Decency Act (CDA) and legal challenges to recent attempts to introduce filtering into public libraries clearly show.[1]

Sex and network connectivity is a compelling combination, a fact underscored in September 1998 when millions of Internet users accessed the Starr Report online to read the prurient details of President Clinton's sexual peccadillos. Just as in France a

Blaise Cronin and Elisabeth Davenport, "E-Rogenous Zones: Positioning Pornography in the Digital Economy," pp. 33–48 from *The Information Society* 17 (2001).

decade or two ago, we are witnessing second-level system effects resulting from the rapid and widespread introduction of a new technology into the public and private spheres (Sproull & Kiesler, 1991). Neither the designers of Minitel nor the inventors of the World Wide Web had sexual communication and commerce as a priority in making their systems available to the public. Nor, previously, was it envisaged that the telephone and video cassette recorder would create massive new markets for phone sex and pornographic videos. In a still earlier age, amorous (and often sexually explicit) exchanges were conducted surreptitiously in code with the help of telegraph operators (Bresnick, 1998) – a belatedly recognized harbinger of things to come. That being the case, the eroticization of more recent information and communication technologies (ICTs) should not surprise us. What does surprise is the elision of this theme (and related subthemes) from many critical analyses of the information society.

Scholarly and Statistical Lacunae

… in the literature on the information society and information economy the subject of sex, and, by extension, pornography, has been undertheorized (e.g., Cooper, 1983; Porat, 1977). … The topic is also conspicuously absent in the North American Industry Classification System (Office of Management and Budget, 1997). Occupational categories such as sex worker, pornographer, striptease artist, and prostitute (and corresponding SIC codes) do not feature, and it must be inferred that they are subsumed under higher level categories (e.g., publishing, industry; other personal care services).

Formulations of the information society have tended to be high level and high-minded. In *The Coming of Post-Industrial Society*, Bell (1973, p. 14) postulated, inter alia, the preeminence of the professional and technical class and the centrality of theoretical knowledge. In like manner, Porat (1977) elevated symbolic processing, as did Reich (1991, p. 229), who stressed the economic importance of symbolic analysis and laid out an educational agenda: "The formal education of a symbolic analyst thus entails refining four basic skills: *abstraction, system thinking, experimentation*, and *collaboration*." Common to these and other studies is a privileging of abstract, or expert, knowledge, and a celebrating of the emerging "cognitariat" (Toffler, 1984, p. 112). Drucker (1987, p. 35), for example, maintains that knowledge workers have become "the center of gravity of the labor force." Carnal knowledge, by contrast, is wholly excluded from the analytic frame. …

Kling's (1996) compendious *Computerization and Controversy* includes two contributions dealing explicitly with the issues of cyber sex and pornography, and, revealingly, those were reprinted, not from academic journals, but from *The Village Voice* and *Ms*. Elsewhere, when the subject is addressed, discussion often centers on criminal activity (Kizza, 1998). Recent comments by Webster (1999, p. 242), a sociologist, on the quality of information available on the Internet illustrate how superficially the subject of pornography has sometimes been approached: "The information it [the Internet] offers is not in and of itself valuable – it may be worthless or even noxious. For instance, it is well known that unscrupulous groups, sinister political schismatics and pornographers – as well as myriad cranks and self-publicists – have websites." Extremists groups have been the subject of serious critical analysis (e.g., Arquilla & Ronfeldt, 1996; Denning, 1999), but online pornographers seem to have been neglected by large segments of the academic community.

Relatively few analyses of e-commerce give serious attention to this pariah industry, as Branwyn (1999) has observed, though many do acknowledge its social and commercial import in passing. Wolf's (1999) critically acclaimed deconstruction of the entertainment economy includes a wittily entitled chapter on hedonomics and the fun-focused consumer, but less than one page of the entire book (p. 205) is actually devoted to the Internet and sex. It may be noted that a recent issue of *The Information Society* (1997) on the topic of e-commerce omitted the sex/pornography sector entirely. Nevertheless, there are clear signs that both the business and popular press are beginning to grasp the significance of the Web for the pornography industry (and vice versa). In the last few years, articles have appeared in a wide range of mainstream magazines and newspapers, including *Time, Forbes, Fortune, The Wall Street Journal, US News & World Report*, and *Wired*, and also in specialty publications devoted to e-commerce (e.g., *The Industry Standard, Business 2.0*). ... There are nascent signs of a willingness in the popular media, at least, to explore the business and cultural politics of pornography. In the next section we propose a theoretical framework, which may explain how the pornography industry is being newly constituted and legitimated in the context of digital commerce.

A Theoretical Framework

If online pornography appears to be invisible in theoretical accounts of the information society (for any number of reasons, including, as we noted earlier, the difficulty of framing it in terms of national accounts data), are there other approaches that may provide an explanation for its increased salience? A framework that draws on studies of the social shaping of technology (SST) may be effective, since our discussion here is of pornography as an electronic product or service, something that is as amenable to social shaping as the technology that articulates that product. Technology, as Fleck (1994) indicates, is an ensemble of needs, users, design objectives, tools, and infrastructural mechanisms, configured jointly by vendors and consumers in a given implementation. A similar framework is offered in the work of Kling (1984), who describes the "production lattice" out of which technologies (viz., ensembles of interests and materials) emerge. Comparable explanatory frameworks have driven several recent studies of technology and organizations, where insight is derived from detailed ethnographic work (e.g., Dutton, 1999).

What behaviors might be illuminated by such a theoretical approach in the context of digital pornography? First, technology is only viable if certain sets of interests can be coopted to induce the desired configuration of resources and assets. From the perspective of the online producer, we suggest that pornographers are exploiting e-commerce (more or less wittingly) to normalize practices that have been stigmatized or proscribed in traditional markets and to achieve presence – to make their products and services more visible and wholesome, like sport or entertainment. Second, from the consumer perspective, the SST approach will allow us to better understand a range of emergent phenomena, such as liberated self-expression, group validation, and what we refer to later as resocialization. Third, the SST lens will enable us to see how e-commerce creates new kinds of producer–consumer interaction and feedback loops that are having a significant impact on business practices, customer behavior, and product line definition within the industry. Finally, our approach throws into relief the complexity of the seemingly simple question, "What is pornography?" In the digital marketspace, pornography has acquired multiple connotations (as entertainment/infotainment, as therapy, as a hobby, as a life-style good, as an art form, etc.), which has a profound effect on the product positioning and legitimation strategies favored by producers and distributors.

E-commerce can be analyzed in ethnographic fashion. In this case, insights may emerge from a myriad of detail captured in, for example, online transaction logs, chat-room archives, or discussion lists. These can provide understanding of the consumer experience that could not be easily gathered in nondigital trading environments by means of conversation analysis of the sort described more generally by Viegas and Donath (1999). In the specific case of pornography there is an added bonus, as gathering data on the traditional trade was made difficult by understandable reticence on the part of the consumer. The archives that digital commerce affords may allow researchers to analyze SST processes in a sector which could not previously be documented. At a local level (the level of the Web site), emerging digital genres (e.g., FAQs) and instruments (e.g., authentication certificates) can be observed that define boundaries (what is acceptable; what is legal) and recurrent practices. The sector has a worldly-wise customer base,[2] which now has sufficient critical mass to encourage pornography suppliers to seek a wider legitimation, articulated in a number of ways – initial public offerings (and all that IPOs imply), feature stories in the mainstream business press, syndicates and potential partnerships with mainstream life-style e-traders.

… Many Web-based pornographic products and services can be sampled, or tested, prior to final purchase/subscription (search goods), which helps reduce consumer uncertainty. Others may only be fully evaluated post consumption (experiential goods), but the online consumer has the added benefit of being able to draw on the opinions, ratings, and recommendations of other, knowledgeable digital consumers to make intelligent and informed choices – the transparency factor. In the case of pornographic goods in the digital economy, we see a new dimension: the input, or information, that the consumer brings to the creation of the product in real-time, by, for example, requesting a specific ingredient or interaction, a phenomenon we refer to later as "constructivist consumption," and a variation on the SST theme. …

E-Commerce in Context

Punditry and media hype nothwithstanding, recent growth in the scale and scope of electronic commerce has been spectacular. As the population of the Internet moves close to the 200 million figure, creating the conditions necessary for global electronic trading, there are those who maintain that we are witnessing the creation of a new industrial order (Hamel & Stamper, 1998) and those who feel that basic economic principles will not change (Shapiro & Varian, 1998). The leading indicators, from the recent spate of IPOs to the astronomical market capitalization of early icons such as Amazon.com, Yahoo!, Priceline.com, or eBay, and consultants' forecasts of market growth are frenetically, if variably, optimistic (Karlgaard, 1999a; Roth, 1999). They are also at odds with most accepted measures of bottom-line profitability and overall business performance: Amazon's market capitalization is greater than major bricks-and-mortar chains like Barnes and Noble, while eBay's is several times that of Sotheby's, the venerable auction house founded 250 years before eBay came into being (Grover, 1999; Karlgaard, 1999). Although e-commerce has been operational for many years as electronic data interchange (e.g., Timmers, 1998), business-to-business trading on the Internet has taken the phenomenon to new heights. According to estimates cited in a June 1999 report from the U.S. Department of Commerce <http://www.ecommerce.gov/ede/edez.pdf>, the emerging digital economy is expected to account for $1.3 trillion worth of business-to-business trading by 2003 – which helps explain why it has been described as the "killer app" of the Internet (Bar & Borrus, 1999).

Digital Consumer Markets

The prospects for digital retailing (business-to-consumer), the primary focus of this paper, are also impressive: Current estimates from market research firms range from $40 billion to $80 billion by 2002, whether it is the delivery of what Kling and Lamb (1999) term "highly digital" goods and services (e.g., software, music, news) or the sale of "mixed digital" goods and services (e.g., flowers, books, education). ...

While there are persistent concerns regarding personal privacy and transaction security (e.g., Hoffman et al., 1999), the generic attractions of electronic commerce for consumers (Table 19.1) are not hard to understand. These include *transparency* (intelligent agents or shopping bots <http://bots.internet.com/search/s-shop.htm > will seek out best value/best buys for the discriminating consumer, or consumers will tap into the expertise, recommendations, and E-pinions of others; Bronson, 1999), *immediacy* (current information, latest versions, and just in-time delivery are the norm), *disintermediation* [middlemen can be bypassed, bringing the supplier and ultimate consumer into direct contact, though "hypermediation" (Carr, 2000, p. 46) may be a more accurate characterization], *price competitiveness* (witness

TABLE 19.1   Generic consumer attractions of e-commerce

Transparency
Immediacy
Disintermediation
Price competitiveness
Convenience
Accessibility
Modularity
Low switching costs
Impersonality

the popularity of online auctions for both commodity and consumer goods, the evolution of customized pricing, and early experimentation with permission advertising and zero-based pricing; Gurley, 1999), *convenience* (shopping can occur around the clock, and smart retailers can offer contoured convenience and richly textured portal sites to attract and retain the consumer's interest in a highly competitive marketspace), *accessibility* (geography drops out of the shopping calculus), *modularity* (consumers can pick and mix from a variety of suppliers), *low switching costs* (if I'm not happy with Amazon.com I can effortlessly take my business to Barnesandnoble.com or Borders.com), and *impersonality* (I can look and buy without having to show my face, which can be a great boon for the socially sensitive or easily embarrassed).

[…]

The Production of Pornography

… In the second half of the 20th century, pornography became a mass consumption phenomenon when, to quote McNair (1996, p. 106), "the mass-reproductive power of media technology could begin to take advantage of the sexual liberalism associated with the late 1960s and thereafter." Pornography, defined here as the market for materials and services depicting or supporting sexual fantasy, is a particularly interesting e-commerce case study, from a business, technical, and social perspective (Lane, 2000). It is a fast-growing, multi-billion-dollar global industry, whose parent, the much larger sex sector, includes everything from adult videos to strip clubs, escort agencies, and brothels. Current revenue estimates for the pornography industry exceed $50 billion, of which some $20 billion is accounted for by the sale of adult videos, a market sector spawned by the development of the video cassette recorder and its rapid incorporation into the domestic sphere. Table 19.2 shows the estimated global revenues for the various segments of the industry. …

TABLE 19.2 The legal sex/pornography industry: estimated global sales ($bil)

Market segment	Sales ($billions)
Adult videos	20.0
Sex clubs	5.0
Magazines	7.5
Phone sex	4.5
Escort services	11.5
Cable/satellite/ Pay-per-view TV	2.5
CD-ROM/DVD	1.5
Internet (sales/memberships)	
Novelties	1.0
Other	1.5
Total	$56.0

This table is reproduced from Morais (1999, p. 218) who sourced the data from Private Media Group Inc. The figures are consistent with those quoted by Rose (1997, p. 221), who sourced his from a range of trade and media organizations.

The boundaries between licit and illicit activity may be blurred in the world of the Internet: An apparently legal Web site may serve as a front for organized crime or other deviant parties to support various dimensions of the global sex trade (e.g., pedophile rings, sex tourism, sexual trafficking). We do not consider here the ways in which inter-networking technologies have been, or might be, appropriated by such groups. The focus of this article is the structure and growth dynamic of the legitimate, online pornography industry. We are interested specifically in the following issues: (a) the similarities between the pornography industry and other life-style/entertainment sectors; (b) the extent to which the Internet is increasing the amount of pornography in the public domain, and whether the presumed volume growth is driven by a wave of new entrants, or by greater diversification and segmentation of existing goods and distribution channels; (c) new forms of service that are being developed and the implications for consumer marketing – whether the emergence of a legitimizing framework comparable to that which surrounds electronic business in other sectors (e.g., certification and authentication; access to investment capital) is conferring mainstream status and financial acceptability on the industry.

A recent article in *Forbes* magazine described in detail how the pornography business is exploiting the massive transport network that is the Internet to repurpose and better target its products at different geographic, content, and consumer segments (Morais, 1999). Traffic to pornography sites between April and September 1999 rose by 140% according to Nielsen (Lake, 1999). Even more remarkable is the increase in the number of providers. It has been calculated that there are somewhere in the region of 30,000 Web sites in the United States alone hosting pornography (Diamond, 1999; Lane, 2000).[3] In their widely quoted February 1999 survey of the publicly indexable Web, Lawrence and Giles (1999) estimated that the total number of pages was about 800 million, of which approximately 1.5% were categorized as pornography. The distribution of unique visitors across adult sites is highly asymmetrical: It follows a universal power law, which is typical of winner-take-all markets (Adamic & Huberman, 1999, p. 1). According to Forrester Research, online earnings for 1998 in the adult entertainment industry have increased 30% from the previous year, reaching approximately $1 billion (or 10% of all Internet sales). Of this, approximately half is generated by subscriptions/memberships, more than a quarter from advertising, and the remainder from merchandising (Rose, 1997, p. 221). However, few pornography sites are grossing more than $5000 per day, and earnings are highly asymmetrical across the industry (Rose, 1997, pp. 220–221). ...

Pornographers are in the business of crafting, packaging, and selling fantasy. Behind this intangible end product lies a production lattice that includes a number of familiar, physical processes. Core creative activities are filmmaking and photo shoots, which can be labor and capital equipment intensive, though decreasingly so with rapid advances in digital technology (O'Toole, 1998; Lane, 2000, pp. 50–53).

Network Advantage

From the viewpoint of pornography producers and distributors, the Internet offers a number of key business attractions. It is an ideal (complementary) distribution channel, allowing goods to be repurposed, cross-sold and up-sold, and differentially priced for a variety of local and international markets, though there has been little if any systematic analysis of price elasticity and price dispersion in this sector. As Wolf (1999, p. 92) rightly observes, "Content is becoming a very liquid asset." Inventory and real estate costs can be controlled with just-in-time delivery of both digital and physical goods directly to the customer. There is no evidence that online sales are being achieved at the expense of fixed-location retailing, which challenges the zero-sum assumption about Internet selling (Peterson et al., 1997, p. 331): "There is no intuitive reason why the Internet, or any service based thereon, will in and of itself cause consumers to spend more. Rather, use of the Internet in marketing to consumers will more likely result in a redistribution of revenues among channels or among members within a channel." In fact, pornography may constitute a positive sum market by converting shy citizens into eager online consumers. Electronic commerce also allows adult entertainment companies to sidestep (for now, at least) some of the the local, legal, and sociocultural constraints (federal statutes, community standards, prohibitions, seizures, injunctions, court proceedings, moral outrage) that have traditionally been part of the cost of doing business in many physical markets.[4] That said, issues of trans-, supra-, and extrajurisdictionality in the inchoate world of global e-commerce are extremely problematic (Clarke, 1999).[5]

New Entrants

The Internet's reach makes it possible for specialty providers (e.g., dealers in antique or period pornography, such as RetroRaunch <http://www.retroraunch.com/main.htm>) to create attractive content destinations and reach a critical mass of customers in thin or niche markets in a way that might not otherwise be possible in land-based markets with their typically higher entry and operating costs (Peterson et al., 1997, p. 333). It also allows independent operators (amateurs, in the correct sense of the term) to set up, host, and deliver their own (and sometimes others') home-based products and services without the intervention of channel intermediaries.[6] It is estimated that 70% of all Web pornography sites are being developed by individuals with no prior experience of the industry (Brown, 1998, p. 2), a phenomenon that recalls the role of independently minded, small business owners in the 19th and early 20th centuries in the distribution of pornographic images (Lane, 2000, p. 44). The high participation rate by startups and new entrants is attributable not only to the low cost of entry, fine-grained stratification and segmentation of the market, and possibly naive assumptions about future revenue streams, but also to a number of other factors, including the following: (1) local sourcing of proprietary materials (the site owner is coextensive with the pornographic content or experience on offer); (2) a desire for novelty and voguish experimentation with new media; and (3) a relatively safe environment for exhibitionism.[7]

... In the case of digital pornography, however, it is quite conceivable that media richness, under certain circumstances, would count for less than, say, convenience or immediacy. Currently, there is a broad spectrum of providers, ranging from the teleworking, sole trader (celebrity porn actress, private escort, or male striptease artist turned self-publicist) to the vertically integrated, publicly quoted corporation, seeking to establish a presence in the expanding marketspace for pornographic products and services. But it is unlikely that revenues will be distributed equally across the various provider categories. Smaller ("labor of love") ventures are likely to deal primarily with intangibles (images, personal service), while larger enterprises will be better able to offer a diversified portfolio of tangible and intangible (interactive and noninteractive) goods for delivery and consumption via the Web.

Branding

Ironically, despite its powerful brand, Playboy Enterprises[8] is not usually spoken of in the same breath as new entrants like Internet Entertainment Group (IEG). Although the company's total annual revenues are in excess of $300 million, only a small proportion of this ($7 million) comes presently from online markets, an increase, nonetheless, of 83% over the previous year (La Franco, 1999, p. 220). Playboy's Web site <http://www.playboy.com/> seeks to reinforce its socially acceptable image as a provider of soft pornography, a continuing basis of differentiation from established rivals such as Larry Flynt's misogynistic *Hustler* magazine and related Web site <http://www.hustler.com/>. ...

In certain cases, brand may be a critical success factor in building a solid online presence (Disney and CNN are two cases in point), but assumptions about easy brand extensibility in digital environments need to be treated with some caution, as Starbucks recently learned in attempting to bridge from vending coffee to selling other life-style products online (Kaplan, 1999). A strong brand is neither sufficient nor necessary reason to guarantee e-commerce success. In the digital economy, nimble startups (like Yahoo!) with no transferrable brand awareness or prior customer base can thrive, if they have innovative business models and enhanced value propositions that resonate with consumers, and if they can exploit the competitive dynamics, rhythms, and cultural value systems of virtual markets (Corcoran, 1999).

Some successful e-commerce pioneers will seek to diversify via branding. For example, Amazon.com has moved into toys, electronics, and auctioneering, three sectors that, in terms of traditional business logic, have nothing in common with bookselling, its core activity.[9] However, the company believes that its first mover advantage and its self-proclaimed customer obsessiveness can be transferred across market and product lines to powerful effect (Weintraut & Davis, 1999). Distributors of pornographic goods, like Playboy and IEG, may emulate this kind of brand extension strategy in an effort to build digital market muscle and durability, based on a more diversified portfolio of lifestyle products and services. Such merchandising moves will help distance them further from pornography's mom-and-pop image and the early swarm of underresourced, new entrants. More generally, established firms will be able to leverage off their extensive archival asset base, networks of industry contacts, existing alliances, and their firsthand familiarity with the subterranean world of pornography praxis to maintain a critical edge over new and inexperienced entrants.

Legitimizing Discourse

This historically stigmatized sector, with its potentially high profit margins and apparently intuitive grasp of networked market dynamics, is proving attractive to some investors. The dual effects of Internet-fueled growth have intensified merger and acquisition activity and indications of a trend toward consolidation within the industry (Greenfield, 1999). The comments of one analyst, quoted in a recent overview of the digital pornography business (Branwyn, 1999, p. 38), are revealing: "What I see when I look at this industry – putting aside any moral judgments about reprehensible content – is an amazing example of an industry that has banded together to protect its business, push revenue across the industry and innovate cutting edge technologies." Certainly, it is universally acknowledged by information technology experts that the adult entertainment industry has been at the leading edge in terms of building high-performance Web sites with state-of-the art features and functionality.

Illustrative of the general trend is Private Media Group (PMG), the first diversified, adult entertainment company to trade on the Nasdaq <www.prvt.com>. The company's stated goal is to be the dominant force in global shopping for the world's mainstream adult community. Its principal business activities include the acquisition, refinement, and delivery of adult feature products and services, including a range of proprietary Web sites, digital video disks, unrated and adult feature films, interactive services, adult novelty products, and the Private Circle fashion line, as well as TV Home Shopping for its proprietary and licensed products (source: company press release, 24 June 1999). The company is developing enhanced state-of-the-art video on-demand with sound and a number of new Web sites to promote worldwide sales of its integrated product lines. Its long-term business strategy is powerfully Internet-focused, a far cry from popular (precorporate) conceptions of pornographers (e.g., McCumber, 1994). Another, albeit smaller, company with a Nasdaq listing is New Frontier Media <http://www.ten.com/index.htm>, a self-described emerging leader in the distribution of adult content. According to its CEO, "We made a decision to be involved in Internet e-commerce in a meaningful way. The Internet represents the single most important means of distribution for content aggregators in the future" (company press release, 29 June 1999). This view is apparently shared by Rick's Cabaret International <http://www.rickscabaret. com>, whose 1995 IPO made it the world's first publicly traded topless entertainment business (Silverman, 1999). The company's share price jumped recently following news of its intention to develop an online presence in conjunction with Quixotic, an Internet marketing and consulting firm (company press release, 29 April 1999).

A fourth example of the new breed is Internet Entertainment Group <http:www.ientertain.com/index07.html>, a much-profiled provider of adult entertainment on the Web. Internet Entertainment Group (IEG) was founded by a youthful entrepreneur, Seth Warshavsky, who has been compared with the patriarchs of the print-based pornography industry, Hugh Hefner (*Playboy*) and Bob Guccione (*Penthouse*). Although its online revenues are fairly modest (approximately $50 million in 1998), the company's tightly focussed and technologically sophisticated marketing strategy has attracted more than its fair share of media attention <http://chat.abcnews.gocom/chat/chat.dll? room=sethwarshavsky>. IEG invests heavily in state-of-the-art technology and uses targeted marketing in an effort to attract and retain customers, and to stay one step ahead of the competition. The company is especially keen to capitalize on its prime mover advantage in order to gradually diversify its operating base.[10]

For some time Internet Entertainment Group has been trying to launch an IPO, but has discovered that underwriters and banks are still reluctant to deal with the adult entertainment sector. According to Bodow (1999), both IEG and Efox.net (a near-market competitor) are exploring creative ways of going public, the former by possibly resorting to a reverse merger (acquire a cheap stock, take over its Nasdaq symbol, and fold IEG into the listed company), the latter <http://www.efox.net/> by doing a self-underwritten public offering (making its stock available directly to the public). Both reportedly acknowledge the difficulties of being perceived to be beyond the investment pale, a view shared by Starnet Communications

<http://www.starnet.ca/index. shtml>, a pornography-turned-online gambling company that decided to concentrate exclusively on gaming in order to attract the necessary levels of institutional investment (Bicknell, 1999). Since making this decision, however, the company has been the the target of a law-enforcement investigation that claims that Starnet has been engaged in a range of illegal activities, including money laundering (Hosenball, 1999). Common to these companies is an apparent desire to create a different kind of business with a different kind of public image, one, for instance, unsullied by presumed ties with organized or opportunistic crime. The principals are presented in the media as professionally credentialed managers, as opposed to hands-on owners personally familiar with the material practices of their industry – the kind of impression perpetuated by movies such as *Boogie Nights*. These companies are taking the idea of the "pornographic establishment" (McNair, 1996, p. 110) to the next level, moving beyond the almost socially acceptable and charismatic founder archetype, be it Paul Raymond in the United Kingdom or Hugh Hefner in the United States, to the new paragon, one who is the epitome of marketing efficiency and moral detachment.

The language of a recent press release from Private Media Group (13 May 1999) is essentially no different from that associated with more socially acceptable forms of business, and indicative of efforts in some quarters to subtly re-engineer perceptions of the industry: "We are committed to meeting our goals to increase shareholder value, on a quarter-by-quarter basis, taking us forward as a complete lifestyle global company, providing our services to the mainstream adult communities of the world." It reads like a mission statement for Body Shop, Habitat, or Martha Stewart. That is not to say that the company's merchandise and content are any softer, less explicit, or less likely to offend certain sensibilities. As Morais (1999, p. 220) notes, "Even as pornography becomes more appallingly graphic, it is becoming more mainstream." Rhetorical reframing is also a feature of the popular business press's coverage of the industry in the past few years. Despite the problematic public image of the pornography business (a feature it shares with the arms industry, among others), it is difficult to ignore a business sector that deals with basic human instincts (palatable or otherwise), exhibits high-revenue growth, is potentially attractive to private and institutional investors, and is astute in its exploitation of embryonic e-commerce structures and mechanisms.

Rehabilitation Strategies

A feature of pornography's rapid move to the virtual arena has been a progressive cleaning up and self-policing of certain segments of the business. Self-regulation is a common response by mature service industries (e.g., finance, law, medicine) to assuage the public's concerns about transparency, integrity, and trustworthiness. United Adult Sites (UAS) is a U.S.-based adult entertainment trade association that seeks to promote responsible and ethical business practices by, for example, agreeing not to trade in images or moving pictures portraying acts of bestiality or child

TABLE 19.3 Pornographers' legitimation strategies

Public flotations
Professional management
Consolidation/diversification
Brand equity building
Media management/PR
Self-regulation
Lobby/trade groups
Product repositioning
Discourse of the mainstream

pornography, and by discouraging many of the dubious technical practices currently associated with the business, such as phony links and pop-up windows. The organization also provides legal advice for its members and seeks to promote interfirm partnering. Details of UAS's goals, code of ethics, and partial list of members can be found at its Web site <http://www.uas.org/>. Founded a few years ago, ASACP (Adult Sites Against Child Pornography) is also a leading campaigner against child pornography, with more than 700 members drawn from the adult entertainment sector <http://www.asacp.com/>.

Another sign of the quest for social acceptability is the Free Speech Coalition <http://www.freespeechcoalition.com/>, a trade organization and lobbying group that represents the interests of the adult entertainment industry with politicians and policymakers, at both the federal and local levels.[11] Notable, too, in the context of image engineering was the invitation extended to the president and CEO of the Internet Entertainment Group by the U.S. Senate Commerce Committee (chaired by Senator John McCain) to testify on how the First Amendment could be preserved without infringing on parents' rights to keep their children from sexually explicit materials. Rehabilitation strategies and public relations instruments such as these (Table 19.3) are likely to become more common, as producers, distributors, and aggregators seek to augment their presence and to enhance their social acceptability and business credibility in order to take full advantage of early e-commerce applications and promise.

The Consumption of Pornography

In this section we continue our exploration of an SST framework to analyze the position of pornography in e-commerce, and we discuss ways in which consumers may be seen to shape pornographic products and services. We outlined earlier some of the problems associated with statistical measurement of the pornography sector and suggested that qualitative data might provide alternative insight into consumer behavior. The difficulties of defining, tracking, and quantifying online trade are widely acknowledged, and sensitivities are understandably high in the wake of the controversy surrounding the publication of the quickly discredited Carnegie Mellon research study, *Marketing Pornography on the Information Superhighway*, conducted by Rimm (1995). This survey attracted much media and political attention, and became synonymous with the erroneous, if (for some) ideologically convenient, statistic that 83.5% of all images on bulletin boards were pornographic in character. It also helped perpetuate some of the mythology surrounding Internet culture and content.[12]

Quantification of Internet and Web usage has proved to be a highly contentious subject in the context of performance-based advertising, whether the issue is web hits, market share, company turnover, or revenues. Nielsen// NetRatings Internet Audience Measurement <http://www. nielsen-netratings.com/default.htm > is a leading market research firm that gathers Internet usage data from a sample of 14,000 individuals nationwide, from which it produces weekly and monthly statistical reports. The top-ranking Web properties typically include AOL, MSN, Yahoo!, Alta Vista, Amazon, and Time Warner, with monthly unique audience figures in the 1 million to 18 million range. Sex sites are noticeable by their absence from these tabulations, but that is not surprising given that the data are based on self-reports and thus likely to seriously underestimate visits to pornographic sites. Tracker <http://www.sextracker.com/about/>, on the other hand, is one of several companies that specialize in logging traffic on pornography sites and ranking/categorizing adult Web pages on a variety of dimensions. The world of cyber pornography is a compelling, impulse-driven market with, by some counts, more than 30 million unique visits being recorded daily. The most frequently visited sites are drawing tens of millions of visitors per month,[13] which mirrors the fact that a small proportion of all retail sites accounts for the bulk of all hits (Adamic & Huberman, 1999). The marketing challenge, of course, is to convert as many as possible of the nonpaying visitors (those who look at the sample images, take the free tours, or experiment with no-charge, temporary memberships) into paying customers, which, given the proliferation of sites, the commodification and duplication of product, and understandably low rates of conversion, means that present revenues may be spread unevenly across the many players, a majority of whom are small businesses or microentrepreneurs (Morais, 1999).

Consumer Behavior

From the consumer's perspective, the Internet and Web offer a rich, if sometimes paradoxical, mix of benefits and advantages. These technologies bring pornography easily and discreetly (inconspicuous consumption) into the consumer's personal space, be it home environment or desktop. They thus bypass many of the social norms and informal controls, in addition to institutionally mandated sanctions, that depress the open circulation and consumption of pornographic materials. Domestication and the resultant (if sometimes false) sense of anonymity (creditcard transactions, e-mails, and cookies all bear witness to one's presence and tracks in cyberspace) are powerful inducements for those who might otherwise have to visit sex shops, clubs, and parlors in person to satisfy their wants. This was a great attraction of the VCR, which offered the coy consumer first-generation portability, privacy, and instant gratification. The sense of social invisibility afforded by the Internet, which certainly helps explain the uninhibitedness and exhibitionism of postings on alt.sex newsgroups or AOL's chat rooms, is, arguably, the most potent driver of this electronic submarket. In some cases, however, online presence may actually be a desideratum for those who do not wish to socialize in the physical realm, but are happy to share interests and experiences openly in cyberspace.

Given widespread concerns about AIDS and other sexually transmissible diseases, it is tempting to speculate on likely future market demand for depersonalized and disintermediated sexual goods and services delivered via the Web. The sleaziness of the red light district is replaced by a much more sanitized and controlled environment, in which the consumer (paying by the minute on his or her credit card) is unlikely to feel physically or socially threatened. The prospect of actions without apparent consequences is a powerful attraction of the virtual environment, where a sense of psychological comfort is complemented by the high level of interactivity, a defining feature of value-added products and services in the digital economy (see http://www.ecommerce. gov/viewhtml.htm). The consumer can, for instance, connect globally with a live sex performance and shape the artist's gyrations in real time by feeding in specific requests, in what might be termed "constructivist consumption." The participant is not just safe from public gaze, but ostensibly in control of the observed spectacle. In addition, the separation of subject and object facilitated by digital technologies may augment the sense of sexual fantasy for both customer and performer.

With the advent of simulators and next-generation Internet bandwidth, we may soon see the emergence of what Grant (1994, p. 252) and others presciently referred to as the virtual reality sex industry (e.g., Chang, 2000). Early experimentation is under way with the commercial sales of "cyberdildonics" and "cyber sex suits," which create sensations produced by touch in the real world (Brunker, 1999; Lane, 2000, pp. 275–280). Futuristic depictions of digitally mediated sex have been provided by Dertouzos (1997, pp. 142– 148), culminating with a description of full-immersion, interactive sex at a distance with a consenting partner. The digital environment blurs the traditional demarcation line between the pornography and sexual performance industries (and between products and services), as distributors use the Web to deliver digitized adult videos (pornographic products) and interactive sex shows (live experiences) to the same or different customer segments. There is no reason to assume that digital pornography will remain the exclusive preserve of the business community. We can expect to see some fusion of the roles of producer and consumer. The advent of the camcorder and digital camera, coupled with the Net's broadband distribution capability, has created an infrastructure for both commercial (Gomes, 1999) and amateur exchange, what O'Toole (1998, p. 276) refers to as the Internet's "self organizing, small-time erotic trading system."[14] As legitimized e-trade in pornography grows, we may also expect to see a shift from mainstream to deviant content (Wallace, 1999, p. 169) and the emergence of a more extreme shadow sex sector, in which customer-to-customer (peer-to-peer) trading and barter will create a covert or black market for obscene and illegal goods.[15]

Experience Goods

The sex industry (not unlike the upscale travel and tourism industry) is one in which longing, expectation, and fantasy-at-a-distance play important parts. Just as holidaymakers invest time and effort in selecting and previewing/sampling their vacation destination/experience (which may involve viewing photographs, videos, or even the use of simulations), consumers of pornography are likely to be satisfied with substitutes or simulacra. Although the Internet allows travel and tourism service providers to intermix traditional marketing channels such as distribution, transaction, and communication (Bonn et al., 1998, p. 305), most consumers will, ultimately, want the real, high-involvement experience. By way of contrast, many consumers of highend pornography may be content to live much of the time with the virtual and vicarious (Dibbell, 1999; Turkle, 1995).

For good or ill, remotely accessed, interactive sex shows are a pornographic phenomenon (with significant new revenue streams) made possible by the Web. They are a striking illustration of the eroticization of advanced ICTs and of how the Internet is set to extend and redefine core (legal) aspects of a long-established business, part of what Wolf (1999, p. 7) presumably implied by the phrase "the entertainmentization of the economy." The Internet promises to do more than increase the size and geographic diversity of the customer base; it both commodifies and renders highly visible a set of consumption practices that, heretofore, have been largely covert in character and, more often than not, conveniently backgrounded in mainstream consumer narratives. But that may change as a result of the progressive corporatization and feminization (both supply side and demand side) of the pornography business.

Gender-Based Market Segmentation

One of the most contested themes in the discussion of pornography is the role of gender in the associated production and consumption processes. The Internet Entertainment Group estimates that 80% at least of its customers are males between the ages of 30 and 45 years with high disposable incomes (source: http://www.ienterain.om/ziff. html).[16] Recent Nielsen data (Lake, 1999) show that three-quarters of visitors to pornographic web sites are male, of whom more than 80% are in the 18–54 years age range. This type of highly skewed demographic profile is still common in the literature. Grant (1994, p. 251), however, speculates that the "raunchy woman ... represents a huge new potential market for capitalism," while others have estimated that more than 20% of all adult video purchases and rentals are made by women, either alone or in the company of men (O'Toole, 1998, p. 55). Gender awareness may prove to an important factor for pornographers hoping to extend their product/service portfolios and market reach. Playboy Enterprises, for instance, is hoping to forge partnerships with female-oriented Web sites where it feels there is scope for crossover and syndication (source: CNET News.com, 10 November 1998). Also noteworthy is the growing number of female-owned/-managed web sites, an incipient trend that could further alter long-held assumptions about, and public perceptions of, the business.[17] The focusing of public attention on the Internet and pornography has brought to light facts (e.g., the sense of satisfaction felt by many female workers in the pornography business) and figures (e.g., on the pornography purchasing and consumption behaviors of women) that challenge some popularly held convictions about the the role and status of women in this sector.

Ideology aside, there is an expanding market for female-oriented pornography, notably magazines and videos. A number of boutique providers, such as Femme Productions <http://www.royalle.com/>, which was established in the 1980s by a former adult movie star, have emerged to fill a niche market need. Predictably, this remains a subject of intensely charged and polemical debate, and the ideological divide is enormous. As Willis (1995, p. 173) points out, pornography has become "a code word for vicious male lust" in the rhetoric of the anti-pornography movement, a form of reductionist reasoning that effectively prevents the subject from being examined "as a cultural genre" (Valverde, 1995, p. 179). Indubitably, consumer practices in the pornography industry are gendered, but that in itself does not legitimate the conception of pornography as necessarily subordinative and dehumanizing of women (Carse, 1999). However, for MacKinnon (1995, p. 59), the adult entertainment industry's most eminent scourge, pornography is nothing less than a civil rights violation: "It eroticizes hierarchy. It sexualizes inequality." In this debate, there is often no middle ground. Despite the demonizing discourse, not all women view pornography negatively, nor wish to have the sale and transmission of pornographic goods outlawed. For example, the National Coalition Against Censorship has a Working Group on Women & "Pornography" that opposes all forms of censorship <http://www.ncac.org/wc&phome.html>, and COYOTE (Call Off Your Old Tired Ethics) is a long-established advocacy group for sex workers on the U.S. West Coast <http://www.bayswan.org/ coyote.html>.[18]

Conclusions: Industry Maturation

The Internet and Web have highlighted afresh the enormous expressed interest in, and persistent demand for, sexual goods, experiences, and services (virtual and real; passive and interactive; pornographic and obscene) among both historically visible and latent market segments. The appetite for novelty continues to accelerate: Pornographic goods have high perishability for most consumers, and providers scramble to generate streams of new images and packaged experiences for their fickle customers to avoid losing market share to more responsive rivals. More significant than the amount of cyber real estate accounted for by pornography is the volume of traffic (one-time and repeat) attracted by such sites. Even allowing for inflation in vendors' claims, and for statistical inaccuracies in market researchers' quantification of Web-page hits and click-throughs, there is no doubt that pornography is an important, yet largely unacknowledged, component in the formation of the digital economy.

We suggest that a social shaping of technology approach can improve our understanding of the positioning of pornography on the Internet and of the associated "reproduction lattice" – the conditions of production and consumption. It helps focus attention on moves made by both producers and consumers to destigmatize the sector (e.g., the public flotations and consumer self-revelation noted earlier) and to achieve presence. It also demonstrates the dialectic between an infinitely extensible digital product base and insatiable consumer appetite, which is propelling industry-wide growth and continuous product and technological innovation.

As we observe, electronic commerce currently offers both producer and consumer a lower risk environment, in which many of the traditional impedimenta associated with the pornography business are being by passed. Digital distribution directly to the consumer's domestic environment or workplace brings a reassuring sense of privacy to a transaction that heretofore has been uncomfortably public for many individuals. The "wonderful cocooning technology that the pornography industry has subsidized" (Long, 1999, p. 49) also allows suppliers to better exploit their digital assets, broaden their product portfolios, and dramatically extend market reach – the extension of (near instant) gratification. It also seems likely to create new market segments: As O'Toole (1998, p. 72) notes, "Couples are porn's dream viewership, bringing mutuality, respectability and a steady inflow of revenue." With interactive digital media, consumers are not simply viewing (passively consuming) materials but, on occasion, participating in the construction, packaging, and consumption of virtual goods and experiences.

We suggest that these are signs of a maturing market. If there is progressive internationalization and capitalization of the pornography industry, it is likely that a more overtly professional and strategically focused business sector will emerge, one acutely mindful of the need for conformance with prevailing legal and cultural norms in its various geographic market segments. This will trigger changes in the ecosystem, as established players broaden their base of operations and move into cognate business streams, whether through organic growth, focused acquisition, or strategic partnerships. The more successful (i.e., profitable) companies will invest heavily in technology and seek to diversify their content and channel reach through strategic alliances and brand extension, just as Amazon.com has begun to transform itself from an online bookseller to an electronic hypermarket, building upon its name recognition and early dominance in the embryonic world of e-commerce.

Though some banks and investment houses may balk at dealing overtly with adult entertainment companies, it will be difficult to claim the moral high ground as several of their blue-chip clients (e.g., cable TV companies and major hotel chains who distribute pornographic goods) will inevitably be part of the production (and distribution) lattice. The activities of the sector will continue to be threatened by the possibility of sudden or unexpected changes in the law, a particular problem for producers, distributors, and retailers in the United States, where there is enormous variability in state legislation, micromoral climates, and prevailing community standards. Cosmetic and substantive changes (ranging from the creation of lobby groups to support for filtering tools like Cybersitter, Net Nanny, and Surfwatch) may not be enough to assuage some public concerns about the effects of pandemic pornography.[19] Specifically, the perceived threat of online seduction and corruption of minors will provide the anti-pornography movement with a powerful weapon in the battle for legislators' hearts and minds. The moves that we ascribe in the previous pages to the producers of pornography can be seen as an attempt to mobilize public and political opinion. Countermeasures will, undoubtedly, be made in an evolving process of the social shaping of pornography and technology-based products and services in the adult entertainment sector. Such dynamics offer a rich agenda for systematic investigation. As pornography is reframed – as a hobby, a lifestyle choice, a social pressure value – unexamined assumptions about the nature of the business and its customers are being called into question. Electronic commerce has highlighted the prominent place of pornography in many people's daily lives – making transparent what was little known or greatly feared. It has also revealed much about the workings of a sector that has historically avoided the limelight.

NOTES

1. Filtering Facts is a nonprofit organization that works to promote the use of filtering software in public libraries, and its web site <http://www.filteringfacts.org/about.htm> is a rich source of information about, and links to, the cast of issues and actors involved, many of which will have a direct, or indirect, impact upon the trading practices and, ultimately, the longer term business viability of the adult entertainment sector.
2. Some idea of the growing, general level of sophistication about online pornography can be had by visiting the YNOT Adult Network <http://www.ynotnetwork.com>, specifically the various discussion sections, such as The Hangout or Affiliate Zone. An illustration of how one facet of the sex trade is being affected by the Web is the emergence of review sites run for, and by, prostitutes' customers (Mersey, 1999).
3. Other estimates are much higher, up to 60,000 <http://www-cse.stanford.edu/classes/cs201/projects/online-pornography/index.html>.
4. Larry Flynt's picaresque confrontations over the years with the US legal system (chronicled in the movie *The People vs. Larry Flynt*) and his continuing high-profile travails in Cincinnati (Roemhildt, 1998) illustrate the nature of the problem.
5. Examples are the contentious conviction of Felix Somm, former manager of CompuServe Deutschland (a leading Internet Service Provider), of complicity in multiple cases of spreading child pornography over the Internet, and the more recent (July 1999), but very different, prosecution of Britain's largest Internet pornographer for publishing obscene materials that were delivered from Web sites based in the United States.
6. Jane Duvall, owner of Jane's Guide <http://www.janesguide.com/navcolumn.html>, a combination of jump site, consumer guide, and community space, is venturing into hosting similarly inclined, noncommercial Web sites.

7. Voyeurdorm <http://www.voyeurdorm.com/> showcases the quotidian and forbidden. Its Web page describes the experience thus: "Peer into the private lives of seven real college coeds. They live In Voyeur Dorm. Their lives are on camera 24 hours a day. You choose the view from 40 LIVE hidden cameras. Enter their bedrooms when they sleep. Spy on them In their bathrooms. Nothing is off limits. There are no taboos. The girls of Voyeur Dorm are fresh, naturally erotic and as young as 18. Catch them in the most intimate acts of youthful indiscretion. Want to find out more? Meet them in live chat sessions. Their privacy is your pleasure. Voyeur Dorm. New secrets are bared every day."

8. The chairman and CEO of Playboy Enterprises is Christie Hefner, daughter of the founder.

9. EasyJet, the low-cost UK carrier, recently extended its brand into easyEverything, a chain of warehouse-sized Internet cafés in shopping areas across London (company press release, 10 May 1999).

10. Copies of the many news and trade articles profiling IEG and its president and CEO can be found at the company's home page <http://www.ientertain.com/index07.html>.

11. This is not an exclusively American phenomenon: The coalition has a small-scale equivalent in Australia, the Eros Foundation <http://www.com.au/eros/erosaims.html>, which is a trade association for almost 200 X-rated video distributors.

12. A useful overview of the thrust of the ensuing debate can be found at the Web site of Hoffman and Novak's Project 2000 (Research Program on Marketing in Computer Mediated Environments) <http://ecommerce.vanderbilt.edu/cyberporn.debate.html>. The issues raised are of particular and general import.

13. PornCity <http://www.porncity.net>, a free site, is estimated to attract more than 50 million unique visitors per month, while Kara's Adult Playground <http://www.karasxxx.com>, a leading pay site, logs almost 6 million customer visits per month. Other statistics are even more arresting: Stephen Cohen, CEO of Sex.com <http://www.sex.com/>, claims between 70 and 120 million hits per day for his high-profile service (Diamond, 1999).

14. The Internet Friends Videochat Network (iFriends.net) claims to put more than 1.5 million Webcam-enabled individuals in touch with one another <http://www.ifriends.net/>.

15. For example, videos depicting chronicled or choreographed death – so-called snuff movies (Svoray, 1998).

16. Caty McPherson of Samantha's Online Galleries <http://juicymango.com/copynotice.html> claimed that three-quarters of all visitors to her web site were males between the ages of 18 and 34 years (Bowman, 1998). She operated Rouze.com <http://www.Rouze.com/>, an online destination site for men that competed with *Playboy* and *Maxim* (Anderson, 1999).

17. For example, at Vivid <http://www.vividweb.com/>, one of the largest pornographic video manufacturing companies in the United States, the head of production, chief financial officer, and foreign sales manager are all women (O'Toole, 1998, p. 52). According to one industry insider, "Virtually every woman in the business now has her own site" (Leland, 1999, p. 61).

18. The advocacy group Feminists Against Censorship compiled the intimate and celebratory volume *Tales From the Clitoris* (Matrix, 1996) to present its side of the argument in the so-called porn wars.

19. Kizza (1998, p. 136) notes that a CNN Interactive survey in the wake of the defeat of the CDA showed that the public "did not consider Internet pornography a serious enough problem to warrant control of the Internet by government, and they believed that the overall responsibility of control of the Internet is with the parents or seniors, like teachers."

REFERENCES

Adamic, L.A., and Huberman, B.A. 1999. The nature of markets in the World Wide Web. *Proceedings of Computing in Economics and Finance 1999*, Meeting of the Society for Computational Economics, 24–26 June. <http://ideas.uqam.ca/ideas/data/Papers/bocbococf521.html>

Anderson, L. 1999. (Birthday) suit gig. *Industry Standard*, 20 September:229–230.

Arquilla, J., and Ronfeldt, D. 1996. *The advent of netwar*. Monterey, CA: RAND.

Bar, F., and Borrus, M. 1999. Innovation and industrial transformation in the e-conomy. In *The digital economy in international perspective: Common construction or regional rivalry? A Conference of the University of California E-conomyTMProject*, held at the Willard Inter Continental Washington, Washington, DC, 27 May 1999, pp. 22–25. Berkeley, CA: Berkeley Round Table on the International Economy (BRIE) and the UC E-conomyTM Project.

Bell, D. 1973. *The coming of post-industrial society: A venture in social forecasting*. New York: Basic Books.

Bicknell, C. 1999. Public porn? No stock answer. *Wired News*. <http:www.wired.com/news/email/explode-infobeat/business/story/21341.html>

Bodow, S. 1999. Initial porno offering. *Wired* 7(8):64.

Bonn, M.A., Furr, L.H., and Susskind, A.M. 1998. Using the Internet as a pleasure travel planning tool: An examination of the sociodemographic and behavioral characteristics among Internet users and nonusers. *Journal of Hospitality & Tourism Research* 22(3):303–317.

Bowman, L.M. 1998. Erotic e-commerce vendors warn against backlash. *ZDNN Tech News Now* 9 October. <http://www.zdnet. com/zdnn/stories/zdnn_smgraph_display/0,443 6,2147505,00.html>

Branwyn, G. 1999. How the porn sites do it. *Industry Standard* 22 March:34, 36–40.

Bresnick, A. 1998. Wired Victorians. *Forbes* 21 September:287.

Bronson, P. 1999. Instant company. *New York Times Magazine* 11 July: 44–47.

Brown, J. 1998. Has the Web made porn respectable? *Salon* 20 October. <http://www.salon-magazine.com/21st/feature/1998/10/cov_20feature.html>

Brunker, M. 1999. Sex toys blaze tactile trail on Net. MSNBC News. <http:www.msnbc.com/news/318124.asp?cp1=1#BODY>

Carr, N.G. 2000. Hypermediation: Commerce as clickstrean. *Harvard Business Review* 78(1):46–47.

Carse, A.L. 1999. Pornography's many meanings: A reply to C. M. Concepcion. *Hypatia* 14(1):101–111.

Chang, Y. 2000. Was it virtually good for you? *Newsweek* 1 January:71.

Clarke, R. 1999. Internet privacy concerns confirm the case for intervention. *Communications of the ACM* 42(2):60–67.

Cooper, M.D. 1983. The structure and future of the information economy. *Information Processing & Management* 19(1):9–26.

Corcoran, E. 1999. The E-gang. *Forbes* 26 July:145–157.

Denning, D.A. 1999. *Information warfare and security*. Reading, MA: Addison-Wesley.

Dertouzos, M.L. 1997. *What will be: How the new world of information will change our lives*. San Francisco, CA: HarperEdge.

Diamond, D. 1999. The sleeze squeeze. *Business 2.0* February.

Dibbell, J. 1999. *My tiny life: Crime and passion in a virtual world*. London: Fourth Estate.

Drucker, P.F. 1987. *The frontiers of management*. London: Heinemann.

Dutton, W.H. 1999. *Society on the line: Information politics in the digital age*. Oxford: Oxford University Press.

Fleck, J. 1994. Learning by trying: The implementation of configurational technology. *Research Policy* 23:637–652.

Gomes, L. 1999. A giant game of "I Spy" on the Web: Netcams bring videoconferences into bedrooms. *Wall Street Journal* 19 July:B1, B4.

Grant, L. 1994. *Sexing the millennium: Women and the sexual revolution*. New York: Grove Press.

Greenfield, K.T. 1999. Taking stock in smut. *Time* 19 April:43.

Grover, M.B. 1999. Lost in cyberspace. *Forbes* 8 March: 124–128.

Gurley, J.W. 1999. How the Net is changing competition. *Fortune* 15 March:168.

Hamel, G., and Stamper, J. 1998. The e-corporation: More than just Web-based, it's building a new industrial order. *Fortune* 7 December:80–92.

Hoffman, D.L., Novak, T.P., and Peralta, M.A. 1999. Information privacy in the marketplace: Implications for the commercial uses of anonymity on the Web. *The Information Society* 15(2):129–139.

Hosenball, M. 1999. Sex, bets and bikers. *Newsweek* 18 October:50–51.

Kaplan, D.A. 1999. Trouble brewing. *Newsweek* 19 July:40–41.

Karlgaard, R. 1999. The Web's fog of war. *Forbes* 26 July:43.

Kizza, J.M. 1998. *Civilizing the Internet: Global concerns and efforts toward regulation*. Jefferson, NC: McFarland.

Kling, R. 1984. Defining the boundaries of computing across complex organizations. In *Critical issues in information systems research*, eds. R. J. Boland and R. A. Hirschelm, pp. 307–362. Chichester: Wiley.

Kling, R., ed. 1996. *Computerization and controversy: Value conflicts and social choices* (2nd ed.). San Diego, CA: Academic Press.

Kling, R., and Lamb, R. 1999. IT and organizational change in digital economies: A socio technical approach. Presented at *Understanding the digital economy – data, tools and research*, 25–26 May 1999, at the U.S. Department of Commerce, Washington DC. <http://www.ecommerce.gov/schedule.htm>

La Franco, R. 1999. The playboy philosophy. *Forbes*, 14 June: 220.

Lake, D. 1999. Industry spotlight: Is porn still the Web's great test bed? *Industry Standard*, 15 November: 172.

Lane, F.S. 2000. *Obscene profits: The entrepreneurs of pornography in the cyber age*. London: Routledge.

Lawrence, S., and Giles, C.L. 1999. Accessibility of information on the web. *Nature* 8 July: 107–109.

Leland, J. 1999. More buck for the bang: How Netsex has transformed the porn industry. *Newsweek* 20 September:61.

Long, R. 1999. Porn on demand. *National Review* 51(10):48–49.

MacKinnon, C.A. 1995. Francis Biddle's sister: Pornography, civil rights, and speech. In: *The problem of pornography*, ed. S. Dwyer, pp. 53–66. New York: Wadsworth.

Matrix, C. 1996. *Tales from the clitoris: A female experience of pornography*. San Francisco, CA: AK Press.

McCumber, D. 1994. *X-rated*. New York: Pinnacle Books.

McNair, B. 1996. *Mediated sex: Pornography and postmodern culture*. London: Arnold.

Mersey, W. 1999. They shoot, they score: Johns post prostitute ratings online. <http://www.villagevoice.com/columns/9926/mersey.shtml>

Morais, R.C. 1999. Porn goes public. *Forbes* 14 June:214–220.

Office of Management and Budget. 1997. *North American Industry Classification System.* Washington, DC: OMB.

O'Toole, L. 1998. *Pornocopia: Porn, sex, technology and desire.* London: Serpent's Tail.

Peterson, R.A., Balasubramanian, S., and Bronnenberg, B. J. 1997. Exploring the implications of the Internet for consumer marketing. *Journal of the Academy of Marketing Science* 25(4):329–346.

Porat, M.U. 1977. *The information economy: Definition and measurement.* Washington, DC: U.S. Department of Telecommunications, Office of Telecommunications.

Reich, R.B. 1991. *The work of nations: Preparing ourselves for 21st century capitalism.* New York: Knopf.

Rimm, M. 1995. Marketing pornography on the Information Super-highway. *Georgetown Law Journal* 83(June):1849–1934.

Roemhildt, R.A. 1998. Americans wouldn't know it, but pornography is illegal. *Washington Times* 14 December.

Rose, F. 1997. Sex sells. *Wired* 5(12):218–224, 276–278, 280, 282, 284.

Roth, D. 1999. My, what big Internet numbers you have! *Fortune* 15 March:114–120.

Shapiro, C., and Varian, H.R. 1998. *Information rules: A strategic guide to the network economy.* Cambridge, MA: Harvard Business School Press.

Silverman, A. 1999. Industry snapshot: adult entertainment. *Hoover's Online.* <http://www.hoovers.com/feature/industry/adult.html>

Sproull, L., and Kiesler, S. 1991. *Connections: New ways of working in the networked organization.* Cambridge, MA: MIT Press.

Svoray, Y. 1998. *Gods of death.* New York: Simon & Schuster.

The Information Society. 1997. Theory and practice of electronic commerce. [Special issue]. 13(1).

Timmers, P. 1998. Business models for electronic markets. *Electronic Markets* 8(2):3–8.

Toffler, A. 1984. *Previews and premises.* London: Pan Books.

Turkle, S. 1995. *Life on the screen: Identity in the age of the Internet.* New York: Simon & Schuster.

Valverde, M. 1995. Beyond gender dangers and private pleasures: theory and ethics in the sex debates. In *The problem of pornography*, ed. S. Dwyer, pp. 177–191. New York: Wadsworth.

Viegas, F.B., and Donath, J.S. 1999. Chat circles. In *CHI 99: The CHI is the limit. Human factors in computing systems*, eds. M. G. Williams, M. W. Attom, K. Ehrlich, and W. Newman, pp. 9–16. New York: ACM.

Wallace, P. 1999. *The psychology of the Internet.* Cambridge: Cambridge University Press.

Webster, F. 1999. Democracy and information in a networked society. In *Information landscapes for a learning society*, eds. S. Criddle, L. Dempsy, and R. Heseltine, pp. 235–253, London: Library Association Publishing.

Weintraut, J.N., and Davis, J. 1999. The startup economy. *Business 2.0* July:61–68.

Willis, E. 1995. Feminism, moralism, and pornography. In *The problem of pornography*, ed. S. Dwyer, pp. 170–176. New York: Wadsworth.

Wolf, M.J. 1999. *The entertainment economy: How mega-media forces are transforming our lives.* New York: Random House.

20 RACE, GENDER AND SEX ON THE NET

Semantic Networks of Selling and Storytelling Sex Tourism

Peter A. Chow-White

Debates about the impact of the internet on society oscillate between utopian and dystopian poles, usually in regards to issues of the digital divide and community building (Burnett and Marshall, 2003). Boosters of the internet predicted it to be a place where social inequalities would be democratized. Individuals and groups would find new spaces for expression and alternative methods of communication that could circumvent dominant forms of mainstream media, state-regulated tele-communications and the technological constraints of old media (Gates, 1996; Gilder, 1994; Rheingold, 1994). Proponents also argued that people could have more control over their own identities, free from the social structures of difference, such as race and gender. These types of debates about the internet often offered prognostications about the solid implications of this emerging technology. Current internet studies, however, have turned the focus of research to what is actually occuring online.

While the networks that preceded the internet were created by agents of state control (Abbate, 1999; Castells, 2001), the rapid diffusion of the internet in the 1990s has enabled marginalized groups to establish URLs and innovate their own forms of community such as e-zines (Cresser et al., 2001), Queer Sisters (Nip, 2004) and Afrofuturism (Eglash, 2002; Nelson, 2002). For instance, Cresser et al. (2001) found that women have been using e-zines to establish an alternative voice to mainstream media discourse and broadcast to a mass audience. Nip (2004) has shown how the Hong Kong-based Queer Sisters bulletin board fosters the building of relationships

Peter A. Chow-White, "Race, Gender and Sex on the Net: Semantic Networks of Selling and Storytelling Sex Tourism," pp. 883–905 from *Media, Culture & Society* 28:6 (2006).

and community. Afrofuturism, a movement made up of a loose collection of artists, musicians, writers and critics, converges on issues of the Black Atlantic communities and technology in digital culture (Eglash, 2002; Nelson, 2002). The internet has also been utilized by right-wing groups to spread messages of white-power (Gabriel, 1998; Ware and Back, 2002).

Although previous studies have made important contributions and insights into dystopian and utopian aspects of the internet, they have given a limited view of identity formation through a focus on single dimensions of difference, such as gender, sexuality or race. Critical scholars have argued that race, gender and sexuality interact to reproduce or challenge structures of difference, often in contradictory ways (Anthias and Yuval-Davis, 1992; Hall, 1996; Hill-Collins, 2000; Mohanty, 2003). This study investigates how discourses of race, gender, sexuality and the market intersect online in the construction of identity through an examination of semantic networks on websites and discussion boards for sex tourism. I argue that the selling of sex tourism and sex tourist storytelling are structured in a manner where neither race, sexuality and gender, nor the market overdetermines the character of the discourse. Foucault has shown how modern social power operates through a web of discourses. Identity formation is not based on a unitary identity but emanates through a number of strategic points of negotiation over the meaning of identification and difference. Using a quantitative approach to usually qualitative concerns, this study investigates Foucault's problematic empirically through a complementary combination of content analysis and network analysis. Content analysis reveals the major themes in the sex tourism semantic network, while the network analysis determines the organization of the themes and the structure of power. Does race, gender or sexuality determine the character of the discussion boards and websites? Or is the structure of the semantic network decentralized?

Sex tourism on the internet is at the confluence of issues of race, gender, sexuality, technology and globalization. Increasingly, information and communication technologies (ICTs), such as the internet, are playing a particularly significant role not only in the promotion and packaging of sex tourism but of a new type of global surveillance of bodies, race and desire (Gabriel, 1998, 2000; Ware and Back, 2002). Cyberspace enables sex tourists to build deeper connections between the racialization, sexualization and commodification of sex workers' bodies and Western masculinity. Like chat rooms (Travers, 2000), MUDs (Turkle, 1995) and MOOs (White, 2002), sex tourists use discussion boards to exchange information and give immediate feedback on their experiences. In this culture of hypertext, users are active contributors to the representation of sex tourism as the recombinant nature of the discussion boards allows them to be consumers and producers (Elmer, 2004: 56; Landow, 1992). The members of this community discuss issues and places with the intention of buying sex and from the experiences of that desire and pursuit. This raises important concerns regarding dystopian and utopian outcomes of internet use. Instead of ICTs making us freer and more democratic, they may be deepening social inequality and structures of difference.

Globalization, Mass Tourism and Sex Tourism

The type of society emerging from globalization has been characterized as one based around flows of information and networks. The crucial pathways to sources of domination and change in globalization lie in having access to the network and its internal logics. In this new, global dynamic 'the power of flows takes precedence over the flows of power' (Castells, 1996: 467). Flows have a number of dimensions that Appadurai (1990) refers to as scapes of ethnicity, technology, finance, media and ideology. Analyses of the economic and political transformations of globalization tend to treat the various scapes as the result of a global pluralism, detached from social processes of gender, race, class and sexuality. While the power of flows may be the defining character of the network, Massey and others have insisted on accounting for the 'power geometry' of global flows, as different people and groups have uneven access and influence to the means of cultural and material production, as well being differentially impacted by them (Massey, 1993; Morely, 2000). Sex tourism on the internet is a strategic site for examining the continuities and discontinuities in the reorganization of power and identity through globalization. Sex tourism and the internet are at the confluence of global flows of information, technology, identity and the new economy.

Sex tourism is a niche market of the global tourism industry. Curiously, tourism itself has largely been omitted from the grand discussions in academia, industry and government about the changing nature and impact of globalization (Enloe, 1989). A set of interconnected industries from the macro level, such as the various airlines, to the meso level, such as local services (restaurants, bars, hotels, beachside rentals, etc.) and the micro, everyday practices of tourists and workers make up the Global Tourism Network (GTN). During the 1990s, academic and private sector observers of the international tourism industry placed it second only to the oil industry (Truong, 1990) and predicted that it would become the dominant global industry in the early 21st century (Apostolopoulos et al., 1996; Crick, 1996; Enloe, 1989; Urry, 1990; World Tourism Organization [WTO], 2000). In the mid 1980s, 200 million people were international tourists (Enloe, 1989: 20). By the end of 2001, this number had risen to 693 million travelers spending US $463 billion worldwide (World Tourism Organization, 2003), rising again in 2002 to 702.6 million travelers spending US $474.2 billion (World Tourism Organization, 2004). The year 2003 showed a slight drop in overall tourist arrivals; however, 2004 finished with a record high of 760 million (World Tourism Organization, 2005). ...

A key component of sex tourism is the movement of symbolic representations of a sexualized and racialized sex worker (Davidson and Taylor, 1999; Enloe, 1989; Mullings, 1999; Truong, 1990). ... Since the mid 1990s, websites have popped up in the internet galaxy as key sites of commerical and information exchange in the development of the sex tourism industry.

Sex tourism websites combine and incorporate features of mainstream commercial sites such as Amazon, Expedia and eBay. The websites are product providers, experience oriented and user driven. They act as a virtual store window for the sex tourism industry while providing points of sale for potential travelers, frequent fliers or those who just want to do some window-shopping. Potential travelers looking for information for their next adventure abroad can find one-time purchase products such as travel literature, guidebooks, newsletters and magazines. For the frequent flier, subscription-based content includes online books, streamed videos, movies and picture galleries with prices ranging from US $5.00 per week to yearly packages at US $59.95. The package tours are all-inclusive and guaranteed for the traveler who likes to leave little risk in their vacation experience:

> Thailand is known Worldwide as the 'Disneyland for adults'. On our Thailand tour you'll stay in a luxurious hotel setting complete with pool and top notch room service. Our experienced Thai guides will take care of your every need and be there for you 24 hours a day. They'll provide **STEP by STEP** instructions and guidance helping you maximize your Thailand tour of time and pleasure. Showing you the best Thailand sex clubs, restaurants, sightseeing and sex entertainment plus explaining the many Thai sex customs and cultures. (www.dexterhorn.com)

A common feature of sex tourism websites is a discussion or message board. Here, sex tourists can provide more detailed information on various aspects of sex travel. The more sophisticated forums are browsable and highly organized by general topic or by continent, with subgroups ranging through countries all the way down to city districts and specific bars. The users of the board do not deal in polite euphemisms about acts of sex, prostitutes and buying sex.

While the internet provides a marketplace for products and services, it also sells something else. At the denotative level are the products and services, the images of sex workers and information about where to go and how to obtain sexual services. They share similar features as mainstream tourism companies such as Lonely Planet, Let's Go, Hotwire.com and Thomas Cook, offering general travel information and the promise of a risk-free travel experience and sun, surf and sand. The added-value offered by sex tourism websites, however, is in myth-making and (male) self-empowerment.

The internet and sex tourism websites are not only tools for information exchange and product distribution, but also structuring devices that create and reproduce myths of sex worker sexuality, race and male dominance. Sex tourism websites entice the consumer to engage in a specific type of travel. There exists a synergy between the sex industry and the travel industry. What distinguishes sex tourism websites is that they are not just selling products and services, places, people and (sexual) adventure, they are selling them through discourses of the marketplace, gender, race and sexuality.

Discursive Formations, Semantic Networks and Power

Male fantasies of the female Other are structured by sexualized and racialized discursive formations. Discursive formations are established hierarchical orders of 'truth' that organize language and determine communicative practices in a particular historical moment (Foucault, 1972; Hall, 1997). … Discourse does not merely reflect social practices, relations and structures. It plays a constitutive role in the construction and reproduction of them (Emirbayer and Goodwin, 1994; Wetherell and Potter, 1992). …

The discussion boards are not only networking people, but ideas and frameworks of understanding or semantic networks. Semantic networks are shared cultural meanings about a particular phenomena; they are meanings by association (Du Gay, 1997: 15). They connect the descriptive or literal meanings of a word or concept with broader connotations and cultural discourses or discursive formations. The stories about sex tourism in the discussion board and websites have their own networks of meaning about female sexuality, male dominance and the market. However, they are connected to broader cultural discourses about orientalism, gender and globalization. From a micro point of view, they are part of a particular discussion string and, at the macro level, each contributes to an evolving discursive formation about sex tourism. The overall narratives that structure sex tourism stories are evolving in the sense that the mechanism of user feedback constantly pushes the discursive possibilities and actual boundaries of the board in terms of its size. The readers are also writers. None of the posts is a self-contained unit. …

Discussion board posts contribute to a larger discussion while, at the same time, being constrained by the topic and the type of storytelling about that topic which is already under way. They are nodes within a broader semantic network, that is, within the broader collection of postings and within broader cultural formations.

Cultural formations are interrelated symbols that have a 'nonmaterial structure' and are organized in a manner similar to material structures while, analytically, being separate from them (Alexander and Smith, 1993). New structural sociology argues for bringing an analytical lens to bear on culture as an autonomous entity in society, calling for an internal analysis of cultural/discursive structures. While human agency has traditionally been dependent on material (meaning economic and network) structures, Emirbayer and Goodwin argue 'cultural formations are significant because they both constrain and enable historical actors, in much the same way as do network structures themselves' (1994: 1440). … In a recursive and relational manner, actors are constrained by a foreclosing of certain options or possibilities for action as well as having to rely on established frames. …

I would argue that Foucault's conceptualization of power can be understood and operationalized as a network theory. Taking the posts on the sex tourism discussion board as a whole, the themes across the different strings and sub-categories of organization can be conceptualized as nodes in a network, a semantic network of sex tourism. ...

Method

This research examines 22 sex tourism websites (STW) and sex tourist discussions on message boards from two of the websites. The data consist of 22 homepages, 1143 discussion board postings from www.dexterhorn.com (DH) and 220 postings from www.worldsexguide.com (WSG) (consulted March and November 2003, respectively). The homepages are the portals to the site and use pictures, descriptions of site and content, and links to attract the traveler/web surfer to the site web pages. The boards are divided into the world's continents and a number of other discussion topics. The semantic network analysis is conducted by taking the output of a computer-assisted content analysis (CACA) and running the data through network analysis software. ...

Network analysis converts the output of the content analysis into a semantic network and measures its structure and the relationship between the themes or nodes. There are three matrices under analysis: the discussion boards from DH, the discussion board from WSG and the homepages from STW. This study is interested in the structure of the matrix and the strength or position of the themes. The structure of the network refers to the relative position of the themes in relation to one another, or how they are connected. ... A highly centralized network indicates that a particular theme is discussed commonly and frequently across the discussion board. A decentralized network would show that the network is characterized by a number of predominant themes. The position of the themes determines which ones characterize the discourse in the semantic network. They are the themes that are most likely to be present in each of the individual posts and would be more likely to frame the discussions. In network analysis, the concept of centrality provides measures of structure and position.

Centrality measures are known as prestige or power measures in network analysis (Monge and Contractor, 2003). This measure determines, at the global level of the semantic network, the degree of centralization of the network and, at the nodal level, which themes hold the most prominent positions. Degree centrality shows the number of direct links a node has with other nodes in the network and indicates prominent positions (Wasserman and Faust, 1994: 172). It is a local measure that shows how well points are connected in their local environments (Scott, 2000: 84). Researchers have used degree centrality as an 'indicator of the node's social capital or centrality' (Monge and Contractor, 2003: 38). While the content analysis shows which themes characterize the discourse on websites, the network analysis shows its semantic structure. ... Centrality measures will show if one theme, a centralized network, or a number of them, a decentralized network, dominate the discussion. If this is the case, then the tendency when talking about and advertising sex tourism involves not solely race or gender, for example, but a combination of both.

Selling and Storytelling Sex Tourism: The Marketplace, Masculinity, Race and Sexuality

The content analysis of the homepages and the discussion boards identified predominant themes found in the literature on sex tourism: the marketplace, gender, race and sexuality. Not surprisingly, these themes dominated the discussions of the users of the discussion boards and the marketing of the homepages. As one of the primary purposes of sex tourism on the web is the instrumental practice of information exchange, sex tourists share stories and experiences about where to go to buy sex, how much one should expect to pay and types of sexual services. Other predominant themes include safety, health, 'packed out' and greedy. The following sections offer a closer reading of the themes.

Health and Safety

Concerns about safety are similar to those of mainstream tourists, from pickpockets to political unrest. Health refers to the hygienic conditions of travel destinations or disease. There is little reference to sexually transmitted diseases (STDs), which is surprising considering the spread of AIDS worldwide. Opinions about 'catching something' range from downplaying risks to outright denial of risk.

> Well, I guess eventually if you hang out long enough and bang enough girls, you're bound to come down with something. If so, you'll need to visit one of the local Clinics. They're easy to find. … Just look for the any of the Red Cross signs and you'll know you're there. Drop you're drawers and take a shot like a man.

Although this message offers advice for curing a disease, it suggests that the actual contracting of an STD is infrequent. The post also implies that sexual experiences are common and numerous.

'Packed out' and Greedy

Simultaneous expressions of desire and deceit underwrite sex tourism discourse. Sex workers are portrayed as both objects of admiration and suspicion as they are to be acquired, but not trusted. This ambivalent characterization of the Other has its roots in colonial conquest and has been well articulated by postcolonial scholars (Bhabha, 1984; Parameswaran, 2002; Said, 1978). Modern Western travelers share a sense of the exotic with their historical counterparts. Sex tourists report to one another on the discussion boards like colonial explorers sending word back home about an untouched and bountiful land of untold riches. …

Unlike the 'empty' lands waiting to be penetrated by colonial conquest, 'women are the earth that is to be discovered, entered, named, inseminated and, above all, owned' (McClintock, 1995: 31). Sex tourists talk about the 'packed out' bars with excitement and anticipation. Always lurking in their boosterism, though, is a sense of *noir*. Along with fascination and desire, there exists a deep suspicion of sex workers. According to sex tourists, they are greedy, tricky and manipulative. …

What begins as a relationship of aid from the point of view of the tourist, 'You feel sorry for them, and you know they're poor. Because you have money, you feel strong' (interview in Seabrook, 1996: 30), becomes one of suspicion. …

In order to 'regain' a position of dominance, sex tourists use money, masculinity, race and sex.

The Marketplace for the Sexual Tourist

Considering the theme of the marketplace, a neoclassical economic approach would suggest that the sex tourist visits sex tourism websites because of the promise of a lower transaction cost for sexual services than could be found in their home, usually an economically developed nation. Here, the logic of a globalized market place in the new economy seeks cheaper sex and better quality in a location different from one's home country. Crick puts it more directly when he argues that tourists 'do not go to these countries because the people are friendly, they go because a holiday there is cheap' (1996: 25). A sex tourist interviewed by British journalist Jeremy Seabrook echoes this rationale and remarks that 'I came because it was cheap. … I use [Thai women] like I might use any other amenity, a restaurant or a public convenience' (1996: 33). Thus, the chief concerns of the sex tourist are low cost and high quality of services.

Re-masculinization

While the actual price of sexual services in many developing countries may indeed be cheaper than the going rate of a sex worker in the US, if the cost of traveling abroad (airfare, hotel, food, etc.) is factored in, the actual price would be much less at home. This points to added-value in the cost of sex tourism. The money sex tourists bring to countries like Cuba, Brazil, India and Thailand affords them something other than cheap sex. There is a performative aspect which makes them feel strong and powerful as the act of traveling for sex can be understood as 'a collective behavior oriented toward the restoration of the "generalized belief" of what it is to be male' (Davidson and Taylor, 1999: 39). This restoration can be viewed as a response to what Castells has called the 'crisis of patriarchy' that has been prompted by second-wave feminism (1997; see also Beynon 2002). Women's challenge to their structural and cultural status was perceived by many men to be an attack on male roles and masculinity in society.

Some argue that there has always been a crisis in masculinity; the 'crisis' is neither new nor unique (Beynon, 2002). However, the association of buying cheap sex for money is viewed by sex tourists as a form of male power. Whereas the meaning of such practices may have been more taken for granted in the past, interviews with sex tourists have revealed that they are actively seeking such practices of domination through economic sexual arrangements (Davidson and Taylor, 1999; Seabrook, 1996). Research has shown that sex tourists perceive a shift in the sex gender system in favor of women and seek to rectify a position of imagined subordination through the act of buying sex cheaply (see Kempadoo, 1999). The reality of a supposed inversion is quite the opposite. While women in the global south experience exploitation and discrimination, there are a number of groups, both at the local and global level, who advocate for sex worker's rights, such as SWEAT (Sex Worker Education and Advocacy Taskforce) in South Africa, COIN (Centro de Orientacíon e Investigación Integral) and MODEMU (Moviemiento de Mujeres Unidas) in the Dominican Republic, La Únion Unica in Mexico and the international NGO Network of Sex Work Projects (NWSP) (Cabezas, 1998, 1999; Kempadoo, 1999; Kempadoo and Doezema, 1998). Individually though, sex tourists mistake any sign of agency on the part of sex workers, whether it be through the advocacy of NGOs or simply in the negotiation over price and other terms of the deal, as an affront to the Western male's position of priviledge and evidence that, in fact, men are the victims. In response to a crisis in patriarchy, a 're-masculinization' (Beynon, 2002: 90) emerged in the 1990s where Western men have attempted to 'reclaim' a position of power that is perceived to be waning with the successes of the second wave of feminism. This response considers the Western woman to have become too independent, too demanding on men and too in control of her own sexuality. A flash-driven advertisement on Bangkok Knight's Global Village website asks:

Know what the difference between sex for money and sex for free is?

Sex for money is a LOT cheaper!

Are you an adventurous, single male?

Recently been FUCKED over in a divorce perhaps?

Or maybe just looking for a good time with women who aren't feminist, Men-hating BITCHES!

Join us on BGV and we'll show you where to have the time of your life!

Learn all you'll need to know to enjoy a vacation or start a new life among beautiful, young, nubile, NON-complaining women! Women whose soul [sic] desire is to please YOU and not THEMSELVES!

The marketing of sex workers, especially Asian woman, is situated in a binary position to the perceived identity of the American woman: dependent/independent, submissive/domineering, sexually available/sexually liberated and domestically inclined/career oriented. ...

The added-value of sex tourism in the exchange of money for sex is the guarantee of submissiveness, traditional gender roles and the 'right' attitude. Beynon argues that the process of re-masculinization has been a national project in response to 'un-masculinizing' historical events, such as men returning from the Second World War in Great Britain, or the election of Ronald Reagan as a response to the hippy 1960s and the 'soft' leadership of Jimmy Carter (2002: 90). Sex tourism becomes a transnational project where the pursuit of unbridled sexuality over women is intended to reassert men's 'proper' place in the social order.

Racialization

Customers of prostitution have often sought out 'sex workers whose racial, national, or class identities [were] different from their own' (Shrage, 1994: 142). The demands by white Western men for prostitutes from Latin America, Africa and Asia may be 'explained in part by culturally produced racial fantasies regarding the sexuality of these women' (Davidson and Taylor, 1999: 48). ... An integral part of the fantasy is the perception that Asian women's sensuality and sexual ability are more 'natural' than that of Western women. ...

While the sexuality of sex workers is perceived as natural and normal, the tourists seek sexual experiences that are quite the contrary.

Transgressive Sexuality

The racialized sexuality of sex workers provides a site for sex tourists to have experiences that they normally would not be able to have at home. Since they are of a different 'race'/culture, the 'exotic' women of the East are to be experienced and, as Enloe explains, 'the male tourist feels he has entered a region where he can shed civilization's constraints, where he is freed from standards of behavior imposed by respectable women back home' (1989: 28). ... Edward Said explains that this realness is actually the construction of myth, however: it is a projection onto Asian women as 'creature[s] of male power fantasy', where they 'express unlimited sensuality, they are more or less stupid, and above all willing' (1978: 207). While re-masculinization has 'caused' Western men to seek empowerment elsewhere, to some extent, sex tourism acts as a time machine for male self-esteem and sexual practices free from cultural attitudes of what is decent sexual behavior. The Other remains a place where taboo sex can be obtained from 'superfeminine, submissive, mysterious, desirable, and docile' women, where 'sexual intercourse [is] cut loose from the ties of conventional, heterosexual monogamy' (Manderson and Jolly, 1997: 125), and the white, male traveler can find his true self.

The content analysis revealed the prevalent themes on the discussion boards and advertising on the homepages. A close reading of the themes illustrated how they are linked to colonial discourses and current discussions of tourism and masculinity. In the next section, the network analysis will show the relationship of the themes to one another and the structure of the semantic network.

Network Analysis of Storytelling and Selling Sex Tourism

Network analysis was conducted on two iterations of DH, WSG and STW. The first iteration (DHa, WSGa and STWa) included the raw themes, many of which indicated the higher-order concepts (race, gender, sexuality, the market) discussed in the previous section. Where appropriate, the indicator concepts were collapsed into the higher-order concepts, producing a second set of matrices (DHb, WSGb and STWb). Normalized centrality measures were conducted only on the first set to find the relative positions of the themes within the network and to find the degree of centralization or decentralization. Confirming Foucault's theory, DHa, WSGa, and STWa proved to be highly decentralized network with equivalent scores among a number of the themes (see Table 20.1).

While the normalized centrality measures show the network at the global level with a number of themes having equivalent positions, it explains little about the relationship between the individual themes.

Naming sex workers, sex acts, price and racialization shared the highest measurements across the matrices. Two messages show how the articulation of the themes changes in different discursive occasions:

> They all come in different sizes, shapes, and colors. Prices range from 50 dollars to 100 dollars. It is up to you to pick the right girl or girls for a good time – I suggest you go for the beautiful ones with a kind and gentle personality who are interested in having pleasing sex with you, and not just in getting your dollars.

The racial referent of 'color' promises a buffet of different, non-white skin tones, while the gendered stereotype of the submissiveness of the female Other promises sexual temptation. The next quote makes a direct connection to purchasing a car and appeals to the racial discourse of sameness:

> Just like Ford said about the Model 'T'. We have any color you want as long as it is black. I don't worry about color. Some of the best lays I've ever had were dark-skinned girls. They're all pink on the inside anyway.

DHa and WSGa are almost identical to one another throughout while sharing the top two positions. In fact, the bottom half and top half of each network have the same themes, with identical positions in some cases. However, the position of racial is a significant difference between the discussion boards and the homepages. Sex tourism websites make more explicit references to race in advertising their services.

Semantic networks DHb, WSGb and STWb contained only the higher-order concepts. … Naming sex workers and sex acts hold the most prominent positions in all three networks, with price dropping only one position in STWb, by a very small margin. … Two significant differences in the results are that pictures with posts and

TABLE 20.1 Normalized centrality measures for DHa, WSGa and STWa

DH		WSG		STW	
Theme	*Degree*	*Theme*	*Degree*	*Theme*	*Degree*
Sex act	100	Sex act	94	Sex act	94
Naming SW*	100	Naming SW	94	Naming SW	94
SW personality	100	SW personality	94	SW personality	94
Quality of service	100	SW body	94	SW body	94
Price	100	Quality of service	94	Quality of service	94
Places to buy sex	100	Price	94	Naming ST	94
Racial	100	Places to buy sex	94	Post with picture	94
SW body	94	Racial	94	Packed out	94
Naming ST*	94	Safety	94	Price	94
Packed out	94	Naming ST	88	Places to buy sex	94
Hygiene	94	Packed out	88	Racial	94
Safety	94	Hygiene	88	Safety	94
Health	94	Greedy	88	Greedy	94
Post with picture	89	Health	88	Hygiene	88
Greedy	89	Post with picture	56	Health	88
Currency	64	Currency	10	Currency	0

*Naming Sex Workers, Naming Sex Tourists.

racial hold much higher positions in STWb than in DHb and WSGb. A comparison of Freeman measures for DHb, WSGb and STWb shows that commodification and sexualization hold the higher positions across the networks. In fact, the structures of the top cohort and bottom cohort of DHb and STWb include the same themes.

Conclusion

The results of the comparison of themes in the sex tourism websites show that discourses of the market, gender, race and transgression structure the ways that sex tourism is sold and talked about. The products and services offered on the sites are packaged in a manner that entices the sex tourists to take a cheap journey into the past where masses of women of color play traditional roles as available and willing servants. The most important discourse is an economic one, as it characterized the websites the most times, followed closely by race and sexuality.

Turning to the discursive formations in the discussion boards, the results show that the structures of the discussion networks are highly decentralized. This is consistent with Foucault's theorizing of social power as a web of discourses. According to the normalized centrality scores, there are a number of themes that hold the more central positions and characterize the discussions, particularly references to sex,

sex worker attitudes, quality of service, price and race. When considering the Freeman degree measures, a more complex picture of the networks emerges. When sex tourism is being marketed and talked about, the discourse is primarily about sex workers, types of sexual services, and quality and cost of buying sex. These discussions are deeply connected to place: knowing which countries to go to for a vacation and where to go for sexual encounters.

Critical race scholars have argued that, in order to properly understand how social power operates, interrogations of the intersections of structures of dominance, such as gender, race and sex, are important starting points. If the DHb and WSGb networks are conceptualized as examples of discursive formations of sex tourism, then one theme does not characterize the network, nor is one most central. Race or gender does not overdetermine the identity of the network. Rather, there are a number of prominent themes that intersect or are closely and widely linked to make up the formation or network. This is an expression of the type of power that Foucault is referring to when he describes modern power operating in network form. The representations of sex workers are formed through the intersection of sexualized, commodified and racialized formations. One reason for the moderate position of the latter theme is that, especially in the case of discussions about Thailand and the Philippines, the largest number of postings, racial identification is largely assumed, as the populations are perceived to be homogeneous by sex travelers.

Discourses of exotic sex, race and commodification constitute the body of the sex worker and the practice of sex tourism. They operate in a manner that limits what can be said, not only about women in the sex trade but all women in developing nations. This is a widespread pattern throughout the discussion boards and websites, as illustrated through the combination of methods. The discourses in the discussion boards are consistent with the themes in the sex tourism websites. The myth-making in the sex tourism websites is intimately related to the practices of sex tourists. The production of discourses of cost and quality, sexual services, female servility and male domination resonate in the consumption of the sex tourists and reproduction of such discourses in the discussion boards. A significant difference is that the marketing of sex tourism through racialized codes on the websites is a much more overt practice. The selling and talk of sex tourism and the sex worker are through the articulation of race, sex and commodity.

The positions of two themes in the Freeman degree scores of DHb, WSGb and STWb point to further theoretical development and empirical investigation. SWNames and STNames code for mentions in the discussion posts of the sex workers and the sex travelers. ... the naming of the former is a very common practice; however, there is little mention of the men who travel for sex and write the posts. Scholars of whiteness have observed that one of the central practices of whiteness is the direction of the gaze. The Other is always in full view, being examined and objectified, but the source of the gaze is seldom revealed (Ashcraft and Allen, 2003; Delgado and Stefanic, 1997; Nakayama and Martin, 1999). The results suggest that the discussion boards and other forms of new media may be new horizons where we can examine practices of whiteness where the new media are being formed.

> The Information age is changing the relationship between time, space, and form in racist culture. New territories of whiteness exceed the boundaries of the nation-state, while supplanting ethnocentric racisms with new translocal forms of narcissism and xenophobia. ... the rhetoric of whiteness becomes the means to combine profoundly local grammars of racial exclusion within a translocal and international reach, which is made viable through digital technology. (Ware and Back, 2002: 3, 98)

Studies of whiteness and the internet are in their early stages and require much more in-depth analysis of the role of information communication technologies in the globalizing process.

This study has examined the ways in which race and gender find new expression through the internet in the employment of the sex tourism industry. The production of knowledge and the economy of products and services in sex tourism websites, and the consumption of sex tourists, have been shown to be sites where racialization and sexualization of sex workers intersect with discourses of the new global economy. Contrary to utopian assertions that the internet will be a new virtual space for social progress, groups such as sex tourists are appropriating the technology in a dystopian manner. The internet does much more than provide another conduit for delivering materials (such as newsletters or videotapes) previously circulated via traditional mail. It marks an intensification and deepening of the development of sex tourism. Because of innovations in computing and networking, the information contained in the websites is cheaper to produce and of higher quality than previous print and analog materials. Digital information, including jpegs and mpegs, can be disseminated much more rapidly and diffused globally. Further, the user-driven message boards disrupt the producer–consumer transmission model of mail-order. Sex tourists are actively involved in a collaborative, real-time mapping of sex tourism routes – often from internet cafes in travel destinations – and the representation of sex workers. Gabriel asks whether new media technologies 'enhance democratic processes, including greater accountability and scope for resistance, or do they merely provide the means for greater surveillance, this time on a global scale?' (1998: 12). The results of this study provide a cautious example of the role of the internet in a global age.

REFERENCES

Abbate, J. (1999) *Inventing the Internet*. Cambridge, MA: MIT Press.

Alexander, J.C. and P. Smith (1993) 'A New Proposal for Cultural Studies', *Theory and Society* 22: 151–207.

Anthias, F. and N. Yuval-Davis (1992) *Racialized Boundaries: Race, Nation, Gender, Colour and Class and the Anti-Racist Struggle*. London: Routledge.

Apostolopoulos, Y., S. Leivadi and A. Yiannakis (1996) *The Sociology of Tourism: Theoretical and Empirical Investigations*. London: Routledge.

Appadurai, A. (1990) 'Disjuncture and Difference in the Global Cultural Economy', pp. 295–310 in M. Featherstone (ed.) *Global Culture: Nationalism, Globalization, and Modernity*. London: Sage.

Ashcraft, K.L. and B.J. Allen (2003) 'The Racial Foundation of Organizational Communication', *Communication Theory* 13: 5–38.

Beynon, J. (2002) *Masculinities and Culture*. London: Open University Press.

Bhabha, H. (1984) 'Of Mimicry and Man: The Ambivalence of Colonial Discourse', *October* 28: 125–33.

Burnett, R. and P.D. Marshall (2003) *Web Theory*. London: Routledge.

Cabezas, A.L. (1998) 'Discourse of Prostitution: The Case of Cuba', in K. Kempadoo and J. Doezema (eds) *Global Sex Workers: Rights, Resistance, and Redefinition*. London: Routledge.

Cabezas, A.L. (1999) 'Women's Work is Never Done: Sex Tourism in Sousa, the Domincan Republic', in K. Kempadoo (ed.) *Sun, Sex, and Gold: Tourism and Sex Work in the Caribbean*. Lanham, MD: Rowman and Littlefield.

Castells, M. (1996) *The Rise of the Network Society*. Oxford: Blackwell Publishers.

Castells, M. (1997) *The Power of Identity*, vol. 2. Oxford: Blackwell.

Castells, M. (2001) *The Internet Galaxy: Reflections on the Internet, Business, and Society*. Oxford: Oxford University Press.

Cresser, F., L. Gunn and H. Balme (2001) 'Women's Experiences of Online E-zine Publication', *Media, Culture & Society* 23: 457–73.

Crick, M. (1996) 'Representations of International Tourism in the Social Sciences: Sun, Sex, Sights, Savings, and Servility', in Y. Apostolopoulos, S. Leivadi and A. Yiannakis (eds) *The Sociology of Tourism: Theoretical and Empirical Investigations*. London: Routledge.

Davidson, J.O.C. and J.S. Taylor (1999) 'Fantasy Islands: Exploring the Demands for Sex Tourism', in K. Kampadoo (ed.) *Sun, Sex, and Gold: Tourism and Sex Work in the Caribbean*. Lanham, MD: Rowman and Littlefield.

Delgado, R. and J. Stefanic (eds) (1997) *Critical White Studies: Looking Behind the Mirror*. Philadelphia, PA: Temple University Press.

Du Gay, P. (1997) *Doing Cultural Studies: The Story of the Sony Walkman*. London: Sage in association with the Open University.

Eglash, R. (2002) 'Race, Sex, and Nerds: From Black Geeks to Asian American Hipsters', *Social Text* 20: 49–64.

Elmer, G. (2004) *Profiling Machines: Mapping the Personal Information Economy*. Cambridge, MA: MIT Press.

Emirbayer, M. and J. Goodwin (1994) 'Network Analysis, Culture, and the Problem of Agency', *American Journal of Sociology* 99: 1411–54.

Enloe, C. (1989) *Bananas, Beaches and Bases: Making Feminist Sense of International Politics*. London: Pandora.

Foucault, M. (1972) *The Archaeology of Knowledge*, trans. A.M. Sheridan. New York: Harper and Row.

Gabriel, J. (1998) *Whitewash: Racialized Politics and the Media*. London: Routledge.

Gabriel, J. (2000) 'Dreaming of a White …', in S. Cottle (ed.) *Ethnic Minorities and the Media*. Buckingham: Open University Press.

Gates, B. (1996) *The Road Ahead*. New York: Penguin.

Gilder, G. (1994) *Life after Television*. New York: W.W. Norton.

Hall, S. (1996) 'New Ethnicities', in D. Morely and K.-H. Chen (eds) *Stuart Hall: Critical Dialogues in Cultural Studies*. London: Routledge.

Hall, S. (1997) '*Representation: Cultural Representations and Signifying Practices*. London: Sage Publications in association with the Open University.

Hill-Collins, P. (2000) *Black Feminist Thought: Knowledge, Consciousness, and the Politics of Empowerment*, 2nd edn. New York: Routledge.

Kempadoo, K. (ed.) (1999) *Sun, Sex, and Gold: Tourism and Sex Work in the Caribbean*. Lanham, MD: Rowman and Littlefield.

Kempadoo, K. and J. Doezema (1998) *Global Sex Workers: Rights, Resistance, and Redefinition*. New York: Routledge.

Landow, G. (1992) *Hypertext: The Convergence of Contemporary Cultural Theory and Technology*. Baltimore, MD: Johns Hopkins University Press.

Manderson, L. and M. Jolly (1997) *Sites of Desire, Economies of Pleasure: Sexualities in Asia and the Pacific*. Chicago, IL: University of Chicago Press.

Massey, D. (1993) 'Power-geometry and a Progressive Sense of Place', in J. Bird, B. Curtis, T. Putnam and G. Roberts (eds) *Mapping the Futures: Local Cultures, Global Change*. London: Routledge.

McClintock, A. (1995) *Imperial Leather: Race, Gender, and Sexuality in the Colonial Conquest*. New York: Routledge.

Mohanty, C.T. (2003) *Feminism without Borders: Decolonizing Theory, Practicing Solidarity*. Durham, NC: Duke University Press.

Monge, P.R. and N.S. Contractor (2003) *Theories of Communication Networks*. Oxford: Oxford University Press.

Morely, D. (2000) *Home Territories: Media, Mobility and Identity*. London: Routledge.

Mullings, B. (1999) 'Globalization, Tourism, and the International Sex Trade', in K. Kempadoo (ed.) *Sun, Sex, and Gold: Tourism and Sex Work in the Caribbean*. Lanham, MD: Rowman and Littlefield.

Nakayama, T.K. and J.N. Martin (eds) (1999) *Whiteness: The Communication of Social Identity*. Thousand Oaks, CA: Sage.

Nelson, A. (2002) 'Introduction: Future Texts', *Social Text* 20: 1–15.

Nip, J.Y.M. (2004) 'The Relationship between Online and Offline Communities: The Case of the Queer Sisters', *Media, Culture & Society* 26: 409–28.

Parameswaran, R. (2002) 'Local Culture in Global Media: Excavating Colonial and Material Discourses in *National Geographic*', *Communication Theory* 12: 287–315.

Rheingold, H. (1994) *The Virtual Community: Homesteading on the Electronic Frontier*. Reading, MA: Addison-Wesley.

Said, E. (1978) *Orientalism*. New York: Vintage.

Scott, J. (2000) *Social Network Analysis: A Handbook*, 2nd edn. London: Sage.

Seabrook, J. (1996) *Travels in the Skin Trade: Tourism and the Sex Industry*. Chicago, IL: Pluto Press.

Shrage, L. (1994) *Moral Dilemmas of Feminism*. London: Routledge.

Travers, A. (2000) *Writing the Public in Cyberspace: Redefining Inclusion on the Net*. New York: Garland.

Truong, T.-D. (1990) *Sex, Money, and Morality: Prostitution and Tourism in Southeast Asia*. Highlands, NJ: Zed Books.

Turkle, S. (1995) *Life on the Screen: Identity in the Age of the Internet*. New York: Simon and Schuster.

Urry, J. (1990) *The Tourist Gaze: Leisure and Travel in Contemporary Societies*. London: Sage.

Ware, V. and L. Back (2002) *Out of Whiteness: Color, Politics, and Culture*. Chicago, IL: University of Chicago Press.

Wasserman, S. and K. Faust (1994) *Social Network Analysis: Methods and Applications*. Cambridge: Cambridge University Press.

Wetherell, M. and J. Potter (1992) *Mapping the Language of Racism: Discourse and the Legitimation of Exploitation*. New York: Columbia University Press.

White, M. (2002) 'Regulating Research: The Problem of Theorizing Community on LambdaMOO', *Ethics and Information Technology* 5: 55–70.

World Tourism Organization (2000, 2003, 2004, 2005) URL: www.world-tourism.org/statistics/index.htm

VI PULITICS, POLITICAL ACTION, ACTIVISM

Introduction

That cyberculture and cyberspace are also political spaces seems to be a truism in the age of online voting, opinion polls, and "hacktivism." Part VI of the book deals with what many thinkers see as the most liberating aspect of cybercultures, and others see as extending the problems and politics of the material world. How does politics from the social and material worlds we occupy transform in cyberspace? Does cyberspace offer a new forum and source for emancipatory politics? Or does it replicate the inequalities of the material world? Most theorists opt for one or the other of these two viewpoints.

Enthusiasts of the internet, from Howard Rheingold onward, have seen cyberspace as a space where the previously marginalized, disempowered, and oppressed can tell their stories, articulate resistance, and gather support. It is a space of "expanding dialogs," with possibilities of transnational linkages that generate a politics beyond the immediate geographical territory. Movements such as environmentalism can now possess a wider support-base where local problems and information can feed into databases and studies that have larger social, political, and economic concerns. Online communities and Diaspora websites seem to suggest that communities and groups have taken to cyberspace. Online existence parallels the material one, and people's lifestyles and ways of working have changed with the advent of the "home office," thereby also altering their social relations.

Online political activism has championed causes of resistance and subversion since the 1990s. Tactical media and activism (electronic civil disobedience) seek to alter power relations via technology. Often, such activism takes the form of direct action against corporate bodies, the state, and other social structures viewed as oppressive. "Hactivism," as this form of cyberculture politics has come to be known, seems to be an extension of the cultures of resistance and action from the material world. Subcultural forms and groups have found cyberspace easier as a less governed and therefore open space to meet like-minded people, generate opinions, and engage in cultural exchanges. Formats such as blogging have helped gather and alter public opinion and fan resistance. The sharing of files and videos online helps communities and groups establish solidarities, and therefore political linkages. Network communities, netdemocracy, and e-governance provide new realms (and versions) of the political.

Others argue that cybercultures only appear to be "free." Thinkers and commentators note that there have been numerous attempts to "regulate" cyberspace, from domain-name restrictions to everyday restrictions such as an employer's right to check their employees' emails. Cyberspace is as subject to systems of governance and control as any public space. Search engines themselves, others have noted, are implicated in capitalist political economy and are never neutral "searches" – especially with their links to commercially viable advertising and propaganda. More left-leaning thinkers note with alarm that the cybercultural economy carries on capitalist forms of exploitation in terms of their labor force.

It could be argued that cyberspace is not a new space for political action, but rather an extension or continuation into another realm of the sites of political action, resistance, and agency that already exists in the current material public sphere. Cyberspace is as contested – commercially, ideologically, politically – a site as any public space. It offers spaces in which to articulate dissent even as it is subject to and becomes an instrument of surveillance.

If the Gulf War altered the role of the media in conflict as never before, post-9/11 the role of information and communications technologies in controlling or spreading terror has been at the forefront, especially in debates about cyberterrorism. David Silver and Alice Marwick note that, since 9/11, companies in Silicon Valley, Boston, and elsewhere have started to receive major federal funding for the development of digital technologies for militaristic purposes. They argue that we are seeing a remilitarization of digital culture, even as the military itself becomes "an industry leader in the sphere of digital marketing." Silver and Marwick suggest that we need to look at a new digital "formation": Dot.mil. Dot.mil is seen in everyday life, politics, computer games and, of course, federal investment in digital cultures. The authors call for an acknowledgment of this new formation: we must historicize it by tracing the genealogies of computers and the internet, theorize the Dot.mil formation and, finally, engineer acts of resistance through what is now called digital activism. Silver and Marwick's article is salutary in its diagnosis of a particular turn in digital cultures, and cautions us to be aware and to resist this turn.

Digital and communications technologies have allowed "free labor" with the availability of website-building tools, programs to create listservs, online activities, the modification of software packages and, more recently, "patches" in computer games. Tiziana Terranova's article notes this shift of labor from factory to society at large. She argues that the internet is permeated with such social and cultural labor. "Digital artisans" constitute the new forms of workers in the digital economy. This new politics of labor, Terranova suggests, relies less on old-fashioned labor than a new form of it: knowledge and cultural labor. The new capitalism incorporates cultural labor into its flows and business practices. The public/user become, in Terranova's argument, productive subjects.

Birgitte Olsen's article looks at the interface of minority rights and the Global Information Society. Olsen moves from looking at conventional structures for minority protection and argues a strong case for regulatory mechanisms that ensure rights of access, transparency in information-gathering about ethnic minorities, and the cultural rights of minorities in cyberspace. This would include, Olsen argues, the troubling question of minority languages, and their persistent absence in cyberdiscourses. However, she believes that the internet offers a structure which could make it easier to access plural information, increase dialog, and address hitherto neglected issues. She calls for new ways of structuring the information society so that it is more pluralistic in its composition but founded on principles shared by all.

Tim Jordan's article deals less with the hacker per se than with the political implications of hacking. Defining hacktivism as "politically motivated hacking," he discusses the work of organizations and groups such as the Critical Arts Ensemble (CAE) and the Electronic Disturbance Theatre (EDT) of the 1990s. Jordan distinguishes between informational politics and a broader non-virtual politics within hacktivism. The former is marked by Mass Virtual Direct Action (MVDA), including denial-of-service attacks, electronic sit-ins, and other hacking procedures, and Jordan sees this as a new form of civil disobedience. In the case of non-virtual politics, groups like Cult of the Dead Cow target state prohibitory and restrictive practices such as censorship. This kind of hacktivism, argues Jordan, seeks a democracy in cyberspace and the free flow of information.

21 INTERNET STUDIES IN TIMES OF TERROR

David Silver and Alice Marwick

Despite the Orwellian memoryhole that infects so much of contemporary American discourse, many of us will remember George W. Bush's *Top Gun*–like landing aboard the USS *Abraham Lincoln* on May 1, 2003. With "Mission Accomplished" as a backdrop, Bush appeared on deck in an outfit heretofore never worn by an American president: a flight suit featuring, among other gadgets, a bulging codpiece. Resembling a *militarized computer game avatar*, Bush praised the troops and declared, "major combat operations have ended in Iraq" (D. Bush 2003).

On the following day, Bush left the USS *Abraham Lincoln* and landed in Silicon Valley, where he would reveal his postwar economic vision for the country. With all major U.S. media outlets in tow, his motorcade ended in Santa Clara, formerly known as the prune capital of America and now a prominent hub of what only a few years ago was called the "new economy." His destination was United Defense Industries, or UDI, a defense contractor specializing in *militarized digital technologies* (DeYoung and Weisman 2003; Sanger 2003).

Like the day before, Bush praised the heroes of the war in Iraq, only this time they included high-tech war machines and the high-profit corporations that build them:

> The new technologies of war help to protect our soldiers and, as importantly, help protect innocent life. You see, new technologies allow us to redefine war on our terms, which makes it more likely the world will be more free and more peaceful. ... You do a lot to keep the American Armed Forces on the leading edge of technological change here at United Defense. And I want to thank you for that. You not only help save lives, but you're an agent for peace. (G. W. Bush 2003)

Before departing, Bush tried his hand at virtual combat, in what UDI calls its "Combat Simulation and Integration Lab," or what digital culture scholars call a first-person shooter game. The computer game gave Bush trouble, and he was unsuccessful in his first few attempts to blow up enemy tanks and helicopters. According to some reports, he finally made a "tank kill"; other reports left the gamer's fate out of the story (DeYoung and Weisman 2003; H. Kennedy 2003).

Bush's landing, his codpiece, his remarks, and his turn at the console were more than merely performance. They signaled a shift in, and full-throttled return to, the military-industrial complex. In 2003, federal military spending reached an all-time high at $401.7 billion a year. Add to that $36.2 billion pumped annually into the Department of Homeland Security (Schrader 2004; Weisman 2003). Encouraged by Defense Secretary Donald Rumsfeld's call for high-tech military strategies, defense contractors like UDI are reaping the spoils of our current climate of fear and its concomitant federal spending priorities.

Of course, defense contractors like UDI and Boeing and Lockheed and Halliburton are not the only ones who stand to gain financially. Indeed, today's U.S. high-tech industry[1] is scrambling to *militarize the new economy*. Witness Microsoft, who last summer made its biggest sale ever: $470 million worth of software to the U.S. Army (Microsoft Wins Biggest Order 2003). Witness Oracle's Information Assurance Center (ICA), a unit that designs homeland security applications and markets them to the federal government. As current head of ICA and former number-three man at the CIA David Carey remarked, "How do you say this without sounding callous? ... In some ways, September 11 made business a bit easier. Previous to September 11, you pretty much had to hype the threat and the problem. ... Now they clamor for it!" (Rosen 2002, p. 49). Witness Jim Opfer, CEO of the Silicon Valley firm LaunchPower, who in 2003 addressed the Tampa Bay Technology Forum. Reminding the audience of the growing budgets of both the Department of Defense and the Department of Homeland Security, Opfer cut to the chase and exclaimed, "Thank God for Osama Bin Laden!" (Leavy 2003).[2]

In a post-9/11, post-dot.com America, high-tech regions like Silicon Valley, Northern Virginia, Redmond/Seattle, and Boston are receiving, once again,[3] major federal funding for their development of *digital technologies for militaristic purposes*. In 2002 alone, over nine hundred Silicon Valley companies received more than $4 billion from the Department of Defense (Baker, Wallack, and Kirby 2003). As the president of the Bay Area Council notes, "What we've seen is a transition from the kind of defense companies we envisioned a decade ago to the new-economy, high-tech applications that are the hallmark of today's military defense" (ibid.). Or, as the publisher of the industry newsletter *Defense Mergers & Acquisitions* explains it, "Just 20 or 30 years ago, the airplane was the thing or the ship was the thing. Now those things are just nodes in the network, and the network is the thing" (Merle 2003).

Along with digital technologies, economies, and geographies, large chunks of *digital culture are being (re)militarized*. In 2003 – the year when computer games became a mainstream phenomena and when, for many, especially young Americans, computer games were digital culture – one of the year's most popular games was

America's Army, created by the U.S. Army.[4] It was also the year that the U.S. military perfected convergent media strategies. For example, the U.S. Army's "An Army of One" television commercials featured reality-show-like settings starring actual recruits solving military problems; for narrative closure (and recruitment hook), viewers were invited to goarmy.com, where they could take virtual tours of U.S. bases, read Army manuals, and peruse job openings. The same year, the Army instituted its "Taking It to the Streets" recruitment tour, driving spray-painted Hummers with computer games and multimedia sound systems into American "urban" areas (city parks, housing projects, and basketball courts) and events (NAACP events, MTV's Spring Break, and BET's Spring Bling). The tour's cosponsor, *The Source*, the oldest and once countercultural hip-hop magazine, eased entrance into particular communities and secured leading rappers and DJs to accompany the tour (Joiner 2003).

Such convergent branding strategies make the U.S. Army an industry leader in the sphere of digital marketing. In June 2002, the American Marketing Association awarded "An Army of One" its Gold Effie in the category of Recruitment Advertising (Army Public Affairs 2002). The same year, the Army's basic-training Web site was a finalist in the Webbys, the self-declared "leading international honor for the worlds [*sic*] best web sites," established in 1996 with a hint of countercultural ethos (Singer 2002).[5] With a brilliant campaign that fuses marketing and recruitment, computer game and computer manual, the Internet and television, the U.S. Army pushes the bar on *militarized guerrilla marketing*. Indeed, throughout 2003, Army recruitment goals were easily met (M. J. Kennedy 2003; Melillo and Barr 2003).[6]

And finally, also in 2003, the Electronic Entertainment Exposition (E3) awarded Full Spectrum Warrior, an X-Box training aid for the U.S. Army, top honors in two categories: Best Original Game and Best Simulation Game. Full Spectrum Warrior was also the most nominated title at E3, garnering votes in Best Console Game and Best of Show (Institute for Creative Technologies 2003). Significantly, Full Spectrum Warrior was designed and developed by the Institute for Creative Technologies (ICT) at the University of Southern California. ICT, a cross-disciplinary enterprise involving USC's School of Cinema-TV, the School of Engineering, and the Annenberg School of Communication, was made possible by a $45 million grant awarded by the U.S. Army in 1999 (Pentagon and Hollywood to Work Together 1999).

Conclusion: Resisting InternetStudies.mil

Dot.mil is the result of a militarized state, a militarized economy, and militarized everyday life. Dot.mil can be seen in the president dressing up as an avatar from a shoot-'em-up computer game. It can be seen in defense contractors rebranding themselves as "system integrators" and in dot.bombs morphing corporate strategies from business-to-business software to surveillance applications. Dot.mil can be perceived geographically with Silicon Valley's shift from venture capital to federal funding. Dot.mil is seen in free and commercial computer games, at goarmy.com (that's.com by the way), in the fully decked Hummers in our (poor, black and Latino) parks and streets. It can be seen, like a spectacle, in the U.S. Army's Gold Effie and runner-up Webby. And dot.mil appears in academia, when military field experiments merge with funded research objectives, when goarmy.com avatars are followed by our students via their computers in the dorms.

If some of the most cutting-edge research, and certainly some of the most well-funded research, is taking place with support from the U.S. military, the question *What can we do about it?* certainly arises. As a means to conclude this essay and to jumpstart a new thread, let us suggest five potential strategies.

The first step is to acknowledge, individually and collectively, .mil. By individually, we mean scholars should begin and continue to address such topics in their research and include them in their syllabi. By collectively, we mean scholars should begin and continue to edit anthologies and special issues of journals around the topics, as Cynthia Enloe did for a recent special issue of *Women's Review of Books*, titled "Women, War, and Peace," and as John Armitage did for a special issue of *Body & Society*, titled "Militarized Bodies." We also must work collectively on an organizational level. It is disconcerting that while the American Studies Association selected the theme of "Violence and Belonging" for its 2003 conference and the Association for Cultural Studies chose "Policing the Crisis" for its 2004 event, the Association of Internet Researchers selected the innocuous theme of "Ubiquity?" for its 2004 event.

The second step is to historicize our object of study and teaching. We must remind our colleagues, our students, and ourselves that .mil is not a new development. While Edwards (1996) offers an excellent history of the development of computers within a militaristic, Cold War environment, Abbate (1999) provides us with a superb early history of the Internet, tracing it to its ARPA roots. Moreover, Borsook (2000) and Winner (1992) remind us that Silicon Valley as we know it has always been .mil, with the Department of Defense supplying the necessary investment to transform the agricultural region into a high-tech mecca. These are the histories we must know. These are the histories we must teach our students. And these are the histories within which our organizations could and should situate our conferences.

The third step is to theorize our topic of study. Although plenty of theory exists around the military-industrial complex, only recently, perhaps starting with De Landa (1991) and Haraway (1991), have we begun to generate theory revolving around the military-entertainment complex, especially as it relates to digital media and technologies (Lenoir 2000; Wark 2003). Der Derian's recent book, *Virtuous War: Mapping the Military-Industrial-Media-Entertainment Network* (2001), is especially effective in not only collecting relevant theory but also in applying it to contemporary digital developments.

Of course, institutes of higher education have always been part of the complex, which leads to the fourth step: a rigorous examination of the intersections between .com, .mil, and .edu. While corporate investment in digital scholarship has decreased since the .com fallout, federal funding, streamed through the Departments of Defense and Homeland Security, is enjoying a mini-renaissance. This has profound implications for all academic fields but especially ours: young fields need money; young fields are more malleable; and young fields can transform more easily to capitalize on current trends in capital investments. As individual scholars, as collective units working within departments, colleges, and universities, and as individual and collective members of academic organizations, we must demand public discourse about funding priorities and insist that research values have as strong a voice as budgetary woes in determining the field's future directions.

Finally, the fifth, and a more hopeful, strategy is to understand, examine, and help build acts of resistance to .mil. These acts come in various shapes and sizes, but particularly relevant to scholars of Internet studies are works of *digital artivism*. By digital artivism, we refer to massively distributed digital artifacts that creatively and intellectually challenge and subvert hegemonic powers. They incorporate multiple elements of digital technologies – the archive, the database, animation, multiple media – and can be found in Open Secrets (www.opensecrets.org), a voluminous archive that allows users to track financial contributions made to specific industries (say, Iraq contracts) and local and national campaigns; Iraq Body Count (www.iraqbodycount.net), an innovative and collaboratively built database charting the number of reported civilian deaths in Iraq; and Cost of War (www.costofwar.com), a script run total of the money spent by the United States to finance the war in Iraq, accompanied by speculative scenarios if the funds were to be spent on things like public education, children's health, and public housing.

The boundaries between .edu, .com, and .mil have always been, for better and for worse, leaky. As academics, we must resist marginalizing ourselves solely with the academy. We must foster and sustain alliances across a spectrum of domains and collaborate with individuals and collectives working in .org, .gov, .net, .art, .green, and .labor. This is no easy task, yet our purpose becomes clearer when we acknowledge where we – and our field of study – currently stand.

NOTES

1. We are aware that calling digital/Internet technologies brought to the market by U.S. companies "American" is problematic, especially when considering the current rate of outsourcing, the manual labor of undocumented citizens, and so forth.
2. While we are at it, let's also witness Aanko Technologies, a company that produces digital anthrax detectors, whose CEO recently noted in *Business 2.0* that his company is "turning risk into revenue" (Hitt 2003, p. 106).
3. It is important to note that Silicon Valley as we know it has always already been dot.mil. For the role of military spending on the development of the hightech region, see Borsook 2000 and Winner 1992.
4. In 2003, two million users downloaded America's Army, making it the number-one free downloadable game and number-five most popular online game (Wooley 2003).

5. Webby Awards, http://www.webbyawards.com. The Web site for U.S. Army Basic Training was nominated for the Best Practices category alongside Amazon.com, Google, National Geographic, and the Peace Corps. Google won.
6. It must be noted that in 2004, a year in which the war in Iraq raged on, recruitment goals were not met.

REFERENCES

Abbate, J. 1999. *Inventing the Internet*. Cambridge, MA: MIT Press.

Army Public Affairs. 2002. Army "Basic Training" Ads Receive Gold Effie Award. June 26. Available at http://www4.army.mil/ocpa/read.php?story_id_key=1315 (accessed February 14, 2004).

Baker, D.R., Wallack, T., and Kirby, C. 2003. Score of Area Businesses Feed Military Machine's Need for Gear. *San Francisco Chronicle*, March 23, p. Ii.

Borsook, P. 2000. *Cyberselfish: A Critical Romp through the Terribly Libertarian Culture of High Tech*. New York: PublicAffairs.

Bush, D. 2003. Bush: Iraq Is One Victory in War on Terror. CNN.com, May 2. Available at http://www.cnn.com/2003/ALLPOLITICS/05/01/sprj.irq.bush.speech.

Bush, G.W. 2003. Remarks to Employees of United Defense Industries in Santa Clara, California. Available at http://frwebgate.access.gpo.gov/cgi-bin/getdoc.cgi? dbname=2003_presiden tial_documents&docid=pdo5my03_txt-28 (accessed September 1, 2003).

De Landa, M. 1991. *War in the Age of Intelligent Machines*. New York: Zone Books.

Der Derian, J. 2001. *Virtuous War: Mapping the Military-Industrial-Media-Entertainment Network*. Boulder, CO: Westview Press.

DeYoung, K., and Weisman, J. 2003. Bush Urges Passage of Tax Plan; President Cites Rising Unemployment in Call for Action. *Washington Post*, May 3, p. A12.

Edwards, P. 1996. *The Closed World: Computers and the Politics of Discourse in Cold War America*. Cambridge, MA: MIT Press.

Haraway, D.J. 1991. *Simians, Cyborgs, and Women: The Reinvention of Nature*. New York: Routledge.

Hitt, J. 2003. The Business of Fear. *Business 2.0*, June, pp. 106–114.

Institute for Creative Technologies. 2003. ICT's New Army Training Aid Wins Best Original Game and Best Simulation Game @ E3. June 10. Available at http:// www.ict.usc.edu/content/view/90/2/ (accessed February 14, 2004).

Joiner, W. 2003. The Army Be Thuggin' It. *Salon*, October 17. Available at http:// archive.salon.com/mwt/feature/2003/10/17/army/index_np.html (accessed January 10, 2004).

Kennedy, H. 2003. Fired-Up W Gives Tanks for Help. *Daily News*, May 3, p. 9.

Kennedy, M.J. 2003. Wanna Play? Military Recruiters Update Their Arsenals to Reach Kids. *Los Angeles Times*, February 26, p. E1.

Leavy, P.G. 2003. Silicon Valley Leader Assesses IT Defense Spending. *Business Journal of Tampa Bay*, February 27. Available at http://tampabay.bizjournals.com/tampabay/stories/2003/02/24/daily35.html (accessed January 10, 2004).

Lenoir, T. 2000. All but War Is Simulation: The Military-Entertainment Complex. *Configurations* 8, pp. 289–335.

Melillo, W., and Barr, A. 2003. U.S. Army Looks to Next Agency Front. *Adweek*, May 5, p. 6.

Merle, R. 2003. Defense Firms Consolidate as War Goes High-Tech. *Washington Post*, May 27, p. A1.

Microsoft Wins Biggest Order. 2003. *Seattle Post-Intelligencer*, June 25, p. C1.

Pentagon and Hollywood to Work Together. 1999. *Agence France Presse*, August 19. Available at http://www.isi.edu/afp_uarc.html (accessed February 14, 2004).

Rosen, J. 2002. Silicon Valley's Spy Game. *New York Times Magazine*, April 14, pp. 47–51.

Sanger, D.E. 2003. Bush Begins Campaign to Sell His Economic Program. *New York Times*, May 3, p. A13.

Schrader, E. 2004. Bush Seeks 7% Boost in Military Spending. *Los Angeles Times*, January 24. Available at http://www.latimes.com/news/nationworld/nation/lana-defense24jan24, 1,4306122.story?coll=la-home-headlines (accessed January 26, 2004).

Singer, M. 2002. Webby Awards Announces Nominees. Atnewyork.com, April 29. Available at http://www.atnewyork.com/news/article.php/1024441 (accessed January 26, 2004).

Wark, M. 2003. Escape from the Dual Empire. *Rhizomes* 6. Available at http:// www.rhizomes. net/issue6/wark.htm (accessed February 9, 2004).

Weisman, J. 2003. Government Outgrows Cap Set by President. *Washington Post*, November 13, p. A01.

Winner, L. 1992. Silicon Valley Mystery House. In *Variations on a Theme Park: The New American City and the End of Public Space*, ed. Michael Sorkin, pp. 31–60. New York: Hill and Wang.

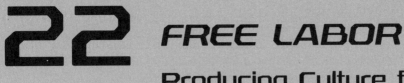

22 FREE LABOR
Producing Culture for the Digital Economy

Tiziana Terranova

> *The real* not-capital *is* labor.
> *Karl Marx, Grundrisse*

Working in the digital media industry is not as much fun as it is made out to be. The "NetSlaves" of the eponymous Webzine are becoming increasingly vociferous about the shamelessly exploitative nature of the job, its punishing work rhythms, and its ruthless casualization (www.disobey.com/netslaves). They talk about "24–7 electronic sweatshops" and complain about the ninety-hour weeks and the "moronic management of new media companies." In early 1999, seven of the fifteen thousand "volunteers" of America Online (AOL) rocked the info-loveboat by asking the Department of Labor to investigate whether AOL owes them back wages for the years of playing chathosts for free.[1] They used to work long hours and love it; now they are starting to feel the pain of being burned by digital media.

These events point to a necessary backlash against the glamorization of digital labor, which highlights its continuities with the modern sweat-shop and points to the increasing degradation of knowledge work. ...

In this essay I understand this relationship as a provision of "free labor," a trait of the cultural economy at large, and an important, and yet undervalued, force in advanced capitalist societies. By looking at the Internet as a specific instance of the fundamental role played by free labor, this essay also tries to highlight the connections between the "digital economy" and what the Italian autonomists have called the "social factory." The "social factory" describes a process whereby "work processes

Tiziana Terranova. "Free Labor: Producing Culture for the Digital Economy," pp. 33–58 from *Social Text* 18.2 (Summer 2000).

have shifted from the factory to society, thereby setting in motion a truly complex machine."[2] Simultaneously voluntarily given and unwaged, enjoyed and exploited, free labor on the Net includes the activity of building Web sites, modifying software packages, reading and participating in mailing lists, and building virtual spaces on MUDs and MOOs. Far from being an "unreal," empty space, the Internet is animated by cultural and technical labor through and through, a continuous production of value that is completely immanent to the flows of the network society at large.

Support for this argument, however, is immediately complicated by the recent history of critical theory. How to speak of labor, especially cultural and technical labor, after the demolition job carried out by thirty years of postmodernism? The postmodern socialist feminism of Donna Haraway's "Cyborg Manifesto" spelled out some of the reasons behind the antipathy of 1980s critical theory for Marxist analyses of labor. Haraway explicitly rejected the humanistic tendencies of theorists who see labor as the "pre-eminently privileged category enabling the Marxist to overcome illusion and find that point of view which is necessary for changing the world."[3] Paul Gilroy similarly expressed his discontent at the inadequacy of Marxist analyses of labor to describe the culture of the descendants of slaves, who value artistic expression as "the means towards both individual self-fashioning and communal liberation."[4] If labor is "the humanizing activity that makes [white] man," then, surely, humanizing labor does not really belong in the age of networked, posthuman intelligence.

… The expansion of the Internet has given ideological and material support to contemporary trends toward increased flexibility of the workforce, continuous reskilling, freelance work, and the diffusion of practices such as "supplementing" (bringing supplementary work home from the conventional office).[5] …

This essay does not seek to offer a judgment on the "effects" of the Internet, but rather to map the way in which the Internet connects to the autonomist "social factory." I am concerned with how the "outernet" – the network of social, cultural, and economic relationships that criss-crosses and exceeds the Internet – surrounds and connects the latter to larger flows of labor, culture, and power. It is fundamental to move beyond the notion that cyberspace is about escaping reality in order to understand how the reality of the Internet is deeply connected to the development of late postindustrial societies as a whole.

Cultural and technical work is central to the Internet but is also a widespread activity throughout advanced capitalist societies. I argue that such labor is not exclusive to the so-called knowledge workers, but is a pervasive feature of the postindustrial economy. The pervasiveness of such production questions the legitimacy of a fixed distinction between production and consumption, labor and culture. It also undermines Gilroy's distinction between work as "servitude, misery and subordination" and artistic expression as the means to self-fashioning and communal liberation. The increasingly blurred territory between production and consumption, work and cultural expression, however, does not signal the recomposition of the alienated Marxist worker. The Internet does not automatically turn every user into an active producer, and every worker into a creative subject. The process whereby production and consumption are reconfigured within the category of free labor signals the unfolding of a different (rather than completely new) logic of value, whose operations need careful analysis.[6]

The Digital Economy

The term *digital economy* has recently emerged as a way to summarize some of the processes described above. As a term, it seems to describe a formation that intersects on the one hand with the postmodern cultural economy (the media, the university, and the arts) and on the other hand with the information industry (the information and communication complex). ...

In Richard Barbrook's definition, the digital economy is characterized by the emergence of new technologies (computer networks) and new types of workers (the digital artisans).[7] According to Barbrook, the digital economy is a mixed economy: it includes a public element (the state's funding of the original research that produced Arpanet, the financial support to academic activities that had a substantial role in shaping the culture of the Internet); a market-driven element (a latecomer that tries to appropriate the digital economy by reintroducing commodification); and a gift economy element, the true expression of the cutting edge of capitalist production that prepares its eventual overcoming into a future "anarcho-communism":

> Within the developed world, most politicians and corporate leaders believe that the future of capitalism lies in the commodification of information. ... Yet at the "cutting-edge" of the emerging information society, money-commodity relations play a secondary role to those created by a really existing form of anarcho-communism. For most of its users, the net is somewhere to work, play, love, learn and discuss with other people. ... Unrestricted by physical distance, they collaborate with each other without the direct mediation of money and politics. Unconcerned about copyright, they give and receive information without thought of payment. In the absence of states or markets to mediate social bonds, network communities are instead formed through the mutual obligations created by gifts of time and ideas.[8]

From a Marxist-Hegelian angle, Barbrook sees the high-tech gift economy as a process of overcoming capitalism from the inside. The high-tech gift economy is a pioneering moment that transcends both the purism of the New Left do-it-yourself culture and the neoliberalism of the free market ideologues: "money-commodity and gift relations are not just in conflict with each other, but also co-exist in symbiosis."[9] ...

I believe that Barbrook overemphasizes the autonomy of the hightech gift economy from capitalism. The processes of exchange that characterize the

Internet are not simply the reemergence of communism within the cutting edge of the economy, a repressed other that resurfaces just at the moment when communism seems defeated. It is important to remember that the gift economy, as part of a larger digital economy, is itself an important force within the reproduction of the labor force in late capitalism as a whole. The provision of "free labor," as we will see later, is a fundamental moment in the creation of value in the digital economies. …

The volunteers for America Online, the NetSlaves, and the amateur Web designers are not working only because capital wants them to; they are acting out a desire for affective and cultural production that is nonetheless real just because it is socially shaped. The cultural, technical, and creative work that supports the digital economy has been made possible by the development of capital beyond the early industrial and Fordist modes of production and therefore is particularly abundant in those areas where post-Fordism has been at work for a few decades. In the overdeveloped countries, the end of the factory has spelled out the obsolescence of the old working class, but it has also produced generations of workers who have been repeatedly addressed as active consumers of meaningful commodities. Free labor is the moment where this knowledgeable consumption of culture is translated into productive activities that are pleasurably embraced and at the same time often shamelessly exploited.

Management theory is also increasingly concerned with the question of knowledge work, that indefinable quality that is essential to the processes of stimulating innovation and achieving the goals of competitiveness. For example, Don Tapscott, in a classic example of managerial literature, *The Digital Economy*, describes the digital economy as a "new economy based on the networking of human intelligence."[10] Human intelligence provides the much needed value-added, which is essential to the economic health of the organization. Human intelligence, however, also poses a problem: it cannot be managed in quite the same way as more traditional types of labor. Knowledge workers need open organizational structures to produce, because the production of knowledge is rooted in collaboration, that is, in what Barbrook defined as the "gift economy":

> The concept of supervision and management is changing to team-based structures. Anyone responsible for managing knowledge workers knows they cannot be "managed" in the traditional sense. Often they have specialized knowledge and skills that cannot be matched or even understood by management. A new challenge to management is first to attract and retain these assets by marketing the organization to them, and second *to provide the creative and open communications environment where such workers can effectively apply and enhance their knowledge.*[11]

For Tapscott, therefore, the digital economy magically resolves the contradictions of industrial societies, such as class struggle: while in the industrial economy the "worker tried to achieve fulfillment through leisure [and] … was alienated from the means of production which were owned and controlled by someone else," in the digital economy the worker achieves fulfillment through work and finds in her brain her own, unalienated means of production.[12] Such means of production need to be cultivated by encouraging the worker to participate in a culture of exchange, whose flows are mainly kept within the company but also need to involve an "outside," a contact with the fast-moving world of knowledge in general. [...]

This essay looks beyond the totalizing hype of the managerial literature but also beyond some of the conceptual limits of Barbrook's work. It looks at some possible explanation for the coexistence, within the debate about the digital economy, of discourses that see it as an oppositional movement and others that see it as a functional development to new mechanisms of extraction of value. Is the end of Marxist alienation wished for by the manager guru the same thing as the gift economy heralded by leftist discourse?

We can start undoing this deadlock by subtracting the label *digital economy* from its exclusive anchorage within advanced forms of labor (we can start then by depioneering it). This essay describes the digital economy as a specific mechanism of internal "capture" of larger pools of social and cultural knowledge. The digital economy is an important area of experimentation with value and free cultural/affective labor. It is about specific forms of production (Web design, multimedia production, digital services, and so on), but is also about forms of labor we do not immediately recognize as such: chat, real-life stories, mailing lists, amateur newsletters, and so on. These types of cultural and technical labor are not produced by capitalism in any direct, cause-and-effect fashion; that is, they have not developed simply as an answer to the economic needs of capital. However, they have developed in relation to the expansion of the cultural industries and are part of a process of economic experimentation with the creation of monetary value out of knowledge/culture/affect.

[...]

Rather than capital "incorporating" from the outside the authentic fruits of the collective imagination, it seems more reasonable to think of cultural flows as originating within a field that is always and already capitalism. Incorporation is not about capital descending on authentic culture but a more immanent process of channeling collective labor (even as cultural labor) into monetary flows and its structuration within capitalist business practices.

Subcultural movements have stuffed the pockets of multinational capitalism for decades. Nurtured by the consumption of earlier cultural moments, subcultures have provided the look, style, and sounds that sell clothes, CDs, video games, films, and advertising slots on television. This has often happened through the active participation of subcultural members in the production of cultural goods (e.g., independent labels in music, small designer shops in fashion).[13] This participation is, as the word suggests, a voluntary phenomenon, although it is regularly accompanied by cries of sellouts. The fruit of collective cultural labor has been not simply appropriated, but voluntarily *channeled* and controversially *structured* within capitalist business practices. The relation between culture, the cultural industry, and labor in these movements is much more complex than the notion of incorporation suggests. In this sense, the digital economy is not a new phenomenon but simply a new phase of this longer history of experimentation.

Knowledge Class and Immaterial Labor

In spite of the numerous, more or less disingenuous endorsements of the democratic potential of the Internet, the links between it and capitalism look a bit too tight for comfort to concerned political minds. It has been very tempting to counteract the naive technological utopianism by pointing out how computer networks are the material and ideological heart of informed capital. The Internet advertised on television and portrayed by print media seems not just the latest incarnation of capital's inexhaustible search for new markets, but also a full consensus-creating machine, which socializes the mass of proletarianized knowledge workers into the economy of continuous innovation.[14] After all, if we do not get on-line soon, the hype suggests, we will become obsolete, unnecessary, disposable. If we do, we are promised, we will become part of the "hive mind," the immaterial economy of networked, intelligent subjects in charge of speeding up the rhythms of capital's "incessant waves of branching innovations."[15] Multimedia artists, writers, journalists, software programmers, graphic designers, and activists together with small and large companies are at the core of this project. For some they are its cultural elite, for others a new form of proletarianized labor.[16] Accordingly, the digital workers are described as resisting or supporting the project of capital, often in direct relation to their positions in the networked, horizontal, and yet hierarchical world of knowledge work.

Any judgment on the political potential of the Internet, then, is tied not only to its much vaunted capacity to allow decentralized access to information but also to the question of who uses the Internet and how. If the decentralized structure of the Net is to count for anything at all, the argument goes, then we need to know about its constituent population (hence the endless statistics about use, income, gender, and race of Internet users, the most polled, probed, and yet opaque survey material of the world). If this population of Internet users is largely made up of "knowledge workers," then it matters whether these are seen as the owners of elitist cultural and economic power or the avant-garde of new configurations of labor that do not automatically guarantee elite status.

As I argue in this essay, this is a necessary question and yet a misleading one. It is necessary because we have to ask who is participating in the digital economy before we can pass a judgment on it. It is misleading because it implies that all we need to know is how to locate the knowledge workers within a "class," and knowing which class it is will give us an answer to the political potential of the Net as a whole. If we can prove that knowledge workers are the avant-garde of labor, then the Net becomes a site of resistance;[17] if we can prove that knowledge workers wield the power in informated societies, then the Net is an extended gated community for the middle classes.[18] Even admitting that knowledge workers are indeed fragmented in terms of hierarchy and status won't help us that much; it will still lead to a simple system of categorization, where the Net becomes a field of struggle between the diverse constituents of the knowledge class.

The question is further complicated by the stubborn resistance of "knowledge" to quantification: knowledge cannot be exclusively pinned down to specific social segments. Although the shift from factory to office work, from production to services is widely acknowledged, it just isn't clear why some people qualify and some others do not.[19] The "knowledge worker" is a very contested sociological category.

A more interesting move, however, is possible by not looking for the knowledge class within quantifiable parameters and concentrating instead on "labor." Although the notion of class retains a material value that is indispensable to make sense of the experience of concrete historical subjects, it also has its limits: for example, it "freezes" the subject, just like a substance within the chemical periodical table, where one is born as a certain element (working-class metal) but then might become something else (middle-class silicon) if submitted to the proper alchemical processes (education and income). Such an understanding of class also freezes out the flows of culture and money that mobilize the labor force as a whole. In terms of Internet use, it gives rise to the generalized endorsements and condemnations that I have described above and does not explain or make sense of the heterogeneity and yet commonalities of Internet users. I have therefore found it more useful to think in terms of what the Italian autonomists, and especially Maurizio Lazzarato, have described as *immaterial labor*. For Lazzarato the concept of immaterial labor refers to *two different aspects* of labor:

> On the one hand, as regards the "informational content" of the commodity, it refers directly to the changes taking place in workers' labor processes … where the skills involved in direct labor are increasingly skills involving cybernetics and computer control (and horizontal and vertical communication). On the other hand, as regards the activity that produces the "cultural content" of the commodity, immaterial labor involves a series of activities that are not normally recognized as "work" – in other words, the kinds of activities involved in defining and fixing cultural and artistic standards, fashions, tastes, consumer norms, and, more strategically, public opinion.[20]

Immaterial labor, unlike the knowledge worker, is not completely confined to a specific class formation. Lazzarato insists that this form of labor power is not limited to highly skilled workers but is a form of activity of every productive subject within postindustrial societies. In the highly skilled worker, these capacities are already there. However, in the young worker, the "precarious worker," and the unemployed youth, these capacities are "virtual," that is they are there but are still undetermined. This means that immaterial labor is a virtuality (an undetermined capacity) that belongs to the postindustrial productive subjectivity as a whole. For example, the obsessive emphasis on education of 1990s governments can be read as an attempt to stop this virtuality from disappearing or from being channeled into places that would not be as acceptable to the current power structures. In spite of all the contradictions of advanced capital and its relation to structural unemployment, postmodern governments do not like the completely unemployable. The potentialities of work must be kept alive, the unemployed must undergo continuous training in order both to be monitored and kept alive as some kind of postindustrial reserve force. Nor can they be allowed to channel their energy into the experimental, nomadic, and antiproductive life-styles which in Britain have been so savagely attacked by the Criminal Justice Act in the mid-1990s.[21]

However, unlike the post-Fordists, and in accordance with his autonomist origins, Lazzarato does not conceive of immaterial labor as purely functional to a new historical phase of capitalism:

> The virtuality of this capacity is neither empty nor ahistoric; it is rather an opening and a potentiality, that have as their historical origins and antecedents the "struggle against work" of the Fordist worker and, in more recent times, the processes of socialization, educational formation, and cultural self-valorization.[22]

This dispersal of immaterial labor (as a virtuality and an actuality) problematizes the idea of the "knowledge worker" as a class in the "industrial" sense of the word. As a collective quality of the labor force, immaterial labor can be understood to pervade the social body with different degrees of intensity. This intensity is produced by the processes of "channeling" a characteristic of the capitalist formation which distributes value according to its logic of profit.[23] If knowledge is inherently collective, it is even more so in the case of the postmodern cultural economy: music, fashion, and information are all produced collectively but are selectively compensated. Only some companies are picked up by corporate distribution chains in the case of fashion and music; only a few sites are invested in by venture capital. However, it is a form of collective cultural labor that makes these products possible even as the profit is disproportionately appropriated by established corporations.

From this point of view, the well-known notion that the Internet materializes a "collective intelligence" is not completely off the mark. The Internet highlights the existence of networks of immaterial labor and speeds up their accretion into a collective entity. The productive capacities of immaterial labor on the Internet encompass the work of writing/reading/managing and participating in mailing lists/Web sites/chatlines. These activities fall outside the concept of "abstract labor," which Marx defined as the provision of time for the production of value regardless of the useful qualities of the product.[24] They witness an investment of desire into production of the kind cultural theorists have mainly theorized in relation to consumption.

This explosion of productive activities is undermined for various commentators by the minoritarian, gendered, and raced character of the Internet population. However, we might also argue that to recognize the existence of immaterial labor as a diffuse, collective quality of postindustrial labor in its entirety does not deny the existence of hierarchies of knowledge (both technical and cultural) which prestructure (but do not determine) the nature of such activities. These hierarchies shape the degrees to which such virtualities become actualities; that is, they go from being potential to being realized as processual, constituting moments of cultural, affective, and technical production. Neither capital nor living labor want a labor force that is permanently excluded from the possibilities of immaterial labor. But this is where their desires stop from coinciding. Capital wants to retain control over the unfolding of these virtualities and the processes of valorization. The relative abundance of cultural/technical/affective production on the Net, then, does not exist as a free-floating postindustrial utopia but in full, mutually constituting interaction with late capitalism, especially in its manifestation as global-venture capital.

Collective Minds

The collective nature of networked, immaterial labor has been simplified by the utopian statements of the cyberlibertarians. Kevin Kelly's popular thesis in *Out of Control*, for example, is that the Internet is a collective "hive mind." According to Kelly, the Internet is another manifestation of a principle of self-organization that is widespread throughout technical, natural, and social systems. The Internet is the material evidence of the existence of the self-organizing, infinitely productive activities of connected human minds.[25] From a different perspective Pierre Levy draws on cognitive anthropology and poststructuralist philosophy to argue that computers and computer networks are sites that enable the emergence of a "collective intelligence." According to Eugene Provenzo, Levy, who is inspired by early computer pioneers such as Douglas Engelbart, argues for a new humanism "that incorporates and enlarges the scope of self-knowledge and collective thought."[26] According to Levy, we are passing from a Cartesian model of thought based on the singular idea of *cogito* (I think) to a collective or plural *cogitamus* (we think).

> What is collective intelligence? It is a form of *universally distributed intelligence*, constantly enhanced, coordinated in real time, and resulting in the effective mobilization of skills. ... The basis and goal of collective intelligence is the mutual recognition and enrichment of individuals rather than the cult of fetishized or hypostatized communities.[27]

Like Kelly, Levy frames his argument within the common rhetoric of competition and flexibility that dominates the hegemonic discourse around digitalization: "The more we are able to form intelligent communities, as open-minded, cognitive subjects capable of initiative, imagination, and rapid response, the more we will be able to ensure our success in a highly competitive environment."[28] In Levy's view, the digital economy highlights the impossibility of absorbing intelligence within the process of automation: unlike the first wave of cybernetics, which displaced workers from the factory, computer networks highlight the unique value of human intelligence as the true creator of value in a knowledge economy. In his opinion, since the economy is increasingly reliant on the production of creative subjectivities, this production is highly likely to engender a new humanism, a new centrality of man's [*sic*] creative potentials.

Especially in Kelly's case, it has been easy to dismiss the notions of a "hive mind" and a self-organizing Internet-as-free-market as euphoric capitalist mumbo jumbo. One cannot help being deeply irritated by the blindness of the digital capitalist to the realities of working in the high-tech industries, from the poisoning world of the silicon chips factories to the electronic sweatshops of America Online, where technical work is downgraded and worker obsolescence is high.[29] How can we hold on to the notion that cultural production and immaterial labor are collective on the Net (both inner and outer) without subscribing to the idealistic cyberdrool of the digerati?

We could start with a simple observation: the self-organizing, collective intelligence of cybercultural thought captures the existence of networked immaterial labor, but also neutralizes the operations of capital. Capital, after all, is the unnatural environment within which the collective intelligence materializes. The collective dimension of networked intelligence needs to be understood historically, as part of a specific momentum of capitalist development. The Italian writers who are identified with the post-Gramscian Marxism of autonomia have consistently engaged with this relationship by focusing on the mutation undergone by labor in the aftermath of the factory. The notion of a self-organizing "collective intelligence" looks uncannily like one of their central concepts, the "general intellect," a notion that the autonomists "extracted" out of the spirit, if not the actual wording, of Marx's *Grundrisse*. The "collective intelligence" or "hive mind" captures some of the spirit of the "general intellect," but removes the autonomists' critical theorization of its relation to capital.

In the autonomists' favorite text, the *Grundrisse*, and especially in the "Fragment on Machines," Marx argues that "knowledge – scientific knowledge in the first place, but not exclusively – tends to become precisely by virtue of its autonomy from production, nothing less than the principal productive force, thus relegating repetitive and compartmentalized labor to a residual position. Here one is dealing with knowledge ... which has become incarnate ... in the automatic system of machines."[30] In the vivid pages of the "Fragment," the "other" Marx of the *Grundrisse* (adopted by the social movements of the 1960s and 1970s against the more orthodox endorsement of *Capital*), describes the system of industrial machines as a horrific monster of metal and flesh:

> The production process has ceased to be a labor process in the sense of a process dominated by labor as its governing unity. Labor appears, rather, merely as a conscious organ, scattered among the individual living workers at numerous points of the mechanical system; subsumed under the total process of the machinery itself, as itself only a link of the system, whose unity exists not in the living workers, but rather in the living, (active) machinery, which confronts his individual, insignificant doings as a mighty organism.[31]

The Italian autonomists extracted from these pages the notion of the "general intellect" as "the ensemble of knowledge … which constitute[s] the epicenter of social production."[32] Unlike Marx's original formulation, however, the autonomists eschewed the modernist imagery of the general intellect as a hellish machine. They claimed that Marx completely identified the general intellect (or knowledge as the principal productive force) with fixed capital (the machine) and thus neglected to account for the fact that the general intellect cannot exist independently of the concrete subjects who mediate the articulation of the machines with each other. The general intellect is an articulation of fixed capital (machines) *and* living labor (the workers). If we see the Internet, and computer networks in general, as the latest machines – the latest manifestation of fixed capital – then it won't be difficult to imagine the general intellect as being well and alive today.

The autonomists, however, did not stop at describing the general intellect as an assemblage of humans and machines at the heart of postindustrial production. If this were the case, the Marxian monster of metal and flesh would just be updated to that of a world-spanning network where computers use human beings as a way to allow the system of machinery (and therefore capitalist production) to function. The visual power of the Marxian description is updated by the cyberpunk snapshots of the immobile bodies of the hackers, electrodes like umbilical cords connecting them to the matrix, appendixes to a living, all-powerful cyberspace. Beyond the special effects bonanza, the box-office success of *The Matrix* validates the popularity of the paranoid interpretation of this mutation.

To the humanism implicit in this description, the autonomists have opposed the notion of a "mass intellectuality," living labor in its function as the determining articulation of the general intellect. Mass intellectuality – as an ensemble, as a social body – "is the repository of the indivisible knowledges of living subjects and of their linguistic cooperation. … An important part of knowledge cannot be deposited in machines, but … it must come into being as the direct interaction of the labor force."[33] As Virno emphasizes, mass intellectuality is not about the various roles of the knowledge workers, but is a "*quality* and a distinctive sign of the *whole* social labor force in the post-Fordist era."[34]

The pervasiveness of the collective intelligence within both the managerial literature and Marxist theory could be seen as the result of a common intuition about the quality of labor in informed societies. Knowledge labor is inherently *collective*, it is always the result of a collective and social production of knowledge.[35] Capital's problem is how to extract as much value as possible (in the autonomists' jargon, to "valorize") out of this abundant, and yet slightly intractable, terrain.

Collective knowledge work, then, is not about those who work in the knowledge industry. But it is also not about employment. The acknowledgment of the collective aspect of labor implies a rejection of the equivalence between labor and employment, which was already stated by Marx and further emphasized by feminism and the post-Gramscian autonomy.[36] Labor is not equivalent to waged labor. Such an understanding might help us to reject some of the hideous rhetoric of unemployment which turns the unemployed person into the object of much patronizing, pushing, and nudging from national governments in industrialized countries. (Accept any available work or else. ...) Often the unemployed are such only in name, in reality being the life-blood of the difficult economy of "under-the-table," badly paid work, some of which also goes into the new media industry.[37] To emphasize how labor is not equivalent to employment also means to acknowledge how important free affective and cultural labor is to the media industry, old and new.

Ephemeral Commodities and Free Labor

There is a continuity, and a break, between older media and new media in terms of their relationship to cultural and affective labor. The continuity seems to lie in their common reliance on their public/users as productive subjects. The difference lies both in the mode of production and in the ways in which power/knowledge works in the two types. In spite of different national histories (some of which stress public service more than others), the television industry, for example, is relatively conservative: writers, producers, performers, managers, and technicians have definite roles within an industry still run by a few established players. The historical legacy of television as a technology for the construction of national identities also means that television is somehow always held more publicly accountable.

This does not mean that old media do not draw on free labor, on the contrary. Television and print media, for example, make abundant use of the free labor of their audiences/readers, but they also tend to structure the latter's contribution much more strictly, both in terms of economic organization and moralistic judgment. The price to pay for all those real-life TV experiences is usually a heavy dose of moralistic scaremongering: criminals are running amok on the freeways and must be stopped by tough police action; wild teenagers lack self-esteem and need tough love. If this does not happen on the Internet, why is it then that the Internet is not the happy island of decentered, dispersed, and pleasurable cultural production that its apologists claimed?

The most obvious answer to such questions came spontaneously to the early Internet users who blamed it on the commercialization of the Internet. E-commerce and the progressive privatization were blamed for disrupting the free economy of the Internet, an economy of exchange that Richard Barbrook described as a "gift economy."[38] Indeed maybe the Internet could have been a different place than what it is now. However, it is almost unthinkable that capitalism could stay forever outside of the network, a mode of communication that is fundamental to its own organizational structure.

The outcome of the explicit interface between capital and the Internet is a digital economy that manifests all the signs of an acceleration of the capitalist logic of production. It might be that the Internet has not stabilized yet, but it seems undeniable that the digital economy is the fastest and most visible zone of production within late capitalist societies. New products and new trends succeed each other at anxiety-inducing pace. After all, this is a business where you need to replace your equipment/knowledges and possibly staff every year or so.

At some point, the speed of the digital economy, its accelerated rhythms of obsolescence, and its reliance on (mostly) "immaterial" products seemed to fit in with the postmodern intuition about the changed status of the commodities whose essence was said to be *meaning* (or lack of) rather than *labor* (as if the two could be separable).[39] The recurrent complaint that the Internet contributes to the disappearance of reality is then based *both* in humanistic concerns about "real life" *and* in the postmodern nihilism of the recombinant commodity.[40] Hyperreality confirms the humanist nightmare of a society without humanity, the culmination of a progressive taking over of the realm of representation. Commodities on the Net are not material and are excessive (there is too much of it, too many Web sites, too much clutter and noise) with relation to the limits of "real" social needs.

It is possible, however, that the disappearance of the commodity is not a material disappearance but its visible subordination to the quality of labor behind it. In this sense the commodity does not disappear as such; rather, it becomes increasingly ephemeral, its duration becomes compressed, and it becomes more of a process than a finished product. The role of continuous, creative, innovative labor as the ground of market value is crucial to the digital economy. The process of valorization (the production of monetary value) happens by foregrounding the quality of the labor that literally animates the commodity.

In my opinion, the digital economy challenges the postmodern assumption that labor disappears while the commodity takes on and dissolves all meaning. In particular, the Internet is about the extraction of value out of continuous, updateable work, and it is extremely labor intensive. It is not enough to produce a good Web site, you need to update it continuously to maintain interest in it and fight off obsolescence. Furthermore, you need updateable equipment (the general intellect is always an assemblage of humans and their machines), in its turn propelled by the intense collective labor of programmers, designers, and workers. It is as if the acceleration of production has pushed to the point where commodities, literally, turn into translucent objects. Commodities do not so much disappear as become more transparent, showing throughout their reliance on the labor that produces and sustains them. It is the labor of the designers and programmers that shows through a successful Web site, and it is the spectacle of that labor changing its product that keeps the users coming back. The commodity, then, is only as good as the labor that goes into it.

As a consequence, the sustainability of the Internet as a medium depends on massive amounts of labor (which is not equivalent to employment, as we said), only some of which is hypercompensated by the capricious logic of venture capitalism. Of the incredible amount of labor that sustains the Internet as a whole (from mailing list traffic to Web sites to infrastructural questions), we can guess that a substantial amount of it is still "free labor."

Free labor, however, is not necessarily exploited labor. Within the early virtual communities, we are told, labor was really free: the labor of building a community was not compensated by great financial rewards (it was therefore "free," unpaid), but it was also willingly conceded in exchange for the pleasures of communication and exchange (it was therefore "free," pleasurable, not imposed). In answer to members' requests, information was quickly posted and shared with a lack of mediation that the early Netizens did not fail to appreciate. Howard Rheingold's book, somehow unfairly accused of middle-class complacency, is the most wellknown account of the good old times of the old Internet, before the Net-tourist overcame the Net-pioneer.[41]

The free labor that sustains the Internet is acknowledged within many different sections of the digital literature. In spite of the volatile nature of the Internet economy (which yesterday was about community, today is about portals, and tomorrow who knows what), the notion of users' labor maintains an ideological and material centrality that runs consistently throughout the turbulent succession of Internet fads. Commentators who would normally disagree, such as Howard Rheingold and Richard Hudson, concur on one thing: the best Web site, the best way to stay visible and thriving on the Web, is to turn your site into a space that is not only accessed, but somehow built by its users.[42] Users keep a site alive through their labor, the cumulative hours of accessing the site (thus generating advertising), writing messages, participating in conversations, and sometimes making the jump to collaborators. Out of the fifteen thousand volunteers that keep AOL running, only a handful turned against it, while the others stayed on. Such a feature seems endemic to the Internet in ways that can be worked on by commercialization, but not substantially altered. The "open source" movement, which relies on the free labor of Internet tinkers, is further evidence of this structural trend within the digital economy.

It is an interesting feature of the Internet debate (and evidence, somehow, of its masculine bias) that users' labor has attracted more attention in the case of the open source movement than in that of mailing lists and Web sites. This betrays the persistence of an attachment to masculine understandings of labor within the digital economy: writing an operating system is still more worthy of attention than just chatting for free for AOL. This in spite of the fact that in 1996 at the peak of the volunteer moment, over thirty thousand "community leaders" were helping AOL to generate at least $7 million a month.[43] Still, the open source movement has drawn much more positive attention than the more diffuse user labor described above. It is worth exploring not because I believe that it will out-last "portals" or "virtual communities" as the latest buzzword, but because of the debates it has provoked and its relation to the digital economy at large.

The open source movement is a variation of the old tradition of shareware and freeware software which substantially contributed to the technical development of the Internet. Freeware software is freely distributed and does not even request a reward from its users. Shareware software is distributed freely, but implies a "moral" obligation for the user to forward a small sum to the producer in order to sustain the shareware movement as an alternative economic model to the copyrighted software of giants such as Microsoft. *Open source* "refers to a model of software development in which the underlying code of a program – the source code, a.k.a. the crown jewels – is by definition made freely available to the general public for modification, alteration, and endless redistribution."[44]

Far from being an idealistic, minoritarian practice, the open source movement has attracted much media and financial attention. Apache, an open source Web server, is the "Web-server program of choice for more than half of all publicly accessible Web servers."[45] In 1999, open source conventions are anxiously attended by venture capitalists, who have been informed by the digerati that the open source movement is a necessity "because you must go open-source to get access to the benefits of the open-source development community – the near-instantaneous bug-fixes, the distributed intellectual resources of the Net, the increasingly large open-source code base."[46] Open source companies such as Cygnus have convinced the market that you do not need to be proprietary about source codes to make a profit: the code might be free, but tech support, packaging, installation software, regular upgrades, office applications, and hardware are not.

In 1998, when Netscape went "open source" and invited the computer tinkers and hobbyists to look at the code of its new browser, fix the bugs, improve the package, and redistribute it, specialized mailing lists exchanged opinions about its implications.[47] Netscape's move rekindled the debate about the peculiar nature of the digital economy. Was it to be read as being in the tradition of the Internet "gift economy"? Or was digital capital hijacking the open source movement exactly against that tradition? Richard Barbrook saluted Netscape's move as a sign of the power intrinsic in the architecture of the medium:

> The technical and social structure of the Net has been developed to encourage open cooperation among its participants. As an everyday activity, users are building the system together. Engaged in "interactive creativity," they send emails, take part in list-servers, contribute to newsgroups, participate within on-line conferences and produce Websites. ... Lacking copyright protection, information can be freely adapted to suit the users' needs. Within the hi-tech gift economy, people successfully work together through "... an open social process involving evaluation, comparison and collaboration."[48]

John Horvarth, however, did not share this opinion. The "free stuff" offered around the Net, he argued, "is either a product that gets you hooked on to another one or makes you just consume more time on the net. After all, the goal of the access people and telecoms is to have users spend as much time on the net as possible, regardless of what they are doing. The objective is to have you consume bandwidth."[49] Far from proving the persistence of the Internet gift economy, Horvarth claimed, Netscape's move is a direct threat to those independent producers for whom shareware and freeware have been a way of surviving exactly those "big boys" that Netscape represents:

Freeware and shareware are the means by which small producers, many of them individuals, were able to offset somewhat the bulldozing effects of the big boys. And now the bulldozers are headed straight for this arena.

As for Netscrape [sic], such a move makes good business sense and spells trouble for workers in the field of software development. The company had a poor last quarter in 1997 and was already hinting at job cuts. Well, what better way to shed staff by having your product taken further by the freeware people, having code-dabbling hobbyists fix and further develop your product? The question for Netscrape now is how to tame the freeware beast so that profits are secured.[50]

Although it is tempting to stake the evidence of Netscape's layoffs against the optimism of Barbrook's gift economy, there might be more productive ways of looking at the increasingly tight relationship between an "idealistic" movement such as open source and the current venture mania for open source companies.[51] Rather than representing a moment of incorporation of a previously authentic moment, the open source question demonstrates the overreliance of the digital economy as such on free labor, both in the sense of not financially rewarded and willingly given. This includes AOL community leaders, the open source programmers, the amateur Web designers, mailing list editors, and the NetSlaves willing to "work for cappuccinos" just for the excitement and the dubious promises of digital work.[52]

Such a reliance, almost a dependency, is part of larger mechanisms of capitalist extraction of value which are fundamental to late capitalism as a whole. That is, such processes are not created outside capital and then reappropriated by capital, but are the results of a complex history where the relation between labor and capital is mutually constitutive, entangled and crucially forged during the crisis of Fordism. Free labor is a desire of labor immanent to late capitalism, and late capitalism is the field that both sustains free labor *and* exhausts it. It exhausts it by subtracting selectively but widely the means through which that labor can reproduce itself: from the burnout syndromes of Internet start-ups to underretribution and exploitation in the cultural economy at large. Late capitalism does not appropriate anything: it nurtures, exploits, and exhausts its labor force and its cultural and affective production. In this sense, it is technically impossible to separate neatly the digital economy of the Net from the larger network economy of late capitalism. Especially since 1994, the Internet is always and simultaneously a gift economy *and* an advanced capitalist economy. The mistake of the neoliberalists (as exemplified by the *Wired* group), is to mistake this coexistence for a benign, unproblematic equivalence.

As I stated before, these processes are far from being confined to the most self-conscious laborers of the digital economy. They are part of a diffuse cultural economy which operates throughout the Internet and beyond. The passage from the pioneeristic days of the Internet to its "venture" days does not seem to have affected these mechanisms, only intensified them and connected them to financial capital. Nowhere is this more evident than in the recent development of the World Wide Web.

Enter the New Web

In the winter of 1999, in what sounds like another of its resounding, short-lived claims, *Wired* magazine announces that the old Web is dead: "The Old Web was a place where the unemployed, the dreamy, and the iconoclastic went to reinvent themselves ... The New Web isn't about dabbling in what you don't know and failing – it's about preparing seriously for the day when television and Web content are delivered over the same digital networks."[53]

The new Web is made of the big players, but also of new ways to make the audience work. In the "new Web," after the pioneering days, television and the Web converge in the one thing they have in common: their reliance on their audiences/users as providers of the cultural labor that goes under the label of "real-life stories." Gerry Laybourne, executive of the Web-based media company Oxygen, thinks of a hypothetical show called *What Are They Thinking?* a reality-based sketch comedy based on stories posted on the Web, because "funny things happen in our lives everyday."[54] As Bayers also adds, "until it's produced, the line separating that concept from more puerile fare dismissed by Gerry, like *America's Funniest*, is hard to see."[55]

The difference between the puerile fare of *America's Funniest* and user-based content seems to lie not so much in the more serious nature of the "new Web" as compared to the vilified output of television's "people shows" (a term that includes docusoaps, docudramas, and talk shows). From an abstract point of view there is no difference between the ways in which people shows rely on the inventiveness of their audiences and the Web site reliance on users' input. People shows rely on the activity (even amidst the most shocking sleaze) of their audience and willing participants to a much larger extent than any other television programs. In a sense, they manage the impossible, creating monetary value out of the most reluctant members of the postmodern cultural economy: those who do not produce marketable style, who are not qualified enough to enter the fast world of the knowledge economy, are converted into monetary value through their capacity to perform their misery.

When compared to the cultural and affective production on the Internet, people shows also seem to embody a different logic of relation between capitalism (the media conglomerates that produce and distribute such shows) and its labor force – the beguiled, dysfunctional citizens of the underdeveloped North. Within people's shows, the valorization of the audience as labor and spectacle always happens somehow within a power/knowledge nexus that does not allow the *immediate* valorization of the talk show participants: you cannot just put a Jerry Springer guest on TV on her own to tell her story with no mediation (indeed, that would look too much like the discredited access slots of public service broadcasting). Between the talk show guest and the apparatus of valorization intervenes a series of knowledges that normalize the dysfunctional subjects through a moral or therapeutic discourse and a more traditional institutional organization of production. So after the performance, the guest must be advised, patronized, questioned, and often bullied by the audience and the host, all in the name of a perfunctory, normalizing morality.

People shows also belong to a different economy of scale: although there are more and more of them, they are still relatively few when compared to the millions of pages on the Web. It is as if the centralized organization of the traditional media does not let them turn people's productions into pure monetary value. People shows must have morals, even as those morals are shattered by the overflowing performances of their subjects.

Within the Internet, however, this process of channeling and adjudicating (responsibilities, duties, and rights) is dispersed to the point where practically anything is tolerated (sadomasochism, bestiality, fetishism, and plain nerdism are not targeted, at least within the Internet, as sites that need to be disciplined or explained away). The qualitative difference between people's shows and a successful Web site, then, does not lie in the latter's democratic tendency as opposed to the former's exploitative nature. It lies in the operation, within people's shows, of moral discursive mechanisms of territorialization, the application of a morality that the "excessive" abundance of material on the Internet renders redundant and even more irrelevant. The digital economy cares only tangentially about morality. What it really cares about is an abundance of production, an immediate interface with cultural and technical labor whose result is a diffuse, nondialectical contradiction.

Conclusion

My hypothesis that free labor is structural to the late capitalist cultural economy is not meant to offer the reader a totalizing understanding of the cultural economy of new and old media. However, it does originate from a need to think beyond the categories that structure much Net debate these days, a process necessarily entailing a good deal of abstraction.

In particular, I have started from the opposition between the Internet as capital and the Internet as the anticapital. This opposition is much more challenging than the easy technophobia/technophilia debate. The question is not so much whether to love or hate technology, but an attempt to understand whether the Internet embodies a continuation of capital or a break with it. As I have argued in this essay, it does neither. It is rather a mutation that is totally immanent to late capitalism, not so much a break as an intensification, and therefore a mutation, of a widespread cultural and economic logic.

In this context, it is not enough just to demystify the Internet as the latest capitalist machination against labor. I have tried to map a different route, an immanent, flat, and yet power-sensitive model of the relationship between labor, politics, and culture. Obviously I owe much of the inspiration for this model to the French/Italian connection, to that line of thought formed by the exchanges between the Foucault/Deleuze/Guattari axis and the Italian Autonomy (Antonio Negri, Maurizio Lazzarato, Paolo Virno, Franco Berardi), a field of exchanges formed through political struggle, exile, and political prosecution right at the heart of the postindustrial society (Italy after all has provided the model of a post-Fordist economy for the influential flexible specialization school). On the other hand, it has been within a praxis informed by the cybernetic intelligence of English-speaking mailing lists and Web sites that this line of thought has acquired its concrete materiality.

This return to immanence, that is, to a flattening out of social, cultural, and political connections, has important consequences for me. As Negri, Haraway, and Deleuze and Guattari have consistently argued, the demolition of the modernist ontology of the Cartesian subject does not have to produce the relativism of the most cynical examples of postmodern theory. The loss of transcendence, of external principles which organize the social world from the outside, does not have to end up in nihilism, a loss of strategies for dealing with power.

Such strategies cannot be conjured by critical theory. As the spectacular failure of the Italian Autonomy reveals,[56] the purpose of critical theory is not to elaborate strategies that then can be used to direct social change. On the contrary, as the tradition of cultural studies has less explicitly argued, it is about working on what already exists, on the lines established by a cultural and material activity that is already happening. In this sense this essay does not so much propose a theory as it identifies a *tendency* that already exists in the Internet literature and on-line exchanges. This tendency is not the truth of the digital economy; it is necessarily partial just as it tries to hold to the need for an overall perspective on an immensely complex range of cultural and economic phenomena. Rather than retracing the holy truths of Marxism on the changing body of late capital, free labor embraces some crucial contradictions without lamenting, celebrating, denying, or synthesizing a complex condition. It is, then, not so much about truth-values as about relevance, the capacity to capture a moment and contribute to the ongoing constitution of a nonunified collective intelligence outside and in between the blind alleys of the silicon age.

NOTES

1. Lisa Margonelli, "Inside AOL's 'Cyber-Sweatshop,'" *Wired*, October 1999, 138.
2. See Paolo Virno and Michael Hardt, *Radical Thought in Italy: A Potential Politics* (Minneapolis: University of Minnesota Press, 1996); and Toni Negri, *The Politics of Subversion: A Manifesto for the Twenty-first Century* (Cambridge: Polity, 1989) and *Marx beyond Marx: Lessons on the "Grundrisse"* (New York: Autonomedia, 1991). The quote is from Negri, *Politics of Subversion*, 92.
3. Donna Haraway, *Simians, Cyborgs, and Women: The Reinvention of Nature* (London: Routledge, 1991), 159.
4. Paul Gilroy, *The Black Atlantic: Modernity and Double Consciousness* (London and New York: Verso, 1993), 40.
5. Manuel Castells, *The Rise of the Network Society* (Cambridge, Mass.: Blackwell, 1996), 395.
6. In discussing these developments, I will also draw on debates circulating across Internet sites. On-line debates in, for example, nettime, telepolis, rhizome and c-theory, are one

of the manifestations of the surplus value engendered by the digital economy, a hyper-production that can only be partly reabsorbed by capital.

7. See Richard Barbrook, "The Digital Economy" (posted to *nettime* on 17 June 1997; also at www.nettime.org; "The High-Tech Gift Economy," in *Readme! Filtered by Nettime: ASCII Culture and the Revenge of Knowledge*, ed. Josephine Bosma et al. (Brooklyn, N.Y.: Autonomedia, 1999), 132–38). Also see Anonymous, "The Digital Artisan Manifesto" (posted to *nettime* on 15 May 1997).

8. Barbrook, "The High-Tech Gift Economy," 135.

9. Ibid., 137.

10. Don Tapscott, *The Digital Economy* (New York: McGraw-Hill, 1996), xiii.

11. Ibid., 35; emphasis added.

12. Ibid., 48.

13. For a discussion of the independent music industry and its relation to corporate culture see David Hesmondalgh, "Indie: The Aesthetics and Institutional Politics of a Popular Music Genre," *Cultural Studies* 13 (January 1999): 34–61. Angela McRobbie has also studied a similar phenomenon in the fashion and design industry in *British Fashion Design: Rag Trade or Image Industry?* (London: Routledge, 1998).

14. See the challenging section on work in the high-tech industry in Bosma et al., *Readme!*

15. Martin Kenney, "Value-Creation in the Late Twentieth Century: The Rise of the Knowledge Worker," in *Cutting Edge: Technology, Information Capitalism and Social Revolution*, ed. Jim Davis, Thomas Hirsch, and Michael Stack (London: Verso, 1997), 93; also see in the same anthology Tessa Morris-Suzuki, "Capitalism in the Computer Age," 57–71.

16. See Darko Suvin, "On Gibson and Cyberpunk SF," in *Storming the Reality Studio*, ed. Larry McCaffery (London: Durham University Press, 1991), 349–65; and Stanley Aronowitz and William DiFazio, *The Jobless Future: Sci-Tech and the Dogma of Work* (Minneapolis: University of Minnesota Press, 1994). According to Andrew Clement, information technologies were introduced as extensions of Taylorist techniques of scientific management to middle-level, rather than clerical, employees. Such technologies responded to a managerial need for efficient ways to manage intellectual labor. Clement, however, seems to connect this scientific management to the workstation, while he is ready to admit that personal computers introduce an element of autonomy much disliked by management. See Andrew Clement, "Office Automation and the Technical Control of Information Workers," in *The Political Economy of Information*, ed. Vincent Mosco and Janet Wasko (Madison: University of Wisconsin Press, 1988).

17. Barbrook, "The High-Tech Gift Economy."

18. See Kevin Robins, "Cyberspace or the World We Live In," in *Fractal Media: New Media in Social Context*, ed. Jon Dovey (London: Lawrence and Wishart, 1996).

19. See Frank Webster, *Theories of the Information Society* (London and New York: Routledge, 1995).

20. Maurizio Lazzarato, "Immaterial Labor," in *Marxism beyond Marxism*, ed. Saree Makdisi, Cesare Casarino, and Rebecca E. Karl for the Polygraph collective (London: Routledge, 1996), 133.

21. The Criminal Justice Act (CJA) was popularly perceived as an antirave legislation, and most of the campaign against it was organized around the "right to party." However, the most devastating effects of the CJA have struck the neotribal, nomadic camps, basically decimated or forced to move to Ireland in the process. See Andrea Natella and Serena Tinari, eds., *Rave Off* (Rome: Castelvecchi, 1996).

22. Lazzarato, "Immaterial Labor," 136.

23. In the two volumes of *Capitalism and Schizophrenia*, Gilles Deleuze and Félix Guattari described the process by which capital unsettles and resettles bodies and cultures as a movement of "decoding" ruled by "axiomatisation." Decoding is the process through which older cultural limits are displaced and removed as with older, local cultures during modernization; the flows of culture and capital unleashed by the decoding are then channeled into a process of axiomatization, an abstract moment of conversion into money and profit. The decoding forces of global capitalism have then opened up the possibilities of immaterial labor. See Gilles Deleuze and Félix Guattari, *Anti-Oedipus: Capitalism and Schizophrenia* (London: Athlone, 1984); and *A Thousand Plateaus: Capitalism and Schizophrenia* (London: Athlone, 1988).

24. See Franco Berardi (Bifo), *La nefasta utopia di potere operaio* (Rome: Castelvecchi/DeriveApprodi, 1998), 43.

25. See Kevin Kelly, *Out of Control* (Reading, Mass.: Addison Wesley, 1994).

26. Eugene Provenzo, foreword to Pierre Levy, *Collective Intelligence: Mankind's Emerging World in Cyberspace* (New York: Plenum, 1995), viii.

27. Levy, *Collective Intelligence*, 13.

28. Ibid., 1.

29. See Little Red Henski, "Insider Report from UUNET" in Bosma et al., *Readme!* 189–91.

30. Paolo Virno, "Notes on the General Intellect," in *Marxism beyond Marxism*, 266.

31. Karl Marx, *Grundrisse* (London: Penguin, 1973), 693.

32. Paolo Virno, "Notes on the General Intellect," in *Marxism beyond Marxism*, 266.

33. Ibid., 270.

34. Ibid., 271.

35. See Lazzarato, "New Forms of Production," in Bosma et al., *Readme!* 159–66; and Tessa Morris-Suzuki, "Robots and Capitalism," in *Cutting Edge*, 13–27.

36. See Toni Negri, "Back to the Future," in Bosma et al., *Readme!* 181–86; and Haraway, *Simians, Cyborgs, Women*.

37. Andrew Ross, *Real Love: In Pursuit of Cultural Justice* (London: Routledge, 1998).

38. See Barbrook, "The High-Tech Gift Economy."

39. The work of Jean-François Lyotard in *The Postmodern Condition* is mainly concerned with *knowledge*, rather than intellectual labor, but still provides a useful conceptualization of the reorganization of labor within the productive structures of late capitalism. See Jean-François Lyotard, *The Postmodern Condition: A Report on Knowledge*, trans. Geoff Bennington and Brian Massumi (Minneapolis: University of Minnesota Press, 1989).

40. See Arthur Kroker and Michael A. Weinstein, *Data Trash: The Theory of the Virtual Class* (New York: St. Martin's, 1994).

41. See Howard Rheingold, *The Virtual Community: Homesteading on the Electronic Frontier* (New York: Harper Perennials, 1994).

42. See Howard Rheingold, "My Experience with Electric Minds," in Bosma et al., *Readme!* 147–50; also David Hudson, *Rewired: A Brief (and Opinionated) Net History* (Indianapolis: Macmillan Technical Publishing, 1997). The expansion of the Net is based on different types of producers adopting different strategies of income generation: some might use more traditional types of financial support (grants, divisions of the public sector, in-house Internet divisions within traditional media companies, businesses' Web

pages which are paid as with traditional forms of advertising); some might generate interest in one's page and then sell the user's profile or advertising space (freelance Web production); or some might use innovative strategies of valorization, such as various types of e-commerce.

43. See Margonelli, "Inside AOL's 'Cyber-Sweatshop.'"
44. Andrew Leonard, "Open Season," in *Wired*, May 1999, 140. Open source harks back to the specific competencies embodied by Internet users in its pre-1994 days. When most Net users were computer experts, the software structure of the medium was developed by way of a continuous interaction of different technical skills. This tradition still survives in institutions like the Internet Engineering Task Force (IETF), which is responsible for a number of important decisions about the technical infrastructure of the Net. Although the IETF is subordinated to a number of professional committees, it has important responsibilities and is also open to anybody who wants to join. The freeware movement has a long tradition, but it has also recently been divided by the polemics between the free software or "copyleft" movement and the open source movement, which is more of a pragmatic attempt to make freeware a business proposition. See debates on-line at www.gnu.org and www.salonmag.com.
45. Leonard, "Open Season."
46. Ibid., 142.
47. It is an established pattern of the computer industry, in fact, that you might have to give away your product if you want to reap the benefits later on. As John Perry Barlow has remarked, "Familiarity is an important asset in the world of information. It may often be the case that the best thing you can do to raise demand for your product is to give it away." See John Perry Barlow, "Selling Wine without Bottles: The Economy of Mind on the Global Net," in *High Noon on the Electronic Frontier: Conceptual Issues in Cyberspace*, ed. Peter Ludlow (Cambridge: MIT Press, 1996), 23. Apple started it by giving free computers to schools, an action that did not determine, but certainly influenced, the subsequent stubborn presence of Apple computers within education; MS-Dos came in for free with IBM computers.
48. Barbrook, "The High-Tech Gift Economy," 135–36.
49. John Horvarth, "Freeware Capitalism," posted on *nettime*, 5 February 1998.
50. Ibid.
51. Netscape started like a lot of other computer companies: its founder, Marc Andreessen, was part of the original research group who developed the structure of the World Wide Web at the CERN laboratory, in Geneva. As with many successful computer entrepreneurs, he developed the browser as an offshoot of the original, state-funded research and soon started his own company. Netscape was also the first company to exceed the economic processes of the computer industry, inasmuch as it was the first successful company to set up shop on the Net itself. As such, Netscape exemplifies some of the problems that even the computer industry meets on the Net and constitutes a good starting point to assess some of the common claims about the digital economy.
52. Ross, *Real Love*.
53. Chip Bayers, "Push Comes to Show," in *Wired*, February 1999, 113.
54. Ibid., 156.
55. Ibid.
56. Berardi, *La nefasta utopia*.

23 ENSURING MINORITY RIGHTS IN A PLURALISTIC AND "LIQUID" INFORMATION SOCIETY

Birgitte Kofod Olsen

Economic, technological, and cultural globalization has led to a world characterized by flexibility and liquidity. The term *liquid*[1] is used to illustrate the form of modernity that we are experiencing today and that is taking us down an avenue of transnationality; increased mobility of money, services, and persons; and restructuring of sovereignty, power, and freedom.[2] This development leaves us in a flux of uncertainty rather than stability in all aspects of life, including marriage, family life, local community, work, and communication. But at the same time, it provides us with the possibility to easily change our residence or location, to engage in work-related migration, to visit places outside our home countries, and to retrieve and disseminate information of all kinds. Distance does not matter any longer. Mobility and accessibility make us capable of staying in touch with family, friends, colleagues, and others with whom we share a common interest.

The information society and the Internet represent a perfect setting for such behavior and needs. They are instrumental for free communication and dialogue across borders, and thus represent efficient tools for maintaining and developing cultural, religious, and social traditions and norms, as well as for preserving

Birgitte Kofod Olsen, "Ensuring Minority Rights in a Pluralistic and 'Liquid' Information Society," pp. 263–80 from Rikke Frank Jørgensen (ed.), *Human Rights in the Global Information Society* (Cambridge, MA: MIT Press, 2006).

language and other elements of identity of persons. At the same time, the internet serves as a platform for accessible pluralistic information, and for dialogue and interchange of such information irrespective of language.

For members of minority groups, this tool is of paramount importance. It enables minority groups to communicate and compare the situations in different countries and – if the groups are spread over a cross-border area – among the jurisdictions they are covered by. Thus a new way of maintaining and developing the common culture within the minority group is possible.

Also, it enhances the possibilities for monitoring the protection and promotion of minority rights by states that have signed legally binding international and regional conventions. International organizations and NGOs may review the situation via access to information made available on the Web by the states and, just as important, by minority groups.

Immediate response to risks of or actual violation of minority rights is made possible via easily accessible digital communication channels, including the internet, satellite TV, and mobile phones. State organs, citizens, and organizations may have instant knowledge about minorities at risk and an opportunity to initiate efficient measures to stop or prevent violations.

Full and effective protection of minority rights presupposes a general acceptance of pluralism in society and of inclusion and equality as basic values and principles. It also requires a willingness to make policy and to adopt legislation, program, and plans of action to implement these standards.

If all this is accomplished, we may, from an optimistic perspective, benefit from the new ways of "liquid" living and the communicative platform given by the Internet, and create a society that exhibits pluralism, tolerance, broad-mindedness, and a common set of values; embraces diversity; and – within this ambit – protects the right to identity of members of minorities and ensures the principle of substantive equality between members of minorities and members of majority populations.

[...]

Traditional Minority Protection

[...]

Within the U.N. system, minority protection has been dealt with in various ways, encompassing human rights initiatives and documents that include the setting up of the Subcommission on Prevention of Discrimination and Protection of Minorities,[3] the appointment in 2001 of a special rapporteur of the U.N. Human Rights Commission on the situation of human rights and fundamental freedoms of indigenous peoples, and the adoption in 1992 by the U.N. General Assembly of a declaration on minority rights.[4] It is, however, noteworthy in this connection that the basic international human rights document, the U.N. Universal Declaration on Human Rights (1948), is silent about minority protection.

If one approaches human rights from the perspective of citizens, and thus seeing them as a vehicle to ensure efficient protection of the individual vis-à-vis the state, it is remarkable that only one provision in a legally binding instrument lays a general obligation on the signatories to protect minorities. The only legally binding international provision on minority rights is found in the U.N. Covenant on Civil and Political Rights (1966, Art, 27).[5] ...

Apart from the general protection of peoples enshrined in the African Charter on Human and People's Rights (1981), a stronger and more specific protection – legally speaking – of minorities is found Europe. An explicit prohibition against discrimination on grounds of membership in a national minority is found in the European Convention on Human Rights and Freedoms (1956, Art. 14). Thus, even though the Convention does not provide for specific minority rights, the prohibition ensures that persons belonging to national minorities have the right to enjoy their civil and political rights without being discriminated against because of their specific status.

[...]

Within the European Union, an obligation to protect national, ethnic, and religious minorities flows from the basic principles of the EU,[6] but is not explicitly identified as a core value or principle in the Treaty of the European Union. This will change if, eventually, the treaty establishing a European Constitution is agreed upon by the EU member states, because this document specifically identifies respect for the rights of persons belonging to minorities as one of the founding values of the EU. Also, the EU European Charter of Fundamental Rights (2000)[7] contains a prohibition against discrimination[8] similar to that of the European Convention on Human Rights, and an obligation to respect cultural, religious, and linguistic diversity.[9]

The Term "Minority": Now and in a Future Perspective

Despite the consensus on both the global and the regional level on the need for protection of minorities, and the efforts of political and monitoring bodies, legal scholars, and others, a clear definition of the term "minority" is not available. A number of criteria have been suggested to distinguish minority populations from the majority, encompassing both objective and subjective criteria. The list includes numerical inferiority; nationality of state of residence; a nondominant position in society; characteristics differing from those of the rest of the population; a sense of solidarity within the group concerning the preservation of their common culture, religion, or language; and stability in the form of long presence in the state.[10]

[...]

Supporting an argument of application of human rights in general to noncitizens is a recent General Comment from the U.N. Committee on the Elimination of Racial Discrimination. The committee recalls in its interpretive comment on discrimination against noncitizens that "although some fundamental rights such as the right to participate in elections, to vote and to stand for election, may be confined to citizens, human rights are, in principle, to be enjoyed by all persons."[11]

As to inclusion of all minorities under the protection found in ICCPR (Art. 27), a General Comment by the U.N. Human Rights Committee suggests this line of thinking by putting forward an interpretation of the provision that rejects the requirement of nationality and states that the length of residence is an irrelevant criterion. On this basis, the committee opens the way for an understanding according to which immigrants and even visitors could qualify as minorities in the sense of Article 27.[12]

It is exactly such inclusive and pragmatic approaches to human rights and minority rights protection that is needed in the information society when it is seen as both pluralistic and "liquid." Transnationality, migration, and cross-border interaction are not easily combined with traditional measures to protect and promote minority rights. On an abstract level, achieving efficient protection of minorities in an information society presupposes an openness in the perception of minority groups and a willingness among states to take responsibility to respect and promote the rights of members of minority groups residing permanently or temporarily within the jurisdiction.

[...]

Basic Principles for Minority Protection

Moving to a more concrete level, existing and applied basic principles are not only necessary but also suitable for application in the information society. As in a traditional setting, protecting minority rights in a pluralistic and liquid setting demands both a prohibition against discrimination and special measures to enable the members of minorities to preserve and develop their own, separate characteristics.[13]

It is clear from the preparatory work of the ICCPR and the legal literature[14] that the obligation which may be derived from Article 27 goes beyond a prohibition of discrimination and contains elements of a right to de facto equality – for instance, by means of positive measures to combat discrimination. The requirement for the states to do more than not interfere has been stressed by the U.N. Human Rights Committee with regard to the horizontal effect of Article 27 (i.e., the application of Article 27 to private interference with protected rights). Hence, the committee has stated that "positive measures of protection are ... required not only against the acts of the State party itself, ... but also against the acts of other persons within the State party."[15]

In Europe, the double approach is directly reflected in Articles 4 and 5 of the European Framework Convention for the Protection of National Minorities. Article 4 contains both a prohibition against discrimination based on belonging to a national minority and an obligation for the state to guarantee the right of equality before the law and to equal protection under the law. Moreover, a positive obligation to promote full and effective equality between persons belonging to national minorities and those belonging to the majority in the state is stipulated in Article 5. According to this provision, the states shall undertake promotional activities to maintain and develop the cultures of persons belonging to national minorities, and to preserve essential elements of their identity, including their religion, language, traditions, and cultural heritage.

Article 6 calls for a commitment by the state parties to encourage a spirit of tolerance and intercultural dialogue. This provision should be read in light of the preamble, which states that "the creation of a climate of tolerance and dialogue is necessary to enable cultural diversity to be a source and a factor, not of division, but of enrichment for each society."

Conceptually linked to the need for cultural diversity is the connection drawn by the European Court of Human Rights between democracy and pluralism. On several occasions, the Court has stated that pluralism is an inherent part of the concept of democracy applied in a European human rights context. This is illustrated below in connection with specific rights relevant to minorities in an information society.

Specific Minority Rights

It seems evident that a minority right of paramount importance in an information society is the freedom of expression and the rights, derived from this freedom, to receive and impart information. Both as a general human right[16] and as a specific minority right,[17] the freedom of expression enables minorities to express themselves and to impart information and ideas in the minority language.

Not only does the freedom of expression give room for expressions of minorities that diverge from those of the majority, but it also plays a vital role for both minorities and the majority in ensuring and facilitating access and dissemination of pluralistic information, and access to receive such information via media[18] and means of information technology, such as satellite television.[19]

In addition, the European Court of Human Rights has frequently stressed the freedom of expression as an imperative in a democratic state and has demonstrated the intimate link between democracy and pluralism. Thus, the Court has stated that freedom of expression applies "not only to 'information' or 'ideas' that are favorably received or regarded as inoffensive or as a matter of indifference, but also to those that offend, shock or disturb; such are the demands of that pluralism, tolerance and broad-mindedness without which there is no 'democratic society.'"[20]

Case law of the Court also reveals that the principle of pluralism should form the basis of all regulation of the freedom of expression.[21] Such a principle may be derived from the *Informationsverein Lentia case*[22] concerning broadcasting of programs via audiovisual media of information and ideas of general interest, in which the Court stated, "Such an undertaking cannot be successfully accomplished unless it is grounded in the principle of pluralism, of which the State is the ultimate guarantor."

The interrelation between the requirement for pluralism and minority protection is not as clear. In two cases against Turkey,[23] the Court stated that "democracy thrives on freedom of expression. From that point of view, there can be no justification for hindering a political group solely because it seeks to debate in public the situation of part of the state's population and to take part in the nation's political life in order to find, according to democratic rules, solutions capable of satisfying everyone concerned." This statement may lead to the assumption that a line can be drawn from the overarching principle of pluralism as an integral part of the European democratic society to actual or potential protection of members of minorities.[24]

[...]

Other specific minority rights that are relevant in the information society cover the right to assembly, the right to establish and maintain free and peaceful contacts across borders, and the right to participate in cultural, social, and economic life. These substantial rights are found in the European Framework Convention for the Protection of National Minorities, but have no equivalents in binding international documents. A right to enjoy cultural life is derived from Article 27 of the U.N. Covenant on Civil and Political Rights.

The impact of these rights in a digitized setting has not yet been tested by human rights monitoring bodies, but does represent a challenge in a society with an increase in the number and diversity of ethnic, religious, and linguistic minorities. Consequently, this will be addressed below.

Challenges of Digitizing Minority Rights

Efficient protection of the right to peaceful assembly and freedom of association for minorities is a prerequisite for the gathering of minorities and their possibility to share common interests and to maintain and develop their specific culture.[25] Also, it contributes to the realization of a pluralist society and thus is instrumental for the development of an information society capable of addressing the needs and interests of a diverse population.

In a future perspective, the right represents a substantial challenge if invoked in cases of protection of virtual associations – and a number of issues will be added to the list of implications if combined with crossborder activities and communication.

The right to enjoy the cultural life of the minority and to participate in the cultural, social, and economic life of society may be effectively facilitated by the Internet and other ICTs. ICT-based reforms of public-sector and government services, including education and health, and of programs aimed at effective public administration within agriculture and taxation, have been carried through in a number of countries worldwide.[26] An inherent risk in initiatives like these is, however, that their full potential is exploited only if a set of demands is met. It must be ensured that everybody with a need to receive services or other forms of government support via ICT systems has access to the Internet. The fulfillment of this demand may require that the state accept a positive obligation to provide public access to call centers, telecenters, or similar operators of telephone, fax, and Internet services, and to complement such services with regulatory and policy initiatives ensuring equal access for members of minorities as well as of the majority.

In some countries, including Estonia, India, and South Africa, so-called community-based multipurpose community telecenters (MCTs) have been established in rural and remote areas that incorporate Internet access, e-mail, and other computer applications into existing community access telephone centers, and also offer educational and cultural services.[27] Similar models are worth considering in the context of maintaining and developing minority cultures, because they seem suitable for ensuring the enjoyment of both specific minority rights and the basic right to equality, and for facilitating intercultural dialogue within communities.

In a broader perspective, ICT may contribute to understanding of and knowledge about diverse cultural traditions among the majority population and, thus, enhance the promotion of a diverse and pluralist society.

A specific right that needs attention in the information society when applying ICT is the human right to (information) privacy in conjunction with nondiscrimination. For many members and groups of minorities it is essential to their daily life, integrity, and participation in society to be able to communicate with private and public actors without the risk of being registered as belonging to an ethnic, religious, or linguistic minority.

On the other hand, states with pluralistic societies are required to combat discrimination, and to achieve this, in many countries registration of ethnicity is seen not only as a legitimate aim but also as a sufficient means to combat discrimination, raise awareness of discrimination as a societal phenomenon, and disseminate knowledge of discriminatory structures and practices.

Monitoring Minority Rights in a Digitized Setting

A central element in safeguarding the adequate fulfillment of the state's obligations to protect and promote minority rights is the monitoring bodies established within the United Nations and regional human rights systems.

Active inclusion of ICT as a means to enhance the enjoyment of minority rights, and to move the pluralistic society toward diversity, tolerance, and mutual respect, has a positive side effect on monitoring mechanisms. The gathering of information from state organs regarding compliance with international and regional standards is easier, since documents, assessments, judicial reviews, and case law in their original form typically are available on the Web sites of state organs. Also, it is possible to have national human rights institutions, NGOs, labor market organizations, minority groups themselves, and other relevant actors submit material in far more easily than today. The huge amount of available material may – on the other hand – give rise to longer and/or more intense preparatory work within the monitoring bodies. It should, however, be seen as a qualitative improvement rather than an obstacle to efficient monitoring.

Multicultural Jurisdictions

A major challenge envisaged by all societies today is represented by the question of how to deal with the consequences of globalization, including cross-border activities and flows of information, within a traditional perception of the nation-state as autonomous both in territorial terms and in legislative, executive, and administrative powers.[28]

Vis-à-vis minority groups this challenge goes to the root of a core issue of minority protection, the possibility – and in reality often barriers – for minorities to achieve acknowledgment of their status as a group and to enjoy their common culture within this group.[29] It is a crucial aspect of the right of minorities to know that the right not only is an individual right but also is closely linked to the existence of the minority as a group. Self-determination and autonomy of the minority group may, as a consequence of this line of thinking, be seen as a sine qua non for efficient and substantive protection and promotion of individual minority rights.[30]

When focusing on the special features of the information society, the Internet and other information and communication devices may play an important role in de facto strengthening and furthering the enjoyment of minority rights. The setting up of Web sites, chat rooms, and virtual conferences enables members of minority groups spread throughout a country or a region, or across borders, to stay in contact and thereby actively maintain and develop their specific identity and culture. Moreover, it creates a basis for a new perspective on structuring a pluralistic society that acknowledges the right of minorities to live in accordance with their own norms and traditions within their ethnic or religious group or community.

A structure that has been suggested as accommodating differences and at the same time respecting human rights is that of jurisdictional authority shared between the state and the minority groups.[31] In such a structure, the minority is allowed, upon delegation of powers from the state, to regulate life within the minority group. ICT would be an excellent instrument to technically support the implementation of shared jurisdiction. Moreover, it could be used to put in place a system that facilitates and contributes to ensuring that basic principles of the rule of law were governing within the minority group.

From a pure minority approach, a society building on diversification of rights and obligations in this way represents a major step forward in the acknowledgment and promotion of minority rights. It does, however, carry a number of serious human rights problems concerning the protection of the rights of the individual. Would it, for instance, be acceptable for the minority group to interfere with the members' individual rights? And, in the affirmative, what would be the limits for such interference? How would we, for instance, handle restrictions on women's rights to participation and nondiscrimination set up as a consequence of jurisdictional authority within the minority group?

Other questions are linked to the delegation itself, and cover principles guiding the delegation, limitations on the ability/power to delegate, subsequent performance of delegated powers, and monitoring of those powers by the delegating state.[32]

Considering the development of populations and societies worldwide, the possibilities offered by the Internet and other ICT devices, and the – however vague – tendency within the international and regional systems to acknowledge the importance of protection and promotion of minority rights, the time may be ripe to introduce and discuss in depth new perspectives on and systems for efficient minority protection in the information society.

Public or Private Governance of the Internet

Yet another challenge that should be mentioned in the context of minority rights in the information society stems from the governance of the Internet. Thus, it cannot be foreclosed that the choice of private or public governance may have an impact on the efficient protection of minority rights. When addressing this issue, the point of departure may be the assumption that the principle of pluralism applies, in the sense that it must form the basis of the regulation of ways and means of expression, communication, and interchange of thoughts and ideas.

If it is made applicable to the basic minority rights to enjoy cultural life, use minority language, and practice the culture's religion, the principle of pluralism would lead to a requirement for the governing actor of the Internet to ensure that communication and interchange of information in minority languages on minority and other issues are not restricted or interfered with in other ways.

Moreover, it may be argued that a positive obligation exists to adopt measures ensuring and enhancing equality between Internet users from minorities and the majority, as well as to promote conditions for participation and for maintenance and development of minority cultures. This is true at least for a public governing actor, but may also follow from the acknowledged horizontal effect of human rights obligations.

Concluding Remarks

The challenges posed by the development in society toward increased communication and interaction, mobility and migration, as well as cultural, ethnic, and linguistic diversity, make it necessary to address minority rights, issues, and conditions from a new perspective. The perils of a new perspective may be set by available ICTs, especially the Internet, which has the potential to serve as an efficient structure for accessible pluralistic information, and for dialogue and interchange of information, irrespective of language, among members of minorities and between minorities and majorities.

Improvement of minority rights also has to take into consideration new ways of structuring an information society that is pluralistic in its composition but founded on basic principles and values that should be shared by everybody. This does indeed present a major challenge, and a focal point here will be to strike a balance between self-determination within a minority group and adequate safeguard mechanisms for external protection against restrictions on the rights of members of minorities set up by internal regulation within the minority group.

In this context the principle of pluralism should be applied in order to ensure that cultural life, religious practice, communication, and interchange of information in minority languages concerning minority and other issues, are not restricted or in other ways interfered with in a way incompatible with international human rights norms and standards. Application of the same principle to governance of the Internet would ensure a similar protection and create a framework for improving the enjoyment of minority rights.

Information technologies are indeed instrumental for the protection and promotion of minority rights and do possess a potential for facilitating the transformation of society into an information society capable of embracing diversity and creating mutual respect for and understanding of differences in traditions, norms, and ways of living. "Liquid" living is a suitable background for addressing traditional concepts of nationality and affiliation of members of minorities from a new perspective. But it requires human beings, resources and reflections to vitalize the vision of efficient minority protection in a pluralistic information society.

NOTES

1. Bauman, *Liquid Modernity*.
2. Bauman, *Globalization*, 57ff.
3. The Subcommission was renamed the Subcommission on the Promotion and Protection of Human Rights in 1999.
4. U.N. Declaration on the Rights of Persons Belonging to National Ethnic, Religious and Linguistic Minorities, GA Res. 47/135, Dec. 18, 1992.
5. Specific protection of indigenous peoples' human rights is found in ILO Indigenous and Tribal Peoples Convention, No. 169, June 27, 1989.
6. See Treaty on European Union, Art. 6, and Network of Independent Experts on Fundamental Rights, Thematic Comment no. 3, "The Protection of Minorities in the European Union, Apr. 25, 2005, p. 6.
7. The Charter is not yet legally binding, but serves as an important political instruments insofar as it is accepted as guiding all EU actions and policies.
8. Art. 21 (Art. II-81 of the Constitution Treaty).
9. Art. 22 (Art. II-82 of the Constitution Treaty).
10. The list builds on the Capotorti–Deschênes standard. For further details and references, see Nowak, *Commentary to ICCPR*, 642ff.; and Henrard, *Devising an Adequate System of Minority Protection*, 16ff.
11. U.N. Committee on the Elimination of Racial Discrimination, General Comment no. 30, para. 5.
12. U.N. Human Rights Committee, General Comment no. 23, para. 27.

13. U.N. Subcommission on the Prevention of Discrimination and the Protection of Minorities, Cf. the Report of the First Session, UN Doc.E/CN.4/52, sec. V.

14. See, e.g., Nowak, *Commentary to ICCPR*, 657ff.

15. General Comment no. 23, para. 6.1.

16. See ICCPR, Art. 19; ECHR, Art. 10; ACHPR, Art. 9.

17. See European Framework Convention, Art. 9.

18. A specific provision on granting the possibility to access to create and use own media is contained in the European Framework Convention for the Protection of National Minorities, Art. 9 (3).

19. In Denmark, the High Court has addressed the issue of compatibility of denial of the right to set up satellite antennas on the balconies of apartments in order to receive programs in Turkish with the right to receive information. In both cases (U99.656V, U97.190V), no violation was found.

20. The principle was introduced in *Handyside v UK*, Eur. Ct. H.R., 7 Dec. 1976, ser. A, no. 24; Eur. Ct. H.R., §49 and reiterated in a number of cases, such as *Incal v Turkey*, Eur. Ct. H.R., 9 June 1998, para. 46.

21. See Cohen-Jonathan, "Article 10"; and Harris et al., *Law of the European Convention on Human Rights*, 384–386.

22. *Inforamtionsverein Lentia and Others v Austria*, Eur. Ct. H.R., 24 Nov. 1993, para. 38.

23. *United Communist Party of Turkey and Others v Turkey*, Eur. Ct. H.R., 30 Jan. 1998, para. 57; *Socialist Party and Others v Turkey*, Eur. Ct. H.R., 25 May 1998, para. 45.

24. See Henrard, *Devising an Adequate System of Minority Protection*, 91.

25. Minority protection is stressed in connection with ECHR, Art. 11, in *Sidiropoulos and Others v Greece*, Eur. Ct. H.R., 10 July 1998, paras. 41, 44.

26. See Grace et al., "Information and Communication Technologies and Broad-Based Development," 32f.

27. Ibid., 37, 38. A plan of action to develop best-practice models of MCT was adopted at the World Telecommunication Development Conference in Buenos Aires in 1994.

28. The concept of autonomy is analyzed in Skurbaty, *Beyond a One-Dimensional State*. The division into forms and types of autonomy is suggested by Max van der Stoel in the book's prolegomenon, xix f.

29. The complexity of combining individual rights with collective rights.

30. Similar viewpoints are found in Henrard, Devising an Adequate System, 2.; and Tomuschat, *Equality and Non-Discrimination*, 966.

31. See Shachar, *Multicultural Jurisdictions*.

32. A discussion is in Martin Scheinin, *How to Resolve Conflicts Between Individual and Collective Rights?*, 219 ff. See also, on autonomy, Skurbaty, *Beyond a One-Dimensional State*, 565 ff.

BIBLIOGRAPHY

Bauman, Zygmunt. *Globalisation: The Human Consequneces*. Cambridge: Polity Press, 1998.

Bauman, Zygmunt. *Liquid Modernity*. Cambridge: Polity Press, 2000.

Cohen-Jonathan, G. "Article 10." In *La Convention Européenne des Droits de l'Homme. Commentaire article par article*. Ed. L.E. Pettiti et al. Paris: Economica, 1995.

Grace, Jeremy, Charles Kenny, and Christine Zhen-Wei, Qiang. "Information and Communication Technologies and Broad-Based Development. A Partial Review of the Evidence," World Bank working paper no. 12. Washington, DC: World Bank, 2004.

Harris, D. J., M. O'Boyle, and C. Warbrick. *Law of the European Convention on Human Rights.* London: Butterworth, 1995.

Henrard, Kristin. *Devising an Adequate System of Minority Protection: Individual Human Rights, Minority Rights and the Right to Self-Determination.* The Hague: Martinus Nijhoff, 2000.

Nowak, Manfred. *U.N. Covenant on Civil and Political Rights: CCPR Commentary*, 2nd rev. ed. Arlington, VA: N. P. Engel, 2005.

Shachar, Ayelet. *Multicultural Jurisdictions: Cultural Differences and Women's Rights.* Cambridge: Cambridge University Press, 2001.

Skurbaty, Zelim A., ed. *Beyond a One-Dimensional State: An Emerging Right to Autonomy?* Leiden: Martinus Nijhoff, 2005.

HACKTIVISM
All Together in the Virtual

Tim Jordan

Hacking, Cracking, Activism and Hacktivism

Hacktivism is politically motivated hacking. Hacktivism is activism! running free in the electronic veins that enliven our 21st-century, global socio-economies.

So many of us now spend time staring at computer screens. Imagine using a networked screen for work or leisure, and it suddenly ceases to function. You try to input commands, but nothing happens. Suddenly, your screen reads 'All files are being deleted. All files are being deleted.' The same thing is happening to everyone else's computer. The message scrolls and scrolls, and there is nothing anyone can do to prevent it – that is, until someone takes emergency action and pulls electric plugs from their sockets, killing the disaster in the crudest way. These actions were played out in 1988 at the National Aeronautical and Space Administration (NASA) in America. Someone had planted a program on their network that continually copied itself to any other computer connected to the NASA network. These files continued to replicate until each computer ceased to function. The message that files were being deleted turned out to be false, a provocation. The program had been planted by someone protesting against NASA launching space probes that included small nuclear reactors, often described by protesters as potential nuclear bombs. This was hacktivism before the term was invented.

[...]

In 1996, the Critical Arts Ensemble (CAE) issued a call for the development of electronic civil disobedience and the politicization of hackers. They argued that power was shifting from physical locations, embodied in slogans about 'power in the

Tim Jordan, "Hacktivism: All Together in the Virtual," pp. 119–35, 161 from Tim Jordan, *Activism! Direct Action, Hacktivism and the Future of Society* (London: Reaktion Books, 2002).

streets', to virtual locations. The élites, they argued, were increasingly making and remaking the world through electronic flows of power, through cyberspace. CAE called for the tactics of blockage and siege developed by civil disobedience to be reinvented in the virtual realm. They pointed out that power derives increasingly from cyberspatial information flows, and these flows can be blocked.[1] By 1998, these ideas had been turned into one kind of reality with the Electronic Disturbance Theatre's (EDT) attempt to support the Zapatistas through online direct action. They launched a software tool called Floodnet that attempted to constantly reload a targeted website (often that of the Mexican President) in an attempt to slow it down by bombarding it with requests. Floodnet also automated the production of satirical messages from the targeted site. For example, someone targeting a computer would see messages reporting a failure to find a page on a site, with the automated message reading something like 'no human rights found on this server' or 'no democracy found on this server.'

Prior to the emergence of hacktivists like EDT, the politics of hacking was almost exclusively focused on virtual issues with an overriding ethic that held free flows of information, securely accessible to all, to be the highest principle. Hacker politics focused on issues such as the security of computer systems and the implications of security for the privacy of individuals. Such politics also concentrated on discovering ways around censorship of the Internet, often utilizing its global nature to undermine attempts by nationstates to censor content. ...

The rise of hacktivism has not superseded or destroyed previous hacker politics, but has reconfigured it within a broader political landscape. This distinction between 'informational politics', traditionally the centre of hacker politics, and a broadening out into non-virtual politics is a useful one, as it separates out the two main streams of hacktivism. To fully explore these transgressions of the information infrastructures of 21st-century socio-economies, I will look at each of these hacktivist strands in turn.

MVDA: Mass Virtual Direct Action

Mass virtual direct action complicates and extends non-violent direct action. Taking notions of violence and action into cyberspace involves a shift of reality. Things are not the same online as they are offline, and the metaphors or analogies so often used to understand virtual life through real life are slippery. For example, hacking is often described as burglary or theft, and some of the descriptions I have given above imply something similar; hacking is illicit, it is intrusion, it cracks someone's computer. However, if a hacker is a thief, then s/he is the strangest of thieves, because no matter what is stolen, an exact copy is also left behind. Which real-world burglar both takes your video and leaves your video behind? This cannot happen, of course, and this distinction means that we should be wary of applying words to the electronic world that make sense when describing the physical one. With this cautionary statement in mind, we can look at some examples of MVDA and then explore each of its constitutent parts.

During the World Trade Organization (WTO) meeting in Seattle in 1999, there were simultaneous online and offline protests. As demonstrators occupied the streets, hacktivists occupied websites. These protests were set up by a group called the Electrohippie Collective (or ehippies). The ehippies created a small software program that was embedded in a webpage. Anyone who chose to go to that webpage to participate in the protest would automatically download a copy of the program and begin using it from their computer. The program repeatedly loaded pages from the WTO network. If enough people went to the ehippies site, if enough computers were thus running the ehippies program, the WTO network would be overwhelmed with requests and brought to a halt. This virtual action was harmonized with the street actions whose aim was to halt the WTO conference. The attempt to physically prevent the conference from occurring was matched by an attempt to block information flows serving WTO delegates. The ehippies claim that around 450,000 computers participated in the action over five days and that the WTO network was halted on two occasions and significantly slowed through much of the conference.[2]

The ehippies action against the WTO was, in some political ways, similar to EDT's Floodnet,[3] in that both targeted a particular website and attempted to make a point by flooding it with requests. However, EDT has not aimed to bring down a targeted website; instead, it has attempted to make a political protest by slowing a target and by ensuring that suddenly increased traffic on a site is clearly related to a political purpose. A later ehippies action used a similar model when protesting against the Free Trade Area of the Americas (FTAA) conference in Quebec in 2001. Rather than trying to bring down the targeted network, the ehippies attempted 'to demonstrate that online action could be constructed to make a point in a directed manner, rather than seeking to cause indiscriminate closure of a site'.[4]

Similar actions have been taken up by other groups with varying levels of technological sophistication. The Italian group Netstrike has the following advice: 'Now insert the target web address in your navigation bar. Keep clicking Reload continuously.'[5] Sitting at your computer repeatedly pressing the reload button may be boring, but it has a similar effect to utilizing software designed to do the same thing automatically (such software is also thoughtfully made available by Netstrike). ...

'Mass' means that these actions are meaningless unless a large number of people participate. This may seem obvious, but large numbers of people mean quite different things in cyberspace, where what 'people' can do can often be done more efficiently by computers. Attacks that aim to slow or stop targeted computers by blockading them require, in MVDA, many individuals, but could also be done by one individual utilizing programs. These are known as denial-of-service (DOS) attacks, because they seek to remove the target from the Internet, denying it service by overwhelming it with masses of requests for information. Such attacks have crippled major online sites such as ebay.com or yahoo.com.[6] They are easily launched if small groups or even individuals use programs such as Stacheldracht. Oxblood Ruffin, foreign minister for the hacktivist group Cult of the Dead Cow, makes the following graphic comparison: 'The only difference between a program like Stacheldraht (a DOS application written by The Mixter) and the … Electrohippies is the difference between blowing something up and being pecked to death by a duck.'

The duck is preferable to the bomb for political, not technical, reasons. MVDA hacktivists seek to engage people, not just stop a targeted site. A mass of people is key, because then the protest is not about one person's technical abilities, but about the choice of many people to protest. This provides the same legitimation for a protest as thousands of people in the street might. It makes the protest a popular protest. The second political aim is to enrol people, to draw them into discussion, reflection and action. Many hacktivists call for debate prior to and after an action, using the communication resources of the Internet. This builds a movement offering many people who might be unable to attend a demonstration, for whatever reason, the chance to participate. It also allows a moment of commitment, perhaps a small one, in which people must decide whether they will or will not participate. A mass event needs the masses. Hacktivists producing denial-of-service actions choose a technically inefficient means to serve politically efficient ends.

However, a problem with the analogy to mass street protest is that when protesters block a street, it is impossible to miss the message and impossible for protesters to miss each other and the feeling of solidarity in the street, while in cyberspace, packets of information flowing across the Net are simply packets of information. Spikes of activity may be recorded on a targeted site, and the site's utility may be impaired by being slowed, but it is unclear whether the meaning of this action will be apparent to those on the receiving end. There are no passers-by in cyberspace. Whereas a street demonstration will reach whoever else happens to be in the vicinity – protesters and passers-by – and whoever watches media reporting, no such chance encounters will occur in cyberspace. Nor might solidarity really be built, as each protester will not know how many others are participating at the same time. Of course, all those who participate have some idea of what they are doing and why, but whether the protest registers more widely is unclear.

Virtual is the second component of MVDA, replacing non-violent when comparing MVDA and NVDA. This transition from violent to virtual needs explanation. The most often used means of explaining what is meant by virtual is to ask, 'When you are on the telephone, where does the conversation take place?' In your living room? But then your partner in communication is not there. In their room? But now you are absent. In the wires? But now both of your bodies are absent, yet still the communication occurs. Virtual communication is like this; it occurs in the wires. Such a place makes the notion of physical violence redundant, but violence may lurk within the virtual in two ways. First, many real-world institutions are affected by cyberspace. Computer networks control all sorts of real-world facilities, from dams and air-traffic control systems to financial institutions. Hacktivists do not automatically escape the possibility of violence by being virtual. Second, violence is not always physical, and damage to emotions and selves can occur in virtual lands. There have been long discussions about various sorts of emotional violence that have been inflicted in cyberspace. As long as an assault has dimensions in addition to physical ones, cyberspace can be home to a virtual version. In both of these ways, violence does not disappear for hacktivists, but must be rethought as they transgress information codes. As we will see later, for example, some argue that the violence hacktivists choose by utilizing denial-of-service attacks constitutes censorship.

Direct action is the third component of MVDA. ... MVDA attempts to take something on directly and prevent it. The clearest example is the attempt to mirror street protests halting the WTO Seattle conference by halting information flows serving that conference. Here, similar direct actions were taken in real and virtual spaces. However, MVDA rarely functions so clearly as a direct action. It can be weak as a direct action, because in cyberspace objects are easily replicated. This means that whereas a sit-in on a street can be difficult to move or a protest camp against a road can occupy a key piece of ground, in cyberspace the targeted computers can move. This can be done more or less simply and more or less expensively, but it is far more easily done in cyberspace than in real space. For example, all sites on the Internet are assigned a unique number that identifies them. When a denial-of-service MVDA is launched, it attacks the unique numbers of the targeted sites. However, it is possible to simply change the numbers and dodge an attack. Problems associated with such shifts should not be underestimated, but they offer opportunities to avoid MVDA that are not available offline. For these reasons, online direct actions may have greater effects as symbolic protests than as direct actions.

MVDA consists of these forces of mass, virtual and direct action. Each force interacts with the others in ways that have created a new class of civil disobedience. These actions bear many of the hallmarks of classic nonviolent direct actions yet are passed through the looking glass of virtuality and become something different as electronic civil disobedience. These are new political moments that did not exist before the crossover of hacking and activism! However, this does not mean that many previously existing actions taken by hackers have either disappeared or are irrelevant to hacktivism. Far from it. Many hacks have been reinvented as hacktivist actions, and an alternate vision of hacktivist politics has emerged with them. The deep concern of hackers for free, secure flows of information forms the second arm of hacktivism.

The Digitally Correct Hacktivist

For a long time, hackers' politics were closely tied to virtual issues – encryption, privacy, access. It is in hacking that we find traditional hacker pursuits such as cracking, developing tools to aid cracking and defending rights to secure, private communication. While these have always been concerns for hackers, the advent of hacktivism has given these actions a new political edge. The hacker group that perhaps best embodies this change is Cult of the Dead Cow (CDC), begun in 1984. The time during which they have been involved in the hacking community and digital issues shows that their work began well before hacktivism, yet they have also embraced it. Two of their projects show how the traditions of hacking have been given a new life with the politicization offered by hacktivism: Peekabooty and Back Orifice.

Peekabooty is the result of a group initiated by CDC working under the banner of Hacktivismo. This group targets censorship of the Internet by legitimating itself on the basis of the United Nations Declaration of Human Rights. This declaration asserts freedom of expression for all, including the freedom to receive as well as offer views. The Hacktivism Declaration states:

> Hacktivismo is a special operations group sponsored by the CULT OF THE DEAD COW (CDC). We view access to information as a basic human right. We are also interested in keeping the Internet free of state-sponsored censorship and corporate chicanery so all opinions can be heard.[7]

The centrality of free flows of information, both to and from everyone, is clear. The concern prompting Hacktivismo is that a number of nation-states are limiting their citizens' access to the Internet. China is the example most often used, but there are other states that have established national firewalls to block politically sensitive material (firewalls are filtering mechanisms that control access to and from the Internet). For example, whether you can access CNN or the BBC online from within China has varied depending on whether the Chinese firewall has been set to allow it. A concrete initiative to address such problems is Peekabooty.

It seems clear that Peekabooty will be a network that anyone can use across the Internet to both bypass national firewalls, thereby gaining access to all information available on the Net, and to anonymize both senders and receivers of data. It is described as a 'distributed collaborative privacy network. It allows the evasion of most forms of … filtering and makes Web page requests directly to a distributed server cloud that processes the requests and trans-serves content back to the requesting client'.[8] Someone who is behind a firewall will be able to make a request to a computer running Peekabooty that will then establish a virtual network to a number of other computers. (it is claimed that it will be difficult to detect whether Peekabooty is running on a network or not, but it may be possible to watch for Peekabooty, which will obviously undermine its utility). These 'other computers' from the 'server cloud', which simply means a number of other computers that transfer requests from the originating computer. Instead of requesting a known Internet site, whose address is blocked by the firewall, the request will be made to a Peekabooty-running computer that is not blocked by a firewall. This Peekabooty-running computer will then connect to the Peekabooty network. One of the computers connected to the network will access the requested material and pass it back through the server cloud to the original requesting computer. There will be no direct connection between requesting and responding computer, and each jump in between will ensure anonymity. These links through the server cloud will also shift dynamically – that is, they will change constantly. This means that a censoring government will have to constantly close down many Peekabooty-running computers to close the Peekabooty network down. Which ultimately means that as long as enough computers participate, closing Peekabooty will be difficult, if not impossible.

Should this network prove successful, it will provide a powerful antidote to national censorship. As Hacktivismo participants recognize, there is no guarantee that governments will not utilize powerful resources to prevent Peekabooty. For example, if a Peekabooty-running computer can be identified, then someone accessing that computer could be traced. Nevertheless, there is, to these hacktivists, a powerful incentive to try, as well as (it currently appears) the technical expertise to succeed.

Peekabooty attempts to prevent the erection of national borders in cyberspace. The focus on ensuring freedom of access to the Internet's huge store of information is also a focus on informational politics. In this sense, it differs from MVDA, which itself attempts to participate in an activist! campaign. The digitally correct hacktivist directly builds a particular informational politics; s/he is not building tools that serve other campaigns. This is similar to the distinction between pleasure politics and pleasure and politics. MVDA-based actions are always for a cause, whereas digitally correct hacktivism is its own cause.

[...]

As with Peekabooty, Back Orifice is a tool focused on the second key arena of hacktivism: ensuring privacy and security online with full access to information. Hacktivismo, as developed by CDC and others, sees little separation between these two issues and for good reason. Providing full access to the Internet in countries that seek to restrict it may be rendered meaningless if people and the sites they visit can be traced. The announcement of Hacktivismo includes this example: 'In August, 1998, eighteen year old Turk Emre Ersoz was found guilty of 'insulting the national police' in an Internet forum after participating in a demonstration that was violently suppressed by the police. His ISP provided the authorities with his address.'[9] Freedom to express your own views and receive all the information available on the Internet can be impaired both by restricting access and by refusing privacy. These two intertwined aims serve a virtual politics that is not restricted to the Internet, but is most at home there. The ability to access and offer information forms the central political principle of this arm of hacktivism.

Information, Irrelevance and Other Interests

Before concluding this chapter, it is important to note that hacktivism, like all the themes of activism!, can fail to develop the politics to which it claims to be committed. Unsurprisingly, MVDA hacktivists and digitally correct hacktivists are prone to different failures. Some of these difficulties have already been mentioned, but it will be useful to draw them together here.

As we have seen, the analogy between MVDA and street protest is ambiguous. While it is true that MVDA's allow many to participate who cannot physically be at a demonstration, at the same time those participating virtually do not take on the risk of the crowd or feel its solidarity. MVDA can perhaps be seen as an easy option. As Oxblood Ruffin said in criticism of an ehippies' MVDA, 'I know from personal experience that there is a difference between street and on-line protest. I have been chased down the street by a baton-wielding police officer on horseback. Believe me, it takes a lot less courage to sit in front of a computer.'[10] Not only might online protests fail to enrol and enthuse participants in the way street protests can; they may also allow those who might have participated to avoid confrontation. MVDA undoubtedly has potential, but it also has pitfalls.

Similarly, digitally correct hacktivism may create tools such as Back Orifice or Peekabooty, but there are also problems. This type of hacktivism aims to provide tools to ensure free flows of secure information; it makes – on a point of principle – little judgement concerning the nature of information sent in these free flows. The Hacktivismo FAQ exhibits this difficulty:

Q: Do you think all information should be accessible?
A: No. That's why we talk about 'lawfully published' information in the Hacktivismo Declaration. Essentially that cuts out things like legitimate government secrets, kiddie porn, matters of personal privacy, and other accepted restrictions. But even the term 'lawfully published' is full of land-mines. Lawful to whom? What is lawful in the United States can get you a bullet in the head in China. At the end of the day we recognize that some information needs to be controlled. But that control falls far short of censoring material that is critical of governments, intellectual and artistic opinion, information relating to women's issues or sexual preference, and religious opinions. That's another way of saying that most information wants to be free; the rest needs a little privacy, even non-existence in the case of things like kiddie porn. Everyone will have to sort the parameters of this one out for themselves.[11]

In this passage, 'lawfully published' information is sanctioned by hacktivism, but immediately this is subject to a critique that asks who defines what is lawful. There is a deep difficulty here between a principle of enabling flows of information and judging some types of information as wrong. The right to free flows of information can only, barely, take a stand against some of the most extreme forms of human exploitation. Digitally correct hacktivism may be a conduit for all sorts of politics, activisms of the past, present and future.

Codes of Information, Coding Transgression

Hacktivism has two currents that intertwine and separate. They also contradict each other. The current that places a premium on free flows of information sometimes sees little sense in the current that generates mass forms of online protest. This can be seen clearly in arguments around denial-of-service attacks. As already noted, denial of service is the restraint of information, the jamming and prevention of someone contributing to or receiving information, by preventing their website or Internet connections from working. CDC's response to the ehippies justification of their distributed denial-of-service actions criticized the ehippies denial of free flows of information:

> Denial of Service, is Denial of Service, is Denial of Service, period ... Denial of Service attacks are a violation of the First Amendment, and of the freedoms of expression and assembly. No rationale, even in the service of the highest ideals, makes them anything than what they are – illegal, unethical, and uncivil. One does not make a better point in a public forum by shouting down one's opponent.[12]

It would be too strong to see such a divergence as some sort of split; hacktivism is not organized enough for such things as splits to appear. But it reflects the fact that two underlying politics of hacktivism may both contradict each other and transgress the information codes of 21st-century societies.

There are other types of hacktivist actions that circulate through and around these two major currents. Culture jamming finds a ready home on the Internet with hacktivists both propagating jams and cracking websites to recreate them jammed. On different occasions, the American Central Intelligence Agency's website has been renamed the Central Stupidity Agency, and political parties have found satirical cartoons inserted on their sites. On different political terrain, cracktivists break into networks to protest. After India tested nuclear weapons, a hacker gained entry to Indian government networks and threatened to trash them if the country persisted. These types of actions continue in and around hacktivism, but if we are seeking to grasp the innovations within activism! that hacktivism brings, then the two currents we have examined closely are key.

Hacktivists developing MVDA are fully immersed in the particular political ethics they support. The ehippies actions have supported the antiglobalization movement, EDT has plunged itself into Zapatista politics, and Netstrike has helped to fight judicial murder in the US. In these circumstances, the information flows are bent and twisted to invent new forms of mass protest that are no longer dependent on the co-presence of many tangible bodies. Here, hacktivism transgresses information codes to reproduce them as protest.

[...]

Hacktivists focusing on the importance of free flows of information are developing a politics in itself. In political terms, Peekabooty and Back Orifice are about nothing other than the virtual politics of secure access to information. The tools serve the ethics in ways that make them almost inextricably the same. Peekabooty, if it works, will embody in its very nature a commitment to the transgressive power of information on the Internet. Here, hacktivists are not so much bending, twisting and reshaping information flows as creating alternative infrastructures to enable new types of flow. Here, hacktivism transgresses information codes to recreate them as a politics of information.

Hacktivists of all types play in the information codes that form the infrastructures of 21st-century socio-economies. They transgress the flows of information both to create new forms of protest and to generate a new, activist politics of information. The geeks have emerged in politics. Activism! has hacktivisms within it.

NOTES

1. CAE (Critical Art Ensemble), *Electronic Civil Disobedience and Other Unpopular Ideas* (New York, 1996).
2. Electrohippies Collective (2000), 'Client-side Distributed Denial-of-Service: Valid Campaign Tactic or Terrorist Act?; Occasional Paper no. 1', available. at http://www.gn.apc.org/pmhp/ehippies
3. Though it should be made clear that the two are technically different.
4. Electrohippies Collective (2001), 'The FTAA Action and May Day "Cyber-Hysteria" communiqué May 2001', available at http://www.gn.apc.org/pmhp/ehippies
5. Quoted from Netstrike website then being mirrored at http://www.contrast.org/netstrike/howto/istruzioni_en.html At the time of writing, the main site, www.netstrike.it, had been blocked by Italian magistrates.
6. O. Ruffin, 'Valid Campaign Tactic or Terrorist Act?: The Cult of the Dead Cow's Response to Client-side Distributed Denial-of-Service 2000', available at http://www.gn.apc.org/pmhp/ehippies
7. Cult of the Dead Cow, 'The Hacktivismo FAQ', available at http://www.cult-deadcow.com/cDc_files/HacktivismoFAQ.html
8. *Ibid.*; for demonstrations of Peekabooty, see TechTV reports available at http://www.techtv.com/print/story/0,23102,3337379,00.html
9. CDC and Hacktivismo (2001), 'A Special Message of Hope', available at http://www.cultdeadcow.com/cDc_files/declaration.html
10. Ruffin, 'Valid Campaign Tactic'.
11. Cult of the Dead Cow, 'The Hacktivismo FAQ'.
12. Ruffin, 'Valid Campaign Tactic'.

VII GAMES, GAMING, META-UNIVERSES

Introduction

While cybercultures have political and financial dimensions, the one that appears most promising in terms of everyday use is the computer game movement.

Computer games of various kinds and the increasing popularity of meta-universes such as *Second Life* constitute the recreational as well as commercially profitable component of ICTs. Games provide narrative form, interactivity, and social linkages for different age groups. Yet these are not about leisure and pleasure alone, as the articles here demonstrate. Computer games and their link to violence, hate crimes, copyright, and community are explored here.

Many of the articles try to provide theoretical frameworks for studying the gameworld. Whether games constitute narratives, the role of stories and temporal organization, the themes of choice, and interactivity are addressed in several of these contributions. Social networks and subcultural groupings are built around networked games, suggest commentators.

Feminist readings of the genre look at the gendered nature of computer and online games, and find that women players often see game expertise as a means of empowerment. In like fashion, critical cyberculture studies looks at race in computer games, noting, in particular, the stereotypes of people of color and sexuality in gameworlds. Bodies, images, and plots in gameworlds invariably reflect and in some cases reinforce existing social prejudices and stereotypes.

Jesper Juul's article examines the debates around the narrative theory of games. Juul first provides a brief summary of the arguments that suggest that games can be read as narratives because most of them possess storylines and characteristics of narratives. He also problematizes the theme of translation – of narratives between different media, for example, *Star Wars* – the movie and the game. Analyzing time in the game, Juul concludes that one cannot have interactivity – which means synchronous time – and narrative (which involves the time of the plot and the time of narration), and that the relationship between reader and story and player and game are completely different.

Torill Mortensen's article is a reading of the successful multiplayer game, World of Warcraft (WoW). From a description of the Multi-User Dungeons (MUDs) and the popularity of multiplayer games, Mortensen draws attention to the parallels between them. An analysis of WoW reveals that the game is primarily social gaming on a scale not achieved by MUDs. Hence, Mortensen argues, role-play games possess their own social rules. Massively Multiplayer Online Role-Playing Games (MMORPGs) help the players develop their own little microgames and universes inside the main game and, like MUDs, encourage players' individual creativity.

It is only in the recent past that the gaming industry has begun to acknowledge women digital gamers. While studies have been made of the representation of women in games, this recent article focuses on women gamers. Pam Royse et al. see women's use of gaming as "technologies of the gendered self," thus expanding the Foucauldian theory. Beginning with the assumption that gaming is a set of technologies through which the self can be constructed, they explore how adult women gamers of various kinds develop their identities. Dealing with constant and "hardened" gamers – termed "power gamers" in the article – moderate gamers, and non-gamers, the authors see a varied response to and appropriation of such technologies. Non-gamers retained the stereotype of the feminine by their rejection of gaming technology. Moderate gamers had an uneasy relationship with the technology, where their aim was a limited amount of control (over the environment and narrative of the game) and escape. Power gamers, on the other hand, were intensely competitive, and were driven by the need to master the skills and technologies needed to win. Pleasure, argue, Royse et al., stems from winning here. Through such victories power gamers assert control and agency and ultimately construct a technologized female self.

Shifting the terrain slightly to video culture, David Leonard's article explores the continuing racialized nature of sports games such as *SSX*, *Tony Hawk*, and *BMX XXX*. Beginning with the "fantasy" of the triumph of white masculinity in the absence of people of color and women, Leonard argues that at the "ideological core" of virtual extreme sport is the white, masculine mastery of untamed space. There exists, he suggests, a hegemonic and unmarked notion of whiteness in such games. Where there are "characters" of color in these games (*SSX* and *SSX Tricky*), they are very often stereotypes or caricatures. Such games, argues Leonard, respond to the crisis of confidence, self-esteem, and masculinity among 1990s white males. Even more racialized are those games set in America's ghettoes. *Thug*, *BMX XXX*, and other games represent ghettoes as exotic spaces to be controlled (from the safety of their white homes) while delinking them from the economic, political, and social contexts that produced the ghettoes. Leonard also addresses the highly sexualized nature of many of these games, noting that the "prize" in most of these games, even in their censored version, is a naked woman. It is significant, notes Leonard, that the black or Asian woman in such games is portrayed in ways in which one cannot ignore the hypersexual body that affirms racial stereotypes.

With *Second Life* moving beyond mere gaming and social space into a space of commerce and profit, its regulation has become a matter of legal debate and concern. Andrew Herman et al. provide one of the most rigorous theoretical frameworks for exploring the virtual world. They argue that intellectual property of consumer-created products (*Second Life* was one of the first to grant rights to users for the products they create in the virtual world) is a performative that generates goodwill. Yet goodwill also, they argue, is produced through power relations. These relations are the effect of "cultures of circulation," specifically the circulation of commodities and cultural forms. With increasing "interactivity," consumers help develop gameplay, and this lends a different dimension to marketing and commerce, state Herman et al. Moving on to the worlds of online gaming, they argue that these are not simply a class of gameplay, but a "variable set of legally structured and contractually bounded computing practices." Varying degrees of extensibility – the ability to customize, control, and elaborate the users' presence – are bound up with property and labor relations. Herman et al. conclude that gameworlds mark the extension of the neoliberal economy into virtual space, where the content and sociability are both governed by the laws of the market economy.

25 GAMES TELLING STORIES
A Brief Note on Games and Narratives

Jesper Juul

Introduction

As questions go, this is not a bad one: Do games tell stories? Answering this should tell us both *how* to study games and *who* should study them. The affirmative answer suggests that games are easily studied from within existing paradigms. The negative implies that we must start afresh.

But the answer depends, of course, on how you define any of the words involved. In this article, I will be examining some of the different ways to discuss this. ...

The operation of framing something as something else works by taking some notions of the source domain (narratives) and applying them to the target domain (games). This is not neutral; it emphasises some traits and suppresses others. Unlike this, the act of *comparing* furthers the understanding of differences and similarities, and may bare hidden assumptions.

The article begins by examining some standard arguments *for* games being narrative. There are at least three common arguments: 1) We use narratives for everything. 2) Most games feature narrative introductions and back-stories. 3) Games share some traits with narratives.

The article then explores three important reasons for describing games as being non-narrative: 1) Games are not part of the narrative media ecology formed by movies, novels, and theatre. 2) Time in games works differently than in narratives. 3) The relation between the reader/viewer and the story world is different than the relation between the player and the game world.

Jesper Juul, "Games Telling stories? A brief note on games and Narratives," from *Game Studies: the international journal of computer game research* 1:1 (July 2001), http://www.gamestudies. org/0101/juul-gts/ © 2001 by Jesper Juul.

The article works with fairly traditional definitions of stories and narratives, so as a final point I will consider whether various experimental narratives of the 20th century can in some reconcile games and narratives.

Telling Stories

Everything Is Narrative/Everything Can be Presented as Narratives

The first argument is a compelling one, as it promises a kind of holistic view of the world: Since we use narratives to make sense of our lives, to process information, and since we can tell stories about a game we have played, no genre or form can be *outside* the narrative.

The problem is that this really is an *a priori* argument. Narratives may be fundamental to human thought, but this does not mean that everything *should* be described in narrative terms. And that something can be presented in narrative form does not mean that it *is* narrative.

Ideal Stories/Back-stories

A more interesting argument centres on the fact that most games have a story written on the package, in the manual, or in intro-sequences, placing the player's playing in the context of a larger story (back-story), and/or creating an ideal story that the player has to realise:

If we play *Space Invaders* (Taito 1977), we are presented with an ideal story that we have to realise using skill. A prehistory is suggested in *Invaders*: An invasion presupposes a situation before the invasion. It is clear from the science fiction we know that these aliens are evil and should be chased away. So the title suggests a simple structure with a positive state broken by an external evil force. It is the role of the player to re-create this original positive state. This is, of course, a sequence often found in folk tales: An initial state, an overturning of this state, and a restoration of the state.

But it works in a different way: If we *play* Space Invaders, we find that we cannot actually restore the initial state; we cannot win since every wave of aliens is followed by another. As players we are fighting to *realise* an ideal sequence of events, but the actual playing is not this sequence.

Most modern, single player non-arcade games such as *Half-Life* (Valve software 1998) actually let you complete the game: through countless saves and reloads it is possible to realise the ideal sequence that Half-life defines. Obviously, only a microscopic fraction of the play sessions actually follow the ideal path, but Half-Life does succeed in presenting a fixed sequence of events that the player can then afterwards retell.[1] This means that some games *use* narratives for some purposes.

Similarities

The above Space Invaders example also means that games share some traits with narratives: Many games feature reversals such as movements from a lack to the lack being resolved. Jens F. Jensen has used this trait of Space Invaders to argue that computer games, while being deviant, are narratives (1988).

Additionally, many games have quest structures, and most computer games have protagonists (though this is less common in non-electronic games). As Janet Murray suggests in *Hamlet on the Holodeck*, such similarities would indicate that there is a promising future for digital storytelling and interactive narratives, that games and narratives are not very far apart.

It is also an oft-repeated but problematic point that game sessions are experienced linearly, just like narratives. (See Aarseth 1997, p.2.) I will return to this but briefly note that this idea ignores the player's experience of being an active participant – this experience is so strong that most people will involuntarily change bodily position when encountering interactivity, from the lean backward position of narratives to the lean forward position of games. And playing a game includes the awareness that the game session is just one out of many possible to be had from *this game*.

Is This It?

It is thus possible, in different ways, to view games as being in some way connected to narratives, but does this really answer the opening question? The above points would indicate that games and narratives do not live in different worlds, but can in some ways work together: A narrative may be used for telling the player what to do or as rewards for playing. Games may spawn narratives that a player can use to tell others of what went on in a game session.

Games and narratives can on some points be said to have similar traits. This does mean that the strong position of claiming games and narratives to be *completely* unrelated (my own text, Juul 1999 is a good example) is untenable.

But we also have to look at differences.

The Problem of Translation

I will now use some narrative theory in an operation for which it was not intended. The basic problem of *the narrative* is the fact that a narrative can never be viewed independently, *an sich*. We can never see the story itself; we can only see it through another medium like oral storytelling, novels, and movies. The classical argument for the existence of narratives is then the fact that a story can be translated from one medium to another: "This transposability of the story is the strongest reason for arguing that narratives are indeed structures independent of any medium" (Chatman 1978, p.20).

Correspondingly, Peter Brooks says: "Narrative may be a special ability or competence that [...] when mastered, allows us to summarise and retransmit narratives in other words and other languages, to transfer them into other media, while remaining recognisably faithful to the original narrative structure and message" (Brooks 1984, pp. 3–4). And this may seem somewhat unproblematic; we can never get everything between media, but at least something seems to get transported from medium to medium. A recounting of Pride and Prejudice the movie will be recognisable to somebody who has read the book.

Translating What?

This brings us to the problem of what we actually mean by saying that something can be translated from one medium to another. In a probably slightly limited view of narratives, narratives can be split into a level of discourse (the telling of the story) and the story (the story told). The story-part can then be split into two parts, *existents* (actors and settings) and *events* (actions and happenings). (Chatman 1978, p.19) A story can then be recognised by having the same existents (with the same names) and the same events; this is what we usually mean by talking of "the same story".

This can be used the other way, as a test of whether the computer game is a narrative medium: If the computer game is a narrative medium, stories from other media must be retellable in computer games, and computer games must be retellable in other media. On a superficial level, this seems straightforward since many commercial movies are repackaged as games, Star Wars is an obvious example. The other way around, games transferred into movies are less common, but examples include Mario Brothers, Mortal Kombat, and Tomb Raider. Upon further examination, we will find the situation to be much more complex:

From Movie to Game: *Star Wars*

The arcade game *Star Wars* (Atari 1983) is based on the George Lucas movie of the same name (1977). In *the movie* Star Wars, an army of rebels fight a heroic battle against the evil galactic empire. The dramatic peak of the movie is when the rebel army and the protagonist *Luke Skywalker* must attack the evil empire's new weapon *the death star*. The Star Wars game is in three phases, in all of which the player controls a spaceship from the inside, presumably as Luke Skywalker. The first phase takes place in space, where we fight hostile spacecraft. The second phase is on the death star, fighting different objects on the death star surface. In the third phase we fly through a tunnel in the death star to attack an exhaust port. This makes the death star explode. First phase corresponds to an in-movie battle before Luke flies to the death star – except that the rebel fleet is absent. Second phase has no clear correlate in the movie. The third phase corresponds to a scene in the movie – again with the rebel fleet being absent. If you complete the mission, the death star explodes. So the game copies a small part of the movie.

The primary thing that encourages the player to connect game and movie is the title "Star Wars" on the machine and on the screen. If we imagine the title removed from the game, the connection would not be at all obvious. It would be a game where one should hit an "exhaust port" (or simply a square), and the player could note a similarity with a scene in Star Wars, but you would not be able to reconstruct the events in the movie from the game. The prehistory is missing, the rest of the movie, all personal relations. Possibly we are even missing the understanding that we are fighting a death star (whatever that is). Finally the most obvious: If you do not complete the mission, this is unlike the movie; if you complete the mission, another death star appears – which is also unlike the movie.

Thus, Star Wars the game can not be said to contain a narrative that can be recognised from Star Wars the movie: Most characters from the movie are missing, and the few events that are included in the game have become simulations where the player can either win or fail. The same thing goes for the second batch of Star Wars games. *Star Wars: Racer* (Lucasarts 1999) features the race sequence of *Star Wars: Episode I* (Lucas 1999), but only that.[2]

From Game to Story

I will only briefly be covering game-story translations, since they are fairly uncommon. If we look at the Mortal Kombat (Midway games 1993) game, it is a fighting game (beat'em'up) where different opponents (humans or computer players) battle in an arena. It is thus a dynamic system that allows many different people to interact with many different outcomes. The Mortal Kombat movie (Anderson 1995) is not a dynamic system, but a story with a specific set of characters entering a Mortal Kombat game and playing through with specific outcomes. The fairly nondescript game characters and open player positions become more detailed movie characters; the simulation is converted into specific events.

Correspondingly, if we recount a game of chess, our playing of the entire Half-Life game or a multi player game of Starcraft, the existents and events will be transferred, but not the dynamic systems.[3] Our retelling will not be a game, and in fact much of the vast journey that it takes to complete Half-life would be excruciatingly dull if retold in any detail.

The concept of existents is best suited for physical games, where the number of manipulable elements is, at least in principle, finite. Problem is that programs are basically existent-creating machines: Computer games allow for the easy production of infinite numbers of existents, many action games in fact come with a infinite number of existents in the form of opponents. The other problem with the concept of existents is that it in itself does not specify what attributes of the existent are important, whereas game rules feature a strict hierarchy of important and non-important features – Erving Goffman calls this the "rules of irrelevance". (Goffman 1961, p.19)

We should also note that most modern games feature cut-scenes, i.e. passages where the player cannot do anything but most simply watch events unfolding.

TABLE 25.1   A table of narrative – game translations

Movies / Novels etc.	Game
Existent	Existent
	or
	Continuous production of existents (i.e. hordes of opponents)
Event	Event (cut-scene)
	or
	Simulation with multiple outcomes
Sequence of events	Selected events as events or simulations
	or
	Ideal sequence of events that the player has to actualise by mastering the simulations[4]
Character	Character (cut-scene)
	or
	Player position (game)

Cut-scenes typically come in the form of introductions and scenes when the player has completed part of the game.

It is then possible to describe in a more general way how games get translated into narratives, and how narratives get translated in to games (see table 25.1).

Note that both directions of the translation leave plenty of room for improvisation and carry many optional operations. In short, games based on movies tend to pick a few select action sequences, which are then simulated in game sequences – as we saw with Star Wars. Character description and development is either ignored or done in cut-scenes (since this is too hard to implement in game form). Working from game to movie, the game is no longer a game, but is rather presented as specific game sessions, played by specific characters, with specific outcomes. The characters also tend to become more developed: Tomb Raider's heroine Lara Croft acquires much more of a past and personality in the Tomb Raider movie.

Time, Game, and Narrative

Narrative is a … double temporal sequence …: There is the time of the thing told and the time of the narrative (the time of the signified and the time of the signifier). This duality not only renders possible all the temporal distortions that are commonplace in narratives (three years of the hero's life summed up in two sentences of a novel or in a few shots of a "frequentative" montage in film, etc.). More basically, it invites us to consider that one of the functions of narrative is to invent one time scheme in terms of another time scheme. (Christian Metz, quoted from Genette 1980, p.33)

In the classical narratological framework, a narrative has two distinct kinds of time, the *story time*, denoting the time of the events told, in their chronological order, and the *discourse time*, denoting the time of the telling of events (in the order in which they are told). To read a novel or watch a movie is to a large extent about reconstructing a story on the basis of the discourse presented.

In a verbal narrative, the grammatical tense will necessarily present a temporal relation between the time of the narration (narrative time) and the events told (story time). Additionally, it is possible to talk of a third time, the reading or viewing time (Genette 1980, p. 34). While movies and theatre do not have a grammatical tense to indicate the temporal relations, they still carry a basic sense that even though the viewer is watching a movie, now, or even though the players are on stage performing, the events told are *not* happening *now*.

"In Eisenstein's account there is the sense that the text before us, the play or the film, is the performance of a "prior" story" (Bordwell 1985, p.15). We cannot necessarily describe this as a specific temporal relation (hence "prior") but there is a fundamental distance between the story time and discourse time. As Christian Metz notes in the above quote, narratives rely heavily on this distance or non-identity between the events and the presentation of these events.

Time in the Computer Game

If we then play an action-based computer game like *Doom II* (ID Software 1994), it is hard to find a distance between story time, narrative time, and reading/viewing time. We may find a representation, and as a player you try to reconstruct some events from this representation: The blocky graphics can be interpreted so far as the player controls a character, whose facial expression is represented in the bottom centre. On the illustration this person has been cornered by a large pink monster, whose hostile intents are clearly identifiable. Players are attacked by monsters; puzzles must be solved to get to the next level.

It is clear that the events represented cannot be *past* or *prior*, since we as players can influence them. By pressing the CTRL key, we fire the current weapon, which influences the game world. In this way, the game constructs the story time as *synchronous* with narrative time and reading/viewing time: the story time is *now*. Now, not just in the sense that the viewer witnesses events now, but in the sense that the events are *happening* now, and that what comes next is not yet determined.

In an "interactive story" game where the user watches video clips and occasionally makes choices, story time, narrative time, and reading/viewing time will move apart, but when the user can act, they must necessarily implode: it is impossible to influence something that has already happened. This means that *you cannot have interactivity and narration at the same time*. And this means in practice that games almost never perform basic narrative operations like flashback and flash forward.[5] Games are almost always chronological.

This article is not about all the intricacies of time in games (see Juul, forthcoming). Let us simply note that games may also have a speed that is not equal to the playing time – a day & night in the online multi player game EverQuest (Verant Interactive 1999) takes 72 actual minutes to complete, and a game played in 2001 may be labelled as taking place in 1941. But playing a game requires at least points or periods of temporal convergence where the time of the game world and the time of the playing merge - and the player can actually *do* something.

The Player and the Game

The next major question is less structural and more oriented towards the reader: How does [sic] the player and the game interact?

Movies and other stories are largely about humans (or anthropomorphic things) that the viewer/reader identifies with cognitively. It is basically boring to view/read fictions without anthropomorphic actors. This is not true for games. Games with no actors represented on screen have appeared throughout the history of the computer game.[6] Many of these have been extremely popular. An early example is *Missile Command* (Atari 1980), where a number of cities are attacked by missiles that you then have to destroy using rockets from three missile batteries. The player is the not represented on screen as an entity or actor, but only sees the results of his/her actions. It would be possible to create a "job description" for the player – a soldier controlling missiles: a typical hero. It is harder to understand *Tetris* (Pazhitnov 1985), where you must combine a series of falling bricks.

Tetris does not have a visible actor either, and it does not seem possible to construct any actor controlling the falling bricks. "Tetris – the movie" does not seem like a viable concept. But Tetris is incredibly popular, and nobody is disputing its status as a computer game.

But how can computer games be abstract and without points of identification, and yet be interesting? – No matter how variable or even absent the protagonist in computer games, the player is always constant. The reader/viewer need an emotional motivation for investing energy in the movie or book; we need a human actant to identify with. This is probably also true for the computer game, only this actant is always present – it is the player. The player is motivated to invest energy in the game because the game evaluates the player's performance. And this is why a game can be much more abstract than a movie or a novel, because games involve the player in a direct way.

This discrepancy raises many issues. In a game, the player works to reach a goal. The thing is then that this goal has to mimic the player's situation. It seems, for example, that a game cannot have the goal that the player should work hard to throw the protagonist under a train.[7] As a player, the goal has to be one that you would conceivably want to work for.[8]

A Final Argument: The Avant-garde Fallacy

There is a final counter-argument to the points set forth here: The problem with my description of story as having existents and events, my description of time, my description of the player/game relation as unique could be this: That I am ignoring the experimental narratives of the 20th century, works that do not simply subscribe to the story/discourse duality, activate the reader much more, and do not have a sense of being past or prior. We can explore this with a few select examples.

Jean-Luc Godard's *Pierrot le fou* would serve as an example of a movie where it is hard to construct a coherent story due to numerous temporal skips and distanciations such as the actor's addressing the camera. This foregrounding of the discourse has a sense of immediacy that would make it ripe for a game adaptation – if only we could figure what the game should be about.

And during the creation of *Naked Lunch*, William Burroughs writes the follow explanation to Allen Ginsberg: "… the usual novel *has happened*. This novel *is happening*" (Burroughs 1993, p. 375).

It may be obvious that the more open a narrative is to interpretation, the more emphasis will be on the reader/viewer's efforts *now*. The difference between the now in narratives and the now in games is that first now concerns the situation where the reader's effort in interpreting obscures the story – the text becomes *all* discourse, and consequently the temporal tensions ease. The now of the game means that story time converge with playing time, *without the story/game world disappearing*.

Games rely on having goals that can be deciphered by the player and something obstructing the player's possibility of reaching the goals. Narratives are basically interpretative, whereas games are formal. Or, in cybertextual terms, stories have an interpretative dominant, whereas games have a configurative dominant. (Eskelinen 2001.) While readers and viewers are clearly more active than some theories have previously assumed, they are active in a different way.

The idea of using experimental narratives to answer the opening question suffers from the problem that the very emphasis on interpretation and ontological instability that would make the narrative more immediate and thus closer to the game, in itself would make a game unplayable.[9]

Conclusion

I would like to repeat that I believe that: 1) The player can tell stories of a game session. 2) Many computer games contain narrative elements, and in many cases the player may play to see a cut-scene or realise a narrative sequence. 3) Games and narratives share some structural traits. Nevertheless, my point is that: 1) Games and stories actually do not translate to each other in the way that novels and movies do. 2) There is an inherent conflict between the *now* of the interaction and the *past* or "*prior*" of the narrative. You can't have narration and interactivity at the same time; there is no such thing as a continuously interactive story. 3) The relations between reader/story and player/game are completely different – the player inhabits a twilight zone where he/she is both an empirical subject outside the game *and* undertakes a role inside the game.

Even if this article has been somewhat structural in its orientation, I would like to state that I think we need to consider games as fairly formal structures that in complex ways spawn and feed player experiences. This means that we cannot afford to ignore the effect of interactivity: The non-determined state of the story/game world and the active state of the player when playing a game has huge implications for how we perceive games. Even if we were to *play* only a single game session of a hypothetical game and end up performing exactly the same sequence of events that constitute *Hamlet*[10], we would not have had the same experience as had we *watched* Hamlet performed. We would also not consider the game to be the same object as the play since we would think of the game as an explorable dynamic system that allowed for a multitude of sequences.

The narrative turn of the last 20 years has seen the concept of narrative emerge as a privileged master concept in the description of all aspects of human society and sign-production. Expanding a concept can in many cases be useful, but the expansion process is also one that blurs boundaries and muddles concepts, be this is desirable or not. With any sufficiently broad definition of *x*, everything will be *x*. This rapidly expands the possible uses of a theory but also brings the danger of exhaustion, the kind of exhaustion that eventually closes departments and feeds indifference: Having established that everything is *x*, there is nothing else to do than to repeat the statement.

Using other media as starting points, we may learn many things about the construction of fictive worlds, characters … but relying too heavily on existing theories will make us forget what makes games games: Such as rules, goals, player activity, the projection of the player's actions into the game world, the way the game defines the possible actions of the player. It is the unique parts that we need to study now.

These are both descriptive and normative issues. It does not make much sense to describe *everything* in the same terms. It also is quite limiting to suppose that all cultural forms *should* work in the same way. The discussion of games and narratives is a relevant one and I can not hope to close it here. This article has argued for telling the difference.

NOTES

1. Note that multi player games rarely contain ideal sequences but rather allow the players to replay the same setting with new results - think of Chess or *Starcraft*. As such they are very far from narratives. On the other hand, the retelling of a game session in a single player game ("*and then I … and then I … and then I …*") is less interesting than the retelling of a multi player game since the latter can include intrigues, lies, and deceit between people ("*we had agreed to combine forces on the eastern front, but only in the end did I realise that she was actually conspiring with Joe*").

2. This also relates to the maturation of the game industry: The first Star Wars movie resulted in one computer game, the latest movie has spawned somewhere around ten different games on different platforms featuring different pieces of the movie or of the Star Wars universe.

3. The other major problem is that games are formalised and rule-bound and as such better suited for physics & firearms than for existential problems, since the latter are not easily formalised. (See Juul 2000) This means that some events are very, very hard to create as dynamic systems.

4. The ideal sequence is much harder to actualise than the numerous non-ideal sequences – this is what makes it a game.

5. Flash forward is more of a problem than flash back, since describing events in the future means that the player cannot do anything.

6. Traditional board and card games tend to be much more abstract than computer games.

7. The Anna Karenina example was presented by Marie-Laure Ryan (2001).

8. This does not rule out ironies, but all examples I know of work by putting the player in an active position doing things normally considered negative: Destroying houses and killing people in *Rampage* (Bally Midway 1986), killing pedestrians in *Death Race* (Exidy 1976) and *Carmageddon* (Sales Curve Interactive 1997). I know of no games where the goal of the player is to die or be destroyed.

9. This still leaves open numerous unexplored possibilities such as multiple contradictory goals, games of Tetris that cause the destruction of famous artworks in another window on the screen etc.. The point is that we should not expect (or demand) that game experiments mimic narrative experiments.

10. *Hamlet* is actually a poor choice for game adaptation since it (like many narratives) has several scenes where the protagonist is absent, and thus gives the audience more information than is available to the characters. Such common devices of knowledge and suspense are not in any obvious way implementable in a game format where audience and protagonist are the same person.

REFERENCES

LITERATURE

Aarseth, Espen J.: *Cybertext: Perspectives on Ergodic Literature*. Baltimore & London: Johns Hopkins University Press, 1997.

Aarseth, Espen J. "Aporia and Epiphany in *Doom* and *The Speaking Clock*: The temporality of Ergodic Art" In: Marie-Laure Ryan (ed.): *Cyberspace Textuality: Computer Technology and Literary Theory*. Bloomington: Indiana Press, 1999.

Bordwell, David: *Narration in the Fiction Film*. Wisconsin: The University of Wisconsin Press, 1985.

Brooks, Peter: *Reading for the Plot*. Cambridge, Massachusetts: Harvard University Paperback Edition, 1992. (New York: Knopf, 1984)

Burroughs, William S.: *The letters of William Burroughs 1945–1959*. Ed. by Oliver Harris. London: Penguin Books, 1993.

Chatman, Seymour: *Story and Discourse: Narrative Structure in Fiction and Film*. Ithaca: Cornell University Press, 1978.

Eskelinen, Markku: *The Gaming Situation*. Paper presented at the Digital Arts and Culture conference, Providence April 2001.
Genette, Gerard: *Narrative Discourse*. Ithaca: Cornell University Press, 1980.
Goffman, Erving: *Encounters: Two studies in the Sociology of Interaction*. London: The Penguin Press, 1972. (The Bobbs-Merril Company, Inc. 1961).
Jensen, Jens F.: "Adventures in Computerville: Games, Inter-Action & High Tech Paranoia i Arkadia". In Kultur & Klasse 63. Copenhagen: Medusa 1988.
Juul, Jesper: *A clash between game and narrative*. M.A. Thesis. 1999. http://www.jesperjuul.dk/thesis.
Juul, Jesper: *What computer games can and can't do*. Paper presented at the Digital Arts and Culture conference, Bergen August 2000. http://www.jesperjuul.dk/text/WCGCACD.html
Juul, Jesper: *Game Time*. (Forthcoming.)
Murray, Janet H.: *Hamlet on the Holodeck: The Future of Narrative in Cyberspace*. New York: The Free Press, 1997.
Ryan, Marie-Laure: *Beyond Myth and Metaphor: The Case of Narrative in Digital Media*. Keynote speech at the Computer Games & Digital Textualities conference, Copenhagen March 2001.

MOVIES

Anderson, Paul: *Mortal Kombat*. 1995.
Godard, Jean-Luc: *Pierrot le Fou*. 1965.
Lucas, George: *Star Wars*. 1977
Lucas, George: *Star Wars: Episode 1*. 1999.
West, Simon: *Tomb Raider*. 2001.

GAMES

Atari: *Missile Command*. 1980.
Atari: *Star Wars*. 1983.
Atari: *Tetris*. 1986.
Bally Midway: *Rampage*. 1986.
Blizzard Entertainment: *Starcraft*. 1998.
Core Design Ltd.: *Tomb Raider*. Eidos Interactive 1996.
Exidy: *Death Race*. 1976.
ID Software: *Doom*. 1994.
Lucascarts: *Star Wars: Episode 1: Racer*. Lucascarts 1999.
Midway Games: *Mortal Kombat*. Acclaim 1993.
Pazhitnov, Alexey: *Tetris*. Spectrum Holobyte, 1985.
Sales Curve Interactive: *Carmageddon*. PC Game, Interplay 1997.
Taito: *Space Invaders*. 1977.
Valve Software: *Half-life*. Sierra 1998.
Verant Interactive: *EverQuest*. Sony Online Entertainment 1999.

26 WOW IS THE NEW MUD
Social Gaming from Text to Video

Torill Elvira Mortensen

In February 2006 I wrote a post on the discussion board of the World of Warcraft (WoW) guild one of my characters is part of. I explained that I am a researcher and told something about my former work on text-based role-playing games – MUDs. It is part of my methodology not to conceal my research as I find that being open about the research process solves more problems than it creates. The next morning I got a private message, asking if the words *Dragon Realms* and *Aarinfel* meant anything to me. It turned out that in 2006 I had ended up in the same faction on the same server and in the same guild as a guild mate from a MUD that closed down in 1999. I have to admit I was surprised but not stunned.[1] I had already registered similarities between the two games and been thinking about this article for a while. The coincidence only confirmed what I already suspected: WoW and MUDs fill much the same niche in the gaming world and have much the same functions.

[…]

What Are MUDs and What Is WoW?

MUDs are early online multiuser games. They are text based, meaning they have no graphics; everything is described in words. These words describe a geographical space that you explore through the metaphors of movement – up, down, north, south, east, west – and your representation or avatar is described through words and numbers, visible to you at certain commands. The input is typed; you cannot use a

Torill Elvira Mortensen, "WoW is the New MUD: Social Gaming from Text to Video," pp. 397–413 from *Games and Culture* 1:4 (2006).

mouse in most MUDs. In recent years there have been some interface modifications done that permit a certain amount of graphics to a MUD (Holmevik & Haynes, 1997), but the rule is that the input and output is all in writing, sometimes with different colors. Some of these MUDs are mainly social spaces with very little that looks like gaming going on: chat, not competition or other strategies of scoring and marking achievement. Others are fiercely competitive and allow for both players-versus-environment (PvE) or player-versus-player (PvP) gaming styles. Mostly these MUDs are noncommercial, they are run by a few administrative staff who are also players, and they are developed and changed through collective effort. The player base is relatively small; 200 players are considered a solid player population that ensures constant around-the-clock adventure and company.

[…]

Games in Current Culture

Online computer games in 2006 have a very different position in culture from what they had in 1997, when I approached my first MUD. From being an obscure activity for geeks, they are now mainstream commercial entertainment. Dragon Realms could have up to 200 players on an exceptionally good day; World of Warcraft had approximately 5 million players in December 2005 (Blizzard, 2005). The economy of game development competes with the film and music industry, and the medium is moving at full speed toward the mainstream of popular culture. The parent generation of today's children has their own computer gaming experiences, even if those were rare occurrences with arcade games. Personal computers even in workspaces come outfitted with some simple standard games, mainly solitaires, and the users are no longer total strangers to the concept of computer gaming the way their parent generation was.

The new media panic discussions, which surface at the launch of all media innovations, have not died down yet (2006), but they are weakened. Henry Jenkins (2004) debunked eight myths of video games, and although his article did not instantly render the myths impotent, the overview is a good list of what people believe about video games in particular and any new media in general. The eight myths Jenkins addressed are:

1. The availability of video games has led to an epidemic of youth violence.
2. Scientific evidence links violent game play with youth aggression.
3. Children are the primary market for video games.
4. Almost no girls play computer games.
5. Because games are used to train soldiers to kill, they have the same impact on the kids who play them.
6. Video games are not a meaningful form of expression.

7. Video game play is socially isolating.
8. Video game play is desensitizing.

... The need for a professor to debunk very similar myths about computer games expresses two important things: Games are treated the same as other, now mainstream media were when they were new. But games are also past the first stigmata of "popular," as they have been discovered, accepted, and are defended by members of academia (writing in academic journals published by reputable publishers).

This means that the potential players of a game such as World of Warcraft are a much larger and diverse segment of the population than the players of MUDs. MUD users were much more heterogeneous, mainly represented by the early users of computers from the period when the 'net was dominated by young White males. The population of current computer/video games is reported to be quite different from the earlier male-dominated space, with 45/55 female/male ratio and ages ranging from 10 to 50+ (ESA, 2006), numbers not deviating too far from the conclusion of a report on U.K. gamers from BBC (Pratchett, 2005):

- 59% of 6- to 65-year-olds in the United Kingdom are gamers: this is equivalent to 26.5 million people;
- 48% of the United Kingdom aged 6 to 65 plays games at least once a week (21.6 million people);
- 100% of 6- to 10-year-olds consider themselves to be gamers;
- a quarter of U.K. game players are aged 36 to 50;
- 18% (or 1.7 million gamers) are aged between 51 and 65;
- the average age of U.K. gamer is approximately 28;
- 45% of all gamers are female.

[...]

One thing is quite immediately recognizable from the MUDs to WoW, and this is the relationship to a fictional genre and the construction of a fictional context for the gameplay. A large number of the MUDs relate to what is known as "high fantasy," and the Warcraft series of games is a series firmly planted in this genre. High fantasy allows magic and different supernatural powers. It also conveniently explains such things as resurrection, instant travel, instant communication without technology (whispers can be heard independent of game geography), why certain quests can be repeated inevitably, and the high density of heroes. Richard Bartle and Roy Trubshaw's original MUD1 is also known as British Legends, which are a common source for high fantasy inspiration – the legends that is. And if you enter MUD1 today you may find this room: "You are lost in a Misty Graveyeard. A headstone to the east bears the inscription, 'OK, so maybe the dragon was a bit of a handful. ...'" This hints at a gothic/fantastic world and one where there are dragons. WoW has plenty of the same, misty graveyards populated with undead, dragons, mysterious paths, and even some of the more technological solutions. Where MUD1 has railroads, WoW has gnome underground inventions like the Deeprun Tram, a railway between two cities.[2]

Both of these relate to a literature starting with the gothic romances of the Victorian age and the monster of Dr. Frankenstein, heavily informed by J. R. R Tolkien and also inspired by science fiction. It is a literature that permits a uniquely playful approach: Rules can be created independent of the physical rules of the universe, and although the universe of both the game and the fantastic literature needs to obey its own rules, it does not have to bend to common conventions. Where technically minded science fiction demands sophisticated knowledge of what may become possible through known technology (e.g., landing on Mars [Robinson, 1992] or creating and entering cyberspace [Gibson, 1993]), the fantastic permits the creator to not just break known rules but also to create new ones, changing any number of known and accepted parameters.

The relation to high fantasy does not count for all games as games to my knowledge draw their fictitious material from every aspect of human experience. But by choosing a high-fantasy setting, Blizzard avoids the controversy that for instance DMA and Rock Star Games has entered into through games such as Grand Theft Auto (GTA), where the setting is the shady side of an American city, and the game entails fictional interaction with the criminal elements of this city. Although we can argue that the GTA context is as unreal to most of the players as is high fantasy, the mafia/underworld setting with recognizable and available weapons, cars, opponents, and victims of GTA is obviously a lot more controversial than the orcs, elves, swords, wands, and maces of WoW. …

The game platform does not discriminate: The player can get the same benefits for any feat, the fictional universe is what decides if the player is to be rewarded for killing trolls, cheating prostitutes, or matching a perfect golf swing. Still, we can assume that the fictional universe influences the behavior of the players and how they create their own stories within the game.

Playing MUDs

A new MUD user is asked to create a character by choosing a name, a password, and certain parameters. The different parameters are set by the game designers, and you choose things like race, class, and gender and manipulate certain statistics. This is popularly known as "rolling" a character, and the process is an automated version of what players of pen-and-paper role-play games do. The *roll* points back to the roll of dice to determine the abilities of the character in pen-and-paper games or live-action role-play games, genres played without computers. In some computer games, rolling is still significant as the character may have different strengths and weaknesses depending on the digitally randomized numbers that appear in the character statistics. For some games, such as WoW, *rolling* merely refers to the process of creation as there is no real randomness to the act.

After creation you find yourself in a starter area. The traditional DIKU-MUD starting area will let you start out in an arena where your character can defeat slugs, snails, and mice – perhaps the occasional bunny – to gather enough experience points to gain a new level. During this process there will be the occasional drop of better equipment from the available monsters: increasingly better equipment as the character gains levels. It also lends a certain humor to the start-up as you can find your character bested by a mouse or a harmless practice dummy.

Death leads to resurrection and subsequent corpse-runs to regain the equipment or even the entire body. It is not uncommon to ask for help from fellow players to find your corpse as part of the culture of assisting and working in groups to solve tasks too tough for the individual players.

Communication in-game between players happens in writing through several different channels: say, yell, tell, whisper, world channel, guild channels, and other channels defined by the Game Masters or developers. Say is heard/read in the same area/room as the character speaking, and the other channels have different range. There is also a system for players to send each other "letters," digitalized simulations of snail mail.

Most gaming MUDs also have storage, a bank where the possible amount of stored items expands as the character gains levels. There are inventories and bags that can be kept in the inventories to expand the storage potential. The characters have a certain amount of slots in the inventory and also a certain amount of slots for equipment that the character can wear. This equipment is visible at certain commands. What distinguishes the character the most is the individual description the player makes to give others an idea about an outer "skin" for the character.

Any WoW player would immediately recognize the previous description as something that can be done in WoW, common features of most role-play games. There are however a few things related to the creation and playing of the character that cannot be repeated in Kalimdor or The Eastern Kingdoms. A MUD character can in most platforms have a written description. Such a description can for instance be: "Spiky hair surrounds a round, moonlike face. Two black eyes and a ruby red mouth stand out against the milky pale skin. The short and chubby body is draped in silky, black material." This allows the player to give a unique, personal touch to the appearance of the character. In WoW the players have certain options, but Blizzard will be hard put to make as many different graphic options as the total open approach of the blank textbox permits.

Both MUD players and WoW players like to show off their equipment. Ducheneaut, Yee, Nickell, and Moore (2006) argued that characters with "epic" equipment like to stand idle in highly trafficked spaces to be admired for their equipment. On the European role-play server Argent Dawn, some of the players of The Onyx Ascendancy, one of the RP focused guilds, replied to my question about this with their interpretation of this behavior. They claimed that the real show-off opportunity was clothing chosen for good looks, not armor. In their opinion, "farmed epics" are bad taste in cities. Epic gear is battle gear, and if you are going to battle or just came from battle that's what you wear while standing in front of the bank or auction house waiting to begin or closing things up before logging off. Good taste and show-off items in their opinion is clothing that makes the character look better than otherwise but has no practical use other than to be admired.[3] Admiration is important, but they expressed admiration for style, taste, and that extra little effort rather than for items that are not all that rare to experienced players. This is the kind of inventiveness that was also appreciated in the MUDs I played and studied (Mortensen, 2003).

Dragon Realms (DR) and Aarinfel (Aa) permitted items to be renamed. Because the appearance of an item was a text line, a player could compose a new text to make a weapon or a piece of armor appear differently. Only administrators with certain authority could do this, and to restrict the practice and demand on these select administrators, the players would have to pay for renames in FPs, favor points. Favor points were earned for good role-play and were distributed by other players through recommendations (Mortensen, 2003). In DR and Aa there was not a lot of gear to choose from; at a certain level there were a couple of good weapons of each type and nothing more. This meant that all players at the same level would be wearing the same gear, and there was little status to be had from acquiring particular items. The prestige was in the elegantly named item: "a sharp dagger" could be changed into "a crystal epee" and "a horned helmet" into "a grinning dragon's head" depending on the player's style.

The FP system does not exist in WoW, and the self-styled renames are not available to regular players. With the larger player base and more intricate issue of graphic design, custom design of armor is pretty much unthinkable in WoW. What does exist is a player-run, player-created system for distributing the epics players have to really work for, the DKP or Dragon Kill Point system (Wikipedia, 2006). This is very different from the FP system in that it does not involve role-play, but at the same time it is a player-administrated reward system that rewards the kind of behavior players want to encourage.

The DKP system rewards attendance and participation in raids for complex, hard-to-master areas in WoW. These raids are from 20 to 40 persons as opposed to the regular 5-person groups, and all players need to cooperate as a unit, filling the different tasks for which their character is most suited. To encourage participation, reliability, and group cooperation, the raid groups need a system for rewards. This system also functions as a system for splitting up the loot: You earn points by participating in a raid and doing your part of the work, you spend points by bidding on the loot that is dropped by the monsters overcome by the raid group. This way, a diligent player has more of a chance at winning a good piece of equipment than a more casual player, and although not always considered fair, the system attempts to reward those who are willing and eager to play by the rules of the other players, and it acts as a social stabilizer. This happens through the way it ensures regular participation by the same group of people in the same kind of tasks, it allows for certain expectations that will be met, and it creates teams in an environment where the potential for being lost and unconnected is very large. This is a way to control and modify the behavior of the players toward each other, and so the DKP system has some of the same flavor as the FP system, although the systems have different goals and encourage or suppress different aspects of human behavior.

Playing WoW

Playing WoW is an overwhelming experience. Where playing MUDs means you have to learn to type really fast, to play WoW you need to be able to move your character around quickly, gauge the distance to nearby dangers, and read and reply to written messages from other players while using several features of your keyboard and your mouse/joystick or whatever input device is your favorite. It encourages and demands multitasking to be played skillfully and well.

It will however soon become evident that it is possible to filter the different experiences out, and the gaming experience can be limited to the level of game intensity you desire. For some, playing WoW is a fully social experience. They adhere to the patterns established by Richard Bartle (1996) with his four much cited and discussed player types and are pure socializers. These players will often gain levels slowly and be more concerned with hanging out, chatting, using the game as a social space rather than a competitive or explorative space. For them, the abilities, armor, and skill of their character are unimportant; what they focus on is to be able to hang out with their friends.

The other three typologies are killers, explorers, and achievers, and Blizzard has even gone so far as to particularly accommodate one of these groups: the killers. With dedicated PvP servers, the killers have whole virtual worlds open to their special version of the game. This consists of testing their skill consistently against other players, not through more subtle means such as showing off role-play skill or elegant gear but directly through player-versus-player combat. On PvP servers players are always vulnerable to attack, and the number of player kills is carefully tracked and displayed on the connected Web sites through the honor system. This suits the killer typology very well as the main pleasure of their gaming is to best others. It is also an example of game development looking at earlier experiences from games like MUDs but also Ultima Online and EverQuest: games where some who fit the killer typology may also have been mistaken for griefers – people who play mainly to ruin the fun of others. As they prey on other players such as the less directly violent or competitive socalizers, they do appear to be malicious rather than friendly, and the solution EverQuest and later Blizzard have chosen with dedicated PvP servers is as much to accommodate those with a desire for challenge as to protect those who do not seek this type of thrill.

This is a major difference from the MUDs and one that is brought about from the magnitude of the player mass. With 200 gamers, a MUD can generate enough company for its participants that they have somebody to play with most of the time. ...

Role-play was the distinctive feature of the games Dragon Realms and Aarinfel. ... This kind of player-driven creativity was the basic structure for game development in MUDs; a group of players would decide that they could make a better game than the current and break out and make one that was configured along the lines of what they considered a good game. The standards of good role-play in Aa was heavily informed by the standards of good role-play in tabletop games and, not the least, in live action role-play games (LARP), where very little is spared to make the illusion of fantasy a reality. This meant that the characters as much as possible acted as if there were no players controlling them, they were not part of a game, and they had no idea about things like levels, hit points, statistics, or other mundane-world references. The characters would not have to leave to have dinner with the family, they had to retreat in the service of the master; they had no homework but meditation in preparation to kill the dragon. And they had their own independent lives, a background, a history, loves, hates, and other experiences that made out their role-played lives. But after the character has said its goodbyes and retreated, there would more often than not be a message over the global OOC (out of character) channel saying: "Thanks for the fun all, but I have got to go do dishes or I will be slain ruthlessly by the mother-dragon."

In WoW we find similar rules for role-play. On the role-play servers there are some common rules for what to discuss in which channels. Say, the channel that appears to those close enough to a character to be within reasonable listening distance, is always supposed to be in character, IC.[4] Many of the global channels – trade, looking for groups, local defense – are considered OOC. An interesting contention is always going on about the general channel – many use that for RP, broadcasting their drama to all. Others use it to make IC comments, or lead long discussions over just about anything, or just to rant. Often one of these groups tries to shut the other down and claim the channel for whatever is their particular interest.

There are some social actions that imitate standard actions: /greet, /goodbye, /hug, /kiss, /smile, /frown, /slap, /spit, and /dance are some of these. The same actions and many many more (where is the /noogie command when you need it?) were available in MUDs to indicate the emotional state of the character. This is why they were called *emotes*. You can however, as in MUDs, also use more elaborate emotes: "/em reaches up to wipe sweat from her eyes, leaving blood from her gauntlet smeared over her forehead." This would be a typical, elaborate emote from a role-player in a MUD – or in WoW – after a battle. The /em part is then translated by the game to being an emote, which means that the sentence will start with the character's name: "Agirra reaches up to wipe sweat from her eyes, leaving blood from her gauntlet smeared over her forehead."

These self-created emotes are highly individual, and so there are few visual aids to them in WoW. Depending on punctuation, there are however a few gestures. In orcs, a period leads to a gesture of closure, a small movement of hands, opening and closing them. An exclamation mark leads to a lifting of arms and hands in a large gesture, whereas a question mark leads to a smaller gesture again, but this time with a little outward circle to the hands, subtly different from the common statement, connoting the lilt of the voice as it rises toward the end of the sentence when asking a question.

A good emote is one that has been created by the player, not a standard expression. In WoW the standardized ones are a bit more acceptable than they were in the MUDs, as they come with animation. For instance, /grieve will show the character crying. They are however more frequently used for ironic, humorous effect than for role-play. When I was applying to be accepted into The Onyx Ascendancy (TOA) I was heavily advised to use emotes to display my role-play abilities: The self-created, text-based emotes are still the most respected tool of role-play despite the sophistication of the graphic universe.

Role-play servers also often have several ways of approaching the storyline. In Aa they tried to solve the issue of repeated quest actions – why can you kill the same mob over and over again, for instance – through making it impossible to repeat quests. WoW does the same thing; once you have finished a quest you are flagged and cannot do it again unless the quest specifically allows for that. But this still does not explain why after you have killed a dragon you can help your friends kill the same dragon over and over again. Why is the dragon always there? Who are you constantly killing?

On Argent Dawn, The Onyx Ascendancy killed a faction leader of the Alliance after many failed attempts. It was a 40-man raid expertly smuggled into the area. The leader was killed, and the group got out safely. This faction leader (Staghelm in Teldrassil) is an NPC, and it was back in place only minutes after TOA had pulled off the assassination. How to explain that the carefully and successfully executed killing had absolutely no impact on the game universe? TOA created its own little story to explain this. In their version of the history of what happens on World of Warcraft, Staghelm is now an imposter, a fake planted by TOA to undermine the Alliance from the inside (Mortensen, 2005). The action was a plan to assassinate the real Staghelm and give the TOA mole a chance to slip in and take over. This has however not gone without discussion. Some found it ludicrous and impossible; some asked if there would be a long line of fake Staghelms now because other guilds might do the same – in general people wanted to know how come one guild felt they had the right to rewrite the game story. TOA answered that they are only rewriting their story, anybody else was free to do their versions.[5]

RP-wise this is a familiar argument. This is the argument that drove at least one player away from DR – he wanted to rewrite the fictitious frame of the world, but his role-play had no impact (Mortensen, 2003). The administrators and creators were more easily available there, so he was less free to create his own little interpretation of the events, although he also had more reason to expect to influence the game as there were other players who did. A computer game is a much more static world than a tabletop game or a LARP. Once something is coded, changing it demands a lot more work than saying "OK, that's a great idea, we go with that from here on, just remember to write it on a piece of paper so we remember what we agreed on." And if you have to recode the game with every little story written by players, it would create a fluidity that is not desirable in a game. All parameters constantly changing means maximum insecurity, the exact opposite of the balance between tension and mastery that constitutes one theory of pleasurable play (Csikszentmihalyi, 1990). This way, an environment that is structured to accommodate role-play is hard to align with an environment that accommodates the kind of play against rules and the game world that constitutes the main gaming events in online worlds. In role-play, rules will have to be broken and can even be changed by the play, in more structured agon-type games. This conflict is very close to one described by Roger Caillois (2001):

> In play and games, *agôn* and *alea* are regulated. Without rules, there can be no competitions or games of chance. At the other extreme, *mimicry* and *ilinx* equally presume a world without rules in which the player constantly improvises, trusting in a guiding fantasy or a supreme inspiration, neither of which is subject to regulation. (p. 75)

Hence, role-play in online worlds demands compromise, whether the world is tiny, with only a few active players who mainly have builder privileges or huge, made up of millions of users, most of whom don't care whether Staghelm really died and was replaced or not. But WoW does develop as a world, sometimes even after player input. The most recent change was to develop a new instance (limited play area with particularly tough NPCs and certain quests) that could be opened early if the players on the server devoted a lot of time and energy to supply "resources" for the defending armies. Although the instance would open sooner or later anyway in all servers, this gave the players a way to influence their game space and feel they had achieved something by accessing the instance early on their server. In MUDs, the potential for influence is much higher as a well-played assassination can lead to the corpse being discovered and disposed of the next day and a new faction leader be built and put in place soon after. With only one game world to look after, the influence of the administrators is much larger, and small-scale changes can be done quickly. But in both cases, these altercations need to be significant events, planned changes that are integrated into the storyline of the role-play world as well as the game fiction and carefully implemented to avoid breaking quest chains or to adhere to the current logic of the known fantastic universe.

The Game Structure

Game-based MUDs such as the DIKU-MUDs and WoW (together with a large percentage of the other computer games out there, particularly of the adventure or role-play type) adhere to a system for calculating the outcome of battles or other contest-flavored conflicts that was not developed for computers but for manual calculation using dice.

This means that even the combat situations in WoW, graphically very differently represented, are familiar. Although the graphic interface is a significant development from the text-based interface, the mechanics of what happens then is not. In a MUD, I can type *cast frostshock skullsplitter* (or most likely *ca fr skull*), and I attack the chosen target in the way I wish. In WoW I hit tab until I see the chosen target represented on top, then I hit the icon for frostshock or I hit a number corresponding to the icon, and I start casting the spell. What happens next is that I am told how much damage I do. In a MUD I am told "Your frostshock does 511 damage on Skullsplitter." In WoW I am told the exact same thing, and I can also have the option of seeing white and yellow numbers running out of the head of the monster I am fighting.[6] …

Other very recognizable issues are death, equipment, quests, and trade. The discussions from the MUDs of the 1990s are resurfacing with the graphic games – or perhaps they never went away. The matters of equipment, trade, and quests are discussed elsewhere (Castranova, 2001; Walker, 2006), but we'll dwell for a moment on the matter of character death, particularly permanent death.

The problem with death is: How do we deal with the death of the character? If death means the character is gone and you have to create a new one and start from scratch (known as permanent death), this means the stakes are just too high. It leaves no room for error, and the tension of the game kills the enjoyment for casual gamers. Less than casual gamers seek this kind of tension, and they keep the desire for permanent death alive. When your skill level is too high for the game you play, you need to make it more complicated. One player I talked to had stopped playing WoW after almost a year because the only things he found to be a challenge in the game were the large, complex dungeons that demand 20 to 40 players cooperating in a large group known as a raid. These raids are very time-consuming both in terms of preparation and in the actual playing.

In any raid like that, your character will however die quite a bit. … By going through a certain set of actions you can regain your former status. In WoW you resurrect wearing your old equipment only with some damage taken to its durability. In a MUD you will often appear in a local designated spot (temple, graveyard) naked, and you have to run and find your corpse to regain your equipment. … this is the paradox that baffles role-players (how to role-play multiple deaths and resurrections?) and other gamers alike – you keep dying but you never die.

This issue is perhaps best solved by the role-players as the role-play solution often is to create rules if the game does not supply them. And so a role-player can for instance say that if he or she dies while in character, the character stays dead and must be deleted (if they are for instance killed by the alliance/enemies while on a role-played mission into enemy territory). Or the role-player can create an explanation: saying they were not really dead but just very badly hurt and needed some time to recover, claiming the Gods refuse to take them from this miserable existence as they still have a mission or explaining it as the matter of joining mind and body through forcing the energies of life back into the body, rather similar to the miraculous rescues in emergency rooms.

This way the player takes control over certain aspects of the game and creates his or her own little game within the game or interpretation of the game. By doing this, the players create microgames or even microuniverses within the massively multiplayer online role-playing games (MMORPGs), where the rules are just a little bit different from what the game developers had planned for. MUDs are microgames compared to a MMORPG, and the MUD player's way of creating a microgame would often be through actually building a whole new game where the rules would be those of the differently minded from the original MUD. Aarinfel was that kind of MUD, and it broke out of Dragon Realms, bringing the bored, the curious, and the discontent over to a slightly different role-play MUD.

Individual Creativity

Both WoW and MUDs show a kind of gamer creativity. A major difference is however in how WoW allows it, whereas MUDs depend on it. The gamer creativity when it comes to coding for WoW is mainly expressed through modifications of the user interface (UI-mods or just mods). There are several available programs that adjust the interface and makes it easier to deal with than what WoW originally planned. Some of these have to a certain degree been integrated in the game, such as the quick loot buttons that allow for a player to pick up available items very quickly and without targeting it by hand or modifications to the raid administration window that makes the groups available for scrutiny directly on the game window without opening the raid group window. But these are all modifications that change the players' interface with the game; it does not (or is not supposed to) interfere with the game.

MUDs were and are made by creative players. New administrators, builders, and developers are recruited from among the player base or from friends of the current developers, friends who dabble in the same as the players and the developers. If the players are not happy with the game as it is played, they develop a new one, and so MUDs are not only run but also renewed and rebuilt by players rather than influenced through long chains of player feedback.

Isn't a Game Just a Game?

The examples I have given of MUDs and WoW can most likely be said about MUDs and most online multiuser games. MUD1 was in many ways the mother of all multiuser games, and that was already just a modification and bastardization of other game genres. What makes WoW different from so many other newer games is that it is so common, so widely spread, and so available. It is a 'net phenomenon that draws all kinds of gamers into it. It is also a game that does not seek to be "pure" in the fashion of first-person shooters, role-play, adventure, action, or any other genre. It is eclectic and opens up for a very diverse set of use – not the least of these the same kind of use as the MUDs are put to.

Possibly the title of this article could have been "WoW Is the New Counter-Strike," but I suspect the protests to that would have been much louder than to this article. Counter-Strike is purely an action game and consistent enough in the way it is played that there can be international competitions at a very high level and it is possible to name a winner. If there are ever to be WoW competitions, they would have to severely limit the play to be only about a small part of what the game contains, for instance the speed of instance runs – which team can get through Molten Core in the shortest amount of time. This would be possible to measure, but all the rest of what is considered WoW play would not be used and expressed, and a very large part of the attraction of WoW to the casual, civilian player would have to be excluded.

WoW is not a winnable game, and neither are MUDs. There can be degrees of mastery of parts of the game, but the measuring sticks for the different parts of the game are not even comparable.

The most important part of this exercise is however not to prove whether WoW really originally is a MUD or not. What I have hoped to show here is that the current, very sophisticated games did not come out of nowhere. They already have a history and have been developing for several decades. They did not suddenly spring to life like Athena out of the forehead of some brilliant Zeus of game creation. They grew, like all other life, out of the mud.

NOTES

1. Not long after, I received an e-mail from a former administrator of one of the games I had played at the turn of the millennium. He invited me to drop by the American World of Warcraft (WoW) server where he and most of the rest of the original admin team are playing. Although there is probably a majority of players from the original MUDs who do not play WoW, there are too many who do to ignore the position of WoW as the new common gaming ground.
2. The railroad is a point of crossing between worlds in fantastic literature, most recently known from Rowling's Harry Potter books where a train carries the children away from the mundane world to the school of wizardry. But the railroad was one of the means of passing from Narnia to our world used by C. S. Lewis and is a common means of fantastic transportation.
3. The Onyx Ascendency, Guild Channel, Argent Dawn Server, March 2006, general response in conversation.
4. *IC* is also the abbreviation for in combat, a use that is confusing on role-play servers but not elsewhere. It has been enforced by the distinction WoW makes between what you can do when you are in combat – attacked or attacking – or what you can do when out of combat – OOC.
5. This discussion happened on the European World of Warcraft discussion boards for Argent Dawn, but these are unreliable sources, and it was impossible to find the thread again a few months later.
6. Note that *frostschock* and *skullsplitter* are terms used in WoW, and to use them in a MUD today would most likely be a copyright infringement. Substitute with your favorite spell and monster names, or just X and Y, to understand the general purpose of the argument.

REFERENCES

Bartle, R. (1996). Hearts, clubs, diamonds, spades: Players who suit MUDs. *Journal of MUD Research, 1*(1). Retrieved August 8, 2006, from http://www.brandeis.edu/pubs/jove/HTML/v1/bartle.html

Bartle, R., & Trubshaw, R. (1980). *MUD1*. Retrieved August 8, 2006, from http://www.british-legends.com/

Blizzard. (2004). *World of Warcraft* [Game]: Blizzard Entertainment Inc.

Blizzard. (2005, December). *World of Warcraft® Surpasses Five Million Customers Worldwide.* Retrieved February 21, 2006, from http://www.blizzard.com/press/051219.shtml

Caillois, R. (2001). *Man, play, and games.* Chicago: University of Illinois.

Castranova, E. (2001). Virtual worlds: A first-hand account of market and society on the cyberian frontier. *The Gruter Institute Working Papers on Law, Economics, and Evolutionary Biology, 2.* Retrieved August 8, 2006, from http://www.bepress.com/giwp/default/vol2/iss1/art1/current_article.html

Csikszentmihalyi, M. (1990). *Flow: The psychology of optimal experience.* New York: HarperPerennial.

DMA design Limited, D. (1997). *Grand Theft Auto* (GTA) [Game]: BMG Interactive.

Ducheneaut, N., Yee, N., Nickell, E., & Moore, R.J. (2006). "Alone together?" Exploring the social dynamics of massively multiplayer online games. Unpublished manuscript.

Entertainment Software Association, ESA. (2006). Game Player Data. Retrieved February 2, 2006, from http://www.theesa.com/facts/gamer_data.php

Gibson, W. (1993). *Burning chrome and other stories.* London: Harper Collins.

Grant, K., South, A., & Dick, M. (1995). *Dragon Realms* [DIKU-MUD, Computer Game].

Holmevik, J.R., & Haynes, C. (1997). *enCore.* Retrieved August 8, 2006, from http://lingua.utdallas.edu/

Jenkins, H. (2004). Reality bytes: Eight myths about video games debunked. Retrieved February 23, 2006, from http://www.pbs.org/kcts/videogamerevolution/impact/myths.html

Mortensen, T.E. (2003). *Pleasures of the player: Flow and control in online games.* Unpublished doctoral dissertation, Department of Humanistic Informatics, University of Bergen and Faculty of Media and Journalism, Volda University College, Norway.

Mortensen, T.E. (2005). The False Arch Druid, in *thinking with my fingers.* Posted December 15, 2005, retrieved August 8, 2006, from http://torillsin.blogspot.com/2005/12/false-arch-druid.html

Pratchett, R. (2005, December). *Gamers in the UK: Digital play, digital lifestyles.* Retrieved March 2, 2006, from http://open.bbc.co.uk/newmediaresearch/files/BBC_UK_Games_Research_2005.pdf

Robinson, K.S. (1992). *Red mars.* London: HarperCollins.

SWOP-USA. (2006). SWOP Statement on Grand Theft Auto. Retrieved February 27, 2006 from http://www.swop-usa.org/

Valve Corporation, V. (2000). *Half-life: Counter-strike* [Game]: Sierra On-Line, Inc.

Walker, J. (2006). A network of quests in World of Warcraft. In N. Wardrip-Fruin & P. Harrigan (Eds.), *Second person: Role-playing and story in games and playable media.* Boston: MIT Press.

Wikipedia. (2006). DKP (Point System). Retrieved April 2, 2006, from http://en.wikipedia.org/wiki/DKP_(Point_System).

27 WOMEN AND GAMES

Technologies of the Gendered Self

Pam Royse, Joon Lee, Baasanjav Undrahbuyan, Mark Hopson, and Mia Consalvo

Introduction

The gaming industry and most popular media have begun to recognize that women play digital games. The rise in 'casual games', coupled with sales of diverse game titles such as *Dance Dance Revolution* and Sony's *Eyetoy* indicate that women and girls are a growing part of the gaming audience. Yet this diverse group is still misunderstood and too often conflated as having a single perspective or experience. This article explores more deeply why some adult women play and how they choose to integrate gaming technologies into their daily lives or reject them.

[…]

In particular, there are two issues of concern. First, when researching female gamers, mention is often made of images of females in games. Although some research reports do make an explicit link between respondent concerns and the importance of these images, other reports seem to mix them together without justification, or through suggestions that the images must be having 'effects' on game players. Second, research on female gamers initially focused on girls and has now broadened to encompass adult women players, but the interests, preferences and play habits of girls and women are usually combined without any discussion of how such conflations might be problematic. …

Pam Royse, Joon Lee, Baasanjav Undrahbuyan, Mark Hopson, and Mia Consalvo, "Women and Games: Technologies of the Gendered Self," pp. 555–75 from *new media & society* 9:4 (2007).

This article seeks to make a more careful examination of women gamers by bracketing the discussion of female representations in games (unless explicitly discussing the comments of female gamers about such images) and focusing exclusively on research done on adult women gamers. This article also approaches the subjects of women and gaming from a feminist, critical-cultural point of view, seeing gender and technology as mutually shaping. Thus, following the work of Yates and Littleton, we view 'computer gaming as something that is constructed out of a set of practices that computer gamers engage in' (2001: 106), and further, that through these constructions gamers also negotiate and create gendered identities.

To do so, this article brings in the work of gender and technology theorists such as Balsamo (1996) and Haraway (1991), but also draws on and expands the work of Foucault (1988), in particular his conceptualization of technologies or techniques of the self. Thus it views computer games and gaming as a set of practices or technologies that multiple individuals use in different and at times contradictory ways to construct a gendered self that is culturally, socially and historically specific.

[...]

Gender and Technology: Relevant Theory

Many, if not most, feminist theorists of gender and technology would argue that these two concepts are socially constructed in specific historical, political and cultural contexts. Further, these two concepts are theoretically intertwined, informing each other in important ways.

One classic example of such mutual shaping is Rakow's (1992) social history of the telephone and her explanation of how it became gendered (as a female medium for socializing) in a specific way and led to particular ways of defining what is (and is not) 'women's work' in relation to family and group communication. Here, gender helps to define a technological medium and a technology is (re)configured gender-wise, to the feminine.

More recent work addresses how technologies that promise greater choice can often end up reifying traditionally gendered body norms. Theorists such as Anne Balsamo (1996) have argued that computer technologies have been employed in the service of redefining appropriately gendered bodies, through such mechanisms as cosmetic surgery. These technologies themselves are bound up in discourses concerning gendered identities of users as well as producers or inventors. Balsamo builds on and expands the (classic) work of Haraway (1991), who argues that women must embrace technology and grapple with its contradictory and potentially dangerous meanings if we are to have a hand in its future development and implementation.

More recently, Liesbet van Zoonen echoed and reinforced these findings, arguing that 'both technology and gender are multidimensional processes that are articulated in complex and contradictory ways which escape straightforward gender definitions' (2002: 6). Further, she makes the pertinent point that 'the decisive moment in the circuit of culture is in the moment of consumption, when technologies are domesticated in everyday lives' (2002: 16). That concern underscores the desire in this article to focus on the consumption (or use) of games, to determine whether and how they may morph from their production culture of a mainly masculine domain to something more complex in gender terms (for more information on the gendered production of games, see Davies, 2002).

Although feminist theorists such as Rakow, Balsamo and van Zoonen have produced critical insights into how gender and technology can mutually shape each other and do so in ways that resist as well as comply with existing (gendered) power hierarchies, their models tend to see the gendered use of technologies in ways that do not account for differences in use – other than in a dualistic use/non-use conceptualization. For example, Balsamo's excellent critique of the rise of digital imaging in cosmetic surgery demonstrates how women's choices reinscribe traditional ideas about female beauty. Yet the analysis is limited to either engaging or not engaging in cosmetic surgery. Similarly, Rakow's inquiry into telephone use mainly focuses on the differences between men and women and does not examine deeply how various women might use the telephone in different frequencies. Although such critiques of differential use are usually related to identity factors such as ethnicity or class, it is also important to look at the level of use of a technology and determine how women who are invested in differential use patterns or practices may come to understand a technology differently and therefore have different attitudes about it, and how they also may see the technology as 'gendered' differently.

Perhaps such concerns can be addressed usefully by integrating Foucault's 'technologies of the self' into the feminist model of 'technologies of gender'. Doing so allows for greater understanding of how individual women, or groups of women, may experience video game play and help us to understand how different women come to have very different patterns of use and attitudes concerning games and game culture.

… Foucault's later theorizing moved to a consideration of the self and how individuals – shaped in specific cultural contexts – could come to choose actions and behaviors knowingly from a range of options, perhaps even choosing actions that would produce sanctions, but doing so willingly. He termed the range of alternatives 'technologies of the self'.

Such a conceptualization can be applied to the study of digital game use by women, and in so doing can help to clarify some of the contradictions found in women's use and interests in games and gaming. Different researchers have identified women with different play frequencies, styles and interests. These differential uses make it impossible for researchers to make ready conclusions about how digital games may operate as 'technologies of gender', for they seem to operate in different ways for different women. Some women, for example, readily play the more 'masculine' first-person shooter (FPS) games and relish the opportunity to 'blow away' other competitors – especially males. Yet, other women play occasionally or sporadically and prefer more 'gender neutral' games such as *The Sims*. A blanket term such as 'technologies of gender' cannot be applied easily here – which is the 'correct' use of the technology in relation to women (or men)?

A better alternative is offered by the combination 'technologies of the gendered self'. This model solves two problems: it allows researchers a way in which to understand differential play patterns and interests among women (and men), and gives us a more useful theoretical tool for understanding how women negotiate particular technologies and how their various work of negotiation can produce different results and different interpretations of the consumption of technology as a gendered practice.

To that end, this study has examined women's experiences of games and gaming from their perspectives, as they seek to integrate (or reject) gaming technology into their lives, in various ways. It examines how games and gaming function as technologies that help them to define their gendered selves. This can be through integration, negotiation or rejection. This investigation looks at women with different levels of play, as well as different interests in genres and individual games. These differences (and their consequences) offer a better picture of both how women define themselves in terms of gaming, and how gaming culture responds. The research questions are as follows.

RQ1: Why do female gamers play digital games?
RQ2: What are female gamers' perceptions of themselves and their gaming experiences? How do these perceptions influence their decisions to play and purchase digital games?
RQ3: How can women's gaming perceptions be understood from the perspective of power dynamics of technologies of the gendered self?
RQ4: Do electronic games influence women's self-identity or self-image, or perception of women in general?

Method

The integration of female gamers into gaming culture is best understood in its 'most complex whole' (Geertz, 1973: 299). As recommended by Geertz, this study strived to create a 'thick description' of how women blend, negotiate and negate digital gaming and gender. This study grew from a graduate methods class which conducted individual in-depth interviews, as well as focus groups with a diverse group of participants in terms of the level of expertise in gaming – from non-players to expert players – and geographic and demographic diversification.

One group of researchers conducted three focus groups to understand the collective processes of interpretations of gaming culture by female gamers and non-gamers among students in the local area. The guided discussions focused on how women described their electronic gaming experiences and how they constructed their own perspectives about gaming culture. Twenty female students from a Midwestern public university were recruited for three separate focus groups: power users, moderate users and non-users. These groups were assembled, based on the number of hours that the participants spent playing digital games and on the level of expertise as determined by the participants in pre-focus group questionnaires. Operationally, non-gamers did not play any games, moderate gamers spent approximately one to three hours a week playing, while power gamers ranged from three to more then 10 hours weekly. The demographic characteristics of the participants for the focus groups reflected the population of the local university town: mostly Caucasian with a few Asians, ages ranging from 18–37 and with annual incomes below $25,000.

The second group of researchers conducted in-depth interviews. In-depth interviews provide a more personal and individualized account compared to focus groups. By asking questions and probing different answers, the researchers captured women's experiences, views, perceptions and the meaning that they give to computer games. In this project, 15 in-depth interviews were conducted using the following interview techniques: face-to-face (FTF); computer-mediated communication (CMC); and telephone. The CMC interviews enhanced the comprehensiveness of this study by allowing the research team to investigate participants who were savvier in regard to online or digital gaming but geographically located as far away as Europe. The participants for the project can be characterized best as evocative. The researchers selected this group to 'provide a flavor' (Mason, 2002: 126) of the different perspectives of female gamers with varying commitments to playing. The demographic characteristics of the informants were similar to those of the focus group interviews, but with a wider age range, from 18–52. The ethnicity and socio-economic status of these participants were not gathered at the time of the original research.

All the interviews and focus groups were conducted in January and February of 2003 and were transcribed by multiple researchers. All the names used in this article are pseudonyms. Although there are many advantages to the interview method, the method relies heavily upon the responses of subjects and does not allow researchers to observe actual behavior of playing digital games. Nonetheless, we believe that the collaborative approach and the use of different qualitative methods have produced data that is rich and reliable.

Findings

While we wish to avoid the suggestion that female gamers can be easily categorized or that their preferences can be predicted, it was revealing that the data cleaved along lines corresponding to the level of play in which the women engaged. Furthermore, these women expressed variations in their definitions of gendered self. Specifically, it was found that gaming technology and gender were most well integrated for power gamers, whereas for moderate gamers, gaming technology and gender is more carefully negotiated, creating an uneasy truce. By comparison, non-gamers asserted themselves – by their very rejection of gaming technology – in ways that might be considered more traditionally feminine. The following discusses the integration, negotiation and rejection of gaming as it is manifested in the women's choice of genre and characters, their attitudes toward the representations of women in game texts and their exercise of control in integrating, negotiating or rejecting gaming technology.

Integration of Gaming: Gender and Technology Fusion

> There are many computer games that portray women as a sex object, but I don't care. You might think I am a little unusual … The games with extreme violence and sexuality are not allowed for those under age to play, so I don't think it matters. (Roselyn, a power-gamer from Korea)

Power gamers place high importance on gaming and engage in it frequently; it is not surprising, then, that these gamers appear more comfortable with gaming technology and game themes and that gaming is better integrated into their lives. The degree of integration is demonstrated not only by the frequency with which they play, but also by their facility with the technology and their revelations that they enjoy multiple genres. The power gamers that were interviewed tended to distinguish between the various pleasures that gaming provides and astutely recognized that different genres promote different pleasures. The women were technologically adept, and consequently reported that they actively choose specific genres to fulfill their desires for particular pleasures, such as sociability, intellectual stimulation and competitive challenge. For example, Kara said:

> I play RPGs [role-playing games] to relax and enjoy, because they tell thrilling stories like interactive storybooks. I play fighting games when I feel the 'urge' or when someone challenges me. I play strategy games to work out my logic.

One particular pleasure which power gamers emphasized is the challenge that certain games provide; these women take pleasure from mastering the skills required by the game and from competing with other players. Several of the participants cited their preferences for online, multiplayer FPS games and they spoke in detail about the pleasures of this particular genre. Kylie, who studies digital game design in the UK, said: '*Counter-Strike* is a hard game to master. If you become very good, you earn the respect of everyone.' *Counter-Strike* requires considerable time and effort to play and requires social and technical skills in order to connect successfully with people on the internet. For the women who play this game, pleasure also stems from their accomplishments in successful competition. Chris, who has played digital games since the second grade, finds *Counter-Strike* to be 'an exhilarating competitive exercise', which she compares to 'scoring a goal in hockey or soccer'. Despite the fact that typically, FPS games are played by males and have violent content, several of the participants indicated that they consciously choose this genre for its unabashed aggressiveness. Ivy, who has played FPS games for seven years, said:

> Sometimes, if I blew up a guy and he would type 'Bitch' … Well, that just makes me smile and go after him more.

Competition provides an arena in which power gamers are able to define and extend their definitions of self and gender. As Taylor (2003) has observed, one of the most salient pleasures for women gamers is the opportunity to engage in game combat, a space which permits them to challenge gender norms by exploring and testing their aggressive potentiality. Indeed, several of the power gamers interviewed take tremendous pleasure in challenging gender norms through their choice of genre. Ivy, for example, said: 'I liked running around with a rocket launcher and shooting people I didn't know.' At the same time, however, Ivy adamantly asserted her femininity, which she marked by such feminine signs as long fingernails, which she referred to at several points in the interview. Ivy refuses to cut her nails and thus we are presented with a paradox of sorts – the gamer who embodies 'femininity', while performing 'masculinity'. For power gamers, digital games are not a problematic technology. Even as they themselves admit to the hypersexualization of some female images in games and the sexism of some male players, they have defined games successfully for themselves as being about pleasure, mastery and control. Technology here is not a problem but an integral part of life.

This paradox crops up in regard to power gamers in a second area. Power gamers also perform their definitions of gender via the representations of the game characters that they employ. Power gamers are certainly not oblivious to the hypersexualized representation of female avatars and they do realize that such representations pander to male fantasies. However, such representations do not necessarily limit the pleasure of this study's participants. On the contrary, such characters appear to enhance pleasure for a number of these women. Several of the power gamers indicated that they purposefully choose and create characters that are feminine and sexy as well as strong. In an online interview, Kara expressed her appreciation for sexualized female characters:

> When I create a character in an RPG, I like to make them as sexy as possible. Haha! I love a sexy and strong female character. A character who is sexy and strong and can still kick a guy's butt 10 ways to Sunday!

Some additional insight was provided by Chris, another power gamer who writes and reviews games and characters for several women's gaming websites:

> It's not like women want to play ugly characters. They just want to be attractive on their own terms.

Those terms appear to combine [feminine] sexy attributes with [masculine] characteristics like 'strength' and 'intelligence'.

The salient factor for the power gamer in this regard appears to involve choice and control. Having a choice of characters, as well as control over their representations, appeared to maximize these women's sense of agency and pleasure. Chris expressed it this way:

> It's not that I don't want to play a sexual character – it's fantasy role-playing after all and I have fantasies, too. It's that I want it to be my own fantasy, not his.

To the extent that games can provide women with a choice of characters, combined with control of their representation, games function as technologies for explorations of the gendered self, producing paradoxical enactments that challenge cultural norms. Furthermore, when power gamers voiced their concerns about gender bias in games, they cited the weaker power levels of stock female characters; this observation signals their desire for more choice and control within the context of game play. The following exchange occurred in the power gamers' focus group and illustrates how their concerns are tied to their desire for control:

> Erin: I wish there were more characters, where they actually did stuff instead of, like, they help the little princesses.
> Linda: Oh, princesses, that's the worst.
> Lauren: Oh, I hate that one. Just like, 'Oh, save me Morion'. I just wish there [were] more words, like you could actually be the person controlling all this stuff.

A little while later, Lauren commented about the Growling Chicken, a stock character in the second *Lord of the Rings* game:

> The second *Lord of the Rings* has a Growling Chicken, which is nice, but she is a lot weaker than the guys. Like her power level is lower and she just can't do as much and she dies faster and it's kinda weird. Just like, she can't do as much as some of the guys can. I wish it wasn't that way, but that's the way they program it … She is in the book; I read about her. She is a strong character. I mean, she's still fighting everything, but she is not powerful. She is just very weak and kind of de-de-de … can't fight this now, and then she is dead.

The desire for control of a character's representation is linked to the pleasure sought from the gaming experience. Female characters might also promote player identification and enhance women's pleasure in this regard.[1] As Kara reported: 'I use my characters to reflect the way I wish I had the courage to be.' It is clear that for Kara, control of the character's representation increases her pleasure and enjoyment. It is significant then, that in role-playing games where she is able to create her own characters, she chooses a combination of (feminine) sexuality and (masculine) strength. For power gamers, technology encourages them to enact new definitions of the gendered self. One might say that they just want to look sexy while they're 'kicking butt'.

Negotiation of Gaming: Gender and Technology in an Uneasy Truce

> I like games where you can control the world. And I just started playing *Civilization*, where you get to control the whole world. I think that's fun and the one that I recently acquired was *The Sims*. You cannot play a short game of *The Sims*. Just controlling them where it's a controlled environment, where in your [real world] environment you cannot control everything. But you can control everything that happens on the screen. It's like an escape, you get to just control it and not worry about other stuff you cannot control in your life. (Jenn, a participant in the moderate gamers' group)

For moderate gamers, as Jenn's comments illustrate, control is once again a salient factor related to the particular pleasures of the gaming experience. However, as Jenn's comments suggest, the nature of control is radically different for this group of women. Whereas control for power gamers relates to the characters that they use to explore new definitions of gender and self, for moderate gamers, control is largely environmental. For a number of the moderate gamers in this study, games provide the pleasure of an ultimately controllable environment. For others in this group, gaming offers an escape or distraction from everyday life, a vehicle used to escape momentarily the gendered role of life's caretaker; here, distraction can be seen as a means of self-control, a way to cope with the demands of women's daily lives.

Commensurate with these particular pleasures and uses, it is not surprising that the moderate gamers expressed preferences for some RPGs, puzzles, cards and problem-solving games. While a few of these women enjoyed competitive games, the moderate gamers as a group tended to reject violent genres such as the FPS games. Kristin's response was typical of this group of women: 'I don't like shooting, zombies, blood here and blood there ... it's not my type of game.' In addition to choosing genres that are less violent, the moderate gamers veered toward games that provide more opportunities to win. Winning for these women does not necessarily mean defeating an opponent; rather, winning can mean beating the game by predicting and making the right moves in order to solve a puzzle or problem. This type of gratification is the reason that Karen, a 52-year-old housewife, prefers to play *Free Cell*. As she explains, 'If you make the right moves, it is never a non-winnable game.' By playing games like *Free Cell*, Karen is able to control even the very experience of gaming in order to ensure that it provides the particular pleasure that she seeks.

Because control is configured differently for moderate gamers than for power gamers, we need to tease the data in order to understand how gaming functions as a technology of gendered self for this group of women. One set of data provides at least two clues to this end. The first we have briefly mentioned already: moderate gamers seek control and/or distraction from their real-life pressures. The second clue concerns the ways in which moderate gamers tended to draw a line between the genres that women play and those that men play. Thus, while these women emphasized control and distraction as their pleasures, they negotiate gaming in ways that tend to reinscribe traditional gender divisions. For example, many moderate gamers assign fantasy games and violent genres to men. Amy, a moderate gamer, said:

> Most of the men I know play Playstations, or Xbox, or Nintendo and they are more into it. They get into a drama, even if it is a shoot 'em up drama. If I'm gonna go to a virtual world, I'm going to go for distraction from my life, but not to replace it.

According to Amy, women play games for distraction. She perceives that men become more fully immersed in the virtual game world – they enter more easily into the fantasy and drama and tend to devote more time to games. This line between reality and fantasy helps to explain other remarks made by moderate gamers such as Kerry, who said: 'I am kind of annoyed by people who talk about video games like real life.' The distinction between women and men and reality and fantasy carried over to a focus group discussion about the representations of women in games:

> I think that most video games are geared towards younger males. They just don't think that there's an audience, like, female. They're geared more towards the man … Anytime you have a female fighter, she's got like huge breasts and a flat stomach and long legs and it's always [an] exact outfit you'll never see in real life. It's all, like, glorified. (Danni)

A little while later, Rachel noted that *The Sims* game that she prefers permits players to choose more realistic characters:

> In *The Sims* you can choose your body. They do have, like, slender, big-boob woman and … the arousing man [who is] rippled out. But they also have, like, the overweight woman-in-her-thirties character.

When asked by the moderator whether they could identify with game characters, or whether some character representations might be empowering for women, the moderate gamers again asserted a difference between the real world and the game world. …

In doubting that such representations might be empowering for women and in denying any identification with the game's characters, moderate gamers provide a clue about how they define gender and self. Inasmuch as self and gender remain tethered to the moderate gamers' realities, their habits of negotiating game technology seem to reinscribe a game technology or gender division for these women. …

With one foot firmly in the 'real world' at all times, it should not be surprising then that moderate gamers talk a lot about the pleasures of control and distraction. In some respects, 'control' would seem to signal an intense involvement with the games, almost diametrically opposed to distraction. However, it can be argued that for the women in this study, control and distraction are two sides of the same coin. In their discussion, control and distraction bracket real life, providing two approaches for coping with its stressors. To demonstrate this, the moderate gamers' 'control' discourse will be vetted further.

For some of the women who expressed pleasure in being able to exercise control over an environment or situation, computer games appear to be useful as a rehearsal for the challenges of life. Eva, for example, faced a daunting cultural adjustment when she came to the USA 10 years ago. When we specifically asked her to compare the difficulties of her real life and the challenges that she finds in computer games, she replied:

> I think it's almost the same thing … Because I tried the game [that] I can do … [In] real life I can do the same thing. I think, almost the same. Whatever I put my effort, I can do in real life and the game.

Eva shares a characteristic with several other gamers who played in order to control an environment – a need to think through problems. Eva prefers war (strategy) games:

> [B]ecause [I] have to think what I have to do … how can I move … how can I improve my characters … how I can win. I have to think.

Many of the moderate gamers indicated that they enjoyed the mental challenge that games provide. Lily spoke about this pleasure as she reflected on her 'role' in the mystery games that she plays:

> You're like, the conscience, you know. You're pretty much in control of his mind. And you get his mind and … all the clues that he knows about to figure it out. And then you have to tell *him* … It puts you up on a pedestal, even over the main character.

We read Lily's comment as further evidence of both gender division and the line that moderate gamers impose between reality and the gameworld. Lily's description of her 'role' as the male character's conscience suggests that she sees herself as positioned outside the game world. It seems likely, then, that the pleasure she derives from this game also works to construct or reinforce her sense of gendered self. By describing her pleasure in the terms of being placed on a pedestal above the main (male) character, we might even read her particular construction of gendered self to be one of superiority. For Lily, the self is constructed as exceedingly competent but nonetheless embedded in the gender conventions of reality.

Although some moderate gamers seek their pleasure in games that help them to think through problems, others among this group play in order to stop thinking about the worries of their daily lives. Michelle, who plays for distraction in order to relieve stress and to stop thinking about her problems and commitments, compared computer games to rock climbing:

> You give all your attention to something, so it is like the rest of the world just, you know, falls away, because you are focusing … so intensely … on this one thing. I heard when people talk about … rock climbing. That is, people like rock climbing so much, because … the only thing they have to think about is the place to put their hand. They don't think about the next mortgage payment, a girlfriend, or whatever; they are, like, just completely taken out by the next motion they have to make.

The moderate gamer uses games in order to cope with her everyday life. For some women, games provide a way to think through and solve various problems and situations; for others, computer games provide a temporary respite from the worries that plague their minds. The desire for control and the desire for distraction are two sides of the same coin, pleasures that bracket the moderate gamer's position. These indicate that the moderate gamer is situated at an intersection where the virtual gameworld intersects with their reality. The moderate gamer negotiates gaming technologies in order to help cope with the routines of their daily life, yet they are not quite fully immersed in the gaming world. …

Rejection of Gaming: Gender Triumphs over Technology of Gaming

> You know, girls, I'm in my mid-20s. The girls I hang out with, they're just way more into going out with friends and doing things, like in their different clubs and organizations. And they have full-time jobs, or they have part-time jobs while they're going to school … Everything they do is more interaction-based. There's not time to be doing something with the computer or with a TV. (Michelle, a participant in the non-gamers' group)

The non-gamers had critical, negative perceptions of gaming. They rejected gaming as a waste of time and were quite vocal about asserting other priorities. In the focus groups, non-gamers expressed the strongest opinions about a perceived 'gaming culture'. They were concerned about the sexualized and violent content of games, but acknowledged that this is a problem with other media products as well. Non-gamers also speculated that players become addicted to computer games. These women viewed gaming as an asocial and solitary activity and believed most gamers to be interpersonally inept. By their implied and expressed comparisons to players, non-gamers define themselves in ways that might be considered more traditionally female: completely grounded in reality, interpersonally competent and with their priorities set on things that really matter.

For non-gamers, the rejection of gaming was expressed as control over time and the assertion of other priorities. The amount of time required to play was discussed at some length in the non-gamers' focus group. Several of the participants stated that the length of time required to play was 'ridiculous'. Speaking about *Final Fantasy*, a role-playing game with which she had some familiarity, Lindsay observed that 'it takes you like 20 hours until you reach the end'. When asked what type of games she might consider playing, Michelle again asserted that time was a primary consideration; if she did decide to play, she would look for games with 'an endpoint' which do not continue 'on for years' and that can be completed 'within a certain amount of time'.

Time appears to be significant in these women's rejection of games because it is a practical obstacle to their participation and because their leisure time is determined largely by family and work responsibilities:

> Women usually have more things to do. I mean, lets face it, they're out there working. Not only do [women] work outside of the home, but then they come in and have to make dinner, do the laundry, get the kids ready for school the next day … They don't have any time for games much less for themselves, to do things they wanna do. (Kathy)

While Kathy's comments demonstrate the practical consequences of limited leisure time, they also suggest that the non-gamer's time is configured in relation to their established gender roles and responsibilities.

According to the non-gamers, their rejection of gaming is not simply a matter of daily responsibilities limiting their available leisure time. While several of the women indicated that they might play games if they could be completed within a short period of time, by and large the non-gamers echoed Michelle, whose comments open this section, in asserting that they choose other priorities.

The choices that non-gamers make appear to align with traditional female expectations, and include interpersonal activities which are 'interaction based'. This particular choice is centered in the way that non-gamers define themselves and is positioned in opposition to their perceptions of players. Non-gamers viewed gaming as a 'solitary' activity which attracts individuals who lack interpersonal skills. For example, Jill observed that players become so absorbed in games that they 'ignore everyone around them'. Similarly, Michelle perceives her own brother and sister, who are both avid gamers, as 'very introverted':

> They are very good at like computer language and decoding this and doing that in the role-playing game, [but] if you take them out to a social event they are not sure how to act with other physical human beings. But put them behind a keyboard and they can talk to people outside of the country, but they can't deal with one-on-one behaviors.

By comparison, then, non-gamers imply their own interpersonal competence. Ironically, despite non-gamers' interpersonal competence, their self-definitions construct a gendered, split-sphere arrangement that is quite long established. It is possible to read how separate spheres conflict with traditionally-gendered interpersonal objectives in Amber's comments:

> If they are my age, which is just under 30, then I'm thinking of the guys in the long, black trench coats who are playing the role-playing games online. Where it's a strangely solitary event, but it's still a group event in a very solitary way. This is why I think that I am still single. Because I think that all the eligible men my age are somewhere in a room playing video games.

We might conclude that non-gamers are playing another game by real-world rules. In addition, non-gamers were more concerned about the sexualized representations of women in computer gamers, but recognized that other media contribute to these stereotypes, creating an intertextual effect:

> I've noticed … that some of the qualities of some of these women, that I've seen in some of these video games or ads, seem to be extremely desirable by men, such as their sluttiness. Uh, and it's just, it's been relationship breakers before and … I don't know where it comes from. I don't know if that's from TV, magazines or it's from these games. (Amber)

Amber and some of the other non-gamers worry that these stereotypes create expectations on the part of men, which spill over into the real world:

> I think that men … It's kind of the virgin – whore dichotomy, in that they'd like to date a nice girl, but really, they'd really like her to act like this … Or do those things in the bedroom that I see on TV. Especially the Japanamation kind of look and those girls seem really domineering, but yet are also coy and shy, but yet very strong sexual overtones. (Amber)

… While non-gamers seem to define themselves in ways that align with traditional ideas of femininity, she insists that she is an interpersonally competent agent who exercises active choice in how she determines priorities and controls her time. She also appears to feel the real effects of sexism most acutely.

Gaming as a Gendered, Technological Practice: Re-integrating Theory

'Technologies of the gendered self' refers to the dynamic relationship between women, gender and technological use. This concept helps us to understand how women negotiate game play, gender expectations and roles in relation to technology use. It acknowledges that practices are often multiple and conflicting and seeks to expand rather than conflate ambiguities and differences. In this way, this concept should be useful in understanding a wider range of technological uses and how gender relates, as it more broadly takes account of active users and multiple uses of technologies.

The results of this research demonstrate that this concept is useful in understanding how female gamers integrate different levels of gaming technologies with their perceptions of gender and self. Additionally, by allowing for variations in the degree of technological integration, the concept allows an exploration of how different gender constructions are implicated in the way that gamers negotiate the tensions of gaming and reality. As part of that negotiation, in fact, gamers create different boundaries for their game-playing activities, with some seeing gaming as squarely separate from 'real life' or reality and others acknowledging that the two overlap and co-constitute each other.

Power gamers who have integrated gaming technologies into their everyday lives construct a gendered self that might be described as more fluid and androgynous, in that it comprises a palette of chosen traits and interests; this contrasts with a gendered female self that embodies 'traditional' norms reflective of a masculine/feminine binary. The integration of gaming technology empowers women with a confidence that prevails in the challenge and competition that they encounter in games. Even 'conventional' signs of femininity, such as long nails and sexualized representations, were viewed by many of these women as pleasurable and emancipating, rather than as subjugating them in male – female power dynamics.

By comparison, the gendered self of moderate gamers is situated in a liminal space between 'real life' and gaming. Although moderate gamers enjoy playing and can be quite good at it, they have not fully integrated gaming technologies with their gendered identity. While power gamers perform a more fluid and androgynous gender in gaming, moderate gamers' self-constructions do not demonstrate this degree of fusion but rather they suggest an uneasy alliance between identity and activity. For them, gaming functions as a coping mechanism, a vehicle of escape from reality, and games provide an opportunity to control an environment on their own terms. For them, gaming is a sphere apart from 'reality'. Moderate gamers perceive gaming as a predominantly male activity and situate themselves as more closely aligned with 'the real world' than the fantasy worlds of particular games. Subsequently, in thus making the distinction and then negotiating reality and gaming, moderate gamers construct a gendered self that appears to be positioned in an uneasy truce between two worlds.

In contrast, non-gamers, who rejected gaming and its culture as totally masculine, positioned themselves as successfully living in the 'real world'. Here again, gameworlds are separate from the 'real' world, as articulated by this group. In this study, these women frequently rejected gaming because it takes too much time, a commodity they perceive as already limited and better spent on 'social' activities – interests and pursuits that are often generalized as more traditionally feminine. The non-gamers studied had less understanding of gaming technologies and tended to depict players as interpersonally inept and 'addicted' to gaming. Unlike power and moderate gamers, the non-gamers did not appear to appreciate the emancipative potential of games, neither did they discern the possibility of negotiating a 'truce' between gaming and reality, or even less likely, see how the two might merge in any way.

Finally, we want to acknowledge that in outlining this conceptualization of 'technologies of the gendered self', this study has relied on three somewhat artificial categories in order to describe female gamers and non-gamers. These categories, and the levels of technological integration that they represent, need not be viewed as a rigid matrix for understanding gender and gaming. With further research, the model can be expanded, modified and refined to represent better the complexities and power dynamics that operate at the intersection of gender and games.

Conclusion

This study began by asking how individual differences in the consumption of computer games intersect with gender and how it is that games and gender mutually constitute each other. To examine this question, its efforts were focused on adult women, seeking to understand the gaming experience from their perspectives, with particular attention to differences in level of play, as well as their genre preferences. Based on the participants' responses, three levels of game consumption were identified. For power gamers, those participants who reported the highest levels of consumption, technology and gender appear to be most highly integrated. These women play more frequently and tended to play multiple genres, deriving different pleasures from different types of games, including the mastery of game-based skills and competition. These women seemed most likely and willing to exploit gaming technology in order to explore different enactments of a gendered self.

By comparison, moderate gamers play games in order to cope with their lives. These women reported that they take pleasure in controlling the gaming environment, or alternately, that games provide a necessary distraction from the pressures of their daily lives. Moderate gamers enjoy games, but negotiate technology in a way that reinscribes the gender divisions that we traditionally associate with the lived world.

The non-gamers who participated in the study expressed strong criticisms about game-playing and gaming culture. For these women, games are a waste of time – a limited commodity better spent on other activities. Their decisions not to play define a self that might be viewed as more traditionally feminine, but which these women insist is interpersonally competent and grounded in the things that matter.

The findings here support the work of other feminist scholars who have previously argued that gender and technology have a reciprocal relationship. This study has tried especially to respond to van Zoonen's (2002) arguments concerning the complexity of technology and gender by accounting for differences in game consumption. By examining three levels of consumption, it has developed a more nuanced understanding of the ways in which gender and technology are articulated. In addition, it has proposed a concept, 'technologies of the gendered self', which offers flexibility and moves us closer to a better understanding of how technology and gender intersect in individuals' resistance or compliance to existing gender hierarchies.

NOTE

1. In this article we do not explore in depth the relationship between identification of players and their avatars, although we do subscribe to Gee's (2003) belief that such relationships are complex in their construction. This limitation is due in part to our lack of specific questioning of women regarding their identification with avatars (or not) – we mainly talked about game-play and representation. In reflecting on the evidence, however, we can see that power gamers are more likely to identify fully with their avatars (viewing themselves as controlling the character, the character in the virtual world and their hopes and plans for the character), while moderate gamers are more conflicted. In using Gee's taxonomy of levels of identification, we could argue that moderate gamers cannot construct a projective identity. That is, they can view themselves as controlling avatars in different games, but do not make a complete interface between 'the real-world person and the virtual character' (2003: 56). For moderate gamers, the avatar (virtual identity) and their own identity (real world) are not meshed, but remain distinct.

REFERENCES

Balsamo, A. (1996) *Technologies of the Gendered Body: Reading Cyborg Women*. Durham, NC: Duke University Press.

Davies, J. (2002) 'Male Dominance of Video Game Production and Consumption: Understanding the Social and Cultural Processes', URL (consulted 30 June 2004): http://www.gamasutra.com/education/theses/20020708/davies_01.shtml

Foucault, M. (1988) 'Technologies of the Self: A Seminar with Michel Foucault', in L.H. Martin, H. Gutman and H. Hutton (eds) *Technologies of the Gendered Self: A Seminar with Michel Foucault*, pp. 16–49. Amherst, MA: University of Massachusetts Press.

Gee, J. (2003) *What Video Games Have to Teach Us about Learning and Literacy*. New York: Palgrave.

Geertz, C. (1973) 'Thick Description: Toward an Interpretive Theory of Culture', in *The Interpretation of Cultures*, pp. 298–320. New York: Harper.

Haraway, D. (1991) *Simians, Cyborgs and Women*. New York: Routledge.

Mason, J. (2002) *Qualitative Researching* (2nd edn). London: Sage.

Rakow, L. (1992) *Gender on the Line: Women, the Telephone and Community Life*. Urbana, IL: University of Illinois Press.

Taylor, T.L. (2003) 'Multiple Pleasures: Women and Online Gaming', *Convergence* 9(1): 21–46.

van Zoonen, L. (2002) 'Gendering the Internet: Claims, Controversies and Cultures', *European Journal of Communication* 17(1): 5–23.

Yates, S. and K. Littleton (2001) 'Understanding Computer Game Cultures: A Situated Approach', in E. Green and A. Adam (eds) *Virtual Gender: Technology, Consumption and Identity*, pp. 103–23. London: Routledge.

28 TO THE WHITE EXTREME
Conquering Athletic Space, White Manhood, and Racing Virtual Reality

David J. Leonard

The sports gaming industry is the crown jewel of the video games world. Sports games account for more than thirty percent of all video games sales. In 2002 alone, EA Sports sold 4.5 million units (Ratliff 96). In total, sports video games represent a one billion dollar industry. While crucial as a source of moneymaking, the popularity and presence of sports embodies a powerful racialized project, offering spaces of racialized play, fantasy and pleasure. Whether reflecting the history of minstrelsy, as evident in games like *NFL Street* or *NBA Ballers*, or efforts to colonize spaces with extreme sports games, sporting virtual realities require ideological and cultural examination.

In a recent interview, Adam Clayton Powell III referred to video games as "high-tech blackface," arguing that "because the players become involved in the action ... they become more aware of the moves that are programmed into the game" (Marriott 2003). Imitation, in both the real and virtual worlds, is not the highest form of flattery. ...

As with the history of minstrelsy, sampling of the other is neither liberatory nor transgressive – it does not unsettle dominant notions through breaking down barriers or increasing exposure. The ideas of blackness introduced through video games reflect dominant ideologies, thereby providing sanction for the status quo, legitimacy for white supremacy and evidence for the common sense ideas of race, gender, sexuality and nation.

David J. Leonard, "To the White Extreme: Conquering Athletic Space, White Manhood, and Racing Virtual Reality," pp. 110–29 from Nate Garrelts (ed.), *Digital Gameplay: Essays on the Nexus of Game and Gamer* (Jefferson, NC: McFarland & Co., 2005).

Sports games represent a site in which white hatred and disdain for blackness and its love and adoration for blackness is revealed through popular culture. In borrowing from Eric Lott's work on minstrelsy, video games reflect, "the dialectical flickering of racial insult and racial envy, moments of domination and moments of liberation, counterfeit and currency" (Lott 18). In other words, these games reveal white supremacy in the form of both contempt and desire. The contempt materializes in different ways, but in reflecting an oppositional binary, sports games legitimize stereotypical ideas about black athletic superiority and white intellectual abilities. The adoration materializes in the approval and value we offer black athletes, whether through financial rewards, posters on our walls, or imitation. The desire to "be black" because of the stereotypical visions of strength, athleticism, power and sexual potency all play out within the virtual reality of sports games. "Today's gaming resides squarely in mainstream America, and for them fantasy means Tigers and Kobes" (Ratliff 96).

In actuality, the fantasy of gaming does not limit the imagination to the virtual embodiment of black athletes, with extreme sports games offering an alternative space in which white masculinity (of player and virtual athletes) is validated in absence of people of color and women as powerful, defiant, courageous and ultimately authentic example of true sportsman. Extreme sports games offers a powerful racialized project of inhabiting the bodies and spaces of extreme sports athletes. The world of extreme sports games represents an increasingly popular genre, offering its participants the ability to embody a virtual white sports rebel. Given the increased value anointed to extreme sports athletes, who are celebrated for their whiteness, rule breaking, and masculinity (ability to get women), it should not be surprising that these games generate significant levels of economic success. Amidst an imagined backlash against white males during 1980s and 1990s (into today), the increasing popularity of the (virtual) white extreme sports rebel reflects an ideological and cultural response to the presumptive pollutant of blackness and femininity on white manhood. The cultural stature of specific extreme sports athletes (Tony Hawk; Dave Mira) and the gendered approval given to mastery over the extreme represent two distinct cues as to why extreme sports games dominate the industry.

At the ideological core of virtual extreme sport is the mastery and conquering of untamed space amidst the hegemony of popular and political protests that imagine the ghetto as a threat to white masculinity. The games offer players the opportunity to play or dominate (black) city spaces in absence of people of color. Those games located outside the city, within the "wild" offer similar ideological and cultural inscriptions, providing a space where an athletic white manhood is validated through domination of the physical landscape. As with extreme sports, the virtual incarnations additionally define this alternative sports world as a space of white masculine dominance, whereupon the entry of women results from male fantasies and sexual needs; moreover, the perceptual presence of people of color legitimizes the space. Hypermasculinity and an excessive female sexuality geared toward male pleasure define *Tony Hawk Underground*, *SSX Tricky* and *Amped*. With this in mind, I argue how these games construct a white masculinity through erasing people of color, commodifying innercity spaces, offering opportunities to dominate nature, all the while rendering females as sexual objects and eye candy. These games personify a powerful racialized/gendered/sexualized project that provides commonsense ideas about race, gender, and sexuality.

With only a few titles exploring the history of video games, and a vast majority uncritically celebrating the explosion in virtual reality, the field of games studies represents a barren wasteland of knowledge. This chapter offers a narrow focus on the intersections of race, gender, and sexuality with extreme sports games. It accepts the task of examining the racialized/gendered content of extreme sports games, paying particular attention to how these games construct a virtual sport dominated by an imagined white masculinity. Specifically examining the popularity of these games, the celebration of rule breaking, and the constructions of white "athletes" as courageous, cool, creative and holding mastery over space/nature, this chapter will defamiliarize the racial construct of whiteness within extreme sports games.

In examining these dimensions, this chapter equally gives voice to the narrative options of these games, in that players can simultaneously engage in a world of extreme sports, challenging mental creativity through imagined stunts, and enter into a world of hypersexuality, in which success leads to the opportunity to consume virtually naked females. In exploring these various narratives, I theorize the ways in which race, gender, and sexuality play into these available choices, each providing pleasure, while accommodating white fantasies and affirming white privilege through virtual gaming.

White Masculinity: The Ultimate Virtual Bond

Both extreme sports and their virtual brethren exist as performative spaces of white male masculinity. These worlds and our understanding of each necessitate a brief discussion of the constructed elements of white male identity. Within this scope, it is impossible to chronicle the expansive and emerging field of whiteness studies. It is important, however, to reflect on "whiteness" as the foundation of this paper (Kusz "Minority," 392). Ruth Frankenberg defines whiteness as a "location of structural advantage," and a "standpoint, a location from which to see selves, others and national and global orders." In her estimation, "whiteness is a site of elaboration or a range of cultural practices and identities, often unmarked and unnamed or named as natural or 'normative' rather than specifically racial" (Frankenberg, "Mirage" 76). While others emphasize the intimate relationship of power and constructions of the other (Kincheloe and Steinberg; hooks), Frankenberg identifies those key elements of whiteness as both wrapped up in privilege and unnoticed.

Although academic discourses have recently sought to render whiteness as a visible racial category of significance, given "the wages of whiteness" and the "possessive investment in whiteness," its meaning and existence tends to remain overlooked as "if it is the natural, inevitable, ordinary way of being" (Dyer, as qtd in Kusz "Minority," 393; Roediger). Dominant discourses and representations render whiteness as "a privileged place of racial normativity" (Wray and Newitz 3). Joe Feagin, Hernan Vera and Andrew Gordon further argue that "one difficulty in studying the white self is that until recently, it was an invisible and non regarded category, even difficult to name and not perceived as a distinctive racial identity. Even today, most white Americans either do not think about whiteness at all or else think of it as a positive or neutral category" (Feagin and Vera 296).

Building on the work of Richard Dyer and James Baldwin, bell hooks argues that the popular imagination has envisioned whiteness as "synonymous with goodness." hooks concludes that whites have been "socialized to believe the fantasy that white-ness represents goodness and all that is benign and non-threatening" (hooks "Representing," 169). Dyer concurs, arguing that "as long as race is something only applied to non white peoples, as long as white people are not racially seen and named, they/we function as a human norm. Other people are raced, we are just people" (Dyer "*White*," 1).

The goal of critical whiteness studies (or a pedagogy of whiteness) and this chapter is to make visible, analyze, and expose "the everyday, invisible and subtle, cultural and social practices, ideas, and codes that discursively secure the power and privilege of white people, but that strategically remains unmarked, unnamed, and unmapped in comparison to society" (Shome 503). As noted by Richard Dyer (1997) and Henry Giroux (1997), a pedagogy of whiteness or explorations into the constructions of whiteness seeks "to make whiteness strange" (Dyer 4).

The textual manifestations of a hegemonic, yet unmarked, notion of whiteness are visible within extreme sports games, which further naturalize whiteness as oriented toward physical dominance, creativity, normalcy, and sexual prowess, while reclaiming whiteness amidst an imagined attack against white masculinity. The result of interrogating textual and contextual renderings of whiteness within extreme sports games is "whiteness unfrozen … as ensembles of local phenomena complexly embedded in socio-economic, socio-cultural and psychic interrelations. Whiteness emerges as a process, not a 'thing,' as plural rather than singular in nature" (Frankenberg "Local," 1).

[…]

A pedagogy of whiteness, evident in this treatment of extreme sports video games, does not simply elucidate the existence or representation of whiteness, but connects its textual utterances in relationship to larger systems of racial formation, power and white supremacy. It is crucial to contextualize examinations of popular culture, or these specific games, within the material conditions that give rise to poverty, inequality, white privilege and state violence. Given these realities and the deleterious effects on people of color, it is futile and contemptible to treat cultural productions as pure texts. To detach popular culture and the dissemination of stereotypes from the conditions of white supremacy reflects the acceptance of studying ethnics, rather than doing ethnic studies.

A dialectical relationship thus exists between the whiteness of virtual athletes and their qualities, actions, and performative identities. In order to understand the racial/cultural/ideological significance of extreme sports games it is important to understand the historical context of the emergence of this sporting field, as well as the discourse's manners of articulation. Following a decade of identity politics (nationality movements), feminist struggles, affirmative action, and several moments of … transgression, the 1980s and 1990s saw "the ascendancy of a new and powerful figure in U.S. culture: the white male as victim" (Savran 4). Popular culture proved particularly powerful in "the production of images and narratives of victimized and disadvantaged young white males that both reflect and reproduce the discursive logics of contemporary white male backlash" (Kusz, "Minority" 392). Specifically, the brand of popular culture evident in Beck's "Loser" (1994), *Sports Illustrated's* "What Happened to the White Athlete?" (1997), *Good Will Hunting* (1997), and a wave of sports films, collectively "imagined … the white male protagonist as under-privileged, lacking social, cultural economic or genetic privileges and under constant siege" (Kusz, "Minority" 396) …

According to Kyle Kusz, Robert Reinhart (1998) and others, the discursive focus and popularity of extreme sports reflects both the increasing visibility of "angry white male/white male backlash" politics and the increasing anxiety over the diminishing power and visibility of white athletes. Given the importance of American sporting spaces as a marker of masculinist prowess, the increasing dominance of African American athletes in the face of a disappearing white athlete, fears about white masculinity were addressed with extreme sports. S.L. Price, in "What Happened to the White Athlete?" identified extreme sports as a response to "the diminishing opportunities for athletic success for white men in 'mainstream' sports such as football, baseball, and basketball: Unsure of his place in a sport world dominated by blacks … the young white male is dropping of the athletic mainstream to pursue success elsewhere.… He is increasingly drawn to … alternative athletic pursuits that are overwhelming white" (Price 31–32). Kusz not only links this discourse to those of "white male as victim," but to a desire to assert a particular vision of white masculinity that imagined white athletes (men) in a "superior and dominant position" (Kusz, "BMX" 166).

Within a context of increasing visibility of feminist and multicultural discourses, and a metamorphasizing sports world – rising player salaries, increasing visibility of black athletes, especially as stars, greater corporate and media interest in sports, and the growth in the visibility and role of female athletes – extreme sports emerged as an alternative sports world that constructed itself as a domain of white mascu-linity, with its emphasis on extreme danger, risk-taking, and performative manli-ness. Those changes inside and outside of traditional sports had "lessened the availability of sportsman as a role that could be unequivocally occupied by those who saw [white] masculinity as under threat in their own lives," to which extreme sports emerged as a source of rectification (Kibby 16). "But if sport, as played out in stadiums and on television screens was occasionally problematic for hegemonic masculinity," extreme sports offered "a productive source of … fulfillment. If con-temporary sport had been fueled by greed, feminism, and social liberalism," extreme sports "safeguarded hegemonic masculinity in providing an arena where individual success, male-male bonds … the rejection of the feminine, could be comfortably accommodated" (Kibby 17). Within this discourse and in response to these ubiquitous political projects, extreme sports games offer an even more pronounced erasure of people of color in the world of athletics.

What Happened to the Black Athlete?

People of color fill one of two roles within the virtual extreme sports world: 1) as virtually absent or lone tokens; or 2) as exotic, racist caricatures. The bulk of extreme sports games lack characters of color, despite their visibility within the world of sports. Within games like *Amped* or *Dave Mira* people of color are totally absent. Both *Tony Hawk* games offer a single character of color who reflects hegemonic visions of blackness. Kareem Campbell, a character based on an actual person, is a well-honed version of the world's street dwellers hopes to someday attain smart, real, and smoothed out style – without the R and B. Unlike his peers who reflect the alternative lifestyles of extreme sports, Campbell embodies its "authentic" rhythms and hip-hop elements. Whether completely absent or existing as hip-hop tokens, the presence of blackness within extreme virtual sports solidifies the meanings of white masculinity.

Games, like *SSX* and *BMX XXX*, which contain several characters of color, do not unsettle this white masculine hegemony, as virtual athletes of color are defined by intensely racist caricatures that add to the exotic and alternative orientation of the extreme sports world. For example, both *SSX 3* and *SSX Tricky* offer extreme (racist) caricatures of people of color: the exotic Asian woman, the Latina (Native American) woman wearing war paint, and the hip-hop, bling-bling black man. Their extreme presentation and stereotypical embodiment signifies the extreme elements of these games. Moreover, the "otherness" of these personages provides meaning to the white characters, which despite their alternative identities, are still clearly white. The baggy pants, defiance of rules, and extreme masculinity, raise little question as to the presence and meaning of their whiteness, given the presence of these stereotypical characters of color. The racialized other marks the visible as invisible, rendering white masculinity as the natural opposition to the exotic, functioning as a defining element in the world of extreme sports.

Despite the transgression of a virtual color line, the world of extreme sports games is ostensibly a world without people of color (particularly males), except the occasional racialized caricature strategically placed to add "exotic flavor" and provide an oppositional binary of legitimacy to the game's visions of whiteness. As part of a larger project to reclaim sports and a white sporting masculinity, male extreme athletes of color virtually disappear, while women of color serve as exotic sexual objects to be consumed by both male characters and game players. The absence of men of color within virtual extreme sports games reflects the larger project of extreme sports.

As a popular cultural site, extreme sports has become involved in a reactionary politics of representation which seeks to represent a "strong, proud, confident, unconstrained, and unapologetic white athletic masculinity whose characteristics, investments, desires and practices would appeal to whites" (Kusz, "BMX" 155). To Kusz, extreme (virtual) sports filled a void, need or panacea to 1990s male anxiety, which "were said to have a crisis of confidence, self-esteem, social status and identity" ("BMX" 155). Extreme sports games fill this persistent void while addressing this imagined crisis. In fact, this constructed world of virtual extreme athleticism offers an "unapologetic white masculinity, defined by alternative values, risk-taking, and extreme sexual prowess" (Kusz, "BMX" 154). More powerful than its real-life brethren, extreme sports games leave few gaps or contradictions. With the ultimate reduction of femininity to sexuality and the complete erasure of men of color, extreme sports games are a space for, by and about white men. Unlike the discourse surrounding real extreme sports games, which emphasizes the whiteness of this alternative world, the fantasy world inscribes people of color as scenery, as racialized caricatures. However, as with ESPN's X-Games or the coverage of extreme sports, these games relate white masculinity to a position of normalcy, as the most desired sporting masculinity. Seen as the pollutants or descriptors of an authentic white masculinity, the absence of people of color and non-sexualized women allow for the production of a particular vision of white masculinity.

We Love the Ghetto, but We Hate Black People

While extreme sports games construct a world defined by white masculinity, a significant number of games take place within America's ghettos. The importance of dominating or mastering space is found in those games located within America's inner cities. Whereas hegemonic projects of the ghettocentric imagination systematic demonize inner-city communities because of the presence of people of color, these extreme sports games construct the ghetto without people of color. Resembling an array of popular cultural projects that glorify/fetishize ghetto spaces, *Tony Hawk Underground, Thug*, and *BMX XXX*, define the ghetto through its aesthetics and an imagined hip-hop culture. Virtual extreme sports games erase "how segregation strips communities of resources and reproduces inequality" (Kelley, "Integration" 18). They, in imagining the ghetto as a cultural signifier and an exotic tourist destination, "[deny] how the decline of decent paying jobs and city services, erosion of public space, deterioration of housing stock and property values, and stark inequalities in education and health care are manifestations of investment strategies under de facto segregation" (Kelley, "Integration" 18). ...

Devoid of political and economic contexts, as well as the realities of American racism, *Tony Hawk* and *BMX XXX* inscribe the ghetto as an exotic locale to be celebrated and conquered. In the context of extreme sports, the ghetto location offers the dangerous elements that legitimize extreme sports as "non-mainstream sporting practices characterized by the valorization of risk-taking behaviors; the emphasis on creativity, individuality and marking oneself as 'different;' and the participation in activities individually performed but practice in small groups that value a sense of community" (Kusz, "BMX" 153).

The valorization of "overcoming one's fear and taking risks" within extreme sport games is especially powerful within these ghettocentric games, in that they allow players/ game characters to conquer dangerous ghetto spaces through performing an extreme, athletic white masculinity. Kusz, in writing about BMX and extreme sports, elucidates this racial context, as evident in both the real and virtual inscriptions of extreme sports. Dominant discourses concerning extreme sports "represents the extreme athlete as an offspring of the American frontiersman (racially coded as white) as both are said to have an insatiable appetite for risk, a thirst for adventure, and a desire to be the embodiment of strength, coolness and confidence" ("BMX" 168). Whereas the frontiersman defied the dangers of the unnamed wilderness guarded by indigenous savages, the extreme virtual skateboarder defies the dangers and geographic obstacles of America's ghetto, conquering this once dangerous space, demonstrating the ultimate "strength, coolness and confidence" of this white masculinity.

For example, *Tony Hawk's Pro Skater 3* offers a series of locations to which players attempt to perform lip tricks and crazy moves within urban centers and suburban locations. Players can skate in Canada or the suburbs. The game insert and visual demarcation of suburbia constructs a banal world without danger or threats: "Did someone say Ice Cream? Explore the neighborhood! Hit the rooftop, ledge grinds, trash the trailer park vert ramps and find your way into the haunted house. ... Who knows, if you are good enough, you own one of these houses some day." The rest of the locations, however, are within city landscapes, offering danger-ous and exotic geographies to physically conquer even without residents of color. In Los Angeles, skaters face the dangers of traffic, with Tokyo affording players the chance to traverse the chaos of city life. As with outdoor extreme sports games, the urban extreme sport location exotifies the urban landscape as a culturally exciting yet dangerous place that challenge and tests the creativity, courage and masculinity of the extreme sports athlete.

White Mastery: Controlling, Dominating and Conquering Untamed Space

Of central importance to the allure and performative attraction of extreme sports games specifically, and video games in general, is the opportunity to control, domi-nate, and conquer space. Henry Jenkins, director of Comparative Media Studies at MIT, encapsulates the celebratory side of the emerging field of game studies through his deployment of historically racialized and problematic language: "Now that we've colonized physical space, the need to have new frontiers is deeply embedded in the games. [Video Games] expand the universe" (Jenkins "Complete"). As the literature connects the popularity of video games to fantasy, "exploration and discovery," colonization and penetrating "the virtual frontier," as if each were raceless projects, it is important to link games and the surrounding discourse to historical projects of white supremacy, based on the power of becoming and occupying the other (Gee; Jenkins; Rheingold).

Additionally, the possibilities of controlling and mastering untamed geographies reflects a profound masculinist project that allows players of extreme sports games to demonstrate their own physical/mental prowess through courage, creativity and physicality. Within both real and virtual extreme sports, representation characterizes white masculinity as "desiring a space where it can reconstruct a sense of superiority and psychic stability by investing in a cultural space and practice it can claim as its own" (Kusz, "BMX" 167).

This emphasis on controlling and dominating space is especially evident within extreme sports games, which offer its primarily white male players the chance to become white male extreme athletes – the chance to master both nature and urban geographies. "All extreme sports are thrill-seeking activities to which psychologies of danger and excitement" guide performative masculinities (Reinehart and Syndor 12). As Reinehart and Syndor note, extreme sports offer a space where courage "can be a vice" (Reinehart and Syndor 12). Yet, Kusz questions how this emphasis on courage and danger reflects a project that seeks to legitimize white masculinity. "The white male [virtual] extreme athlete, being an instrument an effect of representational politics of the white male backlash, … appropriates the logic of identity politics, makes visible and invests" in a particular vision of whiteness." It simultaneously "makes a claim to holding an authentic marginal identity, is figured as overcoming these feelings of fear and insecurity through this practice, which allows him to resecure his manhood and to once again see himself as superior in this racially homogenous cultural site of extreme sports" (Kusz, "BMX" 170).

Within extreme virtual sports, the emphasis on danger and conquering untamed space is particularly powerful. For example, games like *SSX Tricky* or *Amped* not only provide players spaces to exert creativity with tweaks, spins, jibs, jumps, "and insane sick uber tricks" (from *SSX Tricky*), but to face and ultimately conquer all that the wilderness has to offer. No jump is too high; no cliff is too dangerous; no 100-year-old tree is too big an obstacle; nor is the threat of avalanche a deterrent. Each represents a conquerable obstacle to the white male virtual extreme sports athlete. The instructions of *SSX* capture the essence of this element of the game:

> Conquer the Mountain: Overcome everything the mountain throws at you – from fierce snowstorms and breathtaking vertical drops to multipath slope style courses and earth swallowing avalanches – on the quest for the ultimate adrenaline.
>
> Uncover the Mountain's Secret: Explore a huge world of open vistas covered with fresh powder, tick venues, rail parks, racecourses and half pipes with new tricks to master and leave new competitors in the dust.

SSX Tricky, the sequel of *SSX*, offers similar masculine, frontier-related, rhetorical devices that frame virtual extreme sports as a battle between man and nature. "All of your favorite *SSX* courses are tweaked for more speed, more elevation, and more insane thrills, plus two wild new tracks that will blow your mind. Hit the mountain harder with *SSX Tricky* and the sky is your stage." Offering a "mind blowing world," with "near vertical sections and huge drops," *SSX Tricky* validates white male masculinity as unmovable, courageous and up to any test. There is no physical or mental obstacle that the virtual extreme athlete cannot overcome; white masculinity is powerful in the face of a crisis that devalues the visibility of spaces that invoke the productive power of white men. In a sporting world defined by black athletes, and a virtual sports world dominated by these athletes, white virtual extreme sports games elucidate the prowess of white manhood while simultaneously invoking an "identity cloaked in the codes of cultural difference to relieve itself of its feelings of vulnerability, inferiority, and instability and to reclaim its imagined sense of cultural [athletic] superiority and normality" (Kusz "BMX," 167).

Winning a Gold Medal or a Hot Chick?

Just as extreme sports construct a world of white masculinist domination over nature and space, it equally provides an opportunity to conquer women. Given the fact that extreme sports represent a masculinist project, the emphasis on controlling or consuming oversexualized female bodies is of little surprise. In an effort to reconfigure the virtual extreme sport world as a white masculine performative space, females are either erased or reduced to sexual commodities.

Within games like *Tony Hawk* or *Sonny Garcia Surfing*, women are totally absent, virtually erased from this world despite their visibility in the X-games or other extreme sports competitions. Unlike other sporting arenas, which have seen the partial entry of women or the impact of feminism (or at least the imagination of these changes), these virtual extreme worlds remain untouched by the physical or aesthetic presence of females. This erasure signifies the ultimate mastery that successfully conquers/maintains a sporting world without women.

Nonetheless, an intrusion of female bodies is evident within certain games. The inclusion of extreme female athletes in *SSX 3*, *SSX Tricky*, or *BMX XXX* does not, however, unsettle the hegemony of white masculinity, in that these characters exist for the pleasure of both the male virtual athlete and the male game player. Females in these games serve as either the "spoils of victory" within the game itself or the source of pleasure for the game player. For example, games like *SSX Tricky* and *BMX XXX* offer females as prizes for success. In *SSX Tricky*, victories allow players to purchase outfits that are more revealing for its female players, accentuating the already large breasts of the characters. While white male athletes in *SSX 3* wear baggy pants, a standard snowboarder's uniform, the women wear tight, revealing clothing. Elise, who the game describes as 5'11" and 120 lbs, wears an extremely tight one-piece snowsuit that shows off her large breasts. As the announcer introduces her to the fans, she rubs her hands up and down her sides in a highly sexualized way in greeting. In each of these extreme sports games, as with all video games, female athletes are represented by their breasts and tight clothing. Children Now (2001), one of the few quantitative studies concerning race and gender stereotyping within video games, found that ten percent of female characters possessed excessively large breasts and nonexistent waists; twenty percent of female characters had disproportionate body types. Moreover, ten percent of female characters exposed their butts, and an astounding twenty percent of virtual women revealed their breasts (Children Now 13–14).

All of the women in both *SSX* games are large breasted, existing for sexual consumption of their bodies. Similarly, *BMX XXX* offers a strip tease for the completion of a particular mission. In each game, oversexualized, large-breasted sex kitten women, disguised as extreme sports athletes, do not threaten this masculinist space, but rather solidify its orientation, as women function as sexualized window dressing and sources of sexual pleasure as trophies or "athletes."

BMX XXX: *Conquer and You Shall Consume*

The release of *BMX XXX* in 2002 prompted a litany of criticism throughout the entertainment industry. The game was described as "lewd," "raunchy," and as having gone "too far" (Buchanan 5.2; Leahy 46; Snider D05). Levi Buchanan (2002) captures the essence of the reaction that followed the release of *BMX XXX*, which brought bike riding together with "virtual strippers, pimps, and hookers mouthing off" (*Official Playstation Magazine* 60). "On November 19, one of the few remaining taboos in video games will be stripped away, quite literally. Acclaim's *BMX XXX* finally shatters an almost two-decade kibosh on nudity in console gaming, taunting moral watchdogs with plenty of the gratuitous stuff that pulls teenagers into movie theaters or MTV to watch such bizarros as 'Jackass'" (Buchanan 5.2). Both celebratory and in disgust, the critical reception of *BMX XXX* failed to connects its representational strategies of extreme sports to its more subtle brethren. While the ubiquitous outrage focused on the pornographic elements of the game, as well as the game's deployment of "inappropriate language" or its overt sexuality, very little of this condemnation focused on the rampant racial stereotypes and deployment of patriarchal construction of females/femininity within this imaginary world of extreme sports.

Before *BMX XXX* even starts, its orientation is made clear, as a young woman gazes toward the game player. She is wearing pink shorts with her g-string peeking through, a white halter top that exposes her midriff and her erect nipples; she straddles a BMX bike, the lone sign of the forthcoming extreme sports game; pulling her own hair seductively, she exudes sexuality, almost seducing players to continue with the same. This is not the sole signifier of the game's inscription of female sexuality. Each page of the game's instructions contains a scantily dressed woman clearly marked as the prize of the game. *BMX XXX* even includes an insert (to pin on the wall?) of a blonde white woman wearing an almost see-through halter-top, sitting atop a BMX bike. This is no ordinary bike – it has no seat, but rather what appears to be a silver "stripper pole" in its place that strategically sits between her legs. The sexual tone and the clear markers of women as sexualized objects of male consumption are evident in the game's teaser and instructional materials.

The place and function of over-sexualized women is not limited to the enclosed materials and advertising but plays out in the game. Throughout *BMX XXX*, players are advised to complete missions ranging from dropping off prostitutes at a hotel (per request of a black pimp) to picking up recyclable cans for a homeless person. Each mission offers an identical reward: a naked woman. In fact, the game functions with the single goal of accumulating as many points and coins as possible so you can enter Scores, the community strip club. While the Playstation II version offers censored but still overtly sexual images of women donning halter-tops and thongs, the X-Box and Game Cube versions leave little to the imagination, with women stripping completely. Players can also create topless female riders after mastering tricks and obstacles provided by this urban space.

[…]

In *BMX XXX*, as with the bulk of extreme sport games, the virtual game playing space, as well as its performative possibilities, reflect a clearly masculinist space where women are permitted entry only if they are willing and able to elicit pleasure from the male participants. This reality reflects the larger discourse surrounding extreme sports, the historical context and agenda of extreme (virtual) sports to reclaim a sporting world without substantive numbers of men of color and non-sexualized women – a space to reassert the power of an authentic white masculinity.

The inscription of hyper-masculine identity and over-sexualized femininity is not limited by the game's narrative, but is evident in the character descriptions found within the game's instructions/introductions. Each of the female characters reflects a grotesque notion of hypersexuality; their inclusion in the game is clearly linked to their physique and the sexual desirability held by male game players. Mika reflects this prototype better than any of the characters, with her large breasts and exposed nipples and midriff. She exudes a sexuality that marks her difference from her male counterparts. Mika's desirability emanates from her breasts and sexuality, while other white riders are destined to be picked because of their skills or style.

The other female characters reflect this one-dimensional sexuality, albeit through distinct racialized bodies. La'tey and Joy Ride are both black female characters. La'tey appears angry and muscular, exuding a rough sexual exterior. Joy Ride fulfills a similar representation of black femininity. While her image leaves one wondering whether she is a prostitute, with blonde hair, pink shoes, a short mini skirt, leg warmers and a halter top that cannot contain her ample breasts, she embodies not just the hypersexuality of female characters, but the markers of racial difference as well. Karma, a South Asian or Hawaiian, equally reflects this sexualized racial difference.

Unlike Mika, who despite the emphasis on her breasts wears biker gear, Karma wears surfer shorts and a halter top that not only accentuate her dark skin, but her large breasts.

La'tey, Joy Ride and Karma jointly reaffirm the normalcy and desirability of both white masculinity and femininity. The representation of women not only emphasizes their sexuality/body, clearly marking their inclusion as a result of their "assets." However, the game differentiates between the sexualized identity/virtual bodies of its white female characters and those characters of color.

Comparable depictions of masculinity define *BMX XXX*; white male characters wear "traditional" or "normal" bike-rider clothing as characters of color don almost clownish threads. Rave (mohawk, tattoos, Vans and no shirt), Sketcher (cut-offs, sleeveless shirt) and Nutter (jeans, hoodie, green beanie) all reflect the prototypical (white) extreme athlete. They offer a positive, yet oppositional, vision of masculinity. The inscription of an extreme sports identity through representations of whiteness is most evident in comparison to the game's characters of color. Twon is the stereotypical black hip-hop athlete (long purple shorts, bling-bling); Mavel is the proverbial scowling *vato* (baldhead, chinos, white shirt); Triple Dub adds additional favor as the Rasta biker (dreads, Jamaican colors); lastly, Itch, the game's only Asian character, is non-descript yet clearly odd. Each of the characters of color seems out of place. *BMX XXX* uses both the hypersexual female character and racially stereotypical virtual athletes as a means to validate the physical and psychic superiority of white men. Through the naturalization of whiteness and the inscription of extreme sports as a white world, *BMX XXX*, unlike *Tony Hawk*, uses people of color to naturalize the physical and cultural superiority of the white extreme sports athlete.

The arrival of *BMX XXX* in the United States prompted both shock and outrage. Along with loud denunciations and demands for censorship came a discourse that positioned this game as somehow unique. Critics and pundits alike positioned *BMX XXX* as "different" from the rest of the industries' offerings. *BMX XXX*, with its emphasis on conquering deindustrialized urban spaces, its inscribing pimps and homeless as exotic obstacles yearning for white masculine mastery, reflects its links to the genre of extreme sports games. Moreover, its tendency to invoke highly racialized stereotypes, whether through black pimps and prostitutes or the clownish riders of color, *BMX XXX*, like its extreme sports brethren, uses people of color as a representational strategy that legitimizes and naturalizes white masculinity as the marker of a genuine extreme sports athlete. The transparent inclusion of females, whether as prizes in the strip club or topless riders, further links *BMX XXX* to games like *Tony Hawk Underground* and *SSX Tricky*, for each uses both the erasure of women athletes and as appendages, i.e. exposed breasts to fulfill male needs and fantasies. As part of a larger project that validates white masculinity as daring, cool, fearless and able to master any space at the expense of men of color and women who are ridiculed and demonized as hoes, *BMX XXX* is not new, but more of the same.

A Thug Life: White Manhood and the Virtual Extreme Sports Athlete

As I completed an examination of extreme sports games, arguing that virtual reality resembles an extreme manifestation of its real-life incarnation with its construction of a white masculine space, *Tony Hawk Underground II: Thug* arrived in my mailbox. Following in the footsteps of the original, it allows players to conquer urban spaces through tricks and the physical domination of the skateboard. It, too, erases people of color and women, rendering the world of extreme sports as a space of Jim Crow: a virtual athletic world without the intrusion of the racialized other. It, too, imagines America's inner cities as spaces of white play, devoid of poverty, state violence or police brutality. Likewise, this game constructs the ghetto as a space of cultural difference, a destination of virtual tourists needing exotic and dangerous spaces to prove white masculine coolness, courage and domination. Unlike America's actual ghettos, where police brutalize and incarcerate people of color for graffiti, destruction of property and other transgressions of the law, *Tony Hawk Underground II* celebrates these activities as part of an alternative or extreme lifestyle.

It too imagines a space where rules and laws do not pose threats or consequences to white men. In a commercial for the game, Tony Hawk slashes a tire as a voice over announces that it is "not just about skating, but mayhem." In the world of extreme sports, with its celebration of white masculinity, destruction of property represents a signifier of desirable defiance. Yet, in the real world, where black masculinity is demonized, destruction of property garners a sentence of five years inside one of America's finest prisons. *Tony Hawk Underground II* and its peers embody the white male fantasies represented by extreme sports video gaming, where the ultimate reward lies not in a high score or the honing of one's gaming skills, but in the victory of white masculinity over urban spaces, the female body, and the racial Other.

REFERENCES

"BMX PG-13, Did Acclaim take Things too Far? Sony Censors the Racy BMX XXX." *Official U.S. Playstation Magazine: Issue 64*, 1 January 2003: 60.

Buchanan, Levi. "BMX Breaks Barrier with Profanity, Topless Females." *Chicago Tribune* 4 November, 2002: 5.2.

Children Now. *Fair Play? Violence, Gender and Race in Video Games*. Oakland, CA: Children Now, 2001.

Dyer, Richard. "The Matter of Whiteness." *White Privilege: Essential Readings on the Other Side of Racism*. Ed. Paula Rothenberg. New York: Worth Publishers, 2002. 219–223.

Dyer, Richard. *White*. New York: Routledge, 1997.

Feagin, Joe, and Hernan Vera. *White Racism: The Basics*. New York: Routledge, 1995.

Frankenberg, Ruth. "The Mirage of an Unmarked Whiteness." *The Making and Unmaking of Whiteness*. Ed. Birgit Bander Rasmussen, Eric Klinenberg, Irene Nexica, and Matt Wray. Durham: Duke University Press, 2001. 72–96.

Frankenberg, Ruth. "Local Whiteness, Localizing Whiteness." *Displacing Whiteness: Essays in Social and Cultural Criticism*. Ed. Ruth Frankenberg. Durham: Duke University Press, 1997. 1–34.

Gee, James. *What Video Games Have to Teach Us About Learning and Literacy*. New York: Palgrave, 2003.

Giroux, Henry. "Racial Politics and the Pedagogy of Whiteness." *Whiteness: A Critical Reader*. Ed. Mike Hill. New York: New York University Press, 1997. 294–315.

hooks, bell. "Representing Whiteness in the Black Imagination." *Displacing Whiteness: Essays in Social and Cultural Criticism*. Ed. Ruth Frankenberg. Durham: Duke University Press, 1997. 165–179.

hooks, bell. *Black Looks: Race and Representation*. Boston: South End, 1992.

Jenkins, Henry. "Voices from the Combat Zone: Game Grrlz Talk Back." *Barbie to Mortal Kombat: Gender and Computer Games*. Eds. Justice Cassell, and Henry Jenkins. Cambridge: MIT P. 8 July 2003 <http://web.mit.edu/21fms/www/faculty/henry3/gamegrrlz.html>.

Jenkins, Henry. "'Complete Freedom of Movement': Video Games as Gendered Play Spaces." 8 July 2003 <http://web.mit.edu/21fms/www/faculty/henry3/gamegrrlz/pub/complete.html>.

Kelley, Robin. "Integration: What's Left." *The Nation* 14 December, 1998: 18.

Kibby, Marjorie D. "Nostalgia for the Masculine: Onward to the Past in the Sports Films of the Eighties." *Canadian Journal of Film Studies*, 7.1 (1998): 16–28.

Kincheloe, Joe, and Shirley Steinberg. "Addressing the Crisis of Whiteness: Reconfiguring White Identity in a Pedagogy of Whiteness." *White Reign: Deploying Whiteness in America*. Eds. Joe Kincheloe, Shirley R. Steinberg, Nelson M. Rodriguez, and Ronald Chennault. New York: St. Martin's, 1997. 3–31.

Kusz, Kyle. "BMX, Extreme Sports, and the White Male Backlash." *To the Extreme: Alternative Sports, Inside and Out*. Eds. Robert E. Rinehart and Synthia Sydor. Albany: State U of New York P, 2003. 153–178.

Kusz, Kyle. "'I Want to be the Minority': The Politics of Youthful White Masculinities in Sport and Popular Culture in 1990s American," *Journal of Sport and Social Issues* 25.4 (2001): 390–416.

Leahy, Dan. "BMX XXX: Topless Chicks Can't Save Hapless Game." *Game Now* 1 February, 2003: 46.

Lott, Eric. *Love and Theft: Blackface Minstrelsy and the American Working Class*. New York: Oxford University Press, 1993.

Marriott, Michael. Blood, Gore, Sex and Now: Race. *New York Times*, 21 October, 1999. 8 July 2003 <http://query.nytimes.com/gst/abstract.html?res=FA0A14FA385D0C728EDDA90994D1494D81>.

Price, S.L. "What Ever Happened to the White Athlete?" *Sports Illustrated* 8 December 1997: 31–46.

Rat iff, Evan. "Sports Rule!" *Wired* 11.1 (2003) http://wired.com/wired/archive/11.01/sports.html.

Reinhart, Robert E. *Players All: Performances in Contemporary Sport*. Bloomington: Indiana University Press, 1998.

Reinhart, Robert E., and Synthia Sydnor, eds. *To the Extreme: Alternative Sports, Inside and Out*. Albany: State University of New York Press, 2001.

Rheingold, Howard. *The Virtual Community: Homesteading on the Electronic Frontier*. Reading, Massachusetts: Addison-Wesley, 1993.

Roediger, David R. *Colored White: Transcending the Racial Past*. Berkeley and London: University of California Press, 2003.

Savran, David. *Taking It Like a Man: White Masculinity, Masochism and Contemporary American Culture*. Princeton, NJ: Princeton University Press, 1998.

Shome, Raka. "Race and Popular Cinema: The Rhetorical Strategies of Whiteness in *City of Joy*" *Communication Quarterly* 44.4 (1996): 502–518.

Snider, Mike. "Video Games Kicking the Sex up a Notch." *USA Today* 13 November, 2002: D.05.

Wray, Matt, and Annaee Newitz. *White Trash: Race and Class in American*. New York: Routledge, 1997.

29 YOUR SECOND LIFE?
Goodwill and the Performativity of Intellectual Property in Online Digital Gaming

Andrew Herman, Rosemary J. Coombe, and Lewis Kaye

Introduction: Goodwill and the Performativity of Intellectual Properties

Linden Lab, the developers of *Second Life* – a Massively Multi-Player Online Game (MMOG) – transfixed the audience at the 'State of Play' conference in November 2003 with an announcement that literally promised to change the state of play in digital games.[1] They declared that they were prepared to recognize the value of the creative contributions that gameplayers made to the virtual worlds that they, as developers, otherwise controlled. From that moment forward, all players of the game would be granted intellectual property rights in their creations both within the game space and in 'real life'. This was a radical departure for the online gaming industry, where nearly all End User License Agreements (EULA) and Terms of Service (TOS) require players to sign over their intellectual property rights in order to enter into the virtual space of the game.

Although *Second Life* is relatively small by MMOG standards,[2] the implications of Linden Lab's new policy for the electronic gaming industry, and for the entertainment industry in general, are potentially profound. ...

Andrew Herman, Rosemary J. Coombe, and Lewis Kaye, "'Your Second Life? Goodwill and the Performativity of Intellectual Property in Online Digital Gaming," pp, 184–210 from *Cultural Studies* 20:2–3 (March/May 2006).

The increasing value of cultural goods rests upon an ever-expansive regime of intellectual property rights – embodied in copyrights, trademarks, patents, trade secrets, and publicity rights – that enables the cultural industries to exploit the value of their intangible assets in an increasingly global marketplace (cf Coombe *et al.* 2005, Coombe 1998, 2004, Lessig 1999 and 2004, Litman 2001, Rifkin 2000). Scholarly analysis of the centrality of intellectual property regimes in constituting informational capital largely has focused on their globalization, their aggressive assertion by corporations, their legislative extension, and their legitimation in courts of law. Within such analyses, we argue (Coombe and Herman 2004), there is a tendency to construe conflict over intellectual property rights as a Manichean morality play between corporations and creators or consumers valorized as transformative creators of cultural value (McLeod 2001, 2005, Vaidhyanathan 2001, 2004). On the one side, corporations seek to expand indefinitely the territory and temporality of their intellectual property claims in what some scholars have termed a 'second enclosure movement' (Boyle 2003, Hunter 2003). These forces of 'copyright capitalism' (Leyshon 2003) are arrayed against a shifting coalition of artists, programmers, cultural activists, and consumers on the other side, who seek to preserve and expand access to a 'free culture' (Lessig 2004) that is often animated by a rather romantic notion of the public domain or 'commons' of shared cultural goods (Chander and Sunder 2004, Streeter 2003). Such dualistic rhetoric unfortunately obscures the complexity of the politics of intellectual property in digitally constituted social relations of power.

What we seek to explore in this paper is the *performativity* of intellectual property as both a social form and a cultural process in digital contexts. What is at stake in intellectual property as performativity is not simply the expansion of corporate control over cultural goods and resistance to such expansion, but the production of a particular social imaginary regarding the identity, rights, and responsibilities of corporate producers and consumers of cultural goods. One of the key outcomes of the strategic management and negotiation of intellectual properties in the marketplace is the performative production of positively valanced corporate and consumer figures manifested in the accumulation of *goodwill*. This process, we will show, involves considerable misrecognition of the contributions of corporeal effort, the nature of authorship, and the economic value of the social activity of cultural production.

Goodwill is a notoriously slippery concept in discussions of intellectual property; in most critical scholarly discussions, in fact, goodwill is largely ignored as a concept and phenomenon. Often, goodwill is simply listed alongside better-known types of intellectual property such as copyright, trademark, and patents as an intangible asset critical to the well being of the corporation. In accounting terms, goodwill is described merely as the market price of an enterprise above and beyond that of the fair market value of its tangible assets (i.e. real estate, buildings, inventory, cash, credit, etc) less its liabilities (Blair and Wallman 2001, Hand and Lev 2003).[3] Goodwill can encompass the valuation of a happy workforce, a strategic location and, most importantly, customer loyalty. In this respect, the accounting definition of goodwill dovetails with the legal definition of goodwill that recognizes the reputation and symbolic capital of the enterprise in the marketplace. ...

In intellectual property law, goodwill is generated through the strategic management of trademarks, brands, advertising slogans, logos, and the like, as the most visible incarnations of the corporation's persona and moral identity in the marketplace. There have been many conflicts over these manifestations of corporate identity on the Internet (Coombe and Herman 2001a, 2001b). As a social relationship of power and reciprocity between corporations and consumers, however, goodwill may also become a crucial variable in disputes about intellectual property that do not necessarily involve trademarks. For example, copyright disputes between corporations and consumers over file sharing and sampling in the music industry have tarnished the goodwill of consumers towards certain bands (i.e. Metallica), entertainment corporations, and industry associations (i.e. the Recording Industry Association of America), and certain bands (i.e. Metallica) perceived to be overzealous in enforcing their intellectual property rights (Demers 2005, McLeod 2005, Sloop and Herman 1998). In digital games, relations of goodwill usually revolve around the copyright status of materials created in the virtual spaces of gameplay.

Goodwill is produced through relations of power and reciprocity as these are insinuated in the structures of digitally mediated environments that can be understood as having three imbricated registers: a 'culture of circulation' (Gaonkar and Povinelli 2003, Lee and LiPuma 2002) based on 'network sociality' (Wittel 2001); specific 'circuits of interactivity' that shape the quotidian experience of digital gaming and its political economy (Kline *et al.* 2004); and the relative extensibility of the computer/user interface in constraining and enabling player creativity (Johnson 1997, Manovich 2001). We will consider the characteristics of each of these registers before turning to the particularities of *Second Life*.

Cultures of Circulation and Network Sociality

Dillip Gaonkar and Elizabeth Povinelli (2003) open up a more productive pathway for understanding goodwill in digital environments when they urge us to attend critically to the circulation of cultural forms:

> ... it is no longer viable to think of circulation as simply a movement of people, commodities, ideas, and images from one place to another. 'Circulation is a cultural process', say Lee and LiPuma (2002, p. 192), 'with its own forms of abstraction, evaluation, and constraint, which are created by the interactions between specific types of circulating forms and the interpretive communities built around them'. And those interpretive communities, whether they be coffeehouses and publishing firms or banks and stock exchanges, set the protocols for interpretation by inventing forms, recognizing practices, founding institutions, and demarcating boundaries based primarily on their own internal dynamics. (2003, p. 391)

'Cultures of circulation' give shape to the flows of cultural forms, in other words, be they Kentucky Fried Chicken, Nike Shoes, or Mario Brothers Games (and the intellectual property that is manifested in, and in relationship to, each). They should be approached analytically as topographies to be mapped by shifting relations of power-knowledge, which call into being cultural forms and their recognition. The politics of recognizing (and misrecognizing) conflicting claims of intellectual property rights involve the corporate persona as manifested in its claims to ownership, or non-ownership, of intellectual properties and how such claims are legitimated, negotiated, or contested by consumers in digital games. It is the fabrication and transfiguration of goodwill at the point where corporation, commodity, and consumer interact in interpretive communities that define the cultural form of intellectual properties in digital games.

As a culture of circulation, digital gaming is animated by what sociologist Aaron Wittel (2001) terms 'network sociality'. Working with the macro-sociology of the 'network society' first articulated by Castells (1996), Wittel argues that the quotidian performance of personal and social identity is increasingly dislodged from traditional sites of social interaction (i.e. family, work, localized communities, and affiliations) and progressively embedded in the medium of information technology. This is especially the case with the moral identities of corporations and consumers and the social bond manifested in the production of goodwill (Coombe and Herman 2001b). In digital environments, the network sociality that produces the social bond of goodwill is created, as Wittel puts it, 'by the movement of ideas, the establishment of only ever temporary protocols, and the creation and protection of proprietary information … It is informational, ephemeral but intense, and is characterized by the assimilation of work and play' (2001, pp. 51, 71). Apropos, many gamers now consider their activities within the virtual space of the game as creative work, not simply leisurely play, and many are indeed happy to make such play a big part of their life work. This view also underpins their claims to intellectual property rights in their creative contributions.

The interpretive communities that Goankar and Povenelli invoke as the loci of cultures of circulation are not embedded in discrete and localized spaces. Rather, they are increasingly dispersed and distributed across different server nodes and internet protocol addresses, Internet cafes, and wireless hotspots, where imagined communities are virtually and evanescently instantiated at the moment of connectivity and terminated at the moment of logging off. These communities use the dialogic potential of digital technology to establish protocols, create new forms of digital content and, critically, to attempt to negotiate the propriety of the proprietary conditions of digital governance.

Circuits of Interactivity

In their ground-breaking work *Digital Play* (2004), Kline, Dyer-Whitherford, and De Peuter offer a compelling framework for an analysis of the culture of circulation of digital games and its network sociality. As virtual worlds of interactivity, they argue, online digital games represent an 'ideal type of commodity'. This type of commodity expresses the fundamental logic of 'information capital' which maintains growth through the integrated management of technological innovation, cultural creativity, and mediated marketing (p. 29). It also reconfigures the position of the consumer, who no longer simply purchases the game as a product, but is actively engaged in its continued development and marketing, mediated through the feedback loops created by digital technologies which continually circulate information and innovation to feed capital accumulation.

In mapping the topography of these forms of circulation, the authors use the Marxist notion of 'circuits of capital' (production-commodity-consumption) to argue that digital games exist at the intersection of dynamic processes in three specific 'circuits of interactivity': culture, technology, and marketing. Each circuit, they suggest, has its own specific but overlapping social actors and relational structure, as well as its own essential contradiction. The cultural circuit refers to the gaming environment as a semiotic domain in which game designers, players, and games themselves interact to produce a virtual world of meaning and identity. Interactivity involves the agency of players within the semiosis of the game space created by designers. Depending on the game and its interface, players have greater or lesser agency to forge an identity and a unique path through their avatars and the activities in which they choose to engage. Regardless of the degree of agency exercised in this particular circuit however, Kline *et al.* argue that players are always limited by the game's underlying code. We would suggest that although this is indeed true for early 'First Person Shooter' games such as the legendary *Doom* series, digital games that provide greater room for agency and the capacity to modify the underlying code are being developed and attracting greater interest (e.g. the popular Unreal Tournament series, cf Curlew 2005, Nieborg 2005).

The technological circuit refers to the interaction between the programmers, users, computers or gaming consoles, and the underlying software. This interaction encourages the development of particular forms of subjectivity and embodiment particular to the networked telecommunications environment as it 'inculcates the skills, rhythms, speeds and textures of the computerized environment' (2004, p. 55). This circuit entails a continual process of technological innovation and diffusion; as games become goods of mass consumption, new innovations in gameplay are developed and shared. Thus the contradiction here is between 'enclosure' and 'access'. Corporations seek to limit possibilities of interactivity in order to maximize profit, as gamers seek and develop their own uses for the games and the network through practices that range from modifying consoles and 'modding' gaming software to the reproduction and counterfeiting of intellectual property protected software and copyrighted content (cf Banks 2005, Nieborg 2005 and Sotamaa 2005).

In the circuit of marketing, the primary actants are marketers, commodities, and consumers. The vast 'promotional web' of the gaming industry and its branding strategies seek to 'close the loop between corporation and consumer, reinscribing the consumer into the production process by feeding information about his or her preferences back into the design and marketing of new game commodities' (Kline *et al.* 2004, p. 57). The contradiction here is between commodification and play.

The world of gaming promises pleasures of freedom, transgression, and creativity, but these are perpetually incorporated into marketing efforts that may or may not, in turn, incite gamers to find new meanings that escape the corporate gaze.

This framework is useful in so far as it articulates the different roles and agencies that corporations and consumers embody in digital gaming considered as a culture of circulation with multiple registers. It is necessary to take issue with a few of the authors' formulations, however. We would insist that all three circuits of interactivity are cultural in terms of the identities they enable, the properties they produce, the practices they invite, and the politics they engender. Their understanding of the politics of intellectual property in digital games is, moreover, too one-dimensional to adequately account for the dynamism that characterizes this as an issue in virtual worlds. They present gaming companies as inveterate enclosers of an ever-expansive terrain of intellectual property. Although corporations have indeed been stringent in enforcing their intellectual property through digital rights management of gaming consoles, the situation is more complex when it comes to the production of context and content in online games.

Kline, Dyer-Witherford, and De Peuter tend to view users' agency in refashioning games as extrinsic to the flow of capital accumulation; all users' modifications are treated as akin to hacking or piracy (pp. 210–211, 281–282). However, in a growing number of online games, player creativity in deploying the underlying source code is considered to be essential to consumer satisfaction, product development, and marketplace success (Curlew 2005). All of these circuits are domains of cultural contestation in which intellectual property is produced and control over the value of creation is determined in the interplay of designers and players, programmers and users, and companies and consumers. Shifting discourses and evolving practices of authorship/agency and ownership/property cut across all three circuits of interactivity in the online gaming community and are characteristic of it as a culture of circulation. Indeed, we will argue that developments in digital gaming, as embodied in the interface between the different roles played in the various circuits of interactivity, have increasingly 'queered' concepts of producer and consumer, authorship and ownership, and real and virtual forms of property.

The Interfaces of Extensibilities

MMOGs are sociologically distinctive as 'persistent worlds'. Their virtual reality is not dependent upon the active engagement of any one player at any one time but continues as players take breaks, go on vacations, and new players are introduced and socialized. In other words, they function as ongoing social systems replete with their own forms of governance and moral economies of practice that vary depending on the structure of relations established by the respective game's End User License Agreement (EULA) and Terms of Service (TOS). This last point is of crucial importance: MMOGs are not merely a discrete and categorically identifiable class of gameplay, but also, significantly, a variable set of legally structured and contractually bounded computing practices. A thorough consideration of virtual property relations in gaming environments must attend to the external parameters and specificities of these places of digital sociality and the relations, expectations, and practices they engender among the players as an interpretive community in a distinctive culture of circulation. It is precisely this failure to consider the *constitutional* dimensions of gaming worlds that contributes to a tendency either to celebrate players' creative work uncritically as simple contributions to a gift economy (Postigo 2003), or to evaluate it critically in arbitrary terms (e.g. Ondrejka 2005a). Neither approach addresses the crucial issue of where cultural value is being produced and who exercises control over it.

A constitutional perspective permits us to consider the corporate strategies that underpin various regimes of virtual governance, and how these relate to distinctive attitudes that different game publishers and software firms have towards earning goodwill and thus towards player agency. This could be considered to be a question of *interface*. Initially employed by Steve Johnson (1997) to describe the visual, physical, and phenomenological system through which users interact with a particular computing environment, the concept enabled us to see how the powerful visual metaphors of desktops, files, bins, and icons helped to make computer use a more prosaic experience. Johnson was concerned with the success of the modern graphical user interface, the software form that is now familiar to us as the public face of the personal computer operating system. Adapted and extended for the Internet through the related metaphors of links and pages, this interface contributed to making the personal computer the ubiquitous machine it is today.[4]

Computing practices mediated through a software-generated interface have varying degrees of *extensibility* – the ability to customize, control, and elaborate the users digital presence. These levels of extensible interaction are bound up with interrelated property *and* labor relations, many of which are anticipated by, and provided for, the intellectual property rights holders of the underlying code, the programs designed with it, the graphic content it produces, and the symbols used to market it as a distinctive product. The constitutional framework established in EULAs and TOSs varies in complexity depending on the potential extensibility of the interface. The task-specific use of a typical commercial software package (e.g. writing with a word processor) falls towards the non-extensible end of the spectrum. Users are almost completely constrained by a proprietary, programmed interface that supports a one-dimensional, producer/consumer relationship between the user and the software producer. Notions of authorship and intellectual property are predicated on the idea that the software is complete, a finished work, and therefore the property of the publisher (cf Lessig 1999, Litman 2001). Users purchase limited rights to use the software for designed and approved purposes, copying is restricted, and modification is often banned outright. Value is derived from sales of software, and goodwill accrues with an application's reputation for technical integrity and, if fortune or strategy would have it, its ability to become an industry standard.

This basic producer/consumer relationship has been typical of gaming software. Most PC or console games are discrete software applications with limited use provisions. Games were traditionally installed and used locally, with licenses granted on terms similar to other forms of commercial software. The advent of the Internet enabled the introduction of a new range of networked gaming. Many video games now can accommodate networks of two or more players connected to each other over the Internet, yet all running the same software locally. Such network capabilities do not necessarily, however, alter the way the game publishers approach the question of intellectual property.

MMOGs trouble this straightforward relationship between producers and consumers, because the game software ceases to be a complete and inviolable work of authorship. An MMOG environment instead, is always a work-in-progress, dependent to varying degrees on user input. A network game is only as compelling as the community playing it. The size, quality, and active involvement of a game's user base becomes one of its most saleable features. An MMOG interface both demands users' ongoing involvement in a given virtual world and, to greater or lesser degrees, facilitates the modification of this environment to meet players' needs and preferences. If users create content for the game, not surprisingly they often begin to assume a proprietary relationship to the virtual accoutrements they develop through gameplay (Lastowka and Hunter 2004). They come to understand their play as a form of creative labor in which they 'earn' value.

This understanding demands a different constitution with respect to labor and property. As the game's constitution comes to govern a wider set of social relationships in which value is created, it is also increasingly, interpreted, negotiated, and contested by those whom it governs. In these circumstances the narrative of goodwill is inevitably transformed. The story is no longer simply the teleology of consumers' enjoyment of a product that effectively binds them to the corporation. The generation of goodwill takes a different narrative turn wherein the very terms of governance that structure the relation between consumer, game, and corporation, are evaluated in terms of the way they distribute value as well as the pleasures they afford. The characters that enact the story of goodwill – corporation, consumer and commodity – become transmogrified. New notions of authorship and agency are articulated in the enjoyment of digital gaming through the possessive attitudes that it engenders.

Authorship, Agency and Appropriation in Registers of Performativity

The distinctive character of MMOGs interfaces raises new issues of authorship and agency. There is no doubt that the technological circuits comprised by new media have provided the conditions for a new participatory culture involving 'interactive audiences' (Jenkins 2003, p. 215, cf Coombe and Herman 2001b, Jenkins 1992). This can be accounted for by the convergence of three specific sets of developments:

> a) New tools and technologies enable consumers to archive, annotate, appropriate, and re-circulate media content, b) a range of subcultures promote DIY [do-it-yourself] media production and a discourse of how consumers have deployed their technologies, and c) economic trends favoring the horizontally integrated media conglomerates encourage the flow of images, ideas, and narratives across multiple media channels and demand more active modes of spectatorship. (Jenkins 2003, p. 213)

These participatory cultures exist in an uneasy but dynamic relationship with 'commodity culture'. The former continually appropriate and remake what is produced and circulated by media corporations, while media corporations continually try to incorporate consumer productivity and creativity into profitable commodity forms. Jenkins appropriately suggests that a dialectic of resistance and cooptation is not the most fruitful way of understanding this dynamic. Rather, what we are witnessing is a subtle and evolving dance of collaboration and cooperation in which the corporate persona becomes articulated with the creative and interpretive work of the gaming community to generate goodwill.[5]

At the core of the argument for participatory cultures is the idea of 'player-authorship' nominated by Cindy Poremba. As she argues '[P]layers do not use the digital game as a mediated experience, but often as a medium in and of itself' (2003, p. 4). They can deploy this medium to create new aspects, features, and content in the game environment as well as modes of playing (tactics), all of which can be shared with (or sold to) others. However, when players create their own in-game artifacts, they become agents of cultural production. A dialectic of agency and cultural production based on digital interactivity is developed one which uses 'code worlds' that are 'relatively mutable' (3). Players maintain a 'distributed agency' in game contexts, a concept that foregrounds the network sociality of cultural production in digital environments and displaces the traditional idea of the individual originating author. This is also evoked by Lister *et al.*'s (2003, p. 34) concept of the 'prosumer', a hybrid joinder of the positions of producer and consumer enabled by the relative extensibility of digital media (in programs like Photoshop or Garageband for example).

There are at least four different practices of distributed agency that use the medium of digital gaming technologies. The first is the creation of artifacts, avatars, or spaces within the game using digital resources provided by the game space as it has cumulatively evolved. This 'crafting' is best exemplified in the popular game, *The Sims* (see Au 2002, Curlew 2004) where it is estimated that 90 percent of the content is user-crafted (Herz 2001). Second, there is the remediation of other media forms into digital games, such as the creation of movie-like scenarios like *machinima* (cf Curlew 2005). Third is the aforementioned practice of modification, or 'modding' of existing games using software design engines and underlying source code provided by game developers to create entirely new games, such as the creation of *Counter-Strike* out of *Half-life* and *Velvet Strike* out of *Counter-Strike*. Finally, the activity of 'meta-gaming' involves the creation and dissemination of 'mods', patches, and gaming advice through the network interactivity of virtual gaming communities.

All of these practices pose issues of authorship and ownership, but the latter set of practices have produced the most extensive community dialogue about intellectual property rights and what we might consider to be citizen deliberations about the qualities of governance provided by their corporately authored constitutions. Several 'rhetorical visions' of authorship and creativity are operative in these communities of practice, but all of them address players' activities as potential agencies of authorship (Poremba 2003, p. 10). The interpretive community of prosumers in these worlds of 'co-created media' places 'emphasis on the agency of gamers and the power they wield in collaboration, through their play, their community discussions, and, more problematically, when they begin to produce their own content by actively engaging and transforming the texts their communities are centered on' (Nieborg 2005, pp. 2–3).

Despite new visions and understandings of authorship in MMOG communities, the extensibility of the interface won't necessarily be accompanied by constitutional recognition of the agencies enabled by the digital game nor by property rights conceived of in authorial, originary terms. Interfaces were traditionally valued for providing a complete, consistent, and reliable experience for end users. Game publishers thus sought full control over in-game property relations to provide a consistent playing environment. The continual delivery of consistency and reliability to consumers is, in this scenario, the basis for accruing goodwill. Many popular MMOGs, such as Sony Online Entertainment's (SOE) *EverQuest* (a swords and sorcerers-type world) retain this approach to authorship. In the constitution of such environments, player-generated data is treated as just another element of the corporately owned game. All rights associated with in-game, player created content are reserved by the publisher.

Despite corporate disavowal, real-world property relations never have been fully excised from these virtual places. Author Julian Dibbell (2003) reports that the auction market for virtual goods produced for *EverQuest* is about five million US dollars. SOE initially sought to ban the trading of online goods, but the attempt was futile. The company now attempts to control it by granting 'limited licensing' rights to this digital chattel, taking royalties on its trade in online markets. This is a strategy that may well backfire, online commentator 'Cmndr Slack' suggests, providing grounds for the real-world valorization of such data as valuable intellectual property:

> Although SOE can justify the transaction fee for in-game sales for US dollars as a 'service charge', it seems that it is also an acknowledgement of the intrinsic value of virtual chattels. By involving itself in an industry that hinges on the idea that players own their virtual items, coin and characters, SOE's practices may contradict its assertions in its EULA. Describing sanctioned virtual chattel sales as a license transfer may protect SOE in the short term, but since the items behave as property, and because SOE is taking a share of the sale price, it is possible that the EULA could be invalidated under a misrepresentation theory. (2005, n.p.)[6]

This contradictory behavior on the part of the corporation is indicative of the recognition of the radical contingency of goodwill in such contexts and evolving corporate acknowledgment that qualities of governance may shape gamers' loyalty.[7]

Second Life and the Ethics of Virtual Intellectual Property

Obviously, Linden Labs have adopted a very different approach to in-game property in *Second Life*. Rather than ignoring the issue of player authorship, exploiting the creative labor of prosumer communities by seizing their innovations and banning player disposition of online possessions, they have embraced the idea of player-generated intellectual property. Moreover, they have constitutionally transformed *Second Life* to legitimate gamers as creative and collaborative rights holders who possess a genuine financial interest in the products of their efforts. In other words, their play is recognized as a form of authorship that yields the kind of 'work' that intellectual property properly protects under conditions of information capitalism. Indeed, this corporate strategy is built directly into all of the game's circuits of interactivity.

Players are encouraged to change and develop their appearance and identity, build their own virtual domiciles, acquire chattel, automate their creations using a dedicated scripting language, and collaborate with each other in developmental activities (Linden Lab 2005). Such activities are integral to *Second Life* gameplay, which avoids the solitary, task-oriented, level-advancing gameplay characteristic of MMOGs such as *EverQuest*. It is corporate strategy to make the *Second Life* in-game economy as 'real' as possible (Ondrejka 2005b). Not only are intellectual property rights granted to players for their digital creations, players are enabled to transfer Linden Dollars (*Second Life*'s in-game currency) into real US currency. Linden Lab has created perhaps the most extensible interface available to gamers both in its facilitation of distributed developmental agency both inside and outside of the world of digital gaming and in its recognition that the symbolic value created by play has real value. In its first incarnation as Linden Dollars, however, such exchange value is also clearly an innovative new means of accelerating and leveraging the value of goodwill. Through what agencies was this accomplished? What does it portend for the future performativity of intellectual property in digital environments?

Gamers' intellectual property rights were granted in response to extensive criticism by users about the expropriation of their creative labor. As one senior member of the community, 'ZHugh Becqueral' wrote to the online forum:

> I have poured a lot of time in the game. I saw the posts of lots of people demanding more content and then leaving, and I thought, well the game does need content but rather than complaining what I can do is contribute. I have been wrestling with my conscience … about whether or not to stay. I didn't want to leave … but the TOS makes it quite clear that on the one hand all code created in game belongs ultimately to the Linden's and that

on the other we are not Linden employees and are not remunerated ... The in-game *intellectual property* wrestling is silly because every single letter of code belongs to Linden Labs ... either the terms of service will change in order for me to contribute code that I own, or I will wait for Linden Labs to create the code that they own so that the game becomes sufficient and rewarding. (http://forums.secondlife.com/showthread.php?t = 65)

As 'Mark Busch' asserted, however: 'The fun of *Second Life* for me is creating projects that other people enjoy. Who cares if it 'officially' is not mine and Linden are allowed to delete and/or copy it?' (http://forums.secondlife.com/showthread.php?t = 6505). For this player, the labor of creation was indeed a gift with its own intrinsic satisfactions. For most players of online games, however, as Sara Grimes points out, 'resistance to corporate appropriation of online game culture has thus far consisted of little other than the internalization and legitimation of processes of commodification' (Grimes forthcoming). In other words, the only normative issue becomes the question of whose intellectual property it should be.

This disquiet was clearly anticipated by Cory Ondrejka, Vice President of Product Development for Linden Labs, who quickly intervened to declare the debate 'serendipitous'. Realizing that there are 'concerns and stresses between creating interesting and innovative content' and the terms of standard online gaming contracts, the company had decided to revise *Second Life*'s constitution. The new EULA/TOS would guarantee 'real world intellectual property rights to users over their digital creations' (http://forums.secondlife.com/showthread.php?t = 6763). Participants now would have ownership rights with respect to their *Second Life* creations, just as they would with regard to any creations they made offline.[8]

Why did Linden Labs do this? Part of the answer has to do with the peculiar articulation of the circuits of interactivity that characterize MMOGs cultures of circulation of MMOG's. Ondrejka argued that increases in server capacity and technological breakthroughs in programming software had fostered the development of 'atomistic construction' of 'true creativity' in the technological circuit of interactivity, expressing people's desire for agency and authorship: 'It is important to look at the desire of people in general to express themselves through creativity and customization. People want to be perceived as creative by customizing their surroundings, to have their moments on the stage. In many cases, it seems that users are just waiting for the right tools' (2005, p. 86). *Second Life* is designed to be such a tool.

Note that this rationalization involves an acknowledgement of a need for authorial recognition and a transition in the actant of creativity from people to 'users', a territorializing move that is both rhetorical, in that it incorporates the authorial desire to create within the marketing circuit that garners goodwill for the company, and technical, because it involves providing gamers with an even more extensible gaming interface. Ondrejka also emphasizes players' desire to collaborate as a key motivation in programming the game so as to allow real-time interaction (Westerburg 2004). This desire is built into *Second Life*'s semiotic domain, where nearly all of the content is created by prosumers themselves. This content contributes, moreover, to the goodwill accrued by Linden Lab in the MMOG marketplace. When asked why Linden Lab had instituted the new policy, President and CEO Phillip Rosedale explained its most obvious virtue: 'We get the content. We allow people to create a world which will be thousands of times more compelling than we could create ourselves' (Krotoski 2005).

Although the buying and selling of in-game objects was no doubt accelerated by the granting of these new rights, the actual repercussions of *Second Life*'s new constitution only became clear in early 2005. Australian *Second Life*r Nathan Keir licensed a puzzle game developed within *Second Life* to a real-world distributor. The game Keir called *Tringo* combined the early digital gameplay of Alexey Pajitnov's legendary *Tetris* with the classic game of Bingo. After *Tringo* sparked a sensation among residents of *Second Life*, Keir was approached by Donnerwood Media, which bought the rights to the game for 'a fee in the low five-figures' (Grimes 2005, p. B3). It plans to distribute internet and cell-phone based versions of the game. Keir retains the rights to *Tringo* within *Second Life*, where he profits from licensing the game to enterprising players who host tournaments.

Linden Lab responded positively to this news. The company acknowledged that the new constitution allowed for the generous profits Keir earned and will continue to receive from his derivative work. It is important to note, however, that the same constitution enables Linden Lab to use *Tringo* (and its author's success in profiting from it) for the promotion of *Second Life* itself. Indeed, all players' intellectual property (creations and chattel) continues to be constitutionally available to Linden Lab to generate further goodwill. A gamer's good fortune in leveraging activity in *Second Life* into a lucrative asset is an excellent marketing tool and one that is entirely in keeping with the kind of goodwill that Linden Lab seeks to cultivate. *Second Life* distinguishes itself from other MMOGs as a 'development kit and mod environment', a *workspace* where virtual objects and real-world ideas – like the rules of a game – can be conceived, built, and tested. Such features make *Second Life* more akin to programs like Macromedia's Flash than to games like *World of Warcraft* or *Everquest*. Linden Lab actively promotes *Second Life*'s game-developing capacity to draw in new players. As their website states: 'The possibilities are enormous, especially for up-and-coming game developers or professionals on a budget. Build your portfolio – prototype your concept and test it with a live audience, before developing the full version' (http://secondlife.com/games/game_dev.php Game Development).

It would be a mistake, however, to believe that the allocation and determination of appropriate parameters for intellectual property rights are any more settled in *Second Life*'s cultures of circulation than they are elsewhere, or that the means for asserting and ascertaining these are any less ideological. The game world is rife with bootlegged videos; audio streams of popular music pour into its gathering places; and unlicensed corporate logos are reproduced on user-created objects such as lawn chairs and posters. Popular television game shows are reproduced and renamed for in-game participants. Gamers don't necessarily respect the intellectual property rights claimed by their fellow players and there is no consensus around norms of fair use.

When players claim ownership over what they create, it is usually the hegemonic notion of individual creativity they invoke, even as they seem to understand the collaborative nature of creation in the in-game context. However, despite Linden Lab's active encouragement of the use of Creative Commons licenses with respect to online creations – which would, in theory, permit users to use the works of others in their own creative activities provided that they claim no intellectual property rights in the underlying code they create and donate this back to the community – the ethos of Creative Commons licensing has not permeated very far.[9] Disagreements about 'originality' and the disavowal of co-created content in *Second Life* are as common as Lockean arguments about the fruits of labor.[10] In these Lockean arguments we find the basis for our assertion that the evocation and contestation of intellectual property in online environments is a performative speech act.

The vexed relationship between the concepts of performance and performativity has produced heated debate. A long history of performance-based cultural scholarship is ignored by many scholars who, influenced by Judith Butler's work, are nonetheless eager to add the muscular prosthesis of the performative to their theoretical arsenal. The concept of performance is 'central to contemporary views of culture as enacted, rhetorical, contested, and embodied' (Hamera 2006a, p. 2). Performance, which needs to be understood as both a verb and a noun, refers to the embodied processes and practices that simultaneously produce and consume culture (5). The concept refuses the semantic autonomy of the 'work' and insists, instead, on reading, using, and making texts as activities of productive poiesis (Hamera 2006b, p. 17). It is, therefore, particularly appropriate for worlds of digital gaming, where consumers are producing new dimensions for gameworlds in their gaming practices of using, reading, and developing the underlying work, all the while displaying and sharing communicative skills.

Performativity was originally understood as a linguistic means of world-making: a type of utterance that does something as its effect coincides with its use. Butler extends this beyond linguistic instances to suggest that a performative is both an agent and a product of the social and political surroundings in which it circulates. Its effects are reinforced through repetition (Hamera 2006a, p. 6). A performative uses the power of discourse to reproduce particular effects through reiteration, and these effects congeal into socially recognized identities or positivities. Performativity enables us to account, then, for the extra-linguistic effects of linguistic practice. If performativity is indubitably linked to the idea of performance, and performances are necessary for the effects of performativity to be realized, the performative is not simply the accumulation of performances, nor do all performances behave 'performativitily' (if we can coin a phrase).

If theorists of performativity underestimate the conceptual significance and specificity of performance, performance scholars may simplify the concept of performativity by stripping it of features essential to understanding its work. The performative is 'parasitic upon conventional, citational, and socially stratified context … whilst as a theoretical tool or concept, [it] can be used in any given circumstance, its usefulness and what it uncovers and creates are fundamentally specific to the context in which it is sited' (Dewsbury 2000, p. 475). These must be considered as 'authorizing contexts' that enable the utterance to have specific effects. Moreover, 'performativity works by covering over and holding something into place' (Mackenzie 2005, p. 74).

Its constitutive effects are accomplished, in other words, through significant forms of miscrecognition. This dimension of Butler's argument is often elided:

> If a performative provisionally succeeds ... then it is not because an intention successfully governs the action of speech, but only because the action echoes prior actions, and *accumulates the force of authority through the repetition or citation of a prior and authoritative set of practices*. It is not simply that the speech act takes place within a practice, but that the act is itself a ritualized practice. What this means, then, is that a performative 'works' to the extent that it *draws on and covers over* the constitutive conventions by which it is mobilized. (1997, p. 51)

Claims for, evocations of, and negotiations over intellectual property in MMOGs such as *Second Life* must be understood performatively. They are ritualized speech acts that simultaneously invoke and obscure particular authoritative conventions and authorizing contexts. Indeed, these speech acts reiterate and reinforce the authority of one of the dominant ideological narrative contexts that legitimates authorship itself – the Lockean labor theory of value. In the practices we have explored, players routinely assert property rights based on individuated creativity, expenditure of time, effort, and acts of agency understood as acts of creation and authorship. Players, however, don't describe this as work, let alone as labor. Indeed, we would suggest that it is precisely the *embodied* nature of their activity that constitutes one important dimension of several of the constitutive misrecognitions at work here. To reiterate one authorizing context, let us turn to a seminal passage in Locke's *Second Treatise*:

> Though the earth and all inferior creatures, be common to all men, yet every man has a property in his own person: this no body has any right to but himself. The labour of his body, and the work of his hands, we may say, are properly his. Whatsoever then he removes out of the state that Nature hath provided, and left it in, he hath mixed his labour with, and joined it to something that is his own, and thereby makes it his property. It being by him removed from the common state Nature hath placed it in, it hath by this labour something annexed to it, that excludes the common right of other men: for this labour being the unquestionable property of the labourer, no man but he can have a right to what that is once joined to ... (1965, II.5§27)

There is now a large literature appropriately illustrating the limits of using Lockean theory to justify contemporary intellectual properties, its constitutive exclusions, and its inapplicability to contemporary capitalist conditions; no one, however, denies its continuing ideological importance. When invoked in digital contexts, however, the corporeal dimensions of this authorizing context tend to be elided. Players occasionally catch glimpses of the fact that their labor is being expropriated ('we are not Linden employees and are not remunerated') but quickly lose sight of the fact that the extension of the body is the primary interface of extensibility from which the company profits. Rather than insisting on wages, occupational health and safety standards, disability insurance for repetitive stress injuries, or life insurance, the community cathects around the proper distribution of property rights that have market exchange value.

'All Data is Temporary': the Half-life of Your *Second Life*

The representation of forms of personalized computing and game consumption as expressions of creativity in the new constitution of *Second Life* ultimately serves to more fully extend the principles of a neoliberal economy into the game space. Both the creation of content and the collaborative sociality of the game are now wholly governed by the logic of market exchange. Despite the fact that some players disavow financial gain as a motivation for creating content, the desire to create and the desire to collaborate are expressed primarily by engaging in the activities of buying and selling. *Second Life* is so suffused with the ideology of market exchange that ownership of tradable property is a condition for continued residency. In order to maintain a durable presence in the persistent world of *Second Life*, you must purchase a plot of land using Linden Dollars. The company provides a basic stipend, but encourages players to earn money by developing content – a nifty spaceship or clothing line, or perhaps a tattoo for avatars to wear – and selling it to others. This income, in turn, enables you to buy and 'develop' more land which provides the revenue base for Linden Lab – the more land you own, the more 'taxes' you pay (despite a virtual tax revolt, see Grimmelmann 2003).

The ontological nature of Linden Land and its relation to intellectual property is a lively topic of discussion in online circuits of cultural interaction. The relationship between virtual land and intellectual property is a murky one. Virtual land has no exchange value outside of the game space, unlike intellectual property-protected content. As 'Gwyneth Llewlyn' writes on the 'Ownership in SL' forum thread:

> There is a difference between ownership of land on *Second Life* and the ownership of intellectual property of the *content* created on the land. The latter is better defined in the LL TOS – there is absolutely no question about who owns the content (although LL is allowed under the TOS to use that content for their marketing purposes but no more than that). But 'land' is not 'content'; land is the medium that enables you to create the content'. (http://forums.secondlife.com/showthread.php?t = 46662)

The market economy itself is, in a very real sense, the broadest level of interface at work, informing all notions of property, propriety, creativity, and individuality that Linden Lab incorporates in their virtual world. The ownership and modification of virtual land is the *sine qua non* of authorship, creativity, and collaboration, practices that are in effect the social currency of good citizenship.

If we return to Locke, however, another important form of misrecognition becomes evident in these assertions of intellectual property. If the labor of one's body and the work of one's hands are one's own, it is only when one joins this labor or work with an undifferentiated medium held in common (nature), thus removing it from this common state and annexing something one owns to it, that one properly creates property. The 'medium' with which game players mix or join their labor in *Second Life* is neither undifferentiated nor common; Linden 'land' is always already code that is owned by the corporation, a space controlled by the corporation, and one in which all authorial activities first and foremost produce value that accrues to the corporation as goodwill.

What can players actually do with a form of property that is ultimately nothing more than data, given the *Second Life* constitutional claim, that 'All data is temporary?'[11] Current law, at least in North America, does not recognize the status of virtual property in most contexts (despite legal scholar Jack Balkin's [2004] speculative optimism that it soon will). In the absence of legislation, we are left with nothing but contractual interpretation of *Second Life*'s constitution and this baseline assertion. This is not to say the virtual property in *Second Life* has no ontological or moral status. Rather, it is to recognize that its *legal* status is entirely due to a corporate strategy designed to increase Linden Lab's considerable goodwill. The company is free to reclaim, or 'nationalize' if you will, all property in *Second Life*, a strategy real-world liberal democratic governments are also free to pursue under the doctrine of eminent domain. But how would they dispose of it? The corporation would, in all likelihood, so completely have alienated their current user base that they would be left with no market and no market value. This is, however, a strange kind of safety; it provides no insurance for gamers for whom it has indeed become a second life.

Many prosumers of *Second Life* play the game for hours a day; the average player of online games spends 20 to 30 hours a week engaged in these virtual worlds (Yes 2004). The President of Internet Gaming Entertainment even 'estimates that players spend a real world total of $880 million a year for virtual goods and services produced in online games' (Wallace 2005). Jason Ainsworth, for instance, plays *Second Life* four hours a day, running a virtual real estate development business that brings in enough income to pay the mortgage on his Las Vegas home (Wallace 2005). As more and more people turn to online games and gaming markets as a source of income, they will become ever more dependent on the maintenance and development of corporate goodwill. The vast majority of gamers who create this newly recognized intellectual property create content that has use, value, and meaning only within *Second Life*. Their creative labor is valued only insofar as it suits the purposes of Linden Lab and only insofar as the corporate largess represented by their constitutional amendments remains an effective strategy for building goodwill. When and if this ceases to be the case, 'all data is temporary'; a user's second life thus can be terminated, along with all the labor, time, and productive energy that has been mortgaged from the player's first life.

Assertions, negotiations, and contestations of intellectual property are, in summary, performative in the way that they reiterate a Lockean theory of property but nonetheless obscure the corporeal basis of labor and in their constitutive misunderstanding of the conditions under which the value of players' cultural activities accrue to the corporation as the accumulation of goodwill. Such performatives operate to reinforce a reductive understanding of the author as primarily, if not exclusively, a market agent. The nature of the desired activities and responsibilities of the author in a public sphere are not addressed, the author's moral interests in her or his works and the terms of their circulation are not countenanced, and neither public goods nor the public domain appear to be operative as limits to or guiding principles in *Second Life*'s digital sociality.

As a gamer it would appear that you participate in an online 'community' governed entirely by unilateral conditions dictated by the corporate publisher. You have no political rights to participate in the establishment of the constitutional conditions that create the parameters of your second life. Like other consumers you are free to express grievances, but you can do so effectively only in circuits of interactivity controlled by the corporation itself. Even your continued access to these circuits is entirely at the discretion of the company. Goodwill, however, is a benevolent despot; there is always the possibility that the corporate owners of the game will continue to respond to your complaints by modifying the constitutional terms of the game's governance to meet your needs. Ultimately, though, we must ask, is this *your* second life or a half-life of corporate servitude in which fundamental democratic norms of political representation, accountability, and responsibility are ignored, rights of speech and assembly are truncated, and attendance to distributional inequities are unknown? If we are reassured by Philip Rosedale's comment that, 'we like to think of *Second* Life as ostensibly as real as a developing nation' (Krotoski 2005), then we can only hope that goodwill will evolve in digital contexts to accommodate virtual forms of democracy and new norms of digital social justice.

NOTES

1. 'State of Play' is one of the premier academic conferences on digital gaming in the US, bringing together scholars in law, humanities, and social sciences with intellectual property lawyers, new media artists, game developers, and gaming industry executives. It is jointly sponsored by the Berkman Center for Internet and Society at Harvard Law School, the Information Society Project of Yale Law School, and the Institute for Information Law and Policy at New York University Law School. Its proceedings are archived at http://WWW.NYLS.EDU/pages/2396.

2. The most popular MMOG as of July 2005 was *World of Warcraft* with approximately 2,000,000 subscribers; Sony's *Everquest* (to which we compare *Second Life* in terms of player creativity and intellectual property policies) had about 500,000 subscribers; *Second Life* had about 30,000, although it is one of the fastest growing MMOGs. (All figures come from http://www.mmogchart.com, an excellent source of data and analysis on the MMOG industry.) According to Linden Lab, *Second Life* passed the 100,000 'resident' benchmark in January 2006 (http://lindenlab.com/press/releases/01_06_06).

3. The value of goodwill may be enormous and figures prominently in the calculations of mergers and acquisitions. For example, in the recent merger between MBNA and Bank of America, 20 percent of the $35 billion that Bank of America offered was considered to be for MBNA's accumulated goodwill (Talcott 2005).

4. Although Johnson privileges graphics, textual interfaces remain (both as a foundation for graphical interfaces and for greater customization at a deeper level through various forms of scripting and terminal command-line interaction), parallel interfaces that grant deeper levels of access to the computer's basic systems. Even more specialized skills are needed if one is to extend the computer environment further through the authoring and coding of new applications, which requires another software application to act as its own interface

(think, for example of Dreamweaver for website creation, an application that is itself a graphical interface for coding HTML and other web languages).

5. Banks (2005) and Nieborg (2005) add considerable empirical specificity to Jenkins' argument, although their conclusions point in different directions. Banks argues that game developers have an '(im)possible relationship with players', where the sheer pleasure and fecundity of gamer productivity represents an 'excessive, almost perverse enjoyment in the reconfiguration of boundaries and relations between producer and consumer. The fun of playing in the networks of informational capitalism, is a constitutive condition that outgrows and eludes the controlling grasp' (2005, p. 16). Nieborg is more circumspect and ambivalent in his conclusion, remarking that Epic Games easily incorporated the practice of modding into its business model through its *Unreal Tournament* gaming engine (2005, p. 19). Postigo (2003), Taylor (2002, 2006), Terranova (2000), and Grimes (forthcoming) reach conclusions similar to Nieborg to different degrees.

6. It is important to note that creations and chattel are not the same thing: the former involves new object/scenarios that are created in-game, the latter are objects that are created by the developers and acquired by the players through gameplay. However, the legal status of creations and chattel in terms of real-life intellectual property law may be the same (see Lastowka and Hunter [2004], 'CmdrSlack' [2005]). In games like *Quake* or *Everquest*, players sign over rights to their creations and acquisitions in order to gain access to the game. Interestingly, Castronova (2005) argues *in favor* of restrictive EULA's in order to keep the game-space a 'pure' state of play unencumbered by real-life property laws. This argument mirrors our assessment of Sony Online's strategy with respect to controlling in-game chattel transactions within *Everquest*. Castronova is providing a player's perspective on the need to maintain a consistent and predictable player experience, which, we have argued, is not only represented in *Everquest's* EULA but embodied in its interface.

7. In the absence of legislative activity, such issues eventually will be resolved through real-world litigation (Balkin 2004). One of the first cases to address this issue was decided in the People's Republic of China, where the court ordered stolen virtual property to be returned to the gamer who had originally owned it (Xinhua News Agency 2003). In most parts of the world, however, the relation between prosumers' creativity and intellectual property rights in such virtual goods remains subject to the constitutional conditions of governance provided by game-specific EULAs and TOSs.

8. The new policy is phrased as follows on the *Second Life* web site: 'Linden Lab's Terms of Service agreement recognizes Residents' right to retain full intellectual property protection for the digital content they create in *Second Life*, including avatar characters, clothing, scripts, textures, objects, and designs. This right is enforceable and applicable both in-world and offline, both for non-profit and commercial ventures. You create it, you own it – and it's yours to do with as you please' [online] Available at: http://secondlife.com/commerce/ip.php

9. In fact, Linden Lab staged a virtual public discussion in the *Second Life* game-space about the Creative Commons license which featured the appearance of Lawrence Lessig or, rather, his amazingly life-like avatar. It is not known at the time of printing whether he used a Creative Commons license in assigning the publicity rights with respect to his digitally rendered likeness. Discussion of this event can be found at http://secondlife.blogs.com/nwn/2006/01/the_second_life.html

10. For example, resident 'LilyBethFilth' asserts: 'I don't believe that any one who uploads a texture they got from a website can declare themselves a 'creator' … If paying $10L to load into *Second Life* is a 'creation' then it is a poor creation. [The practice] … is a whole moral nightmare … Only people who REALLY make original textures in paint programs have the right to demand copy-right laws' (http://forums.secondlife.com/showthread.php?t=47685).

11. Section 4.3 of the TOS states: 'All Data Is Temporary. When using the Service, you may accumulate treasure, experience points, equipment, or other value or status indicators and contribute to the environment ('Accumulated Status'). THIS DATA, AND ANY OTHER DATA RESIDING ON LINDEN'S SERVERS, MAY BE RESET AT ANY TIME FOR ANY OR NO REASON. ALL CHARACTER HISTORY AND DATA MAY BE ERASED IN WHICH CASE EACH CHARACTER MAY BE RESET TO NOVICE STATUS. YOU ACKNOWLEDGE THAT, NOTWITHSTANDING ANY COPYRIGHT OR OTHER RIGHTS YOU MAY HAVE WITH RESPECT TO ITEMS YOU CREATE USING THE SERVICE, ALL OF YOUR CONTENT AND ACCUMULATED STATUS HAS NO INTRINSIC CASH VALUE AND THAT LINDEN DOES NOT ENDORSE, AND EXPRESSLY DISCLAIMS (SUBJECT TO ANY UNDERLYING RIGHTS IN THE CONTENT), ANY VALUE, CASH OR OTHERWISE, ATTRIBUTED TO CONTENT OR ACCUMULATED STATUS' [online] Available at: http://secondlife.com/corporate/tos.php

REFERENCES

Au, W.J. (2002) 'Triumph of the mod: Player-created additions to lifeblood of the industry', *Salon*, 11 April 2002 [online]. Available at http://www.salon.com/tech/feature/2002/04/16/modding (August 13, 2005).

Balkin, J.M. (2004) 'Virtual Liberty: Freedom to Design and Freedom to Play in Virtual Worlds', *Virginia Law Review*, vol. 90, no. 8, pp. 2243–2298.

Banks, J.A.L. (2005) 'Opening the Production Pipeline: Unruly Creators and Enjoyment', paper presented at the *Changing Views: Worlds of Play Conference of the Digital Games Research Association*, Vancouver, B.C. [online]. Available at: http://www.gamesconference.org/digra2005/viewpaper.php?id = 78&print = 1

Blair, M.M. & Wallman, S.M.H. (2001) *Unseen Wealth*, Brookings Institution Press, Washington DC.

Boyle, J. (2003) 'The Second Enclosure Movement and the Constitution of the Public Domain', *Law and Contemporary Problems*, vol. 66, nos 1–2, pp. 33–74.

Butler, J. (1997) *Excitable Speech: A Politics of the Performative*, Routledge, New York.

Castells, M. (1996) *The Rise of the Network Society*, Basil Blackwell, Malden, MA.

Castronova, E. (2005) 'The Right to Play', *New York Law School Law Review*, vol. 49, no. 1, pp. 185–210.

Chander, A. & Sunder, M. (2004) 'The Romance of the Public Domain', *California Law Review*, vol. 92, no. 5, pp. 1331–1347.

'CmndrSlack' (2005) 'There's Gold In Them Thar Pixels! An Examination of Virtual Chattels and Property Rights' [online] Available at: http://www.grimwell.com/index.php?action = fullnews&id = 284

Coombe, R.J. (1998) *The Cultural Life of Intellectual Properties: Authorship, Appropriation, and the Law*, Duke University Press, Durham, NC.

Coombe, R.J. (2004) 'Commodity Culture, Private Censorship, Branded Environments, and Global Trade Politics: Intellectual Property as a Topic of Law and Society Research', in *The Blackwell Companion to Law and Society*, ed. A. Sarat, Basil Blackwell, Malden, MA, pp. 369–391.

Coombe, R.J. & Herman, A. (2004) 'Rhetorical Virtues: Property, Speech and the Commons on the World-wide Web', *Anthropological Quarterly*, vol. 77, no. 3, pp. 557–572.

Coombe, R.J. & Herman, A. (2001a) 'Culture Wars on the Net: Intellectual Property and Corporate Propriety in Digital Environments', *South Atlantic Quarterly*, vol. 100, no. 4, pp. 919–947.

Coombe, R.J. & Herman, A. (2001b) 'Trademarks, Property and Propriety: The Moral Economy of Consumer Politics and Corporate Accountability on the World Wide Web', *De Paul Law Review*, vol. 50, no. 2, pp. 597–632.

Coombe, R.J., Schnoor, S. & Ahmed, M. Al Attar (2005) 'Bearing Cultural Distinction: Informational Capitalism and New Expectations for Intellectual Property', in *Articles in Intellectual Property: Crossing Borders*, ed. W. Groshiede, Mollengrafica/Intersentia, Utrecht.

Curlew, A.B. (2005) 'Prometheus, Prosumers, Poachers and Property: New Patterns of Cultural Production in the Post-Industrial Digital Age', unpublished manuscript.

Curlew, A.B. (2004) *Oh the Simanity: Reading a Culture of Simulation through 'The Sims'*, MA Thesis, McMaster University.

Demers, J. (2005) *Steal This Music: How Intellectual Property Law Affects Musical Creativity*, University of Georgia Press, Athens.

Dewsbury, J.-D. (2000) 'Performativity and the Event: enacting a philosophy of difference', *Environment and Planning D: Society and Space*, vol. 18, pp. 473–496.

Dibbell, J. (2003) 'The Unreal Estate Boom', *Wired*, 11 (01) January, [online]. Available at: http://wired.com/wired/archive/11.01/gaming.html

Gaonkar, D. & Povinelli, E. (2003) 'Technologies of Public Forms: Circulation, Transfiguration, Recognition', *Public Culture*, vol. 15, no. 3, pp. 385–397.

Grimes, A. (2005) 'Digits', *The Wall Street Journal, (Eastern edition)* 3 Mar., p. B3.

Grimes, S. (forthcoming) 'Online Multiplayer Games: A Virtual Space for Intellectual Property Debates?' *New Media and Society*.

Grimmelmann, J. (2003) 'State of Play: The *Second Life* Tax Revolt' [online]. Available at: http://research.yale.edu/lawmeme/modules.php?name = News&file = article&sid = 1222

Hamera, J. (2006a) 'Opening Opening Acts', in *Opening Acts: Performance in/as Communication and Cultural Studies*, ed. J. Hamera, Sage, Thousand Oaks, CA, pp. 1–10.

Hamera, J. (2006b) 'Introduction: Engaging the Everyday', in *Opening Acts: Performance in/as Communication and Cultural Studies*, ed. J. Hamera, Sage, Thousand Oaks, CA, pp. 12–21.

Hand, J. & Lev, B. (eds) (2003) *Intangible Assets*, Oxford University Press, New York.

Herz, J.C. (2001) 'Learning from the Sims', *The Industry Standard*, 21 Mar., [online]. Available at: http://www.findarticles.com/p/articles/mi_m0HWW/is_12_4/ai_72886914

Hunter, D. (2003) 'Cyberspace as place and the Tragedy of the Digital Anti-Commons', *California Law Review*, vol. 91, no. 2, pp. 438–519.

Jenkins, H. (1992) *Textual poachers: Television fans and participatory culture*, Routledge, Chapman, and Hall, New York.

Jenkins, H. (2003) 'Quentin Tarantino's Star Wars?: Digital cinema, media convergence, and participatory culture', in *Rethinking media change: The aesthetics of transition*, eds D. Thorburn & H. Jenkins, MIT Press, Cambridge, MA, pp. 211–230.

Johnson, S. (1997) *Interface Culture: How New Technology Transforms the Way We Create and Communicate*, HarperEdge, San Francisco, CA.

Kline, S., Dyer-Witheford, N. & de Peuter, G. (2004) *Digital Play: The Interactions Between Technology, Culture and Marketing*, McGill/Queens University Press, Kingston, ON.

Krotoski, A. (2005) 'Second Life and the Virtual Property Boom', *Guardian Unlimited*, 12 Jun., [online]. Available at: http://blogs.guardian.co.uk/games/archives/2005/06/14/second_life_and_the_virtual_property_boom.html#more

Lastowka, F.G. & Hunter, D. (2004) 'The Laws of the Virtual Worlds', *California Law Review*, vol. 92, no. 1, pp. 3–73.

Lee, B. & LiPuma, E. (2002) 'Cultures of circulation: The imaginary of modernity', *Public Culture*, vol. 14, no. 2, pp. 191–213.

Lessig, L. (1999) *Code and Other Laws of Cyberspace*, Basic, New York.

Lessig, L. (2002) *The Future of Ideas: the Fate of the Commons in a Connected World*, Vintage, New York.

Lessig, L. (2004) *Free Culture: How Big Media Uses Technology and the Law to Lock Down Culture and Control Creativity*, Penguin, New York.

Leyshon, A. (2003) 'Scary Monsters? Software formats, peer-to-peer networks and the spectre of the gift', *Environment and Planning D: Society and Space*, vol. 21, no. 5, pp. 533–558.

Linden Lab (2005) 'What is Second Life: Overview' [online]. Available at: http://secondlife.com/whatis/

Lister, M., Dovey, J., Giddings, S., Grant, I. & Kelly, K. (2003) *New Media: A Critical Introduction*, Routledge, New York.

Litman, J. (2001) *Digital Copyright*, Prometheus Books, New York.

Locke, J. (1965) *Two Treatises of Government*, Mentor Books, New York.

Mackenzie, A. (2005) 'The Performativity of Code: Software and Cultures of Circulation', *Theory, Culture and Society*, vol. 22, no. 1, pp. 71–92.

Manovich, L. (2001) *The Language of New Media*, MIT Press, Cambridge, MA.

Mcleod, K. (2005) *Freedom Of Expression (®): Overzealous Copyright Bozos And Other Enemies Of Creativity*, Doubleday, New York.

Mcleod, K. (2001) *Owning Culture: Authorship, Ownership, and Intellectual Property Law*, Peter Lang, New York.

Nieborg, D. (2005) 'Am I a Mod or Not? An Analysis of First Person Shooter Modification Culture' [online]. Available at http://www.gamespace.nl/content/DBNieborg2005_CreativeGamers.pdf

Ondrejka, C.R. (2005a) 'Escaping the Gilded Cage: User Created Content and Building the Metaverse', *New York Law School Law Review*, vol. 49, no. 1, pp. 81–101.

Ondrejka, C.R. (2005b) 'Aviators, Moguls, Fashionistas and Barons: Economics and Ownership in Second Life' [online]. Available at: http://papers.ssrn.com/sol3/papers.cfm?abstract_id = 614663

Poremba, C. (2003) 'Patches of Peace: Tiny Signs of Agency in Digital Games' [online]. Available at: http://www.digra.org/dl/display_html?chid = http://www.digra.org/dl/db/05150.24073 [12 August 2005]

Postigo, H. (2003) 'From PONG to PLANET QUAKE: Post – Industrial Transitions from Leisure to Work', *Information, Communication & Society*, vol. 6, no. 4, pp. 593–607.

Rifkin, J. (2000) *The Age of Access: The New Culture of Hypercapitalism, Where All of Life is a Paid-For Experience*, Tarcher, New York.

Sloop, J. & Herman, A. (1998) 'The Politics of Authenticity in Postmodern Rock Culture', *Critical Studies in Mass Communication*, vol. 15, no. 1, pp. 1–20.

Sotamaa, O. (2005) '"Have Fun Working with Our Product!": Critical Perspectives on Computer Game Mod Competitions' [online]. Available at http://www.gamesconference.org/diagra2005/viewabstract.php?id = 189

Streeter, T. (2003) 'The Romantic Self and the Politics of Internet Commercialization', *Cultural Studies*, vol. 17, no. 5, pp. 648–668.

Talcott, S. (2005) 'Bank of America gets MBNA: $35b deal to create biggest credit card issuer in US', *The Boston Globe*, 1 Jul., [online]. Available at: http://www.boston.com/business/globe/articles/2005/07/01/bank_of_america_gets_mbna/

Taylor, T.L. (2002) 'Whose Game Is This Anyway?': Negotiating Corporate Ownership in a Virtual World, in *Computer Games and Digital Cultures Conference Proceedings*, ed. F. Mäyrä, Tampere University Press, Tampere, pp. 227–242.

Taylor, T.L. (2006) *Play Between Worlds: Exploring Online Game Culture*, MIT Press, Cambridge, MA.

Terranova, T. (2000) 'Free Labor: Producing Culture for the Digital Economy', *Social Text*, vol. 18, no. 2, pp. 33–58.

Vaidhyanathan, S. (2004) *The Anarchist in the Library: How the Clash between Freedom and Control is Hacking the Real World and Crashing the System*, Basic Books, New York.

Vaidhyanathan, S. (2001) *Copyrights and Copywrongs: The Rise of Intellectual Property and How it Threatens Creativity*, New York University Press, New York.

Wallace, M. (2005) 'The Game is Virtual. The Profit is Real', *New York Times*, 29 May, [online]. Available at: http://www.nytimes.com/2005/05/29/business/yourmoney/29game.html?ex = 1123819200&en = 2351fcc00bead9a4&ei = 5070

Westerburg, A. (2004) 'Interview: Cory Linden on IP Issues in Second Life', *The Second Life Herald* [online]. Available at: http://www.alphavilleherald.com/archives/000372.html

Wittel, A. (2001) 'Toward a Network Sociality', *Theory, Culture and Society*, vol. 18, no. 6, pp. 51–76.

Xinhua News Agency (2003) 'On-line game player wins virtual properties dispute', December 19, p. 1.

Yes, N. (2004) 'Hours of Play Per Week' [online]. Available at http://www.nickyee.com/daedalus/archives/000343.php

VIII

THE DIGITAL, THE MOBILE, THE PERSONAL, AND THE EVERYDAY

Introduction

Our experience of everyday life has been transformed by mobile music systems, personal communication devices, GPS, email, and social networking. We occupy multiple spaces when we are on the telephone and commuting to work, and the distinction between various places (of leisure, work, and home) has become blurred. The personalization and customization of cell phones, email, and electronic devices mean that these are now seen as extensions of one's identity. Chatting and networking have shifted the very idea of the social as face-to-face interaction to online "meeting." Relations therefore can begin and end online, and may or may not be carried over into the "real." The personal diary is now online (blogs) and individuals can telecast themselves to the world through "homemade" movies. Corresponding to this shift within the idea of the social and the personal, collective everyday lives have also changed with networking and online religion.

This part of the book deals with the way ICTs have transformed the everyday. The articles here look at the phenomena of social networking, blogging, webcams, online religion, internet dating, and cell-phone culture. In comparison with earlier parts of the book, Part VIII presents the social life of high-tech – to see how people routinely incorporate high-tech into their everyday worlds, spaces, and activities. The assumption determining this part of the book is that our lives are increasingly mediated by and through technology, and we cannot see ICTs as simply sophisticated technology that's out there. The articles show that the personalization and domestication of

ICTs constitute a radical shift in the way we envisage technology itself (what *I* can use) and the user's co-construction of the technology.

Since the beginning of the twenty-first century Orkut, Facebook, YouTube, MySpace, and "social networking" sites have meant a radical change in social relations. These sites are now an integral component of everyday life and association. Sonia Livingstone's article explores the negotiation between "privacy" and risk as embodied in the content of youth sites within social networking sites. She treats the content as a mode of self-expression and identity-creation. Livingstone discovers that the content – including presentation, form, and graphics – of personal pages ("profiles") depends on the age of the person. Younger users tend to use MySpace more and project what they believe are more acceptable identities because, Livingstone argues, their position in the peer network is more important than the information provided. The use of Facebook marks a transition to an older stage among teenagers. Despite the extensive use of these sites, Livingstone argues, there exists considerable concern about privacy and risk among teenagers.

Helene Lawson and Kira Leck's article deals with protocols of internet dating. Examining different kinds of social relationships that develop online – from comfort after a life crisis to companionship – the authors discover that the internet offers individuals the freedom to present themselves in ways they think flattering. Freedom from commitment, relative safety, and a sense of adventure drive people to seek companions online. However, Lawson and Leck note that standard social norms of trust and authenticity inform online social interaction as well. Being lied to in cyberspace, they note, is considered a betrayal. Hence codes of trust and authenticity – such as self-disclosure of details – have developed in internet communication.

Diary writing has a new form: the blog. The personal blog and the politician's blog have become ubiquitous forms of self-display, information dissemination, and community linking. Madeline Sorapure begins by noting the disjunction between the materiality of the online diary form and the author-self. However, she argues, the new technologies enable different modes of self-representation. The fragmented nature of the online diary actually provides, writes Sorapure, "multiple and shifting ways of understanding the self." Also integral to the blog and the online diary is the breakdown of the private/public divide, since, unlike a conventional diary, a blog is available on the Web for anyone to read. The online diary is a "database" (here Sorapure is building on Lev Manovich's work on the language of the new media) rather than a narrative: fragmented, nonlinear, and organizable in any way the reader wants. Sorapure believes that the forms of writing that blogging technology facilitates further marginalize the already marginal diary form.

The cell phone has moved beyond its initial role as a communications device into something more. Mobile weblogs, or moblogs, are modes of archiving everyday lives. Nicola Döring and Axel Gundolf argue that this brings together the internet and communications technologies. They reject the reproach that such social practices are either about exhibitionism or voyeurism. What is interesting, they note, is that developments in moblog technologies came not from the software companies or engineers, but the users. The article demonstrates the social co-constructed nature of technologies. This spontaneous product development, they propose, is itself the consequence of networked cultures.

John Farnsworth and Terry Austrin shift the focus onto portable *sound* technologies (iPods, MP3 players). They propose that sound devices merge public and private spaces and mobilize the arrangement of space and sound. They are also hybrid devices that offer more flexibility to users in terms of connection with local or distant networks. Farnsworth and Austrin identify their main themes in the social consequences and influence on cell phones: assemblage, where social arrangements and technologies combine in particular configurations; the stability or instability of these configurations (especially in the almost continuous process of innovation and improvisation), and the assembly and disassembly of networks (where human interaction is altered through the presence and use of these portable sound technologies).

Vincent Miller's article on social networking notes the dominance of phatic communication in social networking exchanges and networks such as Twitter. Miller notes that much of the communication here serves not the purpose of real communication exchange or even a full dialog, but only the limited purpose of networking. The very process of communication seems to be an end in itself in "network sociality," he argues.

TAKING RISKY OPPORTUNITIES IN YOUTHFUL CONTENT CREATION

Teenagers' Use of Social Networking Sites for Intimacy, Privacy and Self-expression

Sonia Livingstone

Introduction

Young people have always devoted attention to the presentation of self. Friendships have always been made, displayed and broken. Strangers – unknown, weird or frightening – have always hovered on the edge of the group, and often, adult onlookers have been puzzled by youthful peer practices. Yet the recent explosion in online social networking sites such as MySpace, Facebook, Bebo and others has attracted considerable interest from the academy, policymakers, parents and young people themselves, the repeated claim being that something new is taking place. What, then, is distinctive about the youthful construction of self and peer relations, now that this is mediated increasingly by social networking sites?

Sonia Livingstone, "Taking Risky Opportunities in Youthful Content Creation: Teenagers' Use of Social Networking Sites for Intimacy, Privacy and Self-expression," pp. 393–441 from *new media & society* 10:3 (2008).

In terms of their affordances, social networking sites enable communication among ever-widening circles of contacts, inviting convergence among the hitherto separate activities of email, messaging, website creation, diaries, photo albums and music or video uploading and downloading. From the user's viewpoint, more than ever before, using media means creating as well as receiving, with user control extending far beyond selecting ready-made, mass-produced content. The very language of social relationships is being reframed; today, people construct their 'profile', make it 'public' or 'private', they 'comment' or 'message' their 'top friends' on their 'wall', they 'block' or 'add' people to their network and so forth.

It seems that for many, creating and networking online content is becoming an integral means of managing one's identity, lifestyle and social relations. In the UK, MySpace is by far the most popular social network, with 6.5 million unique visitors in May 2007, followed by 4 million for Bebo and 3.2 million for Facebook (Nielsen// Netratings, 2007). US figures are far higher, with 38.4 million unique visitors to MySpace in May 2006 (Nielsen//Netratings, 2006). Young people are in the vanguard of social networking practices: 31 percent of MySpace users are under 18 years, as are 54 percent of Bebo users in the USA (BBC News, 2006); 6.6 million unique users aged 12–17 visited MySpace in August 2006 across Europe (Comscore, 2006), and 32 percent of online 16–24-year-olds use social networking sites at least monthly (EIAA, 2006).

Optimistic accounts stress new opportunities for self-expression, sociability, community engagement, creativity and new literacies. Critical scholars argue that youthful content creation will counter the traditional dominance of consumers by producers and facilitate an innovative peer culture among young people, both locally and globally. Public policymakers hope that media literacy skills developed through social networking will transfer to support online learning and participation and protect youth from the online risks associated with transgressive representations of the self and abusive contact with others. Popular and media discourses all too often reflect a puzzled dismay that young people live in such a different world from the (nostalgically remembered) youth of today's adults.

Media panics amplify the public anxieties associated with social networking. The 'MySpace generation', they suggest, has no sense of privacy or shame. One attention-getting headline read: 'Generation shock finds liberty online: the children of the internet age are ready to bare their bodies and souls in a way their parents never could' (*Sunday Times*, 2007). And another claimed: 'Kids today. They have no sense of shame. They have no sense of privacy' (Nussbaum, 2007) Moreover, social networkers are supposedly wholly narcissistic: 'MySpace is about me, me, me, and look at me and look at me' (Fairfax Digital News, 2007). In short, it is commonly held that at best, social networking is time-wasting and socially isolating, and at worst it allows paedophiles to groom children in their bedroom[1] or sees teenagers lured into suicide pacts while parents think they are doing their homework.

Mediating Social Networking

For once it seems that the academy has kept pace with market innovation and social practice. Usefully countering the hype, a rapidly expanding body of empirical research is examining how people create personal profiles, network with familiar and new contacts and participate in various forms of online community (boyd, 2006; boyd and Ellison, 2007; Hinduja and Patchin, 2008; Lenhart and Madden, 2007). Certain trends are already apparent, challenging the simple distinctions with which new media research began. Notably, despite the potential for global networking, most people's contacts are local, with stronger ties centred on pre-existing study or work contexts (Haythornthwaite, 2001), especially among teenagers (Gross, 2004); although niche networks are often geographically spread, interest in 'strangers' or distant others is minimal (Boneva et al., 2006; Mesch and Talmud, 2007). However, this does not mean that face-to-face communication is being displaced. Indeed, while social networking is displacing other forms of online communication to some degree (email, chatrooms, website creation), it incorporates others (instant messaging, blogging, music downloading) and remediates yet more (most notably, face-to-face and telephone communication; Bolter and Grusin, 1999; Jenkins, 2006). Consequently, the simple distinction between offline and online no longer captures the complex practices associated with online technologies as they become thoroughly embedded in the routines of everyday life (Bakardjieva, 2005; Silverstone, 2006).

These insights centre on emerging social practices with online social networking. Less is known about the specific contribution of social networking sites in shaping these practices, if any. To understand the relation between the two, the notion of mediation – social and technological – permits us to avoid a technologically deterministic account while acknowledging the shaping role of technology and social practices (Bakardjieva, 2005). Hjarvard proposes that

> mediation refers to the communication through one or more media through which the message and the relation between sender and receiver are influenced by the affordances and constraints of the specific media and genres involved. (2006: 5)

… In a complementary fashion, drawing on Gibson's ecological psychology, Hutchby theorizes the mutuality between technological shaping and social practices thus:

> [A]ffordances are functional and relational aspects which frame, while not determining, the possibilities for agentic action in relation to an object. In this way, technologies can be understood as artefacts which may be both shaped by and shaping of the practices humans use in interaction with, around and through them. (2001: 44)

This article combines these perspectives with a child-centred, qualitative methodology (Livingstone, 1998) in order to explore teenagers' practices of social networking.

In addition to understanding the affordances of social networking sites, a child-centred approach means that the analysis should acknowledge young people's experiences, and it should situate their social networking practices within an account of the changing conditions of childhood and youth (James et al., 1998). As has been argued elsewhere, the tensions over children's media use often stem from underlying changes in the positioning of childhood and youth vis-à-vis parents, school and community (Livingstone, 2002). Today's teenagers live through an 'extended youth', historically speaking, staying young for longer in terms of education and economic dependence but becoming independent younger in terms of sexuality, leisure and consumption (Gadlin, 1978).

Hence, for teenagers, the online realm may be adopted enthusiastically because it represents 'their' space, visible to the peer group more than to adult surveillance, an exciting yet relatively safe opportunity to conduct the social psychological task of adolescence – to construct, experiment with and present a reflexive project of the self in a social context (Buchner et al., 1995; Giddens, 1991) as well as (for some) for flouting communicative norms and other risk-taking behaviours (Hope, 2007; Liau et al., 2005; Stattin Kerr, 2000; Wolak et al., 2006). Indeed, it seems that even normatively valued online activities are correlated in practice with risky activities regarding online content, contact and conduct, suggesting that what for an adult observer may seem risky, is for a teenager often precisely the opportunity that they seek (Livingstone and Helsper, 2007); this complicates straightforward policy attempts to maximize the former while minimizing the latter.

The complex relation between opportunity and risk is not distinctive to the internet, rather it is a feature of adolescence. As Erikson (1980[1959]) observed, the adolescent must develop and gain confidence in an ego identity that is simultaneously autonomous and socially valued, and that balances critical judgement and trust, inner unity and acceptance of societal expectations. …

Method

Sample and Interviews

A series of open-ended individual interviews were conducted with 16 teenagers in their homes (see Table 30.1).

Their ages ranged from 13–16 years, half were girls and half boys, most were white but several were black or of mixed ethnicity, and they spanned the range of socio-economic status categories as well as urban, suburban and rural locations in the Greater London area. All had home access to the internet (although in a few cases, this was not working at the time of the interview) and all had their own personal profile on MySpace, Facebook, Bebo, Piczo or similar, which they had visited at least once per week in recent months.

Table 30.1 Participants' details

| School year | Gender | |
	Girls	Boys
Year 9	Danielle, 13, C1, Piczo	Paul, 13, C2, Bebo, ex-MySpace
	Nicki, 14, AB, MySpace	
	Daphne, 14, C2, MySpace, Bebo, ex-Piczo	Joshua, 14, AB, Facebook
		Billy, 14, C2, MySpace
	Jenny, 14, DE, MySpace, Bebo	
	Elena, 14, DE, MySpace, Facebook, Bebo	
Year 10	Ellie, 15, AB, Facebook, ex-MySpace,	Ryan, 15, C1, Bebo, MySpace, ex-Piczo
Year 11	Nina, 15, C1, Facebook, ex-MySpace	Leo, 16, AB, MySpace
	Sophie, 16, C2, MySpace	Danny, 16, C1, MySpace, Facebook
		Simon, 16, DE, MySpace
		Jason, 16, DE, MySpace

Each participant's pseudonym is followed by their age, socioeconomic status (SES), and the social networking site they use/used. Household SES is categorized according to standard UK market research categories – AB (professional middle class), C1 (lower middle class), C2 (skilled working class) and DE (semi/unskilled working class). Year 9 is the third year of secondary school in the UK; year 11 is the final year of compulsory education.

The participants were recruited by a market research agency in July 2007 and interviewed by the author. The teenagers and their parents received a written explanation of the research aims, methods and ethics (addressing the answering of sensitive questions, participant anonymity and confidentiality, data storage and publication of findings) before signing a consent form. Each received a modest honorarium. Interviews lasted around one hour, and comprised a free-flowing, open-ended discussion in front of the computer, while simultaneously going online to visit the participant's personal profile and those of others.

Given the overall concern with online identity and peer relations, as shaped by peer culture and social networking site affordances, along with implications for online opportunities and risks, the interview schedule addressed:

- the choices, motivations and literacies shaping the participant's own profile;
- the semiotic and social 'reading' of others' profiles (in terms of conventions regarding form, identity and peer norms regarding transgressive or risky practices); and
- the social and personal meanings of the contacts sustained online and their relation to offline friends in everyday life.

The interviews were audio-recorded and transcribed before being coded, using Nvivo qualitative coding software, according to categories derived from the issues emerging from the participants' responses as well as from the questions asked in the interviews.

Results and Discussion

Enacting Identity

Strategies for representing the self were found to vary considerably. For example, Danielle's Piczo profile has a big welcome in sparkly pink, with music, photos, a 'love tester', guestbook, dedication pages, etc., all customized down to the scroll bars and cursor with pink candy stripes, glitter, angels, flowers, butterflies, hearts and more (because 'you can just change it all the time [and so] you can show different sides of yourself'). By contrast, Danny has not completed the basic Facebook options of noting his politics, religion or even his network ('I haven't bothered to write about myself'). Most profiles are designed in one way or another to provide 'a way of expressing who you are to other people', as Nina put it. Elena, who spends several hours each day updating and altering her MySpace, Facebook and Piczo profiles, says:

> I think layouts really show like who you are. So look at the rainbow in that. I think that would make you sound very, like, bubbly … I like to have different ones … it's different likes, different fashion, different feelings on that day.

In response to this continual activity of representing the self, Elena's friends have peppered her profile with nice comments – 'I'm always here for you', 'You're gorgeous,' etc. – as part of a reciprocal exchange of mutual support which she appreciates. …

It should not be assumed that profiles are simply read as information about an individual. Jenny, like others, is well aware that people's profiles can be 'just a front'. For several of the participants, it seemed that position in the peer network was more significant than the personal information provided, rendering the profile a placemarker more than a self portrait. Initially, this author misunderstood this – for example, on Leo's site there was a comment from his friend 'Blondie' saying that she's pregnant: when I ask, he observes that, of course, 'she's joking' – the point being to share (and display) their humorous relationship, not a personal self-disclosure. A more sustained and fairly common instance is provided by Paul. A confident and sociable boy who 'got pulled into the world of Bebo' because 'everybody was talking about it', he has constructed his profile as a joke. With a funny photo of himself, it announces him to be 36, married, living in Africa, a person who likes to humiliate people and to get unconscious (there were other examples of teenagers' playful, occasionally resistant style, for example, posting an image of their dog instead of themselves). Yet in the interview, Paul takes little notice of this, since his brothers and friends (with whom he, like some others, has shared his password) have often changed his profile for fun. Thus his profile is meaningful to him not as a means of displaying personal information about him to the world, as often supposed, but precisely because the joky content is evidence of his lively and trusting relations with his brothers and friends.

Pointing to the lack of a one-to-one match between users and profiles, a point also evident in the way that some users maintain several profiles on different sites, Paul explains how the profile may display the peer group more than the individual:

> When we go out together, like they take photos on their phones and stuff and then they upload them on there … So everybody else can see what we've done and, like, see all of our friends and when we're together and it's just like remembering the time when we did it.

Thus although it indeed appears that, for many young people, social networking is 'all about me, me, me', this need not imply narcissistic self-absorption. Rather, following Mead's (1934) fundamental distinction between the 'I' and the 'me' as twin aspects of the self, social networking is about 'me' in the sense that it reveals the self embedded in the peer group, as known to and represented by others, rather than the private 'I' known best by oneself.

[…]

Transitions in Identity Development

Although the intention of this study was to recruit a narrow range of teenagers in terms of age (i.e. 13–16-year-olds, a cohort commonly combined by survey research), it emerged that collectively, the participants had a story to tell about their changing identity. Teenagers are acutely aware of the subtle differences between those a school year younger or older and themselves, indicating perceived differences in identity, social position or maturity, and often media choices are used as markers of relative maturity ('have you got your own television set yet, or seen a film classified for those older than you?'; Livingstone, 2002). Intriguingly, in relation to social networking, such identity development seemed to be expressed in terms of decisions regarding the style or choice of site. Nina, for example, moved from MySpace to Facebook, describing this somewhat tentatively as the transition from elaborate layouts for younger teenagers to the clean profile favoured by older teenagers:

> With profiles, everything [on MySpace] was all about having coloured backgrounds … whereas I just suppose, like Facebook, I prefer to have, like older people, and it was more sophisticated, can I use that word? … I found when I was 14 I always wanted to be like someone that was older than me … When I first got MySpace, I thought it was a really cool

thing because all older people had it, and they were all having their templates and things like that ... but I'm sort of past that stage now, and I'm more into the plain things.

Ellie, 15, points to a similar distinction when comparing her Facebook profile with her 12-year-old sister's use of MySpace:

The reason they [younger girls] like MySpace seems to be because you can decorate your page with flowers and hearts and have glitter on it, whereas on this [Facebook] it's sort of a white background with not so much, it's just a photo and a name, which is pretty much the same for everyone. [Talking of herself] I can't really see the point. This isn't to show off about my personality. I'm not trying to say, oh, I love purple or I love hearts ... It's more just like talking to three friends and, seeing as my friends know me, there's no real need for me to advertise my personality ... On MySpace, everyone's got these things like, I love this, I hate this, and trying to show off who they are, and I just don't think that's necessary if these actually are your friends.

Once sensitized to this stylistic shift, it became apparent to me that some teenagers preferred elaborately customized profiles while others favoured a plain aesthetic. ...

The flexibility of social networking sites in affording revisions of one's identity is welcome. Leo says, of his MySpace profile:

The one I made before I thought I didn't really like it, so I thought I'd start again, I'd start a new one ... [the previous profile] it was just ... people I didn't like had the address, so I thought I should start fresh.

[...]

What might this shift, whether managed by changing one's social networking site or just one's profile, signify for younger and older teenagers? Ziehe argues of lifestyles that these should be recognized as 'collective ways of life ... [which] point to common orientations of taste and interpretations; they demonstrate a certain group-specific succinctness of usage of signs' (1994: 2). ...

Thus Ziehe suggests a way in which the project of the self is represented according to highly coded cultural conventions (here including technological interfaces) and social preferences (here embedded in the norms of consumer culture).

With this in mind, Ellie, Nina and others seem to suggest that for younger teenagers, self-attention is enacted through constructing an elaborate, highly stylized statement of identity as display. ... However, this notion of identity as display – ... is replaced gradually by the mutual construction among peers of a notion of identity through connection. ...

Equally stylized, albeit employing a different aesthetic, and still focused on the reflexive tasks of self-observation and self-assessment, this later phase brings to mind Giddens' (1991: 91) argument that the 'pure relationship' is replacing the traditional relationship long embedded in structures of family, work or community.

As he puts it, 'the pure relationship is reflexively organised, in an open fashion, and on a continuous basis', prioritizing the values of authenticity, reciprocity, recognition and intimacy. Reminiscent of the concerns reflected by teenagers when talking about social networking, continuous revision of the self is hinted at when Leo says, 'I'll always be adding new friends'. ...

In terms of affordances, then, social networking sites frame but do not determine. It remains open to young people to select a more or less complex representation of themselves linked to a more or less wide network of others. These choices pose advantages and disadvantages. Elaborating the presentation of self at the node supports the biographization of the self by prioritizing a managed and stylized display of identity as lifestyle. However, this risks invasion of privacy, since the backstage self is on view (Goffman, 1959), potentially occasioning critical or abusive responses from others. Something of the associated anxiety is evident in Ryan's comment about his profile that 'hopefully people will like it – if they don't, then screw them'. The interlinking of opportunities and risks is also apparent when Danielle discusses how her friend used Piczo to express her unhappiness when her parents separated, 'because other people can advise you what to do or say, "Don't worry, you can go through it"'; yet Danielle is one of the few participants who talked about the risk of hostile comments, noting that 'sometimes the comments are cruel and they're [her friends] all crying and upset'.

Alternatively, identity may be elaborated in terms of the network, the node being relatively unembellished but resonant with meaning through its connections with selected others. As Marwick notes, social networking sites enable people 'to codify, map and view the relational ties between themselves and others' (2005: 3). Here, instead, the project of the self is more at risk in terms of one's standing in the network: do people visit your profile and leave comments, are you listed as anyone's top friend, etc. This concern may explain the routine yet highly absorbing activity of checking people's profiles and, in response, revising one's own, often occupying one or more hours each day. Thus Jenny says of MySpace:

> You look through other people's profiles and look through their pictures, different pictures of their mates and that ... if someone gives me a comment I'll comment them back ... you get, like, addicted to it.

... as with the acts of recognition constitutive of offline social relations, it seems that these are necessary to reaffirm one's place within the peer network.

Creating Private Spaces for Intimacy Among 'Friends'

Creating identity and social relations online is not only time-intensive, and on occasion risky, but also it can be difficult to manage. In the interviews, the topic of privacy tended to point up ways in which the affordances of social networking sites limit teenagers' self-expression. Although there is much they express only offline, and although they generally set their profile to private (Lenhart and Madden, 2007), it is the case that teenagers may disclose personal information with up to several hundred people known only casually. This is in part because social networking sites typically display as standard precisely the personal information that previous generations often have regarded as private (notably age, politics, income, religion, sexual preference). ...

Nonetheless, it would be mistaken to conclude that teenagers are unconcerned about their privacy. ... Teenagers described thoughtful decisions about what, how and to whom they reveal personal information, drawing their own boundaries about what information to post and what to keep off the site, making deliberate choices that match their mode of communication (and its particular affordances) to particular communicative content. This suggests a definition of privacy not tied to the disclosure of certain types of information, rather a definition centred on having control over who knows what about you (Livingstone, 2006). Stein and Sinha put this formally when they define privacy as 'the rights of individuals to enjoy autonomy, to be left alone, and to determine whether and how information about one's self is revealed to others' (2002: 414).

The advantage of this definition is that it resolves the apparent paradox that the 'MySpace Generation' is concerned about privacy yet readily discloses personal information (Barnes, 2006; Dwyer, 2007). The point is that teenagers must and do disclose personal information in order to sustain intimacy, but they wish to be in control of how they manage this disclosure. As Giddens (1991: 94) says, 'intimacy is the other face of privacy'. However, two problems undermine teenagers' control over such disclosure. The first is that their notion of 'friends' is subtle while that of the social networking sites is typically binary, affording only a simple classification of contacts (e.g. for MySpace, your friends versus all users; for Facebook, your network versus all networks). Being required to decide whether personal information should be disclosed to 'friends' or to 'anyone' fails to capture the varieties of privacy that teenagers wish to sustain. Indeed, being visible to strangers (managed through setting one's profile to 'public') is not so much a concern, notwithstanding media panics about 'stranger danger' as that of being visible to known but inappropriate others – especially parents.

[...]

It is unclear to these teenagers how they can reflect such gradations of intimacy in managing who knows what about them, the privacy settings provided seeming inadequate to the task. Fahey argues that:

> Instead of speaking of a single public/private boundary, it may be more accurate to speak of a more complex re-structuring in a series of zones of privacy, not all of which fit easily with our standard images of what the public/private boundary is. (1995: 688)

Since these 'zones of privacy' are now managed partly online, at issue is the (mis) match between technological affordances and teenage conceptions of friendship. Of course, teenagers are not seeking primarily to maintain their privacy from strangers (or else they could simply turn off the computer). Rather, they are seeking to share their private experiences, to create spaces of intimacy, to be themselves in and through their connection with their friends.

Teenagers face another problem in managing their privacy online, which concerns the relation between their internet literacy and the interface design of social networking sites and settings. When asked, a fair proportion of those interviewed hesitated to show how to change their privacy settings, often clicking on the wrong options before managing this task, and showing some nervousness about the unintended consequences of changing settings (both the risk of 'stranger danger' and parental approbation were referred to here, although they also told stories of viruses, crashed computers, unwanted advertising and unpleasant chain messages). ... Unsurprisingly, then, when asked whether they would like to change anything about social networking, the operation of privacy settings and provision of private messaging on the sites are teenagers' top priorities, along with elimination of spam and chain messages – both intrusions of their privacy.

These difficulties in managing privacy via privacy settings reflect broader internet literacy issues. For example, the top bar of a MySpace profile lists 'blog', 'groups', 'forum', 'events', 'music', 'film', and more. While it was observed that most of the teenagers include music on their profile, when asked about blogs, groups or forums, often the question was met with blank looks. Even 16-year-old Danny, whose father works in computers and who says confidently, 'I know a lot about computers', was confused when asked about the group facility, saying: 'I don't know if I've got a group ... I didn't even know there was [sic] groups'. Ellie has joined 163 groups – including the appreciation society for her local bus, one for a favourite programme, another for a charity that she supports, etc. However, she had hardly noticed and certainly does not use the blog, noting that 'I don't think any of my friends have either'. The limits of teenagers' supposedly exploratory and creative approach to social networking are, it seems, easily reached. Pragmatically, such difficulties are 'resolved' often by simply ignoring sites' affordances (irrespective of whether these are well or poorly designed), including not using the detailed privacy options provided by some sites.

... Designing a profile is not solely a matter of individual choice. It is geared towards others through the choice of site (one must select that already used by one's friends), mode of address (most say that they put on their profile the content that they consider their friends would enjoy) and, practically, by the moment of setting up a profile (commonly achieved with the help of a friend who already uses the site). Literacy matters here also, for several of those observed felt limited by the particular way that the profile was set up initially by their friend, not always feeling able to alter this. ...

Conclusion

In late modernity, 'self-actualisation is understood in terms of a balance between opportunity and risk' (Giddens, 1991: 78). Both the opportunities and risks arise because self-actualization is a social process. Selves are constituted through interaction with others and, for today's teenagers, self-actualization increasingly includes a careful negotiation between the opportunities (for identity, intimacy, sociability) and risks (regarding privacy, misunderstanding, abuse) afforded by internet-mediated communication. Among this admittedly small sample of teenagers, younger teenagers were found to relish the opportunities to play and display, continuously recreating a highly-decorated, stylistically-elaborate identity. Having experienced this 'phase', older teenagers tended to favour a plain aesthetic that foregrounds their links to others, expressing a notion of identity lived through authentic relationships with others. As has been previously suggested, this apparent shift in phases of identity development may have implications for teenagers' experience of online opportunities and risks.

Also influencing the balance between opportunities and risks online are the specific affordances of social networking sites, especially their conception of 'friends' and the provision of privacy settings, as has been examined here. Teenagers were found to work with a subtle classification of 'friends', graded in terms of intimacy, which is poorly matched by the notion of 'public' and 'private' designed into social networking sites. While it is teenagers' desire for subtle gradation in levels of intimacy (rather than a desire for publicity or exhibitionism) that guides teenagers' approach to privacy online, it is suggested that in this regard they struggle in terms of internet literacy, impeded in turn by the affordances of the social networking sites.

For those focused on identity as display, online risks may arise from their willing, sometimes naïve, self-display of personal information to a wide circle of contacts, not all of whom are close friends or sometimes even remembered. For those focused on identity as connection, online risks may arise from their very confidence that they can know, judge and trust the people with whom they are intimate, as well as from the possibility of being neglected or excluded from the peer group. Also, risks may arise from the teenagers' limited internet literacy combined with confusing or poorly designed site settings, leaving them unclear regarding their control over who can see what about them. Each of these risks may affect adversely only a minority, but they render public policy measures (improved site design, internet literacy, parental guidance, etc.) appropriate.

Finally, it is worth noting that, rather than compromise their privacy too far, many of those interviewed chose to express their more personal experiences (as defined by them, not by adult society) using other modes of communication, online or offline. Danielle's unhappy friend, noted earlier, seems more the exception than the rule, and most of the teenagers interviewed were clear that they use social networking sites for only part, not all, of their social relations. For example, Ellie uses MSN for private conversations with her best friends and, like many others, for flirting. Nina, Daphne and most others talk to their best friends face-to-face or via MSN. If upset, Joshua turns to neither phone, internet nor even a friend, but rather listens to loud rock music in his room. As Sophie explains:

> When you're moody, MySpace isn't really the best thing to go on … you can't really get across emotions on there because you're writing. It's good for making arrangements and stuff, but it's not good if you want a proper chat.

In other words, although to exist online one must write oneself, and one's friendships and community, into being (boyd, 2006; Sundén, 2003), this does not mean one must include every aspect of oneself. Deciding what not to say about oneself online is, for many teenagers, an agentic act to protect their identity and their spaces of intimacy.

NOTE

1. I do not mean, here, to deny that such cases occur.

REFERENCES

Bakardjieva, M. (2005) *Internet Society: The Internet in Everyday Life*. London: Sage.

Barnes, S.B. (2006) 'A Privacy Paradox: Social Networking in the United States' *First Monday* 11(9), URL (consulted 9 March 2007): http://www.firstmonday.org/ISSUES/issue11_9/barnes/

BBC News (2006) 'Social Sites Wrestle for Top Spot', 24 May, URL (consulted 26 November 2007): http://news.bbc.co.uk/2/hi/technology/5012194.stm

Bolter, J.D. and R. Grusin (1999) *Remediation: Understanding New Media*. Cambridge, MA: MIT Press.

Boneva, B., A. Quinn, R. Kraut, S. Kiesler and I. Shklovski (2006) 'Teenage Communication in the Instant Messaging Era', in R. Kraut, M. Brynin and S. Kiesler (eds) *Computers, Phones, and the Internet: Domesticating Information Technology*, pp. 201–18. Oxford: Oxford University Press.

boyd, d. (2006) 'Friends, Friendsters, and Top 8: Writing Community into Being on Social Network Sites' *First Monday*, 11, URL (consulted 9 March 2007): http://www.firstmonday.org/issues/issue11_12/boyd/

boyd, d. and Ellison, N. (2007) 'Social Network Sites: Definition, History, and Scholarship', *Journal of Computer-Mediated Communication* 13(1), URL (consulted 30 January 2008): http://jcmc.indiana.edu/vol13/issue1/boyd.ellison.html

Buchner, P., M.D. Bois-Reymond and H.-H. Kruger (1995) 'Growing Up in Three European Regions', in L. Chisholm (ed.) *Growing Up in Europe: Contemporary Horizons in Childhood and Youth Studies*, pp. 43–59. Berlin: de Gruyter.

Comscore (2006) 'More than Half of MySpace Visitors Are Now Age 35 or Older', 5 October, URL (consulted 6 July 2007): http://www.comscore.com/press/release.asp?press = 1019

Dwyer, C. (2007) 'Digital Relationships in the "MySpace" Generation: Results from a Qualitative Study', in *Proceedings of the Fortieth Hawaii International Conference on System Sciences*, p. 19. Los Alamitos, CA: IEEE Press.

EIAA (2006) 'Social Networking to Drive Next Wave of Internet Usage', 29 November, URL (consulted 6 July 2007): http://www.eiaa.net/news/eiaa-articles-details.asp?id=106&lang=1

Erikson, E.H. (1980[1959]) *Identity and the Life Cycle*. New York: W.H. Norton and Co.

Fahey, T. (1995) 'Privacy and the Family', *Sociology* 29(4): 687–703.

Fairfax Digital News (2007) 'Turning Japanese', 1 March, URL (consulted 30 January 2008): http://www.theage.com.au/news/web/turning-japanese/2007/02/28/1172338633250.html

Gadlin, H. (1978) 'Child Discipline and the Pursuit of Self: An Historical Interpretation', in H.W. Reese and L.P. Lipsitt (eds) *Advances in Child Development and Behavior*, Vol. 12, pp. 231–61. New York: Academic Press.

Giddens, A. (1991) *Modernity and Self-identity: Self and Society in the Late Modern Age*. Cambridge: Polity Press.

Goffman, E. (1959) *The Presentation of Self in Everyday Life*. Harmondsworth: Penguin.

Gross, E.F. (2004) 'Adolescent Internet Use: What we Expect, What Teens Report', *Journal of Applied Developmental Psychology* 25(6): 633–49.

Hinduja, S. and J.W. Patchin (2008) 'Personal Information of Adolescents on the Internet: A Quantitative Content Analysis of MySpace', *Journal of Adolescence* 31(1): 125–46.

Hjarvard, S. (2006) 'The Mediatization of Religion: A Theory of the Media as an Agent of Religious Change', paper presented at the Fifth International Conference on Media, Religion and Culture, Sweden, 6–9 July.

Hope, A. (2007) 'Risk Taking, Boundary Performance and Intentional School Internet "Misuse"', *Discourse* 28(1): 87–99.

Hutchby, I. (2001) 'Technologies, Texts and Affordances', *Sociology* 35(2): 441–56.

James, A., C. Jenks and A. Prout (1998) *Theorizing Childhood*. Cambridge: Cambridge University Press.

Jenkins, H. (2006) *Convergence Culture: Where Old and New Media Collide*. New York: New York University Press.

Lenhart, A. and M. Madden (2007) 'Social Networking Websites and Teens: an Overview', URL (consulted 20 December 2007): http://www.pewinternet.org/pdfs/PIP_SNS_Data_Memo_Jan_2007.pdf

Liau, A.K., A. Khoo and P.H. Ang (2005) 'Factors Influencing Adolescents' Engagement in Risky Internet Behavior', *CyberPsychology & Behaviour* 8(2): 513–20.

Livingstone, S. (1998) 'Mediated Childhoods: A Comparative Approach to Young People's Changing Media Environment in Europe', *European Journal of Communication* 13(4): 435–56.

Livingstone, S. (2002) *Young People and New Media: Childhood and the Changing Media Environment*. London: Sage.

Livingstone, S. (2006) 'Children's Privacy Online: Experimenting with Boundaries Within and Beyond the Family', in R. Kraut, M. Brynin and S. Kiesler (eds) *Computers, Phones, and the Internet: Domesticating Information Technology*, pp. 128–44. Oxford: Oxford University Press.

Livingstone, S. and E.J. Helsper (2007) 'Taking Risks When Communicating on the Internet: The Role of Offline Social-psychological Factors in Young People's Vulnerability to Online Risks', *Information, Communication and Society* 10(5): 619–44.

Marwick, A. (2005) '"I'm a Lot More Interesting than a Friendster Profile": Identity Presentation, Authenticity and Power in Social Networking Services', paper presented at the Conference of the Association of Internet Researchers 6, Chicago, 5–6 October.

Mead, G.H. (1934) *Mind, Self and Society: From the Standpoint of a Social Behaviourist*. Chicago, IL: University of Chicago Press.

Mesch, G.S. and I. Talmud (2007) 'Similarity and the Quality of Online and Offline Social Relationships among Adolescents in Israel', *Journal of Research on Adolescence* 17(2): 455–66.

Nielsen//Netratings (2006) 'Social Networking Sites Grow 47 Percent, Year over Year, Reaching 45 Percent of Web Users', 11 May, URL (consulted 26 November 2007): http://www.nielsen-netratings.com/pr/pr_060511.pdf

Nielsen//Netratings (2007) 'Facebook and Bebo: The Assault on MySpace', 28 June, URL (consulted 30 January 2008): http://www.nielsen-netratings.com/pr/pr_070628_UK.pdf

Nussbaum, E. (2007) 'Say Everything', *New York Magazine*, 12 February, URL (consulted 6 July 2007): http://nymag.com/news/features/27341/

Silverstone, R. (2006) 'Domesticating Domestication: Reflections on the Life of a Concept', in T. Berker, M. Hartmann, Y. Punie and K.J. Ward (eds) *The Domestication of Media and Technology*, pp. 229–48. Maidenhead: Open University Press.

Stattin Kerr, M.H. (2000) 'What Parents Know, How They Know it, and Several Forms of Adolescent Adjustment: Further Support for a Reinterpretation of Monitoring', *Developmental Psychology* 36(3): 366–80.

Stein, L. and N. Sinha (2002) 'New Global Media and Communication Policy: The Role of the State in Twenty-first Century', in L. Lievrouw and S. Livingstone (eds) *Handbook of New Media: Social Shaping and Consequences of ICTs*, pp. 410–31. London: Sage.

Sunday Times (2007) 'Generation Shock Finds Liberty Online', 25 February, URL (consulted 30 January 2008): http://www.timesonline.co.uk/tol/news/uk/article1433751.ece

Sundén, J. (2003) *Material Virtualities: Approaching Online Textual Embodiment*. New York: Peter Lang.

Wolak, J., K.J. Mitchell and D. Finkelhor (2006) *Online Victimization of Youth: Five Years Later*. Durham, NH: National Center for Missing and Exploited Children, University of New Hampshire.

Ziehe, T. (1994) 'From Living Standard to Life Style', *Young: Nordic Journal of Youth Research* 2(2): 2–16.

31 DYNAMICS OF INTERNET DATING

Helene M. Lawson and Kira Leck

Risk-taking, trust, and serendipity are key ingredients of joy. Without risk, nothing new ever happens. Without trust, fear creeps in. Without serendipity, there are no surprises.
(Rita Golden Gelman (2002))

... Internet dating, which has become increasingly popular in recent times, is an example of an activity that requires taking risks and trusting an unknown person who may be thousands of miles away. These risks are taken in the hope that romance will evolve.

The present research focused on the dynamics of Internet dating, a method of courting used by individuals who meet on the Internet and continue online correspondence in hopes of forming a supportive romantic relationship. It sought to determine why people choose to date online, what aspects of face-to-face relations are reproduced, and the rationales and strategies Internet daters use to negotiate and manage problems of risk accompanying the technology.

[…]

In the 1990s, the Internet became a major vehicle for social encounters. Through the Internet, people can interact over greater distances in a shorter period and at less expense than in the past. Theorists have debated the positive and negative effects this technology has on social interactions. Initially, theorists such as Zuboff (1991) believed "the Internet reduced face-to-face interaction" and created an "uncomfortable isolation" (pp. 479–482) for people at work. Conversely, Raney (2000) argued that online communication expands social networks. According to Raney, the Pew Internet and American Life Project found supporting evidence for this view in a study in which "more than half of Internet users reported that e-mail was strengthening their family ties. And Internet users reported far more offline social contact

Helene M. Lawson and Kira Leck. "Dynamics of Internet Dating," pp. 189–208 from *Social Science Computer Review* 24:2 (summer 2006).

than non-users." (p. G7). Cooper and Sportolari (1997) suggested that the Internet is especially helpful for promoting romantic relationships.

[...]

There is an abundance of literature about social interaction on the Internet (e.g., Baym, 1998, 2000; Bell, 2001; Clark, 1998; Dietrich, 1997; Fernback, 1997; Hardey, 2002, 2004; S. Jones, 1995, 1997; Markham, 1998; Reid, 1997; Slevin, 2000; Strate, 2003; Waskul, 2003; Zimmer & Hunter, 2003), though little attention has been given to the growing significance of Internet courtship. Today Internet video and sound communications are commonplace, and photographs, video, and sound clips can all be altered or fabricated entirely. These new technologies allow Internet daters enormous latitude to prepare their presentations of self.

Using the Internet for Dating

The Internet is a new social institution that has the ability to connect people who have never met face to face and is thus likely to transform the dating process. Beginning with newsgroups such as Usenet and various bulletin boards that operated under the now-obsolete Gopher system, the Internet facilitated the formation of communities. Baym (2000) traced how users of http://rec.arts.tv.soaps, an online newsgroup dealing with soap operas, gradually came to recognize and know each other through their styles of posting. They then began to communicate on personal subjects apart from soap operas. As a result, people who had never met and could not even see each other ceased to be strangers. Internet dating extended this process of incidental acquaintanceship to the specific task of recruiting partners.

We explored the phenomenology of Internet dating, which we defined as the pattern of periodic communication between potential partners using the Internet as a medium. We examined the respondents' concerns over the risk of being deceived, their anxieties about physical appearance, and the hazards of romantic involvement.

Method

Participants

Because we needed a sample of respondents who could be tracked over time and whose reliability could be verified, we began to investigate the phenomenon of Internet dating by interviewing people who were personally accessible, such as coworkers, acquaintances, and students. Soon the sample expanded because respondents told us about people they knew who dated online, which resulted in a snowball sample. It was not a uniform sample with respect to such attributes as race and socioeconomic status because it favored a White middle class and was instead a sample dictated by sampling logistics. However, we believe that the phenomenon of Internet courtship is largely a White, middle-class phenomenon as one can see by examining such public meeting places as hotornot.com. For this reason, we believe our sample to be qualitatively representative: It was composed of 32% students, 24% business and clerical workers, 14% trade workers, and 14% professionals and semiprofessionals. The sample also included unemployed persons, small business owners, and housewives.

Because we were interested in romantic dating relationships that could result in commitment, we did not include people interested only in pornography or online sexual encounters as their primary focus. We defined dating as setting up specific times to mutually disclose personal information with potential romantic partners on an ongoing basis. We did not place any other restrictions on whom we were willing to interview. Consequently, the sample included homosexuals and unhappily married persons. Romance was not necessarily the goal of online dating, but in our sample, three married persons changed partners as a result of Internet interactions.

Interview Questions

Interviews were open-ended and informal. We asked respondents to (a) describe their experiences with Internet dating, (b) state whether these experiences were positive or negative, (c) state how and why they entered the world of online dating, and (d) state whether they used online dating services or met incidentally through chat rooms, online games, or common interest groups. Respondents were eager to relate their experiences, and many interviews lasted an hour or longer.

Interviews were conducted during lunch in restaurants, at respondents' homes, at the home of the first author, in the university cafeteria, and on walks in various neighborhoods. All respondents had ready access to computers in their homes, dorm rooms, or places of work. We watched while they talked back and forth online. In addition, the first author invited three newly paired couples to her home for dinner. Follow-up data were collected in person, on the phone, by e-mail, and by mail. Interviews were later transcribed and coded by keywords according to concepts that emerged through the dialogue, such as trust, time, risk, and need satisfaction.

We limited the number of respondents to 25 men and 25 women because we wanted to compare gender variables in a balanced sample. The men ranged in age from 18 to 58 with a mean age of 32.6. The women ranged in age from 15 to 48 with a mean age of 33. In all, 17 men and 11 women were single (never married), 7 men and 10 women were divorced, and 1 man and 4 women were married. Two men and one woman were gay. Two women and one man were African American. One man was Indian. Six men and seven women were the parents of young children, and as previously stated, five respondents were married when they began to interact romantically online.

Results

Beck (1992) argued that people must risk social dependency on others even though this dependency harms their ability to function independently "in the life that basically must be or ought to be led alone. ... Circles of contact must be built up. ... This requires readiness by people to help bear the burdens of others" (p. 122). Similar to Hardey (2002), respondents revealed multiple affiliation-related motivations for becoming involved in Internet dating.

Companionship

Lonely people tend to report being dissatisfied with their relationships and are often cynical, rejecting, bored, and depressed. They also have difficulty making friends, engaging in conversations, getting involved in social activities, and dating (Chelune, Sultan, & Williams, 1980; W. H. Jones, Hobbs, & Hockenbury, 1982). Their tendency to engage in minimal self-disclosure and be unresponsive to conversational partners often results in poor interactions that are unrewarding for both partners, which leads lonely individuals to feel dissatisfied with their relationships (McAdams, 1989). Both relationship dissatisfaction and difficulty with social behaviors may lead lonely people to seek online relationships.

Regardless of their marital status, respondents of all ages tended to report being lonely. They all talked about needing more communication, emotional support, and companionship. Fred, a 19-year-old student who had never been married, said, "I hate being alone. You want to know someone out there at least cares."

Greta, a 43-year-old, unhappily married mother of a 9-year-old, worked a night shift. Her husband worked during the day, and they both dated others online through chat rooms. Chat rooms often require only token (username) identification. The face presented is largely cloaked, but marital status is usually not hidden. Rather, it is explained:

> I guess the big problem is that my husband works 6 days a week, is gone all day long, and doesn't spend time with me. It is like we are strangers living in the same house. We haven't actually gone out with anyone.

Kelly, a 48-year-old, unhappily married student also blamed her lack of communication with her husband for why she dated online.

[...]

Mary, a 30-year-old, recently divorced student, also blamed loneliness and the lack of communication.

[...]

Regardless of their marital status, all of the above individuals seemed to perceive their social lives as incomplete. This may be a reflection of the separation of family and friends because of current societal structure. Thus, it is not surprising that they were highly motivated to become involved in online relationships with people who were willing to talk, listen, and serve a supportive function.

[...]

Comfort After a Life Crisis

The Internet has been used by people seeking social support and information while coping with cancer (Fogel, Albert, Schnabel, Ditkoff, & Neugut, 2002; Klemm, Hurst, Dearholt, & Trone, 1999; Ljungman et al., 2003), heart disease, (Dickerson, Flaig, & Kennedy, 2000), suicide (Hollander, 2001), and Alzheimer's disease (White & Dorman, 2000). Vanderwerker and Prigerson (2004) found that people with major depressive disorder, post-traumatic stress disorder, and complicated grief who used the Internet and in particular e-mail were more likely to report higher energy levels and a better quality of life after they began using these technologies. Similarly, several respondents in the present sample reported seeking comfort after a life crisis, such as the loss of a job, a divorce, or a death in the family.

[...]

Our society's lack of support structure for individuals who experience life crises may lead them to seek out comfort from online sources. Real-life friends and family members often prejudge and blame people for their predicaments. A desire to avoid being judged may motivate people to seek support in an environment where pre-typed descriptions of self and where true expressions of unhappiness are invisible. The online setting allows them to select which aspects of themselves to reveal to their online companions, which lessens the probability of unfavorable judgment that may be leveled by real-life friends and family members.

Control Over Presentation and Environment

The Internet provides a medium for people to present themselves in a way that that they think is flattering. Clark (1998) reports that girls describe themselves as "thinner and taller" and otherwise prettier in Internet communications than they actually are. Because contact is mediated, individuals do not have to expose themselves directly on the Internet. In general, "the surest way for a person to prevent threats to his face is to avoid contacts in which these threats are likely to occur" (Goffman, 1967, p. 15).

Jean, a 35-year-old, never married woman, said if you were heavy, you could get to know someone who might like you instead of having to attract people with your looks before they wanted to know you.

[...]

Ted, a 40-year-old, never married, legally blind man, said the Internet gave him confidence.

[...]

There is a large body of social psychological literature on social anxiety and dating behavior. In a review of the dating frequency literature, Leck (2003) found:

> Infrequent daters are likely to be shy, introverted, lonely, and have a low sense of self-esteem and self-competence. They also tend to be less attractive, more anxious, less socially skilled, and hold more negative beliefs than do frequent daters. Shy men are sensitive to rejection. (pp. 36–41)

For people who are shy, anxious, and deficient in social skills, use of the Internet may facilitate social interaction because it requires different skills that are necessary for initiating heterosocial interaction in a face-to-face setting. In one study, college students reported using the Internet to meet people because they found it reduced their anxiety about social interaction (Knox, Daniels, Sturdivant, & Zusman, 2001).

Some respondents of both sexes claimed they found it difficult to talk to strangers in social situations such as parties or even in places such as the school cafeteria or a classroom. […]

Men and women respondents complained that bars were not a good place to get to know prospective partners.

[…]

Societal expectations for appearance and behavior can result in individuals who do not fit the norm and perceive themselves as deviants who will not be accepted. Furthermore, they may fear negative reprisals from more mainstream members of society and thus may retreat into an online setting where they feel safer and have control.

Freedom From Commitment and Stereotypic Roles

Clark (1998) found that Internet dating is particularly appealing to teenage girls because it allows them to be aggressive while remaining sheltered. Clark argued that "Internet dating affords teenage girls in particular the opportunity to experiment with and claim power within heterosexual relationships," but she questioned whether the resulting relationships were any more emancipative than those found in the real-life experiences of teenagers. She suggested that "power afforded through self-construction on the Internet does not translate into changed gender roles and expectations in the social world beyond cyberspace." The teenage girls in Clark's study were "not interested in meeting the boys with whom they conversed as they might undermine (their) attractive and aggressive on-line persona" (pp. 160–169).

Danet (1998) suggested that typed text provides a mask for both men and women and found that

> men are curious about what it is like to be a woman or seek the attention that female presenting individuals typically receive. Women want to avoid being harassed sexually or feel free to be more assertive. As a result, some people are leading double or multiple

lives online, even with different gender identities. Others are trying out what it might mean to be gender-free, neither male nor female. ... Masquerading in this fashion promotes consciousness-raising about gender issues and might contribute to the long-term destabilization of the way we currently construct gender. (p. 130)

Traditional gender norms that dictate that women wait for men to ask them out and men be assertive leaders are still common today (Mongeau, Hale, Johnson, & Hillis, 1993; Simmel, 1911). However, some research (e.g., Cooper & Sportolari, 1997) and responses from the interviewees suggest that these norms may not operate online.

Cathryn, a 15-year-old girl, stated,

> I like to play but not really be there. I met this boy and we talked about school and movies, but we didn't meet. We live in different states. I don't know much about him really. He's just fun to talk to. I tease him a lot. Sometimes my friends pretend they are older or even guys instead of girls.

This online interaction is free from commitment.

Five of the respondents, both men and women, talked about freedom from commitment and stereotypic sex roles.

[...]

Although many respondents initially wanted freedom from commitment, they liked spending a lot of time online getting to know each other. Often after a period of months, they decided to meet face to face. Some changed their minds about having no commitment and increased their involvement, whereas others concluded that they had too little in common to justify continuing the relationship. Thus, as with traditional dating, online daters seemed to want to get to know their partners better before committing.

Online Dating as an Adventure

Anyone who has ever experienced a blind date knows it is a gamble. According to Balint (cited in Goffman, 1967), the mere possibility of having a "new sexual partner is a thrill" (p. 197). People have a deep-seated need to experience adventure and excitement (Simmel, 1911). This need was reflected in our respondents' desires to seek dates online for the thrill. One interviewee communicated with five people at a time on the Internet because it was "more exciting." Robert, a 19-year-old, never married student, explained, "For people like me who had never even been to Buffalo, going to meet someone from out of the area was a way out of here."

Greta, the 43-year-old, married woman, described her online partner:

> He e-mailed me a picture of himself, and he was gorgeous! He would send me flowers, you know, over the Internet, and really sweet letters that said a lot of nice things. He said that I was beautiful and that he wanted to meet me in person. Then we exchanged

phone numbers, and he'd call me, or I'd call him when my husband wasn't home. Then I could hear his voice and not just see his face and what he was writing me. He bought me a bracelet for my birthday.

[...]

Online dating allowed some of these individuals to travel to meet their partners. For Greta, who was married, online dating gave her an opportunity to perform behaviors that would have been detrimental to her marriage if she had engaged in them with a real-life boyfriend.

Online Dating as Romantic Fantasy

Internet dating may be construed as a type of romantic fantasy in which individuals construct ideal partners based on their online interactions, which can be very exciting.

Playing a social role on the Internet begins with an online version of constructing a social front. Constructing social fronts is of course not unique to the Internet, but their form is defined by the medium. An Internet social front includes one's averred gender and age, usually as listed in a profile filed with whatever Web institution hosts the social interaction. It may include a Web page containing edited pictures, prose, and in some cases animation and music to project the desired self. These pieces of sign equipment (Goffman, 1959) are supposed to convey something readily recognizable to the respondent. The fronts created by some individuals often appeal to common stereotypes that may reflect the ideals of the individual or group.

The simplification of the perception of online partners resulted in many respondents reporting that they built inaccurate pictures in their minds about the type of people they were interacting with before they met them. Although some said these pictures were put together through interactions taking as long as a year, face-to-face meetings were often not as imagined. Anna felt that visits introduced a different reality:

> I think that because of the way we met and the way we talked to each other that I had confused the fantasy with reality, so I expected him to be more like what we were pretending than everyday life.

[...]

Joyce, a 40-year-old social worker, said,

> There is no real environment. So, people make a fake environment. It's an artificial sense of intimacy. Talk relationships are the drama people are missing in their lives. You can be anything you want to be. It's exciting like a first kiss.

[...]

One of the biggest problems Internet daters face is that there may be no magic when they finally meet. These encounters challenge the roles previously projected online and can give rise to incidents needing solutions that may not be at hand. Joe, a 56-year-old, never married man, said,

> My main thought was she's a nice person but there's not any chemistry and how can I get out of the situation without hurting her and embarrassing myself.

[…]

Joyce, the 40-year-old, never married, heavyset woman, said it was risky to meet offline:

> I take a great risk when I meet someone face-to-face. Not a physical fear, but rejection. I don't want to be rejected.

In real life, people role-play by taking on certain characteristics in some situations and different characteristics in others (Waskul & Lust, 2004). Online dating allows people to create personas that are less constrained than in real life because dating partners know very little about the person on the other side of the screen. Unfortunately, when online partners meet for the first time, both are usually disappointed because the online personas are never identical to the people who created them.

Trust, Risk, and Lying Online

Trust may not be important in an interaction when compared to that of opening an opportunity for taking a gamble. Goffman (1967) believed, "Chance lies in the attitude of the individual himself – his creative capacity to redefine the world around him into its decisional potentialities" (p. 201). Goffman saw all forms of action as gambling. Similarly, Simmel (1911) argued that when a person is offered a token of trust, the recipient is expected to respond in kind. When people place online personals ads, those who respond may be perceived as offering a gift; the implication is made that "I trust you enough to treat me well."

Modern society's values do not foster the development of trusting behavior. In the United States, capitalism and rational choice promote selfish exploitive interactions (Deutsch, 1986; Hardin, 2001). They also encourage "calculating and self-interested modern persons [who] can not be trusted and do not trust others" (Misztal, 1996, pp. 39–40). Beck (1992) observed that our society focuses on technological risk and termed modern America a "risk society." He saw the resulting social dynamic as isolating individuals and creating a large number of unattached people. They are vulnerable, and for them, "an intensification of the friendship network remains indispensable" (p. 122). Even though interacting with strangers online introduces many unknowns, a lack of a friendship network drives people to become involved with Internet dating.

The Internet has been described as a "revolutionary social space" (Hardey, 2002, p. 577) in which old rules for social interaction are discarded in favor of new ones that may be better suited to the technology. However, Hardey (2002) found that Internet daters' interactions are often guided by "rituals and norms that protect the self" (p. 577), which was originally suggested by Goffman (1967). The technology of the Internet may present new challenges to building intimacy and avoiding rejection, but the basic motivations for protecting the self remain. New risks inspire new coping strategies to maintain an environment of trust. Such an environment is necessary to maintain the solidarity of society, according to Simmel (1978). Giddens (1990) emphasized a need to establish trust among individuals and observed that the alternative to trust is inaction, which in itself may be risky because if we do not take the risk of interacting, we will not develop a supportive friendship network. He saw relationships as "ties based upon trust, where trust is not pre-given but worked upon, and where the work involved means a mutual process of self-disclosure" (p. 121).

To establish close relationships within the constraints of the Internet, people use creative methods to identify themselves as cool and trustworthy. Emoticons, abbreviations, unconventional spellings, and specialized grammar are used to weed out people who do not share others' realities or ways of being (Waskul, 2003).[1] Turkle (1995) observed that through photographs, profiles, and narratives, "people create and cycle through a sometimes surprising range of online identities" (p. 10).

Indicators allow people to weigh the goodness of the total strangers with whom they choose to communicate. Daters respond to cues to ascertain another's socioeconomic status, attitude, concept of self, and trustworthiness. Early Internet dating negotiations depend on projecting an alluring social face through the medium. The Internet dater faces an ironic dilemma: The dater's primary task is to meet someone to form a relationship, but that meeting will unmask the dater and destroy any false pretenses. Daters create and invest in a persona while knowing that it may eventually be destroyed.

Online, people commonly misrepresent their appearance, making it more flattering (Clark, 1998). One sample of college students reported lying about their age, weight, and marital status (Knox et al., 2001). They may also misrepresent their gender (Danet, 1998; Knox et al., 2001). Misrepresentation in online social interactions seems so natural that few seem to give much thought to what usually could be dismissed as a makeover of one's persona. Given the limited amount of information available to respondents about each other in Internet interactions and their transitory nature, deception is common.

Most respondents said they had been lied to more than once, and some reported surprise when this happened.

[...]

Ironically, Internet interactions often pose inconsequential risks for the same reasons that their authenticity and veracity are questionable; identities are customarily disguised behind coded usernames, and the distances between the numerous participants are typically great. Much of Internet relating involves sorting through databases. "There is a button you can hit. ... I must have gone through about 10 to

15 different people," remarked Robin. Trust in the people whose Web profiles she accepted or rejected does not seem to have been her first priority. She trusted her search strategy. Instead of trusting others, Robin placed her trust in her system. This system engenders patterns of negotiation.

[…]

Mort, an 18-year-old, gay student, said, "Someone told me, and I found Gerry's [his partner] picture online in a dating service looking to meet someone!" Mort and Gerry broke up over this incident.

Most men and women in this study took physical and emotional risks to gain trust and were willing to continue seeking online relationships even after others had lied to them. A few teenagers and adults who did not want committed relationships took fewer risks by taking on unrealistic roles, not being open, and postponing face-to-face meetings. Others developed symbolic trust indicators to lessen the consequential risks of interacting.

Indicators of Trust

Berger and Luckmann (1967) believed people decide to trust based on intuitive impressions that we refer to as "trust indicators." This research uncovered the presence of early and late trust indicators as part of early and late negotiating strategies that serve to minimize harm to the self.

The development of trust in an online dating relationship requires not only the assurance that the other means no physical harm but also that the other will treat the online persona with ritual deference. A remark such as, "I did not know you were so large; do you use Photoshop?" would be a devastating blow.[2] This is one of the reasons some Internet daters postpone or evade face-to-face meetings.

Susan, a 30-year-old, divorced woman, was asked by her friend Bette to be a chaperone on a first face-to-face meeting between Bette and a prospective male partner. Bette had represented herself as svelte but was actually heavy. After the meeting, the prospective partner broke off the relationship with Bette and e-mailed Susan. Susan admitted she then went out with the man who had dumped her friend.

Younger respondents were concerned with the hermeneutics of keystrokes and codes. Arlene, a 17-year-old interviewed by the first author, used *LOL* (laughing out loud), *BRB* (be right back), and other abbreviations when chatting. We found younger people used this coded language more frequently than did older individuals. Respondents who were not adept in the use of such codes exposed their lack of grace in social interaction and were weeded out. Participants selected for interactions of usually only a few minutes duration were chosen many times based on one word or the speed of their typing. More mature respondents had different early indicators.

Respondents used indicators contained in e-mailed or posted pictures to help evaluate their potential mates and attempted to determine their age and degree of affluence. Clothing, hairstyle, and projected lifestyle were augured from photographs.

[…]

Other indicators deal with time. Through face-to-face relating, we have come to expect a certain pattern of flow through which a relationship develops. This pattern is reflected through the timing of conversation and self-disclosure. Often on the Internet there is a pressure to disclose much in a short time to establish trust and kinship quickly. Some respondents dislike this pressure.

[...]

To develop intimacy to create a bond with an online partner, Internet daters felt pressed to self-disclose as much information as they could in the shortest possible time, though letting people know one's shortcomings begs rejection. Furthermore, disclosing too much too fast violates social conventions and norms. The woman who told Julian, "I think I am ready for a relationship now," scared her potential partner away.

Part of this pressure to relate in a hurry came from the medium itself. The Internet filters out social cues that would be present in face-to-face communication (e.g., Baym, 1998; Hardey, 2002; Waskul, 2003). The lack of nonverbal and paraverbal cues requires Internet daters to use emoticons and other contrivances, which are not necessarily good substitutes for personal presence, to fill the void. In long-term online relationships, telephone conversations augmented the Internet. The telephone felt warmer and less technological to some respondents and was perceived as a transition toward meeting in person. People must not sound "too good to be true," as Phyllis remarked. Ironically, goodness and trueness were not entirely compatible when the faces of both correspondents were at stake.

[...]

Later negotiations were conducted on the telephone and in person, and the trust indicators in these negotiations are familiar to conventional courtship. Goffman's (1959, 1967) frame for social interaction is applicable to describing late negotiations in Internet dating. He argued that social face is customarily seated in face-to-face interactions where the actors can view each other's body language and expression. In daily interactions with strangers, much of our decision to trust depends on how the other presents himself or herself in the theater of social interaction.

Once Internet daters find each other compatible, they move on to the next step of relationship building. This involves spending more time getting to know one another to build trust. Basic interpersonal trust is either contractual trust based on social contracts as in family relationships or trust based on time in relations (Govier, 1992). Most respondents liked the time they spent getting to know each other. They said this time helped develop trust and intimacy.

[...]

When respondents were comfortable with one another online, they wanted to increase their amount of personal contact.

[...]

After interacting on the phone, the next step is meeting in person. The transition from technologically mediated communication to physical encounter is the riskiest step in the process because it requires trust. According to Molm, Takahashi, and

Peterson (2000), the development of trust is an incremental process of reciprocal interactions based on previously established experience:

> Through numerous experiences with specific others who behave in a trustworthy manner under conditions of risk, we may come to expect that others, with whom we have had no direct experience, will also be worthy of our trust. In this way reciprocal exchange relations can contribute to a more generalized sense of trust in others. Establishing such a trusting environment can be a great advantage to society; individuals are free to explore new relations and take advantage of new opportunities. (p. 1425)

[...]

Discussion

The Internet has opened a new avenue for romantic interaction. In the present study, Internet daters reported being able to reach a larger pool of potential partners and experiencing increased freedom of choice among partners. The Internet also raises new issues of negotiating risk and establishing trust. Respondents said they were willing to take risks to take advantage of the new courting opportunities offered by this new technology. Some risks involved physical danger, and others involved loss of face and possible rejection, though interviewees developed rationales and strategies to deal with these risks to trust that they would have positive experiences.

Dating online modified gendered interactions by allowing women to behave more assertively and men to be more open. It also necessitated the development of new strategies based on keystrokes, codes interpreting online photographs, and reading user profiles to develop trust and confirm compatibility. In Internet interactions, gains and losses are only symbolic, and rejection by an online entity identified only as "suv4" can represent no great material loss. It is this very abstraction that motivates people to use the Internet for dating to avoid stereotyped gender roles and the pain of rejection.

The interrelating of Internet daters also reflects old patterns and problems common to all forms of courtship. Even if they do not find objectification and harassment online, meeting offline often brings objectification or harassment into a formerly nonjudgmental relationship. There is irony in seeking a way out of loneliness through a medium that ensures the insularity of participants and perpetuates gender stereotyping once participants meet.

Several old problems remain in Internet dating. It is easy for people to lie to each other, and appearance issues and shyness do not completely disappear when dating online. Rejection and its emotional pain are ultimately a part of Internet dating as much as of dating that is entirely face to face from the start. The fundamental issues of trust, self-presentation, and compatibility carry over from conventional courtship into its Internet variant.

The need to obtain companionship motivates people to seek out romantic relationships in a variety of ways, and the Internet is merely the latest technological development used by people to assist their romantic goals. Participants in the current study reported reducing their loneliness, obtaining comfort, and finding fun and excitement. These benefits appeared to outweigh the risks.

NOTES

1. Emoticons are small icons bearing emotive faces. These can be inserted into text messages.
2. Adobe Photoshop is a very popular photograph manipulation program that allows users to drastically alter photographs and cinematographic video.

REFERENCES

Baym, N.K. (1998). The emergence of community in computer-mediated communication. In S. Jones (Ed.), *Cybersociety 2.0: Revisiting computer-mediated communication and community* (pp. 138–163). Thousand Oaks, CA: Sage.

Baym, N.K. (2000). *Tune in, log on: Soaps, fandom and online community*. Thousand Oaks, CA: Sage.

Beck, U. (1992). *Risk society: Towards a new modernity*. Thousand Oaks, CA: Sage.

Bell, D. (2001). *An introduction to cybercultures*. London: Routledge.

Berger, P.L., & Luckmann, T. (1967). *The social construction of reality: A treatise in the sociology of knowledge*. New York: Anchor.

Chelune, G.J., Sultan, F. E., & Williams, C.L. (1980). Loneliness, self-disclosure, and interpersonal effectiveness. *Journal of Counseling Psychology, 27*, 462–468.

Clark, L.S. (1998). Dating on the Net: Teens and the rise of "pure" relationships. In S. Jones (Ed.), *Cybersociety 2.0: Revisiting computer-mediated communication and community* (pp. 159–181). Thousand Oaks, CA: Sage.

Cooper, A., & Sportolari, L. (1997). Romance in cyberspace: Understanding online attraction. *Journal of Sex Education and Therapy, 22*, 7–14.

Danet, B. (1998). Text as mask: Gender, play, and performance on the Internet. In S. Jones (Ed.), *Cybersociety 2.0: Revisiting computer-mediated communication and community* (pp. 129–157). Thousand Oaks, CA: Sage.

Deutsch, M. (1986). *Distributive justice: A social psychological perspective*. New Haven, CT: Yale University Press.

Dickerson, S.S., Flaig, D.M., & Kennedy, M.C. (2000). Therapeutic connection: Help seeking on the Internet for persons with implantable cardioverter defribrillators. *Heart and Lung, 29*, 248–255.

Dietrich, D. (1997). (Re)-fashioning the techno-erotic woman: Gender and textuality in the cyberculture matrix. In S. Jones (Ed.), *Virtual culture: Identity and communication in cybersociety* (pp. 169–184). Thousand Oaks, CA: Sage.

Fernback, J. (1997). The individual within the collective: Virtual ideology and the realization of collective principles. In S. Jones (Ed.), *Virtual culture: Identity and communication in cybersociety* (pp. 36–54). Thousand Oaks, CA: Sage.

Fogel, J., Albert, S.M., Schnabel, F., Ditkoff, B.A., & Neugut, A.L. (2002). Internet use and social support in women with breast cancer. *Health Psychology, 21,* 398–404.

Gelman, R.G. (2002). *Tales of a female nomad: Living at large in the world.* Three Rivers, MI: Three Rivers Press.

Goffman, E. (1959). *The presentation of self in everyday life.* New York: Doubleday.

Goffman, E. (1967). *Interaction ritual: Essays on face-to-face behavior.* Doubleday.

Govier, T. (1992). Trust, distrust, and feminist theory. *Hypatia, 7,* N1.

Hardey, M. (2002). Life beyond the screen: Embodiment and identity through the Internet. *Sociological Review, 50,* 570–585.

Hardey, M. (2004). Mediated relationships: Authenticity and the possibility of romance. *Information, Communication, & Society, 7,* 207–222.

Hardin, R. (2001). Conceptions and explanations of trust. In K. S. Cook (Ed.), *Trust in society* (pp. 3–39). New York: Russell Sage.

Hollander, E.M. (2001). Cyber community in the valley of the shadow of death. *Journal of Loss and Trauma, 6,* 135–146.

Jones, S. (1995). From where to who knows? In S. Jones (Ed.), *Cybersociety: Computer-mediated communication and community* (pp. 1–9). Thousand Oaks, CA: Sage.

Jones, S. (1997). The Internet and its social landscape. In S. Jones (Ed.), *Virtual culture: Identity and communication in cybersociety* (pp. 7–35). Thousand Oaks, CA: Sage.

Jones, W.H., Hobbs, S.A., & Hockenbury, D. (1982). Loneliness and social skills deficits. *Journal of Personality and Social Psychology, 42,* 682–689.

Klemm, P., Hurst, M., Dearholt, S.L., & Trone, S.R. (1999). Cyber solace: Gender differences on Internet cancer support groups. *Computers in Nursing, 17,* 65–72.

Knox, D., Daniels, V., Sturdivant, L., & Zusman, M. (2001). College student use of the Internet for mate selection. *College Student Journal, 35,* 158–160.

Leck, K. (2003). *A model of dating frequency.* Unpublished manuscript, Department of Psychology, University of Pittsburgh at Bradford.

Ljungman, G., McGrath, P.J., Cooper, E., Widger, K., Ceccolini, J., Fernandez, C.V., et al. (2003). Psychosocial needs of families with a child with cancer. *Journal of Pediatric Hematology/Oncology, 25,* 223–231.

Markham, A. (1998). *Life online.* Walnut Creek, CA: Alta Mira.

McAdams, D.P. (1989). *Intimacy: The need to be close.* New York: Doubleday.

Misztal, B.A. (1996). *Trust in modern society: The search for the bases of social order.* Cambridge, MA: Blackwell.

Molm, L.D., Takahashi, N., & Peterson, G. (2000). Risk and trust in social exchange: An experimental test of a classical proposition. *The American Journal of Sociology, 105,* 1396–1427.

Mongeau, P.A., Hale, J.L., Johnson, K.L., & Hillis, J.D. (1993). Who's wooing whom? An investigation of female initiated dating. In P. J. Kalbfleisch (Ed.), *Interpersonal communication: Evolving interpersonal relationships* (pp. 51–68). Hillsdale, NJ: Lawrence Erlbaum.

Raney, R.F. (2000, May 11). Study finds Internet of social benefit to users. *New York Times,* p. G7.

Reid, E. (1997). Virtual worlds: Culture and imagination. In S. Jones (Ed.), *Cybersociety: Computer-mediated communication and community* (pp. 164–183). Thousand Oaks, CA: Sage.

Simmel, G. (1911). *Phiosophische kultur: Gesammelte essays* [Philosophical culture: Collected essays] (2nd ed.). Leipzig, Germany: Alfred Kroner.

Simmel, G. (1978). *The philosophy of money*. Boston: Routledge Kegan Paul.

Slevin, J. (2000). *The Internet and society*. Cambridge, UK: Polity.

Strate, L. (2003). Cybertime. In L. Strait, R.L. Jacobson, & S.B. Gibson (Eds.), *Communication and cyberspace* (pp. 361–387). Cresskill, NJ: Hampton Press.

Turkle, S. (1995). *Life on the screen: Identity in the age of the Internet*. New York: Simon & Schuster.

Vanderwerker, L.C., & Prigerson, H.G. (2004). Social support and technological connectedness as protective factors in bereavement. *Journal of Loss and Trauma, 9*, 45–57.

Waskul, D. (2003). *Self-games and body-play: Personhood in online chat and cybersex*. New York: Peter Lang.

Waskul, D., & Lust, M. (2004). Role-playing and playing roles: The person, player, and persona in fantasy role-playing. *Symbolic Interaction, 27*, 333–356.

White, M.H., & Dorman, S.M. (2000). Online support for caregivers: Analysis of an Internet Alzheimer mailgroup. *Computers in Nursing, 18*, 168–179.

Zimmer, E.A., & Hunter, C.D. (2003). Risk and the Internet: Perception and reality. In L. Strait, R.L. Jacobson, & S.B. Gibson (Eds.), *Communication and cyberspace* (2nd ed., pp. 183–202). Cresskill, NJ: Hampton Press.

Zuboff, S. (1991). New worlds of computer-mediated work. In J. M. Henslin (Ed.), *Down to earth sociology: Introductory readings* (6th ed., pp. 476–485). New York: Free Press.

32 SCREENING MOMENTS, SCROLLING LIVES

Diary Writing on the Web

Madeleine Sorapure

Alongside the dominant commercial and mass-entertainment applications of the World Wide Web, a number of vibrant forms of self-representation and autobiographical writing have emerged. While complete autobiographies of the kind that define the genre in print do not exist on the Web, there are several types of autobiographical storytelling that are quite popular in this medium.[1] Anthology sites such as *The Fray, The City Stories Project, afterDinner,* and *Noon Quilt* publish short, hypertextual, and sometimes illustrated autobiographical stories. In addition, there are individual autobiographical works on the Web, such as Shelley Jackson's *My Body: A Wunderkammer &,* which Jackson playfully describes as "An autobiography, plus lies," and *Glass Houses* by Jacalyn Lopez Garcia, "a tour of American assimilation from a Mexican-American perspective." Personal home pages are often conceived of by their authors and by the social scientists who have studied them as a space for identity construction and self-presentation.[2] Webcams, video projects, and avatar-style role-playing games can also be seen as forms of autobiographical storytelling unique to the Web. These clearly non-traditional autobiographical acts might best be studied through the kind of "backyard ethnography" Sidonie Smith and Julia Watson describe in *Getting a Life,* as such acts are examples of the "announcing, performing, composing of identity" that is one of the "defining conditions of postmodernity in America" (7). Though Smith and Watson critique the "othering machinery of modern technological culture" (9) that collects, codes, and stores

Madeleine Sorapure, "Screening Moments, Scrolling Lives: Diary Writing on the Web," pp. 1–23 from *Biography* 26:1 (Winter 2003).

medical, educational, occupational, psychological, and financial data about each of us, the proliferation of autobiographical writing on the Web indicates that people are also finding compelling ways to use computer technology to create and perform autobiographical acts.

Of all the forms of Web-based autobiographical writing, the online diary is likely the most popular and well established. Carolyn Burke has been credited with having made the first online diary entry on January 3, 1995; she and other online diary pioneers are interviewed at the *Online Diary History Project*.[3] Even as the Web has become more commercialized, the number of online diaries has grown significantly, thanks to faster connection times, cheaper computers, and increasingly user-friendly Web-authoring software. With the introduction of blogging (or Web logging) sites in 1998, and specifically of *Blogger* in 1999, starting an online diary became a simple point-and-click procedure, and posting entries became a matter of sending an email message.[4] Blogging and diary hosting sites – for instance, *Blogger, Diary-X, Diaryland*, and *LiveJournal* – have themselves become commercial ventures, generally offering some services for free but charging for others. These sites also serve as virtual gathering places for online diarists, offering both technical and creative advice as well as links to myriad online diaries. By contrast, *Diarist.net*, from which most of my examples are drawn, is a non-commercial site produced by online diarists who volunteer to maintain the site and to select the *Diarist.net* Awards, non-monetary awards for excellence in online diary writing given quarterly since 1999. The detailed nomination and judging processes are described at *Diarist.net*, and are refined through mailing list discussions.[5] …

The thousands – possibly tens of thousands – of diaries currently being kept on the Web, and the existence of virtual communities such as *Diarist.net*, suggest that this form and medium are well matched. … Women particularly have found the online diary an inviting way not only to add content to the Web, but also to help shape the medium to further the goals of its users.[6] More generally, online diaries are evidence of this medium's democratic potential: "that everyone could publish, that a thousand voices could flourish, communicate, connect" (Blood).

However, with the exception of Philippe Lejeune in his recent and still untranslated book, "*Cher écran …*," diary and autobiography scholars generally have not ventured into the realm of Web-based life writing. Lejeune's important study, which includes questionnaires, excerpts from Web diarists, and journal entries charting his month-long immersion in the world of French-language online diaries, examines the influence of the computer as a writing technology, and of the Web as an increasingly popular publishing medium for diaries. Lejeune asks, "notre moi, notre intimité ne sont-ils pas façonnés par les moyens d'expression et de communication?" [our sense of self, our intimate being – are they not shaped by the means of expression and communication?] (11). … Comparing this relatively new kind of diary with its print counterparts reveals three important areas in which the computer and the Web remake the practice and product of diary writing, impacting how the diaries are written, what is written, and how they are read. …

Interface

The technologies of computer-based writing and Web publishing make the materiality of the diary and of the act of diary writing significantly different. Lejeune, Suzanne Bunkers, and other diary scholars have stressed the importance of seeing the diary both as artifact and text, of attending to the pen, the page, the book – in short, to the material traces of a writer in a particular context. In Bunkers's words, "When a diary is considered from this dual perspective – as text and as artifact – a thorough exploration requires not only analyzing individual diary entries but also analyzing the size and shape of the diary in an effort to determine how its physical format might have influenced what was or was not written and how it was or was not written" (21–22). For Lejeune, a focus on the material conditions of diary writing guides the investigation that comprises the first part of "*Cher écran ...*," in which he examines the practices of those who use computers to write their diary entries, though without subsequently publishing these entries on the Web. He isolates several key areas in which the computer interface causes changes in diary writing; for instance, in the practices of making corrections and of rereading diary entries. In short, the physical characteristics of the diary influence the act of writing, and the diary as a material artifact contributes to our understanding of the particular context that shapes the writer's life.[7]

... The materiality of an online diary is clearly more difficult to describe than that of a diary written in a notebook. An online diary exists on the hard drive of a server, not in handwriting on a page with a particular shape and feel. At its core, an online diary is a set of ones and zeroes, or even more fundamentally, electrical impulses sent through the circuits of a computer or network. Its author and others read it as flickering signs on a screen; it is perpetually revisable, with revisions leaving no trace of previous versions. The fact that an online diary exists not as a physical artifact but as digital code stored on a distant hard drive problematizes the material relation of writer and text. If nothing else, an online diary foregrounds the fact that its writer lives and writes in a context highly mediated by technology. Aside from this, there is much greater distance, materially speaking, between writer and textual artifact. It is this distance that renders the writing interface visible, or to put it another way, the material separation of writer and text calls attention to the ways in which the interface between writer and text influences the construction of the autobiographical self and story.

Furthermore, while the material conditions of the act of writing influence the print diarist as well as the online diarist, the technologies of the computer and the network provide diary writers with a different set of possibilities and constraints than do the technologies of the pen and the notebook. For instance, at a computer- and network-mediated writing interface, diarists must make decisions about page design and about the overall architecture of the work – considerations not so immediately present for print diarists. Online diarists must also consider the layout of text and image, and decide which, if any, multimedia and interactive elements to use.

For instance, some online diaries feature search engines that allow readers and writers to reorganize diary entries according to keywords or themes, thus generating new connections and associations among entries. At least one Web diarist, "The Gus," has experimented with a program that generates text that is stylistically similar to his own writing, in a kind of cyborg writing or human/computer collaboration that fills in the blanks when Gus is too busy to write.[8] One might say that the interface is more flexible for online than for print diaries because the computer can perform certain organizational and even creative functions. While print diarists can fold or manipulate pages, and can include drawings, photos, and other visual elements, the computer provides a more diverse set of media and more interactive opportunities with which writers can work.

The question of the diary's materiality also involves its permanence, its existence as an artifact that can extend beyond the life of the writer. Because they are physical objects, print documents are generally assumed to be more permanent than computer files and Web sites. In "How Do Diaries End?" Lejeune puts it this way: "Paper has its own biological rhythm. It will long outlive me. It will end up yellowing and crumbling, but the text that it bears will have its own reincarnations, it can change bodies, be recopied, published" (110). As Lejeune also notes, the fate of many print diaries is to be destroyed, intentionally or unintentionally, by their authors or by others. While online diaries can be destroyed (and often are) by being removed from the server at which they are hosted, the recent development of Internet archives gives online diaries the potential to be as permanent as print diaries – and not necessarily with the author's consent. By using the "Wayback Machine" at the *Internet Archive* – a non-profit group site that has archived ten billion Web pages, or one hundred terrabytes of data, representing information on the Web from 1996 to the present – one can, for instance, read pages from Magdalena Donea's 1998–2000 online journal, *Moments*. … So although online diaries do not exist materially in the same way as print diaries do, they may in fact be more permanent in the sense that they can be copied and stored in an archival database. There is, in other words, a "technological rhythm" for online diaries that differs from the "biological rhythm" of paper noted by Lejeune.

How do diarists represent these issues related to the materiality of online diary writing? The *Diarist.net* Awards categories for judging online diaries demonstrate that the considerations discussed above are significant for the writers themselves. Several categories of awards – Best Design, Best Use of Multimedia, and Best Experimental Journal – recognize writers for how well they use the computer and the Web as a publishing medium. For instance, the Best Design category "recognizes both good visual presentation and intuitive organization and navigation" (http://diarist.net/awards/awards.html). The diary here takes on elements of an artwork or performance – and indeed, some of the better-known online diaries are by graphic designers, Web designers, and artists for whom the diary may function as part of their portfolio of work.[9] … The notion of writing is thus redefined for online diarists, as they also "write" with images, navigation choices, and site structure. As in print autobiographies and diaries that include photographs or illustrations, autobiographical expression is not limited to language, although on the Web the means of expression extend beyond visual elements.[10] ...

The winner of the Best Design category for the first quarter of 2002 is an online diary entitled *Random Rain*, created by Sandy, a social worker in her early thirties who lives in Tennessee. The design of the site's home page is quite attractive, with a blue-toned image depicting rain falling on a woman dancing in an open field. The image is segmented into eight parts; rolling the mouse over each part of the image makes that part become lighter, and words appear indicating a link to one of the eight sections of the site: the journal, a calendar-formatted archive of previous journal entries, a Weblog, a gallery of pictures taken by Sandy, "slinging ink" ("collaborations and other projects"), a recipe box (currently empty), a list of links to Sandy's favorite Web sites, and an "about me" page. This multi-part structure is quite common in online diaries; that is, diary sites often contain more than just diary entries. With its single image segmented into parts, the picture on the home page represents this structure.[11]

An "about me" or "bio" page is a standard feature of online diaries, used by writers to provide autobiographical background in a more linear, narrative format than the diary entries allow. ... In contrast to the brief chronological narrative of her life on the "missing pieces" page, Sandy also presents information about herself on a "super-fluous factology" page. Entitled "random facts," this page offers a bulleted list of fifty-five statements written by Sandy about herself: "I believe in God." "I also believe in reincarnation." "I bite my nails." "I am the child of an alcoholic" (http://www.randomrain.net/me/facts.html). Other diary sites also include such "random facts" by the writer about herself.[12]

What we see in these choices of content, presentation, and organization is evidence of the influence of computer technology on the act of diary writing. The "random facts" motif represents a database model of identity, a non-narrative model in which discrete pieces of information are collected and stored. In fact, the diary as a genre, particularly in its online form, constitutes a database of sorts, with information entered in discrete, chronologically-coded units. Similarly, the segmentation common in online diaries, and represented at "Random Rain" by the segmented home page image and the jigsaw puzzle theme, repeats the logic of compartmentalization in the database model. In *The Language of New Media*, Lev Manovich describes the database as one of the two fundamental forms of new media; the database and the algorithm constitute "the ontology of the world according to the computer" (223). ... Representing the self in a database form – creating and coding information about oneself, populating a database that readers subsequently query – develops and reflects a sense of identity as constituted by fragments and segments, each of which is separately meaningful and equally significant. In an online diary, pieces of information about the self may be brought together in different configurations, signifying multiple and shifting ways of understanding the self. ... For online diarists, writing on the computer and publishing on the network, the database form more thoroughly infuses self-representation.

... With its compartmentalization and database structure, the online diary may be well-suited to a person like Sandy, who wishes to represent her own internal sense of emotional fragmentation. It may also be, however, that the database form of online diary writing exacerbates this fragmented (and for Sandy often frustrating) sense of self. … I would suggest that it is not the title of the journal as much as the computer as a writing tool, and the network as a publishing medium, that shape the sense of self that Sandy can represent in her online diary. … Thus, while the writing or reading of Sandy's diary is not a random process, the theme of randomness, along with the diary's database features, combine to shape Sandy's self-representation.

In sum, an online diarist's reasons for writing may be similar to those of her print counterparts. … However, the technological possibilities and constraints of online diary writing also shape and mediate the writer's self-representation, exerting influence over how those "writing muscles" are exercised and how those feelings are "processed."

Interactivity

A second important feature of online diary writing has to do with the private/public dichotomy familiar in the scholarship on print diaries. It is taken as common sense that diaries are private documents, intended to be read by no one besides the author, and for many diarists this privacy is necessary and unquestioned. But as Lynn Z. Bloom notes,

> Contrary to popular perception, not all diaries are written – ultimately or exclusively – for private consumption. … Indeed, it is the audience hovering at the edge of the page that for the sophisticated diarist facilitates the work's ultimate focus, providing the impetus either for the initial writing or for transforming what might have been casual, fragmented jottings into a more carefully crafted, contextually coherent work. (23)

Bloom draws useful distinctions between "truly private diaries" and "public documents" in terms of their purpose, scope, style, form, structure, literary techniques, contextualization, characters, and contemporary value; she shows how these features are shaped differently in the diaries of authors for whom there is an "audience hovering at the edge of the page."

Audience and purpose are clearly important to online diarists, since these writers obviously and intentionally are creating public documents. Even if no one other than the author reads the diary, it is available on the Web for others to read, and is to some extent put on the Web precisely for others to read. … Online diaries therefore not only challenge our current conception of diary writing as a private act, but also compel us to reconsider the boundaries of the private self in a culture characterized by connectivity via cell phones, email, pagers, and other communication technologies.

On the Web, private diaries become not only public but also interactive. In an online diary, each entry is published one at a time, remaking the diary as a serialized form in which readers follow a story that is evolving – and one to which they may contribute.

Most online diaries accept, and many actively solicit, feedback from readers via email links and guestbooks. The Web's interactivity and the immediacy of its publishing enhance that aspect of diary writing concerned not with solitary and private reflection, but with communication and community. Other direct means for diarists to interact with readers and other writers include mailing lists such as *Journals* and *diary-l* that host discussions of online journaling;[13] diary Webrings that provide links to member sites selected for certain characteristics, such as theme, quality, or frequency of writing;[14] and burbs or lists that group together journals according to theme, for instance, or demographic characteristics of the writer.[15] In these venues, online diarists can find links to like-minded fellow writers, and can engage in discussions with their readers. … the fact that these mailing lists, Webrings, and 'burbs even exist is evidence of the desire of online diarists to form a virtual community. "Collaborative writing" projects, for instance, in which a group of online diarists write entries in response to the same prompt, enable writers to share experiences, thoughts, and feelings with one another.[16] …

Analyzing specific online diaries, we see writers taking different approaches to the act of granting public access. In three of the *Diarist.net* award-winning sites for the first quarter of 2002, the authors explicitly address issues of privacy, interaction with readers, and community. *Lexxicon.net*, by Athena, won the Best Journal Overall for this quarter. Married with a nine year-old son and a new baby, Athena has been keeping an online diary since April 1999. On the main page of her site she has a link entitled "please read first," on which she presents a "disclaimer of sorts," explaining why she is keeping an online diary and what she expects of her readers:

> If you know me personally and found this site through happenstance (or a good search engine), please consider whether or not you really want to read what I write. This is a personal journal and some of the things I reveal may or may not be things you want to know. Once you know something you can't un-know it. By keeping this journal online and having it linked to my real name, I know the risk involved with everyone I've ever known possibly reading it. I'm fine with that. I just want to make sure you are too. If I've not told you about this journal, please take no offense. It's nothing personal. I've kept this private in my everyday life for my own reasons. I don't hide this journal; nor do I advertise it.
> If you do make the choice to read, please drop me a line and let me know. (http://www.lexxicon.net/lexxicon/readfirst.shtml)

The main concern for Athena here is not so much the invasion of her own privacy, but rather her need to know who in her offline community is reading her online diary. … Diarists like Athena are therefore not only highly aware of the public nature of their writing but also attempt, in various ways, to modify what they write in direct response to their awareness of the specifics of their multiple audiences.

[…]

Online diarists draw extensively from their daily lives, and discuss their interactions with people who know them; at some sites, we can read descriptions of these friends, family members, and colleagues on a "cast of characters" page. … The act of keeping a diary on the Web is thus both grounded in daily life and dissociated from it.

In *I'd Rather Eat Glass*, the winner of *Diarist.net*'s Best Writing award for the first quarter of 2002, thirty-eight year-old artist Sasha Degn is similarly concerned with controlling access to her diary. Her "Caveat" page invites feedback from readers, but also explains the "rules" for reading her journal entries. Most significantly, she writes, in bold typeface: **"Important: If I know you in real life or if you know Travis** [Degn's husband] **in real life, please email me and let me know that you're reading this journal"** (http://glass.travisasha.com/journal/disclaimer.htm). Degn then notes that people have broken this rule in the past, causing her a "great deal of angst." Perhaps for this reason, Degn has also created a password protected area of the site, "for those times when I need a private place to vent or cry." Only those people who join Degn's "notify list" – a mailing list function that notifies subscribers when there is a new journal entry at the site – can enter this more private area and read the journal entries there. ... Degn has essentially created levels of access to her online diary, sectioning off some material as "more private" – though still on the Web, still public – than other material. ... In Degn's case, though, the more private material is accessible only to those people with whom she has developed an online relationship, providing further evidence of the compartmentalized, segmented sense of self discussed earlier. ... The act of diary writing has shifted here from a solitary venture in which one writes to and for oneself about one's daily life, to a means of reaching beyond the confines of dailyness, beyond the people with whom one has daily contact, perhaps to discover and perform some different version of oneself. The online diary enacts a certain escape from the everyday, even as it takes the everyday as its topic.

Organization and Interpretation

Finally, the structure of the diary and the experience of reading it differ significantly from print to Web. Rebecca Hogan has described the diary as a paratactic form, by which she means that in its grammar, syntax, and content the diary operates on the same principle as grammatical parataxis, in which clauses are joined without connectives or with only coordinating conjunctions. This grammatical structure avoids establishing transitional connectives that would suggest how the items are related. Or as Hogan puts it, "there is no subordination to suggest that one idea or event is more important than another; the clauses are 'equal' in grammatical structure and rhetorical force" (101). ... Parataxis also engages the diary reader in assigning significance, and in the absence of transitions, making meaningful connections within and across entries. This paratactic structure and style distinguish the diary from typical narrative autobiographies. ...

One explanation for the proliferation of online diaries is that because parataxis is also the logic of the database, diaries translate or transcode well into the computer medium. ... Since entries often have narrative elements, the contrast between narrative and database is not this extreme in the diary. But the database form of the computer and new media heightens the sense of diary entries as discrete items, ordered only by chronology. Other paratactic or database-like features also come to the fore. For instance, in contrast to a retrospective, linear narrative that leads up to an ending, a paratactic form doesn't have a logical reason to end, aside from running out of space. For online diaries, this constraint is even less significant than for print diaries.

Perhaps most important in considering the structure of online diaries, though, is the function that links serve. Links can establish connections between entries, and between one site and another; in Manovich's terms, links can provide the narrative that connects different elements in the database of the online diary.[17] Association and juxtaposition can link one page to another just as easily as hierarchy or logic might. When activated, the link simply delivers the page; it is thus a pure expression of the coordinating conjunction "and." To be sure, links can be read as expressing meaningful connections or relations; in online diaries, for instance, "previous" and "next" links indicate chronological relations between entries. In "Rhetorics of the Web," Nicholas Burbules argues that an important component of critical literacy for Web readers is learning how to interpret the link not simply as "and," but as "the elemental structure that represents a hypertext as a semic web of meaningful relations" (105). He argues that "links create significations" (110), and should be understood as "rhetorical moves" (115). The burden of interpretation thus falls on the reader, but as the terminology of Web "surfing" and "browsing" indicates, readers often do not take the time to think about the logic of the transition offered by the links they choose.

Links create literal as well as conceptual transitions in Web sites. Clicking is analogous to turning a page in a book, but because the navigation of a Web site is not as intuitive as the navigation of a book, decisions about how to read an online diary differ from those made in the case of print diaries. … With online diaries, the preferred way of beginning is at the most recent entry, which is usually featured on the home page of the site. Rather than serving as the starting point, as they do in print diaries, past entries are relegated to the archives. After this, there are distinctly different paths to follow online. … In a manner similar to that described by theorists of hypertext fiction, like George Landow, who emphasize the active engagement of the reader in creating the meaning of a story by selecting different pathways through it, each of the methods of reading described above would yield a somewhat different diary, and a somewhat different impression of the writer.

But the most common method among regular readers of online diaries and the diarists themselves is to read across diaries – to move from one online diary to the next, reading only the most recent entries of each. … The fact that many online diaries link to other diaries makes this method of reading quite easy. For Web readers, going to a page in a different diary is as easy as going to the next page in the same diary; this is obviously not the case for print readers, unless they have several books spread out on a desk. While chronology still functions as an organizing principle of diary writing and reading, then, in online diaries time can "vertically" organize the writing of individual diarists, or "horizontally" organize (or anthologize) multiple diarists on a single day. Each entry of an online diary can be thought of as standing on its own; indeed, the *Diarist.net* Awards have eight categories of prizes given for individual entries. And yet, while reading across diaries is a perfectly reasonable approach, given the structure of online diaries and the medium of the Web, it is also quite odd to think of reading a diary entry out of the context of the rest of the diary, and instead in the context of entries by other writers. This common strategy of reading makes the online diary into something like a collaboratively or culturally paratactic form.

Commenting on the structure of online diaries, Lejeune remarks, "C'est mon grand rêve, un texte qui combinerait la structure du journal (fragments datés) et celle de l'autobiographie à la Leiris (réseaux de 'bifurs')" [It is my great dream, a text that would combine the structure of the journal (dated fragments) and that of autobiography à la Leiris (networks of "bifurcations")] (383). Reading across diaries yields something like Lejeune's dream of this hybrid text, possessing both dated entries and "networks of bifurcations" or "forking paths." Another hybrid text that might satisfy Lejeune's wishes is *Ftrain*, which achieves interesting structural and readerly effects through experiments with linking, the database form, and some fairly sophisticated programming. Winner of *Diarist.net*'s Best Experimental Journal award for the first quarter of 1999, *Ftrain* is written by Paul Ford, a twenty-eight-year-old writer and Web designer living in Brooklyn, New York. Ford began working on the site in 1997, and it currently contains more than nine hundred entries. *Ftrain* is quite different from the online diaries discussed previously, and perhaps the term "journal," with its connotations of greater distance and detachment, is a more appropriate description for it than "diary." The content at the site centers on the personal and autobiographical – Ford relates stories from his past and discusses events and experiences in his daily life. But his tone is often ironic, and his writing is very much oriented toward entertaining and otherwise engaging readers. In fact, Ford even solicits donations from readers so that he can devote more time to writing and developing *Ftrain* (http://www.ftrain.com/help_ftrain.html). As well as a venue for personal reflection, then, *Ftrain* is a place for Ford to publish his writing, including intellectual musings in the site's "Theory" section.

It is the structure and navigation paths of *Ftrain*, though, that distinguish it most clearly from other online diaries. Ford has created multiple paths through the site, all of which are available on the left side of each page. There is a "Last 10" list, with links to the ten most recent entries, in reverse chronological order; a Table of Contents; a reverse and a forward chronology of all of the entries at the site; links to a list of indexes for each of the site's sections (Home, Story, Theory, Annex, About, Links); a search engine; and a calendar of entries. Moreover, at the end of each journal entry, Ford provides a description of where that entry is, and thus where the reader is, in the overall hierarchy of the site. For instance, the following text appears below the entry entitled "Cake": "This is **Cake** © Monday, 26 Aug 2002. It is part of The Neighborhood, part of New York City, part of Empire State, part of Location, part of A Sense of Place, part of Story, part of Ftrain.com" (http://ftrain.com/cake_in_rain.html).[18] Each of the underlined words is a link that leads to a page presenting an index of other entries or categories. Clicking on Location, for instance, will lead to a page with the categories Israel (Ford went to Israel in 2001), Keystone State (where Ford grew up), and Empire State (where Ford lives). These category links in turn lead to entries that Ford has written about his experiences in these locations. Finally, Ford includes more navigation options at the end of each entry: Navigate by Hierarchy (Next, Previous, Up), and Navigate by Time (Next, Previous).

The range of options is daunting, but as Ford explains, there are creative and reader-centered reasons for this multiplicity of paths through the site. In an entry appropriately entitled "Making Sense of this Site," Ford describes *Ftrain* as a "layered narrative" of "cross-linked hierarchies," in which one can move laterally as well as linearly.

[…]

By providing readers with many ways to "marry" structure and content in the many paths through the site, Ford does not eliminate linear or chronological connections, but rather suggests that these are not the only possibilities.

[…]

Although the interactive features Ford discusses are not yet functional, and indeed may never be functional, his plans are consistent with the general orientation of his site, and to a lesser extent, of online diaries in general, in which the experience of reading includes both gaining access to the thoughts and experiences of another person, and making decisions that create meaning and enable readers to explore their own interests. Any purely voyeuristic motivation for diary reading is minimized in favor of a more active, playful, and open-ended encounter with the text.

* * * * *

The question of how to read online diaries is closely connected to the question of how to interpret them. What interpretive methods and scholarly approaches are best suited to this form of writing? Lejeune's study brings excerpts from online diaries, interviews and correspondence with diarists, and bibliographic indexing together with a record of his own reactions, observations, and conclusions as he reads online diaries. My approach here has focused in a more detached and systematic way on the question of how online diaries fit into and disrupt frameworks for understanding diary writing and autobiographical writing. For Lejeune, too, print diaries and other autobiographical texts are the points of reference in his interpretation. However, other reference points might yield different insights into the writing and reading of online diaries. As a serialized form that addresses and solicits interaction with a specific group of readers, the online diary is like a letter or an email with multiple recipients who have the option of responding. In its structure, the online diary might be usefully compared to hypertext fiction, about which there is a growing body of scholarship. Those online diaries that integrate photographs, illustrations, animation, audio, and other forms of multimedia might be discussed in terms of autobiographical art or performance. As a computer-based mode of expression and interaction, online diaries might be compared to MUDs or online role-playing games.

The technologies involved in diary writing on the Web raise additional questions for researchers. Online diaries are inherently unstable objects – constantly changing, sometimes disappearing altogether. As studies of hypertext fiction have noted, it is difficult to determine the object of analysis when it is constantly changing, and when moreover, the text itself differs depending on the path the reader has taken through it. The question of access to the technologies necessary for online writing is also significant. A pen and notebook are obviously more affordable than a computer and Internet access. Examples of "best practices" for online diary writing, such as those suggested by the *Diarist.net* Awards, are likely to be drawn from individuals who have the economic wherewithal to access the Internet, learn the necessary skills, and devote time to online diary writing. Research focused on age, gender, class, ethnicity, native language, and disability in autobiographical writing on the Web would undoubtedly yield different conclusions about how people interact with and represent themselves via these new technologies of writing and publishing.

Finally, perhaps the question for some is not how online diaries should be studied, but whether they should be studied. Online diaries reflect potentially disturbing effects of technology on our sense of self, potentially disagreeable shifts in cultural norms of privacy and community, and potentially unwelcome directions for autobiographical writing. Already a marginal form of life writing and literature, the diary edges further into the margins when it goes online, calling into question what it means to write, how we read and make meaning, and how identity is constructed and lived. For me, these very issues constitute the most persuasive reasons to attend to the phenomenon of diary writing on Web.

NOTES

1. On the Web one can find full texts of some classic autobiographies. The non-fiction section of *Bartelby.com* provides the most extensive listing, including such titles as *The Education of Henry Adams, The Confessions* of St. Augustine, Benvenuto Cellini's *Autobiography*, Benjamin Franklin's *Autobiography*, Ulysses S. Grant's *Personal Memoirs*, John Stuart Mill's *Autobiography*, and Booker T. Washington's *Up from Slavery*. These are simply reproductions of print texts on screen; in other words, these works were (obviously) not composed for publication on the Web, and are not altered in any way (with the exception of hypertext footnote links) at *Bartelby.com*.
2. See Döring for a detailed and useful analysis of existing social science research on personal home pages.
3. There is, to be sure, some irony in the fact that the history of online journaling is already being written, after some eight years of existence – evidence of the speed at which Internet past and present move, but also evidence of the ephemerality of Web-based writing. *The Online Diary History Project* exists because online diaries, like other Web documents, regularly disappear.
4. In "Weblogs: A History and Perspective," Rebecca Blood convincingly argues that early interfaces for weblogging restricted writers to creating filter-style Weblogs – in other words, Weblogs that filter other content on the Web by providing links to sites along with brief commentary. *Blogger's* open and non-restrictive interface – "an empty form box into which the blogger can type … anything" – facilitated the development of

journal-style Weblogs. As Blood puts it, "It is this free-form interface combined with absolute ease of use which has, in my opinion, done more to impel the shift from the filter-style weblog to the journal-style blog than any other factor." Although many online diarists use blogging software and hosting for their work, blogs and online diaries are not necessarily the same thing – at least not to purists in both camps. According to Ryan Kawailani Ozawa, the founder and lead editor of *Diarist.net*, "a traditional weblog is focused outside the author and his or her site. A web journal, conversely, looks inward – the author's thoughts, experiences, and opinions." Blood's distinction between filter-style and journal-style Weblogs is similar.

5. *Diarist.net* also includes links to online diary resources, a message forum, news about online diary writing, advice for beginning diarists, reports of online surveys of diarists, a link to the discussion list *diary-l*, and finally, the *Diarist.net* Registry: "The Definitive Directory of Journals, Diaries & Personal Weblogs," listing over six thousand sites (http://diarist.net/registry/).

6. Although the Internet has been regarded as a medium more accommodating to men, most online diarists are women, evidence for what Rebecca Hogan calls the "particular congeniality of diary writing as a preferred form of autobiography for many women" (95).

7. A particularly striking example of the importance of the material conditions of diary writing, and of the diary as a material artifact, appears in Rachael Langford and Russell West's discussion of the Lodz diary in their introduction to *Marginal Voices, Marginal Forms*. This diary, written in four languages, documents the last four months in the life of an unknown writer in the Jewish ghetto of Lodz, Poland before he was deported to Auschwitz in 1944 and eventually killed. Because the writer did not have a blank notebook to write in, the diary was written in the margins and blank spaces of François Coppée's novel *Les Vrais Riches*. As Langford and West point out, "the writing provides an 'indexical' figure of its own space of production: the position of the scrawled entries, squeezed into the margins of the printed text, crammed into 'useless' extremities of the book … figures the cramped conditions of the ghetto writer" (12).

8. This feature, named "RoboGussin'" by its author, is no longer available online; it is described by Nyla Ahmad in "Online Diaries." Gus's current online journal is *Randomly Ever After*.

9. See Claire Robertson's *Loobylu*, Christine Castro's *Maganda.org*, and Lance Arthur's *GlassDog* sites.

10. Perhaps in response to this plethora of media and programming choices, some of the more interesting winners of the Best Experimental Journal award function with self-imposed restrictions. For instance, journal entries at *Until the End of the World* by Claire Wenders are composed simply of fifteen words and a photograph.

11. The main page of *Toasted Spiral*, by Satya (winner of the Best Design award for the fourth quarter of 1999), presents a similar segmentation. Along the left side of the journal entries is a series of black and white photographs of different parts of Satya's body – part of her face, her upper back, one shoulder and upper arm, her face, and what looks like a wrist. In this instance, Satya's segmented body represents the multipart structure of her site.

12. See Christine Castro's "Self-Portrait" at *Maganda.org*, where she presents nine collections of facts about herself, one for each letter of her first name. *Anyone's Any* offers a page of "completely useless trivia" about the writer, Monique, entitled "I didn't learn to whistle until I was 20 …" (http://www.mopie.com/bluegreen/031400.html).

13. See the *Diarist.net* Link Connection Community page (http://diarist.net/links/community.html) for additional mailing lists on the topic of online diaries.

14. *The Amalgam* is a Webring limited to thirty sites that are chosen for "excellence in style and progress"; *Atheist Journals* features fifteen sites (criteria: "You must be an atheist. No back-sliding allowed. Consideration will be given to mere agnostics"); *Journal Babies*, with forty-two members, is a Webring "specifically for online journals that are documenting a pregnancy, birth, and baby"; *Word Goddesses* is an invitation-only Webring (nineteen member sites) for women with online journals.

15. Unlike Webrings, 'burbs or lists simply index similar sites; there are no membership requirements or criteria for selection. Both *Diarist.net* and *Open Pages* offer long lists of 'burbs, including general interest 'burbs and 'burbs based on geography, demographics, or special interests. For instance, *Artists* is a list of seventy-nine online journals maintained by people in the arts. *Autumn Leaves* (thirty-one sites) is "A 'burb for those in their golden years who maintain a diary or journal on the web." *The Bookworm 'Burb*, with ninety-eight sites listed, is for "Journalers who read, and what they read, and how reading plays a part in their lives and journals."

16. See *Dear X, Random Acts of Journaling*, and *The If Project*. At *The Diary Project*, teenagers are invited to "write freely and often about anything that is on your mind, just as you would in your own journal" (http://www.diaryproject.com/about/). *The Diary Project* Web site has posted thousands of entries in twenty-four categories, such as Body Image, Family, Relationships, and School. Also worthy of mention is the *1000 Journals Project*, in which "One thousand blank journals are traveling from hand to hand throughout the world. Those who find them will add stories and drawings, and then pass them along," with the ongoing results of this "collaborative art" project posted on the Web.

17. Manovich draws on semiotic theories of paradigm and syntagm in describing the role that links play in facilitating narrative. In new media, materials exist in database format, while the narrative is only realized through linking items in this database. Therefore, new media reverses the typical relation of paradigm and syntagm: "Database (the paradigm) is given material existence, while narrative (the syntagm) is dematerialized" (231). Since it is a set of links that may or may not be actualized, whereas the database exists materially, the narrative is virtual.

18. The entry itself is a typical Ford offering, telling the story of a concert at Prospect Park that he and a friend attended. The band "Cake" was playing, and it began to rain; Ford turned to his friend and punned, "Someone left the Cake out in the rain." The entry continues with a quotation from Oliver Wendell Holmes, further stories about puns, and Ford's speculations on "Empörunggelächter, disgust-laughter" and "Wortspielabscheu, pun-horror."

REFERENCES

afterDinner. Online publisher and writers' workshop. <http://www.afterdinner.com>.

Ahmad, Nyla. "Online Diaries." <http://exn.ca/Stories/1998/09/17/51.asp>.

The Amalgam. Webring. <http://amalgam.rubyrain.net>.

Arthur, Lance. "GlassDog." <http://www.glassdog.com>.

Artists. 'Burb. <http://www.lunamorena.net/journal/artists.html>.

Athena. *Lexxicon.net*. 16 Aug. 2002. <http://www.lexxicon.net/lexxicon>.

Autumn Leaves. 'Burb. <http://www.themos.org/autumnleaves>.

Bartelby.com. Ebook publisher. <http://www.bartelby.com>.

Blogger. Blogging service. <http://www.blogger.com>.

Blood, Rebecca. "Weblogs: A History and Perspective." 10 Mar. 2002. <http://www.rebeccablood.net/essays/weblog_history.html>.

Bloom, Lynn Z. "'I Write for Myself and Strangers': Private Diaries as Public Documents." *Inscribing the Daily: Critical Essays on Women's Diaries.* Ed. Suzanne Bunkers and Cynthia Huff. Amherst: U of Massachusetts P, 1996. 23–37.

Bookworm 'Burb. 'Burb. <http://www.mopie.com/bookburb.html>.

Bunkers, Suzanne, ed. *Diaries of Girls and Women: A Midwestern American Sampler.* Madison: U of Wisconsin P, 2001.

Burbules, Nicholas C. "Rhetorics of the Web: Hyperreading and Critical Literacy." *Page to Screen: Taking Literacy into the Electronic Era.* Ed. Ilana Snyder. London: Routledge, 1998. 102–122.

Castro, Christine. *Maganda.org.* <http://www.maganda.org>.

The City Stories Project. Journal and city guide. <http://www.citystories.com>.

Dear X. Diary service. <http://www.dearx.com>.

Degn, Sasha. *I'd Rather Eat Glass.* 22 Aug. 2002. <http://glass.travisasha.com>.

Diarist.net. Diary service. 20 Aug. 2002. <http://www.diarist.net>.

Diaryland. Diary service. <http://www.diaryland.com>.

The Diary Project. Diary service. <http://www.diaryproject.com>.

Diary-X. Diary service. <http://www.diary-x.com>.

Donea, Magdalena. *Mimo.* Aug. 2002. <http://www.kia.net/maggy>.

Döring, Nicola. "Personal Home Pages on the Web: A Review of Research." *Journal of Computer-Mediated Communication* 7.3 (Apr. 2002). 10 Aug. 2002. <http://www.ascusc.org/jcmc/vol7/issue3/doering.html>.

Ford, Paul. *Ftrain.com.* 22 Aug. 2002. <http://www.ftrain.com>.

The Fray. Journal anthology. <http://www.fray.com>.

Garcia, Jacalyn Lopez. *Glass Houses: A Tour of Assimilation from a Mexican-American Perspective.* <http://www.cmp.ucr.edu/students/GlassHouses>.

Gus. *Randomly Ever After.* <http://www.spies.com/~gus.ran>.

Hogan, Rebecca. "Engendered Autobiographies: The Diary as a Feminine Form." *Prose Studies* 14 (Sept. 1991): 95–107.

The If Project. Diary service. <http://www.ifproject.com>.

Jackson, Shelley. *My Body: A Wunderkammer &.* <http://www.altx.com/thebody>.

Journal Babies. Webring. <http://www.phaeba.net/jbabies>.

Landow, George P. *Hypertext 2.0: The Convergence of Contemporary Critical Theory and Technology.* Baltimore: Johns Hopkins UP, 1997.

Langford, Rachael, and Russell West. *Marginal Voices, Marginal Forms: Diaries in European Literature and History.* Atlanta: Rodopi, 1999.

Lejeune, Philippe. *"Cher écran …": Journal Personnel, Ordinateur, Internet.* Paris: Éditions du Seuil, 2000.

Lejeune, Philippe. "How Do Diaries End?" *Biography: An Interdisciplinary Quarterly* 24.1 (Winter 2001): 99–112.

LiveJournal. Diary service. <http://www.livejournal.com>.

Manovich, Lev. *The Language of New Media.* Cambridge: MIT Press, 2001.

Noon Quilt. Journal anthology. <http://trace.ntu.ac.uk/quilt/info.htm>.

The Online Diary History Project. Diary archive. <http://www.diaryhistoryproject.com>.

Open Pages. Webring. <http://www.webring.com>.

Random Acts of Journaling. Diary service. <http://www.word-windmill.com/windmills/random/index.html>.

Robertson, Claire. *Loobylu*. <http://www.loobylu.com>.

Sandy. *Random Rain*. 12 Aug. 2002. <http://www.randomrain.net>.

Satya. *Toasted Spiral*. <http://www.toastedspiral.com/journal.html>.

Smith, Sidonie, and Julia Watson, eds. *Getting a Life: Everyday Uses of Autobiography*. Minneapolis: U of Minnesota P, 1996.

1000 Journals Project. Diary service. <http://www.1000journals.com>.

Wenders, Claire. *Until the End of the World*. <http://www.geocities.com/clairewenders>.

Word Goddesses. Webring. <http://www.phaeba.net/wg>.

33 YOUR LIFE IN SNAPSHOTS
Mobile Weblogs

Nicola Döring and Axel Gundolf

Exhibitionism or Journalism?

Julián Gallo is an enthusiastic moblogger. He publicly documents his daily life in minute detail using a camera phone and moblog platform.

> "We used to take some 300 family pictures in a year. Now, with the camera phone, I can reach that number in six weeks. When one of my children comes back from school, when we go for a walk or shopping – I'll always take a picture and publish it on my moblog. If I carry on at this rate and post on average 6.5 family snaps per day, then I'll have 2,372 images in one year. If I had them printed out in a 10 × 15 cm format it would cost me hundreds of dollars. If you put them back to back, there would be a chain of photos 14 miles long. And all of this in just one year!"

Might the cultural critics be right who deem amateurs' publications on the Internet – personal homepages, weblogs or moblogs – in the main boring, useless and often even embarrassing? Who on earth could be interested in where Gallo went for his walk yesterday? More contentious than the banal snapshots of the allotment back home are exhibitionistic photos. This has already led to more than one hundred mobloggers using the moblog platform Yafro to protest against other Yafro members who on a regular basis place online nude pictures of themselves and their partners.

Those criticising this tidal wave of personal content stand on the opposing side of the debate to the prophets of a new democratised civil journalism. They argue that if camera phones, radio networks and moblog platforms enable more and more citizens

Nicola Döring and Axel Gundolf, "Your Life in Snapshots: Mobile Weblogs," pp. 80–90 from *Knowledge, Technology, & Policy* 19:1 (Spring 2006).

to participate at any time in a free exchange of information and opinion, reporting live from important events all over the world, the information monopoly of mass media and professional publicists could be broken. The concept of a moblog carries associations not only with the mobility of keeping a mobile-based logbook but also with the mob as in a 'disorderly crowd of people'. According to Howard Rheingold this crowd may alter, through mobile communication and improved social networking, to become an 'informed mob' that exerts increased political influence (Rheingold 2003a). It was only natural for Internet pioneer Rheingold to encourage US citizens in the summer of 2003 to keep an eye on what was happening with the next presidential elections and to use their camera phones to report live from election events – "Moblog the Conventions!" (Rheingold 2003b). In the summer of 2004 this became reality. The University of South Carolina, among others, organised a major election event moblog – the Wireless Election Connection Moblog (http://wec.text america. com). Here, thanks to industry sponsorship, amateur reporters were given new camera phones, officially accredited as election reporters by both Democrats and Republicans, and interviewed by MTV as media stars in their own right.

From Cult to Commerce

The term "Moblog" or "MoBlog" (short for Mobile Weblog) was used for the first time by web experts Justin Hall (Hall 2002) and Adam Greenfield (http://www.v–2.org). In 2003, the latter organized the first *International Moblogging Conference* "1IMC" in Tokyo. Moblogs are regularly updated web publications comprising a series of chronologically ordered contributions. The crucial difference between moblogs and old-style weblogs that share the same structure is that moblogs may not only be uploaded from stationary computers but also, or exclusively, from mobile technology. . . .

In principle, moblogs serve personal publishing in the same way as homepages; allowing all media consumers to become media producers themselves. Also, Moblogs are part of the social media, as the content of a blog is not produced by a single person; normally several people participate directly and indirectly through links with other blogs and websites as well as public reader comments. *Collective blogs* are published by a team of authors, or are opened up to entries by third parties.

As with old-style weblogs, moblogs have access to specialized online platforms (Application Service Providers) enabling users to send in, save, edit and publish their contributions via e-mail or mobile messaging (SMS, MMS). *Moblog platforms* not only offer publication functions but also various community services. These enable moblog authors to establish personal profiles, exchange messages with other mobloggers (either direct or through forums), mutually list their names in public lists of friends, or form topical moblog circles. Not least, the platforms offer user statistics with information on which moblogs have the highest number of entries, the most up-to-date contributions, or the highest number of visits. The individual contributions eliciting the most comments, or users with the most comments, are registered in Top 10 or Top 100 lists.

... All in all, however, basic moblog platforms offer more limited technical functionality than weblog platforms (see Sauer 2003). In moblog contributions, links to the web, so typical for weblogs, are fairly rare. No wonder: according to Justin Hall (Hall 2002). "A weblog is a record of travels on the Web, so a moblog should be a record of travels in the world".

However, on various platforms – such as German-language providers 20six.de, Blogg.de and Twoday.net – weblogs and moblogs are not accessed separately but in an integrated way. Whoever subscribes as a user for an *advertising-financed simple service* or *a payable premium service* can keep a logbook into which entries are fed by both stationary and mobile technology. Of course, moblogs are of economic interest not only for application service providers but also for the manufacturers of the mobile devices and the network providers who continue looking for killer applications for camera and video phones, broadband mobile phone networks, and related services. Meanwhile, with the 'Lifeblog' software for the Nokia 7610 phone, the Finnish information technology producer has also entered the moblogging market (http://www.nokia.com/lifeblog). Photos, videos, SMS, MMS and personal notes may be archived in chronological order.

Naturally enough, discerning mobloggers are not content with the standardized packages and design templates of the moblog platforms. They would rather use their own web servers to design their mobile logbooks with a higher degree of freedom. This has the additional advantage that they get to keep the exclusive rights to the content they produce, whereas commercial weblog or moblog hosts (e.g. Textamerica) often claim these rights for themselves. Standard blogging systems, typically through Perl, PHP and mySQL, either come with moblog modules (e.g. Pivot: http://www.pivotlog.net and WordPress: http://www.wordpress.org) or complemented by moblog scripts including instructions offered by users with knowledge of programming (e.g. http://www.movabletype.org for MovableType). An open-source system with special moblog support is provided by EasyMoblog (http://www. easymoblog.org). Despite the trend towards commercialisation of the world of blogging, it is possible, with the relevant media expertise, to find and use free platforms, systems and tools. However, apart from the online costs, moblogging does involve substantial financial outlay for high-quality mobile technology as well as the costs of mobile communication.

Niche or Boom?

Current surveys in the US reveal that weblogs are read, either frequently or infrequently, by 11 percent of Internet users, and written by 2–7 percent (Pew Internet & American Life Project 2004). Compared to a killer application such as e-mail, which is used regularly by over 90 percent of online users, weblogs are more of a niche medium. On the other hand, taken in absolute numbers, i.e. hundreds of thousands of bloggers and blogs, the blogosphere has attained remarkable proportions. The Blogcensus project (http://www.blogcensus.com) has registered over two million blogs worldwide, while the Technorati blog index (http://www.technorati.com) records as many as three million. German-speaking countries currently contribute just under 20,000 blogs (http://www.blogstats.de), many of which unsurprisingly progressed no further than the test stage or are barely maintained.

The world of moblogs overlaps to a certain extent with the world of the old-style weblogs, for instance where experienced bloggers now complement uploads previously made from a stationary computer by uploading contributions via mobile technology. Some mobloggers are committed camera phone users who never previously kept a weblog nor appeared in any other way as an Internet or web author.

In recent years, the number of moblogs has increased exponentially worldwide. Whereas in 2001 there were very few moblogs, in 2002 there were dozens, by 2003 hundreds, if not thousands, and now, in 2004, hundreds of thousands. The payable service provider Fotolog.net alone hosts just under half a million moblogs. The Photoblogs.org moblog index currently contains nearly 5,000 registered moblogs from 61 countries in 26 languages, clearly dominated by North America, Japan and Western Europe, and with English the most widely used language by a considerable margin. It is estimated that German-speaking countries are home to several thousand moblogs – with the trend increasing. It can be assumed that in the long term only a minority of Internet and mobile users will be moblogging. However, economically, a lucrative market does seem to be opening up. To illustrate this, the Blog platform www.blogger.com, which also allows mobile add-ins of text, images and sound, was taken over by Google for around US $20 million.

Between Breakfast and the Front Line

The diversity of the contents of weblogs and moblogs matches its quantity. The Austrian moblog index of SMS.at, for instance, is divided thematically into at least 24 main sections such as "Cars and Motorbikes", "Arts & Culture", "Religion & the Spiritual World", "Business" and "Science", with dozens of subcategories. The predominantly young authors of the moblogs administered through SMS.at decide for themselves whether, and in which category, to register their moblog. The 3,000 or so moblogs registered in the index are distributed unevenly between the various sections. The most common are "About Myself" (1,061 moblogs), "Youth" (509), "Sports & Fitness" (245) and "Love & Companionship" (239). On this teenager platform, the sections "State and Politics" (7), "Science" (6) and "Health & Medicine" (3 moblogs) understandably occupy the lowest ranks. What has to be taken into account here is that a thematic division of whole moblogs is problematic because different contributions to the same moblog can deal with very different topics.

Teenagers' moblog contributions – with pictures illustrating their breakfast, their journey to school, their last party, or their pets and siblings – might seem trite, but so is life. They are not targeting a mass audience: most bloggers write, snap and design for themselves, as well as for real-life family and friends and for online acquaintances. Given the subject matter, advertising-style glossy aesthetics or mass appeal are neither possible nor necessary. While many bloggers insist they are publishing for themselves and for a small circle of readers, there are others who aim to generate more *attention*. For example, the administrators of the Fotopages.com moblog platform complained that some users were choosing the sexiest image possible for their most current photo on the platform's start page in order to attract people, even if the picture did not otherwise fit with the rest of the moblog.

[...]

There are *personal weblogs* and there are *topical weblogs*. Subjects around online and mobile communication are favourites; the medium shows itself to be highly self-referential. The scientific research on blogs is also mainly documented and discussed through blogs themselves. No wonder: blog researchers and bloggers are often one and the same person and connect theory to practice. Elizabeth Lawley, Professor of Information Science at the Rochester Institute of Technology and an active blogger herself, criticizes the fact that scientists with no real experience of blogging often view blogs as a homogenous mass and only skim the surface of the medium. To treat all blogs the same, she says, makes as much sense as judging the entire output of books without considering the different genres (Lawley 2004).

In the Blogcensus study, only 6 percent of all blogs surveyed were categorised within the *political blog* section; here the gender balance was reversed from the diary blogs (84 percent male authors, 4 percent female authors, 10 percent group, 2 percent unspecified). Apart from topic-specific asymmetries, the gender balance of the blogosphere is almost equal, which is in complete contrast to nationality or age. Most bloggers live in the western world and are in the first half of their lives.

Amateurs versus Professionals?

A mixture of personal diary and political logbook, frontline moblogs by US soldiers in Iraq are generating considerable interest on the Yafro platform (http://www.yafro.com/frontline.php). The soldiers offer photos of themselves and their comrades, of Iraqi civilians, war wounded and the dead. Moblog readers contribute patriotic slogans as well as anti-war protests, accompanied by jokes, compliments and flirtations ("You look great in your uniform!"). "CrashTheSoldier", who offers his moblog under the keywords "war, Iraq, beer, kill" defends his bloody pictures of the dead and injured by claiming a desire to document the truth of war at close hand and to counter the distorted reporting of the news channel CNN. In this sense he does show the conscience of a civil journalist, although one who naturally is also lobbying his own cause; promoting a more positive image of the US soldiers in Iraq. The "CrashTheSoldier" moblog is registered with Blueherenow. Blueherenow (http://www.blueherenow.com) is a platform for open-source news and moblog journalism reminiscent of Indymedia, but run by a commercial company (http://www.phrint.com). It presents a thematically sectioned mix of links to articles from established press bodies, complemented by links to moblog contributions.

As useful as photos by amateur reporters may be, moblogs alone do not offer a sufficiently sound information base: they can only be put into perspective and interpreted in the context of other journalistic reports. In order for the three-step moblog process ("seen – snapped – posted") to become effective journalistically and politically, moblogs have to be promoted; they need readers in order to have any impact. Blogs only become known through recommendations on the Web and through reports in the mass media. It does not make sense therefore to celebrate moblogs as a replacement for professional journalism; both forms of publication complement and influence each other. It is no coincidence that moblog authors feature many professional publicists, authors, photographers and journalists. Through their personal popularity, as well as the quality of their blogs, they stand a good chance of being read, commented on and linked to frequently, thereby rising to the ranks of an A-list blogger.

Invariably, as in all freely growing networks with self-selecting links, there are a few dominant centres surrounded by large marginal zones. It is clear therefore that there can be no question of equal distribution of publicity influence amongst bloggers. This is not due to a failure on the part of the blogosphere, but more to a consequence of universal network laws (Barabási 2003). The Japanese Internet entrepreneur Joi Ito is without doubt one of the most famous A-list bloggers. Ito runs both a weblog and a moblog (http://joi.ito.com/moblog/) and according to press interviews spends some five hours each day reading and writing blogs.

The mutual surveillance and comments of active bloggers with each other is a form of quality control. For example, the team of the professional weblog *Phototalk* (http://talks.blogs.com/phototalk/) systematically examined Yafro's soldier moblogs in July 2004 in terms of their technical and photographic characteristics. The results showed that the vast majority of supposedly authentic front pictures from so – called amateur reporters in fact came from professional press photographers and had already been published online (Phototalk 2004). The spectacular first-hand reporting revealed itself as *picture piracy*. This means that fakes and falsifications are by no means restricted to the traditional media. To the extent that amateurs act as online and mobile publicists, they not only develop new expertise but also expose the failings that accompany it.

Alongside knowledge of and adherence to legal norms (in respect of issues such as copyright and privacy), arriving at an understanding of the ethical ground rules of blogging is equally important. An online survey conducted by the Massachusetts Institute of Technology in January 2004 amongst 492 bloggers (36 percent female, 84 percent under 40, 66 percent USA) showed that 36 percent of those surveyed had already encountered ethical problems (Viégas 2005). In addition, quite a few of the respondents knew other bloggers who had come into conflict with family and friends because of their blog contents (36 percent), or had even got into professional and legal difficulties (12 percent). Rebecca Blood, who via her blog (http://www.rebec cablood.net) managed the jump to professional author, dedicates a whole chapter of her weblog handbook to blog ethics (Blood 2002). The moblog covering the election event of the University of South Carolina quoted above is already working to jour- nalistic standards.

Freestyle Photography

With camera phones readily on hand in everyday situations and usable where cam- eras are often not an option, the opportunities for image production increase sig- nificantly. This extends to an invasion of the privacy of other people, whether family members at a dinner party, friends at a party, or strangers on the beach who might not appreciate their sun worship being lodged for posterity and commented on in sexually motivated moblogs. On the other hand, Howard Rheingold makes a valid point by referring to the politically emancipating significance of unwanted mobile snapshots. If, for instance, violence against demonstrators or minorities is captured and immediately published on the moblog, then this information cannot be erased even if the camera is confiscated or destroyed.

In contrast to analogue photography, the costs for individual pictures and copies in digital photography are dramatically reduced. Furthermore, the results can be viewed immediately. This accelerates the learning processes of amateur photogra- phers, encouraging photographic experimentation. The camera phone makes these advantages of digital cameras accessible to even more people, and a popularisation of amateur photography can alter the way people perceive reality. Keeping and regu- larly maintaining a moblog means being on the constant lookout for new subjects and becoming more sensitised to interesting details in the environment that might otherwise have been overlooked.

While some amateur photographers only have a patronising smile for the snap- shots of eager camera phone owners, others appreciate this development, as one of the mobloggers in our online-survey commented: "Moblogging means that more people take pictures and start looking at the world rather than just perceiving it. I think that's great because photography is my biggest hobby. When I look at moblogs I like posting motivating comments." Generally, most of us are culturally illiterate at expressing ourselves through pictures. Multimedia messaging, camera phones and moblogs can make a small contribution towards developing more active visual competence and a sense of our own visual voice. This should not be seen as a rival for linguistic compe- tence; in moblogs in particular, choosing the right caption and formulating suitable comments involves an astute handling of text – image combinations (Badger 2004). On the other hand, a purely photographic narrative promises an understanding across linguistic barriers not otherwise available on the text-dominated web.

[…]

A detailed analysis of the content and formal structure of moblog contributions has not yet been conducted. Apart from their photographic content, one particularity of moblogs compared to conventional weblogs lies in their authors' mobility. The method of publishing straight after the event is particularly important for travel, major events, crises and disasters. It can, however, also be used for experimentation, to relieve boredom, to kill time, or to make further use of pictures already shot using the camera phone. Sometimes moblogging has a simple explanation – beyond headline-grabbing speculation about ethically dubious exhibitionism or recommended political activism: "It's a practical way of archiving the pictures taken when the mobile memory is exhausted," was the simple explanation one moblogger gave in our e-mail survey.

Mobloggers and Their Audience

Reading moblogs may be compared to leafing through photo albums of family and friends, or walking through a photography exhibition, or browsing in catalogues and coffee-table books. As there is no editorial selection or control, the differences in quality are as pronounced as on the web in general. Viewers have to decide for themselves what they deem to be *cat content* (bloggers' jargon for content of little interest) or relevant content. Naturally, for animal lovers, pictures of pets on a moblog are worth seeing as much as animals in real life. And apart from any moral criticism of adult content, in a cultural sense it is interesting to explore in more depth how and why men and women present their bodies and sexualities in moblogs. Not only in journalism, but also in the sex industry, online media contributes to increased participation by amateurs – offering specific opportunities and risks.

Moblogs that are regularly updated, gathering a loyal readership from both offline and online existence, develop regular, focused discussions about individual contributions and pictures. These include jokes and ribaldry, criticism and praise for photographers and subjects. "Well, it's just like looking at 'real' holiday snaps together – for instance, a place where you might ask 'where was that?' or comment on how slim the person looks or whatever," explains one female moblogger. For some, reading and commenting on moblogs is closely linked to personal ties; others use the medium out of curiosity or for entertainment ("because I enjoy thinking up 'intelligent' comments and making others smile or reflect", as one of the mobloggers we surveyed put it). The communicative function of moblogs is significant and can sometimes even take on the character of a lonely hearts service.

Other mobloggers are first and foremost interested in creative exchange, allowing themselves to be inspired by the photos other people have taken, and working harder on their own photography projects if they know that their moblog audience is waiting for new material. One of our moblog-survey respondents said: "For me the most important thing is the moment of the picture and the thought that goes with it.

Also, I have all comments to my blog forwarded directly to my mobile; it's important for me to know who is following me 'live'." The desire to communicate cannot simply be dismissed as narcissism – it is one of the most fundamental needs humans have.

As with traditional online diaries (Döring 2001a) and personal homepages (Döring 2001b), moblogs are consciously used to acquire media competence and professionalism. It is no coincidence that the most committed mobloggers include many people involved in the media and photography profession. The compulsive picture-taking of the above-mentioned Julián Gallo is not just an obsession; in his role as photographer and lecturer in New Media at the Universidad de San Andrés in Argentina, Gallo is reflecting the effects of photographic documentation in his moblog. In his own way, he is conducting a scientific experiment on his own person. A convincing moblog project may help a photographer establish himself or herself, as has been the case with some webloggers who are now published authors, have published their blogs as books, or report on blogging in magazines. After eight years of online publishing, Carola Heine (http://www.moving-target.de) describes her "private weblog value-added chain" as follows: "My own column in a PC newspaper, a non-fiction book on setting up a website, two non-fiction titles for young people, and again and again, with great pleasure, freelancing for the publications PCgo! and Internet Magazin."

From Test Account to Moblog Project

A public online logbook allows experiences to be shared with others, may open up new horizons, and can offer backup, encouragement and a sense of satisfaction. Just as in other aspects of life, the possibility of a lack of or undesired feedback cannot be excluded. Participants have the opportunity to operate using pseudonyms and/or to only allow selected persons access to their moblog in order to protect themselves from overexposure. This means that a certain amount of planning is required before launching into a blogging experiment with all its communicative and social dimensions. For pure documentation, traditional online photo albums are sufficient. These also offer the opportunity to order hard copies of the snaps (e.g. with Kodak, Foto Quelle, Media hype.de).

[...]

Is the Future Photo Mobile?

It is unlikely that moblogging addiction will become a problem for society. Some bloggers do have phases of devoting a lot of time and energy to their project, but normally follow this with breaks. As Carola Heine blogs: "Weblogging is addictive but it always calms down again – personally, I have never fought against it but rather just go with the flow. The main thing is not to spend my day running after situations that would be useful for my blog – but to live." And Elizabeth Lawley (http://www.mamamusings.net) recently used her blog to report: "Haven't been blogging much lately. Am busy in the real world and enjoying time with my family."

In a way, in the context of the whole blogosphere, moblogs might be described as "a niche within a niche". They qualify neither for highest praise nor for complete rubbishing. It is all about the details and nuances of this new technical, social and creative form of expression. It makes little sense to pit bloggers against professional photographers, authors and journalists. There is partly an overlap of people involved in any case, and the publication forms are dependent upon each other through co-citation. To a certain extent, mass media and personal publications pursue, independent of each other, completely different goals. If a moblogger says, "My 81-year old mother, who lives 3,000 miles away, is always so pleased to see my pictures", then for her that is the best reason to be moblogging, with no attached thoughts of market share.

The generalised reproach of exhibitionism and voyeurism does not stand up either. The borders of private and public spheres are subject to constant cultural shifts and are shaped very differently depending on the individual. Of course there are dubious moblog contributions, but that holds true for all media – and issues of moblog ethics are under intense scrutiny. Also, blogs should be measured by individual standards instead of overloading them with utopian ideas. Monika Porrman, author and blogger (http://www.dailymo.de), describes the nature of a blog as follows: "A small pin board in a long virtual corridor, in front of which you can stop a while in order to read what's on those little bits of paper hanging there. What goes on there – whether high literature, superficial blah-blah, demanding subjects, jokes, notes or brilliant ideas – is down to the author. The same goes for what is taken off. Nothing has to stay."

REFERENCES

Badger, M. (2004), 'Visual Blogs', http://blog.lib.umn.edu/blogosphere/visual_blogs.html (14 July 2005).

Barabási, A.-L. (2002), *Linked: The New Science of Networks*, Cambridge, MA: Perseus.

Blood, R. (2002) *The Weblog Handbook: Practical Advice on Creating and Maintaining Your Blog*, Cambridge, MA: Perseus.

Döring, N. (2001a) 'Öffentliches Geheimnis. Online-Tagebücher – ein paradoxer Trend im Internet', c't (2), 88–93.

Döring, N. (2001b), 'Persönliche Homepages im WWW. Ein kritischer Überblick über den Forschungsstand', *Medien & Kommunikationswissenschaft*, 49 (3), 325–349.

Gallo, J. (no year) 'Moblogs: The Map of Time', *ZoneZero Magazine*, http://www.zonezero.com/magazine/articles/jgallo/moblogs_time. html (14 July 2005).

Hall, J. (2002) 'From Weblog to Moblog', *TheFeature*, 21 November, http://www.thefeature.com/article?articleid=24815&ref=1858826 (14 July 2005).

Lawley, E. (2004) 'Blog Research Issues', http://www.corante.com/many/archives/2004/06/24/blog_research_issues.php (14 July 2005).

Pew Internet & American Life Project (2004), 'Online Activites & Pursuits', 29 February, http://www.pewInternet.org/report_display.asp ?r=113 (14 July 2005).

Phototalk (2004), 'Soldier Photography/War Photography', 9 July, http://talks.blogs.com/phototalk/2004/07/soldier_photogr.html (14 July 2005).

Rheingold, H. (2003a), *Smart Mobs. The next social revolution*, Cambridge, MA: Perseus.

Rheingold, H. (2003b), 'Moblogs seen as a Crystal Ball for a New Era in Online Journalism', *Online Journalism Review*, 9 July, http://www.ojr.org/ojr/technology/1057780670.php (14 July 2005).

Sauer, M. (2003), 'Jeder ein Publizist. Individuelle Online-Journale mit Blogs', c't (3), 166–169.

Viegás, F.B. (2005), 'Bloggers' Expectations of Privacy and Accountability: An Initial Survey', *Journal of Computer-Mediated Communication*, 10(3), article 12. http://jcmc.indiana.edu/vol10/issue3/viegas.html.

34 ASSEMBLING PORTABLE TALK AND MOBILE WORLDS
Sound Technologies and Mobile Social Networks

John Farnsworth and Terry Austrin

Introduction

Portable sound technologies are now so widespread they have become one of the commonplaces of contemporary society. Most young people in western countries carry mobile phones and many professionals use personal digital assistants (PDAs); iPods and MP3 players are valued fashion accessories; digital radio is in the process of becoming the newest technology in cars.[1] The pocket size and the extreme portability of these technologies facilitate their role as ubiquitous mediators in the growing mobility that characterises modern societies.[2] As numerous studies indicate, such technologies, particularly mobile phones, are reconfiguring work and leisure, and the way social interactions take place.[3]

We propose that two features of portable sound technologies are especially important in these new, increasingly global, arrangements. The first is often overlooked by media researchers. These portable devices are *sound* technologies. Sound instantly crosses conventional social, visual and physical boundaries and, in doing so, opens up the potential for new, often unanticipated networks of connection. Sound, in a

John Farnsworth and Terry Austrin, "Assembling Portable Talk and Mobile Worlds: Sound Technologies and Mobile Social Networks," pp. 14–22 from *Convergence: The International Journal of Research into New Media Technologies* 11:2 (2005).

word, travels. When sound devices travel, they further reconfigure the way private and public space is managed by how they and their user moves through them, and by how this affects hearing or overhearing. Sound, in effect, mobilises both space and social arrangements. We explore this further below.

Secondly, sound technologies are hybrid devices: they are miniaturised assemblages of audio, image and text technologies. Such technologies routinely send, receive, format, edit and store diverse channels that exchange human and digital information. This hybridity enables users enormous flexibility in the way they can connect to diverse local or distant networks. With mobiles, for example, such flexibility comes from the hybrid ensemble of diaries, organisers, browsers, clocks, streaming audio and GPS navigation tools they can carry. Mobiles have become fully multimedia devices.[4] Yet, so too have PDAs, which incorporate most, if not all, of the same technologies. In other words, portable devices are hybrid assemblages whose components can be swopped or recombined according to price, new media functions, market niche or obsolescence.

[...]

The importance of extending media studies attention to these areas is, we believe, increasingly pressing, if only because the industries of which they are part are now so global and dominant. As Geser comments, 'the total number of phones worldwide has for the first time surpassed the number of TV-Sets in 2001'.[5] Likewise in 2001, about 100 nations had more mobile than landline phones in service. Mobile phone technology is viewed as far more effective than computer technology in connecting less privileged populations to the sphere of digitalised information.[6] All sound technologies including mobile phones, CDs, MP3 and other devices are now taken up by literally billions of users worldwide.[7]

Amparo Lasen[8] describes this new reality as 'me and my mobile phone', one of the objects that is not just a device but one which mediates feelings and emotions. It becomes an affective technology. As she puts it:

> Nowadays people are moved and acted upon by their mobile phones. Mobile phone uses are the result of a shared agency. Competences and performances are distributed between people and devices. People and their mobile phones constitute a particular example of the assemblies between the human and non-human, as described by Bruno Latour.[9]

'Me and my mobile phone' with all its companionable associations links human and object together as an increasingly indissoluble unit. This binding takes place because of the multimedia networks such mobile devices access on behalf of their users. Humans and their objects become, in effect, a hybrid entity themselves – an entity connected to, and connecting up, other communities and worlds. For this reason, it makes sense to speak of actor-networks because each half of the term engages with, and assembles, the other.[10] Actor-networks then become a way to track how humans and technologies constantly assemble and reassemble chains of actors, technologies and practices into fluid networks of interaction. Actor-network researchers study how such assemblages translate and mediate these interactions across broadcasting and media industries, music studios and production, technological zones and art worlds.[11]

Bruno Latour describes this aspect of technology as simply 'society made durable'.[12] Achieving such 'durability' cannot, however, be taken for granted. We highlight three processes involved: the first is *assemblage* involving the combination of different technologies and social arrangements into particular configurations. The second is the problem of how such configurations are stabilised or destabilised. This is a key issue in modern societies where change appears to be almost constant. In this respect, devices such as the PDA or the mobile, which are fixed, or stable, in their current material form are already on the road to replacement or reworking by new technological assemblages. We discuss this by pointing to the way that early sound technologies were similarly assembled, reassembled and hybridised in a ceaseless process of innovation and improvisation.

The third theme is the assembly and disassembly of networks. Here, we use the term actor-networks.[13] As we've suggested, human connection is only secured through electronic and digital technology – huge, high-speed asynchronous packet-switching networks. It is these which enable voice, image and data connections along with the social relations they mobilise. More than that, such technologies themselves produce and reconfigure human interaction. Public space, for example, is constantly penetrated and reshaped by private devices – mobiles, beepers and pagers – as any-one who uses public transport can attest. These, in turn, configure the social rules around how such private and public boundaries are negotiated, along with the rituals and ceremonies around the use of these devices.[14] We return to this below.

Assemblage and Personal Digital Devices

Personal digital devices readily suggest how technologies produce forms of sociality: the reshaping of public and private space, modes of conduct, moral orders, and patterns of interaction. Clearly, such miniaturised technologies are also part of very large-scale industries with huge capital infrastructures. These, themselves, are constructed through markets of competing providers and equally by the particular socio-technical configuration of different bands on the frequency spectrum that mobilise them. These networks allow for a hybrid assemblage of texting, phone chatting or video downloading to take place and all within the space of one tiny device. Barry and Callon[15] analyse the complex politics and policy-making this sets in motion through the construction of what they refer to as 'technological zones'. In every case, it is the hybrid arrangements of devices on the one hand, and humans on the other, which produce these contingent, changing and contested landscapes within contemporary mobile societies. Moreover, these arrangements are worked out locally within the context of state and market pressures that change from one society to another.[16]

Stabilisation and Destabilisation: Links between Early and Contemporary Sound Technologies

Susan Douglas[17] describes the shift in radio from point-to-point communication to mass broadcasting, which was unintentionally promoted more by amateur hobbyists than corporations. As she argued:

> The amateurs and their converts had constructed the beginnings of a broadcasting network and audience. They had embedded in radio a set of practices and meanings vastly different from the dominating offices at RCA.[18]

Looked at this way, the distinction between the identity of radio as a project for interactive users and one for mass audiences is a matter of the medium being translated or incorporated into different actor-networks. …

Compare this with the telephone where the same issues of private or mass form emerge from its inception and continue to the present. For instance, Grint and Woolgar comment that telephone technology:

> was used originally to broadcast concert music. It was no[t] axiomatic to its design that the telephone system would ultimately be restricted primarily to two-way personal communication. … The original use of telephone technology, and indeed its use now, was and is the result of interpretations and not negotiations.[19]

Compare this with Lasen's description of the early phone:

> At the end of the 19th century the telephone was a carrier of point-to-point messages to individuals, and a medium of multiple address for public occasions: concerts, theatre, sports, church services and political campaigns. This use as a means of entertainment and broadcasting of news was one of the main uses of the device till the end of the 19th century. The broadcasting of news was both professional and improvised. … Also, people who shared the same line, called party lines, exchanged and asked for news, or maybe more often just eavesdropped in order to be up to date with the current issues.[20]

In other words, neither the radio nor the telephone is a discrete technology; rather, each is a hybrid – an assemblage that is reconstituted to accommodate shifting social and technical demands. More than this, neither technology was even an entirely separate device. The classic overlap is the case of the RT, or radio-telephone, which also began as an amateur device in the 1920s. …[21] In this sense, the radio-telephone illustrates how a technology is both assembled out of other hybrids and itself assembles different networks of professional and lay members. It enables the intersection and production, in effect, of distinct and diverse social worlds. Ironically, radio telephones have themselves just been integrated into mobile phone handsets through new 'push to talk' (PTT) technology. As McKenzie describes it in the New Zealand context, 'the walkie-talkie aspect' allows a trucking team leader to call up group members and find out who can unload a truck 'rather than phoning five or six people'.[22]

Actor-networks and Hybrid Monsters

The focus of our historical discussion is to suggest that the same issues found with contemporary audio devices had already been encountered with early radio and telephone technologies. And, as Boddy[23] describes it, these were present with most other major twentieth-century technologies from the camera to the television. Each new technology destabilises existing cultural arrangements, assembles new industrial forms, occupational practices, problems of regulation and corporate management.

However, following Latour, we go further by pointing to the way that actor-network approaches offer a way of collapsing the common dichotomy between technical and social accounts of new technologies. This, as we have suggested, is what the PDA and the mobile phone illustrate: hybrid devices which enable humans to assemble, and to be assembled by, technologies. Out of this interchange and the configuration of new hybrid monsters, whether the early phone or a contemporary iPod device, these assemblages connect, mobilise or produce new social worlds. Some of this, as Smoreda and Thomas'[24] recent work on cross-national European ICT use shows, serves to reproduce familiar local connections of families, friends and neighbourhoods. To reinforce, in effect, stable forms of networks within everyday life. But equally, they may work to destabilise or remake connections in new or unexpected ways. Haddon,[25] for instance, charts the time-shifting that occurs with mobile use: its impact on children in households and on face-to-face interaction. He and other authors document how both private space in households is reorganised through mobile technologies[26] and how rituals and co-presence are managed in public space.[27] The point, in either case, is that existing worlds are reconfigured through the interaction with particular hybrid assemblages.

The same point is made in a different way by Agre[28] who considers how design, engineering and software communities are mediated through available genres of production in the way they attempt to connect to potential networks of consumers. Such genres, he argues, shape how issues of exterior design (such as skins for mobiles) or internal architecture and software configurations are devised in an attempt to link these networks of professionals to networks of lay or expert users. The iPod is a good example: an iconic white exterior coupled to simple menu-driven software for managing MP3 tracks that has made it the consumer standard in its field.[29] The problem in this case is one of translation from the aesthetics and practices of a highly expert design community to align with the demands of potential users. This involves constant successes and failures, as a glance through the pages of any specialist consumer electronics magazine will indicate. A recent edition of *T3*[30] is typical. This offers page after page of portable machines that couple eye-catching exteriors for young consumers with internal software devices assembled to appeal to a wide range of users. This diverse software connects not only to the private world of the owner's personal PCs, but also to the wider public worlds accessed through internet, SMS, WAP or WiFi networks, exchanging images, text, streaming audio and video in the process. On closer scrutiny, though, many of these portable machines turn out to be simply recombinations of each other. In other words, technical arrays that are temporarily stabilised through particular company designs or specs (e.g. Motorola or Orange), through the patterns of software, network packages (such as Siemens or Vodaphone), or through the handsets and phone features (polyphonic ringtones, changeable covers, triband, memory cards or car kits) in the slowly evolving repertoires of reproducible genres outlined by Agre.[31]

Conclusion

It almost goes without saying that portable sound technologies will become an increasingly integrated part of contemporary societies. In Germany, for instance, mobiles are being trialled as an alternative to parking meters;[32] in Japan, they are often a preferred alternative for young age groups to PCs,[33] while reports suggest a flood of black market mobiles infiltrating North Korea from China have begun to undermine the military regime and are enabling north and south Koreans to reestablish ties.[34]

In these, and related ways, 'me and my mobile phone' becomes a personal, political and socio-cultural phenomenon that connects, interpenetrates and mobilises the societies that take it up. Simultaneously, it reworks the boundaries not only of public or private space, but of the actors, technologies and networks that assemble each other.

NOTES

1. P. Anderson, P. and A. Blackwood, 'Mobile and PDA Technologies and Their Future Use in Education', *JISC Technology and Standards Watch*: 04–03 (November 2004); A. Livingston, 'Smartphones and Other Mobile Devices: The Swiss Army Knives of the 21st Century', *Educause Quarterly*, no. 2 (2004), pp. 48–52; John Tilak, 'Siemens Develops Mobile Navigation System for Java-Capable Mobile Phones', 15 February 2005, http://www.dmeurope.com/default.asp?ArticleID=6058 (accessed 15 February 2005).

2. J. Urry, *Sociology beyond Societies: Mobilities for the Twenty First Century* (London: Routledge, 2000).

3. A. Macgillivray and D. Boyle, 'Sink or Surf? Social Inclusion in the Digital Age', in *Digital Futures, Living in a Dot-Com World*, ed J. Wilsdon (London: Earthscan, 2002); J.E. Katz and M. Aakhus (eds), *Perpetual Contact: Mobile Communication, Private Talk, and Public Performance* (Cambridge: Cambridge University Press 2002).

4. J. Tilak, 'LG Targets European Market with Range of Mobile Phones', 15 February 2005, at http://www.dmeurope.com/default.asp?ArticleID=6073 (accessed 15 February 2005).

5. Geser, ibid.

6. World Telecommunication Development Report "'Reinventing Telecoms" & Trends in Telecommunication Reform 2002 "Effective Regulation"', ITU 15, no. 3 (2002), at http://www.itu.int/newsroom/wtdc2002/backgrounder.html (accessed 12 December 2004).

7. D. Gross, 'How Many Mobile Phones Does the World Need?' 2 June 2004, at http://slate.msn.com/id/2101625 (accessed 12 December 2004).

8. Amparo Lasen, 'Affective Technologies – Emotions and Mobile Phones', *Receiver* 11, 2004, at lang2057 www.receiver.vodafone.com (accessed 12 February 2005).

9. Lasen, p. 1.

10. J. Law and J. Hassard (eds), *Actor Network Theory and After* (Oxford: Blackwell, 1999).

11. A. Hennion and C. Meadel, 'Programming Music. Radio as a Mediator', *Media, Culture and Society*, 8 (1993), pp. 281–303; A. Hennion and C. Meadel, 'The Artisans of Desire: The Mediation of Advertising Between Product and Consumer', *Sociological Theory*, 7, no. 2 (1989), pp. 191–209; Bruno Latour, 'On Technical Mediation – Philosophy, Sociology, Genealogy', *Common Knowledge*, 3, no. 2 (1994), pp. 29–64; Michel Callon, 'Europe Wrestling with Technology', *Economy and Society*, 33, no. 1 (2001), pp. 121–134; B. Latour, 'How to Be Iconophilic in Art, Science, and Religion', in *Picturing Science, Producing Art*, ed, Caroline Jones and Peter Gallison (London: Routledge, 1998).

12. Bruno Latour, 'Technology is Society Made Durable', in *A Sociology of Monsters: Essays on Power, Technology, and Domination*, ed, J. Law (London: Routledge & Kegan Paul, 1991).

13. Law and Hassard.

14. Rich Ling, *The Social Juxtaposition of Mobile Telephone Conversations and Public Spaces. Social Consequences of Mobile Telephones, The Social and Cultural Impact/Meaning of Mobile Communication*, Chunchon, Korea: School of Communication Hallym University, 13–15 July 2002.

15. Andrew Barry, *Political Machines: Governing a Technological Society* (London and New York: Athlone Press, 2001); Callon.

16. Carolyn Marvin, *When Old Technologies Were New: Thinking About Electric Communication in the Late Nineteenth Century* (New York and Oxford: Oxford University Press, 1988); William Boddy, *New Media and Popular Imagination – Launching Radio, Television, and Digital Media in the United States* (New York: Oxford University Press, 2004).

17. Susan Douglas, *Inventing American Broadcasting, 1899–1922* (Baltimore: Johns Hopkins University Press, 1987).

18. Douglas, pp. 185–186.

19. K. Grint and S. Woolgar, *The Machine at Work: Technologies, Work and Organization* (Cambridge: Polity Press, 1997), p. 21.

20. Lasen, p. 22.

21. *Radio Amateur News*, December 1919, p. 260.

22. Dene McKenzie, 'You Can TXT, PXT, and now PTT, too', *Otago Daily Times*, 17 February 2005, p. 27.

23. Boddy.

24. Z. Smoreda and F. Thomas, *Social Networks and Residential ICT Adoption and Use*, EURESCOM Summit, Heidelburg. Stöckler (2001).

25. Leslie Haddon, 'The Social Consequences of Mobile Telephony', 2000, at http://www.telenor.no/fou/prosjekter/Fremtidens_Brukere/seminarer/mobilpresentasjoner/Proceedings%20_FoU%20notat_.pdf (accessed 15 February 2005).

26. N. Dholakia and D. Swick. 'Mobile Technologies and Boundaryless Spaces: Slavish Lifestyles, Seductive Meanderings, or Creative Empowerment', 2003, at http://ritim.cba.uri.edu/wp2003/pdf_format/HOIT-Mobility-Technology-Boundary-Paper-v06.pdf (accessed 9 December 2004).

27. Rich Ling, 'The Social Juxtaposition of Mobile Telephone Conversations and Public Spaces', 2002, at http://www.telenor.no/fou/program/nomadiske/articles/rich/(2002)Juxtaposition.pdf (accessed 12 February 2005).
28. P. Agre, 'Designing Genres for New Media: Social, Economic, and Political Contexts' in *CyberSociety 2.0: Revisiting CMC and Community*, ed, S. Jones (London: Sage, 1998).
29. *Stuff*, December 2004.
30. *T3*, December 2004.
31. Agre.
32. John Tilak, 'Berlin to Trial Country's First Mobile Parking Service', 9 February 2005, at http://www.dmeurope.com/default.asp?ArticleID=5945 (accessed 14 February 2005).
33. Tim Clark, 'Japan's Generation of Computer Refuseniks', 4 April 2003, at http://www.japanmediareview.com:80/japan/wireless/1047257047.php (accessed 16 February 2005).
34. Rebecca Mackinnon, 'Chinese Cellphones Breach the Hermit Kingdom', *The Straits Times*, 22 January 2005.

NEW MEDIA, NETWORKING AND PHATIC CULTURE

35

Vincent Miller

Introduction

> After the first formula, there comes a flow of language, purpose-less expressions of preference or aversion, accounts of irrelevant happenings, comments on what is perfectly obvious. Such gossip, as found in Primitive Societies, differs only a little from our own. Always the same emphasis of affirmation and consent ... Or personal accounts of the speakers' views and life history, to which the hearer listens under some restraint and with slightly veiled impatience, waiting till his own turn arrives to speak. (Malinowski, 1923: 314)

> eating a peanut butter-filled corny dog dipped in queso. mmmmmmm breakfast. 09:48 AM July 19, 2007. ('Twitter' communication from Happywaffle)

This article is a theoretical discussion of blogs, social networking websites and microblogs. I argue that these new media phenomena are symptomatic and illustrative of both technological affordances and larger socio-cultural trends. In particular, it will link the *content* of two major new media products with certain ongoing cultural and technological processes which arguably can be considered problematic: namely a flattening of social bonds as we move into 'networked sociality' (Wittel, 2001), and a similar 'flattening' of communication in these networks towards the non-dialogic and non-informational. What I will call here *phatic culture*.

In that sense, this article has a critical element. Blogging (particularly personal journal blogs), social networking websites and microblogs are used to illustrate these processes, not in the sense that they are seen as inherently deleterious or malevolent, but because these new media objects seem to articulate such processes particularly well.

Vincent Miller, "New Media, Networking and Phatic Culture," pp. 387–400 from *Convergence: The International Journal of Research into New Media Technologies* 14:4 (2008).

There will be four substantive sections to this article, which will demonstrate the move towards a phatic media culture thematically and chronologically. First I will focus on blogging culture and its relationship to the social contexts of individualization. Second, I will discuss the social networking profile within the contexts of 'network sociality' and the rise of database culture. Then I will examine the most recent phenomenon of micro-blogging within the notion of 'connected presence'. In the fourth section I will briefly discuss the encouragement of phatic communication within the context of marketing.

Personal Communication as Commodity: Blogging and Individualization

In any examination of the emergence of a cultural object, it is important to examine the context in which such objects have come into existence. Looking at the environment in which blogging emerged, one of the most relevant sociological developments is the concept of *individualization*. Thus, I would like to start with a very brief review of the concept of 'individualization', particularly as popularized by Giddens and Beck, and its potential relevance in the emergence of blogging (Beck and Beck-Gernsheim, 2002; Giddens, 1992).

In general, individualization refers to a process in which communities and personal relationships, social forms and commitments are less bound by history, place and tradition. That is, individuals, freed from the contexts of tradition, history and, under globalization, space, are free to, and perhaps forced to, actively construct their own biographies and social bonds. Because of the increasingly disembedded nature of late modern life, a major task of the individual is to continually rebuild and maintain social bonds, making individualization by its nature non-linear, open ended, and highly ambivalent (Beck and Beck-Gernsheim, 2002). Within this context of disembeddedness, consumer society offers up to the subject a range of choices from which to create biographies and narratives of the self, in addition to a set of relationships that can be seen as somewhat ephemeral or tenuous (Bauman, 2001).

Anthony Giddens ... argues that in a context of disembeddedness, *trust and security* becomes of paramount importance, and, for Giddens, trust, like the 'reflexive project of the self', is something that must be continually worked at.

In the case of intimate relationships, Giddens of course argues that the late modern social milieu has led to a rise of 'pure' relationships: a social relationship entered into for what can be derived from the other. Such relationships are seen as voluntary, and therefore contingent, and have an intimacy based on the trust of mutual reflexivity and self-disclosure.

One aspect which is particularly important here is the assertion that self-disclosure becomes increasingly important as a means to gain trust and achieve authentic (but contingent) relationships with others. ...

Clay Calvert (2004) … argues that there has been an increasing willingness to 'tell all' or 'expose oneself' in the media, and that this is largely the result of several processes, including an ever increasing need for self-clarification, social validation and relationship development, which are satisfied through acts of self-disclosure.

Similarly, Mestrovic (1997) refers to this more widely as the development of a 'post-emotional society'. … He argues that emotion is increasingly detached from genuine moral commitment and/or from meaningful social action. Thus the overt displays of emotion on talk shows, reality television, in politics and blogging are seen as part of a (cynical) strategy of impression management to the outside world.

[…]

Blogging, for the most part, is based on the notion that information is a commodity that is used to build and maintain relationships. In personal journal blogs, it is personal information, created through relationships of mutual self-disclosure, which attains a commodified status. In the case of other types of blogging (political, news, technological and the like), substantive information is the commodity. In both these cases, this exchange is based on the logic of the 'pure' relationship: an exchange of substantive information achieved through dialogue. This exchange creates tenuous, individually-oriented self-defined communities or networks, which revolve around shared interests and dialogic exchange related to those interests.[1]

Social Networking and Database Culture

For Manuel Castells (1996/2000; Castells et al., 2006), the disembedding and continual deconstruction and reconstruction of social bonds implied by writers such as Giddens, Bauman and Beck is epitomized in the new social morphology of the network society. A morphology that is based less on hierarchical structures and spaces, than on flows across horizontally structured flexible networks. To belong in networks is to achieve a greater measure of security in the 'space of flows'.

In terms of micro-level social relationships, Andreas Wittel (2001) built upon the network society thesis by charting the emergence of what he called 'network sociality': a disembedded intersubjectivity which contrasts the 'belonging' of 'community' with the concept of 'integration' and 'disintegration' in a network. […]

For Wittel, these social relations become primarily 'informational', not 'narrative'. What he means by this is that communications between people become more ephemeral and more akin to an exchange of 'data' than deep, substantive or meaningful communication based on mutual understanding.

Certainly, one can see these actions played out in the rise of social networking websites such as Friendster, MySpace and Facebook since 2003, which really epitomize this 'network sociality' exchange, and in the last three years, the phenomenon of social networking websites has, to a certain extent, surpassed blogging in youth and techno culture.

Social networking profiles push the networking practice to the forefront by placing more prominence on friends and links to others than the text being produced by the author. Where the blog had links to others either on a fairly anonymous list of hyperlinks on one side of the front page, or on a separate profile page, MySpace, Facebook and other networking sites give much more space to friends (including pictures) and thereby much more visual prominence on the profile at the expense of textual material. The overriding point of the networking profile is to reach out and sustain a network through the maintenance of links to others. Thus it is not the text of the author, but the network of friends that takes pride of place on the social networking profile.

Lev Manovich (2001) among others argues that we are in the process of a shift from *narrative* forms (as epitomized by the novel or the cinematic film) as the key form of cultural expression in the modern age, to the *database* as the prominent cultural logic of the digital age. ... In contrast to narratives, the database form, as the foregoing passage suggests, is presented as a collection of somewhat separate, yet relational elements.

[...]

[T]he cultural form of the network struggles with context. The foregoing discussion demonstrated that network sociality is similarly ad-hoc and non-narrative in assemblage. This view has, of course, been put forward by Castells (1996/2000: Wittel, 2001) and many others.

In this respect, social networking websites in particular can be seen as part of the database culture and network sociality. Profile building, while on the one hand enmeshing the profile/self in a network, is essentially the creation of a series of lists; markers which can be called up by others searching for people with similar interests. And of course, in social networking websites, the most important list is the list of 'friends'.

However, social networking websites tend to complicate this notion of 'friend'. For example, Danah Boyd (2006) and Boyd and Heer (2006) discuss the notion of 'friending' and how the concept of a 'friend' on something like MySpace becomes horizontally flattened. Close members of one's inner circle sit alongside strangers under the same banner in an endlessly expanding horizontal network, thus compressing social relations and eliminating context. The only context present is the egocentric nature of the network itself. In other words, friends as a whole create the context in which one's profile sits and from which identity emerges (Boyd, in press).

One step further, the practice of promiscuous 'friending', collecting or 'whoring' on social networking sites such as MySpace or Facebook, (in which users try and indiscriminately collect as many friends as possible)[2] demonstrates the logic of network sociality and the database: endless growth. The larger the network, the more secure the individual.

While the appeal of the blog essentially revolves around a (diary-like) narrative of user-generated content (usually text) and the practices of mutual self-disclosure, sites such as MySpace and Facebook encourage networking and generic 'updates' on status. Blogging features are present on these sites, but are usually marginalized and seldom used, and most text is now generated through passing comments, quiz results, or 'wall' facilities. One can see this type of communicative practice as largely motivated less by having something in particular to say (i.e. communicating some kind of information), as it is by the obligation or encouragement to say 'something' to maintain connections or audiences, to let one's network know that one is still 'there'.

The point of the social networking profile is blatantly to establish (and demonstrate) linkages and connections, rather than dialogic communication. ...

Phatic exchange is a term first used by Malinowski to describe a communicative gesture that does not inform or exchange any meaningful information or facts about the world. Its purpose is a social one, to express sociability and maintain connections or bonds.

[...]

Thus, phatic messages are not intended to carry information or substance for the receiver, but instead concern the *process* of communication. These interactions essentially maintain and strengthen existing relationships in order to facilitate further communication (Vetere et al., 2005).[3] In the next section, I will elaborate on the rise of phatic media culture in more detail.

Microblogging, Connected Presence and the Ascendancy of Phatic Culture

A fundamental aspect of network sociality is its dependency on technological objects to spread networks and to maintain social contacts. An ever-growing network of contacts would not be maintainable without the use of email lists, mobile phones, text messages, business cards, blogrolls and friends lists not only to store and retrieve these contacts, but to maintain 'live' connections to them.

Karin Knorr-Cetina (1997) has used the term 'postsocial' to describe not only the phenomenon of the disembedding of modern selves (and the flattened, thinned out social forms that have resulted), but also the current expansion of object-centred environments. In what amounts to a merging of indvidualization theory and actor-network theory, Knorr-Cetina argues that with individualization we have not experienced a 'desocialization', but a shift in late modern social relations to ones that are increasingly sifted through, or mediated, by objects. This serves to increase the distance of the concept of 'the social' from a focus on human groups to something that takes into account our increasing engagements with a variety of objects, tools and technologies (such as mobile phones, computers, blogs and social networking profiles), which not only allow us, but encourage us, to engage with others through them. ...

Licoppe and Smoreda (2005) note that one way in which these transformations take place is through a change in the notions of 'presence' and 'absence', which occur in an age where many people are continually 'in touch' through networking technologies.

These technologies essentially 'stand in' for them, making one almost continually contactable. Licoppe and Smoreda refer to this blurring of presence and absence as 'connected presence'.[4]

[...]

Licoppe and Smoreda (2005), argue that the technological affordance of connected presence leads to a rise of compressed expressions of intimacy. Non-dialogic means of communication signal recognition and a demand for attention, but allow for the looser commitment of non-intrusive sending of data, and deferred or asynchronous response. Simply put, their findings suggest that there has indeed been a rise of small communicative gestures whose purpose is not to exchange meaningful information, but to express sociability, and maintain social connections. The kinds of communication that Malinowski described as phatic communion.

One should not assume that these phatic communications are 'meaningless', in fact, in many ways they are very meaningful, and imply the recognition, intimacy and sociability in which a strong sense of community is founded. Phatic messages potentially carry a lot more weight to them than the content itself suggests. However, although they may not always be 'meaningless', they are almost always content-less in any substantive sense.

The overall result is that in phatic media culture, content is not king, but 'keeping in touch' is. More important than anything said, it is the *connection* to the other that becomes significant, and the *exchange* of words becomes superfluous. Thus the text message, the short call, the brief email, the short blog update or comment, becomes part of a mediated phatic sociability necessary to maintain a connected presence in an ever-expanding social network.

Indeed, research done by Grinter and Eldridge (2001) on the phenomenal growth of text messaging among UK teens showed that one of the perceived advantages of text messaging was the avoidance of dialogue and conversation when all that is really wanted is a brief exchange of data.

[...]

With the demands of ever expanding networks and of connected presence, dialogue becomes a hindrance pragmatically and the time-saving role of compressed phatic communications increases in importance. This is becoming one of the most interesting features of digital culture: the rise in prominence of phatic media and communication as a way to achieve some form of intimacy and connection with the ever increasing amount of contacts, connections and networks in which we are increasingly embedded.

A more recent, and perhaps the most striking example of the rise of the phatic, and perhaps the next step in this shift, is the increasing popularity of microblogging, and particularly 'Twitter', a microblogging service started in 2006 (Twitter. com). ...

The central theme is 'what are you doing?' One is expected to answer this in a maximum of 140 characters. In comparison to both blogs and social networking profiles, Twitter profiles are stripped down to the minimum. There is much more visual prominence on text, however the text produced, due to the 140 character limitation and the nature of the medium, are stripped down as well. The result is an almost ghostly series of brief texts conveying random thoughts, current activities, or brief greetings. Births of babies are announced alongside random musings and lunch menus, and these messages are sent out to real-time networks of mobile phones, emails and instant messaging, as well as to the 'public timeline' on the twitter main page.

The point of twitter is the maintenance of connected presence, and to sustain this presence, it is necessarily almost completely devoid of substantive content. Thus twitter is currently the best example of 'connected presence' and the phatic culture that results from it. In that way, Twitter is a glimpse into a future media/communications world of connection over content. Even among users, there is a certain amount of trepidation as to the general 'pointlessness' of the messages circulated,[5] at the same time as an appreciation of an overall feeling of intimacy by being connected in real time to many others outside one's geographical location.

The Usefulness of Phatic Media

One question remains … why is phatic communication and media useful? Apart from the demands of connected presence in an increasingly networked world, one has to wonder why phatic communication is being supported, indeed encouraged, by new social media enterprises.

Facebook, for example, encourages phatic communication through sociable add-ons like 'vampire bites', 'zombies', 'hot potatoes' and automating messages encouraging participation between friends in quizzes, film taste reviews and the like.[6] Furthermore, Facebook's new 'beacon' technology creates an environment where one's online purchases and interests get relayed to one's network of friends through automated communication. Twitter encourages phatic communication through the imposed limits of the medium itself. The 160 character limit for messages creates brevity in communication. The lack of a private messaging facility, promotes generic 'announcements' over dialogue or targeted conversation.

To answer this 'why?' question, one has to return to the concept of information as a commodity. In blogging, personal information was used as a commodity to build relationships. Within social networking and microblogging, the value of information is based more on the generation of large amounts of small bits of data, which can be analysed easily in the marketing process. Strategies such as data mining, consumer profiling, 'buzz' monitoring, and reading brand relationships are much more compatible with the small bits of 'data' exchanged in brief phatic exchanges than the narratives and dialogue associated with, for example, blogging. Phatic communication is much easier to put in a database, and much easier to package and sell to those looking to market products or gain consumer insights.

[…]

Conclusion

We are seeing how in many ways the internet has become as much about interaction with others as it has about accessing information. This situation echoes Marshall McLuhan's assertion in the 1970s that the 'the user is content' in electronic media. This has only become more true as we have switched to interactive ICTs and pervasive communication. The massive popularity of blogging, social networking and microblogging on the net and other communication technologies has indeed demonstrated that it is the other *people* in these environments, and the connections to them made in a postsocial world[7] that is increasingly being consumed.

In the drift from blogging, to social networking, to microblogging we see a shift from dialogue and communication between actors in a network, where the point of the network was to facilitate an exchange of substantive content, to a situation where the maintenance of a network itself has become the primary focus. Here communication has been subordinated to the role of the simple maintenance of ever expanding networks and the notion of a connected presence. This has resulted in a rise of what I have called 'phatic media' in which communication without content has taken precedence.

The movement from blogging, to social networking, to microblogging demonstrates the simultaneous movements away from communities, narratives, substantive communication, and towards networks, databases and phatic communion. This is an environment that obliges us to write, speak, link and text others on an almost continual basis to maintain some sense of connection to an ever-expanding social network, while remaining fairly oblivious as to the consumption (and production) of information.

NOTES

1. Hodkinson (2007) provides a good example of such network formation and specialist exchange in his discussion of goth-oriented online journals.
2. Discussed for example in *The Times* article 'Online networkers who click with 1,000 "friends"', Smith (2007).
3. Some classic examples of phatic exchange include 'how's it going?', 'nice day', 'you're welcome', or even nods and winks.
4. They suggest that in these circumstances two dimensions of the social may be transformed. First, the inner disposition to experience and sustain commitment towards relationships, and secondly, the actual work undertaken to accomplish relationships.
5. 'Friends Swap Twitters, and Frustration: New Real-Time Messaging Services Overwhelm Some Users with Mundane Updates From Friends', *New York Times* (Lavallee, 2007).
6. For example, a typical automated message such as '"Mr X" has challenged you to a movie quiz' suggests a personal invitation to compete. However, it is usually the case that if

'Mr X' has participated in a movie quiz, you will, by default, be automatically 'challenged' to the quiz, by virtue of being friends with 'Mr X'.

7. Given McLuhan's tendency to put people in a subordinate position to the technology they use, he might not be impressed.

REFERENCES

Bauman, Z. (2001) *The Individualized Society*. Cambridge: Polity.

Beck, U. and Beck-Gernsheim, E. (2002) *Individualization: Institutionalized Individualism and its Social and Political Consequences*. London: SAGE.

Boyd, D. (2006) 'Friends, Friendsters, and MySpace Top 8: Writing Community Into Being on Social Network Sites'. *First Monday* 11(12), URL (consulted 15 October 2007) http://www.firstmonday.org/issues/issue11_12/boyd/

Boyd, D. (in press) 'Why Youth (Heart) Social Network Sites: The Role of Networked Publics in Teenage Social Life', in David Buckingham (ed.) *MacArthur Foundation Series on Digital Learning, Identity Volume*, URL (consulted 15 October 2007): http://www.danah.org/papers/WhyYouthHeart.pdf

Boyd, D. and Heer, J. (2006) 'Profiles as Conversation: Networked Identity Performances on Friendster', in *Proceedings of the Hawai'i International Conference on System Sciences* (HICSS-39), Persistent Conversation Track, Kaui, HI: IEEE Computer Society, 4–7 January 2006, URL (consulted 15 October 2007): http://www.danah.org/papers/HICSS2006.pdf

Calvert, C. (2004) *Voyeur Nation: Media, Privacy, and Peering in Modern Culture*. Boulder, CO: Westview Press.

Castells, M. (1996/2000) *The Rise of the Network Society*. Oxford: Blackwell.

Castells, M., Linchuan Qiu, J., Fernandez-Ardevol, M. and Sey, A. (2006) *Mobile Communication and Society: A Global Perspective*. Cambridge, MA: MIT Press.

Giddens, A (1992) *The Transformation of Intimacy: Sexuality, Love and Eroticism in Modern Societies*. Cambridge: Polity.

Grinter, D.E. and Eldridge, M. (2001) 'y do tngrs luv 2 txt msg?', in W. Prinz, M. Jarke, Y. Rogers, K. Schmidt and V. Wulf (eds) *Proceedings of the Seventh European Conference on Computer-Supported Cooperative Work* (pp. 219–38). Netherlands: Kluwer Academic Publishers.

Hodkinson, P. (2007) 'Interactive Online Journals and Individualization'. *New Media & Society* 9(4): 625–50.

Knorr-Cetina, K. (1997) 'Sociality with Objects'. *Theory, Culture & Society* 14(4): 1–30.

Lavallee, A. (2007) 'Friends Swap Twitters, and Frustration: New Real-Time Messaging Services Overwhelm Some Users with Mundane Updates From Friends'. *New York Times Online*, 16 March, URL (consulted 1 October 2007): http://online.wsj.com/public/article/SB117373145818634482-ZwdoPQ0PqPrcFMDHDZLz_P6osnl_20080315.html

Licoppe, C. and Smoreda, Z. (2005) 'Are Social Networks Technologically Embedded?', *Social Networks* 27(4): 317–35.

Malinowski, B. (1923) 'Supplement 1: The Problem of Meaning in Primitive Languages', in C. Ogden and I. Richards (eds) *The Meaning of Meaning*, pp. 296–336. London: Routledge & Keegan Paul.

Manovich, L. (2001) *The Language of New Media*. Cambridge, MA and London: MIT Press.

Mestrovic, S. (1997) *Postemotional Society*. London: SAGE.

Putnam, R. (2000) *Bowling Alone: The Collapse and Revival of American Community*. New York and London: Simon & Schuster.

Smith, L. (2007) 'Online Networkers Who Click With 1,000 "Friends"', *The Times* (London), 11 September, on The Times Online, URL (consulted 12 June 2008): http://www.timesonline.co.uk/tol/news/uk/science/article2426229.ece

Vetere, F., Howard, S. and Gibbs, M. (2005) 'Phatic Technologies: Sustaining Sociability Through Ubiquitous Computing'. *Proc. of CHI*, 2005, URL (consulted 15 October 2007): http://www.vs.inf.ethz.ch/events/ubisoc2005/UbiSoc%202005%20submissions/12-Vetere-Frank.pdf

Wittel, A. (2001) 'Toward a Network Sociality'. *Theory, Culture & Society* 18(6): 51–76.

INDEX

Note: Terms and concepts such as "identity," "interactivity," or "consciousness," which occur in almost every chapter, have not been indexed

aesthetics 31–4, 109–16, 434–6
Apparatgeist theory 35–76
architecture and space 79–89 *see also* space and geography
arts (new media) 29–46, 109–16
assemblage (and identity) 262–7

biocolonialism 221–49 *see also* bodies and cyborgs, cybermedicalization, database, Pro-Ana
  population genomics 222–37
  postgenomic collectivities 240–1
blogging 499–514, 515–25, 526–33, 534–43
bodies and cyborgs (in cyberspace) 19–28, 36–7, 185–208, 254–67 *see also* biocolonialism, cybermedicalization

call centers 151–65
community (in cyberspace) 117–27, 268–83
cybermedicalization 209–20 *see also* biocolonialism, bodies and cyborgs
cybertyping 132–50

database 50–64 *see also* biocolonialism
  and narrative 55–7
  and social networking 536–8

digital Cartesianism 185–208
digital divides 144–6
digital economy
  intellectual property 441–63
  labor 335–6
  pedagogy 197–201
digital sexuality 284–306, 307–23
digitextuality 29–46
  click theory 36–43
disembodiment, bodily transcendence, virtual bodies 19–28, 185–208, 257–60

gaming *see also Second Life*
  gender 408–24, 434–7
  intellectual property 441–63
  locative media 109–16
  narratives 382–93
  race 425–40
  social (*World of Warcraft*) 394–407
  social aesthetics 122–4

hacktivism 369–78
hybridity 151–65 *see also* call centers

intellectual property 441–63 *see also* digital economy

internet dating 483–98 *see also* social
networking, youth (and new media)

knowledge (and networks) 117–27

labor (in informational cultures) 335–56
see also digital economy, *Second
Life*
lesbians (on the Internet) 268–83
locative media 109–16 *see also* space and
geography

masculinity (in computer games) 425–40
minorities (and cyberspace) 166–82, 357–68
see also call centers, race (in
cyberspace)
mobile phones 65–76, 526–33 *see also*
Apparatgeist theory, blogging, social
networking

pornography (on the Internet) 284–306 *see
also* sex tourism
posthumanism 19–28
privacy 468–82
Pro-Ana (pro-anorexia) online 209–18
public space 86–8, 109–16, 117–27

race (in cyberspace) 132–50, 225–6, 307–23
see also call centers
remediation 46–9
rights (in information societies) 257–368

Second Life 441–63 *see also* gaming,
social

sex tourism (on the Internet) 307–23 *see
also* digital economy, pornography
social networking 468–82, 526–33, 534–43
see also internet dating, youth (and
new media)
space and geography 79–89, 90–108,
109–16, 117–27 *see also* architecture
and space, locative media
co-evolution of geographical and
electronic space 95–100
relational time-spaces 100–3
spatial transcendence 94–5, 120–1, 190–1,
193–4

terror (and internet studies) 328–34
textuality 29–46 *see also* digitextuality,
remediation
as online diary-writing 499–514
as online profile-making 468–82,
515–24
transnational virtual cultures 158–64
trust and authenticity (in cyberspace)
167–9, 491–5
Twitter 534–43

web sphere 11–18
women (and cyberspace) 166–82, 254–64
see also bodies and cyborgs (in
cyberspace), women and computer
games
women and computer games 408–24

youth (and new media) 468–82 *see also*
internet dating